LINKS FOREVER

ACCESS
SOFTWARE INCORPORATED

4750 Wiley Post Way, Bldg. 1 Ste. 200 SLC, Utah 84116 1-800-800-4880

THE WHOLE PC FAMILY ENCYCLOPEDIA™

THE DEFINITIVE RESOURCE FOR FAMILY COMPUTING

Robert C. Lock
Editor-In-Chief

With Richard T. Mansfield, Senior Editor,

and Steven Anzovin, Charles Brannon, Michael Butters, Scott Clark, Lance Elko, Tom Halfhill, David Haskin, Lisa Iannucci, Jerri Clark Kirby, Thomas Kitrick, Tom Lichty, Jennifer Lock, Vince Matthews, Gary Meredith, Peter Norton, Evangelos Petroutsos, Stephen Poole, Jason Rich, Ralph Roberts, Peter Scisco, *and* William Trotter

PRESS™

Published by The PC Press, Inc. ™
Entire Contents Copyright 1995 The PC Press, Inc.

Library of Congress Cataloging-in-Publication Data

Lock, Robert C.

ISBN 0-9648094-0-0

First Edition

1   2   3   4   5   6   7   8   9   10

The PC Press, Inc.
Post Office Box 13739
Greensboro, North Carolina 27415 USA

Design and pre-press production:
John T. O'Connor
Lightspeed Multimedia Design, Inc.

Manufactured in the United States of America

Front cover logos and trademarks are used by permission of their respective owners. America Online® is a registered trademark of America Online, Inc. Front cover logo and trademark used with permission of America Online, Inc. The CompuServe brandmark is a registered trademark of CompuServe®. Front cover brandmark used with permission. Throughout this book, the use of images, names and logos are solely for editorial purposes and such images, names and logos remain the property of their respective trademark or tradename holders. No other use is implied or intended, and The PC Press, Inc. is not affiliated in any way with the companies mentioned.

Trademarked names that appear within this publication are used only for editorial purposes and to the benefit of the trademark owner with no intention of infringing upon that trademark.

The authors and publisher of this book have made every effort to ensure the accuracy of the information contained herein. The authors and publisher make no warranty of any kind, expressed or implied, with regard to the information contained in this book. The authors and publisher shall not be liable in the event of incidental or consequential damages in connection with, or arising out of, the furnishing, performance or use of the information contained within this publication.

P R E S S ™

THIS BOOK IS FOR PERSONAL COMPUTER USERS EVERYWHERE
WHO HAVE THE PATIENCE AND THE DEDICATION TO USE THEM,
AND TO OUR FAMILIES, WHO HAVE THE PATIENCE
AND DEDICATION TO PUT UP WITH US.

PRESS

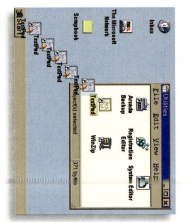
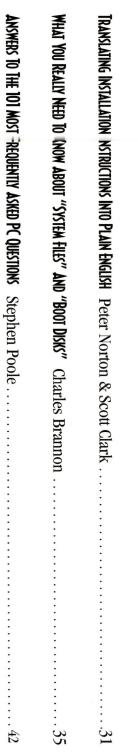

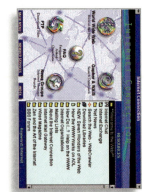

THE ONLINE FAMILY

What's a modem? How does it work? What does "online" mean? What's out there? Incredible sites and resources and interesting places to go. Is the Internet really worth it? Should I worry about what the kids might find?

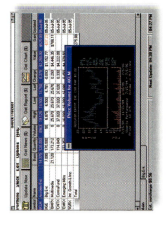

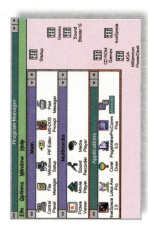

MORE

JUST FOR KIDS

Really fun projects and software for young people. Neat things to do with your computer, and places to explore online.

EDUCATION

Enhancing the educational experience for your kids. Choosing software that works. The key ingredients of effective learning software. Software for all ages and software by age-group.

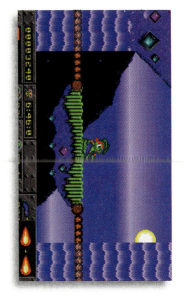

ENTERTAINMENT

PC games. Rating systems explained. Games that every gamer should own. How to pick good games. Where to find hints and tips.

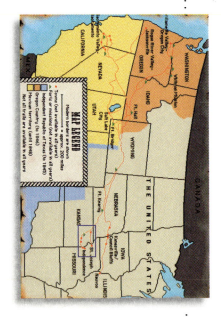

CONTENTS

KIDS TO ADULTS

AGES 6+ ™

HOUSEHOLD PRODUCTIVITY AND THE PC

Beyond games and education. Everything from cooking and designing your landscape to painting and tracking stocks and running your home office. Making your own multimedia.

RESOURCES

For additional copies of this book, see your nearest retailer, or call 1-800-556-9181

By Robert C. Lock

The Whole PC Family Encyclopedia™

A Publication of The PC Press, Inc.

P R E S S™

Robert C. Lock *Editor-in-Chief*
Richard T. Mansfield *Senior Editor*
John T. O'Connor *Art Director*
Charles Brannon *Technical Editor*
Gail Cowper & Meg Smith *Copy Editors*

Contributing Authors: Steven Anglin, Charles Brannon, Michael Butters, Scott Clark, Lance Elko, Tom Halfhill, David Haskin, Lisa Iannucci, Jerri Clark Kirby, Thomas Kitrick, Tom Lichty, Jennifer Lock, Robert Lock, Richard Mansfield, Vince Matthews, Gary Meredith, Peter Norton, Evangelos Petroutsos, Stephen Poole, Jason Rich, Ralph Roberts, Peter Scisco, and William Trotter

Irma Swain *Production Consultant*
Deanne Heffinger *Production Artist*

The PC Press, Inc.
910-A North Elm Street
Greensboro, NC 27401 USA
(910) 272-0083

Robert C. Lock *Chairman & President*
Kathleen Ingram *Marketing Director*

The illustration on page 59 is by **Harry Blair**, former COMPUTE! front cover artist for many years in the early 1980s.

Printed in the United States of America by **World Color Press**.

n 1979, I launched a magazine called *COMPUTE!* COMPUTE! Publications eventually became the largest consumer computing publishing company of the early 1980s. We focused on "home computers" like the Commodore PET, the Apple, Atari, and VIC-20.

One of the few constants in personal computing is the need for helpful advice and hand-holding support. In the pages that follow you'll find just that. Multi-media personal computers now provide a visually rich technology for families to explore and learn and play with. But they can sometimes also be frustrating, seemingly capricious, and difficult.

Many of the best authors in the personal computing field have joined us here to try to demystify, in plain English, many of the trials and tribulations of getting started with—and making productive use of—these incredibly powerful personal computers. This book is intended to be a comprehensive resource you can utilize for many, many months to come.

From conception to publication, this book has been a massive, enjoyable, and fascinating task. I have enjoyed the opportunity to re-establish contacts with authors who I have worked with for many years, and to meet new ones. Many of these authors have been writing about personal computing since, well, since personal computing started in the late 1970's. We all share a common goal in our writing: to help make personal computing easier for everyone. We are exhilarated by the power and potential of family computing; yet we regret that frequently the industry, in its drive to be cutting edge, sometimes embraces the technically advanced at the expense of the novice consumer.

I've never really agreed with the notion that confusion in the marketplace, whether resulting from selecting a new system or installing new software and peripherals, is the customer's fault. I think it's really the result of a technology-based industry that hasn't quite yet figured out how to keep it simple for its customers. The purpose of this book is to help close that gap.

In many ways, this book represents much of the best about personal computing. The book was written on PCs all over the country, and in some cases, around the world. Letters and comments and manuscripts and screen images were passed back and forth around the country through electronic mail on online services and the Internet. I now know some of these new authors quite well, have been in almost daily communication with them for months, but may not meet them in person for many months to come. The book has evolved, grown, been transmitted and retransmitted, all in electronic form, and, as I write, the resulting pages are only now leaving computer systems to take more tangible form as film for printing plates.

> Throughout the book you'll notice words that are underlined and boldfaced in red. This means the word is defined in the glossary. If you already know what it means, fine. If you don't, you can jump to the glossary in back and find the definition.

As I wrote in 1979 in the first issue of *COMPUTE!*, and write again here: we'd love to hear from you. Let us know what you think of *The Whole PC Family Encyclopedia*. Our goal is to help new family multimedia PC users everywhere get started. Have we succeeded? Do you have suggestions about how we can make the book better next year? And if you agree that this is a good book, do us a favor. Stop in at your local bookstore and ask them to stock the book.

Email me on America Online at RobertLock@aol.com, or on the Microsoft Network at PCPRESS@msn.com. Thanks for buying this first edition. We've tried very hard to deliver an exceptional value for an exceptional price.

Robert C. Lock
Chairman & President
The PC Press, Inc.

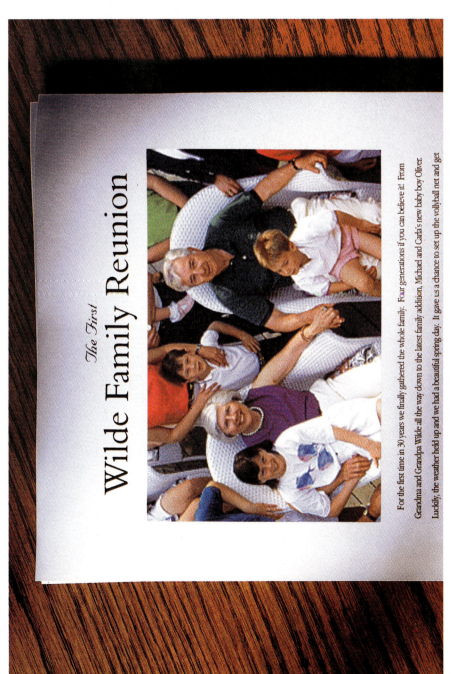

SELECTING A NEW COMPUTER

By Peter Norton and Scott Clark

Buying a personal computer can be heaven, or sometimes something worse. Peter Norton gives you the guidance you need to ensure it's the former.

What could be more fun than gathering the whole family together so that you can all participate in the selection of your new home PC? A root canal, maybe. Walking into a computer store—an be an intimidating experience for anyone, and flipping through one of those huge computer magazines can make you feel a little bit like your kids flipping through a Christmas toy catalog: it sounds like you need everything, so frustration kicks in and you just start picking things at random.

But buying a new computer can be an extremely satisfying and even positive process if you enter into it with some basic guidance under your belt. Despite ever-changing PC technology and the number of options you'll find staring you in the face, you can have some strong concepts in mind that will be very useful to you, regardless of when you jump in to the PC market—today or years from now.

PETER'S PRINCIPLE FOR PURCHASES

Over a decade ago, I wrote down my basic philosophy for buying PCs. Almost everything about PCs is dramatically different than it was back then—except keyboards, perhaps—but fortunately for me, Peter's Principle still works today. In a nutshell, it is this: you should buy the most powerful computer you can comfortably afford.

Tip: In general, buy the most powerful computer you can comfortably afford.

I know it almost sounds sarcastic, but it's really not. The principle is basically an excellent way to buffer your checkbook against the cost of

keeping up with a moving target: that changing technology I mentioned earlier. Keeping up with the Jones' in the PC world could put you into bankruptcy faster than you can imagine. It's not like trying to match their new sports car. You might buy a more powerful car, but you're still only going to get to drive it 55 mph on the highway. Excepting your ego's benefit, you've wasted your money. But there are no speed limits in the world of PCs. And there are very few technical factors restricting what kind of performance is possible.

Your PC salesperson will throw you into the land of superlatives—"faster," "larger," "wider," "higher," and she'll probably be telling you the truth. Everything on the shelves is faster and so on from what she had yesterday. But tomorrow's stock will be faster still, with larger hard disks and higher throughput. Hearing all this jargon might make you want to give up and let the salesperson decide what system you will buy.

Peter's Principle is a guard against that. If you keep Peter's Principle in mind as you start to explore the technical aspects of what you see offered, you will find yourself protected—inasmuch as it's possible to be—against throwing money into a bottomless well.

SELECTING HARDWARE

It used to be that there were some situations in which Peter's Principle seemed like overkill—for example, when buying an office computer for a secretary to type letters. Those exceptions don't really hold true anymore for a number of reasons. A quick glance at Figure 1 will show you one of them: the economics of supply-and-demand.

The amount of money you must spend today to purchase a system with a minimum of acceptable *performance* has plummeted. The 486-DX2/66 that I bought only 18 months ago for $2900.00 you can now pick up for just under $1000.00 at most

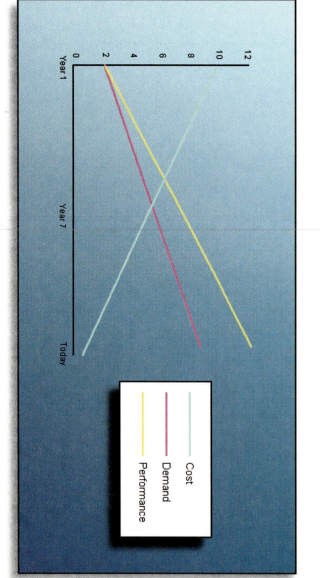

Figure 1: System cost (in blue) has dropped dramatically; in response to surging demand (in pink) and improved technology (in yellow).

Cost
Demand
Performance

0 2 4 6 8 10 12

Year 1   Year 7   Today

discount retailers. Amazing, right? But recall that "minimum acceptable performance" isn't the same thing for everyone. Additionally, the availability of low-cost **power** has raised the bar, so what was minimum performance even a year ago is probably less than adequate today. (You've probably noticed I'm talking about *performance* and *power* interchangeably; the two are essentially the same.)

MAIN PROCESSORS

Let's look at **main processors**, for example. If you're in the market for a PC at the time of this writing, you're facing the option of a 486 or Pentium-class processor. Two years ago, the 486 was definitely the cutting-edge product, with Pentium machines selling for well over three times what they cost today. The performance of those first Pentium machines is the same as that of a low-end Pentium processor today, and today's highest-end desktop Pentium systems cost less than what the low end used to cost, and they accomplish much more.

Today, unless buying the least expensive computer you can possibly find is the only option you have available to you, buying a 486 machine is not a very reasonable option. This is true not only because a 486 system and a Pentium-class system can be had for virtually the same price, it's also true because the 486 is a poor investment in hardware. The time will come—likely within as little as a year of this writing—when a 486 will be antiquated. Why? Well, first of all, the main processor is only one **component** that affects the performance of your PC, as we'll see below. When a 486 system is designed, all of the components on the main system board, or **motherboard**, are selected to work together. However, it's very easy, today, to purchase a modem or a video card that is capable of working much faster than some of the support components on your motherboard can handle. So the little money you might save today will be thrown away tomorrow, first when you buy a modem that works faster than your machine can support, and second when you end up paying significantly higher fees for using more **connect time** on all of your **online services**—which you will do if you have to log on at a slower-than-optimal speed. The Pentium-class processor brings with it a host of support components designed to support both the higher performance of the Pentium itself, and also the performances of all of the other hardware you might connect to your system.

In response to the drop in the cost of Pentium-class performance, software manufacturers have also begun to take advantage of what they can logically assume more and more people will possess. The word processor that I'm using right now is a brand-new version, and it runs noticeably slowly on all but the fastest of the 486s. The manufacturer has assumed that I've kept up with the technology—or will keep up with it soon—and have upgraded to Pentium performance.

COPROCESSORS AND CPU (CENTRAL PROCESSING UNIT) CACHES

Software always pushes hardware—which means that no matter what you buy, you will always find a piece of software out there that will push your hardware to the very edge. That's just how it works. One option for purchasers of 486 systems was a separate chip that helped the 486 perform certain types of mathematical functions. This **math coprocessor** was first sold separately as an upgrade to the standard 486. When the technology was still new and expensive, the separate math chip allowed users to add that power only if they needed it—for a spreadsheet, or for an architectural drawing program, or for scientific work.

As the cost of the technology dropped, math coprocessors were built into all but the slowest 486 chips, and every Pentium-class machine has a math coprocessor already inside. Consequently, more software manufacturers have assumed that your machine will have a coprocessor, and now even some very common graphics painting software will not run unless you do. If you follow Peter's Principle and purchase a Pentium-class machine, a coprocessor is a feature you don't need to think about; every system has one, built in to even the slowest Pentium-class processor.

Every Pentium-class processor has a small amount of memory built right into the processor called an **L1 cache**. Another feature of every Pentium-class machine is an **L2 processor cache**. **L2 cache** memory consists of separate physical memory chips (SRAM, technically) inside your computer that are dedicated to supporting the memory needs of your main processor. Processor cache memory is considerably faster than traditional memory, and it has a direct connection to the processor itself.

Tip: Statistical studies have shown that once your processor uses a given piece of data, it is likely to need to use it again. A processor cache makes that information available at a very high speed.

In most systems, cache memory is currently available in 256K chunks. High-end systems may come with 512K or larger caches. As with conventional memory, generally, more is better. You will also encounter "asynchronous," "synchronous," and "pipeline" caches. Put in practical terms, synchronous caches will give you faster performance than will the asynchronous variety. A pipeline cache is a specific type of synchronous cache, but whether a pipeline cache gives better performance than other synchronous caches hasn't been determined as of this writing.

Cache memory is quite expensive, which explains why this fast memory isn't used for all of your system's memory. But as with conventional memory, the amount of cache memory your system has can give you better system performance, even—in some cases—from a "slower" processor.

MEMORY

Peter's Principle applies to **memory**, too. To get the most for your money, you should buy a system with as much memory as you can afford, and you should buy a system with the ability to accept as much upgrade memory as possible. (The specification will say something like: "Memory expandable to 128M," meaning you are buying the machine with, say, 8M installed but in the future you can add as much as 128M.)

This isn't just because your system will be a better long-term investment—if that was the case, you'd be right in feeling that you could wait and add memory later if you ever needed it. But it's almost always less expensive to purchase memory when you purchase your complete system than it is to add it later. For example, one of the desktop systems that I own came with 8MB of memory. At the time of the system's purchase, the manufacturer allowed me to buy an additional 8MB for only $200.00, bringing the total to 16MB. At the time of this writing, you can't find 8MB of memory available as an add-on for only $200.00. Even from the same manufacturer, adding that memory later would have cost me twice as much.

So how much memory do you need? Well, 16MB is almost universally recommended today for an entry-level desktop configuration. And that's four times the minimum memory of just last year's systems!

The reasons for this are the same reasons behind the whole of Peter's Principle: users want their computers to be able to do more every day. In this case, adding new features to software requires more memory in your system, and the dropping cost of that memory allows software manufacturers to assume that you will buy computers with ever-larger basic amounts of memory.

Tip: Sometimes hardware pushes the hardware, too. Systems with a Pentium-class processor require a minimum of 8MB of memory. This is another example of how all of the components in your system should be balanced to work together optimally. You want to avoid having a significantly weak link in this chain of interdependent hardware.

Not too many years ago, Bill Gates of Microsoft was quoted as saying that no average PC user would ever need more than 640K of memory. Today, Windows 95 alone requires a minimum of 4MB of memory and if all you have is that 4MB, you won't have much real memory left over for your software to use. Consequently, your software will have to run largely in disk swap memory—and your performance will drop to almost nothing, as you'll see below. Memory chips are one of the best investments you can make in your new system.

USING YOUR HARD DISK AS MEMORY

Users of Windows 3.11 are very used to seeing Figures like "33,000KB of memory available" on their screens. That's not because they won the lottery and spent all of the money on memory; it's because they're using a portion of their system's hard disk to provide additional memory space.

Swap memory works by allowing the operating system to behave as though actual space on your hard disk was actual space in memory. Essentially, when physical memory is "full," the operating system can hand-off requirements for more memory to your hard disk. Data is written temporarily into a file on the disk, rather than into locations in physical memory, and when that data is needed again, the operating system knows to read it from the swap file, rather than looking for it in physical memory.

Using your hard disk for memory seems a lot cheaper than buying memory chips, but it's also a great way to throw a lot of the money you've spent on a performance system right into the trash. Why? Disk swap memory is incredibly S-L-O-W. Under even the best of conditions, your hard disk is probably about 300 times slower than your memory chips, and believe me, you will notice the difference. Big time. Swap memory evolved several years ago when physical memory was much more expensive than it is today, and most users simply couldn't afford to buy real memory to accommodate their software requirements. Swap memory will remain useful for a very long time into the future, but because of the way memory is priced, you should not rely on using swap memory in lieu of buying physical RAM for your new system.

HARD DISKS

If memory chips are an almost perfect example of how Peter's Principle can work for

you, hard disks are truly perfection. Make no mistake: regardless of what size of hard disk you purchase, in the lifetime of your computer you will fill all available space. A complete installation of Microsoft Excel 7 requires over 25MB of hard disk space; Microsoft Word 7 requires even more. When you consider that you will have all of the files for Windows 95 itself, plus probably a word processor, a spreadsheet, your online software and all of the files you will download, a drawing program, educational software for your kids, and so on, it's easy to see how hard disks fill up fast. Additionally, many multimedia products, from encyclopedias to games, suggest that you allow a significant amount of hard disk space—frequently greater than 10MB—to be reserved for that product's use. (Windows 95, after you've

larger disk now than to purchase whole additional disks later. At the time of this writing, the smallest new hard disk I would recommend is approximately 720MB. For very little additional money, you can get a 1GB (gigabyte: one million bytes) hard disk that will take you well into the age of multimedia. Still larger disks are available for power-users and, up to a size of about 2.0GB, the cost per megabyte of storage space decreases as the size of the complete disk increases (See Figure 2). Over 2.0GB, the technical requirements of disks cause their price to increase dramatically, but bear in mind that 2.0GB is a moving target. Tomorrow that critical point may be at a much higher capacity.

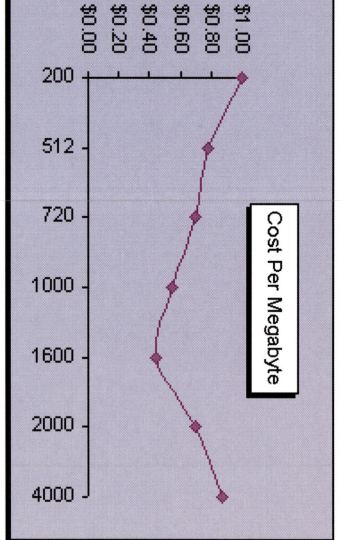

Figure 2: *Hard disk cost per megabyte decreases as you buy ever-larger drives, until you reach a critical point, currently about 2.0GB.*

added extra typefaces, applets, etc., can grow to over 100 megabytes on your hard drive.)

Tip: Your hard disk can move data so much faster than your CD-ROM drive that it is extremely common for a multimedia product to place some of its support files on your hard disk so that the product's performance can be significantly increased.

There are ways to cut down on your hard disk use, of course, and you can read about those later in this book.

The more hard disk space you have to start with, the longer you will put off the inevitable. Certainly, as with memory, you can always purchase another hard disk later, but as with memory, you'll find it far cheaper to purchase a

HARD DISK SPEED

Another factor to consider when you are selecting a hard disk is the speed with which data on that disk can be accessed. In most cases, modern hard disks have an access time of between 11ms and 14ms. Of course, lower is better. High-speed drives may have access times of 9ms or lower, and may additionally have high rotation rates. On a sufficiently fast system, a hard disk with a high rotation rate can move data to and from the hard disk at a significantly accelerated rate. For truly high-end performance—and prices—you will need to consider an SCSI 2 or SCSI 3 hard disk which, in most cases, will also require that you purchase a separate controller card for your system. The difference between a 14ms and an 11ms hard disk might not seem like much, but you will very likely notice a performance difference between even those small rates. The perceived difference between a 9ms and an 11ms is even more dramatic.

BUS ARCHITECTURES

Shopping for a computer used to be additionally complicated by the decision of which bus standard to buy. Many different standards existed (and still do, actually) from ISA to MCI to EISA to VL-Bus, and so on. Well, for the time being at least, that decision has been made simple: the clear winner amongst current bus architectures is the relatively new PCI (Peripheral Component Interconnect) bus. Do not buy a new system that does not come with PCI bus slots.

Most PCI-based systems will come with two or three PCI slots as well as several ISA slots, so that you don't have to purchase a whole new set of cards if you already own a few. The PCI bus is a fast 64-bit bus—as opposed to the slow 16-bit ISA bus—which is truly capable of providing the balance I talked about above among your Pentium-class processor and other system components. While there are several bus architectures currently under development that may out-perform the PCI bus by a factor of 10 or more, the PCI bus today has broad support from the entire computer industry (both PC-compatible and Apple Power Macintosh, incidentally), and will provide you superb performance today and excellent long-term value. The VL-bus (also known as "local bus") options were fine, 32-bit solutions before PCI really got off the ground. But local-bus cards were always relatively expensive and in short supply. Industry-wide adherence to the PCI bus should create market conditions for extremely reasonably-priced PCI cards of all variety.

MONITORS

When it comes to perceived differences, differences in the monitor you select can be some of the most obvious. Today, 14- and 15-inch monitors usually come with most standard systems, and several mail-order manufacturers will allow you to upgrade to a 17-inch monitor at the time of purchase with a considerable discount. Today, cost effectiveness has brought the price of 17-inch monitors down so significantly that you probably don't want to purchase anything smaller, unless absolute cost is your most vital purchasing factor. Twenty-one-inch and larger monitors exist, but their cost is dramatically greater.

Tip: As the size of a monitor's tube increases, retail costs skyrocket because larger tubes are much more fragile during the assembly process and thus are far more costly to produce than smaller tubes. Also, supply-and-demand economics just doesn't warrant a 27-inch computer monitor for $899.00.

While there certainly is a "bigger is always better" aspect to our desire to work with larger monitors, there are real technical advantages as well. If the total physical size of a monitor is only 14 inches, diagonally, a full-screen image under fixed conditions is going to be a lot smaller than the same full-screen image on a larger monitor under the same conditions. Those conditions largely have to do with monitor resolution, which we'll cover in the next paragraph. Suffice it to say, however, that if you operate your small monitor at a high resolution, everything will seem so tiny that you may find yourself experiencing occupational fatigue in the form of the worst headache of your life. Given what is considered standard operating resolution today, a 17-inch monitor is your best choice. Anything smaller than 15 inches is truly a short-sighted investment.

RESOLUTION, DOT PITCH, REFRESH RATE AND COLOR DEPTH

When you shop for a monitor, you'll see resolution and dot pitch discussed everywhere. Dot pitch and refresh rate are actually physical characteristics of the monitor itself: the first is a description of how close together two pixels can be on your monitor; and the second refers to how many times per second the image on your monitor is repainted. As you would expect, the smaller the dot pitch, the less "grainy" or "fuzzy" your monitor's picture will seem. A 0.28 dot pitch (0.28mm between pixels) is the standard as of this writing. Similarly, the more frequently the image on your monitor is rejuvenated, the less likely you are to get eye fatigue from staring at flickering.

Tech Tip: Your monitor works like a television set, with electron beams that cause phosphorous dots to glow briefly. The faster the electron beams move, the more often each glowing pixel is "refreshed," hence the name "refresh rate." If pixels are not refreshed fast enough, the period of time during which their intensity fades will become noticeable to you as a flicker.

VIDEO CARDS

Resolution and color depth, however, are not physical characteristics of your monitor per se, but are instead aspects of how your monitor can interact with your PCI video card (or your built-in video support hardware). To enable monitors and video cards to function reliably, video standards have evolved. Today's lowest-common-denominator video standard is over a decade old. Known as VGA (for Video Graphics Array), this standard specified that a color monitor be capable of displaying 256 colors simultaneously, at a resolution of 640 by 480 pixels.

Tech Tip: The smallest individual single dot of one color that your monitor can produce is called a pixel, which is an abbreviation of "picture element." When you hear that a monitor and video card combination support a resolution of 640 by 480 pixels, you are being told that the monitor can display 640 vertical columns of dots (each column is one dot wide) and 480 dots tall. Take a look at Figure 3 to get a visualization of this.

This level of quality remained the standard for a few years until the SVGA (for "Super-VGA")

Figure 3: *The image on your screen is actually made up of a matrix of individual points of light, called pixels.*

Figure 4: From left to right, the same portrait in 16, 256, and 16 million colors. This image was selected because differences in color depth are particularly obvious in flesh tones. Notice that even resolution appears to suffer at the lowest depth.

standard was defined. To be called SVGA compatible, a monitor must be able to display 256 colors simultaneously at a resolution of 800 by 600 pixels. The advantage of high resolution is obvious: Since you will very likely be working with several different applications at once these days, working at a higher resolution means that you will be able to view more open windows or other information at one time. This means less flipping back and forth between applications will be necessary. For example, will a sufficiently fast system, you could watch CNN, if that's your thing, in a window of its own while you work in another window. Similarly, the greater the number of colors your monitor can display simultaneously, the more realistic the images you view will seem (see Figure 4).

There is a definite cost to higher resolution and color depth, however. Fortunately, it's a performance cost, not a direct cost, and so it's amortized across the price of your entire system. The cost is this: the higher the resolution at which you operate, the slower video performance you'll get. That's not surprising if you think about it. If your video card "paints" a fixed number of pixels per second—and it does—then if you ask it to paint more pixels, it's going to take longer. And, with regards to color depth, the larger the number of colors you ask your system to display, the more memory is required to be able to address the color of each pixel.

In order to compensate for these two performance penalties, video card manufacturers have incorporated dedicated hardware optimizing and acceleration techniques. Video RAM is memory which plugs directly into your video card—or the video support section of your system's motherboard, if you have "on-board video"—which the video card can use entirely to keep track of resolution and color depth data.

If, for example, your video card has 1MB of VRAM, you will likely be able to view resolutions

of up to 1024 by 768 at color depths up to 256 colors. Lowering the resolution to 800 by 600 will allow you to view up to 32,000 or even 16 million colors. Today, your Pentium-class system will likely come with support for SVGA video, with 1MB of video RAM installed and it should support an upgrade to at least 2MB. As with standard memory, you will probably want the additional video memory sooner rather than later, and you will pay less for it if you purchase it as part of your system package. High-end graphics workstations may have between 4 and 8MB of dedicated VRAM and will be able to support 16 million colors or more, at a resolution of 1280 by 1024 or higher.

Video card acceleration and optimization come in a number of flavors. The oldest of these, the Windows Graphics Display Interface (GDI), is a hardware implementation of most of the basic Windows graphics commands, such as "paint a window" or "display this bitmap here," and so on. By putting this kind of Windows instruction in the hardware of the video card itself, much less work is required of the main processor for basic Windows tasks. The processor can simply tell the video card what the running application wants to do with the screen, and can then attend to other tasks while the video card does its thing.

Similarly, motion video playback acceleration is a hardware implementation of specific routines that control vital aspects of multimedia video. Video playback is one of the most demanding tasks that we ask of our PCs today. Video data is so huge that very few video segments can actually be stored in physical memory. Because of this, video playback ends up being a process of many steps:

• The operating system, running on the main processor, asks the processor to control the reading of video data from a long-term storage disk or CD-ROM into main memory.

• The video data is decompressed by running every bit through a decoder which the main processor is also running.

Adjustments must be made if the original video data was stored at a resolution or color depth which is different from that of the current display.

• Data is moved from main memory into video memory, where the video card takes over and displays it.

• The process repeats as necessary.

Bear in mind, of course, that additional requirements will likely be made of the main processor and operating system—handling sound, checking for user input, such as a mouse-click on the "stop playback" button, and any other processes or applications that may be running in the background. As you might expect, it is the disk access operation and the decompression operation which take the greatest amount of time.

A software cache for your CD-ROM can greatly ease the first of these bottlenecks. The decompression issue, however, has been tackled primarily by video card manufacturers. Under Windows 95, rather than asking the main processor to run software which decodes the compressed video data, video cards can now accept the compressed data directly from long-term storage (via the operating system) and the decompression and display instructions all take place very quickly in hardware. The process becomes more like this:

• The operating system asks for data from the disk.

• The operating system sends compressed data directly to the video card, saying "Decode and display this."

• The process repeats as necessary.

By taking the burden of more and more tasks away from the operating system and the main processor, your system is freed to handle the performance-intensive tasks of multimedia, such as allowing you to bring up files on your spreadsheet program while simultaneously spell-checking a final report while you video-conference with your boss to assure her that the report is finished.

Tech Tip: **Some video hardware supports the saving of video material from a video camera or videotape machine onto your hard disk. This is known as "video capture," and may either be part of the same video card that drives your monitor, or may be provided on a separate card. In either case, you will likely encounter the term "hardware codec," which means that video compression ("co-") and decompression ("-dec") are performed by your video hardware.**

THE MPC STANDARDS AND BEYOND

All of these system characteristics, and others, have been put together into sets of collective "standards" over the last few years. Microsoft, in particular, has created the MPC standards (it stands for "Multimedia PC") which have served as very minimal standards to which hardware systems should adhere for a given level of multimedia performance. The standard at the time of this writing, MPC2, is already quite outdated. As you would expect from having read thus far, it is rare for a standard to come into existence before companies are already hard at work making it an antique. When selecting new hardware, you will find yourself well-served if you all but ignore these standards. Any system which you might select today—especially if you follow Peter's Principle—will have gone well beyond the capabilities of an MPC2-compliant system.

Recognizing this fact, Microsoft has released their as-yet unnamed guidelines for manufacturers of hardware on which Windows 95 (and later) will run. Among the new elements of those standards are a recognition that a balance among system components will give you better overall performance—remember, you read it here first—and that previous standards for sound support and CD-ROMs are no longer adequate. We'll look at those two factors next.

SOUND CARDS

Until recently, anything more sophisticated than a "beep" coming out of your PC was exceptional sound, and until very recently, anything that sounded better than music played over a long-distance telephone call was considered phenomenal. No longer. Users have demanded CD-quality sound from their multimedia applications, and manufacturers have provided that quality, in the form of 16-bit **sound cards**.

Not only do these cards provide beautiful playback of any digitally recorded sound, they also use very high-quality digitally sampled instrument sounds to reproduce music which has been saved to disk in one of the standard General MIDI (Musical Instrument Digital Interface) formats. The purpose for this latter technique is simple: to record an entire symphony digitally would take many hundreds of megabytes of storage space. The General MIDI standard allows every note and nuance of a symphonic performance be stored in an extremely compressed format. This is because MIDI functions with the synthesizer built into your computer's sound card much as a roll of punched paper worked in one of the antique player-pianos. A performance is not recorded and played back; it is actually broken down into its component elements and performed anew each time it is heard. All of Beethoven's 5th Symphony can be stored in a file of fewer than 100K, and can be played back in exactly the same way and at exactly the same quality of that hundreds-of-megabytes digital recording.

What brought the world of MIDI from professional musicians to your desktop? An explosion in the demand for high-quality computer games. What caused that explosion?

Figure 5: CD-ROM disks hold huge amounts of information.

CD-ROM

Perhaps more than any other single technology, the appearance of optical storage (**CD-ROM**) has been a turning point in the development of PC's. The breakthrough lies in the ability to distribute hundreds of megabytes of data cheaply. Indeed, why consider producing a video card that can display 16 million colors if a single full-screen image requires more hard-disk space than was available on an entire hard disk? Why create hardware capable of high-quality digital sound if a high-quality digital sound file—a single file—requires over 20 diskettes to distribute?

CD-ROM made those questions obsolete while creating a new set of questions of its own. Initially, you could distribute huge video files on CD, but you couldn't get the data off of the CD fast enough to actually play it back. Technology improved somewhat so that video playback was possible under certain very special conditions—but to ask for synchronized sound playback at the same time was still impossible. The first CD-ROM drives had a **transfer speed** of 150kB per second. That might sound fast, but consider that the fastest hard disks can move 15MB of data per second! That's a factor of one-hundred. Double-speed drives then came on the market, which could consistently transfer 300kB/sec, and which could access data (get to the right place on the CD) noticeably faster (around 250ms seek time) than could the older drives (about 3000ms seek time.)

Today, you should not purchase anything less than a "quad-speed" CD-ROM drive, which is capable of moving 600kB of data per second and has an average access time of less than 200ms. Even 180ms is common. At the time of this writing, 6X drives, capable of moving data at 900kB/sec, are just coming on the market, but the 4X drive will likely be the industry standard for another year.

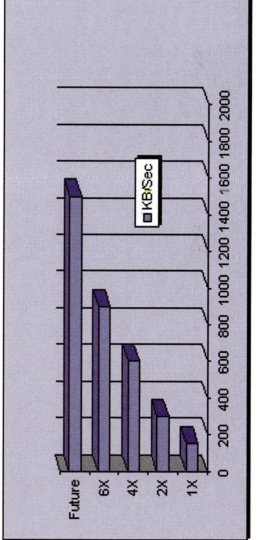

Figure 6: CD-ROM Transfer Rates

Indeed, if you are reading this with interest in buying a new computer today—by the time you are ready for your next major system upgrade, it's likely that technologies will be on the shelves which will provide over twice the current capacity of CD-ROM drives, at an amazing 8X or greater transfer rate (see Figure 6). While the cost of the slowest CD-ROM drives has dropped, the cost of a reasonably performing drive that will be a well-balanced component in your system has stayed relatively steady.

OTHER ASPECTS OF SYSTEM SELECTION

When you are selecting your system, there are a few other pieces of hardware which you will want to consider. For the most part, these are all relatively straightforward, although options do exist.

PORTS

Your PC may come with a variety of different **ports** for connecting external devices, but there is a basic minimum complement that every system should have. Your system should have a minimum of one **serial port**, one **parallel port**, a **mouse** port (or a second serial port), a keyboard port (in a few systems, the mouse will plug into the keyboard, but this is not a standard configuration), a video port for connecting the monitor, and input and output ports for your sound hardware. (This assumes that sound support is included with your system either on the motherboard or on a **bundled card**. If that's not the case, the sound ports will be on the back of the sound card itself.)

FLOPPY DRIVES

Although some manufacturers don't offer them, the most cost-effective **floppy drive** you can purchase is called a double-density drive. This gives you both a 1.44MB 3.5-inch and a 1.2MB 5.25-inch within the space normally required for only a 5.25-inch drive. You will definitely find systems on the market which come with only the physically smaller diskette drive, but for the next year or so, you may want a 5.25-inch drive for greatest compatibility with disks that your friends and small companies might give you, even though these drives are really outdated. (For example, it's now nearly impossible to find software sold on 5.25-inch floppies.) Fortunately, these dual-drives frequently cost as little as $15.00 more than either of the single drives, and their performance is exactly the same as normal diskette drives.

Another available option is the 2.88MB 3.5-inch floppy disk which has recently become available. These devices are reasonably priced, but they have not yet caught on with the market, so low demand has kept pricing significantly higher than their ubiquitous 1.44MB cousins. Additionally, since CD-ROM disks are much cheaper for software manufacturers to distribute than are diskettes, it is expected that the CD-ROM disk will replace the 1.44MB floppy as the medium of choice for professional software distribution. Given the tremendously low cost per megabyte of CD-ROM storage, even recordable CDs may catch the market's favor before larger-capacity floppy disks gain universal favor.

BACKUP OPTIONS

One of the primary uses for recordable CDs in the future will doubtless be **backup**. As you will read elsewhere in this book, keeping a backup, or duplicate copy of your data, is both the most secure and convenient way to protect yourself against losing precious work. At the time of this writing, many businesses are already using recordable CDs to keep track of irreplaceable data.

For most of us, however, today's backup options remain limited to two: floppy disks (or other removable disks like SyQuest or Iomega Zip drives) or **tape** (like QIC-compatible or DAT drives). The floppy disk option is available to every user with no extra hardware whatever. Windows 95 comes with backup software that supports backing-up data to floppy disks (and other media), and every system will have a floppy drive of some kind. However, floppy disks aren't exactly fast, and even if you get very high compression of your data onto the floppy disks, a full backup of your system could easily take well over 100 floppies, making this method costly in terms of both materials and labor. (My current system would require 313 floppy disks and approximately five continuous hours to backup.)

Tape drives offer a vast improvement over floppy disk backups, and their cost effectiveness varies from very good to incomparably better. The common QIC standard tape drive supports capacities of up to 600MB and—though only slightly faster than floppy drives—they work unattended, so that backup can take place both in the background and without requiring any intervention from you.

DAT (Digital Audio Tape) Drives get their name from the music technology that never caught on with you and me, but that is an amazingly cost-effective option for our computer backups. At about $13.00 per tape, with a capacity of up to 8GB (that's gigabytes, not megabytes), DAT tapes have a per-megabyte cost of about 1/10th of a cent! While a DAT drive plus its supporting SCSI controller card will likely cost you just under $800—as opposed to about $200 for a QIC drive—if you do backup your system religiously, you'll find the expense well-justified in terms of the time you'll save, and you'll also discover that a DAT drive's expected life will take you well through this and your next computer system.

QIC drives have a nasty habit of being short-lived, and QIC tapes are far more expensive per megabyte (around $20 for a tape that holds 250MB of compressed data). Although DAT may not be a realistic option for most users' pockets today, you should explore discounts that might be available to you if you **bundle** a DAT drive with your entire system. If you can comfortably afford the cost, you should give serious consideration to it as a backup and long-term storage option.

In either case, you should take the security of your data seriously—consider the amount of work it would take to replace it from scratch, and all of the spreadsheets and love letters and drawings by your kids that you could never replace at all. A backup method should be part of every user's basic philosophy, and bundling either a QIC or a DAT tape drive with your system unit is

Tech Tip: Most non-DAT tape drive options are only slightly faster—in terms of actual data transfer rate—than a floppy disk because most tape drives use your floppy disk controller to connect with your system.

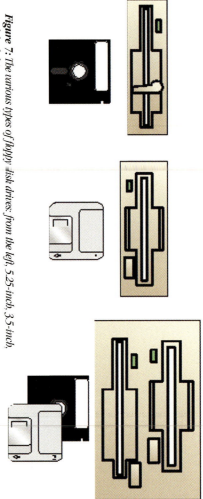

Figure 7: The various types of floppy disk drives; from the left, 5.25-inch, 3.5-inch, and dual-drive.

likely the most cost-effective backup strategy you can choose today.

MAKING THE PURCHASE — A SUMMARY

All of that brings us back to Peter's Principle of purchasing a PC: You should always buy the most computer that you can afford. Don't try to wait for "critical moments in time" to pass fearing that you'll purchase something just before the next new technology makes what you've bought obsolete. If you watch this industry for enough years, you'll learn that your wait will be endless.

For the foreseeable future, computer technology will always be just one step ahead of you. The only reasonable plan of action, therefore, is to get a good sense of what you want to do with your computer today, and what you'll want to be able to do in the future, and add those considerations to the question of how soon you expect to be able to comfortably afford to buy a new basic system. If you're like most people, you'd like a single computer to last your kids through high school or college, about 4 years. Frankly, that's stretching hope a little thin these days, but Peter's Principle will position you well ahead of all of the users who purchase either the least expensive or, indeed, the most expensive computer they can possibly find.

Your needs and desires will likely evolve beyond the capabilities of your computer system. At the same time, new technology will awaken needs and desires that you don't even yet know you'll have. Even ten years ago, who would have thought that commuting to work could be replaced by logging on to a computer? And yet this has been a growing reality for at least the last two years. Even selecting a healthy balance among all of the various components of your new system and always looking at your computer as an investment won't prevent those emotional moments when you realize—as I did—that your $3000 system is now selling for less than $1000. But you will be able to step back from the emotion of that moment and realize that you made the smartest purchase you could have made at the time when you decided you needed to buy a computer. Who could ask for more?

THE IDEAL FAMILY SYSTEM
HOW CAN YOU STAY UP-TO-DATE?

A variety of sources are available to you to help keep you abreast of ever-evolving (or, at least ever-changing) PC technology. The most complete and up-to-date of these are the wide array of magazines and periodicals which will give you both technical and editorial commentary. Checking your public library for recent back issues will almost always provide an article on any aspect of your system that interests you. Many weekly industry periodicals exist for those who want to read about the truly cutting-edge, but a subscription to any one of them can be quite expensive. Additionally, you will find tremendous resources in both the industry-supported and public-discussion forums on online services such as America Online and CompuServe. You'll be able to ask specific questions and get an answer, sometimes in as little as an hour. Happy shopping!

Peter Norton made his mark in the personal computing industry as a programmer, businessman, and author. He is best known for the computer programs, including the famed Norton Utilities, and books that bear his name. Mr. Norton sold his personal computing software business to Symantec Corporation in 1990 and is a noted patron of the arts and humanities in Los Angeles.

Scott Clark is the Editor of Peter Norton's computer book series. He is an accomplished writer and Windows programmer. He recently served as the primary author for the 6th edition of Peter Norton's flagship title, Inside the PC. He is a Windows programmer in Turbo Pascal and Microsoft Visual Basic.

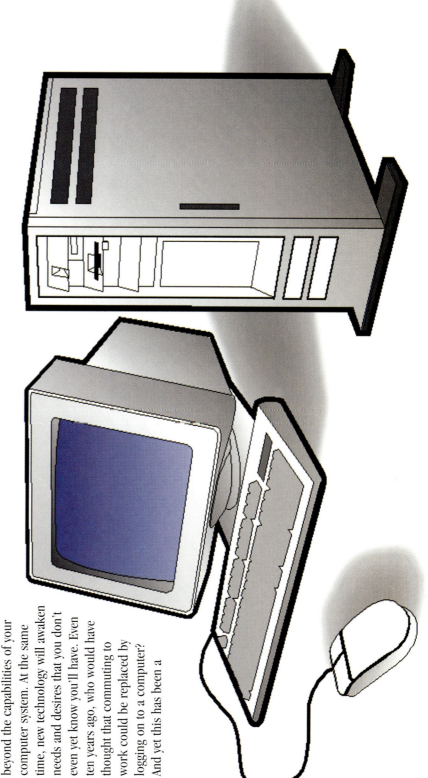

Figure 8: The Ideal Family System

OUT OF THE BOX:
WHAT HAVE I DONE NOW AND WHAT DO I DO NEXT?

By Scott Clark and Peter Norton

Where are the schools? Is there room to work? What are the neighbors like? Can you hear the kids? Can you hear the freeway? It's the same with new computers as it is with real estate: Location, location, location. Here's what to do the day you bring a new computer home.

WHERE DO I PUT IT?

One of the most important decisions you'll make about your new computer—once you've decided what you're going to buy—is where you're going to put it. Luckily, some of the questions you answered to determine what kind of computer you need will also give you the answer to where your new computer should be in your home. Even if you have very limited space for your PC, you'll want to ask some basic questions before you unpack everything. It's much easier to set up a computer than it is to move a computer that's already set up.

HOW AND WHEN WILL IT BE USED?

What are you going to do with your new PC? Are your children old enough to use it? Keep in mind that even very young children can benefit from some of the educational software on the market, so the chances are good that they are old enough to use it. Whether they're old enough to use it *on their own* is another issue, of course. The chances are good that if your child is over five years of age, she's old enough to operate your computer without additional assistance from you. Surprise, surprise. For children this old—and yet, this young—your PC will definitely look like a great toy. If you locate your computer where children have access to it and its components, be sure to teach them about thing like not spilling food and drink into the keyboard and so on.

Will your children use your computer to do homework or term papers? If you only have one computer in the house, the answer to that question is eventually going to be "yes." Many papers to be typed, and typewriters are rather middle- and high-school teachers require term scarce these days. Your children will also definitely benefit from the variety of online research sources available. At the same time, you may well want to be able to easily monitor your

child's use of those same online services, to help teach your children which features are appropriate for them and which are not.

The point, of course, is that the computer should be placed where your kids have access to it without making an unreasonable burden on you. If you live by yourself, the computer can go pretty much wherever you want it to go, with some restrictions that we'll talk about below. But the dining room table is less than a perfect location for a *family* computer. It'll make a terrible centerpiece, and mashed potatoes are hard to get out of the keyboard. Since children commonly do homework around the same time of day that meals are prepared, you can see the conflict. At the same time, if you intend to do serious work at home on your PC, you'll probably want to locate it as far away from the family television set as possible. And yet your older children might want to work on a term paper in the evening when you are doing other work that doesn't require your PC. If the PC is sitting prominently in the center of your desk in a home office, you may have to argue over who gets the chair. And even if you happen to have two chairs, you probably won't want to listen to your kids play video games while you do your taxes.

Even if there are only adults in your home, many of these points still apply. Will one person use the computer while another is watching television? Or studying? Or playing air guitar? Will a computer in the bedroom interfere with

> **Tip:** Bear in mind that to use an online service, you'll need your PC connected to the phone line. If you have only one phone jack in your home, you'll want to consider the impact on your decor of running endless phone wire, and try to place the PC appropriately. More on telephones later.

weekend naps or keep someone awake at night? Will placing the computer in the room where you normally entertain friends open it up to accidents or open you up to domestic discord?

In short, all the issues that impact any common resource in your home will impact your home computer. If it's not a common resource to you now, the computer will almost assuredly evolve into one. And however limited your uses are for it today, you will probably eventually find more uses for it than you ever dreamed. Some of those uses will, in turn, impact your PC itself. You won't be printing reports if you don't own a printer, for example. Statistically, the chances are good that you'll eventually buy a printer, rather than using someone else's constantly. Once you own the printer, you've got to have a place to put it, too. And, as you'll read about below, there are some length limitations to the cords and cables that connect the various pieces of your PC.

WILL IT HURT IF THE CAT SITS THERE?

Fortunately, assuming you have average-sized, housebroken pets, it's almost always safe to let them putter on and around the computer. You might choose not to allow them to do so, but your computer will be safe even if they do. The keyboard is probably not the best place for a catnap, but we've never seen a cat that thought it was a comfortable location, anyway. But don't be a bit surprised if your cat decides that the top of your monitor looks like a bed. It gets pretty warm up there.

If you're concerned about electrical emissions from a video monitor, be assured that today's manufacturing standards against such emissions are very strict. You may want to purchase covers for the pieces of your PC so that animal fur doesn't get into the keyboard or sucked into the PC's cooling fan, but PCs and pets usually get along very well. (Of course, always remove any cover from your monitor or system unit before

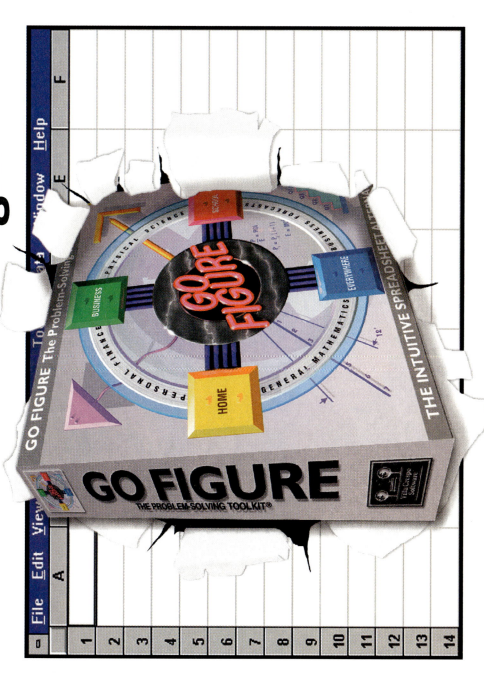

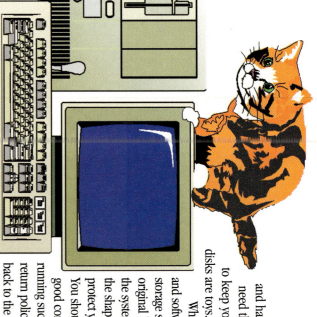

Figure 2: *If kitty decides that this is a good place for a catnap, make sure it's sturdy. Otherwise no harm done.*

and have easy access to them should you need them. There are even lockable boxes to keep young children from deciding that disks are toys.

What about the boxes your hardware and software came in? Well, if you have the storage space, save them. Your hardware's original boxes are the perfect thing to pack the system in should you ever move, because the shaped foam inserts were designed to protect your specific PC and its peripherals. You should certainly save all your boxes in good condition until your PC is set up and running successfully. Even the most generous of return policies will require that your PC come back to the store in the original box. You should expect the same for software as well. If your original diskettes are somehow defective, your retailer will almost always give you an immediate replacement set if you bring back the entire software package—disks, manuals, registration cards, and boxes.

SUPERVISION

Since you don't have to worry about your pets, that leaves you only one worry—your children. Depending on their ages, you may well want to be able to supervise their access and use of the computer. They might know perfectly well how to handle the programs you've shown them, but you may want to check to make sure your checkbook program isn't running "accidentally" some evening when the kids and their friends are gathered around. Young children may need frequent reminders regarding how to operate the computer. Or, if problems arise, they may feel embarrassed to ask for your assistance. Locating the computer where you can occasionally and casually watch their use of it will lighten that burden tremendously.

NEARBY STORAGE

One of the final things to consider about your PC is that it will expand to fill all the space you make available to it, and more. You'll want to have room for the floppy disks, the CDs and the software documentation, an integral part of your computer. True, you'll be installing software and putting the original floppy disks away, but you probably don't want to have to go to the attic and dig through boxes should you ever need those disks again. You definitely won't want to make such an expedition every time you need a manual. So plan for a shelf, to start, for your hardware and software manuals. Additionally, you'll probably want to take all of your original diskettes and keep them together in a diskette box so that you know where they are

POWER AND SAFETY ISSUES

Once you've thought about what and when and who, you'll find that there are some PC power and safety issues to consider as well. First, you should only plug your computer and its components into a grounded three-socket AC outlet (see Figure 3).

If you find the three-socket outlet unavailable in your house, you should contact an electrician to convert at least one of your old-fashioned outlet boxes to the new variety. Please, please resist the temptation to use one of those "converter" plugs to plug your new PC or its components into an old-style socket. That kind of plug can leave your PC ungrounded and could leave it—and you—susceptible to a dangerous shock.

Another electricity-related aspect of your computer is the wattage rating of its power supply. In most cases, your computer will draw between 100 and 200 watts. Nothing more than a light bulb or two. However, your PC is a lot more sensitive to variations in your electricity than are light bulbs. While a lamp might just flicker if you have it plugged into the same circuit as an air conditioner or microwave oven, your PC might shut down, and all your unsaved work could be lost. If you can, you should plug your PC into a circuit that belongs to it alone. If that's not possible, at least try to pick a circuit that has no major appliances plugged into it.

Another inexpensive way to help protect your computer against variations in your electrical supply is to use a surge protector or surge suppressor. You'll see an example in Figure 4.

Figure 3: *On the left, an ungrounded two-socket outlet; a proper, three-socket grounded outlet on the right.*

These devices cost less than $100, but if you are in an area where thunderstorms are common, or if your electric supply is subject to variations—and most are—one of these can save the thousands you've spent on your computer. You simply plug a surge suppressor into the wall socket, and then you can plug your computer, printer, and other devices into the outlets on the suppressor. Some suppressors plug directly into the wall, covering the original wall plate, while others, like the one in the illustration, double as extension cords. Their capacity ranges from as few as two sockets, to as many as eight.

The primary factor to consider when you purchase a suppressor is to be certain that you are actually buying a surge suppressor. Most hardware stores—and even some computer stores—sell multiple-outlet extension cords for only a few dollars that look exactly like a surge suppressor. Some of them even come with their own fuse. But, by the time a large enough (such that a fuse would blow) electrical anomaly passes through the system, your computer could be fried. Make sure that the product you buy indicates that it is a *surge suppressor* or *line conditioner*, suitable for use with electronic equipment. If you're not certain what you're looking at when you're in the computer store, ask the nearest employee to verify that you are indeed looking at real suppressors, not just fuse-protected power outlets.

The most reliable power protection is also the most costly, as you might expect. Emergency backup power supplies serve as line conditioners and surge suppressors. You don't need both. They also contain batteries that will power your computer

RING, RING!!

A final consideration to make about locating your new PC is whether or not you will need access to a phone line for your modem. You probably will. Fortunately, although they're not particularly attractive, phone lines can be run for hundreds and hundreds of feet, so even if you only have one phone jack in your home, you will be able to connect the phone line to your computer. Phone cables are relatively inexpensive and are commonly sold in lengths of up to 100 feet. Couplers are also sold which will allow you to string several phone cables together, making a longer cable. We don't recommend a maximum length of over 500 feet if you're using a high-speed modem, but that is by no means an absolute limit.

Figure 4: On this typical surge suppresser, the green light indicates that the surge suppresser is operating, and the red light flashes when surges are actually being removed from the current. Power "on" is indicated by the large illuminated switch.

minutes in the case of a brown- or black-out. That's long enough for you to save your data safely and shut the computer down. But be careful; some of these types of devices have been known to destroy expensive computer equipment. The safest backup power systems are known as *true sine wave* systems. This means that they actually produce a sine wave output like regular AC current. For several technical reasons, it is difficult and more costly to engineer a DC battery-powered system to produce a true sine wave, and so these are the most expensive of backup systems. At the time of this writing, the least expensive true sine-wave system was $400.

Less expensive and less careful with your hardware are the *modified sine wave* systems. They produce output which looks similar to a sine wave, but which is "squared off," so that it looks like stairsteps. And the least expensive backup systems produce square wave output. We don't recommend that you use a square wave backup system at all. True sine wave systems will identify themselves clearly on their packaging. The manufacturers of these know that they are the best. If you find a backup system that is relatively inexpensive but says nothing at all about the kind of power output it produces, you should assume it is a square wave system, since manufacturers are least likely to advertise that their product is of that type. Stay away.

If several hundred dollars seems like a lot of money for battery backup and surge protection, consider that if your computer shuts off unexpectedly, everything you've been working on that you haven't saved to disk is gone forever. Additionally, files that you had open—even if they were saved—could be permanently damaged. Worst of all, your hardware itself could be damaged or destroyed. If you are doing important work on your PC, a backup power unit is a good investment to consider when you are developing your overall data protection plan. And, of course, that plan should also include manually backing up your data, and we'll get to that important issue shortly.

will mostly be a matter of plugging the right cords into the right sockets properly. This will be easy.

Tip: Another phone-related issue to con-sider is call waiting. If you have call waiting, an incoming call will disconnect your modem. This can be extremely annoying if you're downloading files from an online service or are out there surfing the Net. (Since when do you surf in a net?) Anyway, if you have call waiting, check with your local phone company to obtain the code that will deactivate it for the duration of a single phone call. You can have your modem automatically issue that command as it dials your online service. Of course, anyone calling you while you are online will receive a busy signal.

First, look to see if your computer manual has setup instructions. They almost always do, and many manufacturers have done an absolutely excellent job of writing them. If you're not that fortunate, read on and you'll probably find everything you need to know right here.

Tech Tip: The most important thing to remember about setting up your PC is that the power cable should always be the last cable you plug in. You can seriously damage your PC or peripherals if you plug or unplug cables while the power is on.

BIT BY BIT, PUTTING IT TOGETHER . . .

Once you've decided where it's going to go, you're ready for that intense moment of elation and terror—the moment when you realize that there is "Some assembly required."

Well, relax. This is not like the proverbial child's bicycle that gets assembled at 1:00 a.m. on Christmas Eve. If I tell you that putting your system together is easy, you won't believe me. But you should. It is. First of all, the hardest jobs have already been done for you. The hard disk is connected inside your system, and since you've almost surely bought a complete system, things like the cards that drive your monitor or your communication ports will already be installed. For you, the user, setup

Figure 5: Though the most expensive of the various protection schemes, battery backup is also the safest.

First, take a look at your monitor. If it is a separate unit, it probably has a power socket similar to the one on your PC and either another socket or else a cable permanently attached. If you only have a socket, then look in your monitor packaging for the cable. Look at the cable and the socket on your monitor. You'll immediately see that one end of the cable looks similar to the socket on the monitor. Carefully push those two together. In some cases, PC cables are designed to be screwed in place so that they don't come unplugged accidentally.

Make sure that the cable is plugged in fully, and then gently tighten the screws. Don't overtighten—finger-tight is good enough. If you look at the other end of the monitor cable, you'll see a smaller connector with lots of gold pins inside. This end will plug into the video port on your PC. It may not be labeled, but the monitor cable will only fit into one socket on your computer. Just look carefully for the match, push them together gently, and thumb-tighten the screws. Plug the power cable into your monitor's socket, but don't plug the other end into the wall yet.

Next, unpack your mouse and keyboard. Depending on your particular PC, you may notice that they have exactly the same round connector on their cords, or else one may be round and one rectangular. If they are the same, look at the back of your PC to see if the two matching sockets—and they'll be right next to each other—are labeled. Sometimes one will say "Keyboard," and the other "Mouse." Sometimes there will be a picture of one or the other over the socket. And in some cases, there will be no labeling at all, or else both ports will be labeled with the same picture or words. If the sockets are labeled differently, gently plug the mouse cable into the mouse port and the keyboard cable into the keyboard port. Otherwise, toss a coin and plug in the two devices. Generally, you'll find small arrows on the connectors themselves which will help you orient the connectors—which are generally round—with the sockets. (The arrow usually

Figure 7: A 25-pin COM (serial) port.

plugs in on top.) In a very few cases, your mouse will actually plug into your keyboard.

If your keyboard and mouse have dramatically different connectors, your keyboard port will almost always be labeled "Keyboard." Your mouse port, however, may be labeled "Mouse," or it may be labeled "Serial Port", "COM 1" or "COM-A." In any event, as with your video monitor, there will be exactly one socket into which your mouse connector will fit properly. If your mouse has a rectangular connector, it will also have thumbscrews like the monitor cable. Gently tighten those after plugging in the mouse. You may also notice a larger port labeled "COM-B" or "COM-2". This is your second external serial port, and it is where you will attach any external modem that you may purchase.

Many computer systems are also sold complete with a printer. Printers plug into your PC's parallel port. The parallel port on your PC looks exactly like the 25-pin serial port in Figure 7. It should be labeled "Parallel," or "Printer," however. You'll have one large serial port and one large parallel port, so if one is labeled and the other is not, you still know which is which. The other end of your printer cable will either be a 25-pin screw-in cable like the one that plugs into your computer, or else it will be a large capital-D shaped connector that locks in place on your printer by means of two triangular wire latches. Your printer will also have a power socket and cable like your PC and your monitor.

Believe it or not, if you've just about done. Go back through the steps and gently check that all the connectors are seated properly. Finger-tighten the thumbscrews if you didn't do so earlier. Finally, look on the back of your PC to see if you have a female power socket as well as a male socket. If you do, then your PC is designed to turn your monitor on and off when you turn the computer on and off. Plug the monitor's power cable into the female socket on the back of your PC, and set the switch on your monitor to "on," or the number "1," as you'll often see "on" referred to in computerese. Next, make sure that your printer is turned off, and plug its power cord in. Finally, connect your PC's power cord to the male connector on the back of your PC, and plug the other end into your power source.

Figure 6: With a battery backup when the power goes out—or just goes down to brown—you'll be happy your work is safe.

Figure 8: A male and a female connector.

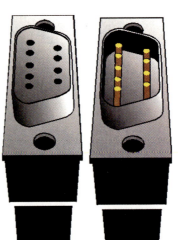

> **Tech Tip:** In computer parlance, a connector that has pins on it, as at the top of Figure 8, is referred to as a "male" connector. The corresponding socket with holes in it, as at the bottom of Figure 8, is called a "female" connector.

> **Tip:** Of course, your power source is coming through a surge-suppressor, right?

YOUR FIRST STARTUP

It's time to hit that power switch. Gather everyone around and—with proper ceremony, of course—punch it! These days, most new PCs are designed to "wow" you with a fancy multimedia presentation the first time that you turn the system on. You may have the option of a guided tour as well. Particularly if you're a new user, sit back and enjoy! You can always re-run these presentations later if you want, so rest assured that each family member can work through the introductory fun. Later, you'll probably want to remove the demonstration files from your hard disk because they inevitably eat up a lot of space. The introduction program will have an option for deleting itself that makes the task a snap.

Figure 9: Finally, it's time to hit the power switch.

> **Tip:** If you get any errors the first time you turn your computer on, turn the power off and re-check your connections. If the specific error you see identifies itself as a keyboard error, chances are very good that you have two similar ports for keyboard and mouse and that you have the devices reversed. Switch those two connections, and try again. If you still get an error, write the error down and call your retailer or manufacturer immediately.

AND YOUR FIRST BACKUP

Most new systems also now give you the option of copying everything on the hard disk onto floppies the first time you turn on the power. Such a copy is called a backup. While this can take between 20 and 30 high-density (1.44MB) floppy diskettes, it's still an excellent idea. Yes, it takes awhile and it's annoying when you want to get right into actually using your computer. But, by backing up everything on your hard disk when the computer is fresh out of the box, you'll be easily able to return your computer to that pristine state should you ever need to do so.

But this is an excellent opportunity for us to plug the idea of backing up your data. Nothing—not a surge protector, not even a backup battery—is ultimately as secure a way to safeguard your data against loss (or theft) than a backup. If your work is lost through either an act of a god or man, your data will still be safe on the backup media. In even a worst-case scenario, such as a fire in the home, if you store your backups at another location or inside a special fireproof data box, the most valuable part of your computer system, your work, will still be safe.

We generally recommend that you back up your important data in this manner: assuming you start this process on a Friday afternoon, first, make a full backup of everything on your hard disk and put that set of disks or tape away safely. Label this tape "Friday #1." You'll use a total of six tapes, incidentally. On Monday and Wednesday, use a second ("Monday #1") and third ("Wednesday #1") tape to make incremental backups. These are a lot quicker than a full backup because you'll only be saving the files that have changed since the previous backup. Then, on Friday, label a new tape "Friday #2" and make a full backup. Repeat the incrementals with new "Monday #2" and "Wednesday #2" tapes. Then, on the third Friday, re-use your "Friday #1" tape.

This cyclical method ensures that, at the most, you will lose only two days' work. Of course, you can make backups every day if you desire. We do. Your incremental backups safeguard the files that you work with during the week. The cyclical method—and the reason you use two sets of tapes—also protects the data on your hard disk that supposedly hasn't changed, for up to two weeks. Of course, you could use three full sets of tapes, and be safeguarded against old data being lost for three weeks, or four, and so on. The amount of effort it takes you to perform regular backups will amount to nothing compared to the stress and effort you'll experience if you lose just one vital file.

Your new system may even have come with a **tape drive** already installed to make backing-up your data less effort-consuming. We talked about these devices in the "Selecting a New Computer" article earlier in

Figure 1: If several family members will be using the computer, decide who gets it when and for how long.

the *Encyclopedia*. High-end systems may even come with **optical disks** or recordable CDs for backup. At the other end of the economic scale, you may have only floppy disks available for use. The backup software that comes with Windows 3 supports backup to floppy disks only. Windows 95 automatically supports backup to floppy disks and the most inexpensive types of tape drive. With either **OS**, you can purchase third-party software that will support backup to the higher-quality and faster **DAT** (Digital Audio Tape) drives and to optical disks. If your system came with DAT or an optical disk pre-installed, that software will already be on your system. All of these technologies are viable backup solutions—but just how viable each is depends on your data.

Certainly, once you have any large amount of data at all, backup to floppy disk is simply too much work to handle. Even with data compression, your 100MB hard disk will still take nearly 50 floppy disks for a full backup. Chances are good, too, that you don't have a 100MB hard disk; you probably have a 840MB hard disk, or larger. You can generally figure two minutes of time per diskette. Talk about a job you can leave to your children! Additionally, at about a dollar per floppy disk, this is some of the most expensive media around, and that's something to consider when you're weighing the cost of different backup options. And if you have a lot of large files, like graphics files often are, you'll find the number of diskettes you need is soaring because graphics files are often already compressed and will not compress much more when the backup program tries to write them to floppy disk. (Text files, on the other hand, shrink dramatically.) A disk-based solution to the "1,001 Diskettes" option is optical disks and recordable CDs. Optical disks themselves are relatively less expensive, but optical disk drives start at about $1,000 and get more expensive from there. They are also very slow.

That leaves tape—and particularly, DAT tape—as your most cost-effective option. First of all, most tape drives can store at least 350MB on one tape, and DAT tapes can hold up to 6GB! Not bad for a $12.00 tape, eh? Additionally, using tape for backup can relieve you of most or all of the work involved. If you have less data to backup than will fit onto a tape, you can start the backup process and leave. Software that supports tape drives

option to read all your data off the tape when the backup is complete to verify that no errors were made during the copy process. If errors did occur, the software will automatically try to eliminate those errors. Fortunately, tape drives of all varieties—and again, particularly DAT—are extremely reliable. We've backed-up over 1.5GB of data every week for two years now and have never experienced an error on any tape. Additionally, no one has to sit and swap hundreds and hundreds of floppy disks for hours to get the job done.

Tape is also far more cost-effective than floppies. DAT drives are more expensive than QIC and other format drives, but the cost of a DAT tape is much more reasonable than other formats (a QIC tape costs about the same as a DAT tape—$12.00—but you'll only get 350MB of storage, instead of up to 6GB).

Figure 10: DAT tape is by far the most cost-effective backup tactic—particularly if you work with graphics. It costs about $2 per gigabyte.

Scott Clark *is the editor of Peter Norton's computer book series. He is an accomplished writer and Windows programmer. He recently served as the primary author for the sixth edition of Peter Norton's flagship title,* Inside The PC. *He is a Windows programmer in Turbo Pascal and Microsoft Visual Basic.*

Peter Norton *made his mark in the personal computing industry as a programmer, businessman and author. He is best known for the computer programs, including the famed Norton Utilities, and books that bear his name. Mr. Norton sold his personal computing software business to Symantec Corporation in 1990 and is a noted patron of the arts and humanities in Los Angeles.*

DID THEY MEAN PLUG & PLAY OR PLUG & PRAY?

By Scott Clark and Peter Norton

If you heard anything about computers in the mid-1990s, you heard about Windows 95 and Plug & Play. Looking at it from one perspective, Windows 95 was supposed to be revolutionary. You'll read about how and how well Windows 95 fulfills its promises elsewhere in this Encyclopedia. Plug & Play, in a manner of speaking, was supposed to do for hardware what Windows 95 was going to do for software.

PLUG & PLAY: HELP OR HYPE?

If you've ever installed a card in a PC, you are already well-aware of the nightmare that it can be. Between IRQ, DMA, and a host of other acronyms and jargon—even the most skilled among us shudders at the thought. In fact, Scott kept himself very busy a few months ago, installing sound cards for a number of skilled users because he was the only one among them who could make the things work properly.

The essential problem is that hardware devices and PC systems are all made by different companies, so there is no standard way to guarantee—or to even *attempt* to guarantee—that they will work together properly. The potential for conflict abounds with multiple devices vying for the same memory locations and the same <u>interrupts</u> within your computer. As Microsoft has correctly observed, the expansion of the market for third-party PC devices has been significantly diminished because many, many users are simply afraid to enter into the process of configuring new hardware—a process which has the potential of rendering your *existing* hardware inoperative.

HOW IT WAS SUPPOSED TO WORK

Plug and Play started out as a dream of how things should be. You plug a peripheral into the computer, and it works. Rather like your toaster, with the threat of jammed, smoking English muffins eliminated. No cumbersome installation instructions, no nightmares, ideally not even any device drivers or installation software to run. By manufacturing devices which adhered to the quickly trademarked Plug & Play standard (developed initially by Microsoft, Compaq, and Intel, and now watchdogged by the independent Plug & Play Association), original equipment manufacturers (OEMs) could produce devices that would tell your computer what they are and what resources they need. Similarly, the computer

> *Tech Tip:* New motherboards and BIOSs are being designed for Pentium- and higher-class future processors which will have at least twice as many interrupts available.

Everywhere You Look: Conflict

A brief illustration will explain what *conflict* means when that word is used to describe a problem between devices attached to your PC. This isn't a perfect analogy; it's more of an allegory. Imagine that you have one of those universal remotes designed to control both your television and your VCR. Those remote controls work because every device they control has a uniquely defined set of commands which the device responds to. Consider how annoyed you'd be if every time you changed the channel on your TV, the VCR started recording, or if fast-forwarding a videotape turned your television off. That's the kind of thing that could happen if the TV and the VCR were responding to the same codes and stepping on each other's toes. Fortunately, there is communication between the various manufacturers of televisions and VCR, and there are also an almost infinite number of digital codes that can be used to control these devices. It's very unlikely, therefore, that a conflict will occur.

Also, the resources inside your PC are anything but infinite. Indeed, there are only *16* channels through which peripherals like a modem or sound card can talk to the microprocessor inside your computer. And most of these channels are already used fulfilling vital tasks like controlling your hard disks, your mouse and printer ports, and so on. (Technically, these channels are referred to as *interrupts*.)

Even though the channels are limited, peripherals nonetheless require unique channels. You can envision the havoc if your hard disk responded to a

modem command and thought it was hearing an "erase everything" command. Fortunately, that kind of mistake is almost impossible, but what is very possible and what has happened often in the past is that your computer will "lock up," and you'll lose any unsaved writing or drawing you've been doing. You have to press Ctrl+Alt+Del to restart the computer and at least prior to Windows 95 this meant that any work in RAM memory that you hadn't saved to a disk just evaporated. (In Windows 95, you can press Ctrl+Alt+Del and generally manage to save data in any running applications except the one that caused the computer to freeze. Sometimes, this technique of shutting down one "task" (program) is a lifesaver.)

There's a similar conflict problem involving computer memory. You probably already know that if two applications try to use the same memory locations at the same time, problems will ensue. It's the same with hardware. If your computer monitor and your sound card try to store their data in the same memory locations, the data of one will replace the data of the other. When the first device tries to access its data, it will find data that makes no sense to it. At the very least, you'll have to restart your PC, again losing everything that's not saved.

Computer cards and peripherals use a special kind of "memory" (not really memory at all, but it's used somewhat similarly) to communicate with the Central Processing Unit (CPU), the computer *inside* your computer. These are the Input/Output Addresses, or simply I/O addresses. Most devices need not only a unique IRQ, but a range of I/O addresses that are not being used by any other device.

would get identifying information from every installed device, and could internally juggle IRQs, memory requirements, and so on to prevent conflicts from happening. And all of this inside the box, with no effort on the user's part.

HOW IT WORKED BEFORE MID-1995

At first things didn't work quite that way for a number of reasons. Many early "Plug and Play Ready" devices didn't adhere to the P&P standard because they were manufactured before the standard existed. Additionally, virtually no PC systems manufactured before the advent of the PCI-bus came with the hardware support necessary to receive and make use of true P&P information that the third party devices provided. While Plug and Play is not actually tied to any given bus standard (like PCI, local bus, ISA, etc.), manufacturers chose to not implement Plug & Play in pre-PCI machines because it was widely believed that the PCI bus would very quickly become the standard of choice at about the same time that true Plug and Play devices would be on the shelves in quantity.

AND NOW...

Plug and Play systems are the obvious new standard at the time of this writing. It seems likely that "how it was supposed to work" and "how it will work" will be one and the same, under certain conditions. Plug and Play compliant systems—when used in conjunction solely with Plug and Play devices—can, in fact, read identifying data from those devices, and can allocate available memory and interrupts as necessary, to make all the devices work harmoniously together. Part of adhering to this new standard is the understanding that no device should insist on having a particular interrupt or a particular location in memory. All such aspects of communication between your P&P PC and its P&P peripherals are supposed to be left to the discretion of the system itself. But what happens if you just bought a new non-Plug and Play internal 28.8 modem? Or if you just bought a new PCI-bus Pentium 120 machine with a non-Plug and Play BIOS? Are you doomed to suffer the same incompatibility nightmares of the past?

Tech Tip: Apple Macintosh computers have had basic plug and play capabilities for over a decade. With the advent of the PCI bus, however, the same Plug and Play-compatible PCI card that works in your PC-compatible will also work in your PCI-bus Macintosh. Similarly, a Plug and Play PCMCIA modem—and even some SRAM cards—bought for your Apple Powerbook will plug directly into your PC, under Windows 95. Depending on exactly how you use your twin-platform system, you may be able to save a lot of money by, for example, buying one PCMCIA modem for the road, and using it in your desktop PC.

WINDOWS 95 BEYOND PLUG AND PLAY

If you're using Windows 95, you aren't doomed to the old plug and pray bad dreams. Obviously, it's likely that even if you did just buy a new Plug and Play computer, you don't want to have to replace all of your existing peripherals as well. Fortunately Windows 95 can bridge the gap between legacy hardware and the P&P future.

Tip: Legacy is the PC industry's polite way of saying old. It's more marketing than it is good English, but, like most jargon, once you know what it means, somehow it seems to make sense.

The Registry

Windows 95 Registry is based on an idea that Microsoft first implemented in **Windows NT**. It is a single database in which is stored both the hardware and software configuration data for your PC and for every peripheral device that you have ever installed in your PC. You can look at the Registry's contents by using the Device Manager. The .INI files used for Windows 3.1 are now obsolete; applications instead register the settings that are used with Windows 95, which updates the Registry. Among other things, this makes it easier for network supervisors to remotely configure your computer—the Registry on any machine is accessible via the network, without the hassle of tracking down all the individual .INI files.

When you install a new device for the first time, all of its installation requirements are stored in the Registry, both to alleviate possible conflicts between devices and also to permit painless removal and reinstallation of devices. When a configured device is removed from your system, the Registry works with Windows 95 to de-allocate that device's resources and make them available.

Additionally, Windows 95 implements a technology called *"Dynaload Drivers."* A *driver* is the system software needed to control a *device* (a piece of hardware.) Information about device drivers required by specific devices is now also stored in the Registry, allowing these drivers to be unloaded. This way, when the device they control is not present, the memory these drivers used can also be made available for other purposes.

A NEW PC AND LEGACY PERIPHERALS

If you have a new Plug and Play system but don't wish to buy all new Plug & Play peripherals—which could cost you half as much again as did your new system—Windows 95 will store information about your legacy devices' requirements (say an old video capture card that must operate on IRQ 7) in the Windows 95 Registry.

Tech Tip: You can access the Device Manager by clicking on the *Start* button, then choosing *Settings, Control Panel.* Finally, double-click on the *System* icon. Power users will prefer a shorter path: just right-click on the *My Computer* desktop icon and choose *Properties* from the pop-up context menu.

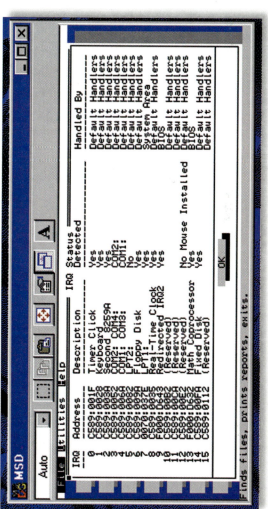

Figure 1: The 16 interrupts and their assignments on a typical PC.

Whenever you unplug or reinsert that video card, Windows 95 will recognize the fact and will aid in the shuffling of resource to accommodate older devices that are not as flexible as the new Plug and Play peripherals.

Of course, if you have a legacy device that requires a specific memory address, and a Plug and Play device is already using that address, Windows 95 will tell your Plug and Play hardware to simply use a different memory location. The basic theory of Plug and Play is if it's in the way, just move it.

Similarly, if you have two legacy devices that both want the same resources by default, but can be set to use other resources, as is most often the case, Windows 95 will notify you of the conflict when you insert the second legacy device. Windows will step you through the short process of telling one of the devices, essentially, to get out of the way, and will store that information in the Registry. The next time you insert that legacy hardware, it automatically reconfigures itself to use the (available) resources you've selected. (Again, if a Plug and Play device has been assigned to that resource while the legacy device was uninstalled, the P&P peripheral will automatically move out of the way, taking the path of least resistance.)

Figure 2: The Device Manager

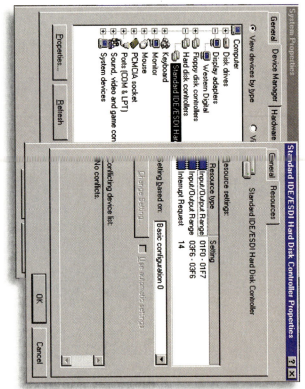

A LEGACY PC WITH P&P PERIPHERALS

If you own a legacy computer which does not have Plug & Play implementation, Windows 95 will do its best to take care of your needs, too. And "its best" is pretty impressive. Windows will compensate for your system's lack of Plug & Play BIOS support by using the Registry to allocate and record information about any Plug and Play peripherals. When a conflict occurs between two devices, Windows 95 will serve the BIOS function of telling one of the devices to "get out of the way," seamlessly. Windows 95 will also accommodate any device that it cannot automatically reconfigure (these should be rare among true Plug and Play peripherals), again taking the path of least resistance. Essentially, by running Windows 95 on a legacy computer, you get a synergy which very closely approximates owning a true Plug and Play computer incorporated into the small cost of Windows 95. This feature is most effective when you use true P&P peripherals, but there is also significant benefit even when installing, removing, or reinstalling legacy peripherals.

LEGACY SOFTWARE AND WINDOWS 95

A small body of legacy software exists which expects to find certain pieces of hardware at certain interrupt or memory locations. Games, in particular, have been infamous for this. Under Windows 95, if, for example, your legacy software is looking for a sound card at interrupt 5 and *only* at interrupt 5, but your sound card has been configured for interrupt 7, Windows 95 can re-route the software's calls to interrupt 7 automatically, so that the software is, essentially, "tricked" into believing that it is still addressing interrupt 5.

TROUBLESHOOTING UNDER WINDOWS 3.1 AND DOS

If you're working on a non-Plug and Play system, and you're not running Windows 95, my first recommendation is to upgrade to Windows 95. If that's not an option, for whatever reason, then sooner or later you'll find yourself wading through at least some of the bad dreams (I won't quite call them all nightmares) that installing things can be. We'll talk about installation of both hardware and software in the next section. First, here are some tips about what to do when something is installed and it doesn't seem to work right.

Multimedia, the wave of the 1990s, brought with it the hidden curse of the "multimedia upgrade kit." I like to abbreviate it MUK and pronounce it *muck*, as in swamp. I realized that MUKs are like a board game; the first person to take a perfectly working computer, add a CD-ROM drive, a sound card, a video accelerator and a pair of speakers, and end up with a perfectly working computer, wins.

It was no surprise, really, when in mid-1995 a computer magazine reported that approximately 75 percent of all products returned to computer stores are multimedia kits that users couldn't install. Some of those users even had to call the manufacturers of the kit or of their PC system to get their *computer* to work again *after* they decided to give up the installation attempt. The first sound card that Scott attempted to install—after working with computers for over a decade—still took him about four hours, and required him to completely reinstall Windows halfway through the process.

There are several solutions to this sort of problem. One tactic is to buy a preconfigured system, with all the options that you want to own preinstalled for you. The manufacturer or retailer plugs everything in and tests it to make certain that it's working before giving you the system.

Regardless of how experienced you are, if you've just purchased a preconfigured system directly from the manufacturer and it doesn't work properly "out of the box," you should stop immediately. If the system doesn't turn on, or if the printer doesn't print at all, or that sort of thing, check first to make certain that all of the cables are tightly in their sockets and are connected in accordance with the setup instructions. If, however, everything seems to be plugged in properly, or if everything works except, for example, the CD-ROM drive doesn't do anything, then it's time to call the manufacturer's technical support department. If you have difficulty reaching them—and you may—then call your salesperson directly and let him know that you're having problems. They may be able to connect you with technical support via an express route. Certainly, your salesman will be aware that you purchased your system with at least a 30-day return policy and that you're free to take your business elsewhere if you don't get satisfaction.

Especially at this very early stage in your ownership of their product, the manufacturer's tech support should be willing to talk you through a step-by-step process of trying to figure out why your new system is faulty. If you have problems "communicating" with a tech support employee, ask to speak with her or his supervisor. Remember that you do always have the option—however inconvenient—of returning the system if there are problems. Some of the largest manufacturers, like IBM and Compaq, even offer technical assistance and repair right in your home or office, free of charge.

Most likely, however, your preconfigured system will run beautifully, at least until you decide to add hardware later. At that point, problems can again arise. While your manufacturer will definitely guarantee that everything he sells you will work together, getting help for adding third-party devices sometimes is another matter.

EXPANDING A PRECONFIGURED SYSTEM

Consider, for example, the purchase made by an attorney friend who bought six preconfigured high-end networked PCs from a major mail-order reseller. These PCs were packed to the gills with all the goodies that the manufacturer offered in a custom preconfiguration. They did not, however, come with SCSI cards to support the external DAT tape backup drives that the law office had to purchase from another source. Hours were spent trying to get the SCSI cards to work properly—normally a comparatively easy task. Eventually, the mail-order tech support was called and told the problem. It turned out that these computers were so packed full of peripherals that one of the resources required by the SCSI cards—an interrupt (IRQ) channel—was not available. All of the available interrupts were already assigned to existing devices! This problem was only solved in a cumbersome and roundabout way. (Ironically, SCSI can help solve the IRQ crunch because you can attach up to seven hardware devices [hard drives, CD-ROMS, scanners, tape drives, and more] to a single SCSI card which only requires one IRQ.)

At the very least, a Plug and Play system or any hardware running Windows 95 would have identified the problem the first time that SCSI card was installed. The hours of checking first to see if one DAT drive, or one SCSI card, or this computer system was defective would have been eliminated. Under Windows 3.1, several steps were necessary to try to isolate the problem, even with the manufacturer's assistance over the phone. These steps approximate the process you will normally go through when troubleshooting hardware under Windows 3.1 and DOS.

IT'S A TWELVE--, UH, THREE-STEP METHOD

The first thing you'll want to do when you encounter what appears to be a hardware malfunction is to look in the documentation for the device to see if there is a troubleshooting section. In a surprisingly high number of cases, you'll find information there that will help you fix the problem. It's true that a minority of troubleshooting sections read like this:

Problem: The device won't turn on.

Solution: Make sure the device is plugged in.

but they are definitely in the minority. More often you will find that manufacturers have performed hours and hours of testing their equipment and have isolated many common difficulties that users have experienced. (They want you happy. And they don't want you tying up their tech support lines with common and easily solved problems.)

It's possible that you may find solutions in the troubleshooting section that seem too technical or complex for you. Don't worry if the manual suggests that you try different combinations of six jumpers and two DIP switches, and you don't know what a jumper is. You always have the third step available to you, so read on.

If you've just finished installing a device for the first time, you should also step yourself back through the installation instructions. Make certain that you haven't inadvertently forgotten to perform any of the steps or a part of a step.

The peripheral probably included some software you have to install. Most do. If you are running under Windows 3.X, try re-running the setup program. If you made any nondefault (or "express" or "typical") installation choices the first time through, this time choose only the default options suggested by the manufacturer. If this first step fails to solve the problem for a first-time installation, move on to step three.

Generally, the second step in the troubleshooting process is useful if you're experiencing only partial performance from a peripheral. If, for example, your sound and video capture card is only capturing video, or if your 64-bit video adapter is only displaying black and white, try *Windows Help.*

In many cases, by using the Search capability of the Windows Help system, you can search through a help document that was stored on your hard disk when you ran an installation program for a particular piece of hardware. Many manufacturers also store trouble-shooting suggestions and important last-minute information about the peripheral in the Help file. (Also look for a file like "README.TXT" or "README.WRI" on the installation disk or CD-ROM.) Often, hardware difficulties stem not from improper installation but from configuring support software incorrectly. While a Plug and Play system would solve the problem of making sure that your modem software knows where your modem is installed, Plug and Play would have no way of knowing that your video card might default to *not* recording sound, to save disk space. That kind of information *will* be available in the product's online help.

The final step in the troubleshooting process is to ask a human being for help. This doesn't necessarily mean that you should call the manufacturer and wait for 30 minutes on long

---

Tech Tip: When stepping through the installation instructions again, if you decide to remove the device and actually reinstall it, make certain that you turn off your computer before you unplug it, whether it is an internal or external device.

Tip: When you're buying a system direct from the manufacturer, remember that system resources—not just physical card slots—determine how many devices your PC can actually support. If you expect to keep the computer for several years and expand it later, you should talk to someone who can advise you regarding how many system resources will be left free after your time-of-purchase devices have been installed.

Read Docs, Read Help, Ask for Help

Figure 3: The Three Steps To Troubleshooting

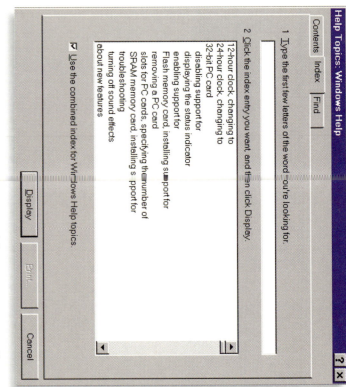

Figure 4: The Windows 95 Help Index allows you to search for answers to common problems.

distance before you get past the voicemail system. Support groups for types of hardware (like modems, sound cards, and so on) and for specific brands and models of hardware exist on every online service. You will find hundreds or thousands of users like yourself who have had a variety of experiences.

So dial-up America Online, CompuServe, Prodigy, or The Microsoft Network. Search the online service for the name of your manufacturer. Sometimes the company-specific support areas—called *forums* or *boards* (from the old Bulletin Board System, or BBS)—are formally or informally monitored by company employees. You can post a question about your problem to see if anyone else has experienced and solved your problem. It's not uncommon for a major online service to find an answer to your question within an hour. (You can even use the board's message search feature to see if the topic of your problem has *already* been discussed.)

Many manufacturers also operate their own BBS systems which are free for their customers. Although these are rarely toll-free calls, you can still log on to their system and post a question. The company's technical support staff will respond to your question, usually within 24 hours. Additionally, manufacturers often accept technical questions via fax. Just fax your question and they will either fax you or call you with a reply.

Tip: Some manufacturers have a voice-mail system you can call and listen to the most commonly asked troubleshooting questions and answers about their products.

Of course, if you choose the online service, or the BBS or fax option, you will have to wait for a reply. And if the reply doesn't solve the problem, you will have to wait again. So, the logical

that your local retailer will suggest you bring the system back to the store for them to examine. There should never be a charge for such an examination, and if you purchased your system under a return policy, the retailer will be responsible for replacing any defective part immediately—assuming the part is in stock—rather than making you resort to the system's warranty repair policy.

If you have purchased your system from a mail-order retailer or manufacturer, their technical support department is the place to call.

If you are adding a device to a system, old or new, the manufacturer of that device will almost always offer technical support. If they don't (as is the case with certain very-low-cost generic peripherals), then you should turn to the store that sold you the product. If they can't or won't help you make it work, they should give you your money back. Generally, however, you will find that a manufacturer is willing to spend the necessary time with you, finding out information about your system and exploring possible problems. This information can help them, too, in the future. You become an unwitting extension of their R&D department.

When you call for technical support, ask first for the support operator's direct extension, or their name so that you can speak directly to them again should you need to call back. It is not unusual for a tech support person to instruct you to perform some lengthy task—say, reinstalling the support software—and then call them back to continue the support process. If you have waited at length on hold to reach that person, verify that you will have immediate access to them when you call back. If they tell you that you will need to wait again, ask to speak to their supervisor. That level of customer support is unacceptable. Particularly if you are paying for the call, the support operator

should be willing to stay on the phone with you while you solve the problem together, or at least answer directly when you call back.

If you are having problems with a system which you bought from a local retailer, call the retailer first. If you are having a conflict between installed devices, the manufacturer of any one of those devices may not be able to get enough information about your system and all its peripherals to solve your problem in a timely fashion. But do be prepared for the possibility

alternative if you need an answer *now* is to call for technical support.

It's also not unusual for a technical support operator to ask you to either read information off of your screen or to use a utility program to print out information about your system and fax it to them. They will talk you through either process, have no fear. Don't feel intimidated by a technical support operator. If you reach an operator who is apparently having a bad day, ask to speak with another operator. You are, after all, their customer. And your problem isn't imbecility; it's merely understandable ignorance of the complexities of their intractable device. Be comfortable insisting on having things explained if you are not comfortable performing them. That is the support operator's job. If it makes you feel any better, consider the fact that computer manuals are some of the worst-written books you'll ever find. More often than not, problems that you encounter are not your fault.

You might also feel intimidated by the length of time it seems to take to solve a hardware problem over the phone. Chances are good that you're simply seeing an indication of how desperately Plug and Play is needed. The operator will work with you even if you need to turn off your computer, remove the device or card, make physical changes to the hardware, reinsert it, and turn your computer on again. And again. That's their job.

For those of us with computers purchased in the last couple of years, our struggle isn't yet over, although Windows 95 goes a long way to making it easier to manage hardware devices. But in the near future, we can look forward to a time when computers are not only easy to use; they're easy to live with, too. Thanks to Plug and Play, that promise may become reality.

Scott Clark is the editor of Peter Norton's computer book series. He is an accomplished writer and Windows programmer. He recently served as the primary author for the sixth edition of Peter Norton's flagship title, Inside The PC. He is a Windows programmer in Turbo Pascal and Microsoft Visual Basic.

Peter Norton made his mark in the personal computing industry as a programmer, businessman and author. He is best known for the computer programs, including the famed Norton Utilities, and books that bear his name. Mr. Norton sold his personal computing software business to Symantec Corporation in 1990 and is a noted patron of the arts and humanities in Los Angeles.

TRANSLATING INSTALLATION INSTRUCTIONS INTO PLAIN ENGLISH

By Peter Norton and Scott Clark

When you wander through the software aisles of your favorite local computer store, do you ever feel as though you need a doctorate in computer science and a masters in advanced linguistics to understand the package information, much less install the software? Here's hope and help...

If you've ever installed a new program or new hardware into your computer, you might have come to the conclusion that the people who write documentation sit around in smoke-filled rooms, sadistically trying to find new ways to make simple jobs difficult.

Most of the time, that's not the case.

Sometimes you have to wonder, though, when you've just been through a 20-step installation process, you didn't understand any of it, the product isn't working properly, and step number 21 says:

> 21) If the widget doesn't seem to be bifurcating properly, simply repeat this installation procedure, using the correct values instead of the values suggested here.

And we're certainly all familiar with the infamous kind of "translated" instructions that read like a Winston Churchill joke:

> Possible greater capacity than the 528MB limit on the drive when jumper 1 is

After over a decade of personal computing, manufacturers are finally realizing that if you and I can't successfully install something, we'll return it to the store. Unfortunately, at least in the case of software manufacturers, they have responded by simply pressuring stores to not accept returns of

opened software. You open it, you can't make it work, you still own it. Combine this with the trend away from toll-free technical support, and it's no wonder that pre-configured systems are selling faster than they can be assembled. Of course, there's simply no chance at all that you'll be able to buy a preconfigured system with every program and device you'll ever want preinstalled. At some point, you'll be opening up the system to add a peripheral, or running a setup program to install the newest version of your word processor.

The key to success is a little learning on everyone's part—yours and the manufacturers. For their part, manufacturers have greatly improved the quality of their instructions over what they were a decade ago. Back then, there was an assumption—more or less correct—that if you were tinkering inside your computer, you already knew what you were doing. That assumption allowed documentation writers to write sentences like:

> Use a generic text editor to modify any settings that do not adhere to the required setup configuration; this must be done manually...

> ...while keeping a straight face. The learning on your part lies in deciphering...

WHAT THEY SAY VS WHAT THEY MEAN

If you've been a doctor all your life, you might not think twice about referring to a *tibia*. Lawyers take a certain glee in discussing *ex parte* matters ad absurdum. If you're in construction you know what R15 refers to and so on. It's not really surprising, then, that computer people—

and by that I mean people who work in the computer industry—get used to thinking in jargon, too. It isn't so much of a problem when it happens amongst a group of friends, one of whom is a doctor or a construction worker, because in a personal setting, you can always ask for an explanation. It's a different matter, however, when it comes to writing instructions for installing software onto one of over 140 million Windows-based PCs——then communication breakdowns become disasters. Very simply put, therefore, installing software just means that you're going to place a copy of it onto your computer's hard disk before you use it the first time. Simple enough. But why is it even necessary?

Years ago, even a word processor was a small program, and everything that went into making up that program could fit in one or two files. Back before hard disks existed—yes, it's true—even professional programs had to fit onto a single floppy disk, along with the entire operating system! If they didn't, the user would have to swap diskettes back and forth so that programs could get whatever resources they needed. We did this a *lot* in the early days of PCs.

Today's applications provide so much power that they are complex and large monsters compared to those early programs. Why, the operating system that I'm running now is using up over 50MB of hard disk space! That's over 100 of those first floppy disks for the operating system alone! Without hard disks for mass storage, nothing like Windows or your 3D chess program or a spreadsheet could have ever existed. The code necessary to make that sort of program available to you just takes up too much space.

But you can't exactly distribute programs on hard disks. Nobody would buy *Stevie Bear Teaches Reading* if that $20.00 program came attached to a $250.00 piece of hardware. And so floppy disks evolved from being the permanent storage medium of choice to a temporary storage format. Temporary because, today, when you buy a new piece of software, the first thing you'll do is copy files off of the original floppy disks copy files off of the original floppy disks onto your hard disk, and then you'll put these floppy disks away. From that moment on—unless you ever need to reinstall the program—you'll work with the copy of the program that is on your hard disk.

Tip: Actually, the first thing many people do when ready to install a new program is make a copy of each of the program's original floppy diskettes. Then, they put the original diskettes in a safe place and install the program from the copies they've just made. That way, if the copies fail or are damaged somehow, they can always bring out their original disks and make a new set of copies. If you use your original diskettes and they get damaged, you may have to wait for the software manufacturer to mail you a new set of disks.

Aside from the space requirements of modern programs, there are two reasons why you'll generally work from programs which are stored on your hard disk: the hard disk installed inside your system's case is a lot more durable, in the long run, than those plastic floppy disks, and it's a *lot* faster, too. Your hard disk is also much faster than your CD-ROM drive, which is why most software that is distributed on CD-ROM is copied—at least in part—to your hard disk before you use it.

Tip: Some programs, especially multimedia games, will copy large quantities of data over to your hard disk so that the excitement of playing doesn't have to diminish while you're waiting for the CD-ROM drive to load and reload frequently used parts of the game. You don't usually have to allow the program to do this. You may be short on hard disk space, for example. But you will usually notice a big degradation in the speed of game play if you don't.

Fortunately, all of this copying and installing is taken care of for you by an installation or setup

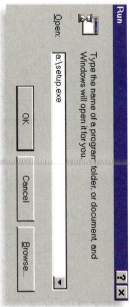

Figure 2: The Run dialog box with an install program ready to run.

Figure 1: Selecting Start /Settings /Control Panel in Windows 95.

program. You'll see both terms now, more out of habit than anything else. Originally, "install," was the common term, and that's all you did: copied the files to your hard disk. Any configuration or "set-up" had to be done the first time you actually ran the program. When those two tasks merged, the first "setup" programs came into being. This type of program lets you specify certain things about the software—such as your favorite font, or how much disk space you want the game to devour for a temporary storage file—while you are copying files to your hard disk. You could argue that either method is a perfectly reasonable one, but at least having a question to answer now and then makes the process of inserting 19 diskettes a little more tolerable.

You start up the installer or setup program differently depending on whether you're running Windows 3 or Windows 95. From the Windows 3 *Program Manager*, you select the *Run* command from the *File* menu. From Windows 95, you select the *Control Panel* menu item from the *Settings* heading under the *Start* menu, as in Figure 1.

If you're running Windows 3, you'll see a dialog box asking you what program you want to run. You'll need to look at your documentation for the exact name of your program's installer, but it's usually either *install.exe* or *setup.exe*. Additionally, you'll need to type the letter of the proper drive. So, for example, if you are installing a Windows 3 program, you might type *a:\setup.exe* (or *b:\setup.exe* if the disk is in your *b:* drive, *d:\setup.exe* if it's on your *d:* CD-ROM drive, and so on). In any case, you will click *OK* or press *Return* after you enter the filename.

Under Windows 95, you don't even have to do that. Once you've brought up

Tip: This is not the place to type in what you think of your boss.

Of course, if you are installing the software on your system at home, you probably don't have a company name to enter. Only the rudest software will require that you type something in the "Company Name" box. Most software, however, will require that you enter your own name. Don't worry if you make a typing error;

immediately after running it, so that nothing on your hard disk will be changed if you ran the installer accidentally. You will also usually be asked where on your hard disk you want a particular piece of software installed. We'll talk a bit about the rules of good hard disk organization at the end of this article, but unless you are an experienced user, you'll probably want to use the location that the install program suggests. There is some software out there that won't let you change where it installs even if you want to, but fortunately that is increasingly rare. As time goes on, proper computing etiquette is evolving, and it's just considered rude to force you or me to put software where we don't really want it.

After asking you, basically, "OK, where do you want this to go?" the install program may guide you through several other steps before you notice the floppy drive doing anything. That's normal. It's pretty common for the software to request your name and the name of your employer. The software will be personalized with whatever information you type at this time, and you will not be able to change it later. In most cases, the information is actually written onto your floppy disk, so even if you reinstall the program entirely, the same information will be used.

the *Control Panel*, just double-click the *Add/Remove Programs* icon. When the window opens, click on the *Install* button, and the process is almost entirely automated from there.

Windows 95 will automatically search your floppy drives and your CD-ROM drive for the installer program and run it for you. Once the install program is running, every piece of software will give you a chance to exit the installer

that you accept the terms of the license. That's another fundamental issue the courts have not yet decided—whether or not clicking your mouse on a screen is as legally binding as, say, your signature on a contract. If you don't agree to the terms of the License, however, the software won't install. We assume that we all intend to make legal uses of the software we purchase, so you'll click on the appropriate button.

Once you've done that, you'll likely be asked what type of installation you want to perform. Common options are to perform a "typical" installation, a "complete" installation, a "portable computer" installation and a "custom" installation. For the "typical" installation, the manufacturer has determined what pieces of the software *most* users will want, and the program will only install those options. The "complete" installation gives you everything, even if you don't have, for example, a network on which to use the network options you will be installing. A "portable" installation usually installs only the minimal software necessary to make the program run because hard disk space is usually at such a premium on portable computers. Finally, the "custom" option allows experienced users to select from a list of all components of the software only the individual pieces of the product that they wish to install.

That all done, you'll see floppy or CD-ROM drive activity. That may continue for some time. During that time, you may see an indicator on

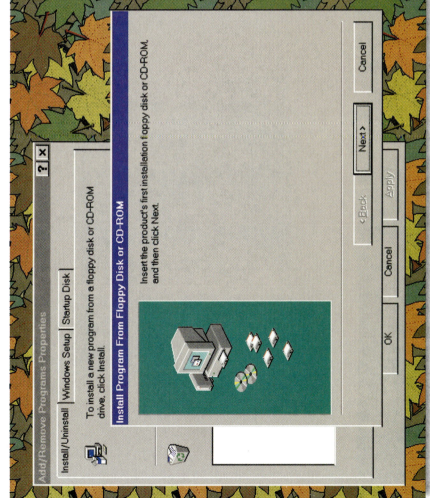

Figure 3: The Windows 95 Add Programs Wizard

you're almost always given the chance to correct any mistakes before your entries are saved.

The next thing you'll likely see is known as a License Agreement. Very briefly put, the License Agreement tells you which ways of using the software are legal and which are not. They really are terribly, terribly complicated, and at the time of this writing, certain fundamental questions about License Agreements are yet to be determined by the courts. Even such basic concepts as "What is 'ownership' of software?" are still matters for debate. In any event, at the bottom of the License screen, you'll be told that clicking *OK*, or *Yes*, is a legally binding indication

Online Registration

One of the facts of life in the software business is that there are two ways to make money doing it. You can sell a million copies of your software, and you can sell lists of your customer's names to other companies that want to target advertising to people who own computers. (And you thought they only wanted to know your household income so they could better their software.) The amount of money to be made through method number two is unbelievable, particularly as customers almost always provide that information—by sending in a registration card—at no cost to the software manufacturer. Now, it is true that major software companies keep track of their customers today so that they can give you discounts on software upgrades and verify that you are entitled to technical support. We can only wonder which motivation is greater, but whatever the case, a new way of obtaining user information has evolved as online systems become ubiquitous and PCs with preinstalled modems become the norm: registration via modem.

Here's how it works. Rather than taking just your name and employer to personalize the software while it installs, the installer program will ask you if you have a modem connected to your computer. If you say you do, you may be asked a quick question or two about whether you need to dial a special code to get an outside line, and so on. Then you'll see a screen like that in Figure 4.

You'll be asked for roughly the same information as on a physical registration card: your name, address, phone, blood type and so on. In this case, however, once you've filled out all of the spaces, you can simply click on the *Register* button, and the software will use your modem to instantly send your registration information to the software manufacturer. This is almost always a toll-free call, and it only takes seconds. In a few cases, the software company may thank you for registering online by sending you some extra files which give their program extra capabilities or show off a particular feature. More often, however, you'll just be saved the time of writing all of that information onto a card and mailing it.

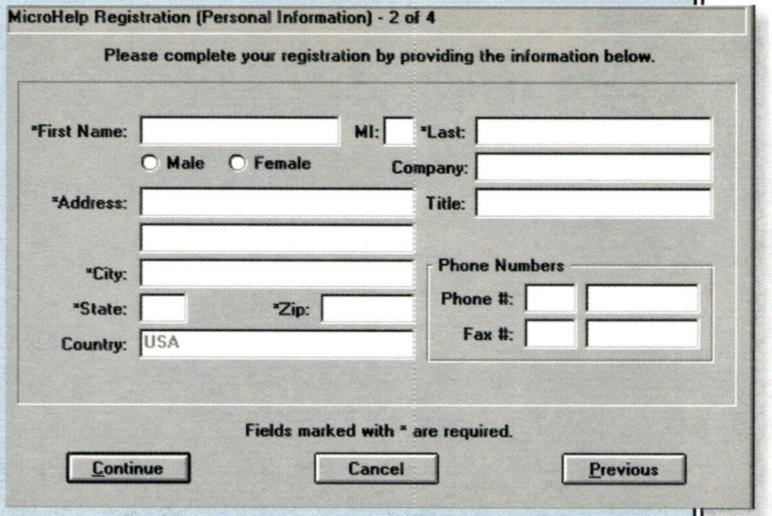

MicroHelp Registration (Personal Information) - 2 of 4

Please complete your registration by providing the information below.

*First Name: MI: *Last:

Male Female Company:

*Address: Title:

*City:

*State: Zip:

Country: USA

Phone Numbers

Phone #:

Fax #:

Fields marked with * are required.

Continue Cancel Previous

Figure 4: An Online Registration Screen

your screen showing you how much of the program has been installed or, more likely, how much of any single floppy disk has been installed. It's also very common today for the installation software to remind you to send in your registration card (see the "Online Registration" sidebar) and to show you a presentation about the features of the product you're installing. While that is happening, the system will be asking you for one diskette after another—unless it's a CD-ROM installation, of course—and the software will wait for you to eject each used disk, insert the next diskette, and click OK.

THE SOFTWARE IS DECOMPRESSING?

Because programs today sometimes take up much, much more space than is even available on the 15 or 20 diskettes on which they are distributed, software is usually put onto those diskettes in a compressed format, using techniques not unlike the way Microsoft DriveSpace can sometimes nearly double your available hard disk space. Even if the software is distributed on CD-ROM, where space is plentiful, it is usually more economical for the software manufacturer to prepare a single installation package that can be delivered either on a bunch of diskettes or one

CD. Therefore, the files on a CD installation disk are probably compressed, too. When the installation program reads these files off of the floppy or CD, it expands their contents before writing the information onto your hard disk.

That might seem bizarre, since the obvious effect is that the files will take up significantly more space on your hard disk once they're expanded. The reason is speed. Your word processor should be able to load its spell check utility whenever you ask for it to do so. And you know how you hate waiting. If the spell checker was stored on your hard disk in compressed form, the amount of time you'd have to wait would be increased by the amount of time it takes your computer to expand the files into memory. And you'd suffer that performance loss every time you used the spell checker. By decompressing files at install time, you only have to wait for the files to be expanded that one time, while they are being put on your computer. The performance you gain is easily worth more than the hard disk space you lose.

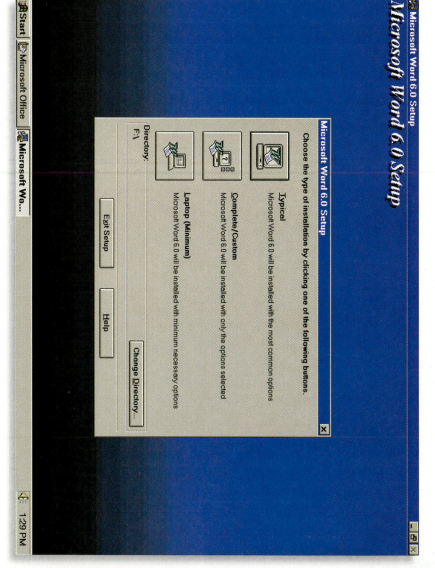

Figure 5: Selecting the type of installation you want to make.

soon as you return to the Windows desktop. If you don't want to restart, you don't have to: just click the *Don't Restart Now* button. But remember to restart Windows before you try to launch the new software for the first time.

In the distant past, there used to be a danger in letting a program restart Windows while other programs were running. If you had any unsaved data in those other programs, that data would disappear forever when Windows restarted. This danger is all but gone now, but it's still a good habit to shut down any programs you may be running before you run any install program.

Peter Norton made his mark in the personal computing industry as a programmer, businessman and author. He is best known for the computer programs, including the famed Norton Utilities, and books that bear his name. Mr. Norton sold his personal computing software business to Symantec Corporation in 1990 and is a noted patron of the arts and humanities in Los Angeles.

Scott Clark is the Editor of Peter Norton's computer book series. He is an accomplished writer and Windows programmer. He recently served as the primary author for the sixth edition of Peter Norton's flagship title, Inside the PC. He is a Windows programmer in Turbo Pascal and Microsoft Visual Basic.

Hard Disk Organization Suggestions

While it's true that you *may* install your software wherever you like, a few good ideas have surfaced over the decade or so that people have been using their PCs. One of these is that you should generally avoid installing software into the root directory of your hard disk (C:\). The reasons for this were largely technical and due to the unsophistication of installer programs all those years ago. Today, particularly under Windows 95, unless you plan to install hundreds and hundreds of pieces of software, it doesn't really matter where you store the files.

Under Windows 3, however, some common sense can help you find things should you ever need to. We like to create folders with names like "Word Processing," "Graphic," "Utilities" and "Games," and we install software into whichever folder fits best. That way, if we ever need to tinker with the files on our hard disk, it's obvious where we should go. For example, if we ever want to delete all the files for a particular game, there's very little danger of deleting the wrong files in a folder named "Graphics." Of course, by using Windows 95's *Add/Remove Programs* control panel, even that danger, too, is largely gone.

IT FINISHED—NOW IT WANTS TO RESTART?

When installation is complete, don't be surprised if you are told that Windows needs to restart before you can use the new product. Regardless of whether you're installing software or hardware, this restart is often necessary because some of that configuration information that you entered is only gathered by Windows when it first starts running. If you want to use the software immediately, allow Windows to restart, and the software will work properly as

WHAT YOU REALLY NEED TO KNOW ABOUT "SYSTEM FILES" AND "BOOT DISKS"

By Charles Brannon

It's not pretty, but there's no escaping it: MS-DOS remains a necessary, although tiresome, part of computing—even with the advent of Windows 95. The good news is that MS-DOS is powerful and sophisticated; the bad news is that it is also complex, difficult to use, and even harder to learn. Yet it's virtually required for the proper operation of your computer.

M S-DOS stands for Microsoft Disk Operating System. (While both IBM and Novell also sell their own versions of DOS, it's **MS-DOS** that runs on 99% of the world's PCs.) The Disk Operating System is a special program that allows programs to access files on your disk drives, adjust the computer's time and date, and perform other low-level but essential functions. From now on, we'll refer to it simply as MS-DOS or DOS (pronounced "doss").

If you only run Windows software, you can disregard DOS most of the time, but you can't ignore it altogether. That's because your computer starts itself (**boots**) using MS-DOS. Only after MS-DOS has booted can it then, in turn, start Windows. Even Windows 95, which doesn't use MS-DOS while running, still requires DOS to kickstart the computer. (There's been some debate about how much, and in what ways, Windows 95 relies on MS-DOS.)

THE BOOT SEQUENCE

We'll now describe the nuts and bolts of what happens when you press the *On* button to fire up your computer. (If this isn't of interest to you, please feel free to skip down to *Your System Files* below.) When you turn your computer on, here's what happens, step-by-step:

1. The computer first runs a program that permanently stored inside one of its **Read Only Memory** (**ROM**) chips. This program is part of the *Basic Input/Output System*, or **BIOS**.

2. The BIOS **initializes** all the hardware in your computer to get it ready for use, and performs a few tests. If your computer beeps several times in a row and doesn't proceed from this step, you have a hardware problem, such as bad memory chips or an incorrectly inserted plug-in card. This problem must be corrected before your computer can start up Windows 95.

3. The BIOS reads a special file that's stored in another type of permanent memory called **CMOS RAM**. This file stores all your computer's setup information, such as the sizes and types of your disk drives.

4. At this point, the BIOS has learned how much memory you have (it gets this from the CMOS), so it performs a basic memory test. You can usually skip this test by pressing the Esc key. RAM memory, the volatile memory that's being checked here, almost never fails.

5. The BIOS can't do much more by itself. It now needs to find a real **Operating System** (**OS**) to load into your computer's **RAM** (**Random Access Memory**). Since RAM is erased when you turn your computer off, the operating system must be kept on a permanent storage device like a floppy disk or hard drive. So the OS must always be moved from the hard drive to your computer's internal RAM before much else can happen.

6. The BIOS attempts to launch a program from your floppy drive to continue booting. This program is stored in a special region of a floppy disk called the **boot sector**.

7. If there is no floppy disk inserted (usually the case), the BIOS attempts to find the boot sector on the first hard drive in your computer (the C: drive in most computers). The meaning of "first" here is that the computer considers drives in a hierarchy—in alphabetical order. So, if you have A:, B:, C:, D: and E: drives, or even some additional ones, the computer looks at them in alphabetical order during the startup process. It's looking for the first boot sector that it can find.

8. The program contained in the boot sector loads into RAM from the floppy disk or a hard drive, and then starts running.

9. Usually, the boot sector's only job is to load a tiny piece of DOS; that, in turn, loads the rest of DOS into RAM.

> **Tip:** If your computer is infected by a virus, that virus can hide in the boot sector, and thereby take control during the boot process before any other legitimate programs on your computer. The virus hides its time until it can copy itself to a floppy disk, reproducing itself to spread further.

10. Assuming all is well, the boot sector loads a file named IO.SYS from the floppy disk or hard drive.

11. IO.SYS now takes over. Its job is to load yet another program, this time called MSDOS.SYS—this is the core DOS program.

12. Once MSDOS.SYS is loaded, it displays the DOS startup screen.

13. If your computer is running MS-DOS version 5.0 or later, you'll then see "Starting MS-DOS." MSDOS.SYS then waits two seconds for you to press a key on the keyboard.

14. If your computer is also running Windows 95, it displays "Starting Windows 95" and waits two seconds for a keystroke.

15. During this brief waiting period, you can press special keys to divert DOS from its usual behavior. For example, if you press Shift+F5, the steps we'll describe below are skipped. Alternatively, pressing F8 puts DOS into a special interactive mode where it walks you through startup step by step.

16. Assuming you didn't press any keys during the previous steps, DOS now loads a file called CONFIG.SYS from the floppy disk or hard drive (whichever it was able to boot from in step 6 or 7). We'll assume that DOS is booting from your hard drive from this

• point, so the CONFIG.SYS file is loaded from your C: drive. (This is almost always what happens.)

17. The lines in CONFIG.SYS are now examined and their "instructions" followed by DOS. For example, the line "FILES=50" tells DOS to set aside enough memory to read up to 50 files at the same time.

18. If there are any lines in CONFIG.SYS that begin with the word "DEVICE," DOS loads the appropriate support programs into memory. These special software programs are usually called device **drivers**.

19. When DOS has finished "obeying" CONFIG.SYS, it then opens the file AUTOEXEC.BAT from the C: drive.

20. Each line in AUTOEXEC.BAT is also examined and acted upon by DOS. For example, the line "ECHO OFF" tells DOS not to display its actions on-screen while it loads—it won't show the commands that are in the AUTOEXEC.BAT file each time it carries one of them out.

21. If the filenames of any programs are present in AUTOEXEC.BAT, the programs are loaded into memory so that they can begin to run.

22. Many of the programs typically listed within AUTOEXEC.BAT don't actually do anything when they first run. They just copy themselves into memory and stay there, ready for use when required by other programs. Programs that just insert themselves into memory, then, without taking any action, return control to AUTOEXEC.BAT, are usually called **Terminate and Stay Resident (TSR)** programs. An example of a TSR program is the program that supports the use of your mouse with DOS programs (MOUSE.EXE). Some of these programs are also called **drivers**.

23. Other programs referenced in AUTOEXEC.BAT can run, perform some operation, then exit to allow the AUTOEXEC.BAT file to continue. An example of this type of utility program is the CHKDSK or SCANDISK program that checks your hard drive for errors. If one of these is in AUTOEXEC.BAT, it runs automatically every time you power up your computer. In other words, utilities like these are not needed (after this point) by other programs, so they don't need to stay resident.

24. When the last line of AUTOEXEC.BAT has been read, DOS then displays its **prompt**, the familiar "C:\>" that tells you that you can now type in DOS commands, such as DIR to see the directory or CD to move to a different directory:

25. There is, though, the possibility that a line in AUTOEXEC.BAT may start a program that doesn't automatically exit. This ends the process of running AUTOEXEC.BAT, at least until you exit this now-active program. If you have such a program, it's usually listed in one of the last remaining lines of AUTOEXEC.BAT. If your computer starts Windows automatically, it's because the last line in AUTOEXEC.BAT is the WIN command, which starts the WIN.COM program from your C:\WINDOWS directory. (Windows 95 doesn't require a WIN command—it's started automatically by the special version of DOS, DOS 7.0, that is installed when you install Windows 95.)

If your computer starts Windows automatically, Windows also triggers and responds to the commands in two special files called SYSTEM.INI and WIN.INI. We'll discuss these shortly. Windows 95 has an additional file, called The Registry, that it looks at for configuration and customization details.

This concludes the process of booting your computer.

YOUR SYSTEM FILES

You can see from the steps above that there are four special files that are required to start your computer: IO.SYS, MSDOS.SYS, CONFIG.SYS and AUTOEXEC.BAT. The first two files never change; they were copied to your hard drive when it was originally set up and they remain in their original form forever unless you upgrade to a new version of DOS or Windows.

Your CONFIG.SYS and AUTOEXEC.BAT files were also preconfigured by the manufacturer before you bought your computer, but that doesn't mean they are static, unchanging files. In fact, you will sometimes need to change the contents of these files to correct problems or optimize your computer. These files are also often modified when you install new software (an application's setup routine usually does this for you). If you add new hardware to your computer, CONFIG.SYS and AUTOEXEC.BAT typically need to be updated to add the necessary software drivers to support your new hardware.

Similarly, the Windows system files (Registry, SYSTEM.INI, and WIN.INI) are often updated when you install new Windows software. Windows also updates these files automatically. For example, if you install fonts, new lines are added to the [Fonts] section of the WIN.INI file.

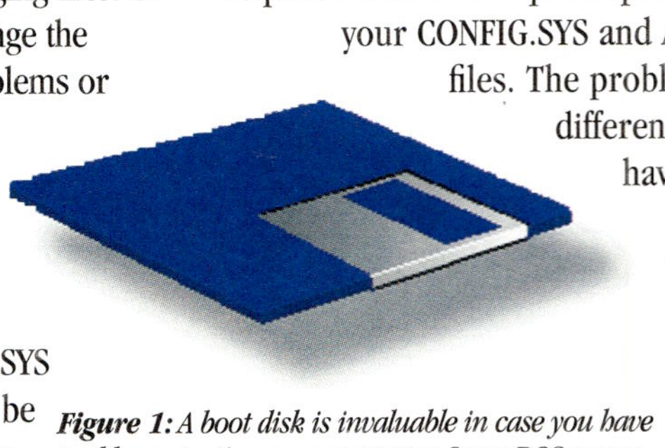

Figure 1: A boot disk is invaluable in case you have problems starting your computer. Some DOS games also require a boot disk for best results.

YOU NEED A BOOT DISK

If something goes drastically wrong with these files, you can start your computer from a **boot disk** and restore your backup copies of these files.

But we're getting ahead of ourselves. What is a boot disk? Recall that your computer can start itself from either a floppy disk or from your hard drive. Usually, if it starts from the floppy disk that's merely because you left a floppy disk inserted in your floppy drive when you last turned off your computer. (If you have two disk drives, named A: and B:, the computer always starts from the A: drive because it is earlier in the hierarchy already described.)

Creating a boot disk should be one of the first things you do after you buy a computer, unpack it, set it up and confirm that it's working. The boot disk is essential in case your computer stops booting from its hard drive. This can happen if any of the system files get scrambled by a buggy program, or if they get deleted accidentally because you made a mistake while managing files with Windows 3 File Manager or Windows 95 Explorer.

If your hard drive won't start, you can then insert your boot disk into A: and start the computer. Booting from a floppy at least gets you to the DOS prompt A:>. From there, it's possible to use the DIR C: command to get a listing of the files on your hard drive, to confirm if C: is even coherent. You can usually also switch to the C: drive by typing its name (C:) and pressing Enter. You may also be able to restore the system files on your hard drive and repair the problem.

Another type of boot disk comes in handy when you're running games designed for DOS. These games often have very finicky requirements that require special changes to your CONFIG.SYS and AUTOEXEC.BAT files. The problem is that different games can have conflicting requirements. The solution is to create a boot disk that's specialized for each game, with the necessary settings for that game stored in the CONFIG.SYS and AUTOEXEC.BAT files on its floppy disk. Don't worry if it isn't entirely clear to you how to configure a boot disk—luckily, many games can create such a disk for you.

Since so much depends on your system files, it's important to save backup copies of these files.

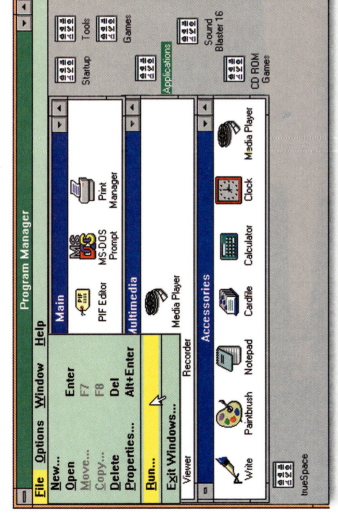

Figure 2: Click the File menu from Program Manager to get to the Run command.

MAKING A BOOT DISK FOR EMERGENCIES

The most straightforward method of creating a boot disk is from the DOS prompt. If your computer starts Windows automatically, choose *Exit* from the *File* menu of Program Manager. (With Windows 95, you can click the *Start* button, then choose *Shutdown*. On the screen that follows, choose *Restart the computer in MS-DOS mode*.)

Tip: If you have Windows 95, there's a much better way to create a boot disk. Click *Start/Settings/Control Panel* to start the Control Panel, then double-click on the *Add/Remove Programs* icon. When *Add/Remove Programs* starts, click on the tab heading for *Startup Disk*. Insert a floppy disk in the drive and click the *Create Disk* button. You can now skip ahead to the section titled, "An Emergency Repair."

To create a boot disk from the C:\ prompt (ordinary DOS), insert a blank (or one you don't mind erasing) floppy disk into the drive and enter the following command *exactly*, then press the *Enter* key:

FORMAT A: /U /S /V:BOOTDISK

You'll be warned that the Format command will erase the floppy disk, and you're asked if you're really sure that you want to format the disk. Type *Y* to begin the format. (**Formatting** prepares a disk for first use, and erases the floppy to make room for new files. WARNING: Make sure you typed *FORMAT A:* above. If you somehow substituted *C:*, your entire hard drive will be erased, assuming you ignore the warnings and proceed anyway.)

When the Format command is finished, you'll be returned to the C:\> prompt. Test the boot disk by restarting your computer with the floppy boot disk inserted in the A: drive. You can restart your computer by turning the power off, then back on; by pressing the *Reset* button on the front of the computer's case; or by holding down the "three-finger salute" of *Ctrl+Alt+Del*.

Tip: If you used a Windows DOS prompt to format the disk instead of first exiting Windows, you'll have to type *EXIT* to end the DOS session, then exit Windows, before you restart your computer.

BOOT DISK FAILURE

If your computer doesn't start from the boot disk, there may be a simple cure. Some computers are set up to boot only from the hard drive. This is to prevent you from accidentally booting from a floppy disk, which is one way computer viruses can be spread. To fix your computer so that it will boot from a boot disk, you'll have to enter the CMOS setup of your computer (described below). You can do this by tapping the *Del* key or the *F1* function key immediately after turning on your computer. We can't tell you what to do after this, since it varies widely from computer to computer; but look for something like "Boot Order" and change it from "C:Only" (or "C:,A:") to read something like "A:,C:"—this tells the computer to now boot from A: first instead of going to C: first.

FINISHING THE BOOT DISK

Once you've confirmed that your computer can start from the boot disk, restart your computer without the floppy disk in the drive so that startup will again be from your hard drive. Exit to DOS again, and finish making your boot disk by typing in the following commands *exactly*. Press *Enter* after you type each line, and wait until the C:\> prompt reappears before you type the next command. (The "\" symbol is usually located underneath the Backspace key—the computer reads this differently from the forward slash "/" that's on the ? key.)

COPY C:\AUTOEXEC.BAT A:\

COPY C:\CONFIG.SYS A:\

COPY C:\WINDOWS\WIN.INI A:\

COPY C:\WINDOWS\SYSTEM.INI A:\

COPY C:\DCS\SYS.COM A:\

COPY C:\DCS\FORMAT.COM A:\

COPY C:\DCS\FDISK.COM A:\

COPY C:\DCS\QBASIC.COM A:\

COPY C:\DCS\EDIT.COM A:\

COPY C:\DCS\SCANDISK.EXE A:\

The commands above copy some useful files to the boot disk that you can use to fix a hard drive that won't boot, or use to reformat your hard drive in case it's been mangled beyond hope of easy repair. Consult a DOS "guru" or repair professional before you take a step as drastic as reformatting your hard drive, however.

Figure 3: With Windows 95, use the Start button to access Run.

The last two steps above copy the EDIT program to your boot disk, which is invaluable in case you need to modify the contents of your CONFIG.SYS or AUTOEXEC.BAT file. The last step transfers SCANDISK, useful for repairing hard drive errors. If you don't have DOS 5.0 or later, you don't have the EDIT command, and you'll get error messages when you type those COPY commands. (No harm done.) If you don't have DOS 6.0 or later, substitute CHKDSK for SCANDISK above.

Tip: Type *VER* at the DOS prompt (C:\>) to display which version of DOS you have on your computer.

You will also get error messages if your DOS files aren't stored in the standard C:\DOS directory. (Windows 95 stores its commands in C:\WINDOWS\COMMAND. But if you followed our advice earlier, you learned about an easier way to create a boot disk with Windows 95, and you don't need to follow the above steps anyway.)

AN EMERGENCY REPAIR

If your computer won't start from the hard drive, insert the special boot disk we just created into the floppy drive and restart the computer. Ignore any error messages that appear when you boot—they may be referring to files that were loaded by your original CONFIG.SYS and AUTOEXEC.BAT files (which you copied to the floppy if you followed the steps above) but that don't exist on the floppy boot disk.

Before going any further, use the SCANDISK command (or CHKDSK/F command if you don't have DOS 6.0 or later) to scan the hard drive for errors. Type *SCANDISK* at the DOS prompt (A:\>) and press *Enter*. Allow SCANDISK to automatically repair any problems that it finds. After SCANDISK finishes, remove the floppy disk from the drive and restart your computer to see if the repair worked.

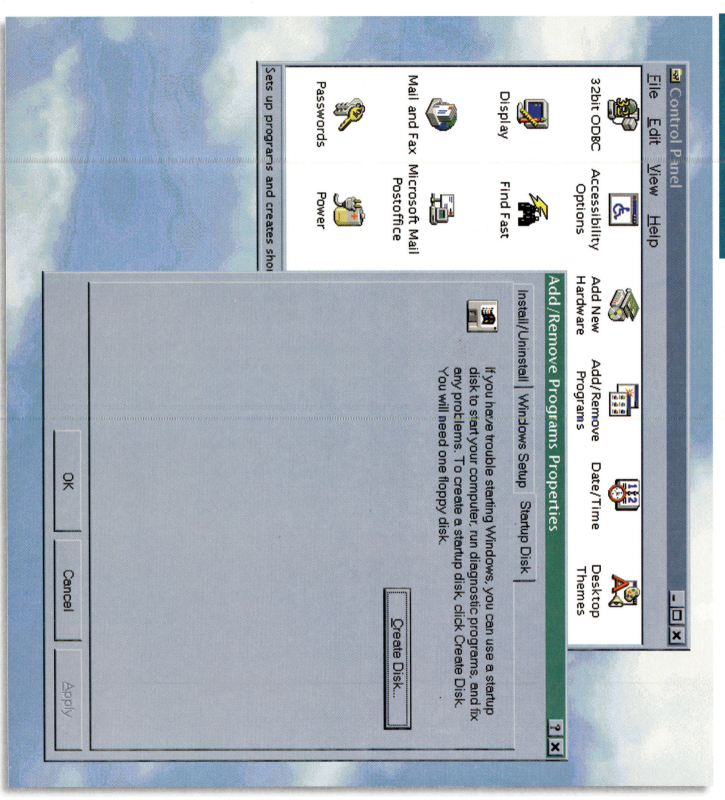

Control Panel

File Edit View Help

32bit ODBC   Accessibility Options   Add New Hardware   Add/Remove Programs   Date/Time   Desktop Themes   Display   Find Fast   Mail and Fax   Microsoft Mail Postoffice   Passwords   Power

Sets up programs and creates sho...

Add/Remove Programs Properties

Install/Uninstall | Windows Setup | Startup Disk

If you have trouble starting Windows, you can use a startup disk to start your computer, run diagnostic programs, and fix any problems. To create a startup disk, click Create Disk.

You will need one floppy disk.

Create Disk...

OK   Cancel   Apply

Figure 4: Use Add/Remove Programs—From Control Panel to create a boot disk with Windows 95.

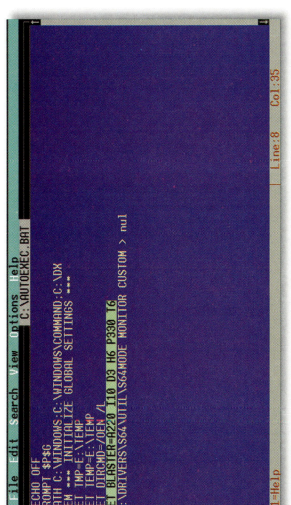

```
C:\AUTOEXEC.BAT
@ECHO OFF
PROMPT $P$G
PATH C:\WINDOWS;C:\WINDOWS\COMMAND;C:\DX
REM *** INITIALIZE GLOBAL SETTINGS ***
SET TMP=E:\TEMP
SET TEMP=E:\TEMP
SET DIRCMD=/OEN /L
SET BLASTER=A220 I10 D3 H6 P330 T6
C:\DRIVERS\S64UTIL\S64MODE MONITOR CUSTOM > nul

F1=Help                                    Line:8   Col:35
```

Figure 5: *The DOS EDIT command makes it easy to change your system files*

NOPE—TRY AGAIN?

If the hard drive still won't boot, insert your boot disk and restart your computer. When you get to the A:\> prompt, try copying the CONFIG.SYS and AUTOEXEC.BAT commands from the boot disk back to your hard drive. But first, we'll make another copy of your existing hard drive boot files, in case the cure is worse than the disease. (This saves a copy of your existing files in two files, each with the suffix .SAV.) Type the following commands *exactly*, pressing *Enter* after each one:

COPY C:\AUTOEXEC.BAT
C:\AUTOEXEC.SAV

COPY C:\CONFIG.SYS
C:\CONFIG.SAV

COPY A:\CONFIG.SYS C:\

COPY A:\AUTOEXEC.BAT C:\

When you're asked if you want to overwrite files, type *Y* and press *Enter* to continue. You can then restart your computer.

If you need to restore your original AUTOEXEC/CONFIG files, use:

COPY C:\CONFIG.SAV
C:\CONFIG.SYS

COPY C:\AUTOEXEC.SAV
C:\AUTOEXEC.BAT

THE COMPUTER STILL WON'T BOOT

If your computer doesn't start successfully after restoring AUTOEXEC/CONFIG from backup, you may need to edit the AUTOEXEC/CONFIG files to correct problems. Skip ahead to "Editing Your Boot Files" below. If you still can't even get your computer to start, boot from your boot disk again, and type the following command from the A:\> prompt:

SYS C:

This recopies the special files IO.SYS and MSDOS.SYS from the boot disk onto your hard drive, replacing those possibly corrupted files on your hard drive. It's important to ensure that your boot disk uses the same version of DOS as your hard drive before you do this. If you ever upgrade the version of DOS you use on your hard disk, be sure to create a new boot disk and get rid of the old one.

In some cases, even the above command won't help, especially if your hard drive has been infected by a malicious computer virus. In this case, you can try the following command to repair the boot sector (or master boot record) of your hard drive. Especially with this command, type it *exactly* as shown, or you could do more harm than good:

FDISK /MBR

If the computer still won't boot, you have a problem so serious that it requires the service of a professional.

EDITING YOUR BOOT FILES

You'll sometimes need to edit your CONFIG.SYS and AUTOEXEC.BAT commands. Perhaps a game tells you that you need to add a line like EMM386, or you've learned that you can use SMARTDRV in your AUTOEXEC.BAT file to speed up your hard drive.

To edit your CONFIG.SYS file, type the following command at the DOS prompt (C:>). (This requires DOS version 5.0 or later.)

EDIT C:\CONFIG.SYS

Use EDIT C:\AUTOEXEC.BAT to edit that file, or use the *Open* command from EDIT's *File* menu to load the file into the editor.

A typical CONFIG.SYS file will look something like this:

FILES=50

BUFFERS=10,0

STACKS 9,256

DEVICE=C:\DOS\HIMEM.SYS

DOS=HIGH

DEVICE=C:\DRIVERS\CDROM.SYS
/D:MSCD01

A typical AUTOEXEC.BAT file might look like:

PROMPT PG

PATH C:\WINDOWS;C:\DOS

SET TEMP=C:\TEMP

C:\DOS\MSCDEX.EXE /M:8
/D:MSCD01

BOOT FILE OPTIMIZATION

To let you practice and gain confidence with editing system files, we'll add two commands that will free up more DOS memory and make your hard drive run faster than ever. Before doing anything else, make sure you've created your boot floppy disk in case you make a mistake that prevents your computer from starting. Any mistake is more likely to result in error messages than in problems restarting, but in computers as in most things, it's always easier to prevent a mistake than to fix one. Your computer may already have these lines in CONFIG.SYS and AUTOEXEC.BAT, so you may just want to follow along. If you're not happy with the changes, use the steps we mentioned earlier to restore your original AUTOEXEC/CONFIG files. (Note: these changes are not recommended for use with Windows 95.)

First open CONFIG.SYS for editing (type: *EDIT CONFIG.SYS*). Use the arrow keys to move to the start of the line that reads DOS=HIGH and type the next two lines (which will be inserted above DOS=HIGH):

DEVICE=C:\DOS\EMM386.EXE

NOEMS

DOS=UMB

Now, change any lines that use DEVICE to DEVICEHIGH. For example, if a line reads:

DEVICE=C:\DRIVERS\CDROM.SYS

Change it to something like

DEVICEHIGH=C:\DRIVERS\CDROM.SYS

Don't change DEVICE=HIMEM.SYS, however. Save your changes by choosing *Save* from the *File* menu. Now let's use *File/Open* to load C:\AUTOEXEC.BAT. Move the cursor to the line below C:\DOS\MSCDEX and type the following line, which will be inserted just prior to PROMPT PG:

C:\DOS\SMARTDRV.EXE /X

Choose *Save* from Edit's *File* menu to write the changed AUTOEXEC.BAT to the hard drive.

Now restart your computer. If your computer lacked the commands you just added, you'll notice that your hard drive runs noticeably faster. (If you have DOS version 6.0 or later, SmartDrive will also speed up your CD-ROM drive.)

You'll also have more memory available because the DEVICE drivers you edited now load into a special area of memory (the upper memory blocks) that don't consume any DOS memory. To see the difference, use the MEM command (type: *MEM*) before you make the changes, and use it again afterward, to see how much DOS memory you have.

WINDOWS SYSTEM FILES

The Windows equivalents of DOS's CONFIG.SYS and AUTOEXEC.BAT are SYSTEM.INI and WIN.INI. Like CONFIG.SYS, SYSTEM.INI loads necessary device drivers for Windows. And WIN.INI has something in common with AUTOEXEC.BAT: it can automatically run certain programs when you start Windows.

Windows also features an easier way to edit your system files. Just choose *Run* from Program Manager's *File* menu, and type *SYSEDIT* as the name of the program to run, and press *Enter*. (With Windows 95, click the *Start* button and choose *Run*.)

SysEdit

SysEdit opens your CONFIG.SYS, AUTOEXEC.BAT, WIN.INI, SYSTEM.INI (and sometimes other files like MSMAIL.INI depending on which version of Windows you use—ignore these other files for now). You can switch between windows by clicking on them or, if a window gets buried, choose it from SysEdit's *Window* menu or use the *Ctrl+Tab* hotkey to switch between the windows.

EDITING WIN.INI

Some of the tips and techniques in this book suggest that you make changes to your SYSTEM.INI or WIN.INI files. Let's make a simple change to practice editing WIN.INI. Use SysEdit to open your system files, and click on the WIN.INI file.

Tip: If you only want to change one file, open it with Notepad. Run Notepad from the Accessories folder, and use its *File/Open* command to load the file you want to edit (such as WIN.INI).

When you make changes to any of the system files, SysEdit automatically makes backup copies. The original version of SYSTEM.INI is stored as SYSTEM.SYD, for example. If you need to reverse your changes, use Notepad to open SYSTEM.SYD and copy the original lines back to SYSTEM.INI.

Use the cursor keys to move down a few lines until you find the section labeled [windows]. Look for a line that reads "LOAD=." You may discover that there are already programs listed after LOAD=. If you want to prevent any of them from running, delete the name of the program you want to prevent from loading.

Move the cursor to the end of the LOAD= line by pressing the *End* key on your keyboard. (End is above the cursor cluster or on the numeric keypad). Type a space after any existing LOAD= programs, and type *CALC*. You don't need to press *Enter*. For example, if WIN.INI looked like this before (simplified):

[windows]

load=dcshkey.exe

It would now read as:

[windows]

load=dcshkey.exe CALC

Now exit Windows, then type *WIN* to restart it, or just restart your computer to reboot and run Windows again. This time, you'll notice that the Windows Calculator accessory automatically starts, ready for use. While you might not want to use this trick with CALC, this exercise shows you how you might use WIN.INI to automate aspects of your computer. To reverse the changes, simply open WIN.INI again and remove CALC from the LOAD= line.

System Configuration Editor

File   Edit   Search   Window

C:\WINDOWS\MSMAIL.INI
C:\WINDOWS\PROTOCOL.INI
C:\WINDOWS\SYSTEM.INI
C:\WINDOWS\WIN.INI
C:\CONFIG.SYS
C:\AUTOEXEC.BAT

```
@ECHO OFF
PROMPT $P$G
REM *** INITIALIZE GLOBAL SETTINGS ***
SET TEMP=E:\TEMP
SET TMP=E:\TEMP
SET DIRCMD=/OEN/L
SET BLASTER=A220 I10 D3 H6 P330 T6
C:\DRIVERS\S64UTILS\S64MODE MONITOR CUSTOM > nul
```

Figure 6: SysEdit is a convenient way to edit all your system files in one place

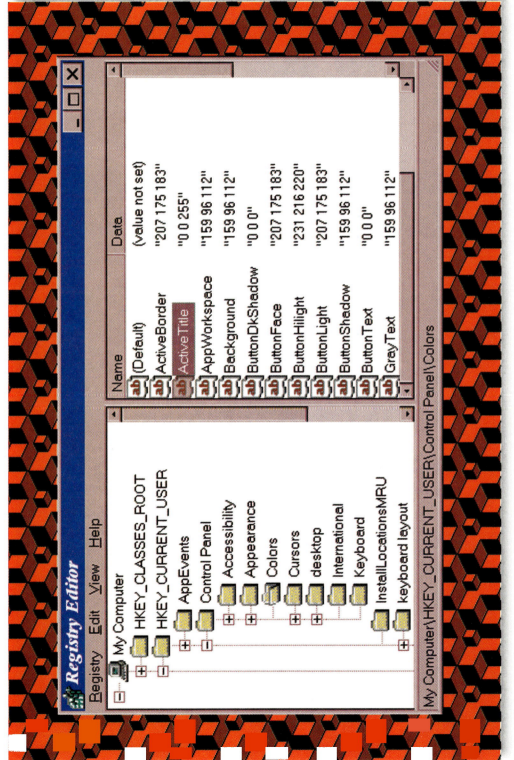

Figure 7: *The Registry is the master control file for Windows 95. Many features of SYSTEM.INI and WIN.INI have been moved to the Registry.*

Tip: The easiest way to start a program automatically with Windows is to copy the program's icon to the Startup group in Program Manager. With Windows 95, copy the Shortcut icon to the Startup folder (C:\Windows\Start Menu\Programs\Startup).

OTHER SYSTEM FILES

We've discussed your most important files, but there are other files that are important, too. SYSTEM.INI and WIN.INI aren't the only "init" files in your Windows directory. If you use File Manager or Windows 95 Explorer to view your hard drive, you'll discover a whole slew of files ending with .INI (Explorer shows them as **configuration files**). Most programs on your computer create these files to store their own custom settings.

Instead of continuing this practice, which clutters up your hard drive, Microsoft now encourages developers to move their system settings into a special file on the hard drive called the **Registry**. Windows 3.1 has a type of registry file called REG.DAT, while Windows 95 uses SYSTEM.DAT and USER.DAT. To view or change these files, you can run **RegEdit** (just as we ran SysEdit above). We recommend that you don't change anything using RegEdit unless

you're given specific directions because the Registry is crucial to the proper operation of Windows (especially with Windows 95). Windows automatically makes backup copies of its Registry, and will restore it from the backup copy in case of a critical failure with the original Registry.

Your hard drive also contains other hidden system files, such as 386SPART.PAR, which is the Windows 3.1 **permanent swap file**. Use the *386 Enhanced* Control Panel **applet** to configure your swap file—never move or delete the permanent swap file manually.

Although we've recommended steps to back up just your system files, there's no substitute for a complete backup of all the files on your computer. At the very least, you should keep copies of all your **data files** on floppy disks. You can always reinstall your programs from the original installation disks or CD-ROMs, but text you've written or spreadsheets you've created—such data files cannot be replaced unless you've backed them up.

TAKING CONTROL

Using the techniques described above can be a lifesaver if you have problems with your computer, and the skills you've learned are valuable—you now have control over some

fundamental aspects of your PC. Now that you know how to edit your system files, you might want to continue to learn more about MS-DOS and ways to optimize and troubleshoot your computer system.

Charles Brannon, previously an editor at COMPUTE magazine and Project Manager for Epyx, now supervises the Novell and Windows for WorkGroups and Windows 95 networks and works as a consultant and freelance writer. He is a co-author of The Windows 95 Book, published in the summer of 1995 by Ventana Press. Charles has been an active editor and writer in the personal computing field since 1980. He is a Contributing Editor and the monthly Windows columnist for CD-ROM Today, and is a Windows 95 Advisor for the Windows User Group Network (WUGNET), a Windows 95 advocacy and member support group.

ANSWERS TO THE 101 MOST FREQUENTLY ASKED PC QUESTIONS

By Steve Poole

You'll find an amazing amount of useful and helpful information here. Good luck!

MAINTENANCE AND CARE OF YOUR PC

1. Is it better to leave my computer running all the time, or turn it off each time I finish a session?

Some people argue that the power that surges through a PC when it's powered up causes wear and tear, albeit slight, to the system components, and can subsequently lead to a premature failure of the power supply or components on the **motherboard**. But unless you turn it on 15 or 20 times a day, little strain is placed on the system by turning it on. And since your PC is much more vulnerable to power surges and spikes when it's up and running, your best bet is to turn it off when it's not in use. Use a quality AC surge-suppressor power strip in any case. (For best protection, unplug your computer during fierce thunderstorms to be on the safe side.) An obvious exception to this rule would be if you use your PC as an answering machine or to receive faxes. You won't wear out your **hard drive** either: most are designed to run continuously for up to five years.

Ideally, your computer will comply with the EPA EnergyStar program, so it can automatically power down your hard drive, **video card** and **monitor** to save electricity when you aren't using your computer. That way you can leave your computer turned on all the time if you prefer without wasting energy. Look for the EnergyStar or other "green" logo when shopping for a new computer or monitor. (You may need to configure your computer's setup to enable power-saving features. See Charles Brannon's article on System Files.

2. How should I clean my monitor?

If you're a stickler for doing things by the book, you should pick up some "monitor wipes" at your local computer store. They're pretty cheap

and have been designed to clean without leaving scratches or streaks. In truth, though, a little glass cleaner sprayed onto a clean, soft cloth works just as well. You can also use isopropyl rubbing alcohol to remove tough residue. The main thing to avoid is spraying any liquid directly onto the display—it could run down the screen and inside the monitor.

3. Should I clean the inside of my computer, and how often should I do it?

Yes, you should. The fan on the back of your PC is constantly sucking in air, along with any dirt and smoke particles floating about. Too much dust can reduce the cooling power of the fan, and that could mean an important chip isn't being adequately cooled. Dust can also collect inside your floppy drives, leading to errors when you later try to retrieve files.

Depending on how dusty your PC's environment is, you should use some sort of vacuum to suck dust and dirt from the outer grill every month or so, and use a can of compressed gas (available from office and computer supply stores) to clean inside your PC once a year. (Don't use compressed gas to clean the outer grill from the outside—it'll blow the dust inside your system.) Make sure you turn off your computer before opening the case.

4. How can I protect my PC against power spikes and surges?

One thing you can do is turn off your PC when you're not using it. Even if power does surge through the line, the fact that the machine is off may prevent extensive damage.

There are two other precautions you can take to ensure your PC isn't damaged by power surges. For around $75, you can buy a high-quality **surge protector**, a **power strip** that's been designed to allow only safe amounts of

power through to your PC. (Less expensive surge strips provide some protection, but like a smaller sponge, their capacity for absorbing surges is limited. Also, you'll have to replace them about every year or so.) The other solution is simple, but a little inconvenient: unplug your computer when it's not in use.

5. How should I clean my mouse?

Remove the ball by flipping the mouse over and rotating the plastic ring holding the ball in place. Alongside the perimeter of the hole where the mouse sat you'll see steel rollers. Take a sharp, flat object (a penknife will do nicely) and carefully scrape off any gunk that has accumulated on the rollers. A can of compressed air also makes it easy to blow off any accumulated dust. Wash the ball in warm soapy water, and then dry it thoroughly. Replace the ball and plastic ring, and everything should work much better.

6. What can I do to reduce the hiss and static I hear through the speakers attached to my PC?

First, make sure your PC is plugged into a **grounded** outlet—don't use an adapter to plug it into a two-prong outlet. If you're using a power strip, you should consider turning off any devices also plugged into the strip. You can also try turning off any appliances in the same room—an air purifier, for instance, or a fan.

You can also get Radio Frequency Interference (RFI) from other equipment, such as a laser printer. This can cause a lower-pitched hum or buzz in your speakers. This can be minimized by using shielded speaker cables.

The best way to decrease hiss is to avoid amplifying the signal too much. Instead of turning up the volume on the speakers or an amplifier,

More Detail! More Power!

Windows® 95 compatible!

Find it...
Map it...
Print it...
and GO!

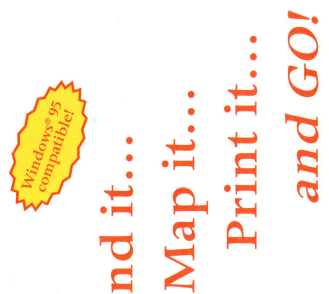

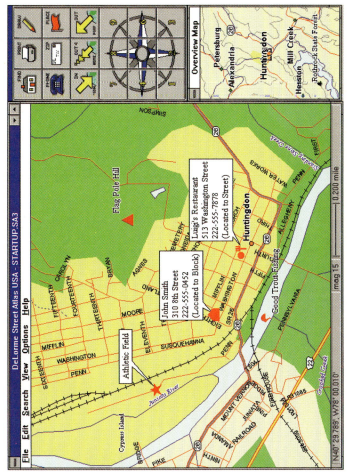

Street Atlas USA®, *America's best-selling mapping program*, lets you zoom in on cities, towns, streets—even specific addresses—anywhere in the country! Now available in **Version 3.0**, it combines unsurpassed detail, street address searching power, and powerful new editing tools to create custom maps.

Phone Search USA™ is a CD-ROM phone directory with *over 80 million* business and residential listings. You can search by name, phone number or business type, and limit your searches to a state, city or ZIP Code. Export your searches to a variety of applications or directly to Street Atlas USA 3.0!

By themselves, both programs help you take control of home or office projects. Or use them together to quickly find phone listings, locate them on a map, add notes and symbols, and print out beautiful, customized maps! You can even e-mail maps to other Street Atlas USA 3.0 users!

Street Atlas USA 3.0

* Search by address, placename, ZIP Code or phone number
* Add symbols and notes with drag-and-drop ease
* ZIP Code, latitude/longitude for any map location
* Select the landscape detail and print layout you want
* Print out beautiful maps or e-mail them to other Street Atlas USA 3.0 users
* Thousands of lakes, rivers, railroads, parks, hospitals, colleges, airports, civic centers and other landmarks
* Lightning fast, easy to use
* Direct link to **Phone Search USA**

Phone Search USA

* Over 80 million business and residential phone listings
* Nationwide phone directory on three CDs
* Search by name, phone number or business type
* Limit searches to state, city or ZIP Code
* Reverse search phone numbers to find addresses
* Export your searches to spreadsheets, word processors, databases or **Street Atlas USA 3.0**

Phone Data supplied by Database America Companies

Street Atlas USA 3.0 and **Phone Search USA** are available at your favorite software retailer, or directly from DeLorme at $79 each (plus $5 shipping per order). Write to the address below; or call or fax toll free! American Express, Discover, Mastercard or Visa welcome.

DELORME

1-800-253-5082

Fax: 1-800-575-2244
P.O. Box 298-206
Freeport, ME 04032
Check out our website!
http://www.delorme.com

increase the volume of your sound card using its mixer utility (or a dial control on the back of the sound card). Windows 95 has a convenient Volume control utility to accomplish the same thing. Click on *Start, Programs, Accessories, Multimedia, Volume Control.*

There's likely to be a small amount of hiss regardless of what you do—after all, the sound card is embedded inside your computer; a fierce storm of electrical signals—so don't be disappointed if you can't eliminate it entirely.

7. What is a boot disk, and why do I need one?

It's a floppy disk that contains files critical for your computer to run, and you should always have one handy in case anything happens to those files on your hard drive. To make a boot disk, insert a disk in the drive and type *FORMAT A: /S.* This copies two hidden files (IO.SYS and MSDOS.SYS) to the floppy disk, along with a file called COMMAND.COM. All three are key to getting your PC up and running. And if you use Windows, you'll also want to put your WIN.INI and SYSTEM.INI files on it—they're in the Windows directory.

If you want to be able to use things like your CD-ROM drive and sound card, you'll want to copy the files CONFIG.SYS and AUTOEXEC.BAT to the boot disk. Also, you can edit the contents of those two files, and consequently configure your PC differently. This is sometimes necessary to open up additional memory for use with DOS-based games (see their manual for instructions).

See the System Files article for complete instructions on how to create an emergency startup disk.

8. How often should I back up my system?

That depends on two things: how often you use your PC, and the sorts of things you use it for. If you just play games, for instance, then you only need to back up files that contain saved-game information. And even that's optional; it just lets you restart a game where you left off.

However, you *should* have a "rescue boot disk" containing your CONFIG.SYS, AUTOEXEC.BAT, WIN.INI, and SYSTEM.INI files. To create this disk from the DOS prompt, type: *FORMAT A: /S* and after the floppy disk has been formatted, copy onto it the four files mentioned above.

But most of us should back up more frequently—say once a week or so. And if that's not enough of a safety cushion, you can do a minimal backup on a daily basis, saving only the files that have changed since the last back up.

At the very least, you should back up any file that *you* create. You can always reinstall your *applications* from the original installation disks or CD-ROMs. (Some computers come with their applications pre-installed and allow you to create the original installation disks optionally; Take advantage of that option.)

9. What's the easiest way to perform back up?

Unless you have a backup tape drive or other unit specifically for backing up, there isn't an easy way. If floppy disks are your only alternative, you may want to back up only certain types of files—the most recent document and data files, for instance—as long as you have the original copy of the program used to create those files.

The best way to back up your system is to add an inexpensive tape drive. A single tape cartridge can store anywhere from 250MB up to 2GB, depending on the type of drive and tape you use.

Tape backup systems make it quick and easy to back up an entire hard drive. Iomega's new Zip Drive will also be a popular alternative for backups and general-purpose storage. It's a removable hard drive system that uses cartridges (similar to floppy disks) with 100MB-plus capacity. You can simply copy your files to the ZIP hard drive. You can also use the Windows DoubleSpace or DriveSpace utilities with a ZIP cartridge to double its capacity.

10. I know that backing up my hard drive is my insurance against corrupted files, but is there any way to retrieve the work I've done in a file that subsequently was corrupted?

Try running a DOS utility called Scandisk or CHKDSK (you'll have one or the other—use *Start/Programs/Accessories/System Tools/ScanDisk* with Windows 95). It'll retrieve any data it can, and save it in a file or files called FILE0001.CHK, FILE0002.CHK, etc. You can then try using the MS-DOS editor (or, preferably, what's called a *hex editor*) to look through the file for data. Another trick you can try is to simply copy the file to another filename; hopefully some of the data will be copied to the new location.

11. While running Scandisk I received a message saying something about lost allocation units and crosslinked files. What does it mean?

Something happened while a program was trying to write data to your hard drive—maybe there was a power outage, or the program simply locked up—and the data was stored in the wrong place on the hard disk. Scandisk will save the information that's been "lost" this way, but unless it was a word-processing document, chances are you won't be able to do anything useful with it. Scandisk repairs the crosslinked files by copying them to new files, but one or more of the crosslinked files has been overwritten by data from the other crosslinked files. To prevent these problems, run Scandisk at least once every other day.

12. Scandisk told me I could use the TYPE command at an MS-DOS prompt to look at the data it tried to save—but when I do that, it scrolls by in a blur. What should I do?

Use the TYPE command, but like this: *TYPE FILE0001.CHK | MORE.* This will display the text one screen at a time. If you see that the file contains data you'll need later, you can use a text-editor or word processor to view and edit the file, then save it with another name. For example, use *EDIT FILE0001.CHK* to leisurely read and scroll through the file, as if it were a document. Then select sections that you want to rescue and save them into a different file.

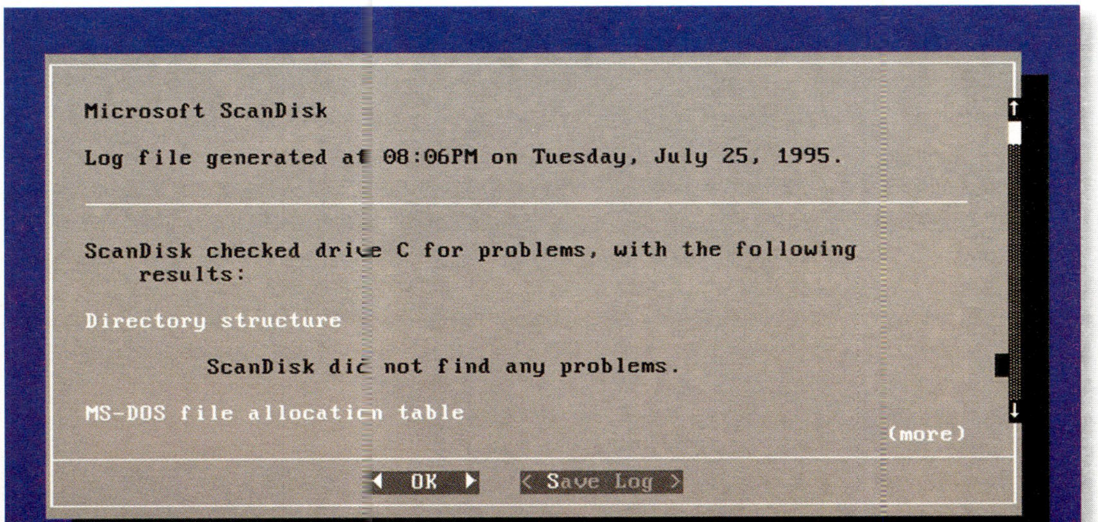

Microsoft ScanDisk

Log file generated at 08:06PM on Tuesday, July 25, 1995.

ScanDisk checked drive C for problems, with the following results:

Directory structure

ScanDisk did not find any problems.

MS-DOS file allocation table

OK   Save Log   (more)

Figure 1: *The MS-DOS utility Scandisk checks for any data that has been corrupted or stored incorrectly; then it tries to retrieve as much of it as possible.*

```
    Changes To "Civil War" since the manual was printed

Version 1.0.38, 2nd June 1995
==============================

Keyboard Shortcuts
==================

Arrow keys : Scroll the map window up/down/left/right
    +      : Zoom in
    -      : Zoom out
    Space  : On the Campaign Screen, toggle between resource and troop mode.
    Return : On most popup boxes Return will be the same as clicking OK.
    Escape : On most popup boxes, Escape will be the same as clicking CANCEL.
    Escape : In other places, Escape will allow you to quit the program.

Serial/Modem Play:

You can change the IRQ settings for the comms ports by clicking on the
-- More --
```

Figure 2: *To view a long text file without opening a text editor or word processor, use the DOS TYPE command followed by the name of the file you want to see and then the command | MORE. For example, enter this:* TYPE AUTOEXEC.BAT | MORE.

13. Is there a way to clean CD-ROMs?

Sure. Take a soft, dry cloth and wipe the data side of the disc in a straight line from the center of the disc to its edge. (If you manage to scratch the disk from center to edge you're cutting into just one or two bits per track, which will be automatically corrected during playback.)

Tempting as it seems, *do not* wipe the disc with a circular motion—a scratch in this direction can wipe out entire data tracks. Circular cleaning was correct for old vinyl LP records; it's completely wrong for CDs.

You can also use cleaning kits designed for audio CDs, as long as you follow the instructions and allow any cleaning liquids to evaporate completely before playing the CD.

14. Is there a way to clean CD-ROM *drives?*

Yes, kits for cleaning your CD-ROM drives are available at most computer outlets. You can also use cleaning kits designed for audio CD players. For best results, store your CDs in the original jewelbox cases to avoid dust. CD-ROM drives actually clean themselves automatically, but you can help out with a blast of compressed air directed into the slot while the CD drawer is open.

15. Where should I position my computer's speakers?

You obviously want to put them far enough apart to fully maximize the stereo effect, but remember that speakers contain magnets—and magnetism can wreak major havoc on floppy disks, hard drives, backup tapes and even a few electronic devices. Put your new speakers too close to the monitor, for instance, and you may see a distortion of color and resolution—*a distortion that can become permanent.*

One solution is to buy speakers that have been "shielded" so they can be placed much closer to monitors and other electrical gadgets. But in any case, don't stack tapes or floppies next to speakers, stereos, the monitor or other electrical devices.

16. Where should I store floppy disks and backup tapes?

In a dry place where they won't be exposed to high temperatures. If you store floppies and tapes in a dry place that gets very cold, wait a few minutes after bringing them into a warm room before you use them. Generally, disks and tapes like to be kept in an environment that's comfortable to you—neither too hot nor too cold, in an area of relatively low humidity. Consider rotating vital backup tapes and installation disks between different locations in case of fire at your primary location.

17. How often should I change the battery in my speakers?

Whenever you notice they aren't providing enough power to the speakers to achieve normal volume levels. If you don't know when that's happening, maybe you should buy an AC adapter for your speakers and forget about batteries altogether.

18. What is a virus?

A program that looks for other programs which it can "infect" by embedding a copy of itself in them, and, often, reproducing itself as well. Whenever the "host" program is run, the virus program also runs—and the end result can vary widely. Some viruses merely reproduce themselves for a while, then die; others display messages on-screen. A few viruses are truly vicious, causing serious damage by deleting files or scrambling information like the File Allocation Table that your computer needs to run.

19. How often should I check my computer to see if it's been infected with a virus?

It depends on several factors. Do you download binary files (i.e., programs rather than simple email) from the bulletin boards? Do you bring disks home from the office? Do you install shareware programs? (Online services like AOL or The Microsoft Network always check programs for viruses before they put them up for public downloading.)

The general rule is: The more often you use software of dubious origin, the more often you should check for viruses. In practice, though, computer viruses are largely a media scare story. Few people ever see one, and fewer still suffer any damage from the relatively rare malicious viruses.

20. When I run *Microsoft Anti-Virus*, I often get messages that certain files have changed, but the program doesn't detect any viruses. What's wrong?

The first time you run *MS AV*, it analyzes your hard drive and creates a summary called a *checksum* for every file that could carry a virus, such as program files (filenames ending in the .EXE or .COM extensions). When you run it the second time, *MS AV* compares the new checksums against the original, and if they don't match you get the "Files have changed" message. Install a new version of *WordPerfect for Windows*, for instance, and *MS AV* might come back and tell you that "File WPWIN.EXE has changed." If, however, you can't think of a good reason why a particular file might have changed its size, you need to get an updated anti-virus program to rule out the possibility that you have a real virus. Most anti-virus software is continually updated because new viruses appear all the time. But remember, your chances of suffering from a damaging virus are about the same as the odds that you'll meet Henry Kissinger.

INSIDE YOUR PC: THE JARGON EXPLAINED

21. What do 386 and 486 mean when describing computers? And is there a 586?

386 is short for 80386, the third in Intel's line of 80 × 86 processors. A 386 is a 32-bit processor (it transmits and receives data in 32-bit chunks—see number 42 below) that has provisions built in to permit efficient multitasking—i.e., running two programs at one time.

486s (i.e., 80486) are very similar to 386s, with the biggest differences being that the 486 has: an improved instruction set (it handles computer programs more effectively); an on-chip **data cache** (to hold recently accessed information and provide it swiftly back to the CPU); an optional on-chip floating-point unit (FPU, or **math coprocessor**); as well as an improved **bus interface** (to send and receive data faster from elsewhere in the computer).

As a result, a 486 performs roughly twice as fast as a 386, if they're both running at, say, a 25MHz clock speed.

There is a 586—it's called a Pentium. Intel avoided the obvious "586" because other manufacturers had already muddied the waters with their own alternative "486" chips. Instead, Intel focused on an extensive marketing campaign for the Pentium, which was only sullied slightly when it was discovered that the Pentium could make an occasional and trivial math error when dividing numbers. The problem has been fixed in new chips, and Intel will replace your Pentium if you request it. However, you're as likely to suffer from this "flaw" in a Pentium as you are to meet Bill Gates. Like viruses, the Pentium bug is another media concoction.

The Pentium has a 64-bit data bus which boosts video and hard drive performance, a fat on-chip cache, as well as new instructions that programs can take advantage of to achieve even higher speeds. We're only now starting to see programs that advertise "Pentium-Optimized" to run faster on Pentium processors, and, wouldn't you know, slightly slower on other **CPU**s.

22. What is the CPU?

The Central Processing Unit (CPU) is your computer's brain—more specifically, it's the part of the computer that *computes*. The CPU interprets and executes computer programming instructions; how fast it does this is determined by the type of processor it is (386, 486 or Pentium), the speed in megahertz at which it's running, and any ultra-high-speed memory (cache memory) attached to the CPU itself.

23. What does megahertz mean—i.e., "a 486/66MHz" computer?

It's a measurement of frequency in millions of cycles per second—i.e., one megahertz is equal to one million cycles per second. All you really need to know is that the bigger the number in front of MHz, the faster your PC should run.

24. What's the difference between DX and SX?

A 486SX is basically the same as a 486DX, with one big exception—it doesn't have a math coprocessor. A coprocessor is a kind of second CPU that takes on the job of solving any math problems involving fractions. The computer finds working with fractions hard, just as humans do—and for the same reasons. This has no bearing on the speed at which most software runs because most programs don't require fractional computation. But a math coprocessor is almost essential to run Computer-Aided Design (**CAD**) software, some flight simulators, and 3D graphics software.

On the other hand, the 386SX chip is a 16-bit version of the 386DX processor (neither have a math coprocessor). The 386SX chip runs Windows 3.1 just as well as the 386DX, but is a stinker when running Windows 95, which uses 32-bit instructions extensively.

25. What is a SIMM?

Single In-Line Memory Module. It's a tiny circuit card with a few **RAM** chips on it that you insert into your motherboard's memory expansion slots to increase the amount of RAM in your system.

26. What is a motherboard?

The motherboard is the large circuit board inside your computer where everything comes together. It's home to the processor, memory and expansion slots for devices such as hard drives, video cards, sound boards and more. How fast the motherboard can funnel data between the processor, memory, and the peripherals determines how fast your PC runs. It's sort of like the nervous system of your PC, responsible for making sure data gets sent to the right place at the right time.

27. What is a bus?

It's a shared pathway built into the motherboard over which data and electrical signals are transferred, either within a computer or between the computer and peripheral devices such as a video card. The type of bus your motherboard has determines how fast data can be sent between the processor and video adapter and the central processing unit. If a bus connects points within the computer itself, it's

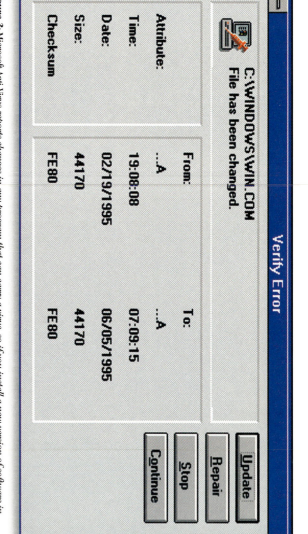

Figure 3: Microsoft Anti-Virus reports changes in any program that can carry a virus, so if you install a new version of software in which the program filename is the same, you'll see this message when you next run MS AV.

Verify Error

C:\WINDOWS\WIN.COM
File has been changed.

	From:	To:
Attribute:	...A	...A
Time:	19:08:08	07:09:15
Date:	02/19/1995	06/05/1995
Size:	44170	44170
Checksum	FE80	FE80

Update | Repair | Stop | Continue

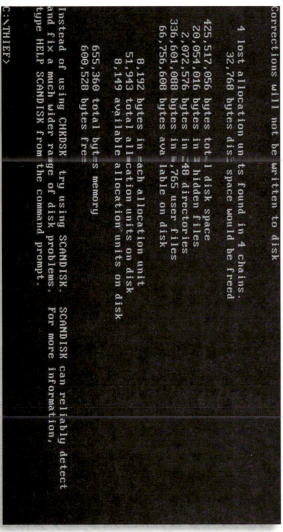

```
Corrections will not be written to disk

4 lost allocation units found in 4 chains.
    32,768 bytes disk space would be freed

425,517,056 bytes total disk space
     20,054,016 bytes in 3 hidden files
      2,072,576 bytes in 48 directories
    336,601,088 bytes in 9,765 user files
     66,756,608 bytes available on disk

      8,192 bytes in each allocation unit
     51,943 total allocation units on disk
      8,149 available allocation units on disk

    655,360 total bytes memory
    600,528 bytes free
```

Instead of using CHKDSK, try using SCANDISK. SCANDISK can reliably detect and fix a much wider range of disk problems. For more information, type HELP SCANDISK from the command prompt.

C:\THIEF>

Figure 4: MS-DOS also features a utility called Checkdisk (CHKDSK) that will locate misplaced or corrupt data. It's not as sophisticated as Scandisk.

called a *data bus*; if it connects the computer peripherals, it's called an *I/O (input/output) bus*.

28. What does VL-Bus mean when referring to a video card? Is it different than PCI?

A VL-Bus card is a video card that's used with a VL-Bus motherboard. VL-Bus (short for VESA local bus—see question 82 to learn about VESA) video cards can process data and send it on to the monitor as quickly as it receives it from the central processing unit.

PCI also describes a type of motherboard and accompanying video card. PCI video cards work much the same as VL-Bus cards, but the PCI motherboard has built-in chips to regulate the flow of information from *all* peripherals (video card, hard drive, floppy-disk drives, etc.) to improve overall performance.

29. What is a serial port?

Serial ports are on the back of your PC (or in some cases on your motherboard inside the computer), and they're designed to accept cables from your mouse, printer or modem. Most PCs come with two types of serial ports—25-pin and 9-pin, called COM1 and COM2—so it's easy to tell into which port an adapter will fit. They're called "serial" because they transmit data one bit at a time, while a parallel port can send several bits simultaneously.

30. What's a parallel port?

An interface from a computer system where data is transferred in or out in parallel—in other words, on more than one wire and thus more swiftly than a single-wire *serial* port.

The main thing you should remember is that your PC's parallel port is also called LPT1, and that it's probably the port to which your printer is connected.

31. What is a Com port?

It's short for communication port, which is another name for serial port (see above). Com ports allow peripheral devices such as modems, mice, scanners, etc. to "talk" to your PC. Most PCs have two external serial ports—COM1 and COM2—for attaching external peripherals such as a mouse or an external modem. If for some reason a new modem card is conflicting with an internal COM port, you may need to configure it as COM3 or COM4. However, you're usually limited to using only two COM ports at a time.

32. I'm shopping for a new hard drive, and keep seeing references to SCSI and IDE. What do these terms mean?

SCSI, or Small Computer Systems Interface (pronounced "scuzzy") and IDE (Integrated Drive Electronics) are two types of interface cards that plug into the motherboard and are connected to hard drives and other peripherals. Because IDE cards can only support two floppy-disk drives and two hard drives, that format is losing ground to SCSI, which can handle up to seven devices—including CD-ROM drives, scanners and optical devices in addition to hard and floppy-disk drives.

Older IDE cards only recognize hard drives that are 512MB or smaller, but a new IDE card called Enhanced IDE (or EIDE) can handle two hard drives up to 7GB in size. And remember: SCSI interface cards only support SCSI hard drives, while IDE interface cards only support IDE hard drives.

33. What does SVGA mean?

It stands for Super Video Graphics Adapter, which in plain English means it can display graphics at much higher resolutions than a VGA card. Any computer manufactured in the past year and a half is almost certain to come with an SVGA card.

34. What is an accelerated video card?

It's a VESA local-bus video card with special chips built in that can take certain kinds of data—usually data associated with Windows applications—and perform additional calculations, lessening the amount of work the CPU has to perform.

Accelerated video cards can really speed up Windows performance, but some of them even slow things up in DOS because they're designed to take over only certain Windows functions, like drawing circles and so on.

35. What does CD-ROM stand for?

Compact Disc - Read Only Memory. The compact disc part is pretty obvious; the ROM part means that once a CD-ROM has been created, you can't store any new data on it. You can now buy CD-R (CD-Recordable) drives for under $2,000. These drives let you create your own CD-ROMs for under $15 per disc. CD-R is a Write-Once, Read-Mostly, or WORM technology.

36. What does it mean when a software package says it requires an "MPC Level 2" system?

MPC stands for Multimedia Personal Computer. An industry consortium called the MPC Council devised standards to define the types of components a PC had to have to be MPC Level 2. The most important requirements of the MPC Level 2 standard are: a 486SX/25MHz; video and color monitor that support at least 65,536 colors at 640 × 480 resolution; a 2X (300KB/sec) CD-ROM drive; and a 16-bit Sound Blaster-compatible sound card with six-voice multi-timbral MIDI synthesis, software volume control and mixing and a microphone input.

37. What are Video for Windows and Quicktime for Windows?

They're programs designed to display video footage and computer-rendered animations inside Windows. If a program uses video footage that's been stored in either of these formats, it usually installs the appropriate program to view the video.

38. What does GUI stand for?

It means Graphical User Interface. A Macintosh computer, for instance, uses a GUI, pronounced "gooey"—you click on folders and icons to activate programs and look inside files instead of typing in commands. Windows works in much the same way.

THANKS FOR THE MEMORY: THE DIFFERENT KINDS OF COMPUTER MEMORY AND HOW THEY WORK

39. What are the different kinds of memory in a computer?

There are three basic types of memory: RAM (Random Access Memory), ROM (Read-Only Memory), and read/write mass storage (on floppy disks or a hard drive). RAM is where programs reside when they're running; data can be stored in RAM, and saved from RAM onto a disk. Programs and data stored in ROM can be copied into RAM for use by the computer; or onto a floppy disk for storage, but no new data can be written into ROM—that's why you can't save files on a CD-ROM (which is a read-only form of mass storage). Your computer starts itself running from its system ROM chips. Read/write mass storage is a kind of memory, too. Data can be read from a floppy disk or hard drive, and you can put data on them for long-term storage.

Data in ROM and on floppy disks or your hard drive remains stored even if the power is turned off, but once you turn off your PC, any data that was in RAM memory is lost. Shut down your PC while a program's running, for instance, and when you turn it back on you won't find that program still running.

40. How much RAM do I need?

If you spend a lot of time in Windows 3.1 or Windows for Workgroups, you should have at least 8MB of RAM—any less and you'll constantly be waiting for programs to load. Also, many entertainment titles run much better with 8MB of RAM instead of 4MB. While Windows 95 will also run with just 4MB of RAM, be realistic. Even Windows 3.1 needs 8MB to perform well, and you'll want at least 8MB with Windows 95, too; 16MB is the "sweet spot" for optimal performance.

Luckily, installing more RAM is a simple procedure. However, RAM isn't cheap, currently running about $35 per megabyte, and if your computer has only four RAM sockets (also called SIMM sockets—see question 25), you'll have to remove your four 1MB SIMMs and replace them with two or more 4MB SIMMs.

41. What's the difference between Expanded Memory and Extended Memory?

Extended memory—called XMS for short—is any memory on IBM PCs above the first ("lowest") megabyte of RAM. Applications such as Microsoft Windows programs and MS-DOS programs that use DOS "extenders" use extended memory. Windows requires the HIMEM.SYS driver to be loaded upon bootup to access extended memory, while MS-DOS programs using DOS extenders may not.

Expanded memory, or EMS, is an earlier, more primitive, approach that is designed to allow IBM-compatible PCs to access memory—RAM—above the first megabyte.

Expanded memory can only be accessed 64kB at a time by MS-DOS programs, and requires the use of an expanded memory manager (a driver) such as EMM386, which comes with MS-DOS and Windows. Since new computers are not limited in their ability to access memory, few programs today use expanded memory.

42. Could you explain the differences between bits, bytes, kilobytes, megabytes and gigabytes?

Bit is short for "binary digit"—either one of the two characters represented by "0" and "1." A bit is the smallest unit of information that can be stored by a computer. A byte is a group of eight adjacent bits handled by the computer as a single

unit of data. For one thing, there's a code whereby every text character (along with the digits and punctuation symbols) can be described by numbers between 0 and 255. It just happens that a single byte can "contain" the numbers 0 and 255.

You might think a kilobyte would mean 1,000 bytes, but it actually means 1,024 bytes. (This is because computers don't use the decimal system like we do, where numbers round off to 10s, 100s and so on. Rather, computers use the binary system and round off at 64, 128... 1,024 and so on—all multiples, you might notice, of eight.) A megabyte is 1,024 kilobytes (or 1,048,576 bytes), and a gigabyte is a kilobyte of kilobytes, roughly a billion bytes (1,073,741,824 bytes to be computer-exact). Hard drive

manufacturers prefer to define a megabyte as 1,000 bytes and a gigabyte as a billion bytes, since it makes their hard drives seem larger. (Divide what's described as a "540MB" hard drive by

Figure 6: Type MEM /C/P at a DOS prompt to get a complete report of memory usage—from how much conventional memory is available to how much memory is being used by each program that's been loaded.

```
C:\GRABBER>mem

Modules using memory below 1 MB:

Name        Total              Conventional        Upper Memory
MSDOS       17,309   (17K)     17,309   (17K)      0    (0K)
HIMEM       1,168    (1K)      1,168    (1K)       0    (0K)
EMM386      8,368    (8K)      8,368    (8K)       0    (0K)
TEAC_CDA    12,464   (12K)     12,464   (12K)      0    (0K)
IFSHLP      3,872    (4K)      3,872    (4K)       0    (0K)
COMMAND     3,760    (4K)      3,760    (4K)       0    (0K)
SMOUSE      9,296    (9K)      9,296    (9K)       0    (0K)
MSCDEX      40,352   (39K)     40,352   (39K)      0    (0K)
MODE        480      (0K)      480      (0K)       0    (0K)
GRABBER     17,184   (17K)     17,184   (17K)      0    (0K)
Free        540,832  (528K)    540,832  (528K)     0    (0K)

Memory Summary:

Type of Memory    Total    =    Used    +    Free
Conventional      655,360       114,528      540,832
Upper             0             0            0
Reserved          131,072       131,072      0
```

Figure 5: If you have EMM386.EXE loaded, it will take Extended Memory (XMS) and turn it into Expanded Memory (EMS).

```
C:\GRABBER>mem

Memory Type        Total    =    Used    +    Free
Conventional       640K          112K         528K
Upper              128K          128K         0K
Reserved           0K            0K           0K
Extended (XMS)*    7,424K        1,536K       5,888K

Total memory       8,192K        1,776K       6,416K

Total under 1 MB   640K          112K         528K

Total Expanded (EMS)             7,744K (7,929,856 bytes)
Free Expanded (EMS)*             6,128K (6,275,072 bytes)

* EMM386 is using XMS memory to simulate EMS memory as needed.
  Free EMS memory may change as free XMS memory changes.

Largest executable program size    528K (540,416 bytes)
Largest free upper memory block     0K  (0 bytes)
MS-DOS is resident in the high memory area.

C:\GRABBER>
```

1,048,576 and you discover that you really bought 515MB of hard drive space.)

43. I'm trying to run a game but it keeps telling me that I don't have enough free conventional memory. How do I find out how much free conventional memory my computer has?

Type MEM at the DOS prompt and you'll get a memory allocation report with a line near the bottom that says "Largest executable program size," followed by the amount of free conventional memory listed in kilobytes (KB) and in thousands of bytes.

44. How can I maximize my amount of free conventional memory (the RAM under 640K)?

The only real way to increase conventional memory is to load some programs into high memory—and to create that high memory you need a memory manager such as EMM386.EXE (which comes with DOS and Windows). DOS's MemMaker utility is fairly good at freeing up conventional memory by altering your CONFIG.SYS and AUTOEXEC.BAT files. (See the System Files article for an introduction to editing and optimizing your system files.)

45. What are drivers?

Every piece of hardware attached to your computer—mouse, keyboard, printer, disk drives, memory boards and more—is a device. MS-DOS and Windows rely on programs called device drivers, or drivers for short, to control each device attached to the system.

MS-DOS has built-in drivers for the keyboard, monitor, hard and floppy disk drives,

PERIPHERAL DEVICES: MONITORS, CD-ROM DRIVES, PRINTERS, MICE, MODEMS AND MORE

and communication ports (COM1, COM2, etc., also known as serial ports). But whenever you add a peripheral that's not supported by MS-DOS drivers—such as a mouse, sound card, CD-ROM drive, etc.—you'll have to add the name of some type of driver program to your CONFIG.SYS file, so MS-DOS will know how to use the device. Generally, the setup software that comes with peripherals will automatically add the necessary line to CONFIG.SYS, and also copy the driver to the right location on your hard drive.

Windows 3.1 uses Windows drivers to control your equipment, often ignoring the DOS drivers. Windows 95 substitutes even more capable drivers—and it uses very few MS-DOS drivers.

It's important to obtain the latest drivers for your video card, printer and other hardware to take advantage of speed improvements and bug fixes. Contact the manufacturer to obtain updated drivers. You can also often find the latest drivers on services like CompuServe, America Online and The Microsoft Network.

46. What's the difference between inkjet and laser printers?

Inkjet printers have nozzles which electrostatically spray small ink droplets onto the paper to print graphics and text. A laser printer uses a rotating mirror to reflect laser beams onto the paper; the beam forms an electrostatic image area which attracts electrically charged toner (dry ink powder), which is then heated (or "fixed") onto the paper to create the desired image.

Laser printers produce higher resolution than inkjet printers, but depending on your needs the improved quality may not be worth the extra cost of a laser printer.

You can also get color-capable inkjet printers for not much more than a black-and-white printer, and for a fraction of the cost of a color laser printer.

47. What is the difference between a "bus mouse" and a "serial mouse?"

A bus mouse plugs into a special adapter on the back of your PC—and nothing else will fit in that adapter. A serial mouse, on the other hand, can be hooked to either of the two serial ports on the back of your PC, both of which can be used for other devices like a modem or scanner. The new PS/2 style mouse is similar to a bus mouse, but you can only plug in PS/2 (mouse port) mice, not a bus mouse or a serial mouse.

48. Aside from cost and where they're located, are there any differences between internal and external modems?

The main difference is in the COM ports they can use. Because an external modem plugs directly into one of the two serial ports on the back of your PC—and because these are automatically set as COM1 and COM2—you have to configure your communications software to use one of those two ports unless you have a special serial-port adapter. Internal serial devices—such as a modem—can be assigned to use those two ports, as well as COM3 and COM4. External modems are also more convenient because you can turn them off separately from your computer in case you need to reset them or force them to hang up the line.

49. While installing the software for my sound card, I was asked to specify an IRQ. What's an IRQ, and what number should I use?

Short for Interrupt Request, IRQ refers to an input found on many processors (a processor is the primary chip inside the computer; the one that does all the calculating) which causes the processor to suspend normal instruction execution temporarily and start executing a request from a peripheral device. Your mouse, for example, uses an interrupt request. Without it, you wouldn't be able to move the mouse pointer to click on the Cancel button and stop the playback of a WAV file until it was finished.

About the only time you're asked to assign an IRQ is when you install your sound card's software. Choose IRQ 5 or 7 and you should have no problems. If you do have problems, though, see the article "Plug & Play or Plug & Pray" elsewhere in this book.

50. I set my sound card's IRQ to 5. Now the installation software for my sound card is asking for a DMA channel. What's a DMA channel, and what number should I use for it?

Direct Memory Access (DMA) is sort of complicated. Perhaps the easiest way to put it is that a peripheral that's been assigned a DMA channel can control the flow of data in and out of the computer's memory, completely bypassing the processor.

About the only time you have to specify a DMA is when you're setting up a sound card. Your safest bet is to specify DMA 1.

51. Can I plug the output of my sound card into my stereo?

Yes, and it's easy. All you need is a cable that plugs into the Line Out plug on your sound card—the one you plug your computer speakers into—and converts the signal into left and right stereo channels. (You'll probably need an adapter with a female 1/8-inch stereo plug on one end, and two RCA plugs on the other, available at Radio Shack if it didn't come with your sound card.) Just attach the two cables as you would any other device running into your stereo system.

52. How do I know if I can use a joystick with my computer?

Most PCs come with a game port, an adapter on the back of the computer that only a PC joystick or hand-held game pad plug can fit into. It's usually located beside one of the serial ports where you plug in a mouse or modem. Also, most sound cards have game ports.

If you don't use the game port located on the sound card, make sure it's been disabled—if it hasn't, it could cause problems when using the other game port. Check in your sound card's manual to find out how to disable the port.

53. What is dpi, and what range should I look for?

It stands for dots per inch. The higher the number of dots per inch for a printer, for example, the better the quality of the image that printer can produce—a document printed at 300 dpi looks a lot better than a document printed at, say, 150 dpi. You can purchase a 600 dpi printer, which has quadruple the resolution of 300 dpi (since the dots are increased both horizontally and vertically), for little more than what you may have paid for a 300 dpi printer a year ago.

Monitors are usually specified in terms of dot pitch instead of dots per inch. The dot pitch is the space between phosphor dots on your screen. Get a 0.28 millimeter (mm) dot pitch monitor in preference to 0.39mm or 0.54mm dot pitch—smaller is better with this specification.

54. What does resolution mean in reference to my monitor's display?

Resolution is the number of pixels—tiny dots—that are displayed on your monitor. A resolution of 640 × 480 means the display includes 640 dots horizontally and 480 dots vertically. The higher the resolution, the sharper the display. Resolution can also refer to the number of colors, or color depth, in a display: 640 × 480 × 64KB means there can be up to 64KB (i.e., a little over 65,000) colors onscreen at any given time.

In order for a monitor to reproduce the resolution being sent to it by a video card, it has to be able to position its pixels precisely. That's where dot pitch comes into play. With 640 × 480 resolution, a dot pitch of 0.39mm is acceptable, but if you want to use 800 × 600, 1024 × 768 or higher resolutions, you'll want a dot pitch of at least 0.28mm. Also, a non-interlaced monitor is preferable to an interlaced monitor, which can cause distracting flicker at higher resolutions. Another factor that effects the quality of a monitor is how fast it updates (refreshes) the screen, measured in updates per second. A plain monitor updates the screen 60 times per second (a refresh rate of 60Hz). A higher refresh rate is easier on your eyes, but it, too, depends on the capabilities of your video card as well as the monitor.

For best results, choose a 0.28mm dot pitch, non-interlaced monitor that supports a refresh rate of 72Hz or better.

55. What do 2X, 3X and 4X mean when used to describe CD-ROM drives?

They refer to how fast the CD-ROM drive can transmit data. Just read "X" as "times," with the X representing a data transfer rate of roughly 150KB/sec—a 2X drive transmits at 300KB/sec, a 3X at around 450KB/sec. A 4X drive transfers data at four times the 150KB/sec speed of an old-fashioned "single speed" CD-ROM, or 600 KB/sec. The newest drives support 6X speeds. However, we don't expect to ever see CD-ROM drives faster than 8X—it's just not feasible to build a motor that can speed up and slow down fast enough to support a speed like 16X. That will have to wait until the CD-ROM format is redesigned entirely.

TROUBLESHOOTING: SOLUTIONS TO COMMON PROBLEMS AND QUESTIONS

56. My communications software displays the current time and date in a corner of the screen—but it's always incorrect. What's wrong?

Your communications software gets its time and date info from your system. To fix the problem, type TIME [Enter] at any DOS prompt, then enter the correct time. (PCs use military time, so 7:30 p.m., for example, would be entered 19:30:00.) To correct the date, type DATE [Enter], and put in the date in month/day/year format—to set it to September 6, 1995, you'd type 09-06-95.

With Windows 3.1, run the Date & Time icon from the Control Panel to set your system's date and time. With Windows 95, just double-click on the clock on the taskbar to set the time and date. (If you're on a network, your date and time are probably reset every time you log in. Contact your network administrator if the file server's date and time need correcting.)

57. OK, I fixed the date and time—but every time I turn off my computer and then come back to it, the time and date are wrong again. What's happening?

Chances are that the tiny lithium battery inside your computer—the one that provides the power your system needs to "remember" a small amount of critical information about your computer while it's turned off—is running out of juice. Replace it as soon as possible; if you don't, your computer can forget more significant information than merely the time and date. If it forgets what type of hard drive is installed, you can face an annoying delay trying to use the Setup routine to restore this information.

58. Is there any way to recover files I've accidentally deleted?

Yes, but how well it works depends on how you've configured Microsoft's Undelete utility in both DOS and Windows. Undelete can be configured in three ways: Delete Sentry, Delete Tracker, and Standard. Standard is the default setting and it works fairly well—unless you copied data to the disk where the deleted files were located before using Undelete. Delete Tracker remembers where deleted files were located, so it offers a better chance of file recovery than Standard Undelete.

If you're really concerned about recovering deleted files, activate Delete Sentry on bootup (each time the computer is turned on) by including the line C:\DOS\UNDELETE /S somewhere in your AUTOEXEC.BAT file. With Delete Sentry loaded, any files you delete are stored in a directory for a specified period of time. One drawback: Deleting files won't free up hard-drive space until you purge the Delete Sentry files by erasing them.

With Windows 95, deleted files are automatically stored in a system folder called the Recycle Bin. The Recycle Bin also appears as a desktop icon. Just double-click the Recycle Bin icon to view its contents, where you can choose to restore any files you've previously deleted. The Recycle Bin only saves files you delete from a folder or from Explorer—it won't catch files deleted by programs or those you delete from the DOS prompt.

In an emergency, you can run the Undelete program with Windows 95, but the only way to do it is to "clean boot" your computer using plain DOS. Turn on your computer and press SHIFT+F5 when you see the "Starting Windows 95" message. If you don't have an Undelete command, copy it to your \Windows\Command folder from the \Other\Oldmsdos folder of the Windows 95 CD-ROM.

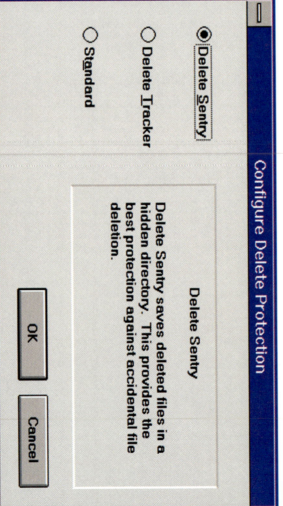

Configure Delete Protection

○ Standard
○ Delete Tracker
● Delete Sentry

Delete Sentry

Delete Sentry saves deleted files in a hidden directory. This provides the best protection against accidental file deletion.

OK   Cancel

Figure 7: Both DOS and Windows have Undelete, a utility program to recover files that have been deleted. How well Undelete works, though, depends on how you've configured it.

59. My mouse works fine in DOS, but not in Windows. What's wrong and how do I fix it?

Make sure that you selected the appropriate mouse when you were setting up Windows. In the Program Manager, double-click on Main, then open Windows Setup. If the mouse type isn't correct, click on Change System Settings and choose the appropriate driver (be sure to have both your Windows disks and the disk on which your mouse driver came).

Another potential cause is if your mouse is using COM3 or COM4; Windows 3.1 can't use mice attached to these ports. The chances of this are very slim unless you've configured an internal modem and some other device to use COM1 and COM2. You'll need to set up the modem to use COM3 or COM4 so the mouse can use COM1 or COM2.

60. Can I change the speed at which the mouse cursor moves?

Often there is a "switch" you can add to the command that loads the DOS mouse driver that determines how fast the cursor moves in proportion to the movement of the mouse. To set the speed of the cursor with a Logitech mouse to

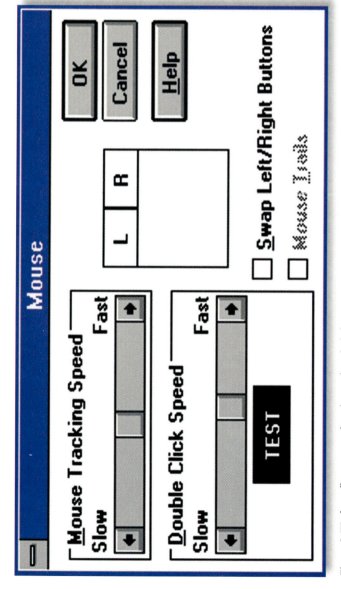

Figure 8: *Windows allows you to adjust the speed at which the mouse cursor moves. You can also tweak how fast you must double-click to activate a program, and even swap the functions of the left and right mouse buttons.*

its lowest level, for instance, you would enter the command *MOUSE /S00* at a DOS prompt; *MOUSE /S10* would cause the cursor to move at the fastest rate.

To change mouse sensitivity in Windows, open the *Control Panel* and double-click on *Mouse*, then use the sliding bar to adjust the cursor speed.

With Windows 95, you also run the Mouse icon from the Control Panel. Click the *Start* button, then the *Settings* menu, and choose *Control Panel*. From the Mouse property sheets, click the tab heading for *Motion*, and adjust the slider to control how fast your mouse moves.

61. Why do I get the message "Invalid drive specification" when I try to switch from my hard drive to the CD-ROM drive I installed?

You're either typing in the wrong drive letter, or the CD-ROM drivers—the programs needed for your PC to talk to the CD-ROM—have not been set up correctly.

To verify both that the CD-ROM driver has been installed and to determine which drive letter your CD-ROM is set up for, look for a line in your CONFIG.SYS file that looks something like this: DEVICE=C:\TSCSI\TSLCDR.SYS /D:TSLCD. The /D:TSLCD is the *device name* of the CD-ROM, used to communicate with the Microsoft CD-ROM Extensions (MSCDEX).

The line in AUTOEXEC.BAT that loads the Microsoft CD-ROM extensions would look something like C:\DOS\MSCDEX.EXE /D:TSLCD /M:10. You can add the switch /L:E to force your CD-ROM to use whatever drive letter you like, in this case, drive E:.

62. After my hard drive failed, I replaced it with a new one. I then turned on my computer and went to the CMOS setup screen and entered the appropriate information about the hard drive—number of cylinders, heads, sectors and so forth. So why doesn't my computer recognize the hard drive?

Before you can tell your system exactly what type of new hard drive you have, you first have to let it know it's there. There's a utility called FDISK that comes with MS-DOS designed to do just this. First, boot your computer with a boot disk that has the FDISK program (it's located in the MS-DOS directory). At the A:> or B:> prompt, enter the command FDISK. This will let the system know there's a hard drive there, and when you enter the appropriate information about your hard drive in the CMOS program the next time you restart your computer you should be up and running just fine.

63. I'm having trouble getting a dial tone from my modem in Windows. What can I do?

Make sure that you've got the phone lines hooked up correctly—there should be a telephone cable running from the LINE jack on your modem to the phone jack in the wall. (The TEL jack is used to attach your telephone itself to the back of the modem.) If you're unsure which serial port (also known as COM1, COM2, etc.) your modem is using, type *ECHO ATDT > COMx* at a DOS prompt, with the *x* representing the serial port you think the modem is using. If you hear a dial tone or some other signal, you know you specified the correct port. (To turn off the dial tone, type *ECHO ATHO > COMx*.)

If you hate using DOS, run the Windows 3.1 Terminal accessory, and try configuring it to any of your COM ports. Use the Ports applet in Control Panel if you don't see all your COM ports listed. With Windows 95, use the Modems applet from Control Panel to auto-matically detect which port is used by your modem.

64. Ever since I installed my modem, my sound card has been silent. What's wrong?

Most likely an IRQ conflict. Solving this kind of "hardware conflict" requires that you follow the series of steps described in the article "Plug & Play or Plug & Pray" by Scott Clark and Peter Norton elsewhere in this book.

65. I just bought a new 14.4 modem, but when I dial into a bulletin board I see the message "CONNECT 9600." What's wrong, and how do I get the modem to run at its maximum speed?

You need to tell your communications software at what speed it should try to connect. To set the baud rate for the Terminal program in Windows, for instance, choose *Communications* from the menu bar, and then pick the appropriate speed. (Note: If you haven't configured Terminal yet, you'll need to select the correct communications port before choosing a baud rate.)

Be forewarned, though, that if the number you're dialing only accepts a 9,600 **baud** connection, then you'll still see the "CONNECT 9600" message even if your communications software is set to a faster baud rate. When your modem talks to a slower modem, it must slow down to make itself understood.

You may also see the term bits per second used instead of baud, and **BPS** is actually a more accurate term. To configure your modem's speed with Windows 95, double-click the *Modem* icon in the Control Panel.

66. Is there a way to keep Call Waiting from disconnecting my modem while I'm online or sending a fax?

Sure. Just type the code that disables Call Waiting in the front of the phone number you're dialing. Let's say I wanted to disable Call Waiting during my CompuServe sessions. I would open *WinCim*, choose *Session Settings*, and insert "*70" in front of the access number at the bottom of the dialog box (check with your local phone company to find out what code disables Call Waiting in your area).

67. Why can I hear sound effects but no music when playing some CD-ROM games?

It's most likely because the CD-ROM drive hasn't been connected to the sound card. You can hear the sound effects because they're being loaded into memory with the other game files, and are then sent directly to the sound card. The music, on the other hand, is played by the CD-ROM the way it would play an audio CD; it's "piped" via a special cable to your sound card.

If you can hear music through headphones connected to the headphone jack on the front of your CD-ROM but not through your speakers, then your CD-ROM drive is definitely not connected to the sound card. You should be able to find a CD-ROM audio cable at a computer store, but if you have trouble, check with the manufacturer of your CD-ROM drive. (Some CD-ROM interface cards and most external CD-ROM drives include left/right RCA phono jacks. If your system has these features, you could buy a cable to route the signal from the RCA phono jacks to the mini phono plug on the back of your sound card, where it's marked LINE INPUT.)

68. What should I do if I'm running a Windows Application and I receive a message saying that it has caused a General Protection Fault?

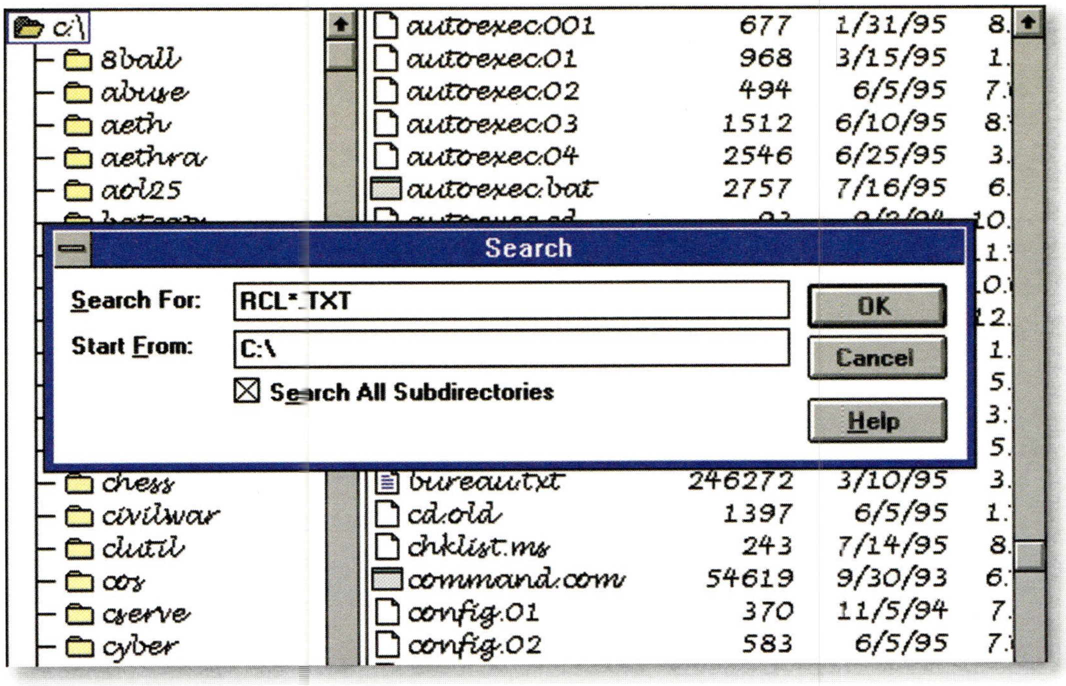

Not much—just click on the OK button and hope that the program shuts down by itself. And if it keeps on happening in one particular program, you might want to call the software publisher's technical support line for advice. A GPF is almost always caused by a bug in a software program, not in Windows itself. However, poor quality video and printer drivers can also cause mysterious GPFs, so you'll want to obtain the latest version of

Figure 10. Use the Search function in File Manager when you can't remember the directory where you saved files. You do need to know part of the filename, though.

Search

Search For: RCL*.TXT
Start From: C:\
☒ Search All Subdirectories

OK   Cancel   Help

c:\

chess		
civilwar		
chsl		
oos		
serve		
cyber		
8ball		
abuse		
aeth		
aethra		
aol25		
autoexec.001	677	1/31/95
autoexec.01	968	3/15/95
autoexec.02	494	6/5/95
autoexec.03	1512	6/10/95
autoexec.04	2546	6/25/95
autoexec.bat	2757	7/16/95
bureau.txt	246272	3/10/95
cd.old	1397	6/5/95
chklist.ms	243	7/14/95
command.com	54619	9/30/93
config.01	370	11/5/94
config.02	583	6/5/95

Figure 9. You can disable Call Waiting (and thereby prevent disconnection while faxing or during an online session) by entering a code in front of the number your communications software is dialing.

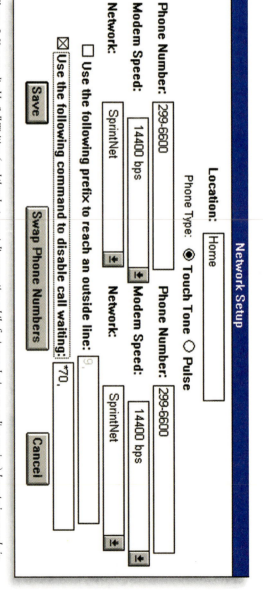

Network Setup

Location: ● Home

Phone Number: 299-6600   Phone Type: ● Touch Tone ○ Pulse
Modem Speed: 14400 bps   Modem Speed: 14400 bps
Network: SprintNet   Network: SprintNet

☐ Use the following prefix to reach an outside line: 9,
☒ Use the following command to disable call waiting: *70,

Phone Number: 299-6600

Save   Swap Phone Numbers   Cancel

the driver for your video card from the vendor. Fortunately, Windows 95 virtually eliminates GPFs, and also isolates programs so effectively that you'll rarely, if ever, have to resort to turning the power off, then back on (rebooting) to regain control of your computer.

69. While running a program in Windows, the hourglass icon appeared—and wouldn't go away. How can I end the program without being able to use the mouse?

There are three ways to shut down a program that's robbed you of the mouse cursor—pressing *Alt+F4*, pressing *Ctrl+Esc* and then selecting *End Task* after you've highlighted the offending program or by pressing *Ctrl+Alt+Del*. You may be able to shut down the offending program. If you resort to the last method, pay careful attention to the on-screen instructions.

70. What does the message "Out of environment space" mean?

Environment space is the amount of memory allocated in your CONFIG.SYS for setting environment variables—the command SET BLASTER A200 I5 D1, for instance, is such a variable. (It lets various programs know that your sound card's Sound Blaster settings are port 220, IRQ 5 and DMA 1.)

By default, you're given 256 bytes of memory as environment space. To eliminate the "Out of environment space" message and ensure that all your SET commands are taking effect, you can insert the line SHELL=C:\DOS\COMMAND.COM C:\DOS\ /E:512 /P into your CONFIG.SYS file (if you have a similar line in your CONFIG.SYS, just increase the number after "E:" to 512). See the article on "System Files" for more information on editing your CONFIG.SYS file.

71. I'm sure I saved the file I was working on, but now I can't locate it. What's the easiest way to find it?

In DOS, type *CD* [Enter] to get to the C:\> prompt, then type *DIR name*.* /S*, where *name* is the first few letters of the missing filename. Your search may return several files, but the one you're looking for will be there somewhere.

In Windows 3.x, open the *File Manager* and click on *File*, then choose *Search*. In the dialog box that appears, type in *name*.* * for filename, backspace over any directory name that appears in the "Search From" box, and make sure you have the "Search All Subdirectories" box checked.

With Windows 95, click the *Start* button, then choose *Find, Files or Folders*. (Alternatively, you can select *Find* from the *Tools* menu of any folder or Explorer. If your keyboard features one of the new "Windows" keys, just hold that key down while pressing the *F* key.) Enter any part of the file you're looking for in the box labeled

Named. You can narrow your search using the *Date & Time* tab heading; use *Advanced* if you need to constrain your search further.

72. I mistakenly deleted a Program Group in Windows. How do I get it back?

Let Windows do it for you. Double-click on *Main*, then on *Windows Setup*. Choose *Options*, then select *Set Up Applications*. If you know the directory where the application in the deleted group resides, choose "Ask you to specify an application"; if you're not sure, pick "Search for applications." (If you used the latter approach, be sure to select "C: A Local Drive.")

When Windows finds applications, it tries to place them in an existing Program Group—make a note of the location. Go to the Program Manager and choose *File*, then *New*. Type in the name of the deleted Program Group, and an empty Program Group appears. Then you can drag-and-drop the application Windows recovered into the new Program Group.

To restore the default Windows program groups, select *Run* from the Program Manager's *File* menu, and enter either *SETUP /P* (for Windows 3.1) or *WINSETUP /P* (for Windows for Workgroups 3.11). With Windows 95, you can click *Start*, then *Run*, then enter *GRPCONV*.

73. I tried to dial into a bulletin board, but all I see are crazy characters on the screen. What's wrong?

You've probably chosen the incorrect communication parameters in your communications software. The most common setting is 8-1-N (which stands for eight data bits, one stop bit, and No Parity); the other popular setting is 7-1-E (seven data bits, one stop bit, and Even Parity). If one of these two settings doesn't work for you, contact the BBS administrator to find out what settings to use. (Some modem

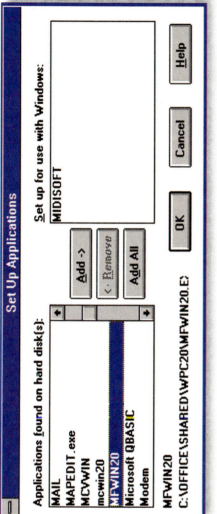

Figure 11: Did you accidentally delete a Program Group? Double-click on Main, then on Windows Setup, then choose Set Up Applications. Windows will do the rest.

programs use a "strip bit 7" feature instead of parity settings to correct this problem.)

74. When I try to install a program on my hard drive, it says I don't have enough space, but when I use the DIR command it shows that I have the required space and then some. What gives?

You've probably compressed your hard drive with DoubleSpace or some other disk-compression utility. Some programs use their own type of data compression after installation, and can't be installed on a compressed hard drive. You'll need to install the program on a part of the drive you didn't compress. This part of the drive will appear to be a different drive (it will use a separate drive designation letter, such as E:) and is often labeled Host.

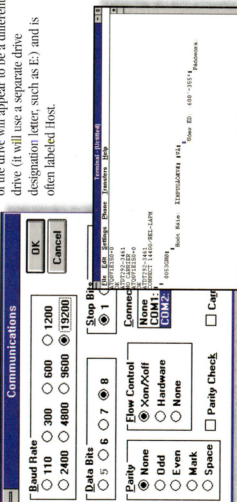

Figure 12, Figure 13: If you see strange characters when you dial into an online service or electronic bulletin board, you're probably using the wrong communications parameters. In the Terminal program that comes with Windows, you can change the parameters in the Communications dialogue box.

75. Why do I see nothing but squiggly lines in Windows after using Setup (from the "C:\>WINDOWS" prompt) to change my display resolution?

You've either chosen the wrong Windows video driver, or your monitor isn't designed to display at the resolution you specified. To ensure you picked the correct video driver, consult the manual that came with your computer (or video card, if you bought it separately).

ENSURING PEAK PERFORMANCE

76. What exactly does defragmenting a hard drive do, and how often should I do it?

A defragmenting utility (such as the Defrag application that comes with MS-DOS 6.0 or the Disk Defragmenter built into Windows 95) reorganizes your hard drive to make it respond more efficiently when you run a program or open a file.

Over time, a file can become split up into sections and these sections will be strewn in various locations on the drive. For example, it might be divided into 12 sections and some of them might be scattered around far apart from each other. (Why? Hard drives put new information into any of its available blank zones when you save a file. Sometimes those blank zones are too small to hold the entire file, so the file is divided up and spread around.)

Fragmentation increases over time, and it slows things down. When you open a badly fragmented file in, say, a word processor, the hard drive has to spend extra time locating all these dispersed pieces of the file. This retards things and it takes lots longer to open that file (or, if an application is fragmented, to start it running).

Generally, you should defragment your hard drive about once a month. *Warning: Never* run a DOS-based defragmentation utility if you're using Windows 95. Instead, click the Windows 95 *Start* button and choose *Programs/Accessories/System Tools/Disk Defragmenter*. If Windows 95 tells you that you don't yet need to defragment, you can skip the defrag and check it again a month later.

77. Why do videos look choppy and slow in Windows, and what can I do to correct the problem?

Video can be slowed down if you have several applications open at once. Even if they're inactive, just having them open is a drain on your system's resources. Close every application except the one displaying the video, and you may get improved performance.

Other likely causes and remedies: You're not using a local-bus video card (you should upgrade if you aren't), your processor isn't powerful enough (a distinct possibility if you're using a 486/25MHz CPU), or your CD-ROM drive isn't fast enough (a single-speed drive is hopelessly outdated).

You may also want to upgrade to the latest version of Microsoft Video for Windows, which is usually included with up-to-date multimedia software. Windows 95 significantly enhances video playback with accelerated video support for even plain SuperVGA display adapters.

78. What is disk-caching software?

Disk-caching software takes information that's been read from the hard drive by a program and temporarily stores it in RAM. This way, if the program tries to read that same information from the hard drive again, the disk-caching software provides it directly from memory instead. Data can move from RAM much faster than it can be pulled off a hard drive.

Obviously, your RAM can't hold all the data on your hard drive. Instead, a cache is designed to keep only the most frequently accessed data on tap—files you haven't used recently are moved from the cache back to your hard drive. Because the cache may contain data that hasn't been written to disk yet, be sure when you exit Windows 3.x or shut down Windows 95 that you wait for the hard disk LED on your front panel to stop flickering before you turn off your computer. (Windows 95 politely displays the message "It's safe to shut down your computer now.")

79. How can I make my computer run faster without buying new hardware?

The first thing to check is the turbo button on the front of your computer. Make sure it's engaged, and that the turbo light is also lit, if your computer has this feature.

Another thing that may help is the Defrag utility that comes with MS-DOS 6.0 and later (see above). You could also try using SmartDrive, a disk-cache utility that uses RAM to store frequently accessed data—if an application needs to retrieve the data again it can pull it much more quickly from RAM instead of the hard drive. (The version of SmartDrive that shipped with DOS 6.x can also speed up your CD-ROM.)

With Windows 3.1, run the 386 Enhanced icon from the Control Panel, and make sure your computer is set up to use a permanent swap file. If not, choose the Permanent Swap File option and set aside half the amount of your RAM for the swap file. Don't use the recommended setting—it's way too high. For example, if your computer has 8MB of RAM, use a 4MB permanent swap file.

- Also use 386 Enhanced to turn on the option for 32-bit Disk Access, and if shown, 32-bit File Access. These techniques can speed up your hard drive access amazingly.

Windows 95 automatically configures your system for optimal speed, so you don't want to use any "accelerator" programs designed for Windows 3.1, nor should you use SmartDrive.

80. I've done everything I can to optimize my PC without buying new hardware, and it's still not fast enough for me. In lieu of buying a new computer, what hardware upgrades should I make, and in what order?

Here are our suggestions, listed in order of the speed improvement you'll achieve. The most important upgrade you can make is to add more RAM. Adding just four more megabytes of RAM to a 4MB machine can practically double its speed when running under Windows. RAM is the single most effective upgrade you can buy (unless you already have 16MB or more installed).

Second, you can install a new, faster processor—from a 486DX2/66MHz to a Pentium, for example. Intel sells upgrade kits designed to make it easy to replace your CPU.

Third, make sure you have both a local-bus motherboard and a local-bus video card—either VESA or PCI, depending on your system—with at least 1MB of Video RAM. This will improve the smoothness of animations and digitized video.

Fourth, step up to a quad-speed CD-ROM or faster. And finally, consider a new, faster hard drive (though this won't necessarily speed up the

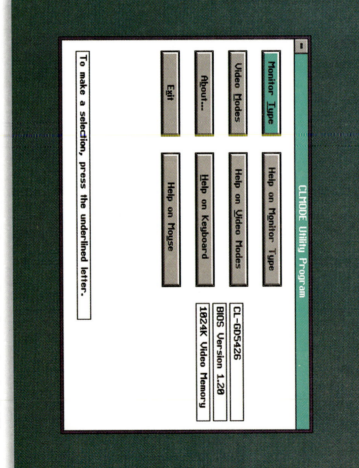

Figure 14: Video cards often come with programs that allow you to choose the type of monitor that'll be attached to the card.

81. What are the advantages of compressing my hard drive? The disadvantages?

There's only one advantage to compressing your hard drive, but it's a big one—increased disk space. That may sound like heaven when you're cramped for space, but compression programs have some drawbacks. For starters, the compression software takes up valuable RAM—the memory that's so crucial to running programs. Some programs simply can't be installed onto a compressed drive (Windows 3.x can't store its swap file on a compressed drive, for instance, although this is not a problem with

Windows 95). If you do opt for compression, be sure to set aside some uncompressed space on the original hard drive.

Compressed drives are also usually slower, although you won't notice this very much with a fast 486 or Pentium-based computer, since the smaller size of the compressed data makes up for the small delay that occurs when compressing the files.

Some people view software compression as potentially unreliable, since all your data is stored in one huge file (a compressed volume file). If anything corrupts that single file, all files on your entire compressed drive can be destroyed. However, even a normal hard drive is vulnerable in this way—it relies on a small area called the File Allocation Table (FAT) to keep track of data. If the FAT is corrupted, even a normal hard drive can be wiped out. Moral: There's no substitute for making sure that you back up your documents regularly.

```
C:\>SMARTDRV /S
Microsoft SMARTDrive Disk Cache version 5.0
Copyright 1991,1993 Microsoft Corp.

Room for   128 elements of  8,192 bytes each
There have been   152 cache hits
     and    33 cache misses

Cache size: 1,048,576 bytes
Cache size while running Windows:  1,048,576 bytes

        Disk Caching Status
drive   read cache   write cache   buffering
----------------------------------------------------
A:        yes            no
B:        yes            no
C:        yes            yes          no

Write behind data will be committed before command prompt returns.

For help, type "Smartdrv /?".

C:\>
```

Figure 15: SmartDrive is a disk-caching program that comes with MS-DOS and Windows. it stores recently accessed information in RAM, so that if a program requests that information again it can pull it from memory. That's much faster than retrieving it from the hard drive.

82. The program I'm installing says it requires a VESA driver. What is it, and how do I know if I have one?

A VESA driver is a small program that's loaded into memory which allows programs to use high-resolution video modes, such as 640 × 480 × 256 colors. They're only used by DOS programs, since video cards come with their own drivers for high-resolution display in Windows.

Don't worry if your video card didn't come with a disk containing a VESA driver; the VESA driver is often built right into the memory on the video adapter card. To find out if your card has a built-in VESA driver, type MSD at a DOS prompt, then click on *Video*.

83. When I type WIN to start Windows, I see the Windows logo, then the screen goes black and nothing happens. What have I done wrong?

Chances are that some type of device has not been configured properly for Windows, and if you've made a rescue diskette (see question eight above) the chances are good that you can at least find out what the source of the problem is.

If you type WIN/B instead of just WIN, Windows will create a text file called BOOTLOG.TXT that displays its progress during startup. Look at the very end of the file, and you'll see what Windows was trying to load when it locked up.

You can also try WIN /D:SVX to disable some of Windows's advanced features. If this solves your problem, try using just one of the letters (S,V or X) to narrow down the problem.

84. My sound card doesn't work. What's wrong?

Whew, that's a tough one. It could be caused by various things, but if you go down through this checklist you should find the problem.

1. *Is there a cable running from your sound card's output to the speakers or some other amplification device?*

2. *If the speakers are powered, do they have batteries, or are they plugged into an outlet? Is the volume control turned up enough?*

3. *Have you loaded the drivers for the sound card (the drivers would be loaded either in the CONFIG.SYS or AUTOEXEC.BAT files).*

4. *Have you configured your sound card to use the same IRQ and DMA as the driver software (or vice-versa)?*

5. *Have you installed the Windows driver for your sound card?*

6. *Is the sound card seated securely in the expansion slot?*

85. The installation instructions for a program I'm trying to load says I should "remove any TSRs." What are TSRs, and how do I remove them?

TSR stands for Terminate and Stay Resident. It's a program such as a mouse driver, memory manager, compression utility, etc. that is usually loaded into memory when your turn on your PC, and which stays there (resident) until you issue a command to remove it. Some TSRs shouldn't be removed—for example, the HIMEM.SYS driver is necessary to run Windows—and TSRs usually can't be removed except by restarting the computer to thereby prevent them from being loaded on bootup. (Press F8 while your computer is starting if you want to step through your startup files a line at a time.) TSRs are installed because they're named on lines within your CONFIG.SYS or AUTOEXEC.BAT files.

86. I accidentally started the CMOS setup program while my PC was booting up. What should I do?

It looks scary, but don't panic—as long as you don't make any changes everything will be okay. To get out of the CMOS setup screen, you can either use the arrow keys to highlight *Do Not Write to CMOS and Exit* and press *Enter*, or simply hit the *Reset* button on the front of your PC. The *Esc* key will also usually get you out of Setup. In any case, if you haven't modified anything in the Setup program, no harm done.

87. When I'm running a certain program, I'm sometimes kicked out to the C:\> prompt and see the message "Stack overflow." What does it mean, and how do I prevent it?

The stack is an area of the computer's internal storage used to temporarily hold a list of data and instructions. (A stack is like a pile of dinner plates. You can add plates to the top of the stack, but you can only get at a buried plate by removing the plates above it.) When the processor receives an interrupt request from the mouse or a sound card, it pushes information about the current status of the program onto the stack. Then it handles the interruption and pulls that status information back off the stack—so it can pick up where it left off. Stack space is limited. If entries ("dinner plates") pile too high, the whole stack is in danger of toppling over, and you get an error message that says the stack has overflowed.

If stack overflow is a frequent problem, here are two solutions you can try. Type the line STACKS=16,256 into your CONFIG.SYS file. Or type this alternative line into CONFIG.SYS:STACKS 0,0. That will bypass the MS-DOS stacks entirely.

88. When I turn on my computer, it automatically loads and runs Windows. How can I change my system so Windows only loads when I want it to?

At a DOS prompt, type *EDIT C:\AUTOEXEC.BAT*, then look for a line in the files that says "win" or "Win"—it'll most likely be one of the last lines in the file. Delete that line, and you'll be taken to the "C:>" prompt each time you turn on your PC. If you decide to start Windows, just type WIN at a DOS prompt.

FILE THIS UNDER "FILES"

89. What does the CONFIG.SYS file do? What about the AUTOEXEC.BAT?

The CONFIG.SYS files tells MS-DOS a lot of things about your computer: how your system's memory should be used; whether or not you have a CD-ROM drive and/or a sound card; and other useful information. If you don't have a CONFIG.SYS file, in fact, most programs won't even know you have more than 640KB of memory.

AUTOEXEC.BAT does things like loading mouse drivers, CD-ROM extensions, sound-card settings, disk-caching software, and other things that you could do yourself one by one at a DOS prompt. See "System Files" for the straight scoop on these important special files.

90. How do I edit my CONFIG.SYS and AUTOEXEC.BAT files?

Just load one of them into your word processor like any other text file, and make the changes. But don't save the edited file. You have to choose Save As from the File menu of your word processor, and then choose the Save as MS-DOS text or Save as text option. If you simply save without specifying that this is plain text, the file will be saved by default in your word processor's format. As a result, the next time you turn your power on, your computer won't know what to make of the now-garbled instructions it finds (word processor formatting codes will be sprinkled throughout the file).

91. What do the WIN.INI and SYSTEM.INI files do?

They are to Windows 3.x what AUTOEXEC.BAT and CONFIG.SYS are to DOS, but they do more. They provide information that Windows needs in order to take advantage of all your system's components. Information regarding the configuration of peripherals like your sound card, video card, mouse, and more are listed here, along with information on fonts, screen colors, resolution and more. Although Windows 95 includes WIN.INI and SYSTEM.INI files, they're present only for backward-compatibility for older Windows 3.x applications expecting to find information within them. Windows 95 relies on a huge file called the Registry—it can be 1MB large—to contain all the configuration and other details previously contained with the .INI files.

It's a good idea to keep a recent copy of CONFIG.SYS, AUTOEXEC.BAT and the two .INI files on a rescue diskette (see question eight).

92. Why are filenames restricted to a maximum of eight characters followed by a period and a three-character extension?

Back when Microsoft created the MS-DOS operating system, 11 letters (eight plus a three-character extension) seemed like more than enough to describe the contents of a computer file. After all, the popular (at the time) CP/M system also used 8+3 filenames, and that's all the designers of MS-DOS expected we'd ever need. They were wrong. (They also expected that 640KB of RAM memory would always be a

generous amount of space. What would they think of the 4MB and 8MB personal computers common today?)

Fortunately, Windows 95 supports filenames of any length (up to 256 characters anyway), and should eliminate the headaches of coming up with descriptive eight-letter "license plate" names.

93. I know how to find out how much space a directory is using, but how do I find out how much space is being taken up by the files in all of its subdirectories?

At the directory prompt—C:\WINDOWS, for instance—type DIR /S /A. You'll get a report listing the total number of files in all the subdirectories, and how much hard-drive space they're using. With Windows 95, you can right-click on any folder and choose Properties to see a complete report of the size of the folder and all files and folders contained within it.

94. Is there a way to sort files (by date, size, etc.) that I've located with the Search command in File Manager?

You can sort files that have been located with the Select command in File Manager, but not those returned after a Search; the problem is that Select only lets you pick files from one directory, while Search can look over the entire hard drive for files.

When you use Start/Find/File or Folders with Windows 95, you get a detailed listing of files, with columns for the name of the program, its size, the date, etc. You can click on any column heading to sort the list by that category.

From a DOS prompt, you can sort files by date, name, size, extension, and more by typing DIR /O, followed by a switch such as D for date. Use DIR /OEN to sort a directory alphabetically, grouped by the three-character file extension.

Type HELP DIR at a DOS prompt to learn all the ways you can sort files.

95. What is a macro?

Most macros are files that consist of nothing more than the "recording" of a series of commands or keystrokes which can then be activated later. In WordPerfect for Windows, for instance, you could turn on the Macro Recorder, then it would watch what you do and save descriptions of those actions until you turned the recorder off. One common macro involves recording yourself while you type in your name and address. Then, forever after—or until you buy a new word processor anyway—you can just select that macro and it will type in your name and address for you.

Anything that you do repeatedly is a good candidate for macro recording, and most major applications contain a recorder. To make invoking a macro even easier, you can usually assign the macro to a particular key combination, like Ctrl+A to trigger the "my address" macro. This way, every time you finish writing a letter, just press Ctrl+A.

96. What is a batch file?

Batch files consist of a series of commands that are all executed by typing in the name of the batch file. Batch files are easy to recognize:

They have the BAT extension, just like your AUTOEXEC.BAT file.

While some batch files are complicated, creating a useful batch file doesn't require a lot of work. Let's say that you've installed a game called Whizzers in a subdirectory on your hard drive called C:\GAMES\WHIZZERS; to start the game, you normally have to enter CD\C:\GAMES\WHIZZERS, then enter the command WHIZZERS. If you'd like to be able to start the game from any DOS prompt by simply typing WHIZ, you would enter EDIT C:\WHIZZERB.BAT at a DOS prompt, then type the

```
File  Utilities                                        Help

Computer............ American Megatrend 486DX    Disk Drives.......... A: B: C: D:
Memory.............. 640K, 742.4K Ext,           LPT Ports............ 1
                     7744K EMS, 5888K XMS
Video............... VGA, Cirrus                 COM Ports............ 2
Network............. MS Client                   Windows.............. 3.11
OS Version.......... MS-DOS Version 6.20         IRQ Status........... Not Active
Mouse............... Logitech Serial Mouse       TSR Programs.........
                     6.02
Other Adapters...... Game Adapter                Device Drivers.......

Press ALT for menu, or press highlighted letter, or F3 to quit MSD.
```

Figure 16: Microsoft Diagnostics can provide vital information regarding your system, from the type of video card you're using to whether or not you have a joystick port.

following commands:

CD\C:\GAMES\WHIZZERS
WHIZZERS

Then select *File* and *Save*. (You could also use a word processor to create this document, as long as you saved it as an ASCII text file.)

97. What is a patch?

Patches are files that are designed to correct problems in an existing application. They usually overwrite one or more of an application's files, though some patches simply add brand-new files for the application to use. (*Patch* also refers to something entirely different: a sound sample for a wavetable sound card or other MIDI instrument.)

98. I downloaded new Windows video drivers for my video card, and now I have two questions—what are ZIP files, and how to I get these video drivers out of the one I downloaded?

A ZIP file is usually several files that have been compressed into one using a program called *PKZIP*—by far the most common compression program in use today. To extract the video drivers from the ZIP file, you'll need to use another program called *PKUNZIP*. *PKZIP* (which includes the *PKUNZIP* utility) is available as shareware on CompuServe, America Online, GEnie, Prodigy, and at many sites on the Internet. Also look for the excellent *WinZIP* program that can easily extract files from a ZIP using Windows 3.1 or Windows 95.

Files are zipped for two reasons. They take up less space on a hard drive and they can be sent more quickly over the phone lines (because they are smaller after the compression).

99. What are *uploading* and *downloading?*

These are terms describing the process of transferring files between different computers, usually via phone lines. When you copy a file from an electronic bulletin board or online service to your hard drive, you are *downloading* the file. Sending a file from your hard drive to another computer is called *uploading*. To keep the terms straight, always imagine that the other computer is located "above" you somewhere up in the sky.

100. What is shareware?

Shareware is software that's sold on a trial basis. Most of the time it works like this: You

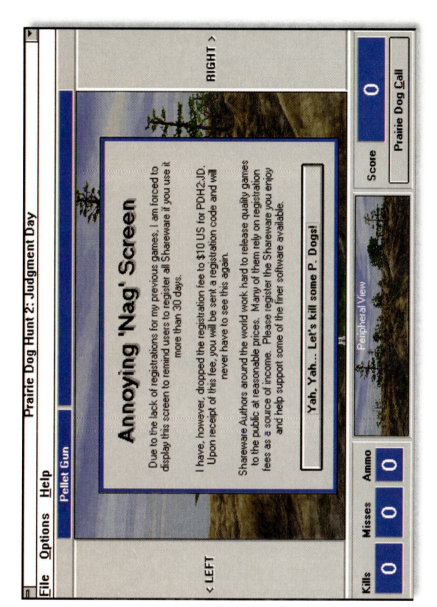

Figure 17: Shareware refers to programs that you can use free of charge on a trial basis. Some shareware programs are "crippled" (i.e., they lack important features), and you must send in a registration fee to receive the complete version. Games are one of the most popular types of shareware.

download a limited (it might do everything except allow you to save files to the disk) version of a program from an online service. If you like it, you can purchase the complete, licensed version from a software vendor (usually the person who programmed the shareware).

Some shareware vendors provide the complete version of the program, then count on the user to be honest and send in a registration fee if he or she continues to use it more than, say, 30 days. The shareware concept only works if everyone (or at least a great many people) pay to register software they decide to use. Many otherwise fine programs have disappeared because too many people took unfair advantage of what they chose to regard as "free" software.

101. I keep hearing about HTML in reference to the Internet. What does it mean?

Hypertext Markup Language, or HTML for short, is a set of codes that tell a program that understands HTML what to do. There are hundreds of codes that affect text display, graphics, background images and more, but the most important aspect of HTML is its ability to highlight (underline) a section of text that you can click on to switch to another document—and on the Internet, that could mean a document on a computer thousands of miles from the one that contained the hypertext link.

You can now create Web documents without learning anything about HTML, thanks to shareware packages like *Hot Metal Pro*, and word processor extensions like Microsoft's *Word Internet Assistant*. You can use them to write your own hypertext-studded documents with hot links to other Internet sites. 🌐

Stephen Poole has been involved with personal computers since 1987. In addition to heading up the Technical Support group at the national online service USA Today Sports Center, he has served as Editor of PC Entertainment and PC Gamer.

WHY DOES MY KID KNOW MORE ABOUT THIS THAN I DO?

OR WHY READING A COMPUTER'S SETUP MANUAL HAPPENS ABOUT AS OFTEN AS ASKING FOR DIRECTIONS ON VACATION.

By Michael Butters

Do you believe that "EIDE" is a southern Appalachian word meaning "an inspiration or thought"? Have you ever lost more than $10 in less than ten minutes at the local arcade while the highest posted score, achieved in eight hours of continuous play, goes to some kid who has spent a single quarter?

I don't know. It's some kind of generational technology thing. The older of my two children, who is now 20, has always thought and processed in digital. At my house, I'm affectionately known as *Analog-Man*.

I used to be smug about it back when I was the "younger generation." My dad used to have me reprogram his VCR every time I visited (he found some ingenious new way to dump the entire program as I was backing out of his driveway after every visit). My mother still prefers less-than-fidelity, all-in-one stereo equipment, not components (the very idea of more than one time have heard Jay Leno talk about his own on/off button mystifies her). And you may at some parents, who won't use an infrared remote control TV for fear of "missing" the set and burning a hole into the wall.

But these days, I'm the dad at my house. I have actually dumped my AUTOEXEC.BAT and CONFIG.SYS files. Three times. Each time for a totally different, more compelling, and even more dunderheaded reason than the time before. I'm beginning to comprehend that trashing these files is a little like donating your liver to science before *you're* actually through with it.

I'm sitting here working on this article and transferring some files to 3.5" floppy disks (they're not particularly floppy, you know, but I guess the cybergenies can only think up so many nifty and confusing robospeak terms at a time). My son wanders through and tosses back over his shoulder: "You're not supposed to touch the little metal disk on the back, you know." He knows this fact much as he knows by heart each and every X-Man or G.I. Joe character, psychosocial histories, special powers, armories and all. Somehow all this was old hat to a fifth-grader, while I, on the other hand, have just spent an entire Sunday afternoon installing a new printer. Which came with its own specially prepared installation disks. And instructions. In very tiny, simple words. The printer also came with these cables. Cables have come a long way since the first time I wrestled with a printer. What was once as complicated as quadruple bypass surgery has now become as simple as ... well, as simple as *double* bypass surgery.

A couple of other reflections on these asides from #1 son. What most frustrates my son is the fact that after immumerable expensive and ridiculous mistakes, I still think I can do this. Now mind you: without ever reading a single word of instruction, I can set up stereo components blindfolded. On intuition alone, I can do inputs and outputs and red and white and yellow interconnection cables and video jacks. I can even make the clock on a state-of-the-art VCR stop blinking 12:00 ... BLINK... BLINK... to do something other than go BLINK... BLINK...

However, give me just two pieces of computer equipment and I suddenly become my father, who had a genetically determined, biological inability to ask for directions on a family vacation. The exact gene is somehow tied to the Y-chromosome, the same one that renders most men incapable of finding their own underwear, locating a jar of mustard in the tiniest of refrigerators, and operating standard household cleaning appliances.

I'm originally from eastern North Carolina. My dad could take us on a family vacation to Carlsbad Caverns and never once ask for directions, even after the family car was securely covered by at least an inch of dust from driving back and forth across endless desert roads. "I know it's right around here somewhere," was a phrase etched in my adolescent brain. "Please, Dad, can't we *please* just stop and *ask* somebody?" Never. It's that Y-chromosome thing again.

That's the genetic flaw. Two or more pieces of unfamiliar computer equipment and I am instantly inflicted with a terminal case of *I Can Do This*. The specific strain is *I-Can-and-Will-Do-This-Without-Any-Help*, the most disabling and virulent form.

I thank my son for his latest reminder about diskettes, which I have needed nearly every day since 1982, when I bought my first computer. I had previously owned a dummy terminal (my kids think it might have been named after me) and got through graduate school by working on the university mainframe via modem. Don't even ask: I once turned in a term paper that turned out to be the most use I had ever made of computer instructions, my abnormal psychology professor remained unimpressed.

There is, however, hope for all of us. The new computers are getting smarter, and easier. I say that before you begin to think of investing that $1,500.00 in a cruise. I say that because there was a time when I was even *more* computer illiterate. Ask my kids. It used to take me a lot longer to dump irreplaceable files. And then I didn't know how to get them back. Now I can execute the latter even more quickly than the former. With greater finesse. And fewer excuses. While I would like to attribute all of this to my greater computer competency, I have to admit a lot of it has to do with the computer having gotten too smart to let me mess up without knowing it, and smart enough to help me clean up what I mess up anyway.

There was a time when all I could run on my megathousand dollar machines was Solitaire, Minesweeper, and various screensavers. Imagine, a $2500 Atari 400.

Finally, I took the plunge for more RAM and nifty new programs that take more headroom than my first computers had for their whole systems. It's a whole new world. Personal and family computing have become activities that can be conducted in *English(1)*, with no master's degree in electronic engineering required.

For one thing, I can run this word processing program like nobody's business. I may even be able to transmit my work to my editor via one of the commercial online services without dumping it into my money management file, or into your living room, by mistake.

For another thing, I love the flexibility of the new CD-ROM programs, which store a virtual Library of Congress of information and programming possibilities. I do **not** love the fact that all CD-ROM programs are not created equal.

I recently bought a megaprogram version of Tetris. It contained about eight different versions of this game (which my wife loves). They ran funny. I couldn't figure out how to move easily from one game to another. Between games, the video on the screen looked a lot like a frog in a blender (as in "What's red and green and goes ninety miles an hour?").

The Tetris thing could use some elaboration. These new multimedia computers have changed our whole involvement with computing. In some ways, it has become the family fireside. We're all involved. My wife is now known as *Analog Woman*. Normally a kind and gentle soul, she becomes so mezmerized by the cute little figures in those fun and clever games that she is totally immune to the fact that billions of them are getting obliterated by the nanosecond, as she marvels at each 256-color macrodeath.

My daughter, who was a Bob Dylan fan from the age of about 10, particularly enjoys the CD-Rom software which explores and recreates the Great One's work and performances. My son set it up for her, on her graduation gift computer, so that The Bob strummed right into an acoustic "Tambourine Man" upon the Windows boot.

Then there's the interactive encyclopedia program, Microsoft Bookshelf, my Seinfeld screensaver and formmaker; and many others. All compelling, entertaining, and even actually useful.

Not to mention the endless possibilities of online communication. I have looked up, and hooked up with, some really special friends, old and new, through America Online. When my son went off to college, we got email almost daily, having just hooked up with the *Prodigy* service. Try that with your typical college freshman on anything less digital (a sheet of processed tree pulp, inscribed with graphite markings, for example) and see where you get. Besides, I could always play ignorant (although I'm not always playing) and insist that I cannot figure out how to send money online.

Looking back over these lines, I begin to realize that we are a more digital family (including Analog Man and Analog Woman) than I had previously realized. It's pretty exciting when your whole family gets into computing, even when most of them are leaving you in the proverbial cyberdust. After all, it's not about competition.

It's about information. And communication. And learning how to transcend the limitations of media and format as this industry continues to grow in exciting new ways.

Mike Butters *is a licensed psychologist in private practice in Chattanooga, TN. Originally from North Carolina, he lives with his wife and two adult offspring, one of whom knows more about computing than the author. Mike started personal-computing with one of the "portable" monochrome Compac "suitcases" in the 1980's (with the USAF), and is presently on his third generation system, a Micron P-75 with the works.*

JUST WHAT DOES MULTIMEDIA MEAN, ANYHOW?

By Evangelos Petroutsos

What is multimedia and how does it work? How do computers handle images and sounds; what's the role of the CD-ROM; what hardware do you need; what's MPEG, and who needs it?

So, you bought this new multimedia computer. Or you're thinking about converting your PC to a multimedia machine. What's multimedia anyway? Why should your computer talk and sing, or why on earth would anyone want to watch TV on their computer monitor? Is it really necessary? Is multimedia marketing hype, a fad that will fade away, or is it the shape of things to come?

Simply put, multimedia is the best way to combine fun with business or education. Entertainment is a huge industry, and for a very good reason—people want to have fun. We spend lots of money on frivolous things. It's no surprise that multimedia is big today, and growing.

WHAT IS MULTIMEDIA ANYHOW?

Any definition of multimedia we might come up with will likely be too narrow. If your computer can handle multiple media—such as text, sounds, images, video—then it's a multimedia computer. Even a computer that displays monochrome text, but beeps every time you commit a major mistake, could qualify as a multimedia computer. Everything else is a question of degree. Grabbing the icon of a file with the mouse and dropping it on a wastebasket icon doesn't qualify as multimedia. It's a simple delete operation. If you hear a burping sound when the icon is dropped in the wastebasket, then it is multimedia. Multimedia is essentially sound and motion video.

Let's take a stab at defining multimedia by looking at the specifications of what's called an MPC, a multimedia PC. This definition will probably not be the same next year, but it's a good starting point. Currently, an MPC is a machine with a 486SX (or better) processor, a 160MB hard disk, 4MB of RAM, a CD-ROM drive, a Super VGA card and a sound card. A joystick wouldn't hurt, and a floppy drive would help in exchanging files with your friends. The actual specifications read "4MB RAM

(8MB recommended)." Since this machine, although an MPC, can hardly run Windows, you'll want to double these recommended memory sizes for a real-life specification.

For all practical purposes, a multimedia computer is one that can display high-quality images, play sounds, show animation, perhaps even record video and live TV. If you need even one of these capabilities, then you need a multimedia computer. And if your computer has at least one of these capabilities, then it's an MPC.

Multimedia is easier to understand if we consider why we use it in the first place. Multimedia is changing the way we interact with computers. If an image is worth a thousand words, our computer should be able to display images. Sounds, too, are an important element of interaction with computers. Even the earliest, most awkward models could emit a beeping sound to warn the user about an abnormal condition. In the near future, sound is likely to become the single most important element of computer interaction. There will be a day when we will be talking to our computers, and they will be actually responding to us.

Figure 1: Zoom deeply into an image and its grain becomes evident.

starts talking to it—but the computer doesn't respond. Cute, but not imaginative. IBM is already advertising on national TV its software that understands six different languages. I believe that efficient ways to interact with computers. It's impossible that we've seen the limits of computer/human interactivity.

Computers are actually capable of talking and responding to voice commands already. This technology has been in the making for many years, but it still isn't quite ready for mass consumption. However, you can experience this technology to a limited extent, even with your PC. All you need is a sound card with a microphone, and the appropriate software. An example of voice recognition software is Microsoft's *Sound System*, which lets you speak the menu commands of all Microsoft applications. For example, you can say, "File open" and you'll see the *File Open* dialog box on your screen, as if you had opened the menu *File* and then selected the *Open* command.

REMINISCENCES FROM THE FUTURE

If you've seen *Star Trek 4: The Voyage Home*, you probably remember the scene where Scotty, travelling back to the twentieth century, attempts to operate a Macintosh computer. He picks up the mouse, holds it upside down and

THE COMPONENTS OF AN MPC

To add sound capabilities to your computer, you need a **sound card**. A sound card can

COMPUTER IMAGES

Let's take a closer look at the various elements of a multimedia computer, the media it handles and how it's done. Let's start with images. Images are traditionally stored on film and paper. If you enlarge a tiny detail of a picture, you will reach a point where the film's grain becomes visible (see Figure 1). Any further enlargements will not reveal more detail, just the grainy structure of the film. However, these grains are so tiny, and so close together, that when you look at a picture at normal magnification they are invisible.

This same effect is true of images stored on your computer. If you zoom into a picture several times, you'll discover that it is made of small squares. On a monitor, these dots are called **pixels**. An image, therefore, is a collection of pixels, arranged in lines and columns.

To simplify the discussion, let's consider monochrome images, which are made up of gray shades. Each pixel represents the intensity of the

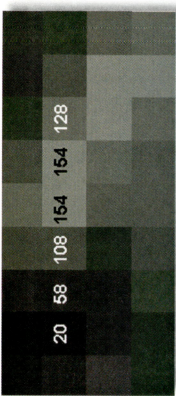

Figure 2: Each square block on this enlarged image is actually a number to the computer: It translates these numbers into shades of gray:

| 20 | 58 | 108 | 154 | 154 | 128 |

record and play back sounds, as well as perform the functions of a synthesizer. To record sounds, you can either plug a stereo or radio directly into the card, or use a microphone. Many cards provide a mike, but any microphone you use with your stereo equipment can be used.

For sound playback, you can either purchase special self-amplifying external speakers, or feed the output of your sound card to your stereo amplifier. Many of these amped external speakers are compact and will fit easily on your desk. They also have their own volume controls, which are usually easier to reach than your stereo's when you're operating your computer.

There are many options for animation playback. The simplest option is to use a **Super VGA** (or SVGA) card, which can display at least 256 colors. *True color* SVGA cards can display nearly 17 million colors and reach resolutions as high as 1280 × 1024—which is more than four times the resolution of a regular VGA card. Most computers now come with SVGA cards and nearly all of them can display 256 colors or more.

You'll probably be using the Windows operating system with your new computer. The current version of Windows is a graphically rich environment, and Windows 95, which is expected this fall, is even richer. Graphics operations are time-consuming and your computer could use some help in handling graphics. To speed up graphics, many video cards include a special chip, the **graphics accelerator**, which handles much of the grudgework of displaying graphics. For a proper multimedia PC, you should buy a graphics accelerator-type video card. Graphics accelerators are more expensive than plain SVGA cards, but are still not out of reach. Without a graphics accelerator, the burden of displaying elaborate graphics is placed on the computer's CPU. Because the accelerator is designed to handle graphics, it not only frees the CPU, it also performs better.

With a SVGA card you can display color images and play back animation and prerecorded video clips, but you can't display or record video. For that, you need a *video grabber*, which is even more expensive (more on this later).

gray at any given area of the image. Black areas have zero intensity, and white areas have full intensity. Black pixels, therefore, can be assigned the value "0" and white pixels can be assigned the value "255" (the maximum value we can store in a byte). All shades between black and white have values in the range from 0 to 255. A medium gray pixel is represented by the value 128. The value 10 is a very dark gray tone, while 240 represents a very light gray tone.

A set of numbers that describes the intensity of the color of each pixel is all the information needed to store a picture in a computer. When we store the monochrome image of the previous example in a file, we only need one byte per pixel (because the numbers 0 to 255 can be held in a byte). Color images are stored in similar forms, but they require three bytes per pixel.

The highest quality color images are called *true color* images. To understand how true color images are stored and manipulated, we must explain how computers handle color. Computer monitors, like TV, understand three basic colors: red, green and blue. Any color can be represented by combining the appropriate percentages of the three basic colors. For example, to display a red pixel, the computer sets the intensity of the red component to its

Figure 3: Images with different color emphases utilize different palettes.

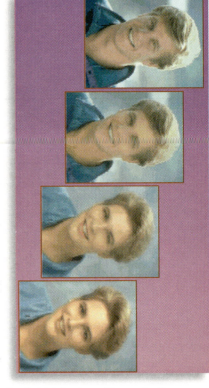

Figure 4: *You provide the first and last stage of the transformation, and the computer performs the morphing. (Graphic courtesy of Lead Systems).*

maximum value and the intensity of the green and blue colors to zero.

To store a true color image in a file, we need three bytes per pixel—one byte for each basic color. A true color image, therefore, takes up three times as much space on the disk (and consequently three times as much to display or copy) as the same image in monochrome. If you are seeking the best picture quality, this is the price you have to pay.

The most common images on current computers are limited to 256 colors because this is how many colors can be displayed on the average computer monitor. The colors of a 256 color image are collected into a palette. With only 256 colors to worry about, we can therefore represent each with a single byte, whose value corresponds to a color, and not a gray value. With this technique, different images can contain different colors, but can contain no more than 256 of them.

For example, to display an image of the ocean, the computer must use a palette with many blue tones; while a park image requires lots of greens. The palette is therefore the 256 colors which best paint a given image. Drastically different images have drastically different palettes.

> **Tip:** Sometimes a color image will take up megabytes—so they can quickly fill up your computer's hard drive. And if you use high-quality color images for Windows wallpaper, the computer will slow down, struggling to redraw the screen every time a window is moved or something else changes against the complex color background. If you have this problem, use small pictures for wallpaper and choose *Tile* rather than *Center* in the Windows wallpaper setup dialog box.

ANIMATION

Since computers can display still pictures, why not motion pictures? Animation is the rapid succession of static images on the screen. If we can display 15 or more images in a second, the eye is fooled into seeing something that fluid movement (though movie-quality smoothness requires 24 pictures, or *frames*, per second).

is created with special programs, entirely within the computer.

One intriguing way to create computer animation is a technique called *morphing*. Remember Michael Jackson turning into a panther? If you give it two pictures, the computer creates in-between frames—or a morph—between a beginning and an ending image.

Yet another way to create animation is to capture live video and store it in your computer. This is called *digital video*. A special video card lets you import sequences of frames from a VCR tape or live TV into your computer. These cards are called video capture boards, or frame grabbers; and good ones are among the most expensive multimedia devices. (For more information on video grabbers, see the section "Adding Video to Your Computer.")

Computer animation uses anywhere from 15 to 30 frames per second, or FPS.

There are two types of animation you can display on your computer: computer-generated animation and digitized video. Computer animation

can't ask the entire population how each is going to vote next Tuesday, we take a "sample." We ask a small number of people and project the results to the entire population. The larger the sample, the more accurate our predictions will be. Likewise, when we sample sounds, we take certain values and throw away the rest.

The quality of the sound when played back depends on the number of samples. The more samples we take, the more accurate our estimation of the original is, and the better the quality of the played-back sound. Of course, if the number of samples is too small, we will not be able to reconstruct the original sound at all. Asking only your immediate family members

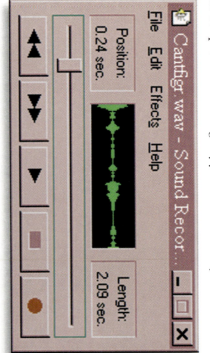

Cantfig.wav - Sound Recor...
File Edit Effects Help
Position: 0.24 sec.   Length: 2.09 sec.

Figure 5: *With Windows's Sound Recorder, you can record, play back and edit sounds.*

about their voting preferences isn't going to give you a clue about the election's outcome.

How frequently should sound be sampled? At the very minimum, there must be 8,000 samples per second. This corresponds to the lowest quality sound and is called telephone quality. To record human voice with a better quality, use 11,000 samples per second. For the best possible quality, take close to 44,000 samples per second. This is referred to as CD quality.

The number of samples per second is called the sampling rate and is expressed in KHz (kilohertz). One KHz is a thousand samples per second (CD quality sound is 44KHz). Higher sampling rates produce better quality sounds. Music, or unusual sounds (with lots of high frequencies), like the sound of a cricket, should be sampled at higher rates. Notice also that stereo requires twice as many numbers for each sample, one set for the left channel and one for the right channel.

Windows provides the Sound Recorder application for recording and playing back sounds. It can also perform special effects on sounds. For example, you can open a WAVE file (they have ".wav" after their name), select the *Echo* special effect from the *Effects* menu and hear the same sound with echo.

Another parameter affecting the quality of the sound is the accuracy with which the values

COMPUTER SOUND

Now let's turn our attention to the second major component of multimedia, the sound. When we talk, we produce variations in the air, which hit our eardrum, producing the sensation of sound. If you could see sounds as they travel through the air, they would resemble ocean waves. The shape of a sound is called its *waveform*. Computers can pick up these variations with the help of a microphone and store them as numbers. These numbers are called *samples*, and they represent the intensity (or amplitude or loudness) of the sound at regular intervals.

When these samples are played back, they reproduce the original sound. Just as we can't distinguish the individual pixels of an image when they are placed very close to each other on the monitor, we can't distinguish the individual samples of a sound when they are played back in rapid succession.

The samples represent the sound, the same way that samples are taken in election polls. Because we

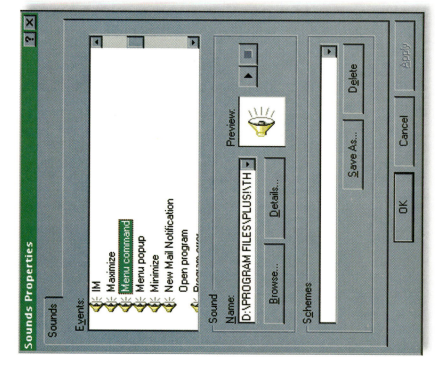

Figure 6: This Windows 95 application assigns sounds to various Windows events.

of the samples are recorded. Computer sound cards offer two options: eight-bit sound and 16-bit sound. Sounds recorded at 16 bits are better because their values are represented with much better accuracy. Eight-bit sounds don't sound bad, but just as you have to go as high as 44KHz to record the sound of breaking glass, you also have to use the most accurate representation for the individual samples. Music CDs are recorded at 44KHz with 16 bits per sample. Your 16-bit sound card, therefore, can likely record sounds with pretty much the same accuracy as they are stored on a CD.

The Sounds application, shown in Figure 6, lets you select sounds and assign them to various computer events—so every time you make a menu selection, or shut down Windows, you'll hear the preselected sound.

Storing such high-quality sounds on your hard disk is going to be a problem, though. If you're using 44,000 samples per second, with 16 bits per sample and stereo quality, each second of sound will take up nearly 200,000 bytes on your disk.

MIDI MUSIC

There's another way to store music on a computer, and it's more efficient than digitizing sound (Windows's .wav). MIDI is a music language used by manufacturers of electronic synthesizers years before computers were equipped with musical capabilities. Music can be written down as a music score in MIDI— sequences of notes and their durations (along with refinements and subtleties like vibrato for a

violin sound or glissando for a steel guitar).

The MIDI language is used by MIDI synthesizers (and computer sound cards equipped with synthesizer capabilities) to reproduce music. In other words, most sound cards sold today can act as a synthesizer in addition to recording and playing back sounds as we described earlier.

The technology used by most sound cards in use today is called *FM synthesis*. This technique imitates the sounds of the various instruments, but anyone who can appreciate music will spot the difference in the sound immediately. Most of the instruments sound computer-generated.

Newer sound cards use a technology based on wavetables to create more natural sounds. A wavetable is a collection of prerecorded, digitized sounds of the various instruments. To reproduce the sound of an instrument, the sound card looks up its wavetable, finds the actual sound of the instrument, adjusts its frequency (pitch) and duration, and then plays it back. If you are into synthesizers, or you want to

experiment with this type of music with your computer, look for a card with the more expensive, but superior, wavetable technology.

MIDI sounds can be stored very efficiently in your computer because MIDI is not an actual recording of sound. Instead, it is a symbolic description. Here's an example. We mentioned earlier that only one second of CD-quality sound uses up nearly 200,000 characters (or bytes) on your hard disk. The MIDI description of the sound of a violin note for one second in MIDI notation takes up a few characters, a few bytes: the name of the instrument, the pitch and the duration of the note. And describing ten seconds of this same note still only takes up that same few bytes in a MIDI disk file (.mid).

The Windows 95 Media Player, which plays sound and animation files, is shown in Figure 7. It can play back sounds and MIDI files, but you need a separate application to create MIDI (music) files. Notice the resemblance of the command buttons to the buttons of your CD player or VCR. In the same figure you see the Volume Control program, which sets the volume for each sound device.

STORAGE REQUIREMENTS

Let's say a computer image is made up of 500 lines, each containing 500 pixels across. This means 500 × 500, or 250,000 pixels. If we allocate one byte per pixel, this image takes up 250KB, or a quarter of a megabyte, of disk space (and memory). If this happens to be part of an

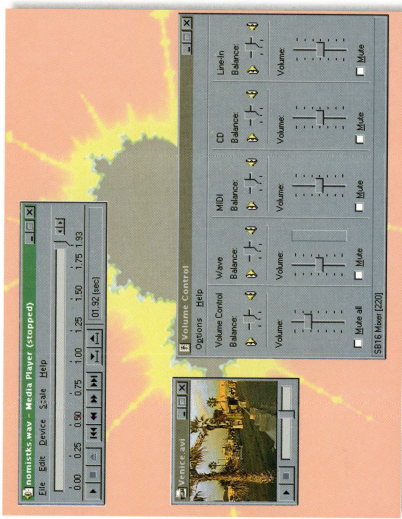

Figure 7: The Media Player and Volume Control applications. An animation file is playing in the small window.

63

Photo CD

The convergence of computer technology and entertainment is demonstrated best by the Photo CD. The Photo CD is a technology developed by Kodak which makes it possible to store photographs on a CD. Instead of having your film printed on paper, you can have the images recorded on a CD. This process is performed by special hardware, but the cost of "burning" the Photo CD is quite reasonable for the average consumer (a little more than printing them on paper). You take the negative to a photo store and the next day you pick up a CD.

A Photo CD looks like any other CD, but it can't be used with your stereo—only with computer CD-ROM drives that support this format. (By the way, you can view Photo CDs on your TV set with a CD-i.) More and more CD-ROM drives support Kodak's Photo CD format, and if you are going to buy a new one and you want to avail yourself of this new technology, make sure it can read Photo CDs as well. You must also go for a "multi-session" CD-ROM drive.

animation sequence, with 20 frames per second, it translates immediately to 5MB of disk space for each second. What if the animation contains a sound track as well? We've seen that sounds can fill up disks rapidly, too.

What does this mean in practice? Obviously, you can't distribute animation or sound files on diskettes. It would take five high-density diskettes for a single, one-second animation file. Moreover, how many users would waste 5MB of valuable disk space to store a few seconds of animation which they'll view once or twice? They can flip on the TV and watch hours of this stuff will no storage penalty.

Distribution of multimedia material, such as images, animation and sound, calls for a new distribution medium. A high capacity, inexpensive medium. And this medium was brought in from the music industry—the **compact disc (CD)**.

THE CD-ROM DRIVE

CDs were developed for storing music. Once the music industry developed efficient techniques for storing information on CDs and the means to reproduce them at a very low cost (less than $1 per CD), the computer industry took advantage of this new medium for its own purposes. This was a fortunate development for the computer industry because storage-media manufacturers could take advantage of the ongoing research in the music industry. Some of the best known CD-ROM drive suppliers today are Philips, Sony and other music industry giants.

To use CDs with your computer, you must have a special device called a **CD-ROM drive**. ROM stands for **Read Only Memory** because CDs can be read, but not written to. However, rewritable CDs are under development and even in limited use. Once their prices drop, they will catch up and you should be able to produce and distribute your own CDs to your friends. The difference between plain CDs and CD-R (for *rewritable*) is not the medium, but the device that reads or writes them. Right now, CD-R drives are very expensive.

Computer CDs are cousins of music CDs. A reasonable question would be, "Can I play music CDs on my computer, or data CDs on my stereo?" The answer is that computers can play musical CDs. However, you can't play a data CD on your stereo. You can't hear digital data (your stereo can't read a sound file the way the computer does; much less animation or text), and you run the risk of destroying your speakers.

Some good news for CD music lovers: You can now buy hybrid portable CD-ROM drives which can either be used with your computer or you can take them with you and listen to music CDs. Portable CD-ROM drives are ideal for notebook computers. If you are using a notebook because you travel a lot, why not have a CD-ROM drive that can keep you company in the airplane or your car?

Another difference between a music CD player and a computer CD-ROM drive is that they operate at different speeds. In the specifications for a CD-ROM drive you will find terms like double-speed (2X), triple-speed (3X) and quad-speed (4X). What do these numbers mean? The first generation CD-ROM drives were spinning at the same speed as music CD players, and they could transfer only 150,000 characters per second to the computer. Considering that a hard disk can easily move a few million characters to and from the computer in a second, it's easy to understand that the speed of the first CD-ROM drives was inadequate.

Manufacturers soon doubled the speed of CD-ROM drives and called them 2X devices. And before you could pay off the 2X drive, a 3X version came out. The fastest CD-ROM drives right now are 4X (which can transfer 600,000 characters per second) and by the time you read this article you may see a 6X drive at your computer store. If you are going to buy a new CD-ROM drive, go for the 4X or better. It will last longer. Double-speed units are very inexpensive, but they may be essentially useless next year.

WHY ARE CD-ROM DRIVES SO IMPORTANT?

The speed of the CD-ROM drive is extremely important because it's not merely another auxiliary storage device. The CD-ROM is the heart of a multimedia PC. To play a movie, for example, the computer should be able to display many frames per second. A fast **CPU** (the **microprocessor**, like a 486 chip, that runs your computer) can do this. But the pictures must flow into the computer (from storage on a CD) at a fast enough rate that the CPU can then display them seamlessly.

It just wouldn't make sense to have a computer fast enough to handle animation and a CD-ROM drive that couldn't provide the frames fast enough. The computer will try to compensate for the slow transfer, sure. It will do its best. But the animation will be jerky and the display will even freeze while the computer waits for the CD-ROM drive to furnish the next frame. This will surely ruin your enjoyment of the latest generation of cinematic computer games. Even if your current games or other multimedia programs work fine with a double-speed CD-ROM drive, you should consider investing sooner or later in a faster unit. If you can't afford it, check out some programs that speed up the transfer rate of a slow CD-ROM drive. *d-Time 10* is a speed-up utility that retails for less than $50, and you can find it at any major computer store.

Another reason for the popularity of the CD is the freedom it offers to game developers. Games distributed on CDs can include large animated sequences, sounds and, in general, material that could not possibly fit on diskettes. The CD-based games are much more exciting and fun to play. And coming down the pike is a new standard called **MPEG (Motion Picture Experts Group)** that can fit a whole movie onto a CD, complete with CD-grade sound, and full-screen 30FPS quality. More on this shortly.

Tech Tip: A Photo CD can hold up to 100 images, so it would be a waste to have a new CD made for each 24- or 36-picture roll of film you shoot. You'll probably add new pictures to a Photo CD several times. Only multisession CD-ROM drives will read the pictures you've added after the first time.

ADDING VIDEO TO YOUR COMPUTER

The last multimedia component we're going to explore here is video recording. To bring video into your computer, you'll need a **video capture** card, and they come in two flavors: **frame grabbers**, which can display continuous TV but capture single frames, and **video grabbers**, which, if the system allowed, could capture entire movies. (Recall that you can't possibly capture an entire movie because of hard disk limitations.) A video grabber is really useful for recording short video segments. Video grabbers are more expensive, of course. Their prices start at around $400, but a good video grabber can exceed $1,000.

Typically, you'll just feed a video signal from your cable or a camcorder into the video capture card. A video capture card can also accept an S-*video signal*—a special, slightly superior kind of video signal

video at resolution 720 × 480 and at 30 frames per second. This represents a compression ratio of 100 to one. A 10MB video file can be reduced down to 100KB. There are actually feature films available on CD that can be played on your computer screen with the help of the MPEG playback cards.

Tech Tip: MPEG is the solution to current inadequate, tiny or jumpy computer animation—as long as your ambitions are limited to watching prerecorded video. If you want to record your own videos at MPEG quality, you're out of luck. Guess why these boards are called MPEG playback or MPEG decoders? Recording (or encoding) MPEG video is very expensive and only manufacturers who distribute digital videos on a massive scale can afford it.

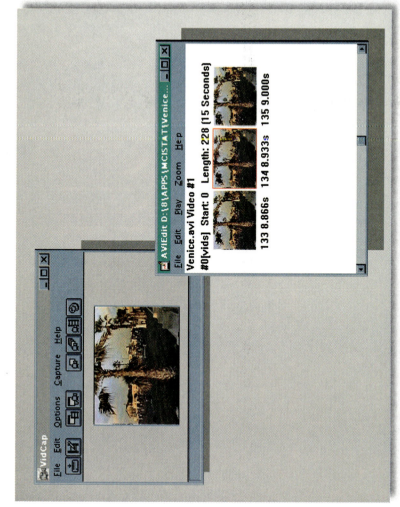

Figure 8: *The VidCapture function lets you capture video from your VCR. AviEdit is a video-editing application.*

connection requiring a Super VHS camcorder or another video source with an S-video output. Once the video source (VCR, camcorder, TV) is connected to the video capture card, you can view the video on your computer's monitor. Then, with the appropriate software (it comes with the capture hardware), you can start capturing video images and save them to disk. The quality of the recorded video, however, may disappoint you. It just can't come close to your TV. This is a technology that's essentially not yet ready for consumer applications.

MPEG COMPRESSION

If you are already using a multimedia computer, you have certainly noticed that its animation is pretty crude. Some critics call it "video in a stamp," and they are quite right. Is that the best your expensive multimedia computer can do? The answer for now is, unfortunately, yes. Without any assistance from specialized hardware, your multimedia PC can't handle serious animation.

The specialized hardware that will help you play good-quality animation on your computer is an **MPEG decoder**, or MPEG playback card. Recall that your computer must not only read 15 or more images in a second, but display them as well.

To overcome this limitation, animation files can be compressed before being saved to disk. To play back a compressed file, the MPEG decoder decompresses the file "on the fly" and displays the successive frames on the monitor. MPEG is a very effective compression/decompression technique, yet too intensive for your computer to manage all by itself. That's why you need specialized hardware.

Many video cards are capable of displaying MPEG compressed animation files. Their prices are between $300 and $400. Their capabilities, though, are impressive. They can play back

THE FUTURE

So what does the future hold for multimedia? For one thing, multimedia technology will be with us forever. It has already become a mainstream technology, and this is just the beginning. It won't be long before video will be played back in full size and rewritable CDs will allow us to store enormous amounts of information on inexpensive media. CDs may well become to the next generation of computers what diskettes are today. The cost of MPEG technology will drop substantially to the point where it will eventually be possible to both record and play back MPEG videos without the need for MPEG decoders. We also expect significant advances in sound manipulation, too. Voice recognition will enable us to interact with our computer by voice—won't that be a kick!

A drastic shift in the way we use this technology will occur when it becomes possible for us to connect to other computers at very high speeds. Then we'll be able to watch video brought to our computer from any other, or communicate with other users with sound and video. Video-conferencing with anyone on the planet will become as popular as today's electronic conferencing, and distances will become even smaller. Your multimedia PC will truly become your "window to the world."

Evangelos Petroutsos *has a degree in Computer Engineering from the University of California and works as an author and consultant. He is co-author of the best-selling book Visual Basic Power Toolkit.*

COMMON MULTIMEDIA FILE EXTENSIONS

Extension	Description
AVI (Audio Video Interleave)	*AVI files contain mostly digitized video, but computer-generated animation can be stored in AVI files as well.*
FLI, FLC	*Contain computer-generated animation. A file format used by Autodesk, which has become the de facto standard for storing animation sequences.*
WAV (Waveform)	*Contain sounds. The file format used by most Windows applications.*
VOC	*Contain sounds, but in a different format than WAV files. This file format is used by Sound Blaster.*
MID (MIDI)	*Contain MIDI music files.*
TGA, BMP, TIF	*Some of the most common image file formats.*

This table shows how you can tell the type of a multimedia file, based on its extension.

EXPANDING YOUR SYSTEM

By Richard Mansfield and Evangelos Petroutsos

Want to know what you can do to make your computer even more useful, faster and fun? We'll discuss which add-ons, peripherals and upgrades do the most to improve your machine. We'll describe each peripheral and what it can do for you. At the end, we'll list these customizations in order of difficulty—which installations are a relative snap, and which ones can drive you up the wall.

A fter you've used your personal computer for a couple of months, if you're like most people you discover that it's both fun and useful. Then you wonder what you can do to make it *more* fun and useful.

The first and most obvious answer is to get more software. Buying new programs can give you whole new capabilities and whole new worlds to explore.

But eventually you start to think about adding new hardware as well (**peripherals**). A new video card or a faster CPU chip can make *all* your software more responsive. A CD-ROM drive immediately doubles the software you can select from. A second hard drive can triple your storage space. What to do?

What's the single best enhancement you can make to your computer? If you're running Windows 95, the greatest improvement will probably result if you buy a new, accelerated video card. (If you're not running Windows, or are using Windows 3.1, the most significant improvement would probably be to switch to Windows 95.)

The second-best improvement would likely be to buy a CD-ROM drive for all the new CD-ROM-only software you can then enjoy.

However, as with most things in life, there's a dark side to this customization and amplification of your computer. You have to somehow attach new peripherals to the machine *physically*; and you usually also have to integrate them via **software drivers** into the **operating system** (so Windows knows they are physically attached, and how they do their job).

Some peripherals are quite easy to attach to your machine and quite easy to tell Windows about. Others are bears. This article describes the most popular hardware add-ons; explains what each unit does and how it does it; and, at the end, lists them in order of the difficulty you're likely to

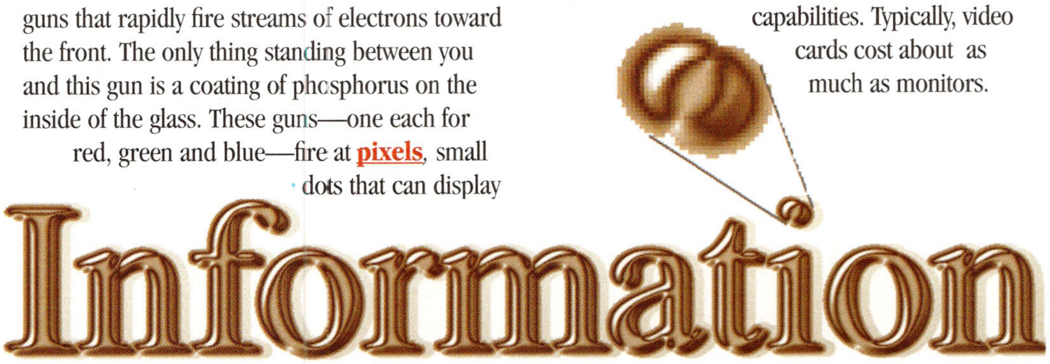

Figure 1: Pixels are tiny, but when we magnify the dot over the "i" you can see they're discrete, not continuous.

experience when bringing them home and trying to physically integrate them into your system.

MONITORS

Compared to ordinary TV's, computer **monitors** are visually far superior. They display more detail and are more stable (hardly any jitter). You're expected to read text on a computer screen, and if you work with graphics, you should be able to see photographs at photorealistic resolutions.

But the size and quality of computer monitors differ, so if you're considering upgrading your monitor, you've come to the conclusion that your current monitor is inadequate. Let's see how monitors work, and the various options to consider when buying a new one.

There are four main considerations, four main specifications that describe the quality of a monitor: **vertical refresh rate** (how many frames of video are displayed per second), **dot pitch** (resolution or "sharpness"), **interlacing** (whether or not it redraws each line or only every other line during a single frame) and physical size. Let's consider each spec in turn.

FAST REFRESH AVOIDS FLICKER

At the back of a monitor are three electron guns that rapidly fire streams of electrons toward the front. The only thing standing between you and this gun is a coating of phosphorus on the inside of the glass. These guns—one each for red, green and blue—fire at **pixels**, small dots that can display

red, green and blue. By adjusting the intensity with which the electrons strike, various colors and shades can be created.

The beams move horizontally, illuminating a line across the screen, then return (with the guns turned off) to the left of the screen to start illuminating the next line. Finally, after lighting up these lines across the whole screen like a set of electric venetian blinds, the guns are turned off at the lower right corner and moved back to the upper left to restart the whole process.

All this must take place rapidly, essentially continuously, because the phosphors fade, and because things change when you type or watch a video. The guns, then, are constantly rotating the beams from left to right, then swinging back again one line down. The time it takes the guns to completely illuminate the entire screen is called the vertical refresh rate. Typically, this measurement ranges between 60 and 72 times per second (expressed in specifications as 60, 70 or 72Hz). The higher the refresh, the better. At 70 or 72Hz, annoying flicker virtually disappears.

Monitors come in two flavors, the less expensive fixed refresh rate types and the **multisync** monitors. You're better off getting a multisync model because you can then upgrade your **video card** if you wish, without having to buy a new monitor that can accommodate its capabilities. Typically, video cards cost about as much as monitors.

other line of dots. Then on the next pass they hit those lines, but skip the other group. Obviously, this tactic cuts the job in half, but there's a penalty. The screen *swims* slightly, waves crawl across the screen. It's not as bad as watching TV through a fish tank, but it's distracting. If you plan to use the computer much at all, spend a little more to get a non-interlaced (no line skipping) model.

People generally think of resolution in terms of the sharpness of an image—can you see the individual blades of grass? But having enough different colors is an equally important factor—the more colors your monitor can display the more realistic things like bowling balls and pearls will look.

Oddly, smoothness is an aspect of detail—a gradient from the light gray shadow at the bottom of a pearl to the pure white highlight at the top should be continuous. Viewed on a low resolution monitor, a pearl will appear to be layered, like rice paddies or a topographical map. There will be abrupt changes of shading, simply because the monitor cannot display enough colors to achieve a steady unbroken gradation from dark to light.

Resolution in a monitor is measured by **dot pitch**—how closely together the phosphor dots are positioned. That, and the sheer number of pixels on the entire screen, combine to produce the sharpness of the image. You should look for a dot-pitch of 0.28mm or smaller for a 15" monitor. (On larger 17" or 21" monitors, the pitch can be somewhat larger for equivalent resolution.) The monitor should also feature at least 600 × 800 pixels, with 768 × 1024 preferable.

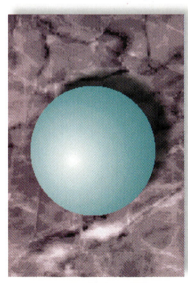

Figure 2: High resolution means smooth transitions from light to dark, and fine detail like the veins in this marble.

Figure 3: Lower resolution results in layered shading and blurred detail.

RESOLUTION MEANS DETAIL

If you spread Vaseline on your car's windshield, things will appear drastically less detailed. You'll see blurry tree-like and house-like shapes and a blue smudge for the sky, and an oncoming car will look like a growing dot. This is low resolution. Brush cooking oil on the windows instead and it gets better. You can see more detail, but colors will still be unrealistically velvety and everything will still smear: objects like houses will have fuzzy outlines.

Sparkling clean windows let through what's really there, in all its various colors and sharp detail. That's high resolution, and that's what you want in a monitor.

BIGGER'S ALWAYS BETTER

The final consideration is size, and a larger monitor is of course better. But monitors quickly escalate in price when you move from the most common 15" model up to 17" or 21". Because the quality of the video image on a computer monitor is so superior to ordinary TV, the support electronics within a monitor are necessarily of higher grade. You can get a 21" TV for under $300, but a 17" monitor is more than double that price.

The actual display is considerably smaller than the advertised size. Following the dubious practices of the television industry, computer monitors are measured from somewhere inside the tube, resulting in significant inflation of the true, usable surface. For instance, a 17" monitor (they're all measured diagonally) results in roughly 14" of display. Expect to see 20 to 25% less than the size you think you'll be getting.

Tip: To reduce fatigue, position the monitor slightly lower than your eye level, and at least 16" from your face. In other words, don't put it on top of the computer.

INTERLACING CAUSES FALSE MOTION

Recall that the guns have a rough job—hitting as many as 786,432 dots (on a 768 × 1024 monitor) 72 times every second (with a 72Hz vertical refresh rate). Some monitors cheat a bit—they skip every

Tech Tip: It's no good having a high-resolution monitor if the video card feeding it signals is inferior. You wouldn't use a bent coat hanger as an antenna for a quality large-screen TV. The video card must match or exceed the specifications of your monitor. We'll deal with cards below.

VIDEO CARDS

Although a computer monitor resembles a TV set, it doesn't get its video signal through an antenna. Instead, the computer sends the images to a board with printed circuits and chips on it called a **video card** which, in turn, translates the computer codes into a video signal. (Some PC manufacturers put the electronics for video directly on the main circuit board, the **motherboard**. However, if you decide to upgrade and install a card, you can disable the motherboard video—see your PC manual for instructions.)

The specifications for a video card are similar to those for a monitor. And remember that either the card or the monitor can be the weak link in the chain. They work together, so it's no use having a high-resolution monitor being fed medium-resolution signals by the card. The specifications we'll look at for the video card are resolution, memory and speed (or acceleration).

RESOLUTION AGAIN

Resolution involves both the number of pixels that can be displayed (commonly 480 × 640,

Figure 4: Interlacing doesn't cause this much distortion, but it's fatiguing and distracting

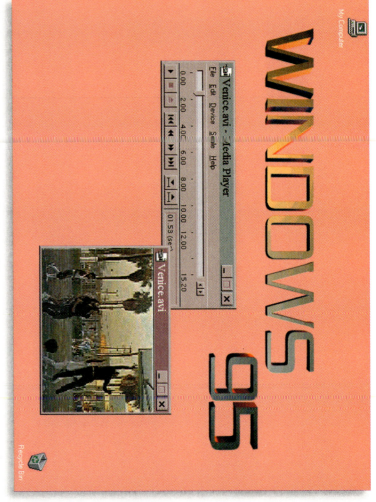

Figure 5: *Until MPEG, computer animation was slow, fuzzy and tiny:*

600 × 800, and 768 × 1024) and the number of colors. (Technically, the number of colors is **color depth**.) Today's video cards are capable of displaying either 256 (also known as 8-bit color), 65,536 (16-bit, or *high color*) or 16,777,216 (24-bit or *true color*) simultaneous colors. As Figures 2 and 3 illustrate, your best bet is to get the highest resolution and greatest number of colors possible. Video cards are generally quite affordable, though cards with identical specifications can range quite a bit in price, so shop around.

MEMORY VARIES

Video cards, like printers, contain some RAM memory of their own. However, the amount of RAM is variable. Often you'll see the same card sold with 1MB or 2MB of memory, with the greater memory adding perhaps $100 to the cost. Why extra memory? The card must maintain the image in RAM before displaying it, so higher resolutions with greater numbers of colors require additional RAM. For this reason, you might see specifications for card X which say it displays 16/256/65,536 colors at 768 × 1024, or 16.7 million colors at 768 × 1024 with the addition of 2MB of RAM to the card.

ACCELERATORS: SPECIAL FOR WINDOWS

If you use Windows, and 80% of PC users do, consider getting a video card that features an **accelerator**. This is a special chip that "knows" how to do some common graphics manipulations

Figure 6: *Look at the bottom of a card to match it to a slot in your computer. This is the bottom edge of an 8-bit card.*

such as drawing circles, moving windows, filling areas with color and so on. Because the tools for accomplishing these common graphics tasks reside on the card (and don't require the computer to calculate), and are optimized for Windows, the screen redraws more quickly.

Redraw isn't the same as *refresh*. Redraw means repainting when something has changed: a window when you scroll text, the whole screen when you maximize a window, etc. If repainting is noticeable on your screen—if, for example, a picture seems to unroll slowly from the top rather than flash at once onto the screen—you'll benefit from acceleration. Certain other graphics-intensive jobs also benefit from accelerated video. Among these are 3D rendering, desktop publishing and computer-aided design (**CAD**).

MPEG: FULL-MOTION VIDEO

Related to acceleration is the latest computer video buzzword: **MPEG** (meaning Motion Pictures Experts Group). MPEG is a technique and a technology that displays high-quality video and audio in full motion on a computer.

Useful for games, education and business, indeed anywhere multimedia makes sense, MPEG-capable video cards will doubtless be the rage during the next year or so. MPEG compresses video primarily by refusing to record every pixel in every frame. When the horses gallop up the hill in the movie *Legends of the Fall*, sure, the horses move, but the hill and the huge blue sky don't change from frame to frame.

INSTALLING THE CARD

Adding a video card is no different from adding any other card—modem, scanner, sound, whatever. You take the following steps:

1. *Turn off the computer and unplug the computer from the wall.*
2. *Detach any plugs going into the computer (such as phone lines to the modem, the*

In fact, though there seems to be a lot of motion in motion pictures, much remains static between frames, MPEG takes advantage of this by storing only pixels that need to be redrawn.

MPEG video comes on a CD. A single CD can hold 74 minutes of video. This is full-motion, 30 frames per second, just like the movies. What's more, it's full screen—not the little fluttering 12-frames-per-second 4" movies we're used to with earlier multimedia video. And the audio is CD-quality (16-bit stereo). There are movies on the format, like *Goldfinger, Star Trek IV* and *Top Gun*. There are also golf lessons, Bon Jovi and Eric Clapton, an atlas, games (of course) and much more. The average MPEG CD movie costs under $25.

BUSSES, ISA & VESA

When you buy a card, make sure it's compatible with your computer's **expansion slots**. Some slots are for **8-bit cards**, with 32 little sockets located over an inch away from the back of the computer. On an 8-bit card, look at the connector—you'll see 32 little metal spots on a protruding lip on the bottom of the card. This lip is in the middle of the card.

A **16-bit card** or socket (called **ISA**) has this same 32-spot plug, but it's located right against the back of the computer, and there's a second lip, half as large with 16 spots, located in the middle.

There's a **32-bit card** (called **EISA**), which looks pretty much like a 16-bit card, but has 64 connector spots, and the first of the two lips is located about 3/4" away from the back of the computer.

You might see only 16-bit plugs in your computer, but 8-bit cards can be plugged into them. Likewise, a 16-bit card can be plugged into a 32-bit slot.

Finally, there's a special kind of connector called a **local bus** (or **VESA** or **VL-bus**) that speeds things up by being able to "talk" directly to the computer's microprocessor. Before buying a VESA card, check your manual or with your computer's manufacturer to see if your machine accepts this kind of card.

cord that goes between the monitor and the old video card, and so on).

3. *Put the computer up on a table.*

4. *Unscrew the screws holding the cover on the computer, and slide the cover off, exposing the innards.*

5. *Unscrew the old video card—there will be one screw at the back of the computer holding the card in place.*

6. *Pull the video card out of its socket (the expansion slot, as it's called).*

7. *Find an empty socket that matches the 8-, 16-, or 32-bit plugs on the bottom of your new card. Ease it in—sometimes you have to rock it a little, the long way; to get it seated.*

8. *Now work backward from steps 5 to 1 to restore the computer to working status.*

IF YOU HAVE TROUBLE

When you've finished installing a new card, turn on the computer and you should see the usual memory display (like 8,192 or whatever you usually first see). If you see it, all's well. If you don't see anything, turn off the power and make sure the cable from your monitor is plugged snugly into the new video card. Turn it on again. If this fails, you'll have to remove the cover of the computer again. Pull out the new card and re-seat it, making sure that it's securely against the bottom of the slot, and that all the plugs are in the correct sockets. If this fails to produce results, one of your other expansion cards might be interfering. Try removing them, one at a time, until the video card works. At this point, you know which card—sound, modem?—doesn't want to work in harmony with your new video card. The best bet if this happens is to call the store where you bought the card, or the technical support number of the card's manufacturer.

KEYBOARDS & MICE

It looks like a squared-off lima bean, but Microsoft's mouse is ergonomically designed to fit well in most any hand. Likewise, the Microsoft "Natural" keyboard looks like a free-form swimming pool, but it, too, has been torture tested extensively in many focus groups and usability tests. Most people find them comfortable, and that's what you should look for in mice and keyboards.

There are other ergonomic input devices from companies like Logitech. For instance, you can get a nice upside-down mouse called a "trackball" where you rotate a ball with your fingers rather than slide a mouse around on the ball beneath. There are also wireless mice, huge mice, and specialized pointers for detailed drawing and so on. But the essential question remains—does it feel good in your hand?

DO YOU NEED BOTH?

If you use Windows, you probably will want to use both a mouse and a keyboard. It's true that nearly anything can be accomplished with either a mouse or a keyboard. For example, you can press *Alt+F* to drop down the *File* menu in most applications. Or you can just click on the *File* menu. But a keyboard is clearly superior for writing text and mouse excels when you're "physically" interacting with graphics—moving, resizing, selecting an area and so on.

When you're working with the computer, you're often editing, fixing things up in an existing document. And most editing of either text or graphics involves selecting (choosing a zone within a large document), cutting, pasting, copying or moving ("moving" means copying, then deleting the original, and pasting it somewhere new). And, of course if you goof, there's undo. You'll find the common techniques for both keyboard and mouse in the table below.

Of course there is additional redundancy. For instance, you can use the keyboard to access a menu: you could copy by pressing *Ctrl+C,* which drops down the Edit menu, then press *C* to choose *Copy* from within that menu. Likewise, some applications—like *Word for Windows* and graphics programs—permit you to move a selected zone by dragging it. But even with all this duplication, you're likely to find yourself relying on both keyboard and mouse for their particular specialties.

SHOULD YOU UPGRADE?

The mouse and keyboard that came with your computer probably work OK. They're likely not top of the line, but if you're happy with them, keep them. However, if you spend a lot of time with the computer, consider upgrading. We've tried a variety of keyboards and mice over the years and can recommend the Microsoft Mouse and Microsoft Natural keyboard for heavy-duty use.

They're not only well designed and sturdy, they also come with software that adds some useful features. For example, you can turn on

Snap To, which moves the mouse pointer automatically to the most likely used button when a dialog pops up. For instance, when you select Print in most applications, a Printer dialog pops up where you can change page orientation, number of copies, etc. You usually just click on the OK button to start printing. That button is where the mouse pointer will be "snapped to." So you just click—you don't have to move the mouse. Also included is Wrap, which causes the mouse pointer to reappear on the opposite side of the screen when you move it off-screen. For example, move it off the top and the pointer appears at the bottom.

The Microsoft Natural Keyboard looks at first glance bizarre. The keys are split into two angled sections. However, after using it an hour you'll probably forget about this rift and notice that your hands are resting more, well, *naturally* on the keyboard. An ordinary keyboard forces you to hold your wrists close together. On the Natural Keyboard you position your hands the way you'd rest them on your stomach when taking a nap.

JOYSTICKS

A joystick is strictly used with games, and then only with some games. In fact, you don't really need a joystick—games can also be played with the keyboard or mouse. But some gamers find a joystick indispensable—particularly for flight simulations and action games like *Doom.*

The simplest models are under $20 and are merely a four-position switch with a button for firing at the enemy. There's a stick that you grab with one hand and move in various directions. The fire button is usually on top of the stick and you press it with your thumb.

But you can spend thousands of dollars for a "joystick" or, more properly speaking, a **game controller.** Some flight simulator enthusiasts want their simulations as real as possible. There are chairs that tilt and vibrate; aviation-quality flight sticks; and foot pedals to control additional factors such as the elevators of a plane. There are headsets that respond to the tilt of your face or the movements of your eyes. There are gloves that

FUNCTION	KEYBOARD	MOUSE
Select	Shift-Arrow Keys	Drag mouse across text or graphics
Copy	Ctrl+C or Ctrl+Ins	Click on the Edit menu, select Copy
Cut	Ctrl+X or Shift+Del	Click on the Edit menu, then select Cut
Clear	Del	Click on the Edit menu, select Clear
Paste	Ctrl+V or Shift+Ins	Click on the Edit menu, select Paste
Move	Cut, then Paste	Click on the Edit Menu, Cut, then Paste
Undo	Ctrl+Z	Click on the Edit Menu, Undo

Table 1: The most common editing—for keyboard or mouse.

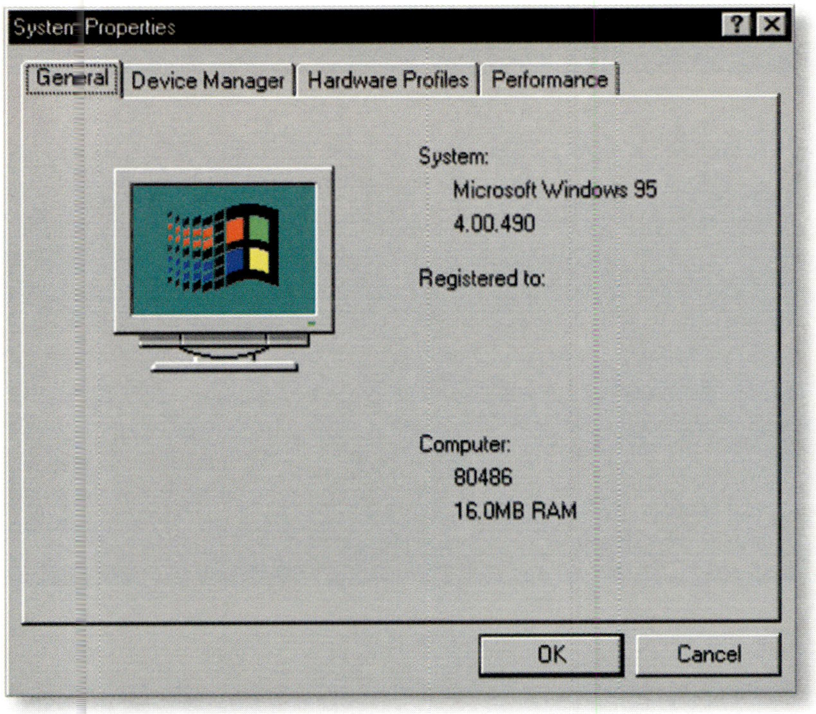

sense hand movements. If this kind of gear interests you, you'll find some multi-button, multi-feature joysticks at your local computer dealer. You'll find greater variety sold through computer magazines. For the truly extravagant models, look in magazines like *Computer Gaming World* that specialize in computer games.

To add a joystick in Windows 95, click on the *Start* button, then *Settings*, then *Control Panel*. Double-click on the joystick icon and select your joystick type. Next, click the *Calibrate* button. Each brand of joystick sends different information to the computer, so you have to calibrate. Calibration lets Windows 95 memorize the values that the joystick sends to represent its various possible positions when you move it around.

CPU AND MEMORY UPGRADES

In a sense, the two most important components of your computer are its **CPU** (Central Processing Unit) and its memory, called **RAM** for Random Access Memory. The CPU

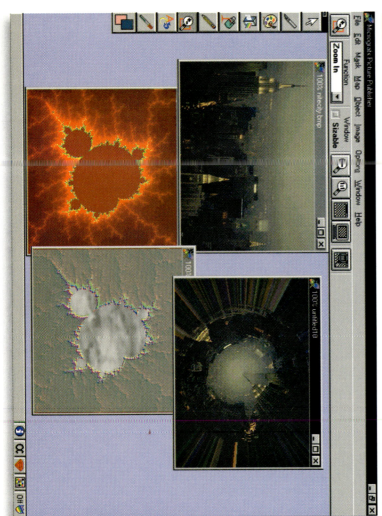

performs all the calculations. The memory is where the data to be processed and the programs reside. All the "information processing" takes place between the CPU and RAM, and together they determine the performance of the entire system more than any other components. The faster the CPU and the more memory on your system, the faster and smoother it will work.

Figure 7 To find out which processor and how much memory are on your computer, click on the System icon in the Settings folder.

REPLACING THE CPU

The fastest PCs on the market today run on the Pentium (586) processor. Most computers sold today use the Intel 486 processor. Older PCs have the 386 processor. These numbers represent succeeding models, and larger numbers correspond to faster processors. There are also speed variations within each family due to the speed of the **clock**. The clock controls the operations of the CPU and synchronizes the computer's electronic components. The clock controls the speed of the ... The faster the clock, the faster each instruction is executed. The higher the speed of the clock, the faster the processor. A 486 processor with a clock at 100 MHz (or 486/100) is approximately 50% faster than a 486 processor running at 66MHz. The most common processor today is the 486, at 66MHz (or 486/66). There are also the designations **SX** and **DX**—SX models are somewhat less expensive, but avoid them. Buy a DX.

If you want more speed from your old 386 machine, consider a CPU upgrade. You can make the old computer run at least twice as fast.

Processor upgrades are offered by a few manufacturers, like Cyrix and Evergreen Technologies. The upgrade is a new processor (a chip) that replaces the old one and runs at twice the speed of the old processor. By upgrading a 386 processor to a 486, your programs will run much faster—especially if the old system didn't have a co-processor (a special processor that handles tough math problems).

Another option is the OverDrive chip from Intel itself. Intel is the maker of the original processors used in PCs and when they came up with the Pentium processor, they offered an upgrade for the existing 486 machines. This chip is called Pentium OverDrive and can bring the performance of a 486 computer close to that of a Pentium computer.

A new microprocessor chip can cost several hundred dollars, so before you update your processor, make sure it will pay off. If you have a 386SX machine, with a 100MB hard disk and 2MB of RAM, upgrading the processor isn't going to help much. You will soon realize that you need a new disk and extra memory in addition to the processor, so the cost of upgrading your computer will become comparable to the cost of just buying a new computer.

Tip: Upgrading your PC may not always be your best bet. It's only a way to postpone the inevitable. If you are considering major upgrades, like the CPU, compare the cost of the upgrade to the cost of a new system, and find out whether it's better to upgrade, or just let the old war-horse go.

ADDING MORE MEMORY

At other times, the bottleneck isn't due to the CPU, but rather to the amount of memory installed on your system. If you are running Windows, as most people do today, and you like

Figure 8 It's great fun to process images with your computer, but images eat memory.

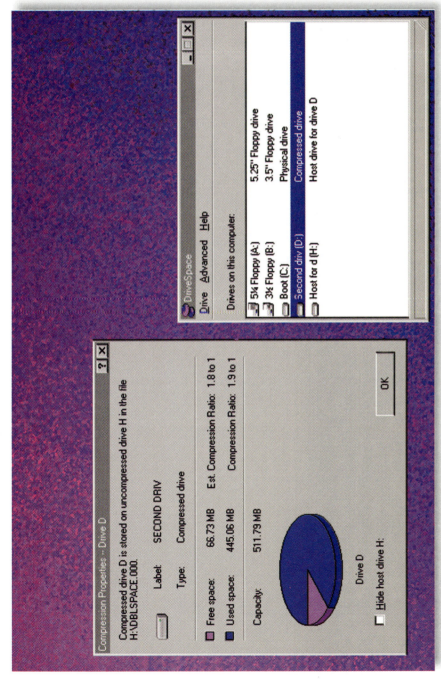

Figure 9: Windows 95 can significantly increase the capacity of your hard disk by compressing the information stored in it.

to have several programs running simultaneously, you may notice that while you switch among applications the disk starts spinning and nothing happens for several seconds. Or when you open a new application, the disk works hard for a while. This means that there's not enough memory on your PC to accommodate all open applications, and Windows has to store information on the disk temporarily. The computer might be trying to make room for a new application, or a data file. This is called **disk swapping** and it can bring your computer down to a crawl.

To minimize swapping, add more memory to your computer. If you're running Windows 3.1, your computer is probably equipped with 4MB of RAM, possibly more. This is the minimum amount of memory required to run Windows 95—but you shouldn't even attempt to run Windows 95 on a system with less than 6MB or 8MB of RAM. If you are using painting or image processing applications and you need to have several images open at once, even 8MB of RAM will be consumed very quickly.

When reading computer **specifications**, you will see listed the amount of memory installed on the computer, followed by a number in parentheses, like "4MB(32)." This means that the computer comes with 4MB of RAM, but if you later decide to add memory, the maximum amount of RAM it can hold is 32MB.

But there's a catch. To add, you might have to subtract. Memory comes on small boards, called **SIMMs** (**S**ingle **I**nline **M**emory **M**odule). These boards fit into special slots, and there are only a few SIMM slots in your computer. The amount of memory on each SIMM board ranges from 1MB up to 16MB. Your computer may support higher capacity SIMMs as well, but you must check it out.

Let's say your computer has four slots and a maximum RAM capacity of 16MB. To achieve this maximum capacity, you must put one 4MB SIMM in each slot. But what if your computer had two 1MB SIMMs when you bought it? Two of the slots are taken, so you can only upgrade it to 10MB, by adding two 4MB SIMMs. To further increase its memory, you must get rid of the low capacity 1MB SIMMs and replace them with 4MB SIMMs. (Selling these 1MB SIMMs isn't easy, either.)

You must, therefore, go for the maximum capacity SIMMs your computer can support. If you are buying a new computer, ask that it be equipped with the highest capacity memory modules, so there will be room for expansion without sacrificing the memory you've paid for. Base models (the ones manufacturers advertise as great deals) are usually equipped with low capacity memory modules because they are slightly less expensive.

If you are going to buy your new computer from a store like CompUSA, you can specify what you really want to end up with. Many mail order distributors will also provide customized systems. Although you will pay more for the initial configuration, you will not have to waste perfectly good (and paid for) memory modules in order to achieve your computer's maximum memory a year or two down the road. Also, go for a model that can support more memory than you think you need. Is 16MB of RAM too much for you? Once you start using Windows 95 and multimedia applications, you might want more. Also, software is growing larger every year, and requiring more RAM.

If you have a computer already and you plan to upgrade its memory, check out the ads of some manufacturers who specialize in memory modules. You will find many ads in magazines like *PC Magazine* or *Computer Shopper*, and their prices are usually much better than the prices offered by your computer's manufacturer. On the other hand, you'll frequently find competitive memory prices at your local computer store, especially when you factor in the benefits of store installation, proper specification (for your particular system) and testing.

Also make sure that you buy the same *speed* of RAM chips (typically ranging from 50 to 70ns, or nanoseconds) because most computers require all RAM to be of the same speed. Further, check to be sure that the *style* of SIMM is the same. The easiest approach is to check that the SIMMs you buy are listed as compatible with your computer make and model.

Finally, if you can't afford more memory, or if your computer can't support more memory, you can increase the amount of memory your computer sees without actually adding more physical memory. You can buy a **RAM doubling utility** for less than $100 that doubles the amount of RAM in your system, just like disk compression utilities double your hard disk's capacity without additional hardware.

Modern computers require large amounts of fast memory. Don't plan to use RAM doubling software to go from 4MB to 8MB—install the extra memory chips. However, if you have already 16 or 20MB of RAM in your system and you can't add more physical memory, consider doubling it with software. *SoftRAM* and *MagnaRAM* are two utilities that will double your computer's RAM and cost around $60 each. There's some penalty in speed, but it beats disk-swapping. At the time of this writing, these programs are not yet compatible with Windows 95, but upgrades are promised. However, it's difficult to say how useful these doublers will be with Windows 95, because the new operating system itself incorporates some of the efficiencies offered by the doublers. In addition, software designers are increasingly incorporating compression into their applications.

HARD DISKS

The hard disk is where programs and files (all the information your computer can hold) are stored when the power is off. They are moved from the hard disk to RAM memory as needed. Unlike memory, hard disks are permanent, or non-volatile, media. This means that the information stored on the disk is maintained even when the power is turned off.

There are many ways to classify hard disks, but let's start with the basic characteristic, their capacity. Like memory, hard disk capacity is measured in millions of characters (megabytes, or MB). A disk capacity of 20 to 300MB is quite common today, even for notebooks. If you are about to buy a new computer or update an existing one, go for the highest capacity you can afford. You can buy a hard disk that holds up to 1,000MB (that's one gigabyte, or a billion characters) for approximately $1,000.

The size of the new drive should be at least twice the capacity you need. Let's say you are currently running Windows 3.1 and you plan to upgrade to Windows 95. The operating system itself can consume as much as 80MB on your disk (depending on the options you install). Now figure about 15MB for each software application. This is a reasonable size for typical word processing, drawing, spreadsheet, etc., applications. If you are using *AutoCAD*, or any other specialized application with very large hard disk requirements, adjust your calculations accordingly.

Whatever number you come up with, triple it to be sure that the disk is going to last for a couple of years. If you need 100MB of storage today, go for a 300MB drive. Don't forget that applications generate documents—and they can take up lots of space, too—particularly graphics.) And if you are going to work with multimedia files, go for 500MB or more, even if

most of the disk will be empty for a while. You'll be surprised how quickly you can fill it.

There are a few more hard disk specifications to consider as well. One of them is the access time, which is given in milliseconds. The access time is how long it takes the hard disk circuitry to locate any given piece of information on the disk, and the smaller this number is, the better. A typical access time for a hard disk today is anywhere from 10 to 14msec. Large capacity disks, which are more expensive, have smaller access times—sometimes even less than 10msec.

Hard disks can also be classified according to the way they are connected to the computer's motherboard. There are three types of hard drives: ESDI, IDE and SCSI. ESDI (Enhanced Small Device Interface) disks require a disk controller (a card that fits in one of the computer's expansion slots.) An ESDI controller supports two hard disks, so if you already have a hard drive, you don't need another controller to add a second drive.

IDE stands for Integrated Device Electronics and, as the name suggests, the controller is built into the drive. In other words, you can connect this drive directly to your system's motherboard.

SCSI (Small Computer Systems Interface) drives are the fastest, but they require a SCSI port. Some of the most expensive computers come with a SCSI port. If your computer doesn't have a SCSI port, you will have to install a SCSI adapter (another expansion card) as well. A SCSI adapter lets you connect up to seven devices to your computer. The devices are "daisy-chained," connected in a serial fashion, one after the other.

Before you order a new drive, you *must* find out the type of drives your computer supports. If you need a very large and fast hard drive, you should consider adding a SCSI drive, even if your computer's prime drive is a different type.

If you need more disk space, but can't afford a new disk, or for any other reason you want to get more out of your existing disk, use a disk compression utility. This program squeezes the information stored on the disk, effectively increasing the disk's capacity.

Compression utilities were developed by several manufacturers and have been in use for several years. Microsoft decided to include a compression utility in its Windows 95 operating system. When you install Windows 95, you can ask the operating system to compress the information down by as much as 3:1. This means a threefold increase in your disk's capacity—not bad at all if you consider that it is costing you absolutely nothing.

Tech Tip: After installing a new hard disk, you must provide some parameters (such as number of cylinders, tracks, etc.) so that the computer knows this information. Most people don't know about the low level details of their hard drives, because they are generally never needed after the installation. If you are not sure how to do it, you should ask a friend who knows, or have it installed at the computer store where you bought it for an additional fee. (Of course, this situation will change with the proliferation of the Plug and Play technology employed in the Windows 95 operating system.)

Before you take your computer in for a new hard drive installation, make backup copies of all the files on the hard disk. The new drive will not interfere with the existing one, but things can go wrong during installation, so best be prepared.

CD-ROM DRIVES

The CD-ROM drive is a relatively new peripheral, but it has already changed the computer landscape. A CD-ROM is just like a music CD, except that it contains computer programming or data. Each CD-ROM can hold 650MB worth of information. They are significantly slower than the hard disk, but less expensive, too.

CD-ROMs are read-only devices (their name stands for Read Only Memory). You can read the information stored on a CD, but you can't write on it. (Some rewritable CDs have already hit the market, but they are still too expensive for most users.)

Despite this limitation, CD-ROMs turned out to be extremely useful. Just as music CDs replaced records, computer CD-ROMs are replacing diskettes as a distribution medium. An entire encyclopedia can be stored on a single CD, and the manufacturing cost of a CD is less than a diskette. Program manufacturers stuff CDs with large amounts of auxiliary data (clip art, samples, extensive on-line help systems, etc.). The CD-ROM drive is not just another storage device; it is swiftly becoming a necessary part of every computer sold today.

As with hard disks, the most important specification of a CD-ROM is its speed (the capacity is just as important, but it's fixed). Unlike hard disks, where the most important speed indication is the access time, the speed of a CD-ROM device is best measured by its transfer rate: how fast it can supply information to the CPU. A CD-ROM device can have an access time of 200msec and not be considered slow. When you play back an animation

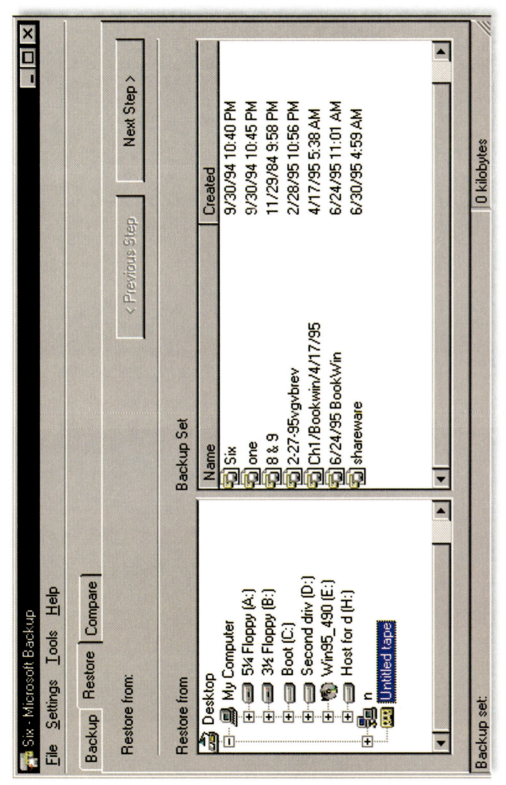

Figure 10: This backup utility comes with Windows 95 and works with many backup units.

file from the CD, for example, you aren't interested in how long it takes to locate the beginning of the file (it will be less than a second anyway), but whether the drive can supply all the information needed by the CPU in a timely manner.

The first generation of CD-ROM drives—called 1X, and practically extinct—could transfer data at the rate of 150kB per second. Today, you can buy a 2X CD-ROM drive for approximately $100, while a quad speed CD-ROM (4X), which transfers data at 600kB per second, costs between $200 and $400.

Speed is a very important factor when you buy a CD-ROM. If you can't afford a 4X unit (or you really hate to throw away the 2X CD-ROM you bought last year), check out some inexpensive software that doubles the speed of a CD-ROM drive. Even if it doesn't quite live up to its promise, it will be a great help for that old double speed CD-ROM you are currently using. *d-Time 10* is one CD speed-up utility that retails for less than $50 and you can find it at any major computer store.

Another aspect of a CD-ROM is how it is connected to the computer. Most CD-ROMs are internal, and they are connected to your sound card's SCSI port. If you don't have a sound card, the CD-ROM comes with its own card, which

must be installed in one of your computer's slots. If you own neither a sound card nor a CD-ROM, you are better off buying a so-called multimedia kit, which contains both the card and the CD-ROM device. Installation is also then simpler, because the factory default settings will most likely work. Besides, you can usually get a good deal on a pair of compact speakers with the multimedia kit, as well as a few free CDs.

Tech Tip: **The SCSI port of a sound card isn't a true SCSI port. In other words, you can't connect a SCSI hard drive on it.**

External CDs plug into your computer's parallel port (daisy-chained with the printer). External peripherals can be very convenient, because you can take them with you, and connect them to any computer. No expansion cards, no jumpers, no hassle. However, they are not as fast as internal ones, especially if your computer doesn't have an **enhanced parallel port**—and most older computers don't.

BACKUP UNITS

An extremely practical and useful expansion to your system is a **backup** device. Think of it as a slow hard disk.

There are two reasons for using backup devices. The first, and most important, is safety. Your hard disk may fail at any time. Hard disks are very reliable devices, but they may fail, just like any other mechanical or electronic device. Even if the disk itself doesn't fail, a virus may destroy information you have stored on it. Also—and more likely than viruses or drive crashes—files can be accidentally erased, or can become "cross-linked" and unusable.

The second reason for buying a backup unit is convenience. As your hard disk fills up, you may have to make room for new data or new programs. In other words, delete files you don't need anymore to free valuable disk space. But can you be absolutely certain which files are not needed any longer? Just dump a large number of old files on a tape and free up your disk. If you need some of them in the future, you can always restore them from the tape.

The classic media for backing up files were diskettes. With today's file sizes, however, diskettes are out of the question. They are too slow, take up too much space and for one reason or another you will eventually overwrite one of them.

There are many types of backup devices. The most common ones use tape cartridges.

They are called **tape backup units** and they start at under $200. A tape backup unit can connect to your computer's SCSI port or the parallel port. The SCSI port is faster and should be preferred. However, if you think you may have to transfer large volumes of data between computers, you should consider a unit that can connect to the parallel port, because it can work with any computer. Just take the unit with you, connect it to any other computer's parallel port, load in the backup software (or use Windows 95's built-in backup utility) and you're in business. Moreover, the backup device has an additional parallel port, to which you can connect the printer, so that the printer you had connected to the parallel port will still work.

The capacity of the tapes varies and many manufacturers use compression techniques too. In general, you can easily fit 350 MB worth of information on a $16 tape.

Another option is a removable hard disk, in addition to the primary hard disk. This unit itself doesn't cost more than a tape backup unit, but the disks are more expensive than tapes. A removable hard disk, however, offers additional benefits. For one thing, it's secure. You can store your data on it and then lock it somewhere. When you need the data, just insert the appropriate hard disk. No time-consuming backup or restore procedures.

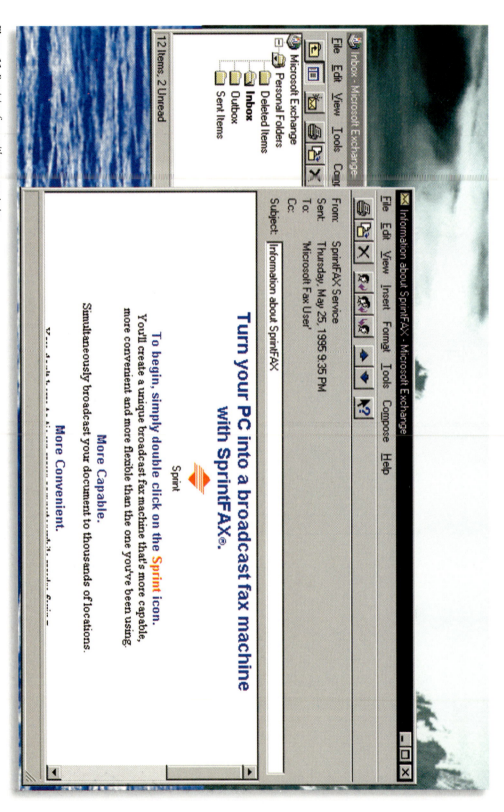

Figure 11: *Receiving faxes with your computer.*

If your children are using your home computer too, a removable disk will allow you to create a totally different environment for yourself, and a separate one for your kids. Even if they know more about computers than you do, you can't trust your livelihood to them. So, why not yourself? Every time you want to work on the computer, plug in your disk and there you are. A totally new computer. Removable hard disks are especially handy if you are the type of person who habitually brings work home.

A very popular product in this category is the new Zip Drive, from Iomega. Zip Drive costs around $200 and is a cross between a hard disk and a backup unit. It uses cartridges that can hold 100MB worth of data (they cost less than $20), and it has an access time of 19msec. It's not the perfect choice for a hard disk, but it's a very fast backup device, which can also be used as an additional hard disk should you need one. Always consider the *media* (tapes or disks, etc.) when evaluating backup hardware. It's not smart to buy a $200 backup peripheral if the media costs $75 per unit and only holds 75MB. If you have a very large hard disk and perform backups regularly (as you should), then check out backup units that use DAT tapes (the same ones that are used to record music digitally).

The unit itself is expensive (close to $800), but it lets you store 4GB (that's 4,000MB) worth of data per $15 tape. And they're very fast, too.

MODEMS

A **modem** is your gateway to the world. No matter how fast your computer is, or how much you can accomplish with your software, there will always be a need to communicate with other people electronically, instantly locate hard-to-find information on the **Net**, or simply work out of the office. The computer community has become global and you don't want to miss this opportunity. Think of the modem as a way of greatly expanding your computer—reaching out beyond the walls of your home or office and contacting computers worldwide.

A modem is likely one of the least expensive peripherals on your computer, yet you'll get much use out of it. You will use it to send files or email to your company's computer, or to your friends' computers. Or you can connect to an online service, such as CompuServe or AOL, where you can find incredible amounts of information. You can read the latest news, see the latest pictures from the space shuttle or the Hubble telescope, or download all kinds of free software for your computer. You can also send and receive faxes.

There are several aspects to consider before buying a modem. Is it going to be an internal or external one? An internal modem will cost less and will not take up your serial port. External modems communicate with your computer via the serial port, which is usually taken by the mouse. If you opt for an external modem (because you want to use it with more than one computer, for example) make sure your computer has a second serial port to which you can connect the mouse.

A modem transfers data over telephone lines. The more quickly it can transfer data, the better. Modem speeds are measured in Bits Per Second, or BPS. Your new modem should operate at the speed of 9,600BPS or higher. Slow modems are adequate for exchanging text messages, but if you want to take advantage of the best resources out there you must get a fast modem. An internal 9,600BPS modem costs less than $100. The fastest modems, which operate at 28,800BPS, are closer to $300.

The more expensive a modem is, the more options it offers. If you plan to use your notebook to send messages via a cellular phone, make sure your modem supports the MNP10 protocol for reliable cellular connections. These are called cellular modems. Some manufacturers advertise their modems as "cellular upgradable." Before you buy such a modem, find out how much the upgrade costs, and whether it's available yet.

OF BLACKOUTS AND BROWNOUTS

Your computer, like any other electrical device, requires power. When you plug your computer's cable into the wall socket, you are actually plugging in the power supply, the device that distributes power to all computer components. All computers sold today have adequate power supplies and you'll probably never have to change the power supply. If it fails, though, purchase a new 200W (or larger) power supply.

There are two more related devices you should consider: the Uninterruptible Power Supply (UPS), and the surge protector (or surge suppresser). The less expensive device is the surge suppresser. This device sits between the wall plug and your computer's power supply and controls the quality of the electricity that flows into your computer. Under normal conditions it doesn't do anything. However, it can save your computer if lightning hits the power lines close to home. When lightning hits, power surges travel through the lines and can reach your computer (lightning is the most common, but not the only, source of surges). A power surge is a large amount of energy, which can cause all kinds of problems in electronic devices. The memory could lose its contents, the hard drive might be destroyed, the CPU might even burn up. A surge suppresser will block the surge before it reaches your computer's power supply. Read the specs carefully when selecting one. Their speed and capabilities vary widely.

A UPS is like a battery that can power your computer in the case of a power failure. It normally sits between the power plug and your computer and regulates the current that goes into the computer, just like a surge protector. If the power goes down, though, the UPS kicks in instantly and starts supplying power to your computer. Some UPS's can go on for half an hour before they are discharged.

The basic reason to use a UPS is to avoid an abnormal shutdown of the computer. A computer should be shut down in an orderly fashion: first close all the applications, then save the data files, exit Windows and finally shut the computer down.

In the case of a power failure, the computer may shut down in the middle of an operation. If the computer happened to be defragmenting, or compressing the disk at the moment of the failure, there's a chance some of your files will be lost for good. A UPS can cost as little as $100, but you should be ready to invest $200 or more for a good one.

Neither suppressers nor UPS units are in common use with home computers, but they can save you hours of work, and sometimes save the computer itself. Your computer doesn't need a total blackout to shut down. A brownout—a split second "sink" of the power, when the lights go dim for a moment in the house—can cause the computer to restart. And this may cause your computer to shut down abnormally.

A surge suppresser looks like a power strip with many outlets, and can cost around $20. Buy one with several outlets to accommodate all of your equipment. For $100, or a little more, you can buy a UPS that will not only regulate the electric signal, it will also protect the equipment from blackouts and brownouts. Like surge suppressers, UPS's come with many outlets, to which you can also connect your monitor, printer and so on.

SHOW IT TO THE WORLD

No computer system is complete without a printer, even a crude dot matrix model. The most popular printers sold today are laser printers and ink jet printers. Laser printers work like photocopiers and they are based on the same principle. The actual pattern to be printed (text and/or graphics) is first stored in the printer's memory, similar to the way the monitor's image is stored in the display card's memory. Then it is transferred to paper with the help of tiny particles which stick to the paper. A laser printer must have enough memory to accommodate large, complex images. Also, for all practical purposes, laser printers are restricted to monochrome images. Color laser printers exist, but their prices start at $5,000.

CMYK PRINTING

Ink jet printers are similar to dot-matrix printers, only instead of firing pins for each tiny dot on the page, they spray (squirt) ink on the page. The ink is held in small containers, called ink cartridges. Black-and-white ink jet printers use a single container of black ink. Color ink jets use three different ink colors: cyan, magenta and yellow.

We mentioned earlier that monitors use three primary colors as well, but different ones: red, green and blue. Because of the different media, printers can't use the same three colors. Where minimizing all three primary colors on a monitor produces black, minimizing on a printer produces white. The color model used in monitors is called RGB and the color model used in printing is called CMYK.

What's the K in CMYK? It is a fourth component, black. Most inexpensive color printers today use the other three primary colors to produce black. But the result is not a clear black—it's more like a muddy, very dark brown. By adding a cartridge with black ink, you can print true black on the page.

PRINTER RESOLUTION

Another factor affecting the quality of the printout is resolution. Both laser and ink jet printers reproduce the image (or text) with tiny dots. The smaller and closer to each other these dots are, the better the quality of the printout. The minimum resolution you will get on a typical laser printer is 300 dots per inch (or DPI), but some feature 400 or 600DPI. If you want magazine-quality output, look for a printer capable of 1,200DPI.

Ink jet printers have a resolution of 300DPI too, and the most expensive ones can reach 600DPI. Sometimes you'll see specifications like 600×300DPI. This means that the horizontal resolution is 600DPI and the vertical resolution is 300DPI. A notable exception is the Epson Stylus, which can reach a resolution of 720DPI and produce near-photographic quality printouts.

You may have heard of bubble jet printers, too. They are basically ink jet printers, but some companies, Canon for one, prefer the other name.

Prices of ink jet printers start at $300 and you can buy a very good one (600DPI, four color) for about $500. You can also buy a monochrome ink jet printer for a little less than $300 today and upgrade it to a color model for another $200. Laser printers are more expensive. They start at $400 and depending on the resolution they can easily exceed $1,000.

Another consideration when buying a printer is its speed, measured in pages per minute. Laser printers can print from four to ten pages per minute. Ink jet printers are slower, sometimes less than a page per minute. Color printouts also take longer than black and white ones, but most people can tolerate the delay in anticipation of a colorful page.

THE REAL COST OF PRINTING

Since cost is the bottom line, the most important consideration before buying a new printer is the cost of each printed page. Both laser and ink jet printers use cartridges, which must be replaced every now and then. A laser toner cartridge lasts 3,000 to 4,000 pages and costs $70 to $100. Ink cartridge's cost around $10 to $30, but they only last about 100 pages. Some companies will refill your toner and ink cartridges for approximately half the price of a new replacement cartridge.

The cost of the paper can be a consideration too. Laser printers work fine with regular paper (also called plain copier paper). Ink jets can't produce optimal results on this paper, because the ink bubbles sprayed on the page tend to leak and spread. For the best color reproduction, you must use a special coated, glossy paper which looks almost like a photograph but is quite expensive.

HOOKING THEM UP

A joystick is easy—you just plug it into the joystick receptacle (usually on your sound card). But some peripherals are much more difficult to add to your computer system. There are many different computer models in the PC world— different case sizes, various types of expansion slots and various numbers of bays for hard drives and CD-ROM units. And when you decide to add a new peripheral to your machine, you'll find that there are often dozens of different models to choose among.

Fortunately, each computer and each peripheral comes with a manual to give you guidelines about how to insert, plug in and activate your new peripheral. Unfortunately, these manuals are often written by people who are technically adept but not strong writers. What to do?

If you get stuck, one resource is the manufacturer's "Technical Staff" phone number at the back of the equipment's manual. There are three drawbacks to calling them: (1) It's rarely an 800 number, so you pay; (2) You usually have to pay quite a bit because you often wait 20 minutes on hold listening to somebody's idea of

MODERATE ONES

Ordinary cards—modems, sound cards, scanner cards, video cards—are all fairly easy to upgrade. You do have the hassle of removing the

THE HARD ONES

Don't even think about changing the motherboard—that's equivalent to replacing the motor in a car. You've got to know what you're doing to pull out the main printed circuit board of your computer and put in a new one. This tactic is sometimes advertised as a way to "upgrade" your whole computer, but it's not for amateurs.

Hard and diskette drives, tape backup drives and CD-ROM units are all at pretty much the same difficulty level. They're not impossible, but you've got to physically get them into a "bay" which isn't always easy. Machine tooling in computers isn't perfect and things can get tight. We're not talking about the space shuttle here— personal computer hardware is mass-produced and screw holes don't always line up, space between bays can be close and so on. But even when you get the unit inserted physically, you've then got to attach it electronically. The plugs for disk drives are particularly badly designed. Most of them can be attached any which way, but must be attached a particular way. There's a "red stain" on one side of the ribbon wire. That's a clue. And CD-ROM units usually have to be attached to your sound card with an additional separate cord. Basically, your local store with its own service center is still your best, hassle-free way to accomplish error-free results.

music; (3) Finally, no company in its right mind puts its crack engineers on customer service duty, so the person you're talking to is as a rule looking up your query in a database. If your problem isn't written down in this database, or if something unusual comes up, your guess is as good as theirs.

> **Tip:** If you've got an extra $20 to $100 lying around, you can always buy a peripheral from the local computer store and pay that extra money to have them install and test the new peripheral on your system. If it doesn't fit or doesn't work—that's then their problem. If you buy the peripheral locally, they'll often install it for you for a reasonable fee. This is often the headache-free way to go.

If you decide to tackle the job of accessorizing your machine, what follows is our personal list of how tough installing the various peripherals are for us amateurs. Some peripherals are easy to install; some are real headbangers.

THE EASY ONES

The rest are relatively effortless. Anything that simply plugs into the back of your machine is painless. For one thing, these kinds of peripherals are *outboard*—meaning that they don't generally require that you get inside the machine and push in a circuit board or, worse, an entire new unit. A new printer is plugged into the printer port on the back of the computer; a new keyboard, mouse, monitor or joystick—each has its port, too. All you have to do in these cases is look at the plug on your new peripheral and then find, on the back of the computer, a matching receptacle. And most of them are asymmetrical so you can't plug them in the wrong way.

cover; but pulling the old card out and inserting the new one is fairly foolproof. Just make sure you line up the plugs on the card with the socket in the computer. And if it's a tight fit, try rocking the card gently to pull it out or insert it. Windows 95 makes the software aspect of upgrading fairly painless. Just click on *Start/Settings/Control Panel*, then select *Add/Remove Hardware* and follow the instructions of the "Wizard" that pops up to assist.

Equally moderate are adding extra memory and upgrading your CPU. Memory resides within a series of small slots on the motherboard. Once you've made sure that the speed and size of the memory fits in with the other memory you've already got, inserting new cards of chips isn't too tough. Likewise, on contemporary computers, adding a faster CPU is usually a matter of pulling a lever to "unseat" the existing CPU, positioning the new faster "brain chip," then pushing the lever back down. (One caution: Check first with the company that made your computer before you add memory or upgrade the CPU. There are sometimes peculiar difficulties—incompatible memory sizes or hard-wired CPUs.)

Richard Mansfield's books on personal computing have sold over 350,000 copies worldwide. He is the author of two current bestsellers: The Visual Guide to Visual Basic and The Visual Basic Power Toolkit. Richard was Senior Editor of COMPUTE! Publications from 1982 through 1987, and Senior Editor of Game Players Publications from 1988 to 1992.

Evangelos Petroutsos has a degree in Computer Engineering from the University of California and works as an author and consultant. He is co-author of the best-selling book Visual Basic Power Toolkit.

WHY WINDOWS?

By Richard Mansfield

To understand the features and utilities of Windows 95, we'll first take a brief tour of its precursors—DOS and the 12 years of ancestor versions of Windows itself. Then we'll take Windows 95 for a test drive. We'll look at the major new features in Windows 95, and by the end of this article, you should be able to judge whether upgrading to Windows 95 is worth your while.

First introduced in 1983, Windows languished for nearly a decade. It wasn't until the early 90's that Windows really took off.

Just as early radio was noisy, often boring and hard to tune, early computing was awkward, colorless and frequently confusing. **DOS** (Microsoft's <u>Disk Operating System</u>) made its first appearance in 1981. Like any computer **operating system**, its primary job was to manage disk files by saving and retrieving information. It also kept track of the time via a little battery-powered clock; accepted key presses if the user started typing; displayed characters on screen; managed memory so programs and information didn't get put in the same places inside the machine; and performed other housekeeping tasks. DOS worked, but by today's standards it was primitive.

You worked at a screen with white text on a black background. Something as simple as copying a file was complicated—many people had difficulty remembering all the cryptic DOS commands and rules of punctuation. The

their value in communicating with 30 students, a blackboard and a piece of chalk are not the best tools for composing personal documents or organizing files.

People use personal computers for many things—learning, creating, analyzing, preparing reports, playing games, storing and retrieving information and so on. It became obvious that a *desktop* is a better, more typical environment to accomplish these various tasks than a blackboard. People are more familiar with, and work more efficiently within, a desktop setting.

Unfortunately, computers were physically incapable of simulating a realistic desktop during the first decade of personal computing. Apple, Atari, Commodore, IBM and others tried to add color and a sense of depth, but the hardware wasn't fast enough and computer memory wasn't large enough. Probably Apple came closest with its offerings: the Lisa and later the Macintosh operating systems. But they were expensive, difficult to customize and also colorless.

Windows was introduced by Microsoft in 1983, but it too was feeble and inadequate. Compared to DOS, Windows was slower, there were few visual improvements, it easily ran out of memory, was problematic with

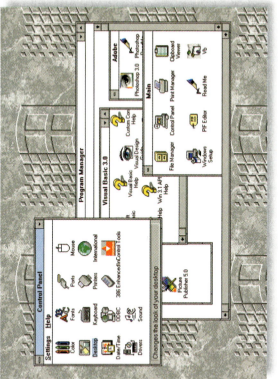

Figure 2: In the early 90's, Windows finally came into its own with Version 3.0.

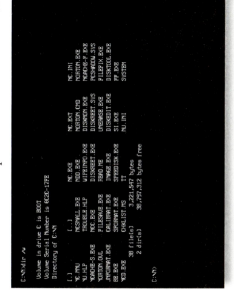

Figure 1: The DOS world was monochromatic, flat and difficult to use.

networks and crashed (froze up and refused to respond) relatively often. The marketplace reacted to these problems by more or less ignoring Windows. Few people were willing to leave the visually restrictive but nonetheless reliable and swift world of DOS. Besides, there were few applications that took advantage of Windows's visual features.

THE FIRST GREAT MIGRATION

Then, finally, Windows 3.0 appeared in May 1990. It was followed two years later by Windows 3.1. This time around, the hardware was powerful enough to make a Graphical User Interface (GUI) usable. And the Windows 3 software was swift and robust enough to make the transition from DOS worthwhile. The tidal wave of migration began. People moved happily to this new, easier way to compute. Today there are very few holdouts still using DOS. Almost everyone who moved from DOS to Windows 3.0 or later agrees that computing became easier and more enjoyable.

Monospaced Proportional

Figure 3: The proportional typeface on the bottom is easier to read because the word's shape is unique.

WINDOWS'S QUALITIES

What are the qualities of Windows that make it easier to use than DOS? First and foremost, things are easier to see. There's color, of course, which adds many additional visual clues. Second, computer **video cards** and **monitors** have become capable of superior, more detailed display—more colors (over 2½ million colors is not uncommon today); finer dots (**pixels**); and better typefaces (fonts) so you can read more text on the screen at a time.

DOS permitted only a single typeface on-screen at any give time. And the typeface was monospaced (each character takes up the same amount of space—I is as wide as a W). Books, newspapers and magazines are all printed in *proportional* typefaces where the spacing within a word depends on actual letter widths. This is important because people don' read individual characters—they read by recognizing word shapes. Clearly, a proportional typeface results in more unique word shapes (see Figure 3).

THE AGE OF RODENTS

The mouse was in limited use in the world of DOS, but Windows virtually requires a mouse. Its advantages? Unlimited mobility across the entire screen, making it easier to select, move and otherwise manipulate visual objects. A mouse is physical—your hand motions are reflected by the pointer on the screen. It's true that most anything can be accomplished with *either* a keyboard or a mouse, but for specific situations, usually one or the other is better. For example, the keyboard is best for entering text, but the mouse is best when working with graphics.

Windows is a graphical interface, like the real world. It includes text, of course, but isn't limited to text. In Windows, you start the Notepad running by clicking (with the mouse) on a visual icon that *looks* like a notepad. Objects have shape, position, size, dimension. Things overlap.

Windows is also a *Multiple Document Interface*, meaning that you can have more than a single file or application active at the same time. This makes it much easier to tackle such common jobs as cutting, pasting and moving information. The Clipboard is a special area in memory where you can temporarily put text or graphics, then copy them into other documents or applications. All this was nearly impossible in

DOS but is quite simple in Windows. To copy, just select a document or a zone in a document by dragging the mouse over it, then press *Ctrl+C*. It's now in the Clipboard. To paste it elsewhere, just point (click) with the mouse on where you want it to go, and press *Ctrl+V*.

You can still run DOS programs within a window in Windows. You can even cut and paste between Windows and DOS, but there are now so many Windows applications that you might find yourself going down into DOS rarely, if ever. And file management (opening, saving, moving, deleting and copying whole file documents) is simplified in Windows—the File Manager and Program Manager were great improvements over the "command line" codes you had to type in when managing files in

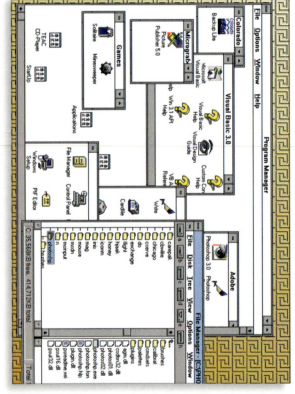

Figure 4: In Windows you manage files with both text labels and graphic symbols.

DOS. In Windows you can get physical, you can drag a file and drop it elsewhere to move it to a new directory. To drag, click on a file's icon but don't release the mouse button. Then slide the mouse to move the file. When you're over your target location, release the button to drop the file.

Windows 3 introduced various other efficiencies. Control Panel allowed you to conveniently adjust such things as the speed at which your keys repeated, the sensitivity of your mouse and so on. The Windows Setup icon made changing screen modes and resolutions convenient. Memory management was improved, even including an area on your hard drive to provide extensive "virtual" memory—making it seem that your computer had, say, 20 megabytes of usable memory instead of the four megabytes it really had.

SmartDrive speeds up disk access by keeping recently used data in RAM memory. This way, when you want to move to page 25 of a document, it's already there in the computer's RAM memory (fast) rather than requiring a second disk read (slow). A dental assistant doesn't just put a pick on the tray; even though that's the first tool the dentist will use. The tray is filled with pliers, wedges, grinders and whatever else might be needed. This apparent improvement in disk response was perhaps the single most impressive "tweak" to personal computer performance since the introduction of color monitors.

Windows also included elementary but frequently useful applications. Cardfile was a simple database manager for storing limited information, like names and addresses or recipes. Write was a word processor of modest abilities. Notepad was even less elaborate, but when you wanted to jot down an idea or look at a small document, nothing worked better.

Paintbrush was an undorned drawing and re-touching program. All in all, Windows 3 was quite a package—the first usable graphical interface for IBM-style personal computers. And its advantages over DOS were so conspicuous that almost everyone migrated from DOS to this new, colorful surface. At the time of this writing, over 85% of all the world's computers display Microsoft's Windows 3 (or the later version, 3.1) Program Manager when you turn them on.

MAKING THE MOVE

What about moving from Windows 3.1 to Windows 95, the decision many people must make today? Is it worth it? I was one of the original beta testers for Windows 95 and began using it daily in late 1993. Almost immediately I felt comfortable in the Windows 95 atmosphere—at first it doesn't appear all that different from what you're used to in Windows 3.1. Yet many significant and fundamental changes have been made.

Even after nearly two years of constant use, I'm still discovering new ways of doing things, new shortcuts, alternatives and conveniences. Windows 95—in spite of its sleeker but still familiar surface appearance—is simultaneously simpler and more powerful than Windows 3.1.

It's difficult to resist the rich new set of accessories; the smooth and effective tools and

Figure 7: On the left Windows 3.1; on the right Windows 95. Note the additional detail, shading and subtle realism.

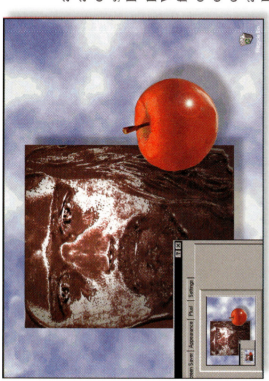

Figure 5: You can create amazing backgrounds like this for Windows 95 by using programs such as Photoshop.

features; and above all, the sense that you're in command of a thoughtfully designed and carefully crafted system. If forced to choose a single word to describe the difference I would choose *smooth*.

Are there hidden risks in upgrading to Windows 95? Will your trustworthy tried-and-true word processor still work? Is there an increased hazard of unexplained shutdowns and freeze-outs? Not at all—in fact, Windows 95 is considerably sturdier and more reliable than Windows 3.1. Windows 95 is much less likely to crash or run out of system resources than earlier versions. (Running low on system resources makes Windows 3 slow down because things get too crowded; too many applications are running at the same time.)

gracefully withdraws with no harm done.

Also take comfort in the knowledge that no previous product in history—hardware, software, truck or jet fighter—has been as widely and exhaustively tested as Windows 95. Nearly half-a-million users have been pushing it to its limits and stress-testing it on nearly all possible hardware and with nearly all known programs. It supports over 1,900 hardware items and over 3,500 applications and other software. So rest easy.

A DIMENSIONAL SURFACE

The first thing you notice when Windows 95 fires up on your screen is that it looks dimensional; it has a subtle 3D quality. It's in the details—the surface has been polished.

In Figure 6, notice the new detail: there are icons in the listings; the arrows on the scroll bars are more refined; the framing around the status bars along the bottom is more detailed; there's a delicate rough spot in the lower right, showing where you can drag the window to resize it; the entire window is quietly divided visually into more zones (note the difference between the zone that displays the name of the current drive "C:(BOOT)" versus "C:\".

To really see the many subtle

Windows 3.1 version has a too-fat bottom line on the "2." And see how finer detailing in the pages of the calendar make them look more like actual sheets of paper. The open file folders in the middle have been replaced by icons that look like diskette and hard drives. And the file folders at the top are improved by removing the solid black line and adding a drop shadow.

Why get so close to these details? To demonstrate the results of the years that Microsoft has spent refining and burnishing the visuals. A team of designers has made great efforts to make the surface of Windows 95 more inviting and realistic, within the constraints of current personal computer video power. Obviously one day we'll enjoy photo-realistic icons, and the desktop metaphor will give way to a dimensional space that we can move into and around (rather than just across vertically and horizontally).

An individual detail is, admittedly, trivial. Cumulatively, though, the fine points of design and the restructuring of the entire Windows interface have resulted in what most critics are calling the premier personal computer operating system. At first glance, Windows 95 might seem merely somewhat improved visually, but as you get to know it, as you work with it, you'll begin to see its considerable depth.

And it's not just the visual details that Microsoft has been working on all these years. Many "focus groups" have sat in front of computers interacting with the operating system while programmers and program designers watched what they did—what confused them, what was intuitive, what meant nothing at all. The result is a new graphical user interface that differs in hundreds of ways from Windows 3.1, yet feels and looks markedly familiar.

SMART ASSISTANCE

One example involves renaming a folder (what used to be called a "directory"). Windows 95 is just plain smarter than Windows 3.1. Say that you have an icon that, when clicked, starts CompuServe running. If you change the name of the CompuServe directory from *CSERVE* (which is the name the icon

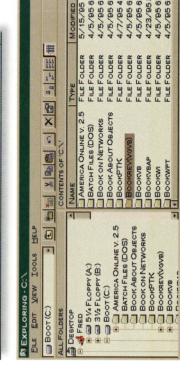

Figure 6: Windows 95, on the bottom, adds many subtle visual clues to the File Manager.

changes, look at Figure 7.

In Figure 7—icons representing the same thing in both versions of Windows—compare the quality of the numbers in the calendars. The

The Windows 95 setup process is safe and clean. Assuming you're installing over an existing version of Windows, Setup will search out and discover your current applications, preferences

and hardware, then accommodate them. It will organize Windows 95 similarly to the way you had organized your program groups in Windows 3.1. It even features an Uninstall option that restores your earlier computer configuration and removes all traces of Windows 95. In the unlikely event that you do decide you don't like it, Windows 95

"knows" to look under for the CompuServe program) to *COMPU*, Windows 3.1 will lock up and report that it cannot find the application. Windows 95, by contrast, will search your hard drive for the application, then it will change the reference in the icon and start CompuServe running—all automatically and without complaint.

You won't notice all the smaller mutations the first few weeks, but you'll certainly feel the focus on several of the most significant—the largest structural adjustments.

In Windows 3.1, holding down the *Alt* key and repeatedly pressing *Tab* cycled you through the active applications. It was annoying and, let's be honest, silly, that when you wanted to switch between running programs you could only see their icons one at a time in this fashion. Why not simply display a bar that showed all running programs so you could quickly move to that icon? Why not indeed? That's precisely what Windows 95 does—and it does it in two locations. If you use the *Alt+Tab* shortcut, you'll see all the active applications at once, and if you look down at the bottom of the screen, you'll see the same applications on the Task Bar where you can click with the mouse to activate one of them (see Figure 9).

Microsoft, like the designers of space vehicles and medical tools, believes in redundancy. In general, you'll find two or more ways to accomplish everything in Windows 95. To switch between currently running programs, you can press *Alt+Tab* or, if you prefer to do it via the mouse, move to the bottom of the screen. You'll see the new Taskbar, as illustrated in Figure 9. To use the Taskbar, you merely move to the program you want to switch to, then click on it.

EVEN MORE ELEMENTARY

Microsoft's studies, focus groups and discussions convinced them that there had to be some clear, memorable locations on the screen. They decided that when you first turned on the computer, there should be a thing called *Start*. This is unambiguous, even for a first-timer: Click here to begin.

Also, even after you've been working for a while, *Start* is still always there down in the left corner. And if you hesitate, with your mouse on top of the *Start* button, a little message appears: Click here to begin.

When you do click on *Start*, up pops a menu like the one shown in Figure 10.

Tip: There are three things that you most often want a computer operating system to do for you, that must happen all the time: start another application running, switch to another application that's already running, and locate something on your hard drive. Windows 95 makes all three jobs as easy and as close-to-hand as possible:

1. Starting another application running: *Click on the Start button, then click on the Run option.* (Shortcut: If you have the Microsoft Natural Keyboard, press the Windows key+R.) *Alternative: Click on the Start button, then move your mouse over Programs (you don't have to click it). A new menu will pop up and the Windows Explorer will be listed directly to the right of Programs. Click on Windows Explorer* and you've got the best of File Manager and Program Manager at your disposal. (Shortcut: Press the Windows key+E.)

2. Switching to another running application: *Press Alt+Tab or move your mouse to the bottom of the screen and select from the Taskbar.*

3. Locating a file on your hard drive: *Click on the Start button, then choose Find.* Alternative: *Start Explorer running* (see #1 above) *and click on folders (directories) or drive icons until you locate the file.* Alternative: *under Explorer's Tools menu, select Find.* Explorer's Find utility is extremely fast and flexible. (Shortcut: Press the Windows key+F.)

Figure 8: This Windows 95 carousel merely moves the frame among all running applications. You can see at a glance where you're going.

Figure 9: The Taskbar duplicates the information shown in Figure 8, but is for those who prefer to switch with their mouse.

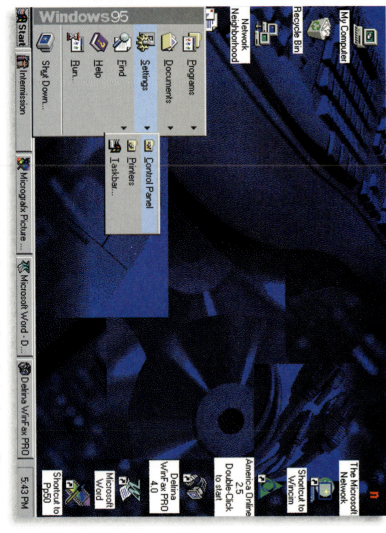

Figure 10: Any time you click on Start (or press the Windows key on a Microsoft Natural Keyboard), up pops this menu.

THE START BUTTON

Notice that after you click the *Start* button, a menu pops up. Two lines divide it into three sections. The lowest item is *Shutdown*, which you should click on when you want to turn the computer off. This allows Windows 95 to gracefully take care of a few details (like memorizing the size and position of your applications on-screen, warning you of any active but unsaved documents, etc.). Don't just turn off the power to the computer—wait until Windows 95 gives you the go-ahead.

Clustered within the next zone on the *Start* menu are: *Run, Help, Find, Settings, Documents* and *Programs*. Moving your mouse to *Settings* reveals *Control Panel, Printers* and *Taskbar. Control Panel* is where you can adjust various parameters—add or remove fonts, sounds, hardware, software and so on. It's similar to the Windows 3 *Control Panel. Printers* and *Taskbar* permit you to adjust various behaviors of those objects.

The *Documents* selection displays the 15 most recently edited text, graphic, multimedia or any other kind of document (file) that you've been working on lately. Click on one of those and the document, plus the program that edited it (like a word processor), are activated for you to resume working.

The *Programs* selection displays a set of new selections equivalent to Windows 3's Program Groups—related files and programs that are within a single folder. When you install a new application, it will usually create a Program Group for itself. This group can then be accessed here via *Start/Programs*. At the very top of this *Programs* list you'll see *Accessories*, which contains all the applets (like Notepad, Calculator, etc.) that are bundled with Windows 95. The *Programs* selection also displays, at the bottom of its list, *Microsoft Exchange* (a beefed-up, feature-

packed email application); the MS-DOS gateway (so you can go back to DOS temporarily, should you wish); *Microsoft Network* (an online service); and the *Explorer.*

Finally, as you can see in Figure 10, you can add your own most-often-used applications to the Start menu. They'll go above the line at the top. To add an application to the Start menu:

1. First find the application on the disk (it will have a name like WINWORD.EXE or NOTEPAD.EXE). You can use Explorer or Find to locate the application you're after.

2. Then create a shortcut to this application. Right-click (not the usual left-click) on the icon or title of the application. A menu will pop out. Select Create Shortcut and a duplicate icon (with a small arrow added) will appear. This is a "pointer" to your application, not the application itself. In other words, you can delete this pointer without deleting the application on the hard drive. However, double-clicking on the shortcut's icon is as good as double-clicking on the actual application's icon—in both cases the application will start running.

Tip: The distinction between an actual application or document icon and a shortcut pointer is like the difference in Windows 3 between items in File Manager and Program Manager. File Manager contained the "actual" programs and documents—deleting one removed the object from the hard drive. Program Manager, however, contained only pointers and deleting or moving these icons had no effect on the hard drive.

3. Now that you've got a shortcut, you can either copy it or move it into your Windows/Start Menu folder. To copy it you could drag it within Explorer (drag with the right button, then drop into the Start Menu folder, then choose Move or Copy). Or, perhaps even easier, click on it once to "select it" so the shortcut icon goes gray and its title reverses colors. Then press Ctrl+C to copy it. Now, in Explorer, move into the Windows/Start Menu folder and press Ctrl+V to paste it in the new location.

NEW-WAVE CLICKING

You might have noticed that we've been suggesting you try some pretty peculiar clicking moves—single-clicking, right-clicking, right-dragging, even hovering. In Windows 95, these are all now highly useful maneuvers and the mouse is that much more flexible.

In Windows 3, there *was* a right-button on every mouse, but it was inert and did nothing. Like a little toe, you could see it hanging there but it served absolutely no purpose other than to make you wonder *why* it was there.

SINGLE-CLICK

Several contexts that used to require a double-click now react to a single-click. For example, a single-click opens a folder in the left pane of Explorer; closes a window via the X button on the top right; and launches a program or opens a folder displayed anywhere on the *Start* button menu hierarchy or on the Taskbar.

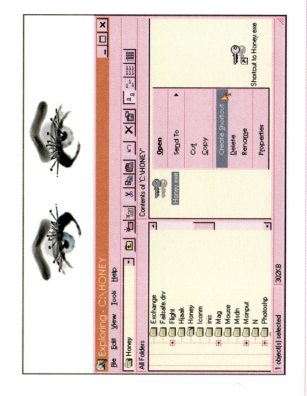

Figure 11: Create a Shortcut by right-clicking on an icon.

RIGHT-CLICK

Right-clicking on nearly any object in Windows 95—a running application; a blank spot on a title bar, button bar or 'Taskbar; or on an icon—drops down a menu including several useful options. Which options are displayed depends on the object, and are up to the designers of individual applications. What they all generally have in common, though, is that they are actions you can perform on the object: copying, cutting, deleting and pasting; adjusting its qualities (Properties); renaming, resizing or repositioning; creating a shortcut; and so on. You can even right-click on an empty spot on the Windows 95 desktop itself. Try it, then select *Properties* to see how many ways you can adjust and personalize your workspace.

Figure 12: Right-clicking pops up these useful options for managing disk files.

application menus as well as on the *Start* button and other Windows 95 menus.

THE RECYCLE BIN

The Recycle Bin is another useful tool embedded in Windows 95. Instead of deleting files from your hard drive, never to be seen again, Windows 95 expects that you, being human, might accidentally delete a file from time to time. Or you might *think* you'll never need it again, but then later you do. Who among us hasn't done this?

Recycle Bin to the rescue. When you delete a file from within Explorer, you'll see a message asking you to confirm that you "really want to send this file to the Recycle Bin." If you say no, nothing is done—the file stays where it was. If you say yes, the file still isn't really deleted—it's just moved from wherever it was to a new folder called Recycled. This folder, like the Windows folder, is on your hard drive, probably C:\.

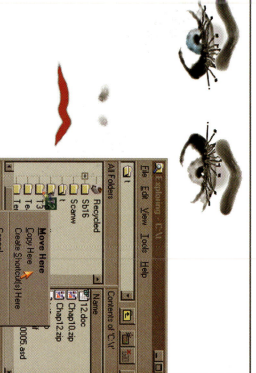

point—all to let you know you're about to do something extreme.

Of course, you can't ignore the Recycle Bin forever; it will become huge and eventually your hard drive will fill up. Every week or so you can empty the Recycle Bin, after you're sure that you won't need the files and folders you've sent to it. Right-click on the *Recycle Bin* icon, then click on the *Empty Recycle Bin* option. The icon will change from its "filled" to "empty" version, as shown in Figure 15.

MY COMPUTER

You can change the names of desktop icons by *slowly* double-clicking on the title underneath the icon, then typing in a new title, like changing "My Computer" to "I." Or you can move them around the desktop. You can even squeeze them so close to the

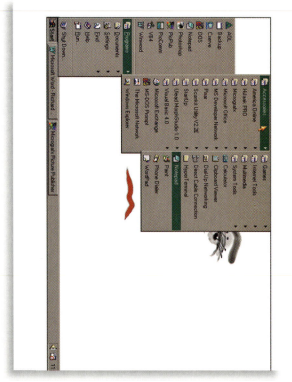

Figure 13: Hovering—merely holding the mouse pointer over a parent menu—pops out the child menu.

bottom of the screen that the title disappears, like the Recycle Bin in Figure 16.

But you can't delete them. They're *The Persistent Icons.* Microsoft, in its wisdom, has decided to put a few icons on your desktop and nail them there so you can't remove them. Several Windows 95 icons, like Microsoft Network, can be deleted (right-click on them, then choose *Delete* if you want to get rid of them).

But four of them are permanent. Like tattoos, you can't get them off. The Network Neighborhood Recycle Bin, In-box and My Computer icons don't react to the Delete key. If you like a clean workspace, this will annoy you. The best you can do is drag these permanent icons way over to the sides of the screen, as shown in Figure 16. If, on the other hand, your refrigerator is bristling with post-it notes and magnets, you might think the more icons the merrier.

RIGHT-DRAGGING

In Windows 3 you can drag and drop various items. This is a highly visual, nearly physical way of reorganizing your disk files. You just click on an icon, hold down the left button while moving the mouse to move the icon, then, when it's over the target (a different directory in File Manager for instance), you release the mouse button and the icon is 'dropped' into the new location.

In Windows 95, you do this reorganizing with the right button on the mouse. *Right-dragging* means holding down the right mouse key while dragging. This is an improvement. When you drop it in the new location, a menu pops up like the one shown in Figure 12. Single-click to move (first it copies, then deletes the original), copy (create two instances of the object in different locations), create a Shortcut (a pointer to the original) or cancel the operation.

HOVERING

Merely holding your mouse pointer on top of a menu item can cause a new, subsidiary menu to pop out. Menu items that contain other menus are indicated by a black triangle, as you can see in Figure 12. Merely keeping the pointer over such an item pops out its child menu, no clicking required. This works in

Figure 14: Deleting from the Recycle folder brings up this warning message.

Confirm File Delete

Are you sure you want to delete Zgdw95.zip?

Yes   No

If you delete a file from the Recycled folder, it will really be gone for good. You'll see the message in Figure 14, complete with an evaporating document/folder icon and a red exclamation

like error checking and **defragmentation** (a reorganization that tightens things up and improves performance).

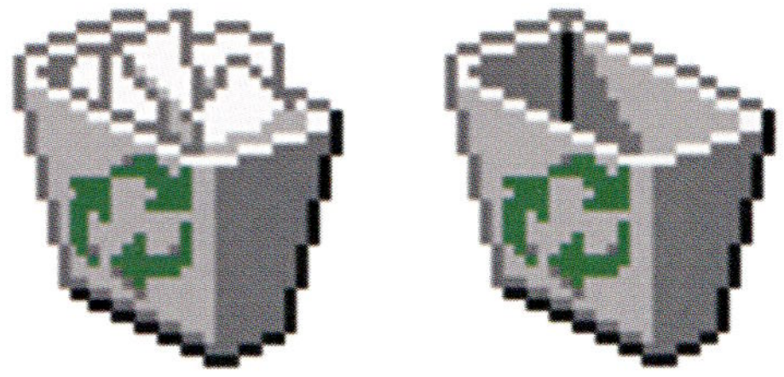

Defragmentation is only one of the new utilities that are bundled with

you use the DriveSpace utility to increase your disk capacity. More on this below.) Finally, there's a CD-ROM called E: and three folders where you can adjust properties of your system, your printer or the network.

In general, the My Computer icon is a gateway to particular zones of your system—the

Figure 15: The filled and empty versions of the Recycle Bin icon.

Tip: Another tactic if you don't care to see clutter on your desktop is to select *None* for desktop wallpaper, then change the background color to match the color of your blank desktop.

Or you can use wallpaper, but set the background color to match it as closely as possible. To do this, right-click on the *Desktop*, then select *Properties* from the drop-down menu. Click on *Appearance* and change the background color (select *Desktop* from the drop-down list). When you change the desktop color, you also change the icon title color. We did that in Figure 16 to match, as best as possible, the grays in our wallpaper.

The My Computer icon is another gateway into the Explorer. It's related to the Start button, but My Computer gives you a bird's eye view of your computer.

Figure 17 shows that this machine has two floppy drives: one large, one small. It also has two hard drives, C: and D:, plus one called H: "Host." (This last one, H:, is a "virtual drive," really a partition of D:. This is necessary when

My Computer

File Edit View Help

5¼ Floppy (A:)   3½ Floppy (B:)   Boot (C:)   Second driv (D:)   (E:)

Host for d (H:)   Control Panel   Printers   Dial-Up Networking

9 object(s)

Figure 17: *Double-click on the My Computer icon to see your entire hardware configuration at a glance.*

disk drives, CD-ROM, printer and the other miscellaneous accessories and features collected within Control Panel. Double-clicking on any of the drive icons contained within My Computer brings you into an abbreviated, single-pane version of Explorer. *Right*-clicking on any of the drive icons brings up several options, including Explorer, Format and Properties, plus some disk management tools

Windows 95. Many handy applications that you previously had to buy separately from third-party software companies are now included free with Windows 95. There's a Backup utility that compresses and saves files to a high-capacity tape drive or other medium. There's ScanDisk, a program that checks for bad spots on the hard drive, or locates and fixes faulty files. You'll also find other valuable free tools like Briefcase, a utility that ensures you're using the most recent version of documents that you transfer between your main computer and a portable.

Some of these extra programs (Microsoft calls them "applets" or "accessories") are installed when you run Windows 95 setup. Some aren't. To see all the available applets, and install additional ones if you decide to—click on the *Start* button, then *Settings*. Choose *Control Panel* and double-click on the *Add/Remove Programs* icon. Finally, click on the *Windows Setup* tab, click on *Accessories*, then click the *Details* button. You'll see the list box shown in Figure 18. While you're here, look for useful applets under the other categories, too—such as Disk Tools, Communications and Multimedia.

COMMUNICATION WITH THE WORLD

The Microsoft Network (MSN) is part of Windows 95, so give it a try. It boasts several features unavailable on CompuServe, America Online or any other competitor.

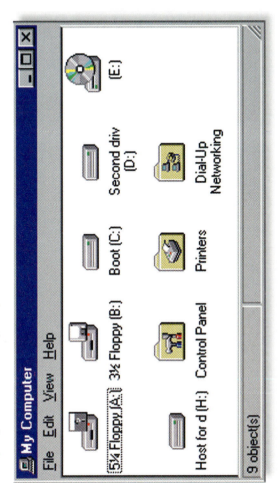

Figure 16: *There are four permanent icons here, but three of them have been dragged over to the far left side of the screen and are nearly invisible. Only the Recycle Bin remains fully visible.*

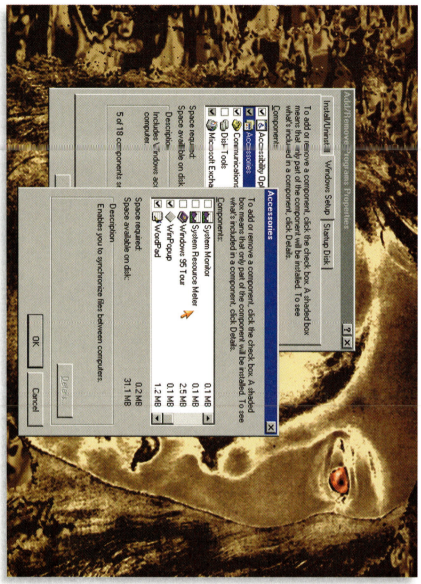

Figure 18: *Here's where you can add new, free accessories to Windows 95.*

Trial versions of Microsoft's reference libraries are there (*Encarta, Bookshelf*) and, as you might expect, a superior interface for you to work with. In fact, the interface is the same that you use in Windows 95 itself—Explorer-like windows, a Find feature and so on.

Among MSN's exceptional qualities are the ability to put pictures and even music into messages that you *email* (electronic mail) to other people. Notice in Figure 19 that we were able to use varying fonts, font sizes, italics and color—and a drop in a photo.

Supplementing MSN is the new Microsoft Exchange, a feature-packed application for sending and receiving email and the In-box, which alerts you to received messages. Internet and fax capabilities are also part of the central messaging system, and the system is fully a part of the Windows 95 operating system itself. With Microsoft Exchange you can get messages from someone at the next desk via your office network, or from Tokyo. This is leading-edge technology. For example, ordinary faxes are *pictures* of text. You can't load them into your word processor and edit them. Faxes sent via Windows 95, however, if received by another computer running Windows 95, are *true text* and can be manipulated in Notepad or any other text or word processor.

CUTTING EDGE TECHNOLOGY

Windows 95 boasts many cutting-edge features in addition to editable faxes and multimedia-ready

email. Much of what's new is "under the hood" and most users won't need or want to understand precisely what's going on down there in the engine room. However, they will notice that they can easily do several things at once—send email, start writing in their word processor and listen to a tune on their CD-ROM player simultaneously. This is called *multitasking* and Windows 95 supports it in ways superior to the limited multitasking available in Windows 3.

You'll also notice that Windows 95 is faster than Windows 3. Print jobs are sent to the printer faster, the screen redraws more quickly, the disk drive and CD-ROM are accessed more swiftly and so on. Speed without safety, though, is a mixed blessing. Fortunately, several changes in Windows 95 make it fairly crash-proof. You'll likely rarely experience one of those mysterious "General Protection Faults" or other inexplicable crack-ups that plagued Windows 3, requiring you to

restart the computer (and lose some of your work).

Should you upgrade to Windows 95? If you want your computer to work faster, be easier to use, run more reliably and also get lots of solid applications thrown into the bargain for free, the answer is clearly, yes. **PC**

Richard Mansfield's books on personal computing have sold over 350,000 copies worldwide. He is the author of two current bestsellers: The Visual Guide to Visual Basic and The Visual Power Toolkit. Richard was Senior Editor of COMPUTE! Publications from 1982 through 1987, and Senior Editor of Game Players Publications from 1988 to 1992.

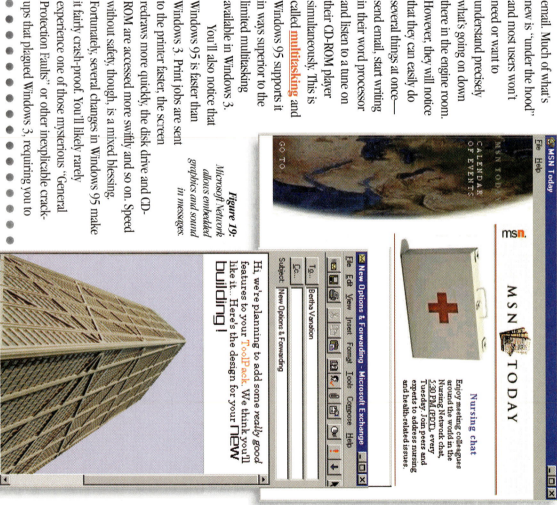

Figure 19: *Microsoft Network allows embedded graphics and sound in messages.*

84

100 GREAT TIPS
FOR WINDOWS 3.1 AND WINDOWS 95

By Charles Brannon

There's a lot to learn about Windows. We've gathered together here our favorite tips, techniques and shortcuts that no Windows users should be without. You'll find some that have never before been published, including special bonus tips for new Windows 95 users.

Note: When referring to menus, we'll use the format FileOpen, which means click on the File menu, then choose Open. Keyboard hotkeys are described as Alt+Enter, which means hold down the Alt key while you press Enter. Mouse combinations such as Alt+Double-Click means to hold down Alt while you double-click the left mouse button.

MANAGING WINDOWS'S WINDOWS

1. *Hold down the Alt key while you press the Tab key to switch between running applications.* Keep holding down Alt so that each time you press Tab, you switch to the next window—don't let go of Alt until you see the name of the program you want. (Windows 3.1 shows you the name of each, one at a time, so just hold down Alt and keep pressing Tab until you've arrived at the window displaying the application you want to use. With Windows 95, you'll see the icons for all open windows while you press Alt+Tab. A gray box surrounds the current target.)

2. For windows within windows (known as *child windows*), use Ctrl+Tab or Ctrl+F6 to cycle between them, or choose the name of a child window from an application's **Window** menu. Also try Alt+Esc as an alternative to Alt+Tab.

3. *Double-click on any empty part of the desktop to open the Windows Task Manager.* (The desktop is the background of your screen—the place where there are no windows or icons, just blank space or wallpaper.) You can then choose any running program from Task Manager's list to quickly switch to it.

4. *Press Ctrl+Esc to pop open the Task Manager at any time.* Instead of Task Manager, use the taskbar with Windows 95. Just click on any program's "button" at the bottom of the

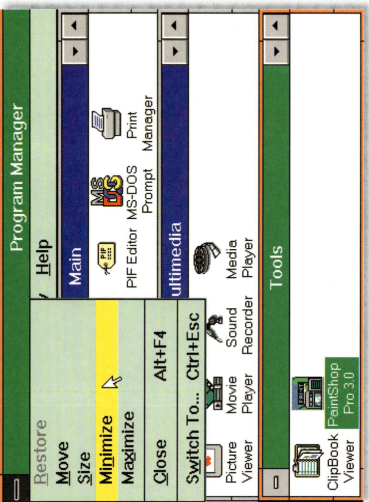

Figure 1: *Alt+Spacebar is the keyboard hotkey that drops down the Control Menu, handy for precise positioning of windows.*

screen to quickly switch to that program and pop it to the top of all other windows. (Ctrl+Esc opens the Windows 95 Start button menu instead of Task Manager. If you want to open Task Manager in Windows 95, click on the Start button, select Run, then type "TASKMAN.")

5. *Use Use Task Manager to arrange your desktop windows.* With Task Manager visible, the Cascade option in the Windows menu lays all open windows on top of each other, but staggered so you can see all the title bars. Use the Tile option to arrange all open windows side by side or in rows and columns (depending on how many windows you have open). Use Arrange Icons to line up the minimized program icons at the bottom of the screen. Windows 95

users can right-click anywhere on the taskbar to tile or cascade windows, or arrange icons.

6. Windows 95 Only: *Right-click on any empty part of the taskbar and choose Minimize All Windows to reveal your desktop icons.* Right-click again on the taskbar and choose Undo Minimize All to restore all your windows. If you have a Microsoft Natural Keyboard or other 104-key Windows keyboard, you can use ⊞+M to minimize all, and Shift+ ⊞+M to undo minimize all.

7. *Double-click the ▭ symbol in the upper-left corner of a window to close that window.* Windows 95 uses the program's own icon or a Windows logo symbol instead of the ▭ symbol

used in Windows 3.1. If you close the main window of a program, you'll exit the program and free up the memory and other resources it was using. You'll be reminded to save any work you have open before the program ends:

8. Click the ▭ symbol just once to show the Control Menu, which includes choices for Restore, Move, Size, Minimize, and Close. (You'll get additional choices including Edit and Font if you're using a DOS window.) The minimize, maximize, and restore choices are shown as buttons on the right-hand side of a window's title bar. With Windows 95, you can also choose the ✕ (Close) box to quickly close a window. You can use Alt+Spacebar to open the control menu with the keyboard (Alt+Hyphen for "child" windows). Bonus tip: you can double-click on the title bar of any window to maximize it. Double-click again to restore it to normal size. (The title bar is the band across the top of a window that displays the name of the application the window contains.)

9. *Press Alt+Spacebar and choose Move to position a window precisely using the arrows keys on your keyboard.* You can choose Resize to size your window with the keyboard. These maneuvers can be especially handy if the program window has moved off the edge of the screen, but you can still get to it with Alt+Tab. (A window can also become inaccessible if you were viewing a window at a higher resolution, and then switch to a lower resolution.) Press Alt+Hyphen (the minus key) if you want to control a window within a window (a child window).

10. *If you open a dialog box window to view its current settings, it's faster to choose Cancel instead of OK to close the window.* You can also press Esc instead of Cancel, and Enter instead of OK (or whatever the default button is—the default button is shown with a heavier outline.) A dialog box asks questions of the user, or provides information. For example, when you shut down a program a dialog box can pop up asking if you want to save your work.

11. *Type the first letter of any item in a list box to skip quickly to that item.* For example, if you select File|Open from within an application, you can quickly jump to any file in the list of files by typing the first letter of the file you're looking for. If there is more than one item with the same first letter, you'll move from one to the next each time you press the key, thereby closing in on your target. Windows 95: Some list boxes (such as in the Help index) now let you enter any part of an item's name to jump to that item. This happens automatically as you type—each character you type leads you to the closest match.

12. *Look for underlined letters on a menu bar.* You can hold down Alt and type the underlined letter to open the menu and pick menu choices using the keyboard. If a menu choice is not underlined, you can select it by just typing the first letter of the menu choice.

13. *Instead of using the scroll bars to move within a document, try dragging the mouse through the text.* Click the mouse within the document and hold it down while moving the mouse up or down. The document auto-scrolls as you move the mouse. Move the mouse just off the visible text window to scroll slowly, further below or above to scroll more quickly. You can also use this trick in list boxes and drop-down lists to more quickly move downward in the list. Release the mouse and click again to turn off the highlighting when you want to stop scrolling.

14. *Use Ctrl+Click and Shift+Click to select multiple items in a list box.* A list box is like a menu, containing a list of choices, such as installation options. Some programs allow you to choose multiple items in any order by Ctrl+Clicking to select items (the items need not be contiguous). Ctrl+Click on a selected item to un-select it. You can also set a range of selections by clicking on the first item and then Shift+Clicking on the last item. All entries between are selected automatically. You can extend this selection from another position (without losing your current selection) by Ctrl+Clicking on the first item and Shift+Ctrl+Clicking on the last item.

15. *Click on any visible part of an obscured window to bring it to the top of the stack.* Or press the Minimize button to hide a window that's on top of a window you want to use. A minimized folder becomes an icon at the bottom of the desktop. These minimized icons can become hidden themselves if you've maximized any of your desktop windows. Press the restore button to "un-maximize" a window. To restore a minimized icon, just double-click it. Windows 95 users can simply use the taskbar, even if another window is running maximized.

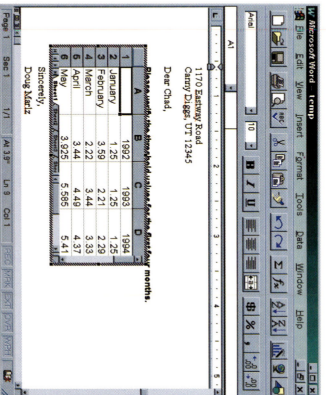

Figure 2: *Double-click on an embedded spreadsheet to graft Excel's toolbar onto the word processor.*

16. *Take a "snapshot" of your screen by pressing the PrintScrn key.* You can then paste (Edit|Paste or Shift+Ins) the image into any program that accepts graphics, including Windows's own Paintbrush applet. (From Paintbrush, you can print the image, the original purpose of the PrintScrn key.) Use Alt+PrintScrn to capture just the currently active window instead of the entire screen.

17. *Use Cut and Paste for compound documents.* You've probably used the Edit|Cut (Ctrl+X), Copy (Ctrl+C), and Paste (Ctrl+V) commands when working within a document, but you can also cut and paste between different applications. For example, copy a range of cells from a spreadsheet and paste it into your word processor. Many applications also let you simply drag a selection (a section you've highlighted by dragging the mouse across it) from one program into another. (Windows 95 users can also drag selections onto the desktop itself to create *scraps.* You can then drag a scrap into another application.) If a program supports Object Linking and Embedding (OLE), you can double-click on the pasted item to edit the "object" using the original program— some programs sneakily add their menus and toolbars to your current application for *in-place editing.* Experiment with other Edit options including Paste Special, Paste Link (which pastes a *reference* to the original object instead of a copy of it), and Edit Object.

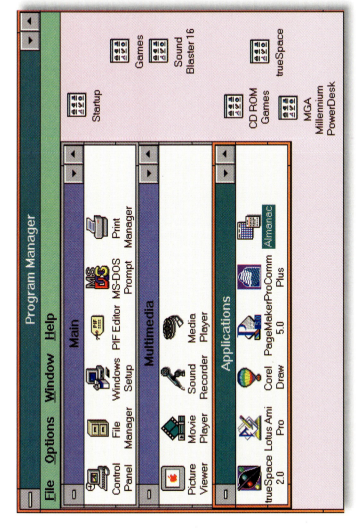

Figure 3: *A carefully laid out Program Manager is much easier to work with.*

BEST PROGRAM MANAGER TIPS

18. *To avoid clutter, consolidate your Program Manager icons.* Use File|New to create a new group called Applications and drag into it the icons for all your favorite programs. (You can save resources by deleting icons you never use, such as Help and "Read Me" icons.) You can then delete the individual group folders created by each application. Similarly, organize all your utilities into a Tools group, keep your games in a group together, etc.

19. Windows 95 users can organize the Start menu's Programs menu by rearranging the icons in the Windows\Start Menu\Programs folder and subfolders. Right-click on the Start button and choose Open to get started.

20. *Turn off Options|Save Settings on Exit once you've arranged your icons and folders to your liking.* This prevents an inadvertent change from becoming permanent. Instead, use Shift+Alt+F4 to force Program Manager to memorize its layout. Once you've done this, Program Manager will return to this layout every time you start Windows, even if you accidentally rearranged the layout the last time you ran Windows.

21. *While you can choose Window|Arrange Icons to line up your Program Manager icons into neat rows and columns, you may find it more convenient to simply choose Auto Arrange from Program Manager's Options menu to keep your icons locked into place at all times. You can still move them around, but they snap into alignment automatically.

22. Another way to keep your screen clean is to choose Options|Minimize on use. Whenever you run a program by double-clicking its Program Manager icon, Program Manager disappears and becomes an icon at the bottom of your desktop. To get it back, just double-click on the minimized Program Manager icon.

23. *You can run programs even if they don't have a Program Manager icon.* Click on Program Manager's File menu, and choose Run. You can now type the name of a program (including the full path that specifies the program's location on your hard disk) and press Enter to run it. For example, you can use File|Run and enter SYSEDIT to conveniently edit all your system files. Use File|Run and enter A:\SETUP to install most software from floppy disk. (Use D:\SETUP if installing from a CD-ROM. Change the D:\ to the actual drive letter of your CD-ROM, if necessary.) File Manager also has a Run option. Windows 95 users can choose the Run command from the Start menu, or press ⊞ + R.

24. *Hold down Alt and double-click within an open group window to create a new icon* (a shortcut for File|New Item). If you click on an icon and then use Alt+Double-click, you can edit the properties for that icon. Or just press Alt+Enter.

25. *Take advantage of "freebie" icons.* Alt+Double-Click on a Program Manager icon and click the Icon button to edit the item's icon. For the name of the icon file, try PROGMAN.EXE for some nifty icon choices. Try MORICONS.DLL for icons especially made for DOS applications (which normally lack icons). You can also "steal"

icons from any program by using that program's name as the name of the icon file.

26. *Press the F7 function key to move an icon to a different group* or just drag the icon to the other group (if it's not open, just drag it on top of the group's icon). Use F8 if you just want to copy the icon.

27. *When dragging icons between groups, hold down the Ctrl key if you want to keep a copy of the icon in its original place.* (Windows 95 users can also use Ctrl to copy instead of moving when dragging and dropping files. But it's easier just to drag with the *right* mouse button: it pops up a list of choices when you drop the file.)

28. *Copy icons to your Startup group to run them automatically every time you turn on your computer.* You can hold down the Shift key while Windows is loading if you want to bypass these automatically run programs.

29. *Windows 95 users can copy shortcuts to the Windows\Start Menu\Programs\Startup folder* and can also hold down Shift during Windows startup to skip the "autostart" programs or documents. Hold down Shift while Windows 95 begins to bypass Startup icons and to get a clean desktop—uncluttered by any folders that you left open in a previous session.

30. *Create "hotkeys" for your favorite programs.* Click on an icon then use Alt+Enter to view its properties. Click on the box labeled "Shortcut key" and type any key on the keyboard. Windows automatically adds Ctrl+Alt to your choice. For example, could assign Ctrl+Alt+N to Notepad. These hotkeys may not always work unless you switch to Program Manager first with Alt+Tab. (They always work in Windows 95.)

31. *For added convenience, create a hotkey for Program Manager.* Open your Startup group and use File|New Item (or Alt+Double-Click) to create a new program item (icon). Fill in the command line with PROGMAN.EXE, and assign a hotkey like P to the "Shortcut key" entry. After you restart Windows, you can use Alt+Ctrl+P to pop up Program Manager at any time.

32. Similarly, *Windows 95 users can edit the shortcut key for any shortcut within any of the Programs folders* (\Windows\Start Menu\Programs), or on the desktop, to assign hotkeys to programs and other shortcuts. (Note that the use of "shortcut keys" has nothing else in common with "shortcuts," which are pointers

87

to files similar to Program Manager icons. That's why we prefer the term "hotkey" to avoid confusion.) Just right-click on a shortcut and choose Properties, and click on the Shortcut tab heading. Then click on the box labeled "Shortcut key" and press the key you want to use. From then on, you can use Ctrl+Alt+<the key you choose> to launch that program.

33. *Click on an icon, then press Enter.* This is a good alternative to double-clicking when your mouse finger gets tired. You can also "jump" to any icon in a group by typing the first letter of the icon's label.

34. *If you accidentally remove the default Windows groups (Main, Accessories, Games), you can restore then by choosing Run from the File Menu and typing SETUP /P.* Use WINSETUP /P if you're using Windows for Workgroups 3.11.

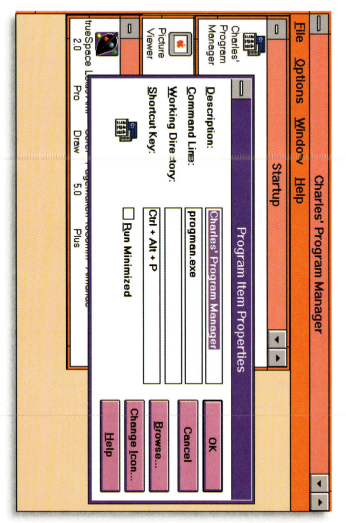

Program Item Properties

Description: Charles' Program Manager
Command Line: progman.exe
Working Directory:
Shortcut Key: Ctrl + Alt + P
☐ Run Minimized

OK · Cancel · Browse... · Change Icon... · Help

Charles' Program Manager
File · Options · Window · Help
Startup

trueSpace Level 2.0 · Pro · Draw 5.0 · Plus

Figure 4: Adding Program Manager to the Startup folder lets you press CTRL+ALT+P to recall Program Manager at any time.

35. *You can back up your program groups for safekeeping by opening a DOS prompt and typing in something similar to* COPY \WINDOWS*.GRP \BACKUP. This copies all your group folders to the Backup directory on your hard drive. (It's helpful to create a directory called BACKUP, to hold copies of your AUTOEXEC.BAT, CONFIG.SYS, and other essential initialization files—in case of disaster.) If a group is deleted or corrupted, try copying it back to your Windows directory from its backup. You may also want to copy *.INI files to your Backup folder to protect your program's .INI file.

36. *Control access to your computer by adding restrictions to Program Manager.* Use Notepad to edit your PROGMAN.INI file and add a [restrictions] section. Use some or all of the following:

```
[restrictions]
NoRun=1           ;Disables Run on the File Menu
NoClose=1         ;Prevents closing Program
                   Manager
NoSaveSettings=1  ;Prevents users from saving
                   changes
NoFileMenu=1      ;Removes the File menu
                   altogether
EditLevel=0       ;Unrestricted access (default)
EditLevel=1       ;Users can no longer add,
                   delete, or change groups.
EditLevel=2       ;Users also can't change the
                   command line of any Program
                   Manager item (icons)
EditLevel=3       ;Users also can't change any
                   Program Manager item
                   (icon) properties
```

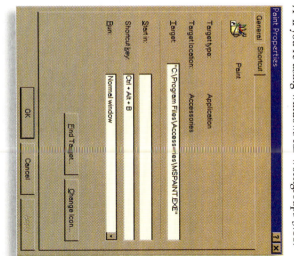

Paint Properties

General | Shortcut

Paint

Target type: Application
Target location: Accessories
Target: "C:\Program Files\Accessories\MSPAINT.EXE"
Start in:
Shortcut Key: Ctrl + Alt + B
Run: Normal window

Find Target... · Change Icon...

OK · Cancel · Apply

Figure 5: Windows 95 users can also trigger shortcut keys (hotkeys) for their favorite programs.

Windows 95 users can take advantage of the Policy Editor (POLEDIT) is in the \Admin\Apptools\Poledit folder of the Windows 95 CD-ROM) to customize and restrict access to their computer.

FILE MANAGER FAVORITES

37. *Click on a drive icon to change the File Manager window to a view of that drive.* Double-click on a drive icon to open a separate folder view of that drive.

38. *Or use Ctrl+<drive letter> to instantly open that drive's window.* For example, use Ctrl+A to open a window for your A: drive.

39. *Hold down the Ctrl key while you drag and drop to copy a file instead of moving it.* (This behavior is reversed when you drag and drop between different drives—Ctrl moves the file instead of copying it.)

40. *Make drag and drop easier by opening*

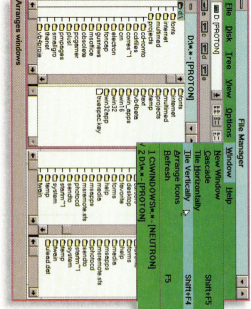

Figure 6: Tiling makes drag and drop copying much easier.

two drive windows (just double-click again on a drive icon) and choose Tile Horizontal or Tile Vertical from File Manager's Window menu.

41. *Press Tab to switch between the left (tree) pane and the right (files) pane.* Use Shift+Tab to reverse direction. Press Tab again to get to the drive icons.

42. *You can use the arrow keys to move up and down within the tree pane.* Press + to expand a folder to show all its subfolders, press the hyphen (-) key to collapse a branch of the tree (hiding subfolders). Press * to expand a branch of a tree, expanding the folder and all its subfolders. Or use Ctrl+* to expand all folders and subfolders. You can also double-click on a folder icon to expand

or collapse it. (These keys also work with Windows 95 Explorer.)

43. *Press the Backspace key to move "back" to the parent folder of the current folder.* If you're viewing \Windows\System, Backspace moves you up to \Windows. Press it several times to move to the *root* (the topmost level) of your drive.

44. *Drag programs and documents from a File Manager window to a Program Manager group to create an instant icon.* Double-click the File Manager icon and browse your hard drive for programs that you'd like to create icons for. When you find an application's file (which ends with the letters .EXE), click on the file and hold down the mouse button while you drag the file toward Program Manager. (For this to work, make sure File Manager is not overlapping the Program Manager group window that you're using to hold the icon.) Release the mouse button when the pointer is hovering over an open Program Manager group window. The icon takes on the name of the program file. If you want to change the name, click on the icon and choose Properties from Program Manager's File menu. With Windows 95: Drag a program file to the desktop or any open folder to create a *shortcut* icon for that program.

45. *Drag any document from File Manager onto the open window of an application.* Or drop it on the minimized icon for that application. (You can't drop it on a Program Manager icon, however.) With Windows 95, you can open a file by dragging it from a folder view or Explorer onto a shortcut for an application. You can also drop a document file into an open application window, but you can't simply drop it on the taskbar button as you might suspect. Instead, drag it to the taskbar button and let it hover there for a moment without releasing the button. This causes that program to pop to the top of all other windows, which makes it easy to then drop the file into the open window.

46. *Drag and drop printing is easy.* Just Shift+Double-Click on the Print Manager icon (or just run it, then minimize it.) You can print any file from File Manager by dragging the file and dropping it onto the Print Manager icon. Or perhaps more simply, just use File|Print. (With Windows 95, you can copy a shortcut to your favorite printer and put it right on your desktop for convenient drag and drop printing. You can also right-click on most document icons and choose Print.)

47. *Double-click on a file to launch the program associated with that type of application or file.* For example, double-click on MOOCOW.BMP to open that picture using Paintbrush.

48. *Use FileAssociate to link a file to whatever program you like.* The last three letters after the period in a filename are the file's *extension*, and determine which program works with that type of file. You can also use this trick to reassign an association to a different program. (Windows 95 users will turn to View|Options, File Types to edit their associations.)

49. *You can use File Manager as your primary Windows 3.1 user interface instead of Program Manager.* Use Notepad to open your SYSTEM.INI file. Look for a line that reads SHELL=PROGMAN.EXE. Change it to read SHELL=WINFILE.EXE. You can still run Program Manager. Just use File|Run from File Manager and enter PROGMAN. Closing Program Manager no longer shuts down Windows, but closing File Manager will exit Windows. (Don't try this with Windows 95: you should use Explorer as your shell to retain full functionality.)

50. *Don't forget that you can customize your fonts with File Manager.* Just use Options|Fonts. Use a small font if you want lots of room for file details, or a large, bold font if you prefer greater legibility. TrueType fonts are the most pleasing to the eye, although screen fonts like MS Sans Serif, Small Fonts, and Courier display text onscreen somewhat more quickly.

51. *Use File|Search to look for any type of file, opening a custom drive window containing related files.* For example, use *.TXT to search for text files. Click the check box for "Search all subdirectories" to get a more complete search: If you search from the "top" of your drive (C:\ for example) you'll get a list of all the text files on your hard drive. To search within the current folder, use View|By File Type to filter your view, showing only certain files or file types. View|By File Type also lets you turn on an option to view hidden files.

52. *You can work with several files at once.* Use Ctrl+Click to select files out of sequence. Ctrl+Click again to "unselect" a selected file. Or click on the first file in a list and Shift+Click on another file to select those two files and all files listed between them. You can even extend this range by Ctrl+Clicking on another file and using Shift+Ctrl+Click to select another series of files. When you have a range of files selected, you can move or copy them *en masse*, or delete them all in a stroke. Another way to select files is to use File|Select Files. Choose something like *.DOC to

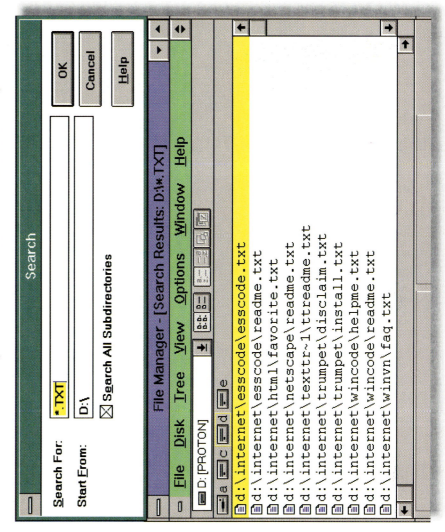

Figure 7: Organize related files in a single window using File|Search.

select all document files, or ~.* to select all files that begin with X.

53. More File Manager keyboard shortcuts:

DEL:	Deletes the current file
F1:	File Manager Help
Shift+F4:	Cascade all open windows
F5 function key:	"Refreshes" (forces a redisplay) of a drive window.
Shift+F5:	Tile Vertically all open windows
F7:	Moves a file or files to a different directory
F8:	Same as F7 but copies the files, leaving the originals alone
Alt+Enter:	Same as File|Properties. Shows you details such as the date the file was created, and lets you turn on or off file attributes such as Read Only, System, and Hidden.

APPLET TRICKS

54. *Cheat at Minesweeper:* When you turn on "cheat mode," look for a tiny pixel in the upper-leftcorner of the Minesweeper window. This pixel turns white whenever the mouse pointer is hovering over a safe square. To amaze your friends, start Minesweeper and type XYZZY, then press the Shift key (don't let them catch you doing this!).

55. *Look up computer terms:* Press F1 while viewing Program Manager and choose Glossary from the index to get a list of common computer and technical words, along with pop-up definitions. (Not available with Windows 95.)

56. *Add the date and time to Notepad.* Choose Edit|Date/Time to insert the current date and time into the current text file.

57. *Automatically load your favorite card file and calendar.* You can edit the command line of your CardFile and Calendar applets to add the

name of any card file or calendar you've saved to your hard drive. Open your Accessories group and click on the Card File icon, and press Alt+Enter (or choose File|Properties). Replace the entry CARDFILE.EXE with something like CARDFILE.EXE MYCARD.CRD, or the name of whatever .CRD file you want loaded.

58. *Exploit Character Mapper to make the most of your fonts.* The WingDings TrueType font and others (such as Symbol, Monotype Sorts, MT Extras) are a rich source of simple clipart symbols. Run Character Map from the Accessories group to make it easy to copy and paste these special symbols into any word processor or desktop publishing program.

59. *Multimedia E-Mail and More:* Open a multimedia file with Media Player, and use Edit|Options to turn off the options for *Caption* and *Border around object.* Turn on the option for *Play in client window.* Use Edit|Copy and use Paste to put the multimedia object into an e-mail message or other document that you want to share with others. You can also run Sound Recorder to insert "voice mail" notes. If you turn on Edit|Picture using Cardfile, you can use Cardfile to store graphics and multimedia images—just use Edit|Paste to place them on any card.

60. *Increase Sound Recorder's length limit.* By default, Sound Recorder only lets you record up to one minute. To get around this, record a minute of silence and save it as QUIET.WAV. Then use Edit|Insert File to add QUIET.WAV to the current sound file. Each time you Insert File, you get an extra minute of recording time. Then rewind to the start and record whatever you like on top of this chain of silence.

61. *Double-click on the title bar of the Clock applet to turn off its title bar and menu,* making it a free-floating clock.

62. *PaintBrush Tricks:* Select part of an image with Paintbrush then hold down Ctrl as you drag it to leave a copy of it behind. Hold down Shift to "paint" with the image. Fill the background by right-clicking on any color in the palette and double-clicking the eraser tool. You can change any color into any other by left-clicking on the color you want to change (in the palette) and right-clicking on the color you want to

63. *Create Program Manager icons for your favorite Control Panel items.* Press Alt+Double-Click within any program group window to create a new item. Fill in the command line with CONTROL and the name of the control panel applet you want to use. For example, use CONTROL.DESKTOP to create an icon that jumps you directly to Desktop Settings. (This works with Windows 95 too, but there's a better way: just drag and drop a Control Panel icon from Control Panel into a folder, such as one of the Programs folders, to create a shortcut to it.)

64. *Optimize your computer with 386 Enhanced mode.* Double-click on the "386" icon in Control Panel, then click the Virtual Memory button. Make sure you're using a Permanent Swap file set to half the size of your actual memory size. If you have 16 Megabytes of RAM, set the Swap file to 8 Megabytes. And make sure the Swap file located on an *uncompressed* hard drive (as opposed to a Stacker or Doublespace volume). Turn on 32-bit Disk Access to speed up your hard drive. If you have Windows for Workgroups 3.11, also turn on 32-bit File Access. You can then remove SmartDrive from your AUTOEXEC.BAT and enjoy a noticeable speed increase. (This tip is not applicable to Windows 95, which automatically configures your computer for optimal performance.)

65. *Play sound effects without a sound card.* Download the PC Speaker Driver from Microsoft Downloads at (206) 936-6735. (You can also get it from most online services. Search for SPEAKER.DRV.) Once you've installed it, use the Drivers option in Control Panel to set the volume and speed for the speaker driver, which uses your PC's tiny internal speaker to produce sound effects. The speaker driver is limited—it freezes your computer while playing sound, and is no substitute for a sound card for multimedia applications. But it's a good place to start. (The driver is also compatible with Windows 95.)

66. *Speed up your keyboard.* Run the Keyboard applet from Control Panel and decrease the Keyboard Delay setting and increase the Keyboard Speed setting. This is

53. More File Manager keyboard shortcuts:

CONTROL PANEL SECRETS

replace it with. Then use the color eraser to selectively change colors, or double-click the color eraser to change the entire image. (Windows 95 users can't use all these tricks, but they do get another bonus: use File|Set As Wallpaper to turn your design into instant wallpaper.)

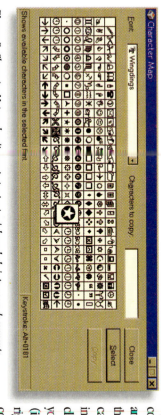

Figure 8. *Character Map makes it easy to paste special symbols into your documents.*

Shows available characters in the selected font

Character Map

Font: Wingdings

Characters to copy:

Help   Close   Select   Copy

Keystroke Alt+0181

Figure 9: Many computers, like this one, have far too many fonts installed. Limit yourself to just your favorite ones to save memory and resources, which is important even with Windows 95.

especially handy when using the arrow keys to scroll through text.

TWEAKS AND TUNE-UPS

67. *Remove unnecessary fonts.* Many applications automatically install dozens, even hundreds of fonts, and you may have installed fonts in the past that you never use anymore. Having too many installed TrueType fonts is a common problem; it's easy to forget you've got them all sitting there. But font-glut leads to sluggish Windows startup and reduces Windows' resources. Run the Fonts applet from Control Panel and remove any you don't use frequently (you don't need to actually delete them from your hard drive).

68. *If in doubt, reboot.* Many computer problems can be solved simply by exiting all your applications, exiting Windows, and restarting your computer. One reason this helps is that rebooting reinitializes everything, freeing up lost system resources that many programs don't return to Windows when they exit. (When using Shut Down in Windows 95, hold down the shift key while clicking Yes to restart Windows.)

69. *Run SETUP from DOS.* With Windows 3.1, the safest way to change your system settings, such as your video card driver, is to exit Windows and run SETUP (do it from within the Windows directory, but while in DOS). This avoids conflicts that can occur when files are running as Windows attempts to update them. Also, if you install a new video card or sound card, remove the drivers for the old card *before you remove the old card.* Similarly, reset your video driver to plain VGA before you remove the old video card, so that Windows will be "clean" for the new video driver.

70. *Speed up your hard drive by optimizing the layout of its files.* If you have DOS 5.0 or later, exit Windows and use the DEFRAG command. Windows 95 users should click Start, then Programs\Accessories\System Tools\Disk Defragmenter—never run a DOS optimizer or other disk utilities with Windows 95, to prevent damage to the new long file names.

71. *Speed up your hard drive* by adding SmartDrive to your C:\AUTOEXEC.BAT file. Edit your AUTOEXEC.BAT file with Notepad (or use the DOS EDIT command). Look for a line containing SMARTDRV. If it's not listed, add the line SMARTDRV. You can follow SMARTDRV with two numbers. The first number sets the size of the SmartDrive cache for DOS. The second number sets its size for Windows. You don't need to use SmartDrive if you've enabled 32-bit File Access with Windows for Workgroups 3.11 (and it would waste memory to use both)—see below.

72. *Double the size of your hard drive (in effect) by deploying DoubleSpace.* Upgrade to at least version 6.2 of MS-DOS for best results. DOS 6.22 replaced DoubleSpace with DriveSpace, but it works the same way. Exit Windows and type either DBLSPACE or DRVSPACE to get started—DOS will lead you through the steps to compress your existing drive (recommended) or create a new compressed drive out of the empty space on your drive. You can also compress floppy disks to get nearly 3 MB of removable storage, readable by anyone who also uses DoubleSpace or DriveSpace. Windows 95 users should turn to Start\Programs\Accessories\System Tools\DriveSpace.

73. *Free up conventional memory with MEMMAKER.* Exit Windows and type MEMMAKER at the DOS prompt to optimize the

loading of your DOS drivers and TSRs in CONFIG.SYS and AUTOEXEC.BAT. (DOS 5.0 or later required.) Windows needs plenty of conventional memory to run well, especially if you have lots of multimedia drivers. This can avoid mysterious OUT OF MEMORY errors which can be confusing when you know you have lots of memory free. (Memmaker is often unnecessary with Windows 95 which replaces most DOS drivers.)

74. *Remind yourself that you're running DOS from Windows.* Edit your AUTOEXEC.BAT file and customize the WINPMT setting. (It works just like the DOS PROMPT statement, but only applies when running DOS from Windows.) For example, use the following in AUTOEXEC.BAT:
SET WINPMT=Type 'EXIT' to return to Windows$_$P$G

75. *Use SYSEDIT to edit your system .INI files.* Click File\Run from Program Manager and type in SYSEDIT to run the System Files Editor. Or use File\New Item to create a new Program Manager icon for SYSEDIT. You can then use the System Files Editor to make some of the following changes to your system files. (Our examples start with a section heading, such as [386Enh]. Look for that section in the system file we discuss and add the subsequent lines below.)

System Configuration Editor

File Edit Search Window

C:\WIN311\SYSTEM.INI
C:\WIN311\WIN.INI
C:\CONFIG.SYS
C:\AUTOEXEC.BAT

```
@ECHO OFF
PROMPT $P$G
PATH C:\WINDOWS;C:\WINDOWS\COMMAND;C:\DX
REM *** INITIALIZE GLOBAL SETTINGS ***
SET TMP=E:\TEMP
SET TEMP=E:\TEMP
SET DIRCMD=/OEN /LA /P
SET BLASTER=A220 I10 D1 H5 P330 T6
```

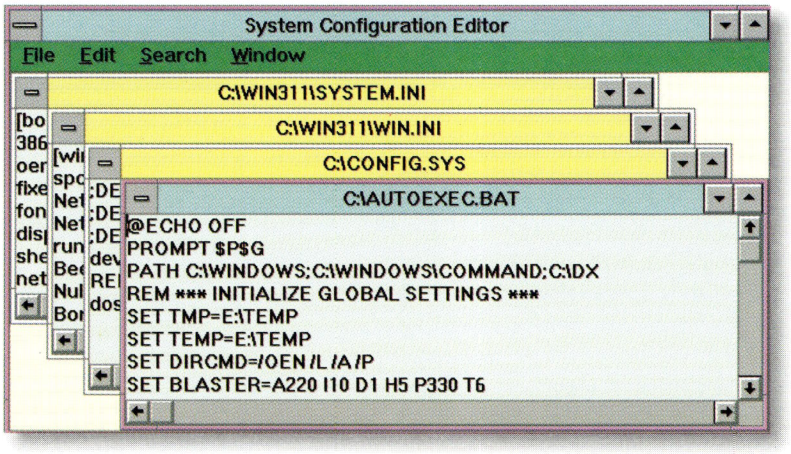

Figure 10: The System Files Editor gathers all your system files together in one place for convenient editing.

anywhere after that section heading.) You can also use Notepad to open any of these .INI file. Warning: it's always a good idea to make copies of WIN.INI or SYSTEM.INI files before you do any editing to them. This way, if things don't work out the way you like, you can restore to your original settings.

76. *Make double-click easier.* You can use the Mouse applet in Control Panel to adjust the speed of your mouse and set the delay between double-clicks. But you can also add the following two

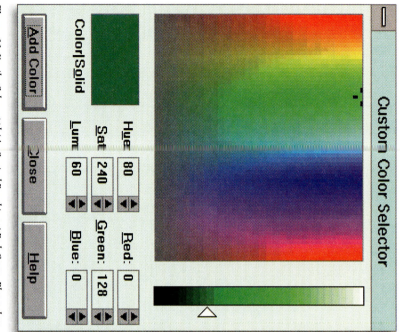

Custom Color Selector

Color|Solid

Hue 80 · Red: 0 ·
Sat 240 · Green: 128 ·
Lum 60 · Blue: 0 ·

Add Color · Close · Help

Figure 11: Use the Colors applet in Control Panel to get Red, Green, Blue values.

---

lines to your WIN.INI file if you tend to move the mouse too much when you try to double-click.

[windows]
DoubleClickHeight=8
DoubleClickWidth=8

77. Take control of Window automation. Recall that you can put icons in your Startup group to load them automatically when Windows starts. Another way to do this is to add the path and name of a program to the LOAD= line in WIN.INI. Although you probably won't prefer this method, you may need to edit your LOAD= line if you want to remove a program that is set to start automatically. Programs in the LOAD= line automatically start up as minimized icons. Use the RUN= line to start them in a normal window.

78. Improve HELP readability. The Windows 3.1 help system uses underlined text (jumps) to let you skip from one section of a help file to another. The default light green color is hard to read. Change it to a darker color by replacing the following line in WIN.INI. (The three numbers correspond to the red, green and blue components of the color. To create custom colors, use the Colors applet from Control Panel and write down the numbers shown for Red, Green, and Blue. You can then type these numbers into the WIN.INI file.) You can also change the colors for other Help features, such as IfJumpColor, IfPopupColor, MacroColor, and PopupColor.

[WindowsHelp]
JumpColor=0 128 0

---

is MS Sans Serif IconTitleSize=9 ;Default is 8

With Windows 95, you can set these options and more using the Appearances tab from the Display applet in Control Panel. (Or right-click on the desktop, and select Properties.)

79. Access any undocumented desktop settings. You can control most Desktop attributes using the Desktop applet in Control Panel. For example, increase your border width to make it easier to "grab" and resize windows. You can also increase the horizontal spacing for icons using Desktop. But there's no way to adjust the vertical spacing for Program Manager icons, unless you add the following line to WIN.INI:

[desktop]
IconVerticalSpacing=54 ;this value is in number of pixels.

80. Change the icon caption font. Add or change the following line in WIN.INI:

[desktop]
IconTitleFaceName=Arial ;Default

---

81. Use any bitmap file as Wallpaper. Normally the Desktop applet in Control Panel only allows bitmap files for wallpaper if they're relocated in the \WINDOWS or \WINDOWS\SYSTEM directories. You can edit the following line in WIN.INI to point to any bitmap graphic on your hard drive, instead of copying it to your Windows directory. (Windows 95 lets you browse for wallpaper anywhere on your hard drive.)

[desktop]
Wallpaper=C:\ART\BMP\TROLLS.BMP

82. Copy custom colors from one computer to another. It can be tedious to customize the colors on more than one computer. Instead, customize one computer and copy the entire [Colors] section from its WIN.INI to the WIN.INI on another computer. You can use this trick elsewhere too. If all the computers have access to the same set of fonts (such as on a network drive), you can copy the [Fonts] section in WIN.INI to another computer's WIN.INI to create standardized font lists for all computers in your company. You can also copy the [Color Schemes] section from CONTROL.INI if you want to move not just the current set of colors, but all custom color schemes too.

83. Make it easy to print to a file, or to bypass Windows for printing. Edit WIN.INI using

---

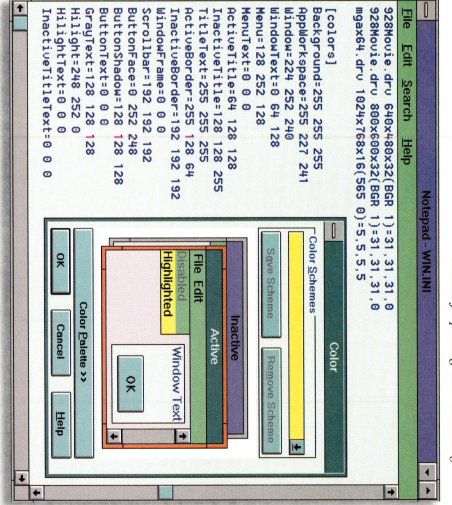

Notepad - WIN.INI
File Edit Search Help

928Movie.dru 640x480x32(BGR 1)=31,31,31,0
928Movie.dru 800x600x32(BGR 1)=31,31,31,0
mgax64.dru 1024x768x16(565 0)=5,5,5,5

[colors]
Background=255 255 255
AppWorkspace=255 227 241
Window=224 252 240
WindowText=0 64 128
Menu=128 252 128
MenuText=0 0 0
ActiveTitle=64 128 128
InactiveTitle=128 128 128
TitleText=255 255 255
ActiveBorder=255 255 255
InactiveBorder=192 192 192
WindowFrame=0 0 0
Scrollbar=192 192 192
ButtonFace=0 252 248
ButtonShadow=128 128 128
ButtonText=0 0 0
GrayText=128 128 128
Hilight=248 252 128
HilightText=0 0 0
InactiveTitleText=0 0 0

Color Schemes
Save Scheme · Remove Scheme

Color
Color Palette >>
Window Text
Active · Inactive
File Edit
Highlighted · Disabled
OK · Cancel · Help

Figure 12: The Red, Green, Blue values in WIN.INI correspond to the color scheme shown on the right.

Notepad or SYSEDIT. Under the section [ports], add the following entries:

[ports]
LPT1.DOS=
FILE:==

You can then use the Printers applet from Control Panel to connect a printer driver to the FILE: "port" if you want to save the printed output to a file, which is handy if you want to print to someone else's non-networked printer. You can transfer the file to the other computer and use the DOS command COPY /B filename LPT1: to print your file. If you connect a printer driver to the LPT1.DOS port, Windows doesn't manage the printing. This can sometimes cure printing problems.

84. *Customize third-party sound effects.* Use the Sounds applet in Control Panel to change the Windows sound effects, such as the sound that plays when Windows starts, or the default beep sound effect. Other programs, such as the America Online software, also add sound effects to your computer. Edit WIN.INI and look for the [Sounds] section if you want to replace the default sounds with your own custom .WAV files.

85. *Defeat screen saver password protection.* Don't tell everyone about this trick! Use it if you forget your screen saver password. First start your computer without Windows. You may need to remove the line WIN from AUTOEXEC.BAT. Then use the following DOS command: EDIT \WINDOWS\CONTROL.INI. Look for a line in CONTROL.INI labeled PASSWORD= and delete the text after the = sign. Save the modified CONTROL.INI and restart your computer. (There may be more than one PASSWORD entry.)

86. *Improve multimedia reliability.* Add the entry DMABufferSize=32 to the [386Enh] section of SYSTEM.INI. This helps some sound cards to avoid breaking up sound effects. Try a value of 64 if you still have problems.

SYSTEM.INI:
[386Enh]
DMABufferSize=32

87. *Improve DOS game playability.* Some DOS games will run better in a Windows 3.1 DOS box if you add or change the following line in

SYSTEM.INI:
[386Enh]
TrapTimerPorts=Off

This can lead to somewhat inaccurate timekeeping, which can be alleviated by adding the line SyncTime=On. (Don't bother with this tip if you're using Windows 95—it plays DOS games very nicely.)

88. *Improve modem reliability.* Add or change the line COMxBuffer (replacing x with the COMM port used by your modem) to the [386Enh] section of SYSTEM.INI. Use the value 2048 to start with, and try increasing it if necessary to avoid dropping characters. To improve DOS modem apps, add the line COMBoostTime=4.

[386Enh]
COM2Buffer=2048
COMBoostTime=4

89. *Investigate hardware conflicts with MSD.* The Microsoft Diagnostics program should be run from DOS (exit Windows first and type MSD at the DOS prompt). Use the IRQ feature to find out which Interrupt Request lines are in use before you install new hardware. (Some new hardware will ask for this information during setup.) The Memory feature gives you a visual map of your memory layout. Windows 95 users will prefer the much more detailed and accurate Device Manager, available via the System icon in Control Panel or by right-clicking on the My Computer desktop icon.

90. *Get ready to upgrade to Windows 95.* If you haven't already upgraded, following this tip can be the most rewarding of all. Windows 95 improves Window's capacity, reliability, flexibility, and productivity—and it's a whole lot of fun, too, once you recover from the brief "future shock" of the new user interface. For best results, install at least 8 MB of memory (12 to 16 MB is better), and make sure you have at least 100 MB of free hard disk space and a fast 486 computer (although a fast 386 will work fine too). Use a commercial uninstaller program to clean up your system and remove obsolete drivers and applications. While you can upgrade your existing Windows 3.1 directory, which is convenient, you may get best results by installing Windows to a new directory (a "clean" installation) and reinstalling only the applications you *really* use.

TOP 10 WINDOWS 95 TIPS

91. Right-click on My Computer and choose Explore—or just Shift+Double-Click on it, and you'll get the far more versatile and useful Explorer view instead of a plain folder view. Be sure to use View|Toolbar to turn on the toolbar. You can also run Explorer with Start|Programs|Windows Explorer.

92. *Try the right mouse button every time you encounter a new icon or control*—you'll be surprised at the numerous power-user features available this way. You can also use the right mouse button to drag and drop files and get a choice of Copy, Move, or Create Shortcut. While drag and drop is sometimes convenient, get in the habit of using Edit|Copy or Edit|Cut and Edit|Paste to copy or move files—it's more efficient and requires less futzing around with the mouse. Remember that there are three ways to copy, cut or paste a selected file or group of files. 1. From the edit menu. 2. Using Ctrl+C, Ctrl+X, and Ctrl+V. 3. Using Ctrl+Ins, Ctrl+Del and Shift+Ins.

93. *Right-click on items in property sheets to get instant "What's This?" help.* You can do the same thing by clicking the ? symbol in the upper-right corner, then using the help cursor to click on items you want to learn about.

94. *Copy your favorite shortcuts to the \Windows\SendTo folder.* You can then right-click on any

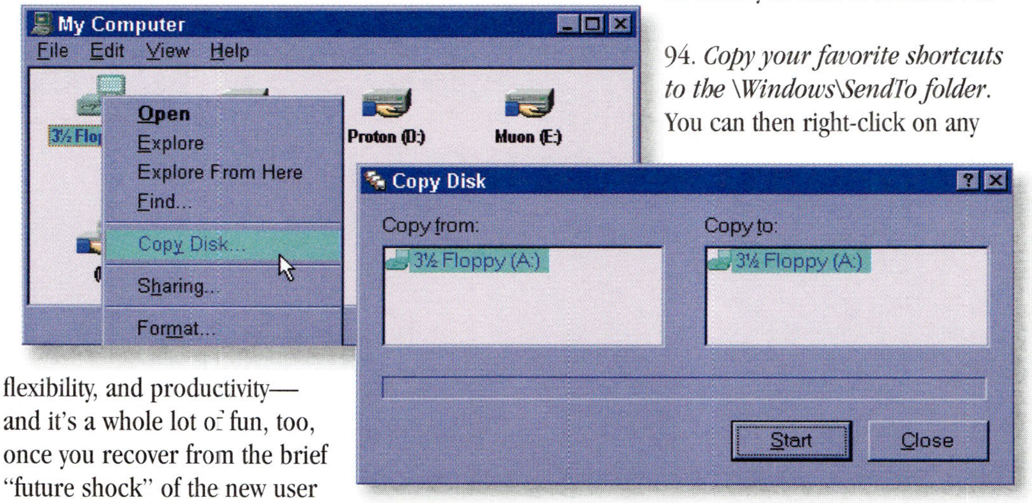

Figure 13: *Open* My Computer *and right-click on a floppy disk icon to copy the disk.*

file and use SendTo to "send" the file to any program you like, even if the file is normally associated with a different program.

95. The new Open and Save As dialog boxes are actually folder views, so you can take the opportunity to create a new folder, rename, delete, even copy and move files, all from within the Open or Save As dialog box. For example, when you click on the File menu in a word processor, then choose Open, you'll be seeing a Windows 95 *folder.* From within this window you

96. *Always make backup copies of installation diskettes*—just right-click on the floppy drive icon in My Computer and choose Copy Disk.

97. *Run Add/Remove Programs from Control Panel if you want to uninstall a Windows 95 application easily.* Click the *Windows Setup* tab to add Windows components you originally left out when you installed Windows 95. For example, click on Disk Tools and then click Details. You can then turn on the checkbox for Microsoft Backup, a convenient way to back up applications and files to either floppy disks or onto a tape drive.

98. Windows 95 lets you change your video resolution without rebooting as long as you don't change the number of colors or change from small fonts to large fonts or vice-versa. You can run games and multimedia applications at 640x480 for best results, then return to 1024x768 for word processing and graphics. Right-click on the desktop and choose Properties for convenient access to the Display properties.

99. Favorite Windows 95 Keyboard Hotkeys:

Alt+Enter	Properties
Alt+Double-Click	Properties
Shift+Double-Click	Explore a folder
Ctrl+Double-Click	Open a subfolder, reusing the same window
Ctrl+Tab	Switch to next tab heading (property sheet)
Backspace	Delete a file and put it in the Recycle Bin
Shift+Delete	Delete permanently without storing in Recycle Bin
Shift+F10	Same as right-clicking
Ctrl+Esc	Open Start button and reveal taskbar if hidden

Explorer or folder view:

F4	Drops down the list of drives
F5	Refreshes (updates) the file and folder views
CTRL+A	Select all files in current view
CTRL+Z	Undo (reverse) last file operation
Backspace	"Back up" to previous (parent) folder
Shift+Close box	Closes all subfolders that have been opened

Hold down Shift while inserting a CD-ROM to bypass the Autorun feature.

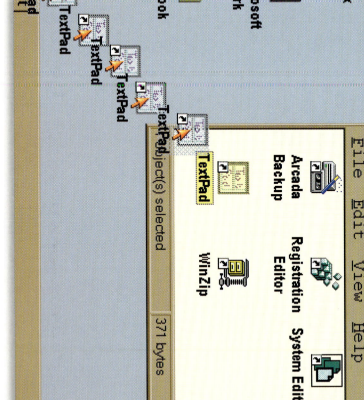
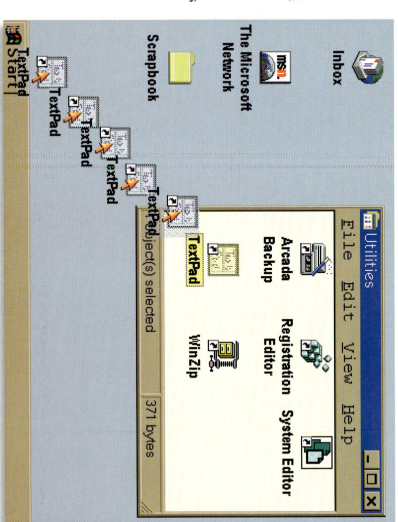

***Figure 15:** Drag and drop a shortcut onto the Start button for convenient access to your favorite programs.*

can manage files just as if you were working in Explorer or a normal opened folder.

100. *Drag and drop any icon or shortcut onto the Start menu icon to create an instant Start button icon.*
Right-click on Start and choose Open or Explore if you want to remove these shortcuts, or right-click on the taskbar and choose Properties, Start Menu Programs.

Discover any new tips lately? Send them via electronic mail to Charles Brannon at 70720,462 on CompuServe, Ceemeister on America Online, or Charles_Brannon@msn.com. If we use your tip, you'll receive a free copy of the next edition of The Whole PC Family Encyclopedia. (IC)

Charles Brannon, previously an editor at COMPUTE magazine and Project Manager for Epyx, now supervises the Novell and WorkGroups networks and works as a consultant and freelance writer. He is the co-author of "The Windows 95 Book," published in the summer of 1995 by Ventana Press. Charles has been an active editor and writer in the personal computing field since 1980. He is a Contributing Editor of the monthly Windows, columnist for CD-ROM Today, and is a Windows 95 Advisor for the Windows User Group Network (WUGNET), a Windows 95 advocacy and member support group.

***Figure 14:** Right-click on the empty desktop background and choose Properties, then the Settings tab to quickly change your video card settings.*

HOW TO BUY SOFTWARE

By Peter Norton And Scott Clark

Finding a piece of software that does exactly what you want it to do can be incredibly rewarding. And even as an experienced user, I still grin and laugh at software that is so elegant, it surprises me. Software like that is out there. Finding elegant programs is a matter of keeping your eyes and ears open. Finding rewarding programs is mostly a matter of knowing what you want.

WHAT ABOUT MY NEEDS?

Knowing what you want might sound easy. Perhaps you want a word processor. Straightforward and simple. But when you get to the store, you discover that there are 20 different word processors available, and that their prices range from $19.95 to nearly $750. When you tell a salesperson that you just want to write letters at home, she tells you to use "Write," which comes free with Windows. So how are you supposed to know what you need? What if *Write* is right for you? (It isn't. Trust me.) The only thing worse than spending more money than you need to is to spend money only to find that you haven't bought what you need. While it is true that the major applications in each software category compete closely (which means that they will have similar features and will be priced similarly), the major players may still not be what you want.

Consider the two most prominent players in the word processing market. Both are very powerful programs. You could create almost any professional document that you can conceive of on either of them, so long as you don't need high-end typesetting power. But what if you do most of your writing at work, and your primary goal at home is to spark your daughter's interest in the computer by showing her that she can write letters to Grandma? Neither Microsoft *Word* nor Novell *WordPerfect* will be a particularly pleasant learning experience for a very young child. Nor will you likely enjoy the process of trying to teach her how to use them. In a relatively unsurprising situation like this one, however much you would spend on either of the two largest performers would be a waste because they wouldn't perform in the way you want and need them to perform. (Just so you know, both companies have recognized this particular fact and have released word processors for children.)

And so the first thing to focus on when you're selecting software is not the software—it's you. You'll want to spend a little time thinking about what you actually want to *do* with your computer. Once you begin exploring and seeing what software exists and what it *can* do, you'll find yourself discovering entirely new things that you'll want to do that *never* occurred to you previously. Getting there, as they say, is half the fun. Fortunately, getting there doesn't require that you go out and blindly purchase software. There are a wide variety of inexpensive—or even free—resources available to you.

GREAT RESOURCES AND REVIEWS

The first place to start exploring software is probably your PC itself. If you purchased a complete multimedia system, it very likely came with at least two or three major pieces of software pre-installed. It's not uncommon to find "suites" of integrated programs waiting for you to use them. These generally consist of at least a word processor, a spreadsheet and a database program of moderate power. Remember, though, that these are scaled-down applications, so you shouldn't use these suites to judge the quality of a company's more advanced products. However, you *can* make some subjective judgments based on them.

Do the menus seem to be organized intelligently? Do you find commands located where you think they make sense? Is the online

Help actually useful? If you call the company for technical support, what is the quality of that support? These sorts of questions can give you some insight into the programming philosophy of the company itself. Issues like how their designers and programmers think and whether you think very differently can give you some forewarning of products that might drive you crazy. Keep in mind that this method is entirely subjective, but it has worked for me.

> *Tip:* By exploring the capabilities of the software that comes with your system, you will continue to develop a better sense of the features that you like, and what you want and need from any additional software that you buy later. Windows comes bundled with two mini-word processors and several other accessories you can try for free.

FRIENDS AND COUNTRYMEN

The next place to look for recommendations or warnings is among your computer-using friends and associates. Speak to people whom you know and with whom you have rapport. If you have a close friend and the two of you "think a lot alike," her or his comments may be some of the best you'll find anywhere. Those friends will also let you try out their software, so you can get some hands-on experience. With the variety of software titles expanding every day, it is increasingly rare to find computer stores that have demonstrations or will let you use the software before you buy. At the most, you might find a multimedia "advertisement" that will try to impress you with a long list of jargon and features, but that will give you little or no sense of what it's actually like to use the program. As I sit here, I can see a 3D modeling program that was demonstrated in just such a way. It turned out to be so complicated to use that I've never produced anything with it.

Figure 1: Try to determine your needs before buying or you might wind up with software too complex (and too costly).

The real beauty of these sources of reviews is that they're free, and you are likely to know if your best friend has a million copies of *WonderWriter* in his basement—or any other particular bias or agenda. Probably the next best place to look for software reviews is among people you probably don't know, but with whom you can at least converse: the online community.

DISTANT FRIENDS AND OTHER COUNTRYMEN

One of the greatest strengths of the online world has always been the wealth of computer-related newsgroups or **forums** which exist. As **online services** have evolved, so have these forums, from groups of very few individuals interminably discussing arcane issues to huge collections of users and interested others doing everything from still having the endless debates to asking a simple question about a particular product, and getting a single—and correct—answer.

Today you can find forums about particular kinds of software—say, desktop publishing—as well as forums that discuss one single company's products—say, Symantec or Microsoft or Turtle Beach. In either kind of forum, you can freely post questions you may have about a particular product, a particular feature and so on, and other users from all over the world can post answers to your questions or questions of their own. By following the online conversations, called *threads*, you'll be amazed at the information you can find. If someone else has already asked the same thing you want to know, your answers may be waiting for you before you even pose a question. If a long discussion took place some time ago about a particularly nasty quirk of a program or about the particular need for a certain type of feature to be developed, that entire conversation may be archived in a file that you can download and read at your leisure.

Additionally, most of the company-specific forums are moderated. That means that company employees regularly—usually daily—monitor the discussions and very willingly jump in when a particularly technical or difficult question gets asked. These moderators can also send additional information about a product to you through **email**. Of course, anything such a person sends you will be marketing from the company itself, and moderators have been known to make particularly critical discussions "disappear" from forums. However, the majority moderate with a surprisingly light hand. Perhaps those individuals know that their companies will learn far more from thoughtful criticism than from praise.

Speaking of marketing, that's another thing you'll find a ton of—usually available for you to download from a file library that is connected to each forum or discussion group. Press releases, extensive product descriptions and technical documents can all be found, and they can make your job of selecting software a *lot* easier. If you're tossing and turning between two or three products over their list of features, you can probably download exactly that—a list of features—for each of the products and can compare them side-by-side.

Look in computer magazines for side-by-side comparisons already done for you. Magazines are often the most valuable source of this kind of information.

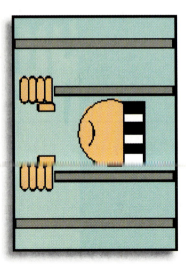

Figure 2: Software piracy is theft—and like any other theft, it costs us all money.

Figure 3: The Industry Connection on America Online.

I DIDN'T KNOW I NEEDED IT

G. K. Chesterton said of journalism that it, "...consists largely in saying 'Lord Jones died,' to people who never knew that Lord Jones was alive." Curmudgeonry aside, if you read enough computer magazines, you'll be amazed at the number of products that you didn't know existed, and that now, knowing of their existence, you can't live without. On the other hand, you'll find no better source of mostly objective commentary anywhere. True, you can't easily have a conversation with most writers, and magazines certainly aren't free. But there are some real advantages to magazines that none of the other sources can touch.

First, there's money. Computer magazines can be extremely profitable ventures. That's one reason why there are so many of them. But a lot of that profit goes right back into the magazines' research and testing labs—independent facilities stacked to the gills with large enough collections of hardware and software that the subjective ("This is too slow!") becomes objective ("This is exactly 3 milliseconds too slow!"). That kind of information might sound arcane to you, but when you collect enough of it together, you'll find yourself in the enviable position of converting knowledge into wisdom.

Many computer magazine writers are experts at exactly that. Since they're not affiliated with any company that produces software—with some exceptions, of course—they're often in the best position to look at reams and reams of technical information and feature lists, and spend hours running program after program to come up with an analysis that says, roughly, "Look, I've tried them all. If you want to do *this*, buy this. If *that's* what you really need, then this other product is stronger. If cost is your bottom line, then *this* product gives you the most for your money," and so on. If you love to write and you love computers, it's a pretty enviable job.

Most computer magazines come out monthly, which has its advantages and disadvantages. Consider the sorts of problems than can occur if you read a weekly news magazine instead of a daily newspaper. By the time you read the news, it's already history. Technology doesn't move quite as fast as international politics, but it can happen that—

Figure 4: Technology moves fast. This month's magazine review of a piece of software can be out-of-date next month.

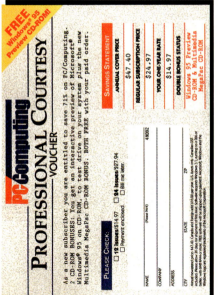

Figure 6: A computer magazine subscription is often an excellent place to find out about software in-depth.

because of deadlines—the latest and greatest product in *this* month's issue is replaced by a new version or a more competitive product by the time you read about it. Of course, this is where these sources become circular, because the thing to do after reading a magazine sing the praises of some piece of software is to ask around and to look at other magazines to see if there's a more up-to-date opinion, or perhaps a dissenting voice.

When software is as complex as it is today, it's perfectly possible that one single aspect of a given piece of software might drive you crazy. Better to know that before you buy, and by looking at a number of resources, you increase your chances of finding a writer or other user with a personality and foibles like your own.

Tech Tip: **There are industry trade magazines which are published weekly. They contain the most up-to-date news available, but they are very expensive to subscribe to as a member of the general public. Still, they are available if you have a need that justifies spending $100 or more a year. Additionally, some of these trade papers are available for free to the public in an excerpted form via online services like Ziff-Net (which is available on CompuServe).**

The primary advantage to monthly distribution, on the other hand, is that magazines have the time to research and develop exactly the kinds of investigative reports that make them so useful. Additionally, computer magazines are always on the inside track when it comes to obtaining new information about new software. They'll have a pre-release copy of that new spreadsheet or that new game, and so by the time it's available for you to actually purchase, you can have read an article—or several—about it to decide if it's really for you.

While it is certainly possible to come to understand particular writers' personalities over time, getting a grasp on an entire magazine can be difficult. Computer magazines are as susceptible to changes in publishers and editors as are any other kind of magazine or newspaper, and sometimes those changes are dramatic. Recently, for example, a magazine that had had a reputation for ten years as being one of the most accurate and technical of all computer magazines, has turned into pop-culture garbage.

The best way to start "getting into" computer magazines is to visit your local newsstand and check out the contents of several different issues. Find individual articles on topics that interest you and purchase those magazines. Once you've read those articles, check out the rest of the magazine to see if the whole package sets a tone that speaks to you and your interests. You may discover a magazine or two that you like so well, you'll subscribe. For example, you might want to keep as close to the cutting edge as you can, and you'll find one magazine that devotes over half of its editorial space to new product reviews. Such a match would certainly justify subscribing, and a subscription is almost always less expensive than purchasing single issues. Or, you might decide that you would rather take the time to browse through each issue of several different magazines and continue purchasing on an issue-by-issue basis. Your local university or public library probably subscribes to several of the most popular titles as well.

GOING SHOPPING

The final place you will want to take a look at software—unless you're browsing for serendipity, of course—is your computer store itself. Software packaging, like all packaging, is designed to sell the product. "Being informative" comes in as a distant second goal. Nevertheless, you'll find an awful lot of writing on most software packaging, and even if most of it is just printed "sound bites," some of it can be very useful.

FIGURING OUT THE FINE PRINT

Walk into a local computer store, pick up any software product at random and read the box. You'll generally find yourself reading about the subset of features that the manufacturer feels is most likely to sell the product. Remember that those are not necessarily the features that the product does best, or even necessarily well. They're simply the features that the product does have. Whether you'd have to be a power-user to even begin to take advantage of them is another story entirely. Consider this copy from a popular database application: "A Powerful Script Maker. Automate routine tasks, menu operations and procedures with unique point-and-click script creation." Sounds great, right? Easy? Exciting? As it turns out, I don't know of a single person who actually uses this feature. Most of us have looked at the "unique" point-and-click script creator and found that it is much more efficient to just perform our tasks manually. Perhaps an extreme example, but you get the point.

Another bit of fine print to look for is marketing copy which says something like, "...and this program easily integrates with this other program of ours to do great things!" To do those great things, you'll need to buy each program separately, and install them separately. You'll also be at the mercy of whoever designed the "integration" scheme for the two products. You could be in for a very frustrating time—you could even lose data—if the method for using the two products together is inexplicable.

CD-ROM has also added another bit of fine print to many software boxes. First, you should know that distributing software on a CD-ROM disc is *significantly* cheaper than distributing the same software on floppy disks. Additionally, the manufacturing method of making a CD means that it doesn't cost any more to produce a "full" CD-ROM (about 600MB of data) than it does to produce a nearly empty one. Contrast that, again, with the low capacity of diskettes and the need to spread a large program across as many as 30 floppy disks.

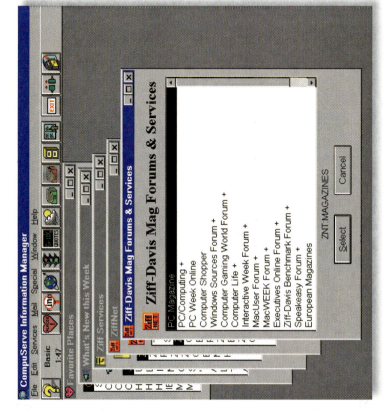

Figure 5: Electronic versions of magazines, like ZiffNet on CompuServe, can provide the most up-to-date information about software.

Several software manufacturers have owned-up to these facts, and are passing their lower costs on to you and me. Take, for example, a popular suite of drawing and graphics tools. If you purchase this software on a CD-ROM, it will cost you nearly $100 *less* than if you purchase it on floppy disks. Additionally, the manufacturer further "thanks" its CD-ROM customers by packing the CD full of free fonts, textures and

On CD-ROM
13,740 clip art symbols, 290 Type One and 289 True Type Fonts, and over 200 photos.

On disk
1,200 clip art symbols, 120 Type One Fonts, and 25 photos.

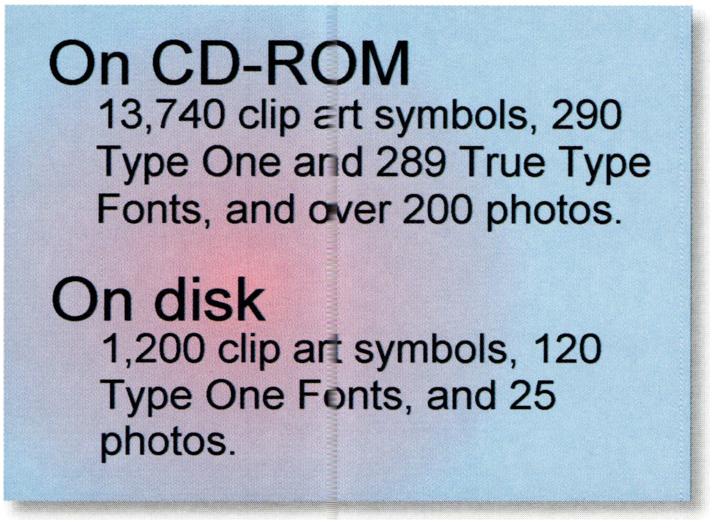

Figure 7: *CD-ROMs are not only less expensive to produce than diskettes, they also provide room for much more information.*

hundreds of megabytes of clip art that are simply absent from the floppy disk version of the product. This kind of thing certainly makes a CD-ROM drive pay for itself quickly!

In fact, CD-ROM disks are so inexpensive to produce that the CD-ROM version of this particular product includes two additional CD disks packed with goodies. But wait! There's still more. The process of installing software from one CD takes only a fraction of the time required to perform the same task from 25 or 30 floppy disks, and it's *infinitely* less annoying. And (yes, more!) this product can be run entirely from its original CD-ROM disk, so that it uses almost *no* space on your hard disk at all!

It's also common for games to be released in two versions: a full multimedia version on CD-ROM with digital video and sound, and a dramatically less impressive version that comes on floppy disks and has neither digital music nor video. I purchased both versions of a highly advertised game recently, just to explore the differences. It was like playing two entirely different games! The CD-ROM multimedia version was very engaging, and the floppy disk version was intolerable. Both versions sold for the same price. So if you have a CD-ROM drive, you'll want to be aware that in some circumstances you'll get a lot more, sometimes for a lot less, by reading the fine print and selecting the CD-ROM version of the product.

Figure 8: *It's a good idea to look for "competitive upgrades" which can cost as much as 75 percent less than the full retail price of an application.*

Competitive upgrades most commonly exist where they can be of particular financial benefit to you: in the case of the most popular software products, which almost always have a high full-retail price. Competition between these products is especially fierce, and the reality is that a huge number of users own both products and keep both products current. It's a little bit like the eternal battle between Coca-Cola and Pepsi. A few people can't stand one or the other; and a lot of us just drink whatever's most convenient. Software manufacturers know that, in the long run, they will make far more money by selling you a deeply discounted upgrade once a year, every year, than they'll make if they only sell you a very expensive program every four or five years.

There are other factors involved, too. Technology has

	Minimum	Recommended
1.	286-based processor	486-SX25 or greater
2.	4MB RAM	8MB RAM (12MB for network)
3.	Windows 3.0 in standard mode	Same
4.	20MB free hard disk space	45MB free hard disk space for complete install
5.	VGA video adapter and monitor	SVGA video adapter and monitor
6.	Mouse or other pointing device	Same

Table 1: *A typical list of minimum and recommended system requirements.*

Another cost-saving option that you may find sequestered away in the smaller print is a version of software known as the *competitive upgrade*. This is a full version of a piece of software which is being sold, often at a dramatic discount, to anyone who already owns a competing product. At the time of this writing, for example, Adobe *Photoshop* sells to a new user for over $500. However, if you own Aldus *Photostyler*, you can "competitively upgrade" to *Photoshop* for only $148. 70 percent off is indeed a sale worth looking for! Sometimes the manufacturer of the competitive upgrade will request that you send in some form of proof of purchase of the original product with your registration card. In some cases, the software itself may search your hard disk to see if you actually own the competitive product that you are upgrading. Sometimes that original product might have even been included free with your computer system.

MINIMUM AND RECOMMENDED SYSTEM REQUIREMENTS

Go back in to your computer store and pick up another piece of software. Somewhere on the box—in *small* print—you'll find the minimum and recommended system requirements for the software. The reason this information is printed so small is because it has never sold a single piece of software, and it has probably *unsold* quite a few.

Here's why: the minimum system requirements for a piece of software make up the list of characteristics that your system must match—at least—to obtain some absolute minimum level of "acceptable" performance from the program. You'll see a sample list in Table 1.

What *does* all that really mean? Well, line one tells you that the software will "run" on a 286-based PC. When you consider, however, that the recommended processor is a 486, you would probably be correct in concluding that cheese grows mold faster than the program will run under the "minimal" conditions. Line 2 lets you know that you only need 4MB of RAM to run the program, but that you'll probably want 8MB. If your PC happens to be on a network, and you want to make use of the networking features in this particular program, you'll need a minimum of 12MB of RAM. In this instance, major features of the program—like network support—will be entirely unavailable to you unless you have the

changed so much in the very recent past that annual upgrades of many programs have been warranted. Additionally, it appears that individuals are quite willing to purchase a relatively inexpensive upgrade while they are far more likely to obtain very expensive software through less legal methods. Further, as computer hardware becomes more ubiquitous, so must software. People who simply couldn't afford to buy a $600 word processor are happy to pay for a $100 "competitive upgrade." And, by selling the software as a discounted upgrade to individuals, manufacturers are still able to get the full-retail price from their large corporate and government clients.

A final bit of small print can be so important that we'll look at it separately.

12MB of RAM required. And even then, that 12MB of RAM is the *minimum* RAM required to use the network features. Performance from this program might be unbearably slow if run on a system with the minimum specifications suggested because the program will start using virtual memory on your hard disk if it ever runs out of the real thing.

Line 3 doesn't tell you much, except that this program, like most, requires Windows to run. By the time this book is in your hands, you will likely see the first fully 32-bit software products with the words, "Windows 95," in the "Minimum" column. By then, the Windows 95 logo will have replaced the current Microsoft Windows logo, indicating that software is compatible with that new operating system.

Line 4 is the really scary line. This program takes 20MB of **hard disk** space for an absolutely minimum installation. To give you some idea of what that means, you should know that a "minimum" installation of a popular word processing program doesn't include that program's spell-checker, its dictionary, thesaurus, grammar-checker, help files, support for importing other types of files or for opening files created by other word processors. Truly a *minimal* installation. That observation is further supported when you notice that a complete installation of the program requires over twice the minimum space. Finally, lines 5 and 6 let you know that you'll probably want to use a resolution higher than the standard 640 × 480-pixel VGA screen (although you can use that resolution), and that a mouse is required to operate at least some portion of the program.

Fear not. We picked a particularly horrifying example so you'd get a dramatic glimpse of how you can read between the lines of fine print to get a good estimate of how the program will actually perform for you. Computer magazines also provide some great insights in this department because they have the opportunity to install and run the software on a number of different systems, with different processors, video displays and memory configurations.

OK, you've done your homework and you went out and bought a product for your computer, and either you can't make it work or you hate it. What can you do?

HARDWARE VS SOFTWARE

Some time ago, we went on record saying that you should never buy hardware or software without a 30-day return policy. While we still believe that, industry pressures have dictated otherwise. At one of the country's largest chains of computer superstores, any hardware product—including printers—may be returned

Figure 9: *Check for this logo on the box—it shows that the software is compatible with the new Windows 95 operating system.*

for full refund up to 30 days after you buy it. Many stores offer the same policy, but make an exception for a laser printer. They may not take them back at all if you've opened the toner cartridge. (This is primarily because there is nothing "wrong" with a lot of hardware that gets returned to stores, and so it is simply repackaged and sold to someone else. But a printer that is full of toner can't be sold as new.) Software, however, is another story.

A very few computer software manufacturers will allow you to open and use their products and then return them to the manufacturer for a refund if you're not satisfied. In general, however, the major superstores will allow you to return *unopened* software for up to either 15 or 30 days after you purchase the product. In most cases, "unopened" doesn't refer to the box, but instead refers to the sealed envelope inside which actually contains the disks. This allows you to open the package and read the manual to verify that you have, indeed, purchased the right program for you, and to return the software if you realize you've made a mistake. In almost all cases now, however, if you break the seal on the diskette or CD-ROM envelope, the store will not take the product back at all for anything other than an exact exchange of another copy because the one you bought was defective. There are some stores that do mean the outer box when they say "unopened" software, but some of these will allow you to open the software in the store under employee supervision and examine the manual *before* you ever buy anything.

Don't be afraid to ask to look at the manual in the store before you make a purchase. You may need to ask to speak with the store manager; but most stores will allow you to do this. They, too, would rather foster goodwill and make you a longtime customer of theirs. You'd be amazed at some of the great news of forthcoming "goodies" you can find out about once you become buddies with the manager of your local computer superstore.

MAIL ORDER REGRETS

If you purchase software through the mail, be certain to read the return policy carefully. As with the different stores, you may be allowed, in rare cases, to actually open and use the software and still return it if it's not right for you, or you may not even be able to open the *shipping box* in which the software arrives. Scott ordered software from a midwestern discounter once who had that latter policy. If the outer FedEx box was opened, the software was not returnable, even if the product was still sealed inside its own box. Now, it's true that if you purchase software through the mail and use a major credit card to pay for it, the credit card company may work on your behalf to get your money back if you've returned the product clearly in good faith—even if you have technically "voided" the return policy—but taking that route can be time-consuming and frustrating. Your best bet is to be certain you're aware of the return policy before you hear that cash-register ring. (For those of you like me who remember when cash-registers actually rang).

Purchasing hardware through the mail can offer its own set of unhappy surprises. For example, it's very unlikely that software will "break" in shipping. That's not necessarily true of that brand-new 21-inch monitor, however. Always arrange for hardware to be delivered at a time and

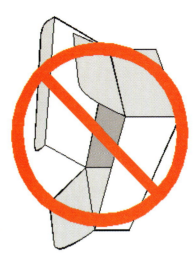

Figure 10: *In some cases, you can't return software even if only the outer box has been opened.*

location where a responsible adult will be available to check the outer packing box for any damage. If you see any damage, you should refuse to take the delivery. The company that sold you the product will investigate the matter along with the shipping company's insurance agent, but you won't have to be involved in that process. Similarly, if the outer shipping box seems fine, but you discover concealed damage inside, stop what you're doing right away and telephone the shipping company. Let them know that you have found concealed damage and they'll tell you what to do. In either case, you may want to make a telephone call to your mail-order company so that they can immediately send you a replacement product.

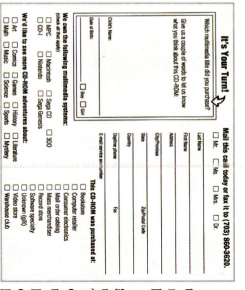

Figure 11: It's important to fill out the registration card and send it in.

than 24 hours after I made my phone call to report that we had encountered the problem, we had a new set of disks.

Some companies—most, in fact, will not give you technical support for their products unless they have you listed as a registered owner. There's a good reason for this, and it really comes down to an issue of fairness. Providing technical support for software is a very expensive prospect. If technical support phone lines are clogged with questions from people who don't have the software instruction manuals (because the software is, in fact, stolen rather than purchased), all the rightful users who paid for the product are the ones who will suffer. The most reliable way to handle that problem is for the support operator to ask for your name or your customer serial number before they answer your questions. Many companies will let you register your software right over the phone if you have technical problems right after purchasing the product and the registration card information has not yet been entered into the support database. In those circumstances, the support operator will want all of the information that was requested on the card, as well as—most likely—the product serial number, to verify that you do actually own it.

Almost universally, software companies recognize that their products are complicated beasts, and that everyone has a question now and then. The support departments of most companies will stay on the line at length—even if it is at their expense—to bring your difficulties to a positive conclusion. It doesn't seem terribly unreasonable for them to ask that only legal users of their products ask for assistance.

Figure 14: Most technical support is helpful—and they'll stick with you until your problem is solved.

In addition to technical support and technical support, so on, you do, in fact, also get your name on another company's junk mail list. And, if you get your name on their list, you'll eventually end up with your name spread all over when the first company sells its user list to another company—and almost all of them do exactly that.

In the past ten years, however, I've received surprisingly few computer-related materials that would actually qualify as junk mail. For the most part I've received upgrade offers and competitive upgrade offers that have been very advantageous to me. I've also received some really cool stuff, like the customer magazines published by companies like Sega, Sierra On-Line, CompuServe, Adobe, Aldus and Paper Direct. These magazines themselves are often just stuffed with great news and information about new products, about new features of online services and so on. CompuServe always features some very interesting subscribers who are using online services in a particularly unique or creative way. The Adobe and Aldus magazines usually contain several very good articles on the subject of desktop publishing or making a productive use of fonts; and these are some of the best freebies to be had. And it's not uncommon for these magazines to contain coupons for in-store discounts or mail-in rebates for the products of the magazine's host company as well as other participating companies. For the trivial cost of taking a minute or two to fill out a card, it's a real bargain!

Figure 12: Consider a trip on the information highway if you're looking for information before making a purchase.

Scott Clark is the editor of Peter Norton's computer book series. He is an accomplished writer and Windows programmer. He recently served as the primary author for the sixth edition of Peter Norton's flagship title, Inside The PC. He is a Windows programmer in Turbo Pascal and Microsoft Visual Basic.

Peter Norton made his mark in the personal computing industry as a programmer, businessman and author. He recently served as the computer author for the sixth edition of Peter Norton's flagship title, Inside The PC. He is best known for the computer programs, including the famed Norton Utilities, and books that bear his name. Mr. Norton sold his personal computing business to Symantec Corporation in 1990 and is a noted patron of the arts and humanities in Los Angeles.

WARRANTY AND REGISTRATION CARD

Tip: If you discover that some part of your new hardware has obviously been damaged in shipping, but that all of it isn't damaged, your best option is still to report the damage to the shipping company and to ask your mail-order seller to send you a complete replacement. Getting a replacement from the mail-order house might only take 24 hours. Ordering a replacement part from the manufacturer could take weeks. If the product still doesn't work when that replacement part arrives, your return-policy period will be gone and you will have to make arrangements—with shipping usually at your cost—for the device to be repaired under the manufacturer's warranty.

Speaking of warranty repair brings us to our final topic: should you, or should you not, fill out and return those pesky warranty and registration cards?

Putting it directly: yes, you should. Here's why. Registration cards do a lot more than just add your name to another company's junk mail list. Most companies offer large discounts on product upgrades to registered users. That alone will absolutely pay you back for the time it takes you to fill out a prepaid postcard. Additionally, if there are hidden problems in the software—bugs—the company may automatically send a new, "fixed" copy of the program to registered users, free of charge. Microsoft did this for us, recently, when a version of Microsoft Word conflicted with a version of Microsoft Windows by accident. Fewer users of Microsoft Windows for Workgroups...

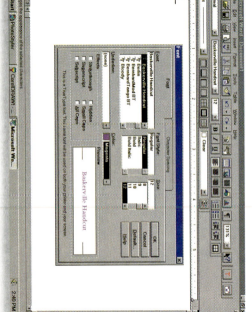

Figure 13: Software can be complicated, but help is usually only a free phone call away.

WHAT IS A PROGRAM?

By Richard Mansfield

Computer programs are stored on disks along with ordinary document files. Here's how to tell them apart; how to understand what, precisely, a program is; and suggestions on how to get started if you want to try programming yourself.

A computer **program** is a tool—it does a job. We're surrounded by familiar tools—from simple tools like forks to complex machines like cars. Most tools expand the capabilities of our bodies. A fork is a specialized "finger" that is superior to eating with our own fingers. A car is untiring and far swifter than our own legs. But until the computer, there were few tools to expand our brain.

There were, of course, recording things on paper by writing them down as a way to improve on our memory, and primitive devices like the abacus to speed up calculating with numbers. But like most traditional physical tools, all these were *dedicated* devices—they did one thing. Indeed they did their job better than we could by ourselves, but they remained highly specialized. That's how we moved from cave drawings to ink pens to the typewriter. You can't write letters with an abacus and a fork can't take you for a ride.

EARLY COMPUTERS WERE HARD-WIRED

Early computers were like that too: made up of wires soldered to other wires, surrounded by vacuum tubes and switches. If you wanted to solve a problem like "2 × 2," you heated up your soldering gun and rewired the machine, or moved plugs around until the device was capable of multiplying two numbers. Like nearly every tool used since the beginning of human history, early computers were *hard-wired*. Put another way, tanks and knives and other implements are **hardware**; it's not easy to change their purpose or their abilities.

Scientists early in this century realized that the computer should be able to "learn" to do new things. Unlike traditional tools, it should be capable of a great variety of behaviors. A finger remains a finger, but the human brain can expand by learning new techniques. A computer should be highly flexible too.

THEY LEARNED FROM LOOMS

One of the first steps in this direction came about when they looked at how cloth was woven. Early in the Nineteenth Century, a Frenchman named Jacquard made a great improvement to the loom. This tool had been used for weaving for thousands of years without many improvements. But Jacquard attached a set of vertical wires that governed how threads are fed into the cloth being woven. More importantly, the various colored threads that made the pattern in the cloth were controlled by wooden cards with holes punched in them. A hole in a particular position lifted the wire that fed a particular thread—omitting it from the weave pattern at that location in the cloth.

This seemingly simple invention permitted far more complex patterns in woven cloth. And it made a loom more useful—patterns could be "remembered" on the cards and reproduced flawlessly and endlessly.

The player piano, like the Jacquard loom, recreates patterns by reading the bumps on a metal cylinder or the holes in a roll of paper.

At the turn of the century, comparatively crude

Figure 1: *An invention that greatly improved weaving was an important early contribution to the notion that machines could "think" and "remember."*

Figure 2: *Player pianos recall the "memory" of music by "reading" bumps on cylinders or paper.*

computers were constructed that analyzed data like the census. They, too, were fed information pretty much the same way that looms and player pianos were—on cards with holes punched in them. Stacks of these cards, each the size of a bank check, were fed into the machine and in this way it received data that it could manipulate. Later, banks had giant machines wired to add and subtract. The bank could feed it all the "punchcards" representing your deposits and withdrawals, and the machine would calculate your balance.

Then computer scientists had an important idea: the general-purpose computer. If you could feed in data, why couldn't you also feed in a program? In other words, you wouldn't be limited to only one or a few computer jobs the way the old hard-wired machines were. Instead, you could store the patterns of various programs outside the machine. This way, if you wanted to calculate a bank balance, you would first feed in the program that did this kind of job, then feed in the data, in this case a set of deposits and withdrawals. But this same machine, when provided with a different program, could alphabetize names.

IT'S A PATHWAY, A RECIPE

So, a program is like a pathway that manipulates information: a set of steps that when applied to data, change that data. (The words **application** and **software** mean the same thing as program.)

Data is like raw material and a program is like a factory that transforms the raw material. One easily understood example of the distinction between data (information) and a program is to visualize this set of raw materials:

- flour
- water
- salt
- sugar
- yeast

This data (raw material) is "acted" on by the following series of steps (the program) that change the data into something else:

1. Heat the water.
2. Mix all ingredients well by squeezing them with your hands for ten minutes.
3. Let sit one hour.
4. Push out all air.
5. Let sit 40 minutes.
6. Heat in the oven 40 minutes.

A program is a pre-arranged series of instructions that, when followed (and when provided with appropriate data) produces a predictable result. A program isn't fundamentally different from the patterns punched into Jacquard's cards. In essence, a program says: do this first, then do this, then this, then stop.

A computer program that figures the average of two numbers works like this:

1. Get a number.
2. Get a second number.
3. Add the two numbers.
4. Divide the result by two.
5. Display the result.
6. Stop.

Something like this list of instructions is buried inside every spreadsheet program. When you click on an **icon** (or **button** or **menu** item) labeled *Average*, the program has a list of addresses (locations inside the program itself) where various smaller programs reside. (These smaller programs are called **subroutines**.) It finds the address associated with *Average* and follows the list of instructions.

A computer program as large as a spreadsheet can do many things. It has many small subroutines inside it that can transform data in a variety of ways. Just as a cook could make various things out of flour and water—cookies, paste, crackers—a spreadsheet program has various sets of instructions that permit it to combine numbers in various ways. Likewise, a word processor can manipulate words in many ways and a graphics program can take an image and resize it, color it different, even make it look like a mosaic or a watercolor.

THEY BUILT THE FIRST ONE IN 1945

The first truly modern computer was built in 1945. It contained internal "memory." There wasn't much memory, hundreds rather than the millions of bytes you have in your personal computer today. And that early computer, named ENIAC, was composed of metal rings the size of quarters suspended in a matrix of wires. But the patterns that previously had to be fed on paper tape could now be transferred into the machine itself. The holes in the paper caused some of the rings to be magnetized, while the rest of the rings remained unchanged. In other words, the image of the paper holes had been transferred into the machine itself. This greatly speeded things up. If your program has to be fed into the machine each time you use the program, things slow down quite a bit.

Today most programs flow off of our **hard disk** and into our computer's memory in a matter of seconds. They're ready almost instantly to accept data that we type in or files of data that we load in from the hard disk.

Remember, however, that even though data files and program files both reside on your **hard drive**, there is an important distinction. A data file might be a list of the addresses of all your friends and relatives. It's just information, a list of names and places. It can't do a job inside the computer the way a program can. By contrast, a program is a list of instructions that tell the computer how to accomplish tasks, how to manipulate or process raw data.

WHERE DO PROGRAMS COME FROM?

People write programs using a language that the computer can understand. There are many programming languages and different programmers prefer different languages, but the computer can understand them all. Programming languages range from the near-mathematical complexity of "assembly language" to the near-English clarity of Basic. Our averaging program looks very different, for example, when written in Basic. (*This program, and the program later in the article, has line breaks that should be ignored when typing it in. "Please enter a number...", would all be on one line before pressing Enter.*)

```
1 Input "Please enter a
  number...", FirstNumber
2 Input "Please enter
  another number...",
  SecondNumber
3 Total = SecondNumber
  + FirstNumber
4 Answer = Total / 2
  'Average the two numbers
5 Print Answer  ' Display
  the answer
6 Stop
```

The comments following the apostrophe on a line of programming are ignored by the computer. They are English and today's computers wouldn't understand them. Comments are for the benefit of the programmer, to explain the meaning of instructions that aren't, in themselves, obvious. Then, if the programmer later wants to make changes, the program is easier to read.

HOW DO YOU RECOGNIZE A PROGRAM?

In DOS and Windows 3.1, filenames have **extensions**, and the extension is the giveaway that a disk file is a program and not a data file. An extension is a three-letter identifier tacked onto the end of a filename, the ".TXT" in: MYDOC.TXT. Ordinary data has all kinds of extensions (or possibly no extension): MYFILE.DOC, MYPICTR.BMP, ANIMAGE.TIF and so on.

Programs, however, nearly always have the extension ".EXE": WINWORD.EXE, PHOTOSHP.EXE. A few programs have a ".COM" extension, and there are also program-like "script files" with the extension ".BAT".

In Windows 3.1, there are two ways to look at the files on your hard drive: File Manager and Program Manager. File Manager provides you with a list like a DOS DIR list. Programs have the .EXE extension.

However, when looking in Windows 3.1's Program Manager, all you'll see are icons and titles.

```
:\SCAN
            <DIR>
MSCAN    ICO        766  04-19-95  11:00a
TEST     ICO        766  12-31-92   1:47p
README   ICO      1,086  12-31-92   1:48p
README2  DOC      9,799  12-30-92   5:01p
README   DOC      8,554  02-22-94   9:53a
CONTROL  DLL     17,213  02-24-94  10:59a
METER    DLL      9,728  03-18-93   3:43p
INSTALL  HLP     31,891  01-28-92  10:23a
SCANTEST INF      1,579  02-05-93   5:50p
M1904    SYS     22,915  07-09-93   9:16a
M1906    SYS     14,962  02-10-93  10:34a
PRINSCAN SYS     14,188  01-21-93   1:35p
PSCAN3   SYS     26,025  01-21-93  12:52p
STITCH   DLL     36,864  10-13-93  10:47a
SCANW    HLP    229,888  10-11-92  11:02a
SCANW    EXE    184,832  01-25-94   4:47p
SCANTEST EXE     87,040  01-26-94   5:53p
TWAIN    DLL    146,432  05-10-94   2:36p
MUSTEK   DS
PRINSCAN DS
    20 file(s)    903,856 bytes
               84,262,912 bytes free
     2 dir(s)
```

Figure 3: When you type DIR in DOS, you'll find that programs almost always have an .EXE extension.

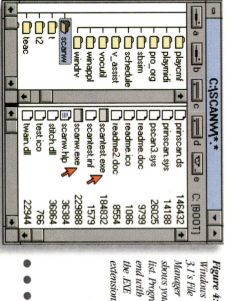

Figure 4: Windows 3.1's File Manager shows you a list. Programs end with the .EXE extension.

The title usually won't include an extension to provide a clue to whether it represents a program. You just have to remember: In Figure 5, Calendar, CdPlayer and Backup Lite are programs; Readme is a Notepad text file and TE.TIF is a graphic image.

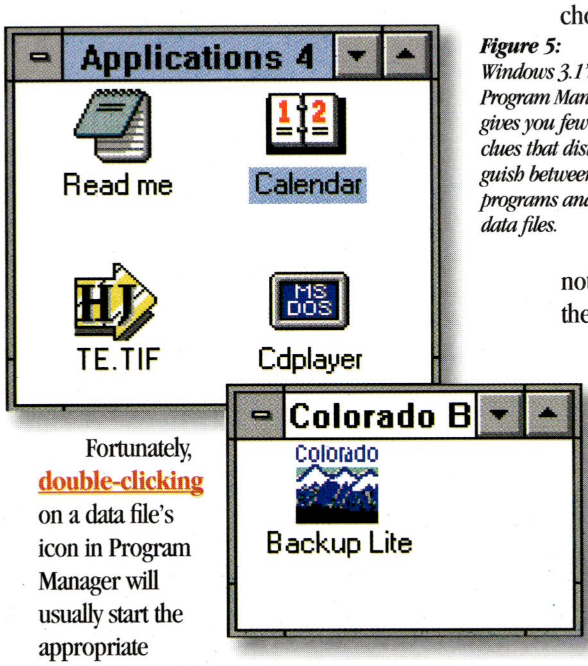

Fortunately, **double-clicking** on a data file's icon in Program Manager will usually start the appropriate application running anyway. If, for example, you double click on the Readme icon shown in Figure 5, Windows will automatically start the Notepad program running, and load in the Readme data file for you to look at. Windows allows you to associate data file extensions (such as .TXT) with the appropriate program that displays them. For more on this, look in Windows Help under "associations." And remember, no matter what you do, double-clicking on an icon or filename isn't going to do any damage to the computer.

Figure 5:
Windows 3.1's Program Manager gives you few clues that distinguish between programs and data files.

Windows 95 is quite a bit more helpful, in many ways, than previous versions of Windows or, of course, DOS. For one thing, the new Explorer combines the best features of Windows 3.1's File Manager and Program Manager into a more efficient and more logical assistant. You can choose whether you want Explorer to display the file extensions visible in Figure 6. (To do this, click on the Explorer *View* menu and select *Options*. Then click to select, or deselect, the *Hide MS-DOS file extensions* option.)

If you really want all the details about a given file (including whether or not it's a program), just **right-click** on its icon, then select *Properties*, as shown in Figure 7.

THE FIVE KINDS OF PROGRAMS

Programs fall into five general categories:

Applications—full-fledged, generally large programs that perform some useful job. The The four main types of applications are graphics, word processing, spreadsheets and databases.

Languages—Basic, C, Pascal and others are programs with which you can construct other programs. These are called higher level languages because they have an English language-like structure.

Games—educational or just plain fun, there are thousands of computer games. Categories here include adventure (novel-like stories); action (shoot, stomp and run), simulation (fly an airplane, design a city) and traditional (bridge, chess, pinball).

Networking & Telecommunications—allow your computer to communicate with other computers in the same office via wires, or around the world via the telephone.

Utilities—generally smaller, highly specific programs that usually perform "housekeeping" tasks within the computer. Examples include File Finders, File Compressors, and Backup programs.

Programs can also be categorized by how or where you get them:

Commercial Software—ranging in price from $2 to $100,000, the average computer program costs under $100. Available from stores or via mail order.

Freeware—programs given away (they're quite rare). Available on bulletin boards, telecommunication services like America Online or CompuServe and on CD or disk in magazines.

Shareware—try it out, if you like it send some money to the author. There are many shareware programs and some of them rival or exceed the quality of commercial software. Available in the same places as freeware.

Vaporware—commercial programs that come out long after their expected date of release, or never appear at all.

Viruses—distributed hidden within authentic programs. Far more scarce than their reputation would suggest, a truly destructive virus can nonetheless wreak havoc on your hard drive, erasing files, filling it up with nonsense or even requiring that you get professional help to regain control of your computer. Some are harmless and merely display the perpetrator's name on your screen; others can destroy many weeks of work by damaging your document files. That's why we need virus-checking programs on our systems. These highly specialized programs scan the programs you're loading into memory and watch for viruses.

DO YOU WANT TO WRITE YOUR OWN?

Programming can be great fun. It can range from simple time-saving routines to massive, complex applications. You could write

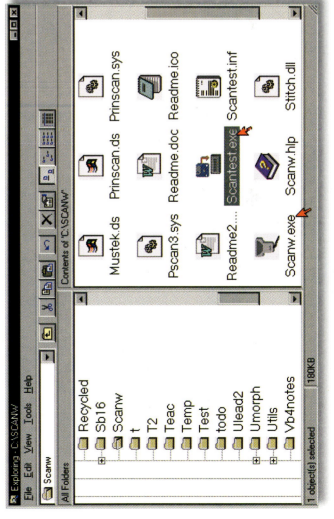

Figure 6: *Windows 95's Explorer makes it easy to tell the difference between data files and runnable programs.*

a little program in a few minutes, or join a team of other programmers and spend years writing a full-featured word processor or photo-retouching application.

If you want to get your feet wet, by far the best place to start is by recording a **macro**. Major applications include their own built-in programming language. This allows you to customize the application. Here's an example using *Word for Windows.*

MACROS ARE EASY

Click on the *Tools* menu, then click on *Macro* and select *Record.* Name it "MyName" and press *Enter.* Now type in your name and address. Click again on the *Tools* menu, then click on *Macro* and select *Stop Recording.* That's it. Word watched what you clicked and what you typed and translated your actions into a program. Click on *Edit* in the Macro window and look at the program you just created:

```
Sub MAIN
Insert "Richard Mansfield"
InsertPara
Insert "200 Poterio Court"
InsertPara
Insert "Anywhere, USA 12443"
End Sub
```

Now, any time you wan to run this macro, select *Tools/Macro*, locate the "MyName" macro, and click on *Run.* You can even assign this shortcut to a key combination like Ctrl+N. Every time you're finishing up a letter and want your name and address typed in for you, just press *Ctrl+N* (see "Shortcut Keys" in *Word's* Help for instructions).

Notice that you didn't actually write this program, but you could. While in the Macro window, type in the name you want to give it, then select *Create.* You can then just type in the lines above between Sub MAIN and End Sub. Either way, you've created a useful tool. You could even edit your macro replacing it with a friend's name and address, and give him or her a custom macro to use.

HELPFUL BOOKS

Good first books on programming Visual Basic include these two tutorials: *Learn Visual Basic in 21 Days* (Sams), *The Beginner's Guide to Visual Basic* (Wrox). Fortunately the definitive reference to Visual Basic is also quite easy-to-understand: *The Visual Guide to Visual Basic* (Ventana).

Richard Mansfield's books on personal computing have sold over 350,000 copies worldwide. He is the author of two current bestsellers: The Visual Guide to Visual Basic and The Visual Power Toolkit. Richard was

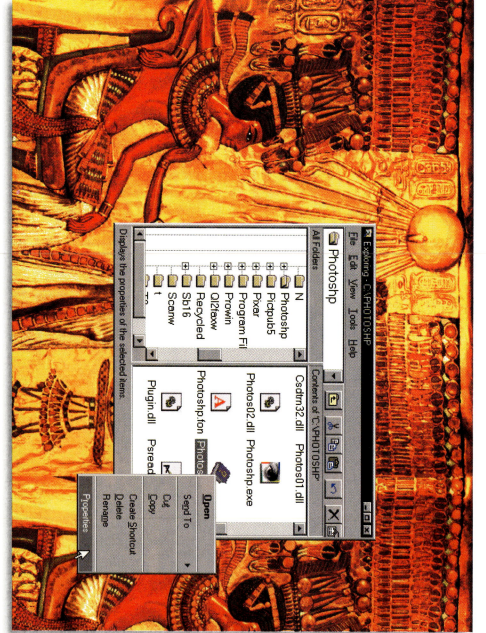

Figure 7: Right-clicking on an icon allows you to see its "Properties"—a comprehensive description of the file.

If you want to write programs that will run by themselves under Windows 95 (instead of within an application), get a copy of *Visual Basic* (Microsoft). Basic is the easiest computer language to learn, and *Visual Basic* gives you all kinds of help. To create **windows**, text-input boxes, labels, pictures, **scroll bars** and dozens of other visual elements—you just drag them with your mouse and position and size them to suit yourself. All this without even writing your first word of programming.

Senior Editor of COMPUTE! Publications from 1982 through 1987, and Senior Editor of Game Players Publications from 1988 to 1992.

Figure 8: Windows 95's Explorer provides an exhaustive description, including a file's type. Recall that application means the same thing as program.

CONNECTING TO THE WORLD

By Evangelos Petroutsos

Here's a quick guide to your modem and what it does for you: how data is communicated and transferred; what actually happens; what a modem does; the importance of speed for image transfers and the Web and the online services; modems and communications software; fax packages; the difference between internal and external modems.

Welcome to the world of computer communications, the amazing world of the future! Whether you are adding communication capabilities to your computer because you want to exchange files with a friend, or you're about to become a cybernaut, this article will help you get started. Computer communications are shaping the future, and our little world will never be the same again.

Communication has been an issue in every human community. Today, as communities become global, the need for efficient, speedy, effective communications is even more pressing. Computer technology doesn't ignore this need. Indeed, it makes it possible to be in touch with the rest of the world, anytime, from anywhere, and at a very small cost. All you need is a personal computer, a modem and a telephone jack.

WHAT IS A MODEM

A **modem** is a small device that lets computers talk to each other via the telephone. People use telephones to talk to each other, and so do computers. The difference is that computers can transmit complicated information, like documents, programs, charts and images. And they can send these things very fast.

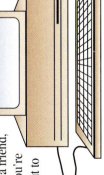

Figure 1: *Computers can communicate through the telephone lines with the help of modems—the one shown here is external.*

In Figure 1, you see a typical modem connection. Each computer is connected to the telephone network via a modem. What's between the modems? Whatever is between you and the person you call. If you are talking to another person in the same town, it is the local telephone company. If you are calling a friend out of state, it is your long-distance telephone company.

To make a phone call, all you need to know is how to dial your party's number. Establishing a computer communication is just as simple, and is accomplished with the help of an inexpensive communications program.

To better exploit the capabilities of your new modem, however, you should know a few things about its operation. At the very least, you should be able to understand the specifications of a modem. Things like *9,600BPS* or *V.42bis*, or terms like *compression* and *error detection*. We'll take a look at how information is transmitted through the telephone network, what happens to it when it leaves your computer, how it travels through the wires and how to make sense out of these specifications. Understanding all of this will help you know what modem to buy.

Telephones were designed to transfer voice—in other words, analog signals like those shown in Figure 2. The top signal is called **analog** because its amplitude varies. The amplitude is the intensity of the signal, or, put another way, how

loud or soft your voice is at any given time. As you talk, the microphone picks up the loudness variations in your voice and transmits them to the other end of the connection, where they hit that telephone's speaker and are then heard by the other person.

The **digital** signal on the bottom of Figure 2 has only two possible values: 0 and 1 (or off and on). At the most elementary level, "on" and "off" are the only two qualities computers can understand. To make it possible for a computer to use the telephone network, the digital signals produced by the computer must be converted to analog signals. These analog signals can then move through the telephone network just like voice.

TELEPHONE COMPANY

DO YOU SPEAK DIGITESE?

Have you ever called a company after hours and had a fax machine answer your call? This hissing, buzzing, screeching and ultimately *annoying* noise you hear is the analog representation of a digital signal—the kind of signals computers understand and we don't.

It's like eavesdropping on a conversation between two people speaking in a foreign language. You know the computers are talking in their native language, but it's all Greek to you. It's computer *digitese*.

The modem's job is to convert the digital signal at your computer's end to an analog signal suitable for transmission through telephone lines. The process of translating a digital signal into analog is called **modulation**. The reverse process at the other end is, understandably, called **demodulation** (translation of the analog signal back to digital). The modem is a modulation/demodulation device and that's where its name came from.

Analog Signal
Digital Signal

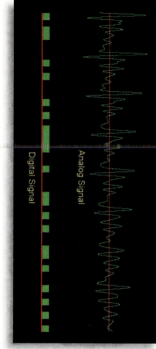

Figure 2: *Analog signals vary in loudness. Digital signals, used by computers, have only two states, on and off.*

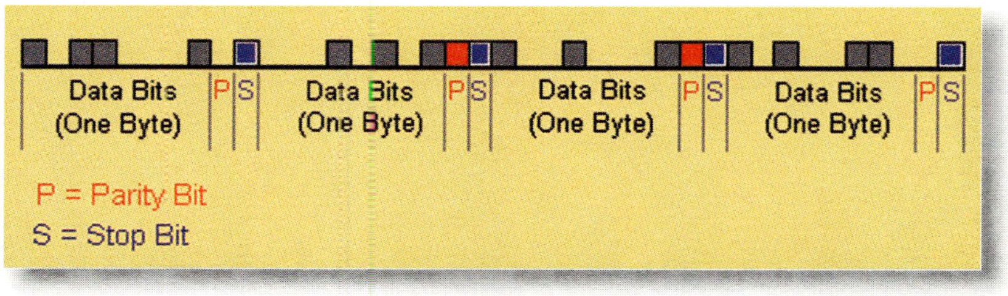

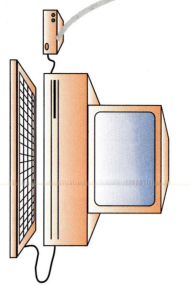

Speedy Modems

The single most important feature of a modem is its speed, the amount of data it can move in a second. (It's much faster than we can talk!) Digital signals are made up of bits, 0s and 1s. These bits are transmitted one after the other. If you could watch what goes down the wire from your computer to your modem, you'd see a train of pulses (as in Figure 3). Each pulse is a bit, and every eight bits forms a byte. This is also how

information is represented in your computer. Each letter of the alphabet (and other characters like the ten numeric digits and punctuation, like a comma or a period) is stored as a byte. While your computer moves multiple bytes to and from its internal memory and other devices (like CD-ROM) all at once, modems transmit information one bit at a time, in a series.

Not all these bits carry information, though. After each byte there is always an extra bit, called the **stop bit**. It is used to synchronize the transmitting and receiving modems. When the receiving modem sees the stop bit, it knows a byte has ended and a new one is beginning.

Data Bits (One Byte)
P S
Data Bits (One Byte)
P S
Data Bits (One Byte)
P S
Data Bits (One Byte)
P S
P = Parity Bit
S = Stop Bit

Figure 3: *The information is transmitted through the modem one bit at a time, not unlike the old telegraph. Each character is composed of eight successive bits. The stop bits help the two modems stay in sync.*

The first modems could move information at the rate of 300 bits per second, or **BPS**. Considering that there are eight bits in a character, they were limited to fewer than 40 characters per second. Today's modems can go up to 2,400 bits per second (or roughly 300 characters per second), 9,600BPS (or 1,200 characters per second) or even as high as 28,800BPS. Although the speed of a modem is always given in bits per second, you can divide it by eight to reduce it to characters per second, which is a more meaningful unit.

Moving bits around inside a computer at speeds of 9,600BPS is very slow for even the least expensive personal computer. How come a computer can move 300,000 bytes from your CD and over 1,000,000 characters to and from its hard disk in a second, but only 1,000 or so characters a second to and from the modem?

The speed of a modem is not limited by the computer. Rather, the problem is the telephone line. Telephones were designed to transmit voice and are very inefficient at transmitting digital data. A similar limitation applies to printers. Computers are capable of sending information very rapidly, but a printer, working in the physical world, can only print so fast.

Modems try to squeeze through as much information as they can, but only to the point where this information can be transmitted reliably over the telephone lines. Now, you know what happens if you attempt to talk very fast: the same information is heard over a shorter period of time and the sound you produce contains more and more high frequencies (a Donald Duck kind of sound). It's like playing a record or tape at a speed higher than normal. You still understand the words, but can't recognize the voice tones anymore, so you don't know who's talking. Speeded up, everybody sounds like a duck. If you increase the speed even more, you will reach a point where you can't even understand the individual words.

Something similar happens with telephone lines. Because they were designed to transmit voice, they can't handle very high frequencies. Modems are designed to operate close to this limit without exceeding it. The latest generation of modems can go up to 28,800BPS. But the phone line limitations explain why their speeds still seem so inadequate in comparison to the transfer speed of other computer operations.

Tech Tip: **Although a fast modem is desirable, a modem connection may not always work at maximum speed unless the modem on the other end is just as fast. Once you connect to a bulletin board with your 9,600BPS modem, you may see a message like "Communication established at 2,400." This means that the modem at the other end simply can't operate at any speed higher than 2,400BPS so yours had to adjust itself downward to accommodate the limitation.**

America Online - [NASA Jet Propulsion Laboratory]
File Edit Go To Mail Members Window Help
Back Reload Forward Favorite Places Home Help Stop
http://www.jpl.nasa.gov/
JPL
National Aeronautics and Space Administration
California Institute of Technology
Jet Propulsion Laboratory
News flashes

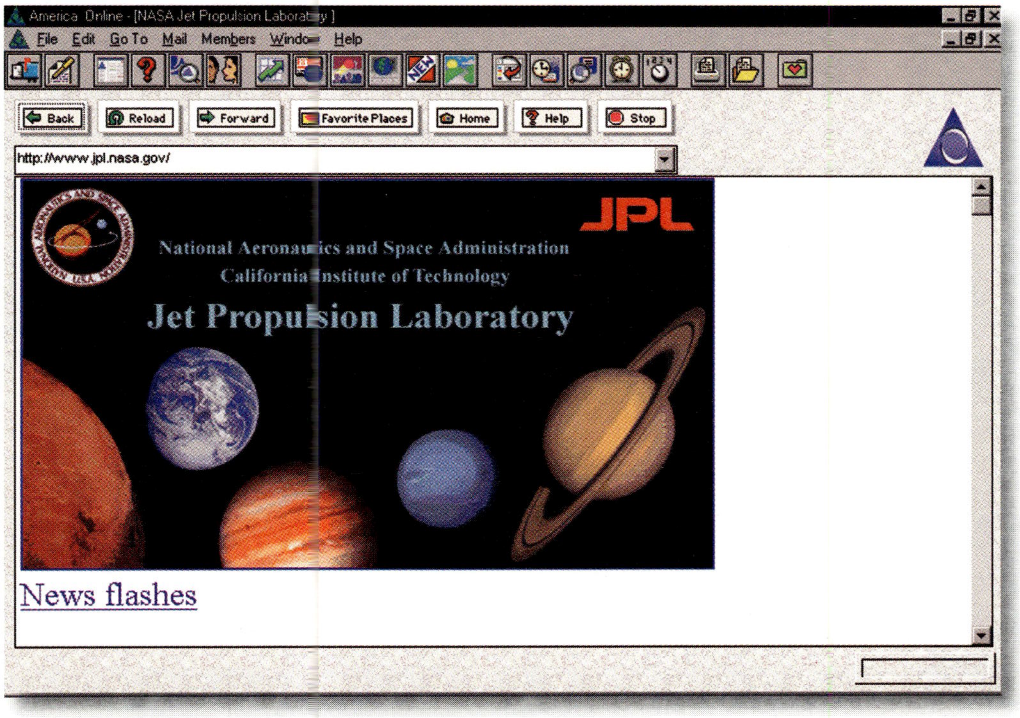

Figure 4: *Today's computer programs employ rich color graphics that necessitate high communication speeds.*

COMPRESS FOR FASTER TRANSMISSION

To overcome this inherent speed limitation, modems use special programs to **compress** the information to be transmitted. Compression became popular in personal computers as a way to increase the capacity of hard disks. If you are not familiar with compression techniques, you may be surprised that they can reduce the size of a file without losing any information. It's really a very simple principle.

There was a time when telegraph was the dominant form of fast communication. Compression of information was used routinely even back in those days. For example, one wouldn't send a telegram saying, "HEATHER JUST GAVE BIRTH TO A BABY GIRL. MOM AND DAUGHTER ARE IN GOOD HEALTH. BYE." The telegram would say, "BABY GIRL ARRIVED. BOTH FINE. BI" The second message conveys the same information, but costs less. Of course, a telegram might convey no information at all to persons other than the intended receiver. That's why a compression program is always accompanied by a

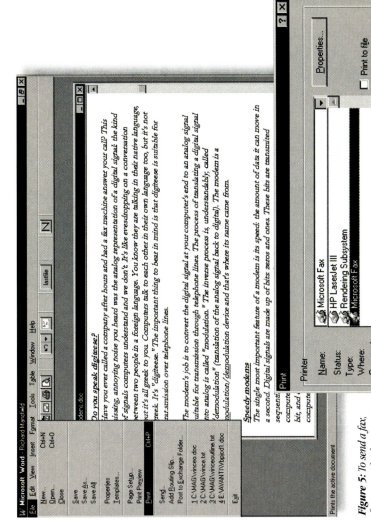

Figure 5: To send a fax, first create the document with a word processor, print it with the Print command and...

decompression program, which knows how to restore the compressed information to its original form.

Computers use a similar principle; they just employ more efficient techniques. Consider an image, for example, whose top is made up of blue **pixels** like a cloudless sky. Let's say this color blue is represented by the number 4. We could transmit this color value of each dot in the picture over and over: 444444444444... However, we could compress by merely storing the color value, followed by the *number of repetitions of this same color:* 4 (2,304). To the decompressor, this means "Print 2,304 blue dots." A typical image can easily be compressed down to one-tenth of its original size. All the original information is still there, it's just communicated more efficiently than simple, blind repetition of every single dot of color in the picture.

A modem that uses compression is only good if used with a modem on the other end that supports the same compression technique, and therefore knows how to decompress the information it receives. Fortunately, compression standards exist so all modems can understand each other's shorthand. In the specifications of a modem, you will see some codes like *V.21, V.32* and *V.42.* These are the compression protocols. The fastest modems today are rated at 28,800BPS, which corresponds to roughly 3,500 characters per second. However, when using the V.42 compression

Figure 6: ...then select the FAX printer

protocol, that same modem can transfer nearly 30,000 characters per second—nearly ten times more. Of course, this is a best-case scenario, as advertised by manufacturers. Not all pictures have cloudless blue skies. And, of course, if you are sending a file that you've already compressed using the popular PKZIP utility, you can't expect any additional compression. Any repetitiveness will have already been wrung out of the file.

HANDLING NOISE

The telephone network is not perfect. Every now and then, errors creep in and they can disturb your conversation. These disturbances are called *noise*. Like a clicking noise every second or so, which obviously isn't part of the conversation. Or an echo effect.

With human voice communication, this isn't much of a problem because we can ignore noise. With computers, though, it's a whole different story. It doesn't take more than garbling a single bit to create havoc. Instead of receiving the digit 3, your computer may receive the digit 1. If this error goes undetected, there might be problems—especially if this happens to be the left-most digit in your bank account balance.

Figure 7: If you don't want to dial (or wrong number again, let your computer do it, by connecting your telephone to the modem.

before the next one is transmitted. This way, the computer doesn't have to re-transmit the entire message if it contains errors—only the zone that was corrupted during transmission need be repeated. In addition, there are even more advanced techniques for not only detecting, but correcting errors as well. Modems that support the V.42bis protocol can correct many transmission errors without even needing to re-transmit the problem packet. What this means in practice is that even with a noisy connection, corrupted packets are not repeated.

SETTING UP YOUR MODEM

There are two types of modems: internal and external. Internal modems fit in one of your computer's internal slots and provide two telephone jacks: one called LINE and one called PHONE. You connect the line jack to the telephone line coming out of your wall. The cable you need usually comes with the modem, or you can buy them at any CompUSA or Radio Shack store.

If you want, you can connect your telephone to the modem, too, through the phone jack on the back of the modem card. Using this type of connection, you can have your modem answer phone calls, or dial a number from within your computer. The computer dials the number and you pick up the phone when you hear the calling signal. It will even keep dialing if it gets a busy signal.

External modems provide the same two connections, as well as a cable to connect to your computer's serial port. Here's a potential problem: many computers and notebooks are notorious for having only a single serial port, and this single serial port is usually taken up by the mouse. It's true most modern notebooks provide an alternative pointing device, but you may not find it as convenient as a mouse. If your computer has a single serial port, you should consider an internal modem. Fortunately, most notebooks have the option of an internal modem, but it will cost you more than an external one.

There are three vital parameters for the proper operation of a modem: speed, parity bit and stop bit. Your modem's parameters must match those of the other modem, or else they will not be able to communicate. Another parameter is the number of data bits, which is seven or eight. Your communications software will usually set these parameters for you, but there are occasions when you may have to do it yourself. Many bulletin boards specify the values of these parameters in the form 2400-8-N-1. This means that you must connect at 2,400 BPS, with eight data bits, no parity and one stop bit. You must

use the modem's setup program to set the values of the corresponding parameters before you attempt to connect. If you connect and still have problems, try adjusting these values. The speed, however, is usually adjusted automatically by your modem when it realizes that it's "talking to" a slower modem.

THE SKY'S THE LIMIT

So, what can you do with the modem you just bought? There's practically no end to the possibilities. You can connect to any other user on the globe—people you know, or people you've never met who share your interests. You can participate in a multi-user action game, or explore a dungeon with friends and enemies. You can play chess with a novice or an expert, or, along with other chess lovers, watch a chess game between two experts. There are more practical things you can do as well: You can seek advice from experts, screen job descriptions, even sell your skills to those who need them.

If you are a freelancer, your modem is your gate to the world. You can find new customers and new resources, even work from home. Telecommuting is not just a future possibility or a fad; it's a working reality for many already.

If this sounds so exciting that you can't wait to jump into the global network, give it a try. This article should serve as your technical introduction to computer communications. Luckily, "going online" is not very complicated. Once you familiarize yourself with online services like AOL, and a few basic concepts, you'll be surprised by how easy it is to locate information you need, join discussions that interest you, locate beautiful graphics, connect to NASA and much, much more.

You'll get help along the way, too—if you have a question, just ask anyone you "meet" online. Don't forget, even the most experienced net-surfers were beginners at some point, and so many of them will be willing to help. You'll quickly meet many people on the global network, the network you are about to become part of.

A good book on modems is *Modems for Dummies* from IDG Books Worldwide. If you're interested in a specific online service, like AOL or Compuserve, any good book describing it will contain information about the necessary modem settings.

So, how do modems deal with noise? In principle, the same way humans do. When you give someone your telephone number, or an account number over the phone, they usually repeat it back to make sure they heard it right. When you make a flight reservation, your agent gives you back a code, such as "1,100." The travel agent will read it out as "Lima one hundred," or "1, as in Lima, one, zero, zero" to make sure you will not hear it as N100, or something else. The basic idea is that in order to secure the integrity of data transmission, be it from one human to another, or between computers, some redundancy must be introduced.

A simple technique for checking the integrity of the transmitted information is the parity bit. One approach is to make the parity bit a 1 if the number of bits set to 1 is odd, and a 0 otherwise. For example, the byte 10011001, because it has four 1s in it, would result in a parity bit of 0. The parity bit is then attached to each byte of information along with the stop bit mentioned earlier (see Figure 3).

There are other, more complicated techniques for checking the integrity of a message, but they are all based on this basic principle. A number called a checksum is extracted from the message and attached to the message. A checksum can be calculated at the receiving end and then compared to the transmitted checksum. If they match, the message was correct and communication proceeds. If not, the receiving modem requests re-transmission of the corrupted message.

Messages are not transmitted in their entirety. Instead, they are broken into smaller chunks, called blocks or packets. Each packet is verified separately with a checksum or by some other error-detecting technique. That is, each packet has its own error-detecting information, and is verified, or repeated,

Evangelos Petroutsos has a degree in Computer Engineering from the University of California and works as an author and consultant. He is co-author of the best-selling book Visual Basic Power Toolkit.

AMERICA ONLINE

By Tom Lichty

AOL is one of the fastest-growing and most popular online services. Here are some reasons why:

n 1919, Don Francisco, working for the California Fruit Growers Exchange, burned the name "Sunkist" into the skin of a California orange with a heated fly swatter. Francisco's was the kind of entrepreneurism that arises from neighborhood lemonade stands.

Steve Case probably had a lemonade stand. Steve Case is the founder of America Online, and his "lemonade stand," started in 1985, took the form of a niche **commercial online service** for Commodore computers called *Q-Link*. Ten years later, America Online—Q-Link's precocious progeny—boasts over three million members and is well on its way to becoming the Sunkist of the online telecommunications industry.

What Don Francisco did right was to put a trademark on a commodity. What Steve Case did right was to make telecommunications easy. Both had unique strategies for their day. Case's strategy was to give away his software for the Commodore. Once installed on a home computer, the software automatically "phoned home"—established contact with the parent **mainframe**—adjusted all of the necessary protocols to suit the user's Commodore, found a local phone number, and stored all of its settings on the Commodore's disks, ready for use the next time the user wanted to sign on. This automation was a significant departure from other online services of the day. Before Case's Q-Link, the user was expected to provide software of his or her own—software that required familiarity with the arcane science of parity, stop bits, baud rates, and transfer protocols. The kind of people who would

rather *eat* an orange than grow one became attracted to the Q-Link philosophy where everything was familiar, predictable, and easy to use.

A few years later, Q-Link changed its name, software was offered for the Apple Macintosh and PCs running Windows, and Steve Case's lemonade stand became **AOL** (for America Online, as it's known). AOL is a publicly owned company, traded on the NASDAQ stock exchange, with headquarters in Vienna, Virginia—a suburb of Washington, DC.

AOL'S FEATURES

America Online's meteoric rise in popularity (growth in the mid-1990s is almost 300 percent a year) can be attributed to a number of factors beyond the increase in popularity of online services in general—an increase for which AOL is at least partly responsible.

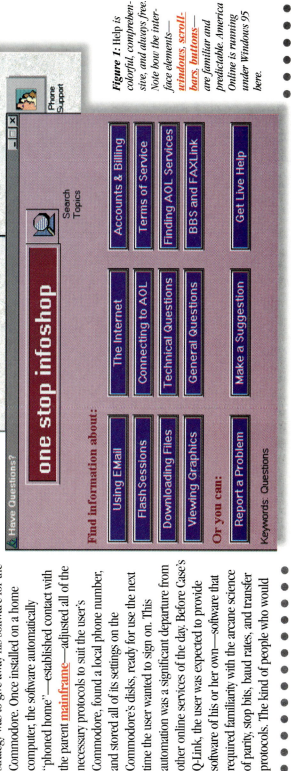

Figure 1: Help is colorful, comprehensive, and always free. Note how the interface elements—*windows, scroll-bars, buttons*—are familiar and predictable. America Online is running under Windows 95 here.

GETTING HELP

Perhaps nowhere is the interface more evident than in getting help. Though we'll discuss help later in this article, a look at it now gives indication of the appearance of the interface (see Figure 1).

ACCESSING THE INTERNET

The **Internet** clamors for an effective interface. Any mortal who has struggled with arcane **UNIX** commands to direct an **FTP** (file transfer protocol)

THE INTERFACE

Perhaps most important is that effortless **interface**—the software for Macs and PCs that AOL still gives away. If you're familiar with your computer, you're already familiar with America Online. Menus pull down, windows resize, **scrollbars** scroll—it's all very predictable. It's also very common now, but it hasn't always been that way, and AOL's early pioneering ventures were what won its acclaim in the early 1990s.

download or conduct a **Telnet** session can attest to the benefit of an intuitive interface.

AOL's "client" software—the software that runs on your PC or Mac—offers an especially effective interface for the **World Wide Web**, the

Internet's *pièce de résistance* (see Figure 2). Using proprietary compression and decompression schemes, AOL's graphics transmit demonstrably faster than most other Internet providers, and AOL's local **cache** of recently accessed Web pages often provides Web access directly from your own hard disk, rather than from a sluggish telephone line.

SIMPLE PRICING

With an outrageous disdain for tradition, AOL has always preferred a one-price strategy, where everyone pays the same rate for access regardless of which features of the service are used or what time of day they prefer to use them. Though AOL first appeared with a "prime time" rate premium, and though it once favored "charter members" over others, both policies have been phased out. At this writing, AOL charges $9.95 a month, which includes five hours of access and *Multimedia Online*, the service's monthly magazine. Members who spend more than five hours a month online pay $2.95 per hour—regardless of the time of day—for every hour thereafter. There are no quotas on mail sent or received, even Internet mail, and there is no surcharge for Internet access.

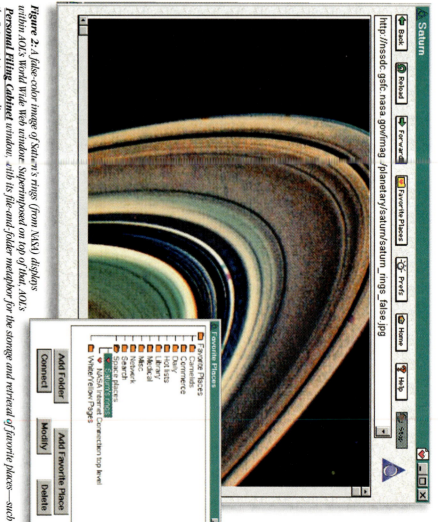

Figure 2: *A false-color image of Saturn's rings (from NASA) displays within AOL's World Wide Web window. Superimposed on top of that, AOL's* Personal Filing Cabinet *window, with its file-and-folder metaphor for the storage and retrieval of favorite places—such as the Saturn picture—online.*

Saturn — Back — Reload — Forward — Favorite Places — Prefs — Home — Help

http://nssdc.gsfc.nasa.gov/mag_-/planetary/saturn/saturn_rings_false.jpg

Favorite Places — Add Folder — Add Favorite Place — Delete — Connect — Modify — Favorite Places — Cannels — Commerce — Daily — Hot lists — Library — Medical — Misc. — Network — Search — Space places — Saturn's rings — NASA Internet Connection top level — White/Yellow Pages

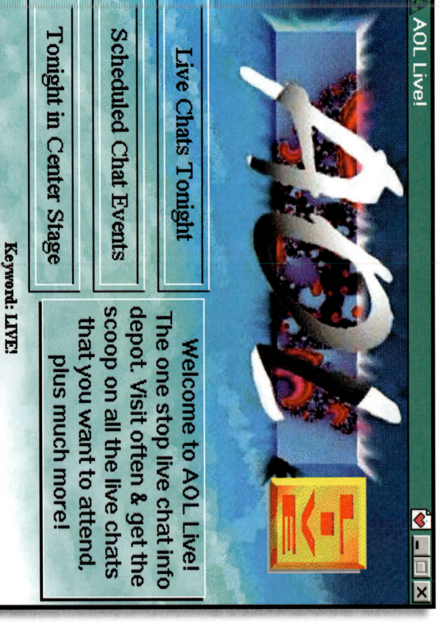

AOL Live!

Live Chats Tonight

Scheduled Chat Events

Tonight in Center Stage

Welcome to AOL Live! The one stop live chat info depot. Visit often & get the scoop on all the live chats that you want to attend, plus much more!

Keyword: LIVE!

Figure 3: *AOL Live! lists guests and meeting places for the upcoming week.*

How AOL Compares

Like cars and colas, online services are becoming increasingly difficult to tell apart. The differences are subtle, though they're evident enough to spawn legions of vehement supporters and detractors—not unlike...well...cars and colas.

Recall that America Online's primary emphasis is on community. At any one moment, thousands of people are to be found in AOL's People Connection—the area of the service where live conversations take place between members, or members and guests. Roaming among them is a small army of Guides, who are paid to provide assistance to any member in need. In addition, a number of TOS Advisors play a policing roll, standing by to discipline any member who abuses the rights of others.

AOL also provides a number of Parental Controls that allow parents to restrict access to certain areas of both AOL and the Internet. Rather than ignore the censorial potential of an online provider, and rather than provide censure itself, AOL prefers to leave the decision up to the parent. It's a defensible and effective solution to a quandary that pesters all online services.

Community aside, a number of other factors differentiate AOL from its competitors:

- A single-price strategy, with no surcharges for Internet or prime-time access.
- A simple installation and an excellent, intuitive interface; built-in graphics viewers, sound and video players.
- Financial chart animation.
- **FlashSessions** to automate most everyday mail and Internet **newsgroup** activity and minimize online time.
- Real-time **Roadtrips**— guided tours conducted by staff or members—to familiarize the newcomer with the service.
- A "Favorite Places" hierarchy for the storage of site information from both the World Wide Web and AOL itself.
- An extensive **Personal Filing Cabinet** for the storage and retrieval of mail and Internet newsgroup postings.
- A personal **News Agent**, to search AOL's information services and forward articles to you (via email) that match your specified criteria.

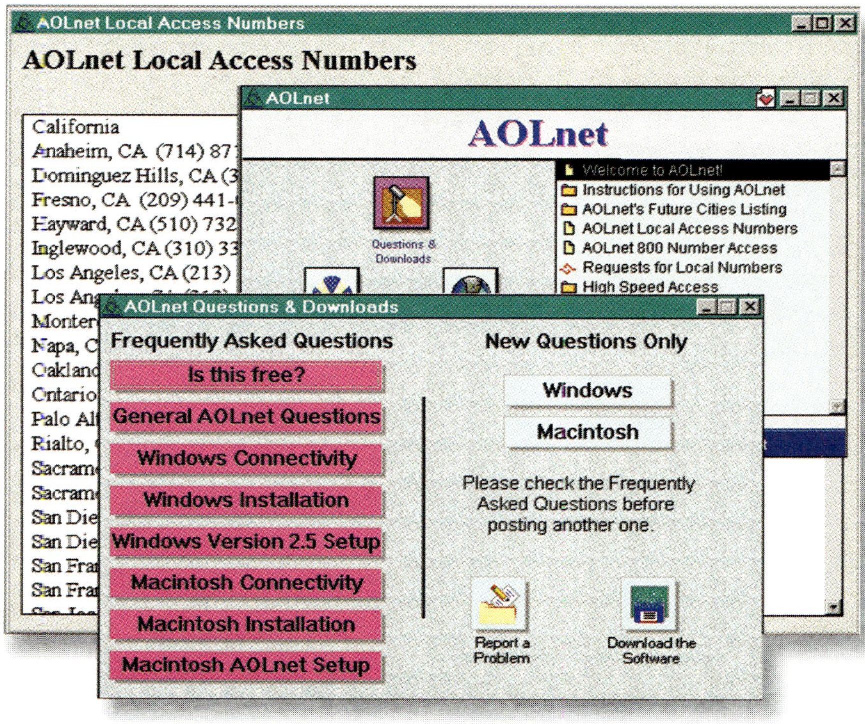

There is one significant exception, and that's long-distance access. Though AOL offers local telephone numbers in thousands of cities, there are some communities that are simply too small to justify the expense. America Online offers toll-free "800 number" access for these members, though there's a surcharge—currently $4.80 an hour—for its use.

Figure 4: AOLnet is America Online's answer to dwindling telecommunications resources.

COMMUNITY

People join online services for all kinds of reasons—curiosity, access to files, the Internet—but what brings them back month after month, year after year, is *community*. Most of us make friends and associations while we're online, whether intentional or not, and these people are why we sign on each day, to stay in touch. America Online knows that, and their emphasis on community is the consequence.

Figure 5: AOL's News Agent searches newswires for stories that meet your personal criteria. Qualifying articles are forwarded to you via email each day.

CHAT ROOMS

For many AOL members, community happens in **chat rooms**. Chat rooms are virtual "rooms" where people gather to discuss subjects of common interest in real time. They're a haven for shy people in particular, since each member is allowed as many as five **screen names**—names by which they're known online—and the screen names can be anything the member chooses (as long as the choice is unique, falls within the ten-character limit, and doesn't violate

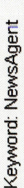

common decency) Thus, members enjoy a certain anonymity: there are no age, race, gender or political barriers.

To encourage participation in chat rooms, AOL schedules dozens of special guests each week. The guests interact with members, answering questions and making general conversation. David Bowie, Billy Graham, Garth Brooks have all appeared as AOL guests. In July of 1995, members participated in the first live online chat with astronauts aboard the Shuttle in outer space.

FORUMS AND MESSAGE BOARDS

Thousands of **forums** populate the service. Essentially, a forum is an area where people with common interests and concerns gather to exchange resources, ideas and conversation.

All forums offer a library of files—articles to read, computer programs, artwork—but the **message boards** are often the primary calling card. Message boards allow members to interact on specific subjects: the Pet Care Forum, for example, offers separate message boards not just for, say, cats, but for kittens, cat software, cat names, cat nutrition, cats and the law, and hundreds of categories of breeds, both pedigree and non-pedigree.

Unlike chat rooms, there are no temporal restraints on message boards: members interact by posting messages and returning later to read replies. Many online friendships come about this way.

ACCESS

To connect to America Online, your computer uses a modem and standard telephone lines to make a call. Proprietary software is required, but it's readily available and always free.

INSTALLATION AND SETUP

In addition to its user-friendly interface, AOL takes pride in its installation routine. For most computer configurations, all you need to do is insert the program disk, double-click an icon, and the installation program takes it from there. Not only is the program installed and configured to match your system, the installation routine even places a call to Virginia to consult AOL's database of phone numbers to find those closest to you. You will be asked to provide your name, address and billing information (AOL accepts most major credit and debit cards, or funds monthly directly from your checking account), but for the most part, all you have to do is watch. Should anything go awry, the installation program halts and offers a special toll-free telephone number for you to call for installation assistance.

AOLNET

The greatest threat to online services—indeed, the entire telecommunications industry—is the resource called **bandwidth**. As little as five years ago, nearly all online communication was just text. Today, however, graphics, sound, video—even three-dimensional **virtual realities**—are becoming the norm. While these features are exhilarating, they squander resources. Just ten seconds of sound requires almost half a megabyte

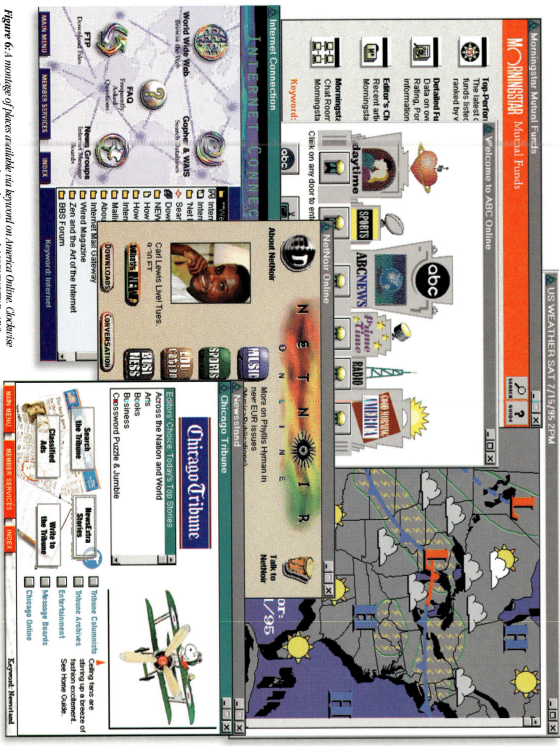

Figure 6: A montage of places available via keyword on America Online. Clockwise from the upper left: Morningstar Mutual Funds, at Keyword: MORNINGSTAR; ABC, the city weather map, at Keyword: WEATHER; Net Noir for the online African-American community, at Keyword: NET NOIR; the Chicago Tribune, at Keyword: TRIBUNE; and AOL's Internet Connection—home of all Internet activities—at Keyword: INTERNET.

of data—that's equal to 500 pages of text! As you can imagine, video and 3D are another order of magnitude (or two) beyond that.

Transferring this much information from Virginia to members' computers requires a lot of fat wires, and the scarcity of these wires—bandwidth—is the threat. The threat extends beyond America Online: every telecommunications service—from your local telephone company to the Internet—is threatened similarly. Recognizing this problem, AOL began stringing its own network of cables as early as 1994. They call this network AOLNet, and the number of cities it services is multiplying every day.

FINDING YOUR WAY AROUND

Online services suffer a common malady: If a broad variety of people are to be served, an extensive pool of resources must be available. But if the pool is adequate to serve every conceivable interest, its sheer depth—the volume of information available—becomes unwieldy and intimidating. Fortunately, AOL, like most online services, offers a number of tools—roadmaps—to assist the online explorer.

KEYWORDS

All the online services have them: a sequence of typed characters to get you from one place to another *fast!* America Online calls theirs keywords. There are thousands of them, of course, and the list is searchable. Press *Ctrl+K* (or *Command+K* on the Macintosh), or choose *Keyword* from AOL's *GoTo* menu.

THE DIRECTORY OF SERVICES

Keywords are primarily for those who know where they want to go. If you're not sure where you want to go or how to get there, you need something akin to a roadmap. Perhaps AOL's most widely promoted roadmap is the *Directory of Services* (Keyword: SERVICES). The Directory is, in fact, a searchable database of AOL's resources. You identify your criteria—the subjects that interest you—and the Directory of Services provides a listing of those AOL areas that correspond with that criteria.

WHAT'S HOT! AND WHAT'S NEW

The keywords *HOT* and *NEW* take you to areas that are being promoted, or are new to the service, respectively. It's always wise to check these periodically. Even the staff does.

SEARCHING THE LIBRARIES

Libraries, as AOL refers to them, are collections of files available for downloading onto your hard disk. *Keyword: FILE SEARCH* offers a searchable database of most of the 60,000+ files now available.

THE MEMBER DIRECTORY

A directory of AOL's members is available, and it can be searched using a variety of criteria: interests, locale, type of computer, birthdate. Participation in the directory, however, is voluntary and the information that's posted isn't checked for accuracy. This is the only way to search the AOL membership, and it's far from all-inclusive.

GETTING HELP

Any service that prides itself on "community" had better offer an abundance of help, and AOL certainly does. Moreover, help is always free: AOL stops the clock whenever you enter a help area.

The help topics below are listed in order. Try Number 1 first, then Number 2, and so on.

1. Run the AOL software and choose Search for Help On from the Help menu. You can do this without signing on. Off-line help offers an extensive searchable list of topics and will often answer your question, especially if it has to do with the most commonly asked AOL questions.

2. Go online and use Keyword: HELP. *This will take you to AOL's Member Services, a particularly comprehensive resource.*

3. Go online and use Keyword: MHM. *This will take you to AOL's Members Helping Members message board. Post your question in the appropriate folder there. Within a day or so you will have a response to your question from another member. Peer help is often the best help you can find.*

4. Go online and use Keyword: TECHLIVE. *This will take you to Tech Support Live, where you can consult AOL's Technical Support staff. This feature is available from 6 a.m. to 4 a.m. (Eastern time) seven days a week.*

5. Ask a Guide. Choose Lobby from the Go To menu, and once you arrive, look around for someone with the word "Guide" in their name. Guides are a particularly friendly form of help, and they're on duty 24 hours a day, seven days a week, 365 days a year.

6. Send email to Customer Relations. Use the Keyword: HELP. In the Help window, click the Have Questions? button. You'll hear back from them in a day or two.

7. Call Customer Relations at 1-800-827-3338 or 1-800-827-6364. They're open from 6 a.m. to 4 a.m. (Eastern time) seven days a week. It's a toll-free call in the continental US, and there's no charge for this service.

HOW TO SIGN UP

As do most online services, America Online offers a trial period whereby you can go online and get a feel for the place without paying. In fact, trials are the best way to choose an online service: join one for a month, then quit. Do this for each service that interests you. When you've seen them all, you'll know which one suits you best, and your research won't have cost you a dime.

REFERRALS

This is the best way to join America Online. If you know someone who is a member, ask them for a referral. If they don't know how to do referrals, tell them to use *Keyword: FRIEND*.

Why is this the best method? Because your colleague will receive free online time (currently ten hours) if you join. It's a nice thing to do for a friend.

REQUEST A SIGN-UP KIT

If you don't know of anyone who is an AOL member, or if you want software right now, call 1-800-827-3338 and ask for a startup kit. It's free.

LOOK FOR FREE DISKS IN MAGAZINES

AOL gives away more disks than a politician gives handshakes. Visit your favorite newsstand and look for AOL disks packaged with computer or online magazines.

THE OFFICIAL AMERICA ONLINE TOUR GUIDE & MEMBERSHIP KIT

If you're sure you want to join the service, visit your local bookstore and obtain a copy of *The Official America Online Tour Guide and Membership Kit*. The kit is complete with a 500-page Tour Guide, software, and 20 hours of online time, which offsets the cost of the kit nicely.

Tom Lichty is author of six computer books, including Design Principles for Desktop Publishers *(voted Book of the Year by the Computer Press Association in 1988),* America Online's Internet, *and* The America Online Tour Guide, *(an alternate of the Book-of-the-Month Club in December, 1992, and the featured offering of the Quality Paperback Book Club in February, 1993). Tom lives at the base of Oregon's Mount Hood, where he specializes in the design, desktop publishing and online communications fields of the computer industry.*

UPLOADING AND DOWNLOADING FILES ON AMERICA ONLINE

If you want to add formatting (or even graphics) to your email, download your messages.

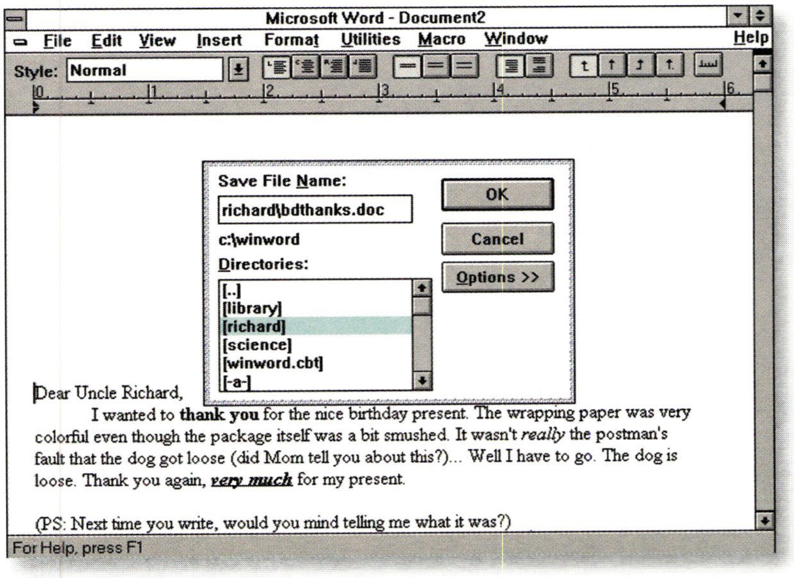

By Robert Lock

Composing and sending short email letters on America Online is easy and convenient. You can compose mail **offline** (meaning you're in the AOL software that's on your computer, but not connected to the AOL host computer) or you can compose it **online** while the AOL meter is running.

Writing long email letters on AOL, whether composed offline or online, has several disadvantages. One is that you can't **spell check** your work. For some of us, that's a big disadvantage. Another disadvantage is that you can't format your work. Long email compositions are entered and transmitted on AOL as running text. You can't use *italics* or **boldface** or even tabs. If you're used to punching the tab key to create an indented line in a letter, and try that while writing an AOL email online, you may accidentally send your letter before it's even finished.

IT'S EASY TO CREATE AND SEND LETTERS FROM YOUR WORD PROCESSOR

You can create your letter, complete with formatting and tabs and the opportunity to use your spell checker, on your own word processor. Let's say you're using *Word for Windows* to write your letter. Once you're finished, save it. Make a note to yourself on where you're saving it. Your version of *Word* is in a **directory**, and will have **subdirectories**. It doesn't matter where you save it, but it does matter that you know where it is.

Now go to America Online and open it up. In AOL, go to *Compose Mail.* You can do this offline or online. Select your friend's name from the *Address Book* and enter it on your mail by clicking *To:* Then enter your heading. In the message field say something like, "Here's a letter for you in *Word for Windows*, version 2 format." Now comes the *Attach File* icon. Click the *Attach File* icon. A window will open that shows you a directory. It will probably look like Figure 2.

Now you have to find your letter. Click on *C:*, and the screen will change to a list of directories. Click on the down arrow until you come to your word processor directory. (My directory, where *Word for Windows* resides, is called Winword.) Then find your file and click on it. You may have to go one layer deeper if you have several subdirectories. When the name of the correct file appears in the box, click on it and it will reappear in the file name line at the top. Now click *OK*. The icon in your *Compose Mail* window will change from *Attach* to *Detach.* That means your *Word* file containing your letter is now "attached" to your email note. Click *Send.* After a moment, a box will appear that says *Now Uploading File, X minutes remaining.* Wait patiently, and you're done.

When your friend next logs on, he or she will get email from you with an icon selection that says *Download Now.* When they click on it, a box will appear that says *Now Downloading File, about X minutes remaining.* This box shows the name of the file, and they should write that down or remember it, including the directory where it is being stored.

Dear Uncle Richard,

I wanted to **thank you** for the nice birthday present. The wrapping paper was very colorful even though the package itself was a bit smushed. It wasn't *really* the postman's fault that the dog got loose (did Mom tell you about this?)... Well I have to go. The dog is loose. Thank you again, *very much* for my present.

(PS: Next time you write, would you mind telling me what it was?)

Figure 1: Here are the subdirectories presently in the directory Winword. Note the **c:\winword.** This tells you where you are within your disk's file structure. In this case, our read letter is named **baltbanks.doc.** Everything else is there just to tell us how to find it: **c:\winword\richard\baltbanks.doc** means we're on the **c:** disk drive; on the **c:** disk drive we're in a directory called **winword;** within the winword directory we're in a subdirectory called **richard,** and inside that subdirectory we're pointing at a file named **baltbanks.doc.** By following these naming conventions we can find any file, anywhere on our disks.

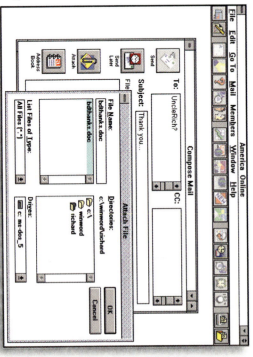

Figure 2: Here's our file, after we've first clicked on **c:,** then on **winword,** then on **richard;** then on **baltbanks.doc.**

Directories And Subdirectories

The file structure in your computer is organized like a big tree. You might have hundreds and even thousands of files on your hard disk drive, and your computer helps keeps track of them for you. One problem with files under early versions of DOS and Windows is that the prefix on a filename is limited to eight characters. This means you end up with a lot of files with cryptic names that you always forget two hours after you make them up. Fortunately Windows 95 addresses that problem by allowing you to have very long file names of over 200 characters. Instead of

LETRM610.DOC

I could name my file

LETTER TO RICHARD MANSFIELD JUNE 10 95.DOC

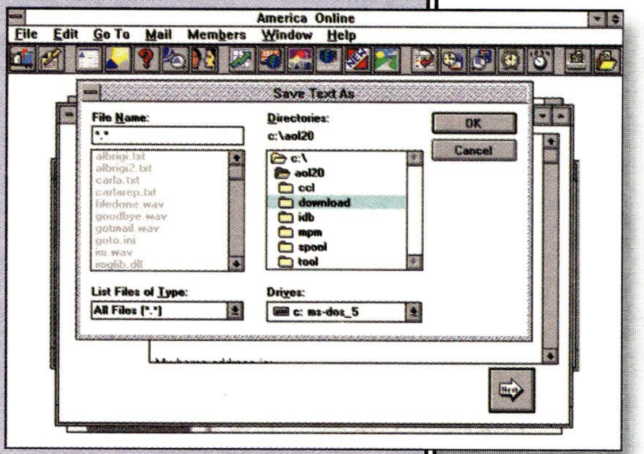

One way to help organize files, and to make them easier to keep up with, is to make wise use of directories and subdirectories. If you imagine a big tree in your front yard, the trunk would be the main directory, in most computers it's the C: directory. As we go up the trunk, major branches go off in different directions. These are like your primary directories, say, those of *Windows* and *Lotus* and DOS and *WordPerfect* and AOL. If we then follow any one of these major branches, we come to smaller branches and twigs. When we need to save a file, the computer does it for us, after we give the file a name. But when we need to find that file, it hasn't always been saved in a way that's convenient for us to quickly find. That's why we humans need to have a basic understanding of where (down which twig on which branch) the computer has saved a file.

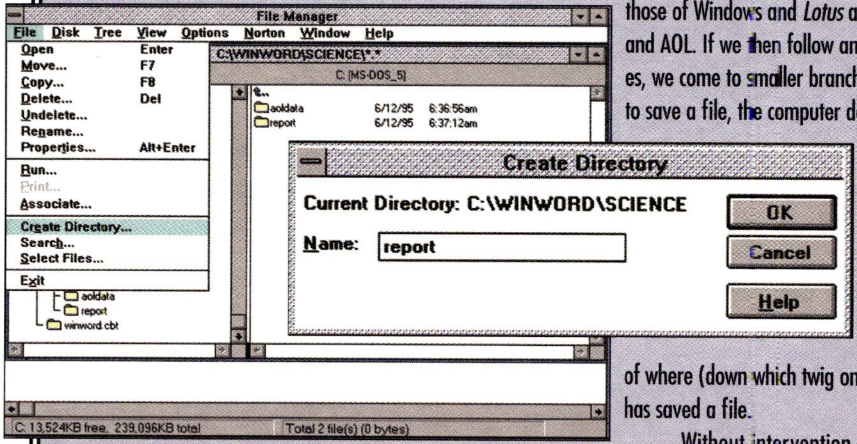

Without intervention from you, AOL will probably put any files you download in **C:\AOL25\DOWN-LOAD*.*** (where *.* is the file name, prefix + extension you've chosen).

Fortunately, we can also choose where to put it. If you're using AOL to do research for your science project, it might be a lot easier to decide beforehand that you want

and you're writing your science project in *Word for Windows*, it might be a lot easier to end up with everything in one place. Whether you're downloading a file from AOL or simply saving some research you've called up on your screen, you'll do this the same way. In your *Word* directory (the main branch), you might previously define a subdirectory named **SCIENCE**.

In that directory (a branch in our analogy), you might create the two more subdirectories called **AOLDATA** and **REPORT**. Then you could save all of the files and information you find in the subdirectory **C:\WORD\SCIENCE\AOLDATA*.***, and you could save your own writing and revisions in **C:\WORD\SCI-ENCE\REPORT*.***. To learn how to create your own subdirectories, go to the File Manager in your *Windows Accessories* or *Main* icon and click on *File Manager*. You can use the ^ function to get more specific instructions if you find you need them.

You should plan this out before you start. It's a lot easier to establish these branches and twigs before you're in America Online and have to save something. Once they're established, you can easily get to them when you're looking at the directory box AOL presents you when you select *Save* or *Download*. Using directories and subdirectories thoughtfully is a good way to keep things more organized than having them all around your computer and trying to find them later. This is especially true if you're having to decipher those little eight-character filenames you made up and no longer remember.

After signing off, the recipient will need to go to Word's *File* menu and click *Open*. Then, they should select the AOL:Download directory, and click on the file from you. And there will be your letter, just like you sent it.

If you're sending a file in a word processor format, your friend doesn't have to have the same word processing software can open files in other formats. Most word processing software can open files in other formats. That's why your friend has to know in which format you've sent your letter, or you have to know what word processor they use. *Word for Windows*, for example, can save a file in a *WordPerfect* format. (To do this, you'll use the *Save As* command, instead of *Save*. Use the *Help* (F1) feature and then *Search* for *Save As* in your word processor if you don't yet know how.)

This sounds complicated, but once you've done it a few times it's easy. You can also send other documents this way, including things that are too long for email, formatted lists where the formatting is an important part of the message—even graphics.

Figure 3: When you have a file to download, you can create your own name. Make sure you keep the appropriate extension. If it's a .doc file, keep that extension so the person you're sending it to can easily recognize it as a word processor file.

Figures 4 & 5: In a program like File Manager, you can create additional subdirectories (branches) as places to save, and more easily find, your files. Within the Winword directory, we've created a subdirectory named science. One more layer down, inside the science subdirectory, we're creating a subdirectory called report.

Robert Lock is the Chairman and President of **The PC Press, Inc.** He founded COMPUTE! Publications in 1979. COMPUTE! became the fastest growing home-computing publisher in the US during the early 1980s. The company's magazines achieved a combined circulation of over 1,000,000 by 1985, and COMPUTE! Books published over 200 titles. COMPUTE! launched the first "beginner's guide" series of books in 1982 and was the first publishing company to bind diskettes into newsstand magazines. Mr. Lock sold the company to the American Broadcasting Companies in 1983. In 1987, he co-founded and launched the Game Player's family of electronic gaming publications.

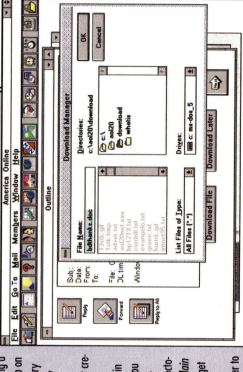

Figure 6: Here's what Uncle Richard sees when he's ready to download your file.

COMPUSERVE

By David Haskin

CompuServe is the oldest online service. And if you're doing research or otherwise require considerable depth of information—CompuServe is still the best.

COMPUSERVE INFORMATION SERVICE BASICS

CompuServe is the oldest online service, dating back to 1979. By high-tech standards, that's ancient—it is well before the introduction of the IBM PC.

These days, CompuServe runs neck and neck with America Online for the honor of having the largest number of subscribers (about 3 million each). Depending on the day and whom you talk to, one service will have surged ahead of the other.

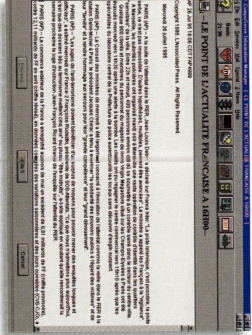

Figure 1: *CompuServe's international presence means that its forums get input from around the world. It also has features like news from the French Associated Press.*

But those two services—and Prodigy—all look and feel different and have different strengths and weaknesses. It would be wrong to take the following analogy too seriously, but if the other online services' environments feel like prosperous, friendly, mid-America communities (think sunny spring weekend in Des Moines), CompuServe would be a university town (think Boston). CompuServe, being the oldest, offers greater depth and variety to scientists, researchers, intellectuals, computer enthusiasts

or anyone else looking for a large, thorough, organized, world-class information resource as an alternative to the still-chaotic Internet. But CompuServe is frivolous or whimsical only here and there.

PRODUCT SUPPORT

Perhaps one of CompuServe's greatest assets is its product support forums. More than 900 hardware and software companies offer customer assistance on CompuServe—more than any other service or even on the Internet. The chances are good that if you have difficulty with a software or hardware product, you can find answers and get results on CompuServe.

In each support forum, you can leave messages for the vendor's technical support staff. This is an efficient way to communicate if your problem isn't urgent. In fact, it also can be faster if your vendor's support lines are busy and you can't get through. You also can post questions and have other users of the product answer. Finally, you can download software to support your product. Sometimes that software fixes your existing software or hardware and other times it adds new speed or features to it.

WORLD-WIDE COVERAGE

CompuServe also is the only commercial service with a truly world-wide presence. The company claims to have paying subscribers in 150 countries, with direct connections to CompuServe from most of those nations. This international presence is significant.

First, it gives the forums a decidedly international flavor that can be both useful and fascinating. Say you want to take a bicycle trip in Australia. Chances are that, if you log on to CompuServe's bicycling forum, you can ask an Australian about the best places to ride.

This international presence also is important during a trip. You can log onto CompuServe from virtually any place in the world and check your email and forum messages. And, if you access the Internet via CompuServe, you also can log on to that sprawling online world from anywhere in the real world. Traveling cyber-citizens will tell you that without CompuServe this is usually a daunting task.

Finally, you can keep track of news in foreign countries in which you might have a special interest. Included in the CompuServe service are a number of international news services. You also can discuss events first-hand with CompuServe subscribers from those countries.

EXTENSIVE REFERENCE

Since its inception, CompuServe has had a reputation as an excellent place to do research. It features several online encyclopedias, including Grolier's and the Academic American Encyclo-

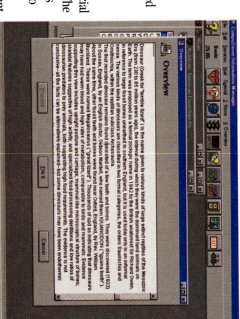

Figure 2: *CompuServe is extremely information-rich. This is the online ver...*
Grolier's Encyclopedia.

118

logging on to CompuServe (using special software you can download from CompuServe. Go NLSupport).

CompuServe's basic hardware and communications capabilities have at times been out of date in the fast-moving field of online services. However, the company is fighting to catch up. Most notably, until recently the fastest connections available to CompuServe were at 14,400 baud, with many cities having only 9,600 baud connections. Internet surfers quickly become frustrated with such slow speeds.

CompuServe claims that by mid-1996 all dial-in connections will be capable of 28,800 baud. If you're looking to subscribe to a service and CompuServe's other advantages attract you, make sure the connections in your area are fast enough to suit you.

Like the other online services, Net addicts can spend quite a bit of money on online fees accessing the Internet through CompuServe. If you spend much time on the Net, you'll get off more inexpensively using a dedicated Internet service provider.

Figure 3: CompuServe offers reasonably complete access to the Internet. However, it has been slow to offer high-speed connections to the Internet. And, like the other commercial online services, you can wind up spending a lot of money surfing the Net.

pedia. It also includes a wide variety of other resources, including the Information Please almanacs and several online services that scan through dozens of sources for the information you request.

Many of these information resources will cost you additional online fees and some are not easy to navigate. But, overall, CompuServe currently does a better job than its competitors at putting a world of information at your fingertips.

ACCESSING THE NET

CompuServe's legacy as the oldest online service doesn't mean that it always reacts quickly to change. It has been, for example, slow to provide the level of connections to the Internet that its competitors provide, although it is racing furiously to catch up. It recently acquired a large Internet-related firm, Spry Communications, to aid it in its struggle.

CompuServe's Internet access is decent and is improving quickly. Like other services with more thorough Internet access, such as America Online, you can directly access the Internet after you've logged on to CompuServe. You also can log on to the Internet separately without first

popular services. For example, most of the product support forums are extended services. Also, you'll pay extended online fees for almost all the areas from which you download software.

• Internet services. Like other commercial online vendors, CompuServe charges you extra for accessing the Internet. You get some free hours each month (currently three free hours). After you use those up, you'll pay an additional fee (currently $2.50 per hour) for Internet access. By comparison, depending on your location, you can buy virtually unlimited Internet access from Internet-only providers for between $15 and $25 per month. And often at 28,800 baud.

Technically, CompuServe's electronic mail service isn't free. But you do receive a free credit each month for the equivalent of 90 three-page letters, which makes the service essentially free for most users. If you use up your credit, CompuServe charges a nominal amount per-character in your messages. If you send computer files, such as a shareware game to a friend, CompuServe also charges extra.

To repeat an important caveat, these fees are changing rapidly, as are the fees at the other commercial online services. Everyone's waiting to see what Microsoft will do with its new service.

GETTING AROUND

To navigate CompuServe, you use CompuServe Information Manager (CIM). Most people now use the version of CIM for Windows, called WinCIM. WinCIM is icon-based—you can click on an icon to go from one area to another. However, WinCIM isn't as straightforward or as well-organized as America Online's or The Microsoft Network's user interface.

Figure 5: The Favorite Places window lists the CompuServe resources you use most often, and speeds you on your way to them.

FEES AND CHARGES

Discussions of fees charged by any commercial online service quickly become out of date. That's because the commercial online world is highly competitive and subject to rapid change.

The same is true of CompuServe—even company officials acknowledge that prices in effect at this writing will change soon. Still, CompuServe currently has a three-tier pricing system. Those tiers are:

• Basic services. This is basic news, weather, sports, travel and reference services. For a flat monthly fee (at this writing, the fee is $9.95 per month) you can use these services to your heart's content.

• Extended services. This includes all the rest of CompuServe's non-Internet services. CompuServe charges you an additional hourly fee for access to them (at this writing, $4.80 per hour). Not surprisingly, the extended fees apply to some CompuServe's more

Figure 4: WinCIM's opening screen includes icons that lead you to the major areas of the service.

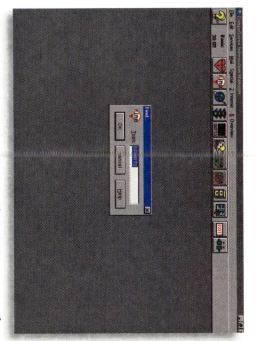

Figure 6: The Find dialog helps you locate specific CompuServe resources if you don't otherwise know where to go.

In fairness, while WinCIM doesn't offer quite as smooth an interface as others, it's not difficult to use. As with most areas in which CompuServe has fallen behind, the company claims it is working hard to make WinCIM easier to use.

And, beyond its considerable depth of information, there are a couple of additional clear advantages to CIM. First, it's multi-lingual—it is available in a number of other languages such as Spanish. Also, it's available for DOS for those who wish to keep using that operating system.

There are several ways to find your way around CompuServe. First, the opening screen of WinCIM displays icons for the broad areas of the service. Clicking on an icon leads you to a window that offers more choices. Often, clicking on a choice in that window leads to more choices still—you can descend through many layers of CompuServe in this way.

To find a resource on CompuServe, use the Find dialog box, accessed from the Services menu. Here's where navigation can get a bit tricky. If your search is simple, the Find command is easy to use. For example, if you open the Find dialog box and type "games," it lists all CompuServe resources that relate to games. However, say you're looking for a forum or other resource to help you figure out an obscure DOS command. It's not obvious what you should type into the Find dialog box as your query, nor is it obvious which of the hits you'll see listed after you run Find is the correct one.

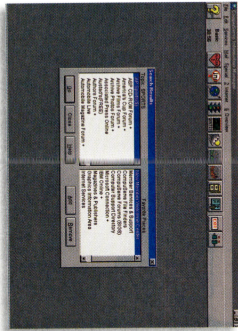

Figure 7: Use Find to see a list of all the CompuServe resources that may be related to your request. This isn't a particularly efficient way of finding things, however.

You can, of course, download as many files as you want.

- Double-click on an intriguing file to read a description.
- Click on the Retrieve button if you decide to download that file.
- Click on the icon to show the libraries window for that forum.

GETTING THE GOODS

Downloading files, like so much on CompuServe, isn't difficult. The procedure goes something like this:

- Using the FIND or GO commands, you go to the forum you're interested in.

---

date with CompuServe is the attractive, helpful and free *CompuServe Magazine*.

COMPUSERVE FOR FAMILIES

By their own admission, CompuServe had fallen behind America Online in content of interest to families. This is another area in which the company claims it is working overtime to catch up. For example, CompuServe is beefing up its collection of online magazines. They recently added People Magazine, Sports Illustrated and Rolling Stone. Also, CNN's new site is large and elaborate.

Among CompuServe's 900 forums, there are many that appeal to both kids and their parents. Some of the more popular forums include gardening, home fix-ups, health and genealogy. There also are forums devoted strictly to teens, and chat rooms where teens can talk with each other online in real time.

One area where you shouldn't expect much improvement—resources for pre-schoolers. Currently, there are no such resources on CompuServe, and they don't seem intent on improving that situation.

STRENGTHS:

- Great resource for researchers and others looking for a massive and varied amount of well-organized information.
- Product support.
- International coverage.

WEAKNESSES:

- Navigation and visual interface is not elegant (they're working on it).
- Interface is not as intuitive as other services. (ditto)
- A little behind in some of its technical capabilities. (ditto)

Use the GO command if you know the name of the section to which you'd like to go. Just click on the GO button in the toolbar (it looks like a traffic light) and type the name of the resource.

CompuServe is growing fast and is adding new features every day. To keep track, check out its New section, which the service updates every day. Another way to keep up-to-

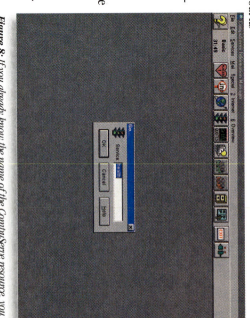

Figure 8: If you already know the name of the CompuServe resource, you can move there directly with the GO command.

CompuServe Information Service
5000 Arlington Center Blvd.
Columbus, OH 43220
800-848-8199;
Email: CompuServe: 70006,101
Internet home page: http://www.com
puserve.com

David Haskin *is a writer specializing in computer-related topics. Formerly a newspaper journalist and software executive, David is a regular contributor to PC Magazine, Computer Life and Computer Shopper. He is the author of six books about computers including* The Complete Idiot's Guide to Multimedia, The Complete Idiot's Guide to PC Games *and* Using PC Tools for Windows.

EXPLORING PRODIGY

By Jerri Clark Kirby

Co-owned by Sears and I.B.M., Prodigy went online in 1988. There are versions for DOS, Macintosh and Windows. For a free, 10-hour trial membership kit, phone 1-800-PRODIGY.

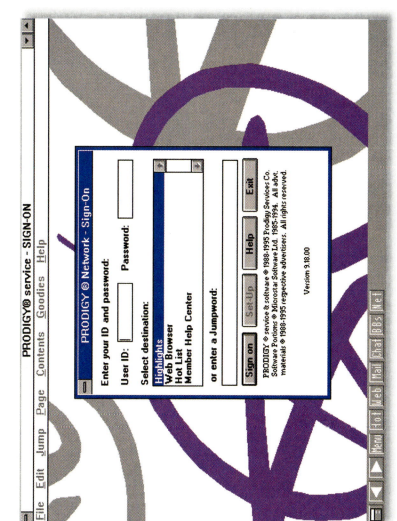

Figure 1: *Prodigy Sign-On Screen will look like this once you've installed your Prodigy software.*

CURRENT MEMBERSHIP PLANS: AN OVERVIEW

BASIC PLAN: $ 9.95/mo. Five free hours. Prodigy features: 2400 / 9600 / 14,400 (where available) BPS: Enrollment for up to six family members; $ 2.95/hr. For usage beyond five hours 30/30 PLAN: $29.95/mo. Thirty free hours. Note that this plan is popular with people who spend a lot of time on CHAT, WWW or writing **email online**.

Commercial and Member Help features are not timed. Fees are charged for premium features like Baseball Manager, Newspapers Online, Strategic Investor and Ziffnet for Prodigy. Each premium feature provider has a customer service section with details. No timed charges apply while you shop, view commercial advertising, use Member Services or Member Help, or use most features listed in the Prodigy Fees Section under "Extra-fee Services," because these are already billed separately. You may change to another plan anytime, online, effective with the starting of your next billing period.

A billing symbol appears in the lower right hand corner of your screen when you are online. If the feature you are using is free, or an extra-fee feature, the symbol is [****]. That means that your time isn't currently being charged against your basic Plan. However, when no symbol appears, [ ], you are being timed under your Plan.

The person responsible for the account is the "A" member. This person's credit card is billed, and he or she controls all access by household members to specific features which may be adult in nature or incur charges. The "A" member can see how much online time each person has used, up to and including the previous day. All members can check their own usage plus the overall time used by the household. For full access information, Jump: Member Access. (In Prodigy, you can always leap to another location within the service by typing in a Jump target.)

SIGNING ON

Free software from Prodigy contains easy installation instructions. When you've installed the software and reached the sign-on screen, you are ready to enroll, which occurs automatically the first time you connect with Prodigy online. Prompts allow you to choose a local phone number; provide Prodigy with information about yourself; indicate that you understand and agree to membership rules; and create your own **password**.

Tab to or place the cursor in the flashing I.D. box. Enter the temporary I.D. number and password, provided with your membership kit. Once online, you'll be given a new, permanent number and you wil be asked to create your own password. Press Enter. Click Sign-on to connect to Prodigy.

ONLINE

The Welcome screen will direct you to choose the local phone number that your **modem** will dial to connect with Prodigy. You will be asked to enter your area code and phone number prefix. In a series of very easy-to-follow set-up screens, you'll provide phone/modem information. Try to choose a local number to avoid long distance charges. You'll also choose an alternate number.

Follow the screens, click on flashing screens and fill in information, push Enter and it will be recorded. The final screen asks you to accept the Member Agreement; after reading it, click on I Accept. You can print the Member Agreement by selecting the File Menu (upper left screen); click to open the options. Be sure your printer is on. Click on Print.

You now create your own password. It can have six to ten letters or numbers. Create a word known only to you. You will be asked to type in

prodigy®

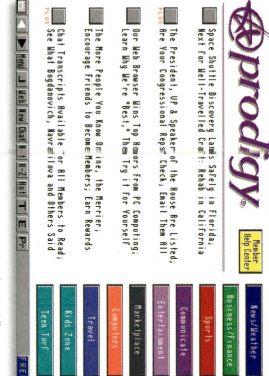

Figure 2: *This is Prodigy's Main Highlights screen. You may choose from 15 different screens: (Jump: Change Highlights)*

- Space Shuttle Discovery Lands Safely in Florida; Next for Well-Travelled Craft: Rehab in California
- The President, UP & Speaker of the House Are Listed, Are Your Congressional Reps? Check; Email Them All
  - PLUS
- Our Web Browser Wins Top Honors From PC Computing; Learn Why We're "Best," Then Try it for Yourself
- The More People You Know Online, the Merrier; Encourage Friends to Become Members; Earn Rewards
- Chat Transcripts Available for All Members to Read; See What Bogdanovich, Navratilova and Others Said
  - PLUS

News/Weather · Business/Finance · Sports · Communicate · Entertainment · Marketplace · Computers · Travel · Kids Zone · Teen Turf · FREE

the password twice, pressing Enter each time. A screen will now welcome you as the newest Prodigy member.

HIGHLIGHTS PAGES

When you connect to Prodigy, you'll see Prodigy's main Highlights screen. You may change to another screen by Jump: Change Highlights. You'll get a screen with button for the 15 Highlights screens currently available. Click on each button to see its screen. Some choices are: Sports, Shopping, Home/Family/Kids, News/Weather, Reference. After you choose a screen, click twice on Menu on the bottom Tool Bar to return to the main Highlights screen.

COMMUNICATING ON PRODIGY

EMAIL

Private messages can be sent to any Prodigy member, in the same house or across the continent. It is received from others, can be downloaded into a file or printed out. Each time you sign onto Prodigy, your Highlights screen will flash an envelope if you have new mail. You simply click on the envelope and the mail menu will pop up. Click on Open to read your new mail. Click on Write to respond. The Write screen will appear.

In July 1995, Prodigy upgraded its system to enable its members to check spelling, format or mark messages "urgent," and send carbon copies. You can also now send messages that are about seven times the previous length, and scroll text and list boxes. Step-by-step screens prompt the user and make it a snap to do whatever you're interested in doing.

MEMBER LIST

You can locate another Prodigy member's online address by Jump: Member List. Select the By Name option, type two or more letters of a member's last name or full last name, and part of first name. Select OK. A list of names that match your request will appear. Click on any name to get more information and/or the Prodigy address.

If you want to search by state and/or city, select Search by State. You'll be given a choice to search all states or to select a state (by clicking on the name of the state). Then you'll have the option to search all cities or one city; again, click on any name to get more information.

Compatible listings will appear. Click on any name to get more information.

You must enter your own name and address in the Member List to be listed. Simply Jump: Member List; follow the prompts to create your own directory listing.

INTERNET ACCESS

Jump INTERNET to access World Wide Web (WWW), USENET news services, to send Internet Email, to use FTP/Gopher, for a glossary of net definitions and answers to common questions. Prodigy provides a quick tutorial and information on system requirements.

Anytime a word is highlighted, as shown in Figure 4, you can click on that word and you will be taken to further information on that subject. To return to the home screen, you simply click on the Back button at the top of the page. To visit a new place, click on the Document URL: block, highlight it, press your enter key to remove the address. Type in the new address. Suppose you want to go to a travel magazine online called

BULLETIN BOARDS

Prodigy has almost 70 bulletin boards, covering over 2,000 subjects. Messages you post on a bulletin board are public—any Prodigy member can read them. Special interest bulletin boards cover games, pet care, health care, aviation, genealogy, music, food, computing, careers and many other topics. You can download free information, photos, maps, software, games—the list is long. Once you find the board you like, just use the Jump command to get to it. To learn about Bulletin Boards, Jump; Board Questions. Click on BB Guidelines, Jump; Bulletin Boards for an A-Z list of all boards.

Tip: Bulletin Boards are a timed feature, meaning that after you've used the free time allocated to you through your payment plan, you will be charged for time spent online at these boards.

CHAT

In CHAT, you talk to other Prodigy members live. You can type messages back and forth with up to 25 people at once in a normal CHAT room. You can also exchange IM's (Instant Messages) in a private screen with another person. There are auditoriums for guest speakers provided by Prodigy at scheduled times. Prodigy schedules frequent guest sessions, free of charge, for users to ask questions about using Prodigy. All speakers are advertised on sign-on screens well ahead of time. To learn about CHAT, Jump: CHAT. Click on the information buttons on the right hand side of the screen to get full details. Warning: CHAT is a timed feature and is extremely addictive! An appealing feature of CHAT is that you select a nickname which prevents other chatters from knowing your real identity. You may also elect to conceal your Prodigy ID number from chatters.

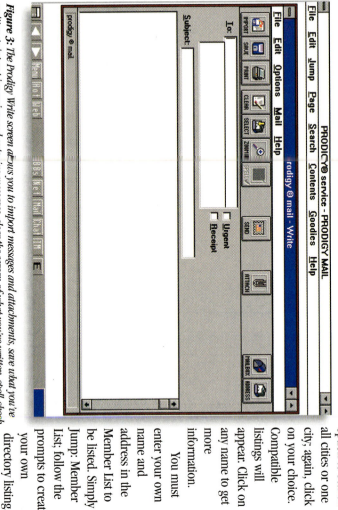

Figure 3: *The Prodigy Write screen allows you to import messages and attachments, save what you've written, print out incoming and outgoing messages, clear the screen of what you've written, spell-check your outgoing email, send your mail with attachments, check your mailbox and use your address book. Click on the button for the feature you want. If you cannot understand the instructions, click on Help at the top of the screen.*

TravelASSIST. Simply remove, by highlighting and pressing Enter, "http://antares.prodigy.com/welcome.htm", and type in:http://travelassist.com; press your Enter key. You will be taken to the home page of TravelASSIST Magazine.

Like Chat, exploring the WEB can be fascinating and time consuming. After your initial membership time is used each month, the WEB becomes a timed feature. Also it's a good idea to take Prodigy's free tutorial **before** you start to explore the Internet. An Internet Forum Bulletin Board enables you to keep up-to-date, share Internet finds and hints, and get questions answered. Jump: Internet.

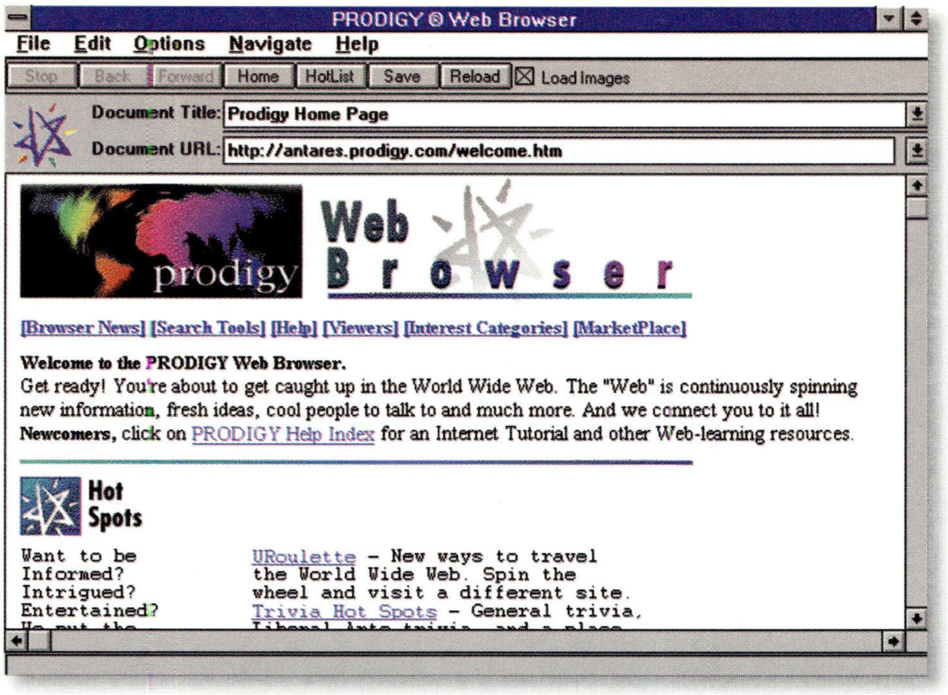

GETTING AROUND PRODIGY

When you sign on to Prodigy, the Highlights screen has buttons representing features available. Each Highlights page offers different features. To the left of the screen, numbered gray buttons indicate the day's headlines on the right. A black frame flashes around the first headline button when you sign on. You can either tab to and Enter, or click on any numbered button to get the story page. Clicking on the Menu button at the bottom of the page, or on the Highlights button in the lower left hand corner, will take you back to the first Highlights screen..

FUNCTION KEYS

Function keys can be used instead of clicking with the mouse or using the tool bar for specific actions. To learn more, Jump: Function keys. Uses are:

F1 – Help Offline, topics for signing on; online, help on current page.
F2 – Action Help with complete order process when you purchase online.
F3 – ViewPath Opens window list of JumpWords in pathlist.

Figure 4: Prodigy's Home Web page. To read the page, you click on the down arrow on the lower right hand side, or use the Page Down button on your keyboard.

F4 – Path Goes to up to 20 features in your chosen order.
F5 – Highlights Goes to main Highlights from wherever you are online.
F6 – Jump To Goes to any feature for which you type a jumpword.
F7 – A-Z Index An Alphabetical listing of all jumpwords.
F8 – Xref Allows you to view information related to feature you are in.
F9 – Menu Goes from current page back through all pages you've visited, to the page where you made a menu choice. stopping at main Highlights.

Tip: The JUMP function is perhaps the most valuable. Use F6 or click on J at screen bottom for a Jump screen to type a jumpword. Use F7 or click on A-Z for a complete list.

TOOL BAR

With a click, the Tool Bar gives quick access to many commands.

Each family member may customize Tool Bar settings for personal preferences. Sign on to Prodigy; click on the Goodies Menu at the top, follow instructions to add, arrange or remove commands from your personal Tool Bar. Then, click the button for the command of your choice. You may modify your Tool Bar anytime.

CUSTOM CHOICES

You may choose many activities requiring additional fees. Choices available include investment tools, stock market analysis programs, computer games, fantasy sports, (you may own, manage and control your own sports team), extended research facilities, downloading computer software and reference material, and access to other online services and newspapers. All features must be ordered by the "A" member. For information on features and costs, Jump: Custom Choice.

DOWNLOADING INFORMATION ON PRODIGY

Jump to the page you want to copy. Click on the EDIT menu on upper left top of screen. Click on the COPY command. Prodigy will give you an option screen to copy a single page or an entire article, (called 'story'). Click on the story button for all or on the page button for one page. The copy box will show the text that you've copied in a few seconds. Click on the copy button to move text to the Windows Clipboard. Click on Cancel to close the copy box.

Click on the upper right hand corner arrow to make the screen smaller. Start another program, such as Paintbrush. Click on Edit again, choose Paste. The information will be copied onto the screen. You can now save the file for reading, editing or printing. Close the Windows Paintbrush file, click on the arrow of your smaller screen to return it to full size.

For downloading email and attachments, simply click on Save and follow screen prompts. Prodigy's instructions are clear.

To take a full picture of a screen, click on Edit. Choose the Snapshot command. Select Clipboard, Printer or File option. Click OK. The image will be sent to the Clipboard, Printed out (this may take quite a while), or to the designated file.

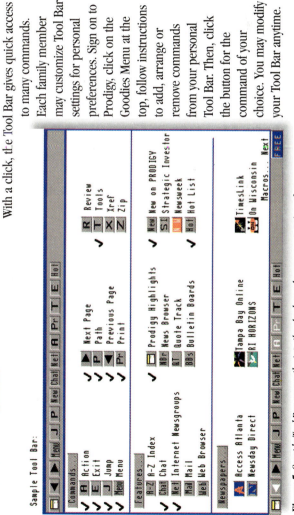

Figure 5: Sample Tool Bar across the top; the check marks represent options that are on. Choose your favorites and change them anytime.

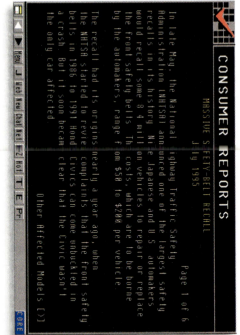

In late May, the National Highway Traffic Safety Administration (NHTSA) announced one of the largest safety recalls in its history. Nine Japanese and US automakers would recall some 8.4 million vehicles to repair or replace the front safety belts. In costs, which are to be borne by the automakers, range from $58 to $208 per vehicle.

The recall had its origins nearly a year ago, when complaints that the front safety belts in 1986 to 1991 Honda Civics can come unbuckled in a crash. But it soon became clear that the Civic wasn't the only car affected.

Other Affected Models [>]

Figure 6: This is a SNAPSHOT of a screen, instructions below

ONLINE HELP

For account information, tutorials on working Prodigy software, explanations of timed and free features, phone numbers, sending messages to Prodigy and getting the most out of your membership,

Jump: Member Help.

If you click on the 3 button on the left of the above screen, you'll get the following screen:

FREQUENTLY ASKED QUESTIONS

What is Jump? How do you use it?
Jump is the command used to go to a specific area on Prodigy. Try Jump: quick start for some tips on using Jump.

How do I return to a previous screen?
Select M or Menu at the bottom of the current screen, click on the button and you will be back at your last screen.

How do I get to the next page or the rest of the article I am reading?
Click on the right hand arrow key to scroll down or use the **page up** or **page down** keyboard buttons to go to the previous or next page.

What is a Path?
Path brings the information you want to see to your screen fast and in the order you want it. Your personal Pathlist can include up to 20 destinations on Prodigy. Jump: Path

What is ZIP?
The **Zip** key on the Command Bar is used when you have looked at an ad and and want to go back to where you were.

How do I know what Jumpwords to use?
Select A-Z from the bottom of the screen. Click. This gives you a list of **Jumpwords**. You can move through this Index with the next and back arrow keys or you can use **page up** or **page down**.

Is Prodigy available 24 hours a day?
Prodigy is available 24 hours a day except from 4:00 am - 7:00 am ET on Wednesday and Thursday when the service is down for maintenance.

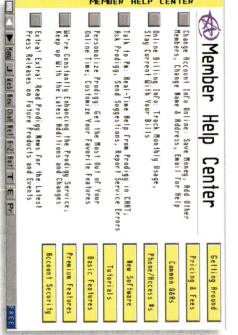

Figure 8: "Ask Us for Help." Click on the appropriate button on the right to pull up a screen to send a free message to Prodigy. Usually, a response comes within 24-48 hours. They'll answer your question and invite you to contact them at the appropriate number or email address if you have further questions.

Yes. Your Prodigy address is your member ID XXXX11A

Can I get a virus from the Prodigy service?
Not from Prodigy directly. However, any data that is received from sources outside of Prodigy, such as a file transfer or Internet email, could contain a virus. You may want to scan all files you receive from non-Prodigy sources as a precaution.

What speed can I use to connect to Prodigy?
You can connect with a 2400 or 9600 BPS modem. Many areas now have 14,400 BPS modem and want 9600 access, Jump: 9600 setup.

Is there an additional charge for 14,400 BPS service?
No.

Can I write to someone on another online service?
Yes, if you know their address on the other service.

What are the hours for Member Services?
Member Services are always available, never closed.

Can I receive Internet Mail; if so, what is my Prodigy Internet address:

Jerri Clark Kirby, a freelance author focusing on travel, food and health, has traveled to more than 60 countries, writing for publications in the US and eight other countries. She is a regular contributor to TravelASSIST Magazine on the World Wide Web. In 1986, she replaced her portable typewriter with a new computer. Uneducated in computer technology, she relies on husband Jim, her computer "guru," to keep her computer running smoothly. She roams the Internet daily for research, entertainment and adventure.

Tip: You can use other Windows programs while you are online. Simply hold down the ALT key and press TAB repeatedly to see the programs currently being run. Each time you press TAB, a screen icon will show to indicate any program that is in use. Remember, however, that you are always on a clock when on an online service. Prodigy will display a disconnect screen after a few minutes; if you don't respond to it quickly, it will automatically disconnect you from the service.

PROBLEM SOLVING

The first thing to remember is **1-800-PRODIGY.** A touch-tone phone will enable you to check a long list of menus, which give you information to locate what you need online. A dial phone will get a voice response-controlled menu. Both options give plenty of direction to find the information you need. You will have a long wait if you elect to reach a service representative in person. If you can connect to Prodigy online, you will save a lot of time and online help is readily available.

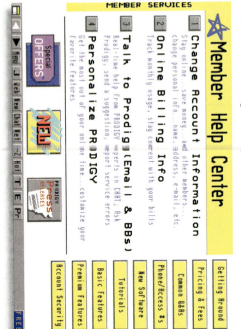

Figure 7: Member Help Screen. Click numbers or buttons for the information you want. Note the three buttons at the bottom of the screen. "Special Offers" keeps you current on offers to get new members, to get free hours for giving friends and family trial membership, and other incentives. "NEW" keeps you current on the latest free Prodigy software upgrades. "Press Releases" keeps you current on latest features, latest software and anything related to up and coming enhancements for the service.

THE MICROSOFT NETWORK

By Richard Mansfield

Microsoft's new online service appeared within Windows 95 on August 24, a major bundling event all its own, packaged in the launch of a significant new operating system. Here a beta tester who's been using the network for many months offers an overview.

The Microsoft Network (MSN) offers some extraordinary features—both technological and stylistic. MSN is structured following the Windows 95 paradigm, and boasts the Windows 95 look and feel. If you know how to get around in the Windows 95 file system (Explorer), you know how to get around in MSN. The Find utility will search for data either on your hard drive, or within MSN—as if the one were an extension of the other. The toolbars and buttons and keyboard shortcuts are similar, often indistinguishable. In sum, if you ignore the sound of your **modem**, MSN acts just like another zone within the Windows 95 milieu.

Let's take a tour of the world of The Microsoft Network. The first thing most people will notice is the high-resolution pictures. They appear gradually. First they are rather blurry but then after a few seconds they sharpen.

MORE THAN A PRETTY FACE

But of course beauty without substance is evanescent. Fortunately, MSN's structure and thoughtful, logical design matches the quality of its surface. After all, MSN is quite Windows 95-like, and Windows 95 has been more thoroughly tested by more people than any consumer product in history. Countless man- and woman-years of focus groups, meetings, trial designs, and redesigns have culminated in an operating system that many critics consider unsurpassed.

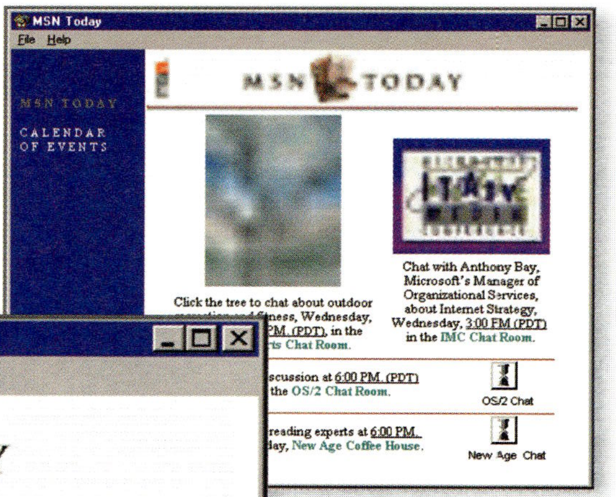

When you first click on the MSN icon, you're asked to type your onscreen name (a "handle" or nickname that will be displayed to other users). It's a good idea to use some false sobriquet rather than your true name. As in the real world, most people you'll meet on MSN are fine people. And then there are some others.

Likewise, there's a "Member Information" page you can fill out. Here you can describe your interests and so on, so other members can contact you if they wish. But here too it's a good idea to avoid giving out your address or phone number.

When you first sign up for MSN, you're asked to provide a credit card for payment, and this sort of information is of course kept confidential. However, if you went on to fill in your "Member Information" sheet with explicit details about your location, you might want to erase your real name, address and phone number. Here's how. In MSN Central (see Figure 3), click on *Email*. In the *Tools* menu of the Email window, click on *Address Book*. Now select *The Microsoft Network* under *Show Names From the*. Find your name in the list of members,

Figure 1: *At first, MSN's high-res pictures are fuzzy;*

Figure 2: *Then they sharpen up into quality color graphics.*

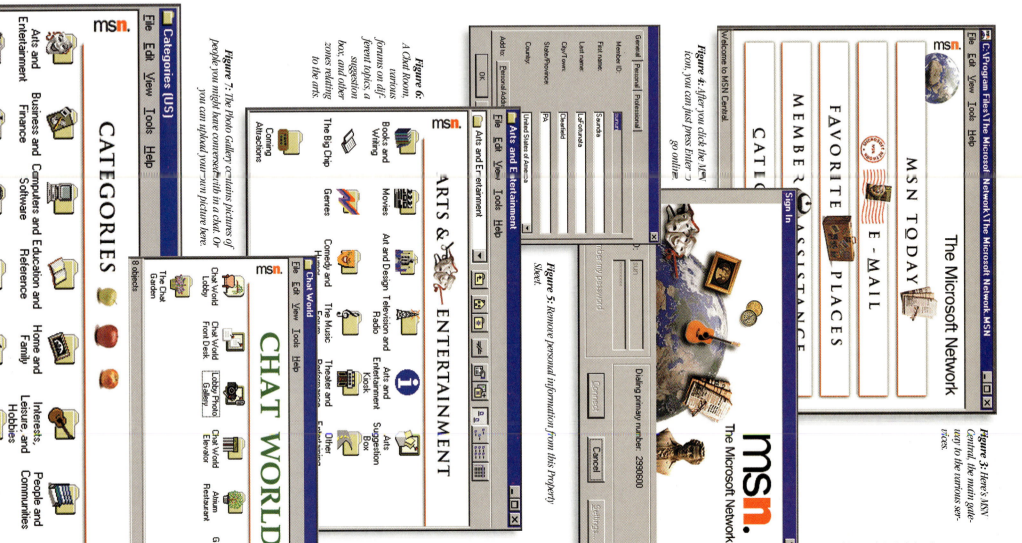

The Microsoft Network

msn.

MSN TODAY

E-MAIL

FAVORITE PLACES

MEMBER ASSISTANCE

CATEGORIES

Figure 3: Here's MSN Central, the main gateway to the various services.

Welcome to MSN Central.

Figure 4: After you click the MSN icon, you can just press Enter to go online.

Dialing primary number. 2990600

Connect   Cancel   Settings...

msn.
The Microsoft Network

Sign In

Enter my password

C:\Program Files\The Microsoft Network\The Microsoft Network.MSN
File Edit View Tools Help

Member ID: starter
First name: Saundra
Last name: LaFortunata
City/Town: Clearfield
State/Province: PA
Country: United States of America

Add to: Personal Address

General | Personal | Professional

Figure 5: Remove personal information from this Property Sheet.

Arts and Entertainment
File Edit View Tools Help

Arts and Entertainment

Coming Attractions   The Big Chip   Genres   Movies   Books and Writing

Figure 6: A Chat Room, various forums on different topics; a suggestion box, and other zones relating to the arts.

ARTS & ENTERTAINMENT
File Edit View Tools Help

Arts and Entertainment

Art and Design   Television and Radio   Arts and Entertainment Kiosk   Arts Suggestion Box   Other

Comedy and Humor   The Music Forum   Theater and Performance

8 objects

Figure 7: The Photo Gallery contains pictures of people you might have conversed with in a chat. Or you can upload your own picture here.

CHAT WORLD
File Edit View Tools Help

Chat World

The Chat Garden   Chat World Lobby   Chat World Front Desk   Lobby Photo Gallery   Chat World Elevator   Atrium Restaurant   Games and Casino   Pool and Spa

Categories (US)
File Edit View Tools Help

msn.

CATEGORIES

Arts and Entertainment   Business and Finance   Computers and Software   Education and Reference   Home and Family   Interests, Leisure, and Hobbies   People and Communities

Public Affairs   Science and Technology   Special Events Sports, Health, and Fitness   The Internet Center   The MSN Member Lobby

Figure 8: You can narrow down your search for areas of your personal interest by clicking on an icon here.

then double-click on your name. You'll see the property sheet in Figure 5. To make any changes, just type over the existing information. Note that your *Member ID* is the handle that others will see when you chat, post messages in forums, or otherwise interact on MSN. However, anyone can click on that handle in, say, a message you've posted. If they do, they'll then see the data you've entered into the Member Information sheets shown in Figure 5.

After your modem dials the local access number, you're put through to MSN and you'll shortly see the two main screens. First, shown in Figure 2, is MSN Today: notices about current chats, meetings, conferences, a famous visitor to one of the "Pavilions," or other current events. Second, shown in Figure 3, is MSN Central, the top level of The Microsoft Network. From MSN Central, you can go burrowing down into several lower levels.

DEEP INTO MEDIA

It's easy to get back to Windows. Say you locate in an MSN music forum a good sound file, a premium rendition of Schubert's Trout Quintet or the definitive instrumental version of Willie Nelson's "Crazy." Want to hear it? Double-click on it, then choose *Download & Open*. Next thing you know you're back in Windows 95 (you never really left it), and the Media Player accessory is pumping out the music through your speakers.

Where are you? Are you now in Windows 95 or still in MSN? Both, really. While the music multitasks (plays in the background), you can start a program running in Windows 95 or press Alt+Tab and do something in MSN. We're talking serious *integration* here. Information, as Bill Gates says, at your fingertips.

MSN also boasts some of the best research tools available today—Microsoft's Encarta and BookShelf. Are you in your word processor doing a report on hummingbirds? Want a picture of one, or some more information about them? It's at your fingertips. Click on the *Tools* menu in Explorer or some other MSN or Windows 95 window. Choose *Find* and search for Encarta, Microsoft's multimedia encyclopedia.

Figure 9: *Click on the Books & Writing folder and you go down yet another level.*

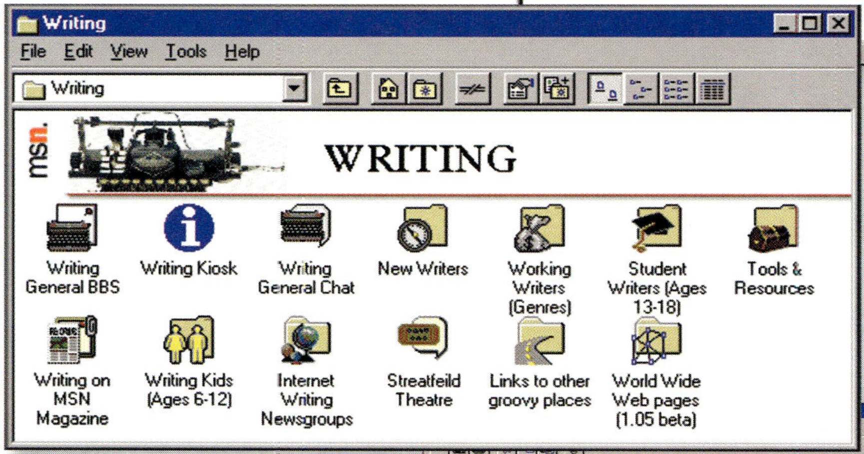

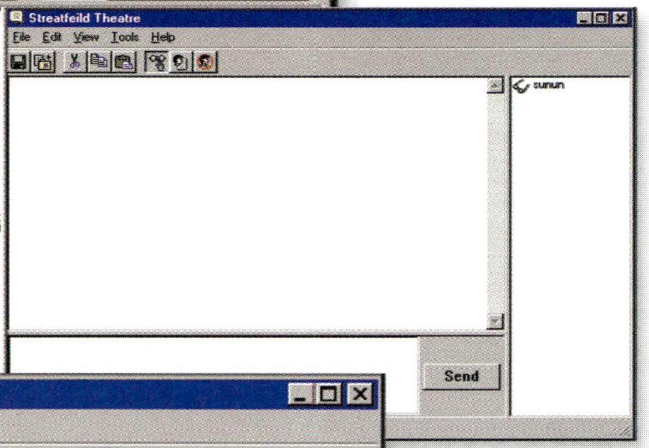

Figure 11: *Click on Writing and you'll see yet another set of folders and other elements.*

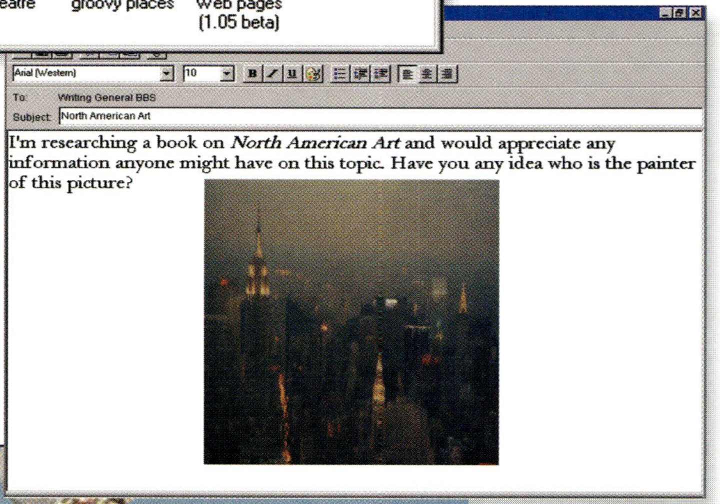

Figure 10: *Here's where you can interact with the celebrated guests who'll drop in from time to time to talk about books. Right now, we're all alone.*

Figure 12: *You can embed high-resolution graphics in your messages.*

Figure 13: *Encarta: pictures and information available to you within MSN.*

So far, we've been hovering like a helicopter and viewing the general landscape, the big picture. Now let's zero in on just one zone within MSN, to experience its depth up close. And remember, there will be much more to this online service over time—MSN is only months old. We'll take a detailed look at how MSN deals with *chatting*—members communicating.

You can meet with other users and "chat" by typing messages back and forth—and get reactions immediately. These aren't messages that you've posted in a BBS or sent via email. Instead, you're having a keyboard conversation because these other people are online right now too. Join a chat in a "Lounge" like the one shown in Figure 15; a "Chat Room" within a forum; or a Pavilion where you can chat with famous guests.

Below the main dialog pane is where you write messages that you want to send into the dialog above. When you click on the *Send* button, or just press Enter, your remarks will be added at the bottom of the large pane. You can edit the send pane, but not the main one—so don't send until you're happy that what you've typed what you meant and you meant what you typed. There's no taking it back.

The pane on the right shows who's in the "room." Notice that we've silenced JIF because, well, her comments were tedious and unpleasant and, more to the point, directed at us. Whatever she might say from now on will be visible to her and the others in the room, but not to us. You can blank out harassing or untoward people by merely clicking on the ignore button (first click on that person's name to highlight it).

MSN Chat includes several features either rare or entirely absent on competing online services. For one thing, there's that seemingly measureless history. And, as usual with Microsoft prod- ucts, the chat structure is highly user-customizable. On the *Edit* menu you can choose to clear the history. On the *View* menu, you can choose to adjust the relative sizes of the three panes—even eliminating one or two of them from view entirely if you want.

Right-click (or double-click) on a member's name in

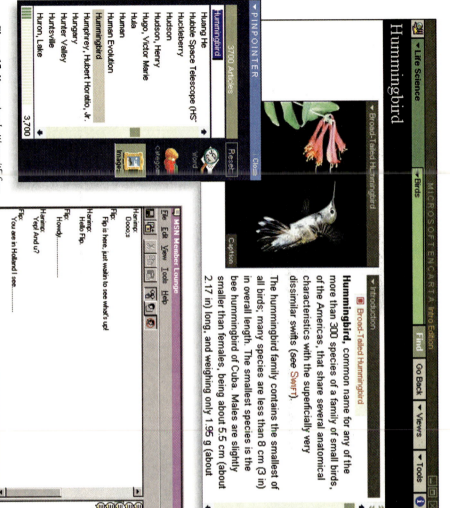

Hummingbird

Hummingbird, common name for any of the more than 300 species of a family of small birds, of the Americas, that share several anatomical characteristics with the superficially very dissimilar swifts (see Swift).

The hummingbird family contains the smallest of all birds; many species are less than 8 cm (3 in) in overall length. The smallest species is the bee hummingbird of Cuba. Males are slightly smaller than females, being about 5.5 cm (about 2.17 in) long, and weighing only 1.95 g (about

Figure 14: Want to know more about hummingbirds and even see one? No problem.

the right pane where all participants are listed. You can then see that member's online Profile—information they provide about their location, interests, age or anything else. This could be entirely fiction, though. Nobody checks it.

The Chat World Lobby is a general-interest chat room that can include 50 members at any given time, and it's monitored 24 hours per day by Hosts. The Front Desk is the equivalent of the message boards in other forums. Here you can read or post messages (this isn't realtime chat—it's like a bulletin board in a supermarket or the corkboard in an office lounge). You put messages here and others can read them next time they log onto MSN. The Elevator is for private chatting. It moves you to "floors" within the hotel you can conduct *unmonitored* chats with others. You tell someone in a general chat to meet you on a particular "floor" (like Floor 3) for a private conversation.

Microsoft describes the Restaurant like this: "The Atrium Restaurant is a friendly place to meet and chat with old and new friends in a quiet and serene 'garden' setting. Rooms in this 'restaurant' are not monitored." It's another place for private interaction, like the

"floors" described above. But the Atria can hold thousands, each engaged in a private chat with the others.

The Games & Casino is like a game room in a hotel. Take it easy and converse with others interested in "Trivia" or pinball here. These are chat rooms. The Pool & Spa and the Chat Garden are also private chat rooms—unmonitored and accommodating various numbers of private chats.

The next step is up to you. If you have Windows 95, you might want to click on the MSN desktop icon and sign up. After you've filled in your credit card information, walk right into a  nt, colorful, ever-changing world.

YOU BE THE JUDGE

Richard Mansfield's books on personal computing have sold over 350,000 copies worldwide. He is the author of two current bestsellers: The Visual Guide to Visual Basic and The Visual Basic Power Toolkit. Richard was Senior Editor of COMPUTE! Publications from 1982 through 1987, and Senior Editor of Game Players Publications from 1988 to 1992.

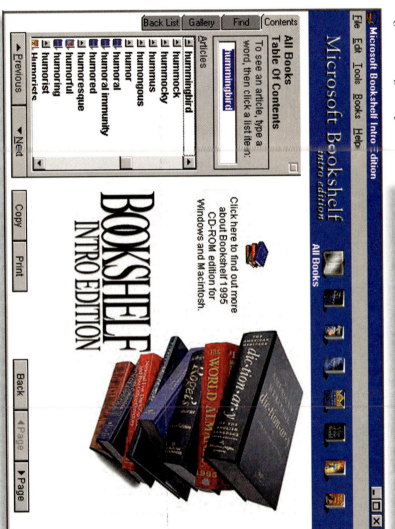

Microsoft Bookshelf Intro Edition

File Edit Tools Books Help

Microsoft Bookshelf
intro edition

All Books

All Books — Table Of Contents

hummingbird

Articles

- hummingbird
- hummock
- hummocky
- hummus
- humongous
- humor
- humoral
- humoral immunity
- humored
- humoresque
- humorful
- humoring
- humorist
- Humorists

To see an article, type a word, then click a list item.

Back List | Gallery | Find | Contents

◄ Previous | ▼ Next

Click here to find out more about Bookshelf 1995 CD-ROM edition for Windows and Macintosh.

Copy | Print | Back | ◄ Page | ► Page

Figure 15: Here we're chatting with four other members. Notice that we clicked on the button on the far right of the toolbar. This prevents you from seeing any comments made by the member whose name is highlighted on the right side of the screen.

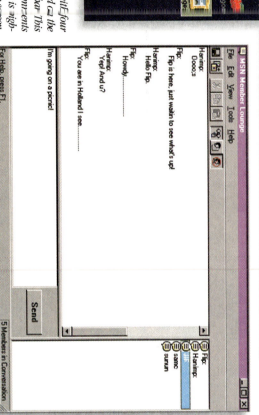

PINPOINTER

Hummingbird — 3700 Articles

- Huang He
- Hubble Space Telescope (HS...
- Huckleberry
- Hudson
- Hudson, Henry
- Hugo, Victor Marie
- Hula
- Human
- Human Evolution
- Hummingbird
- Humphrey, Hubert Horatio, Jr.
- Hungary
- Hunter Valley
- Huntsville
- Huron, Lake

3,700

MSN Member Lounge

File Edit View Tools Help

Harimp: 0:00:...
Flip: Flip is here, just waitin to see what's up!
Harimp: Hello Flip.
Flip: Howdy.....
Harimp: Yep! And u?
Flip: You are in Holland I see....
Flip: I'm going on a picnic!

Send

5 Members in Conversation

For Help, press F1.

Figure 16: Look in the Bookshelf for hummingbird info.

Dial into Chat World, our new online chat resort.

Figure 17: If you're interested in chatting, use the Find utility to search for "Chat World." You can do lots of things there—and get to any chat.

THE BEST OF ONLINE

By William R. Trotter, David Haskin, and Jerri Clark-Kirby

We asked several of our authors to recommend great sites for new online families. Their recommendations are just the beginning. Many new computers and software packages have bundled online access software. You can usually try one or more of the online services for a month at little initial expense. There are certainly similarities across the major online services (for example, all have weather sites and all have news sites). We haven't tried to compare them here but instead present some of the sites that our group of authors like. Have fun!

Many of the America Online sites listed here are accessible from the *Discover AOL* icon that appears in the Main Menu; click there to start, then click on the *Best of AOL* icon (the two hearts) to see the most popular destinations.

A logical AOL starting place, given the title of the book you're reading at this moment, is the **Family Computing Forum.** Some of the categories found there overlap with other selections in this list, but this is a great place to start your first **surfing** expedition.

artwork on *The Refrigerator Door* (in the *Rec Room*) for everyone to see.

The heart of this forum is the *Family Room,* where users can chat with visiting speakers, leaf through or contribute to the Family Photo Album, and check the calendar for future events and classes.

CompuServe is the oldest of the on-line services and it has a rich assortment of features. The CompuServe selections in this section don't include CompuServe's game-related

the "extended services" realm—they cost extra for each minute you access them. As a result, each of the descriptions for CompuServe throughout this article ends with either the word *Basic* or *Extended.*

The Family Handyman Forum (GO HANDYMAN) is a quite busy place on CompuServe. It's where to go for questions about maintaining your house. Want to know the best way to build a deck or remodel your kitchen? Just ask, and plenty of handy forum members will be happy to help. The coverage here is extensive. When we looked in recently, subjects ranged from software to home construction to repairing concrete. *Extended.*

Over on AOL, if you want to start (or end) your day with a chuckle, or update your repertoire of snappy one-liners, spend some time with *Jokes, etc.* Jokes are arranged by topic ("Lightbulb Jokes", "Clinton Jokes", "Blondes", "Knock-Knocks", even a file of "Libertarian" jokes!), and there's also a special file of "Bumper Sticker" messages. Some of the material is mildly off-color, but nothing obscene is allowed, so you

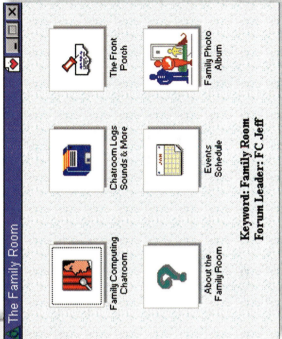

Keyword: **Family Room**
Forum Leader: **FC Jeff**

Figure 1: Look in AOL's Family Room for friendly chats and special events

Keyword: **FC**

From here on AOL, you can post messages, browse among family-oriented computer information or sample software demos in *Lifestyles & Computing,* try your luck at an ever-changing array of contests and easy-to-play games in the *Rec Room,* and find much more of interest to you and your family. Your kids can even post their

topics—those are described elsewhere in this book. CompuServe charges a base fee that entitles you to unlimited use of its so-called basic services. However, many of CompuServe's services are in

FINANCIAL NEWSSTAND

Business News

Business News
Market News
BusinessWeek Online
Chicago Tribune Business
Inc. Online
Investors Business Daily
New York Times Business
The Nightly Business Report
Orlando Sentinel Business
Worth Magazine
San Jose/Mercury Business
********Suggested Internet Sites********
Singapore Business Times - WEB
Financial Times - WEB
The Nando Times Financial Report - WEB

Figure 2: There's a wealth of financial information on AOL.

useful clearinghouse of information.

Two interesting sections on CompuServe are **The Health and Fitness Forum** and **FundWatch Online by Money Magazine** (GO BASICMONEY) is an excellent way to find a mutual fund in which to invest or to track the progress of funds you already own. You can search for funds by name or get a listing of the best-performing funds. This isn't as comprehensive as some financial services, but it is free and it is more than thorough enough for casual investors. *Basic*.

The Health and Fitness Forum (GO GOODHEALTH) is a thorough set of resources for issues ranging from mental health, addiction and recovery to martial arts and body building. The only commonality between some of these areas is that they concern your good health. Some of the topics are touching—we checked in on one area lately in which a depressed and suicidal person received strong, forthright support from those who had been through similar problems. Another section deals with physical health problems. If good health is important to you, this is a lively, exciting place to be. *Extended*.

Also on CompuServe you'll find **HealthNet** (GO HNT-289). This site provides volumes of health-related information. It is divided into two extremely thorough parts: the reference library and a section on sports medicine. The reference library includes extensive details about diseases, drugs and medical procedures. It also includes information about first aid and a comprehensive listing of symptoms if you don't feel quite right. The sports medicine section covers the basics of how exercise affects

your body. It also has a section on nutrition and information about specific sports. *Basic*.

Choosing *Newsstand* from AOL's Main Menu takes you to a veritable smorgasbord of information sources. Besides up-to-the-minute weather information and financial data, you can obtain breaking stories straight from Reuters or peruse the new issue of *Time Magazine* (updated every Sunday at 4 pm).

Want the latest national and international weather information? On Prodigy, Jump: Weather. You'll see national and regional maps for the entire U.S.; get forecasts for major U.S. cities as well as cities around the world.

In AOL's Newsstand, you'll find some of the nation's most respected newspapers (*The New York Times*, *The Chicago Tribune*, the *San Jose Mercury*), and once you've clicked on their names, you can access sports, business news or entertainment features just as though you were turning the pages. You can also tap into the resources of ABC network news, and post email messages to put in your own two-cents-worth. The latest issue of *The Atlantic Monthly* is yours

don't have to worry about the kids peeking over your shoulder. To get there, click on the *Go To* button in the Menu Bar at the top of the screen, scroll down to *Keyword* and type in *Jokes*.

If you want more passive humor, look at CompuServe's **Comics** (GO SSN-16). Here you'll find just what the name implies: comic strips. You've probably seen some of these in your newspaper, but here you can view them on-line and even download them to look at later. At last count, there were four comics in the Basic services section and four that cost extra.

One of the free comics is Bizarro, a funny, off-kilter strip. Two of the fee-based comics are extremely popular—Doonesbury and Cathy. By the way, this is a great place to come after you return from vacation. It contains strips dating back two to three weeks, so you can catch up on your reading. Basic and Extended.

The online services are a rich source of timely news and information. For the latest financial news on America Online, as well as financial information of all kinds, choose *Personal Finance* from the Main Menu. The *Financial Newsstand* has up-to-the-minute financial data and offers access to the business pages of the newspapers AOL carries. Special interests are well catered-to. The "Small Business Center" is a highly

HOW DO THESE ANIMALS BEAT THE HEAT?

Fennec Fox
Thorny Devil Lizard
Bactrian Camel
Sidewinder Rattlesnake
Map

Figure 3: Want to learn about the habits of various animals? Click on flashing boxes and follow instructions to see and learn.

to read, as are all the publications of the armed services. Under *Columnists and Features Online* you not only get to read the musings of well-known syndicated pundits, but you can also write and post your own columns. Subject to AOL's rules of decorum, the entire spectrum of political beliefs is represented.

On CompuServe, whether you want to meet people who agree with you or rail against those who don't, rush to the **Issues Forum** (GO ISSUESFORUM). The subject matter here is wide open, ranging from issues between the sexes to events on Capitol Hill. If you really want to get things hopping, simply say something either positive or nasty about Rush Limbaugh.

Sometimes there's more smoke than fire (or substance) in these discussions, but they're never boring. One thing to remember, though: Some of

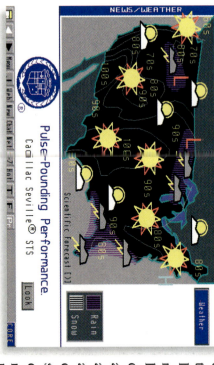

NEWS/WEATHER

Weather

AccuWeather's Wednesday Forecast

Pulse-Pounding Performance.
Cadillac Seville® STS
Scientific Performance

Rain
Snow

LOOK

Figure 4: Weather map of U.S. on June 12, 1995. Note the ad below for Cadillac automobiles. By clicking on LOOK, you can access the rest of the ad. Prodigy's paid advertisers display doorways to their ads at the bottom of feature screens.

Selected Prodigy Sites

While many of the online services are experimenting with some form of revenue generating commercials, Prodigy has embedded them since the beginning. You'll see them as an integral part of the service. Here is a list of recommended sites from our Prodigy author, Jerri Clark Kirby.

• **Jump: Soaps**
Get daily updates on soap opera story lines, gossip about the stars and join bulletin board discussions where you can ask and answer questions.

• **Jump: Consumer Reports**
Read what consumer guide says about products you want to buy. Research household appliances, cars and many other consumer goods.

• **Jump: Prodigy Poll**
Find out how other Prodigy members responded to polls on current topics and controversial issues. Results are presented by age, gender and geographic regions of poll respondents.

• **Jump: Classifieds**
Buy, sell or window-shop using these ads.

• **Jump: Cars**
Browse reviews of the latest car models; get information on parts, service, recalls, safety features, auto events and owners' clubs. You can also request brochures directly from car companies.

• **Jump: Free Store**
Get free information, free catalogs and free products.

• **Jump: Horoscope**
Read Jeane Dixon's forecast for you, or anyone, for today or in the past or future.

• **Jump: CBS**
Check out your favorite shows; get tips, program listings; join the bulletin board; shop in the CBS store; find out what's happening on late night TV.

• **Jump: Political Profiles**
Learn about Congress; download biographies of Congress members; check voting records, committee assignments, major campaign contributors. Send a letter to a Senator or Representative (fee involved).

• **Jump: Computer Basics**
Baffled by computer technology? Look at the glossary of computer terms; learn about computers.

• **Jump: Family Travel**
Plan a family vacation; get advice from expert Alfred Borcover.

• **Jump: Cooking Class**
Cookbook author Ellen Brown gives recipes and lessons on cooking techniques.

Figure 5: The CBS Welcome screen. Click on a button to explore further:

current cover and save it if you want. Note, though, that while the basic People service is free, if you want some specific information, such as celebrity gossip, you'll pay extra. *Basic and Extended.*

Also on CompuServe, you'll find **CNN** and **AP Online** (GO AP) is a comprehensive online source of news, updated hourly by the Associated Press. It includes national, international, business, sports, weather and entertainment stories. It also includes science and health news and features.

AP has reporters located around the world and also draws information from local newspapers that subscribe to its service. The

coverage here is quite complete. This is great site if you just want to keep up with the day's events or if there's a breaking story that you want to track on a moment-to-moment basis. *Basic.*

CNN Online (GO CNN) doesn't provide as many stories as does AP Online, but it offers many other opportunities. For example, it provides a forum in which people can discuss the news. In fact, during the trial of O.J. Simpson, the forum devoted to discussing that case was one of the most heavily used on all of CompuServe. It also is an excellent place to gather images of top stories and to give feedback to CNN. The basic CNN service is free, but some of the areas to which it leads, like the discussion forums, will cost you extra. *Basic and Extended.*

For the younger members of the America Online family, *Tomorrow's Morning in Kids Only Online* (KOOL), which is found in the *Leisure and Recreation* section from the Main Menu, is a lively source of information and features.

On Prodigy, Jump: National Geographic to find educational games, articles, and interactive activities for the whole family.

Back on CompuServe, you can explore a full range of interesting places. The magazine you read before you buy anything, **Consumer Reports** (GO CSR-1), is online. This is a thorough compendium of current tests. Through the years, millions of families have come to rely on these tests for unbiased information to help

these discussions have been raging for a long time, so it can be difficult to figure out the gist if you jump into the middle. *Extended.*

If you like the magazine, you'll love Compuserve's **People Magazine Daily Edition** (GO PEOPLE). This is thorough online coverage of Liz, Michael, Chuck and Di, celebrity weddings and inspirational stories of personal courage. In other words, it's *People Magazine* in all its celebrity-packed glory. You can even view the

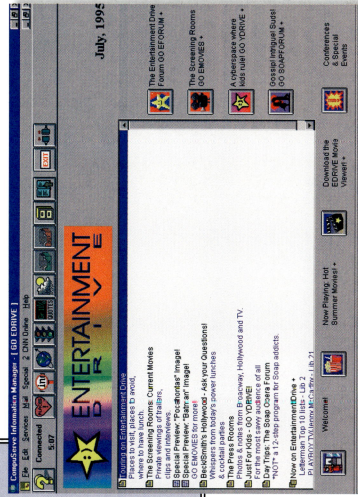

Figure 6: E-Drive is the place to catch up on the latest entertainment news. This site is jam-packed with entertainment news, whether you want to see a collection of David Letterman's Top 10 lists or download clips of the hottest movies.

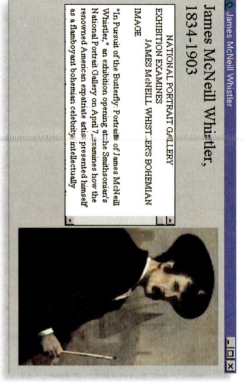

NATIONAL PORTRAIT GALLERY
EXHIBITION EXAMINES
JAMES McNEILL WHISTLER'S BOHEMIAN
IMAGE

"In Pursuit of the Butterfly: Portrait of James McNeill Whistler," an exhibition opening at the Smithsonian's National Portrait Gallery on April 7, examines how the renowned American expatriate artist presented himself as a flamboyant bohemian celebrity, intellectually...

James McNeill Whistler, 1834-1903

Figure 7: *In AOL's Smithsonian Museum online forum, you'll find lots of exhibits like this one from the National Portrait Gallery.*

them make better buying decisions. *Basic.*

There's nothing unusual about CompuServe's **Electronic Mall** (GO MALL)—all online services have shopping areas. However, CompuServe's was the first of its kind and it also is very large, with 170 vendors. It's well organized—you can easily find the products you want with the mall's hierarchical set of menus. *Free.*

Entertainment Drive (GO EDRIVE) is like a super version of about ten separate World Wide Web sites devoted to entertainment. It has a vast amount of information about movies and television. It even has libraries of David Letterman's Top 10 lists and loads of information about soap operas. You also can download clips of all the hot movies. E-Drive does not forget the kids. It's **Youth Entertainment Drive** (GO YDRIVE) Forum is run by kids, for kids. The subjects range from music and bands, to sports, hobbies and computers. It's a great (and safe) place for kids to hang out together on-line. *Extended.*

On America Online, similar resources available in the *Education* site (from Main Menu) are the meat-and-potatoes of general research. The *Congressional Quarterly* resides here, as do the recent issues of *Consumer Reports* and *The National Geographic.* The entire Library of Congress isn't accessible via AOL (not yet, anyhow), but selected exhibits are, and reproductions of historic documents, artwork, and manuscripts can be downloaded easily.

The Smithsonian museums have a site here; in it you can visit the National Portrait Gallery, among others, and obtain information and download pictures.

A very special feature of AOL's *Education* area is the *KIDSNET*, a non-profit clearinghouse devoted to children's media programming. All the major networks contribute, and their information forms a continually updated KIDSNET database. By inputting a key word ("dinosaurs", for instance), you can call up a listing of all programs, in all media, relating to that topic, along with any information needed to access them.

Can't start the day without a visit from the Cookie Monster? On Prodigy, Jump: Sesame Street. Here's a great place to spend time with your kids: read a story, play with Big Bird, Oscar and, yes, even the Cookie Monster. PC owners with a taste for the finer things in life will find a veritable smorgasbord of goodies online. On America Online, try the **Food and Drink Online** department of *Clubs and Interests.* Can't think of something new for dinner? Check out the *Recipe Exchange,* where users post their favorite menus (on one recent visit I found no fewer than 74 recipes based on Spam!).

Traveling gourmets will appreciate the literally hundreds of restaurant reviews posted by diners. Listed according to cities and states, these reviews

Figure 8: *Sesame Street's sign-on page. Click on the blinking numbers to join the Sesame Street gang for lots of family fun.*

This is the online version of the popular nationwide book of restaurant reviews. Want the best seafood in Boston or the best pizza in Chicago? Look here and your questions will be answered. The list is reasonably comprehensive and it isn't snooty—it covers as many delis and pizza joints as it does haute cuisine. Each listing includes average prices and basic information like which credit cards the restaurant accepts. *Free.*

Another useful CompuServe site is **Roger Ebert's Movie Reviews** (GO EBERT). Here you'll find a collection of movie reviews from the well-known movie critic. While Ebert's frequent partner, Gene Siskel, isn't part of these reviews, Roger still is well-qualified to give films the old thumbs up or down treatment all by himself.

The site provides much more than just movie reviews. Also included are Ebert's glossary of movie terms, his lists of best movies, interviews he conducts with celebrities and film news. This is a must for film fans. The only downside: you can't take this resource with you to the video store. *Basic.*

AOL sports fans will love the *Sports* section accessible from the Main Menu. Specialized

range from the short and pithy ("Avoid this dump like the plague!") to minutely detailed course-by-course critiques, including prices, service and waiting-times.

And if a knowledgeable friend gives you a bottle of, say, Mondavi Pinot Noir Reserve, 1992, you can consult the *Wine Dictionary* to learn everything you could conceivably want to know, including the location and reputation of the vineyard that produced it.

On CompuServe, **Cooks Online** (GO COOKS) is a delicious site. Just browsing the message subjects and recipes is enough to make you ready for dinner. If you want good food—and plenty of recipes—sit down at the table of the *Cooks Forum. Basic.*

When CompuServe subscribers eat out, they consult **Zagat Restaurant Survey** (GO ZAGAT).

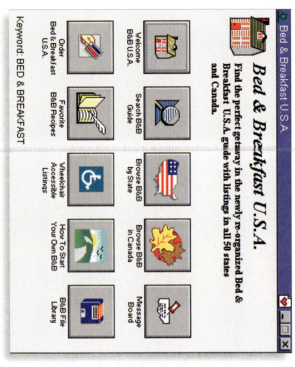

Bed & Breakfast U.S.A.

Bed & Breakfast U.S.A.
Find the perfect getaway in the newly re-organized Bed & Breakfast U.S.A. guide with listings in all 50 states and Canada.

Figure 9: *AOL's travel information is extensive and often quite helpful.*

Keyword: BED & BREAKFAST

Omni Magazine Online

One of the newest and most unusual AOL features is *Omni Magazine Online*, which you can reach by using *Keyword: Omni* in the *Go To* menu. In 1994, *Omni*'s publisher and editor made a bold decision: to change their printed edition to a quarterly and make their monthly edition online-specific. The verdict is not yet in, but the online *Omni* certainly offers all the major attractions of the old magazine.

You can read the first-rate science fiction, the cutting-edge science fact, the stimulating interviews, that made the newsstand version so highly regarded (and you can print it out or save-to-file anything you want to keep permanently).

Check into the *Auditorium* to chat with writers, scientists and other fans. Here you will find raging discussions of cults, psychics, Loch Ness sightings, NASA projects, quantum physics, fusion technology, time-travel, UFO abductions—you name it, sooner or later somebody will get a discussion going about it.

Under *Resources*, you'll find a fascinating array of information. Want to contact all the major UFO societies? Learn about cryonics? Get on the mailing list of the Office of Paranormal Investigations or the Aerospace Medical Association? Or maybe you'd like to send an email letter to former President Jimmy Carter? Whatever your special interest in the fields of science, science fiction, unexplained phenomena or futurism in all its multifaceted aspects, this is the place to get the appropriate names and addresses.

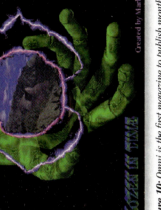

Figure 10: *Omni* is the first magazine to publish monthly online instead of on paper. Look on AOL for Omni's award-winning art.

forums and information sources are plentiful. In its *Sports News* you'll find all the data you'd expect from a newspaper sports section (game recaps, statistics, standings, etc.), as well as injury reports and the latest updates on contract disputes.

Naturally, the major "ball" sports get the most coverage, but more esoteric activities are also well covered. Want to know the result of the latest cricket match between Glamorgen and Lancashire, or the latest rankings in the World Cup Luge championships in Koenigsee, Germany? It's here. If you have school-age kids at home, you'll probably find numerous occasions to check out the *Academic Assistance Center* in America

Online's *Education* site. Under the heading *Exam Prep Center*, for instance, you'll find hundreds of tips on SATs, MCATs, and other standardized tests. There are also user-posted *Cramming Tips* for those last-minute pre-exam panic sessions.

A unique and very helpful feature is the *Teacher Pager*. After selecting this option, simply type in the topic you need help on, select a grade level (grade school, middle school, high school or college), list the subject of your inquiry (math, biology, history, etc.), then click on *Send*. Your request will automatically be forwarded to an expert in that field, and a short time later you'll receive a reply, usually with suggestions for reference materials.

Speaking of kids, not to mention adults with an interest in pop culture, *MTV Online* in the *Education* section lets you stay hip with a few mouse-clicks. Under the MTV *Red Alert* icon, you can get the latest updates on tour itineraries, TV specials and user-supplied reviews of musical acts. Other MTV features include downloadable audio and video clips, a list of musical stars' birthdays and fan clubs, even a broad selection of "Beavis and Butthead" screensavers.

Online computing is generally a secular environment, but AOL also offers *Christianity Online*. The aim of this service is to connect Christians around the world through electronic means, and to provide a wide array of Christian information.

In this forum, the interested browser will find media reviews, chat rooms (atheists and skeptics are not excluded from the debates, provided the discourse is civil and conducted without profanity), online Christian magazines and databases listing Christian-oriented resource centers and

educational facilities. *Christianity Online* is one of the newest AOL services that , fills a cultural and social niche; it is also a non-profit service.

AOL's *Travel* is a very useful department (reach it from the Main Menu) where you can make reservations, check out foreign exchange rates—even read the latest State Department advisories concerning global danger-spots. The information available here goes far beyond the basics, however. You'll find a state-by-state directory of wheelchair-accessible bed-and-breakfast inns, for instance, as well as a comprehensive list of site-specific recipes.

Many of these entries are posted by veteran travelers who speak with hard-won authority on such topics as "The Top Ten Overrated Destinations," or the best places to go horseback riding in Patagonia. There are also dozens of ever-changing reviews of resorts, travel agencies, and hotels, often scathingly candid, occasionally side-splittingly funny. 🌐

Figure 11: *MTV Online boasts some of the most radical graphics you'll ever see.*

David Haskin *is a writer specializing in computer-related topics. Formerly a newspaper journalist and software executive, David is a regular contributor to* PC Magazine, Computer Life *and* Computer Shopper. *He is the author of six books about computers including* The Complete Idiot's Guide to Multimedia, The Complete Idiot's Guide to PC Games *and* Using PC Tools for Windows.

Jerri Clark Kirby*, a freelance author focusing on travel, food and health, has traveled to more than 60 countries, writing for publications in the US and eight other countries. She is a regular contributor to* TravelASSIST Magazine on the World Wide Web. *In 1986, she replaced her portable typewriter with a new computer. Uneducated in computer technology; she relies on husband Jim, her computer "guru," to keep her computer running smoothly. She roams the internet daily for research, entertainment and adventure.*

William R. Trotter *has been a senior writer and reviewer for* PC Gamer *magazine since 1987. He has published hundreds of articles and reviews on personal computer gaming, and has written the monthly* PC Gamer *column, "The Desktop General," since 1989. He is the author of eight published books.*

THE SMART TEENAGER'S GUIDE TO ONLINE CHATTING

By Jennifer Lock

Online chatting is a good way to meet new friends, but you should keep some basic cautions in mind. Here's the definitive guide to an America Online chat session.

Figure 1: *At the Main Menu, click on the People Connection box to get to a Chat Lobby.*

Chatting on online services can be a rewarding pastime. It's an ideal way to make new friends from all over the country, or to keep in touch with old ones. Chat Rooms are good places to talk with people close to your own age who may be from different backgrounds and have interesting ideas and opinions to share with you. **Chatting** is also an exciting way to meet others with your same interests. It's fun to talk with people you otherwise would not be able to meet.

America Online is a great place for inexperienced chatters to start out. It is so easy to use that in almost no time you'll get the hang of chatting, **emailing** and **surfing** the net.

Getting to a Chat Room is very easy. Once you have signed online, a *Welcome* screen will show up, and behind that you will see a menu. The menu has many boxes that offer places to go. Click on the button marked *People Connection,* and you will enter a Chat Lobby.

Lobbies have people of all different ages in them, and they often have interesting conversations. How-ever, if you would like to chat with people closer to your own age, click on the button marked *List Rooms.* This will take you to a directory of Chat Rooms. If you scroll down this directory, you will see a room labeled *Teen Chat.* Double-click on this room to enter it. You may then get a screen that says the room is full and asks if you would like to go to another room like it. If you click on yes, it will put you into another Teen Chat Room.

In order to talk with others in your Chat Room, simply type what you want to say in the box at the bottom of the screen, and click *Send* or press *Enter* on your keyboard. As everyone's messages **scroll** along the screen as they're sent. If you're not ready to chat yet, you can just follow the conversation.

A more private way to talk with someone in your Chat Room is to send them an *Instant Message.* This is frequently abbreviated *IM.* There are two basic ways to send an IM to someone: you can go to the *Members* heading at the top of your screen, pull it down, and click on *Send an Instant Message,* or you can go to the list of people in your Chat Room (in the top right-hand corner of your screen), scroll down the list to the person's **screen name,** and double-click on it.

Either of these methods will display a small, blank Instant Message screen. Type in the person's screen name and your message, and click *Send.* It's possible to IM with as many people as you like at any given time. However, if you fall behind and want to know if someone sent you an IM that you happened to miss, just pull down the Windows directory from the top of the screen and it will show you who has sent you an IM. Then simply double-click on the IM you want to respond to. IMs are an easy and efficient way to chat privately with one or more people at one time, without having to leave your Chat Room.

If you want to find out more information about someone on America Online, reading their

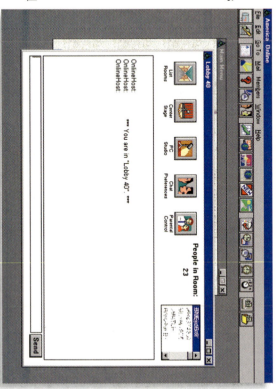

Figure 2: *This is a Chat Lobby. We're making the screen names unreadable for the same reason a newspaper wouldn't print phone numbers: to protect people's privacy.*

your screen, and scroll down to *Keyword*. Then, type in *GuidePager*. This will bring up a form for you to fill out, and your complaint will be registered.

Another way to deal with obnoxious or harassing people in a Chat Room is to "ignore" them. The *Ignore* button is handy with scrollers or otherwise unwanted people in your room. To get to this button, you go once more to the small box at the top right-hand corner of your screen, go down to the person's screen name, and double-click on it. Then just click the space beside the *Ignore* button and you will no longer see anything they type even though they are still in the Chat Room with you.

If you have met someone in your Chat

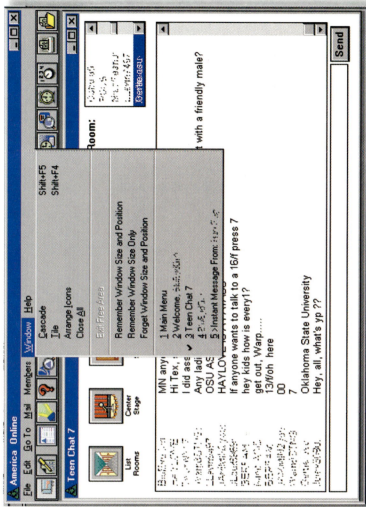

Figure 4: Here's how to pull down Window to see previous IMs.

Room with whom you would like to chat away from everyone else in your Chat Room, you can go to a *private room*. This is another kind of Chat Room that you can create to chat privately with one other person or, if you like, several. To get to a private room, click on the *List Rooms* button at the top left of your screen, and then

Figure 3: The Information box includes the options IM, Profile and Ignore.

Member Profile is a good way to start. There are two ways to access the Member Profiles of people in your Chat Room. First, you can go back to the box at the top right-hand corner of the screen, scroll down the list to their screen name, and double-click on it. This double-click will bring up the same screen you could use to send them an IM, but if you click the *Get Info* button, you will get their profile.

The other method is also similar to the way you send an IM. Go to *Members* at the top of the screen, and scroll down to *Get a Member's Profile*. Not everyone chooses to create a profile, so you might not get any information, but many people do have one, so it's always worth checking.

To make your own profile, go to *Members* at the top of your screen, and scroll down to *Edit Your Own Profile*. Then type in as much information as you would like. A note of caution, however: it's best not to type in your last name. Just provide your first name and any information you'd like to include about your hobbies, job and some interests.

If someone in your Chat Room is making a nuisance of themselves by *scrolling* (entering a message repeatedly, or so fast that it is interrupting the regular talk of the Chat Room), by harassing someone or doing anything else you don't feel is appropriate, you can page a *Guide*.

A Guide on America Online is a person who checks to make sure things are running smoothly throughout the Chat Rooms. They have the power to give offenders warnings if their behavior warrants it. Three warnings can result in the cancellation of a person's online account. To page a Guide, simply go to *Go To* at the top of

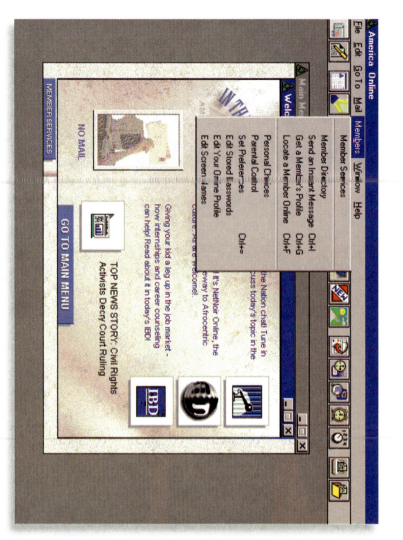

Figure 5: Pull down the Members directory to IM someone or to get their profile.

room very easily by just clicking on the *Create Room* button.

One of the most popular features of any online service is **electronic mail**. More commonly referred to as **email**, it's an easy way to communicate with others all over the world. To email someone on America Online, just go to *Go To* at the top of your screen, and scroll down to *Compose Mail*. Then type in the screen name of the

person you're writing; add a title for your letter and write whatever you want to say to the person. When you receive mail, a sign will come up on your Welcome screen to tell you that you have new mail.

Tip: It is always important to remember that however truthful you might be when talking with others on America Online, they are not necessarily being as truthful with you. People sometimes lie about their age, gender, location, hobbies and so on, in order to make you want to talk to them. It's important never to give out your full name, address or phone number to anyone on America Online, unless you know you can completely trust them with this information. Giving out this information can be very dangerous. Also, no one who really works for America Online will ever ask you for your password. No matter what anyone says to you, don't give them this information, because anyone who has your password can use your account and the resulting bills would show up as yours. If you just follow these safety guidelines, chatting on any online service will be safe as well as lots of fun.

As a *newbie* (a person who is new to online chatting), you are entering a whole new world of experiences. With America Online, or a similar online service, you are right at the forefront of technology.

You'll quickly discover all the advantages such a service can give you. I hope you have a good experience with your online service, and I wish you many years of happy chatting

Jennifer Lock is a 16-year-old high-school student. The daughter of **The PC Press, Inc.**'s *founder, Robert Lock, Jennifer has been an active personal computer user for many years, and an avid online chatter since 1992.*

Figure 6: Use Keyword: GuidePager to get a guide if there are problems.

click *Private Room* on the right of this new screen. Then you just name the room.

Another, more personal form of chatting is in *member rooms*. These are rooms that have been created by someone else online, but you can enter them whenever you want to. To get to the directory of member rooms, go to the *List Rooms* button, and then just click on *Member Rooms*. You can also create your own member

Keyword

To quickly access an area, type its keyword below and click Go. To locate areas that match your topic of interest, type words that describe what you are looking for and click Search.

Enter word(s): GUIDEPAGER

Go   Search

A PARENT'S GUIDE TO ONLINE CHATTING

By Lisa Iannucci

The world can be a dangerous place, and the virtual world of telecommunications can also be hazardous. In either world you can keep yourself and your loved ones safe by using a bit of common sense. Here are the rules of the virtual road.

As a parent, when you subscribe to an online service, you will probably look forward to the vast array of educational materials available to help your children achieve their academic goals. Online services also offer your child social opportunities as well. There are many specialized forums for children and teenagers where they can meet other children of the same age with the same interests. They can exchange public and private messages, and engage in live conversation.

For the most part, this is a terrific learning experience. Children make friends, explore different cultures, and expand their hobbies. However, while there are many benefits from being online, children need supervision to make sure that these online experiences are positive and rewarding.

DARK CORNERS

Although you would like to believe that your children are engaging in enjoyable conversations with kids their own age, it isn't always true. There are dangers and risks to being online, and it's important to know what these risks are so you can protect your child. You also need to educate your children about these potential dangers.

You've taught your children not to talk to strangers, go for a ride in their car or let anyone in the house when they are alone. You want to be introduced to their new friends before they go out, and you always try to know where your children are. These same rules are appropriate when your children spend time online.

- After exchanging messages with older men, a 13-year old girl was missing for two weeks from her home in Kentucky. She was picked up in Los Angeles two weeks later. Her parents found sexually explicit images had been transmitted through her computer.

- A 15-year-old Seattle teen ran away to San Francisco using a bus ticket mailed to him by another teen he met in an electronic chat room for gays. He returned home two weeks later.

- Thinking she was talking to another teenage girl, a 15-year-old gave out her home telephone number. A 50-year-old called and wanted to meet with her in person.

- A young man arranges to meet an online teen. It turns out to be an older man who attacks him

These cases are startling and severe, but things like this happen online, just as they do in the real world. Children and teenagers tend to be trusting and curious. They sometimes give out too much personal information. As a result, your child might be harassed or put in a dangerous situation by arranging a face-to-face meeting.

PARENTAL CONTROLS

You can restrict access to certain online areas and features. For example, America Online (AOL) allows you to block instant messages and prevent children from entering live chat areas that might be adult-oriented. Prodigy screens bulletin board messages and returns any inappropriate messages to the writer. On CompuServe, you can block instant messages and solicitations to engage in a private conference. You can also prohibit your child from entering individual forums or bulletin boards.

On Prodigy and AOL, your child has his or her own member name, but your master account can block what the other users have access to. On CompuServe, your children share your account with you, including your mailbox. This may discourage inappropriate activity.

It's important to know that your children can also use the Internet through your online service provider. The Internet is not generally monitored. Recently, however, several companies have created special software packages that will help you to restrict your children's access on various services, including sites on the Internet.

OFF LIMITS

Besides chatting with other members through bulletins, email messages or live chat, your children may also be exposed to inappropriate material of a sexual or violent nature. There are many areas on private bulletin boards and the Internet that are specifically designed for adults who want to read, post or download sexually explicit material. Although these forums are open only to adults, be aware that computer-literate children can locate them and may view this material.

Pictures and articles can also be sent via email messages. This is another dark corner of online services. Your children may be sent sexually graphic material in a private message. They may also be asked to exchange photos with another member. If your children are familiar with downloading and scanners, make sure they *never* send pictures of themselves to another person or upload them into a forum library without your permission.

WHO ARE YOU REALLY?

Remember the girl who gave out her telephone number to someone she thought was another teenage girl? It turned out to be a middle-age male. Depending on what online name you choose. no one knows how old you are or whether you are male or female. For example, when you sign on to America Online, you can choose the name WOW. This doesn't tell

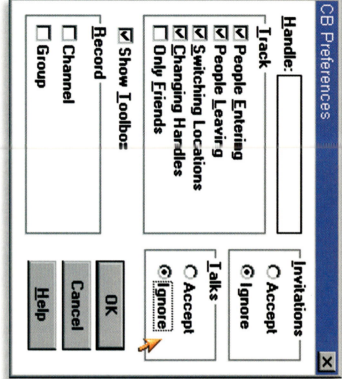

Figure 1: *Both invitations and talks can be ignored in CompuServe's CB Simulator.*

CB Preferences

Handle: _____

Track
☑ People Entering
☑ People Leaving
☑ Switching Locations
☑ Changing Handles
☐ Only Friends

☑ Show Toolbox

Record
☐ Channel
☐ Group

Invitations
○ Accept
● Ignore

Talks
○ Accept
● Ignore

OK Cancel Help

The research can be done any time of the day or night and in any weather. For fun, your child can download computer games or challenge a child in another state to a game. They can find someone their own age who wants to talk about POGS, now that you've had enough.

Most people exploring the information highway and chatting with your children are not interested in harming them. However, it's important to know the risks involved when you're introducing your child to this wonderful technology that connects all the corners of the world. Here's a brief checklist:

• Talk to your children before you sign up with an online service. Make sure they understand that meeting and chatting with people can be dangerous if they're not careful.

• Learn how to log on and find your child's chat and bulletin board areas. If you don't know how, ask your child to show you.

• Set rules for computer time. Limit the hours the service can be used for live chatting.

• Make sure you and your child agree never to give out the following information:
- telephone number
- home or school address
- name of school
- where the parents work
- your online password
- financial information

• Never allow a child to have a face-to-face meeting unless you are present. Make the first meeting in a public spot.

• Your child should never give out pictures of themselves or any family members without your permission.

• Your child should never respond to threatening or harassing messages or any messages that make them feel uncomfortable.

• Don't let your child explore the services on their own. Sit down with them and find out what the proper areas are for your child's age.

• Although children need their privacy, look through their hard drive and floppy disks for questionable material. Make unexpected visits while they are online and see what's on the screen.

• Monitor your phone bill to see how much time your child is spending online.

• Consider putting the computer in a family room or other public place in the house.

• SurfWatch can block more than fifteen hundred Internet sites that contain material you would not want your child to see. They also offer a subscription service which updates the list of unwanted sites. SurfWatch screens for newsgroups likely to contain sexually explicit material, and prevents your computer from accessing specified Internet sites. A password protected on/off switch gives you the ability to allow or prevent access.

• Net Censor, written for Windows 3.1, is the first add-on product to Internet In A Box that allows a user to restrict children's access to sensitive material. Created by New York Net Works, Net Censor will also include a free newsletter that discusses children's online safety issues.

SurfWatch Software, Inc., 105 Fremont Avenue, Suite E, Los Altos, CA 94022; 415-948-9500; fax: 415-948-9577.

info/www.surfwatch.com; $49.95 for the software and the base list, an additional $5.95 a month for the subscription program updates.

Net Censor retails for $29.95. It also includes a free newsletter that discusses children's safety issues on the Internet. For more information or to place an order, call 1-800-94-NYNET.

HOW TO RECOGNIZE A PICTURE FILE

If you're downloading a picture of a football, the filename may look like this: Ftball.gif. GIF means the football is a digitized photograph in graphical interchange format. There are other extensions that tell you whether the file is a picture: gif, jpg, bmp, tif, pcs, dl, and gl. This will help you monitor what, and how many, pictures your child is downloading.

Lisa Iannucci has published in Parenting, Practical Homeowner, New Body, Home Mechanix, Writer's Digest, Bride's, American Health *and* Weight Watchers. *She is Executive Editor of* New York's Westchester Health Review. *She began computing ten years ago. A member of* The American Society of Journalists and Authors, *she regularly reviews software for ASJA and the* CompuServe Journalism *forum.*

---

anyone who you really are. You can join any conference or forum. However, this provides safety as well. By allowing your child to have a nickname, for example TuffGuy, no one knows your child's real name, sex or age. Unfortunately, some people change their name to pose as children or teenagers and gain the trust of a child. Warn your children that not everyone is who they say they are.

WHAT IF YOU HAVE A PROBLEM?

In a live conference on CompuServe, someone solicited a young woman and used offensive language. That person was warned. When he continued, he was locked out of the conference and lost access to that section of CompuServe. Obscene, threatening or sexually explicit language is not tolerated in any message board, live chat area, email or instant messages. Most live chat is usually monitored by a sysop. However there are times when live conferencing will not be supervised, and your child may be subjected to this type of language.

If your child is being harassed in any manner by instant messages, use the block-out function and let the sysop know immediately. Write down the person's name or ID number. If you are sent obscene email material, don't discard it. Keep a copy of the note or file as proof. Report them immediately and don't respond to the person.

IT'S NOT THAT BAD

Online services offer wonderful educational tools. Your child can explore the world without leaving your home, learn a language or find information on presidents for a school project.

THE INTERNET:
WHAT IT IS, HOW TO CONNECT, WHAT IT COSTS

By Stephen Poole

You've heard about the Information Superhighway, but do you really know what it is, how it works, and how to get started exploring in cyberspace?

ENTER THE INTERNET

There's been enough hype about the Internet over the past couple of years to last us well into the 21st century. You can't turn on the television or read a newspaper or magazine without seeing something about the "Information Superhighway" or "Cyberspace," and nearly every company involved in computer software or telecommunications is hopping on the Internet bandwagon.

IBM uses "easy Internet access" as a selling point for OS/2; Microsoft plans to provide full Internet access as part of its upcoming online service, and will ship Word with a feature that allows users to create World Wide Web sites (don't worry—we'll explain the Web later!); America Online, CompuServe, Delphi, Prodigy, and other existing commercial online services now offer or plan to offer full Internet access; major broadcast and cable television networks like CBS and ESPN have their own Internet sites—the list goes on and on.

But even with all the media attention, little effort has been made to explain just exactly what the Internet really is, how it works, what can be found there, and how much it costs the average user. We'll try to answer those questions and more over the next few pages, and hopefully make it easier for you to decide if, when, and how you want to become part of this rapidly expanding virtual world.

THE NATURE OF THE BEAST

Simply put, the Internet is a network of computer networks that communicate with each other using the Transmission Control Protocol/Internet Protocol, or TCP/IP for short. All you really need to know about TCP/IP is that it allows any kind of computer to send and receive data from any other kind of computer.

Many of the computers with direct, full-time connections to the Internet are running Unix, an operating system (like MS-DOS) that's used in everything from desktop PCs to huge mainframe computers. Until just recently, taking advantage of the Internet's vast resources meant learning at least some Unix commands. But thanks to the arrival of Windows-based Internet software, the only thing you need to know in order to travel the Internet is how to point and click.

Because the Internet is growing at such an explosive rate, it's hard to say exactly how many computers are connected to this "network of networks"; estimates range from between four and five million, with between 20 to 30 million people having some form of Internet access.

How does it work? Well, to someone like you or me it's similar in many ways to logging onto a commercial online service like CompuServe or America Online. Just as with those services, you must have an account to log onto the Internet, and unless you're a college student, government worker, or an employee at a company that has a computer hooked directly to the Internet, you'll have to pay for account setup and monthly usage charges. (We'll look at the various ways to get an Internet account a little later.)

After being given a name and password, you use your modem to dial into a computer that's directly connected to the Internet on a full-time basis—again, very similar to logging onto a commercial online service. And once your modem is connected to that computer, you can then "travel" to any of the millions of computers that make up the Internet.

When you "visit" a site on the Internet, your PC is communicating directly with another computer—one that might be thousands of miles away. What you're able to do once connected to a particular computer hooked to the Internet (also known as a "site" or "server") depends on what that computer has been configured to do. Some sites you link to may only allow you to upload or download files; some allow you to use a program residing on the remote computer as if it were on your own PC; some allow you to send email; and still others transport you to yet another site with the click of a button.

What makes all this even more amazing is that just a few short years ago the Internet was a mere fraction of its current size. The fact that it works as well as it does is a testament to the Internet's basic design, which becomes clearer if we look at how the Internet first started and how it evolved into the technological marvel it is today.

CHILD OF WAR

As strange as it seems now, the Internet was created in response to the possibility of a foreign attack on the U.S. You see, if several computers are linked together in serial fashion by a single wire and a bomb hits that wire (or something else breaks the line), then many of the computers will have lost the ability to communicate with each other. This inability to communicate could have disastrous import during a time of crisis, particularly during a military emergency where communications are of the utmost importance.

To address the question of how to link computer networks dispersed over a large area and still ensure proper connections even with major breaks in data lines, the Department of Defense created ARPANET in 1969 (ARPA stands for the Advanced Research Projects Agency). In its original incarnation, ARPANET consisted of only four computers.

ARPANET arrived at a solution based on several simple principles: that there must be many routes of communication between computers; that communication should occur directly between two computers; that the computers on the network (instead of the network itself) would be responsible for knowing where to send data and then transmitting over whatever route is available; and that all the computers on the network would use the same rules, or protocols, when talking to each other. The first protocol used by ARPANET was called the Host-to-Host protocol, but because it limited the numbers that could be on the network, research began in 1972 to develop a new protocol. The result was TCP/IP and by the early 80's TCP/IP was the protocol for ARPANET.

Other networks started appearing in the late 70's and early 80's: UUCP (a network of Unix-based computers), USENET (User's Network), CSNET (Computer Science Network), BITNET (Because It's Time Network), and more. Some of these were private, while others were paid for by the government. Then came MILNET, a Department of Defense offshoot of ARPANET; the two networks were collectively called DARPANET (Defense Advanced Research Projects Agency Network), and eventually became known as the Internet.

In the late 80's, the National Science Foundation created NSFNET (red tape prevented NSF from using the Internet) to link its five supercomputers so their resources could be easily shared. NSFNET used the same TCP/IP employed by the Internet, and relied on a series of regional networks to connect the supercomputers.

To make a long story short, all the private and public networks joined the regional networks managed by the NSF; the network was opened up to accommodate a few of the larger commercial networks, and networks outside the U.S. were

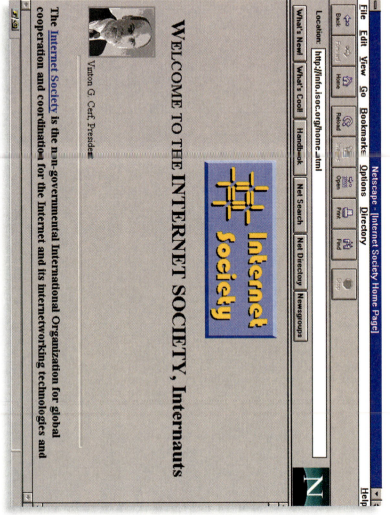

Netscape - [Internet Society Home Page]

File   Edit   View   Go   Bookmarks   Options   Directory   Help

Back   Forward   Home   Reload   Images   Open   Print   Find   Stop

Location: http://info.isoc.org/home.html

What's New!   What's Cool!   Handbook   Net Search   Net Directory   Newsgroups

WELCOME TO THE INTERNET SOCIETY, Internauts

Vinton G. Cerf, President

The **Internet Society** is the non-governmental International Organization for global cooperation and coordination for the Internet and its internetworking technologies and

Figure 1: Surprisingly, no one really "owns" the Internet. The closest thing to an executive board is the Internet Society, which helps implement technical standards and promotes cooperation between the various networks that comprised by the Internet.

allowed to become part of the Internet. And with the lessening of restrictions on commercial sites in 1992, the Internet began the incredible growth spurt that has made it a household world. Ah, capitalism!

WHO'S THE BOSS?

There's a lot of money tied up in the Internet these days, and you'd think that whoever owned it would be sitting back watching the dollars pour in. But the fact is that no one "owns" the Internet. That doesn't mean people aren't making money off of the Internet; commercial Internet providers exist because they can charge you a fee for access. Once an Internet provider has collected your fees, however, it doesn't have to turn over any of that money to a higher authority (except to pay for phone lines, equipment, etc.).

The only real governing body on the Internet is the Internet Society, or ISOC. The ISOC was created "for global cooperation and coordination for the Internet and its internetworking technologies and applications" (their words, not mine). There are several organizations associated with the ISOC that develop and implement technical standards, keep track of computer addresses, and other functions crucial to the smooth working of the Internet, but about the only time you'll run into them is if you're interested in starting and maintaining an Internet site.

THE WORLD IS YOUR (VIRTUAL) OYSTER

What all this means is that, for a very modest price, you can take advantage of the incredible

resources and tools of the Net. Here are some of the things you'll be able to do online:

• **Electronic mail** (email). One of the most useful features of an Internet account is the ability to send email to any of the millions of people with Internet accounts. What's more, all the major commercial online services and email companies have Internet mail gateways—which means you can send email to someone whether they're on CompuServe, America Online, Prodigy, Delphi, GEnie, MCI Mail, AT&T Mail, and others.

• **Participate in Discussion Groups.** There are thousands and thousands of forums—called "newsgroups"—covering almost any conceivable topic where you can read others' messages and post your own. There are even newsgroups that are set up to have messages from other newsgroup members sent to you directly via email. If you can't find a newsgroup dedicated to, say, 1969 Goldtop Les Paul guitars, the solution is simple—start it yourself! It's not that hard to do. Even though newsgroups only support ASCII text, there's a way of posting binary files—graphics, programs, sound clips, and more—by "encoding" them so that the binary data is translated into ASCII text and back again after downloading.

Besides allowing you to discuss your interests with people from around the world, newsgroups can also be a great resource. If you're having problems with a certain software package, or if your monitor display went bonkers after you installed a new video card, you'll find that posting a message detailing your problem will elicit advice—often very good advice—in an amazingly short period of time. And if you decide to sell that software or monitor instead of working out the problem, then you can even post a "For Sale" message in the appropriate newsgroup.

• **Download Files.** There's a veritable mountain of software just waiting to be downloaded on the Internet. Of course there's a lot of Internet-related software available (newsgroup readers, Web browsers, email programs, programming tools), but you'll also find games, updates to productivity software, screensavers, disk-compression utilities, programs to test your PC's performance, and much more. You can also upload files from your PC to an Internet site, so if you've created a shareware game, for instance, you could easily post it online for the whole world to try.

• **Browse Information Resources.** Nearly every university in the United States

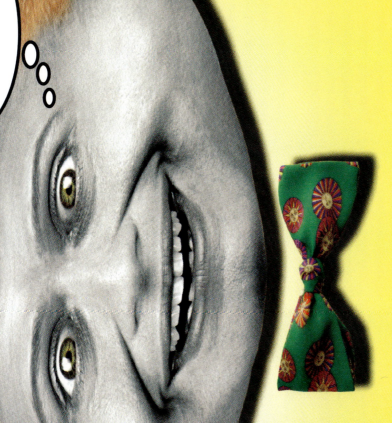

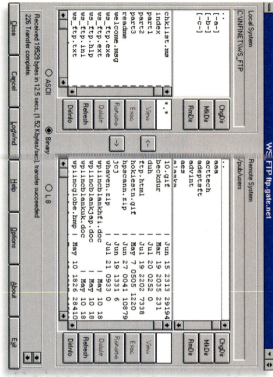

Figure 2: *Using File Transfer Protocol, you connect directly to another computer on the Internet—at which point you can view the contents of that machine's hard drive, and pick the files you'd like to download.*

• **Keep Up With the News.** Every day, more and more magazines are bringing their wares to the Internet. Mainstream publications like *Time, Sports Illustrated, The Wall Street Journal,* and more have their own sites on the World Wide Web, and niche titles like *Wired, Mother Jones,* and others can also be

found on the Web. Naturally, computer magazines are represented quite well here, especially magazines dealing with the Internet. Why buy it at the newsstand when you can find it on the Internet at a mere fraction of the cost?

• **Play Games.** You'll find dozens of games to play online, ranging from classics like chess, checkers, Othello, Hangman, and others to online versions of "Name That Tune" and "Battleship." Another popular type of game takes place in a MUD, short for Multi-User Dungeon or Multi-User Dimension. Participating in a MUD is similar to being part of a role-playing game such as Dungeons & Dragons—and, just like a

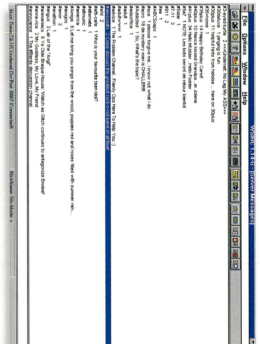

Figure 3: *Hundreds of topics are available on Internet Relay Chat (IRC) servers, and the conversations take place in real time.*

game of Dungeons & Dragons, the action in a MUD takes place in real time (though almost all MUDs are text-based games).

In the future, you can expect to see more top-notch computer games being played on the Net. Already there are versions of the classic computer game *Civilization* and the highly popular board game *Power* that can be played on the Internet, and over the coming

months they'll be joined by flight simulations, racing games, fighting games, hunt-and-kill extravaganzas like *Doom,* and more.

• **Experience Multimedia.** If you have a Web browser—and if you have an Internet account, they're yours for the asking—you can view graphics, hear digitized audio, and see video clips. And very soon you can expect to start seeing stuff on the Internet that you used to see on television: in early 1995, for instance, the Rolling Stones did a concert that was broadcast over the Internet using a technology called MBone.

• **Shop.** There are now more commercial Internet sites than all other types of sites combined. In many instances, it's in a company's interest to have an Internet site regardless of the costs; but the fact is someone's got to foot

the bill for the development and upkeep of these sites—and many of the companies are hoping that someone will be you.

What this means is that, using your credit card, you'll soon be able to purchase nearly anything online, from luggage and sporting goods to jewelry and airplane tickets. There are already places online where you can make purchases; one of the biggest is called the Internet Shopping Network. It's sort of like QVC or the Home Shopping Network, except you choose what item's for sale at any given time. It's probably safe to say that within a few years, anything that can be bought in a store or through mail order can also be purchased online.

GOING ONLINE: DIRECT INTERNET ACCESS VERSUS COMMERCIAL ONLINE SERVICES

Sound good? Then the next step is deciding just how you're going to hook up to the Internet. Only a few short years ago, Internet access was limited to a relatively small number of people;

is linked to the Internet, and as a result there's information available on almost any subject imaginable. University and government databases, the Library of Congress Catalogue, U.S. State Department Travel Advisories, sports schedules, Supreme Court rulings, MIT Media Lab projects—these are a mere smattering of what you can access with a few mouse clicks.

• **Chat With People Around the World.** By logging onto one of the many servers on the Net that support IRC (Internet Relay Chat), you can send typed messages to one or many people in real time. And that's not all: new software has just been developed that will allow you to carry on spoken conversations with anyone on the Internet—i.e., anywhere in the whole world. It doesn't take a professor of economics to realize how much money you could save by paying Internet access rates to talk instead of using a long-distance carrier.

Extra! Extra! Read all about it! Our electronic newsstand will keep you up-to-date with the latest online versions of top computer publications:

Click on the Link Below to View:

• **Wired Magazine**
  HotWired is the place for electronic arts and culture
• **In, Around and Online**
  News of the online industry.
• **Internet World**
  That thing with the coming
• **Windows Magazine**

Figure 4: *You'll find dozens of magazines online, ranging from computer-oriented publications (there's a lot of those) to investigative periodicals like Mother Jones to the hip but informative Wired. Of course, mainstream publications such as Time, Sports Illustrated, and The Wall Street Journal are also represented, with more joining their ranks every month.*

researchers, students, government employees, and the like. Thankfully, that's all changed, and now almost anyone with a computer and a modem can tap into the almost mind-boggling information and resources the Internet offers. There are now a wide variety of options when it comes to setting up an Internet account, each with its own advantages and disadvantages.

Probably the simplest and most hassle-free way to jump on the Information Superhighway is through one of the major commercial online services, all of which now offer access to all the Internet's services. And with the explosion of interest in the Net, there are now more dedicated Internet providers—services that link you directly to the Internet, instead of going through another service to get there—than ever before. Which method is best for you? We'll compare the Internet features of three of the most popular online services—America Online, CompuServe, and Prodigy—then take a look at what you can expect to get from a dedicated Internet provider, and how much each costs. After that, the choice is yours.

America Online

Thanks to a combination of shrewd marketing techniques, a simple user interface, and comparatively low rates, America Online (AOL) has experienced the most phenomenal growth in the history of online services. Since its inception in 1990, AOL has become the most popular online service the world, with a current membership of over two million people. (For complete details on services and features indigenous to AOL, see "The Online Family.")

AOL first started offering its users limited Internet access in 1994; now, AOL members can access almost every nook and cranny of this network of networks. And in keeping with the user-friendly nature of AOL, you don't need to know all the different Internet protocols to cruise the Net.

Using the keyword Internet, you're immediately taken to the Internet Connection menu; once there, you'll find an easy-to-use menu system that lets you access a wide variety of Internet services.

All of AOL's major Internet resources are accessible through clearly labeled globe icons, and since the software is integrated fully into the AOL Interface, dashing all through cyberspace won't seem a lot different from visiting other areas of AOL.

Advantages and Disadvantages

How you rate America Online as an Internet provider depends on several things. If your main concern is getting on the Information Superhighway as quickly and painlessly as possible, and you don't plan on spending more than a few hours of month online, then AOL is the

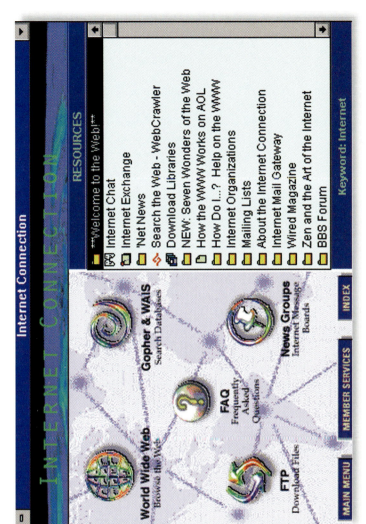

Figure 5: America Online's Internet connection puts the power of the Internet at your fingertips, thanks largely to a system of icons and menus that makes finding your way around a breeze.

service for you. Because all of AOL's Internet resources have been fully integrated into the standard AOL interface, you'll be able to use powerful Internet tools such as FTP, WWW, and Gopher in a minimal amount of time; with an account through a dedicated Internet provider, you must learn the nuances of individual software packages just to get up and running.

come with ten free hours of access, the company's regular rates for Internet access are the highest among all the leading commercial online services. There's a standard monthly membership fee of $9.95, which covers the first five hours of online time; any time spent online beyond five hours is billed at $2.95 an hour. At those rates you're looking at some

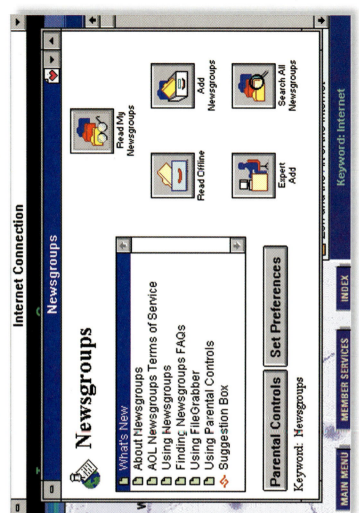

Figure 6: AOL's news reader is a fairly decent tool, but in keeping with the family-oriented nature of the service you must manually enter the names of newsgroups that are considered provocative or controversial.

fairly high monthly Internet bills — $24.70 for 10 hours, $54.20 for 20 hours, and a whopping $83.70 if you spend 30 hours online each month. These prices and pricing plans do

But that ease of use brings with it several disadvantages, the first and most noticeable of which is monthly cost. While there's no setup charge for America Online accounts and they

change frequently. On all of the services you should check the latest pricing.

Then there are AOL's Internet features, all of which are adequate for beginners but which aren't nearly as flexible as what you'll find offered by a dedicated Internet provider or even other commercial online services. Why? Because AOL's Internet resources are integrated directly into the service, which precludes you from using, say, a third-party Telnet package. So if there isn't a menu option for a particular Internet feature, you can't access it through America Online.

Take AOL's Internet chat, for instance. While jumping into or starting a chat only requires a couple of mouse-clicks, you don't have the option to log onto one of the dozens of available IRC servers around the world—you must use AOL's Internet chat server.

Another area where ease of use detracts from your Internet capabilities is Telnet. AOL's Internet Connection currently doesn't support the Telnet protocol, which prevents you from logging on to many MUDSs, as well as any future multi-player games that will rely on the Telnet protocol. America Online's Web Browser program, while certainly functional, lacks the power and options of standalone programs. One important feature it does share with better web browsers, however, is a local disk-cache; set it for, say, 12MB of hard-drive space, and it "remembers" the last 12MB of images and data you've accessed with the Browser. What this means is that when you return to a spot you've recently

visited, the browser will load all relevant data and images from the hard drive, instead of waiting for it to be sent over phone lines—and that helps you be more productive while you're connected.

One AOL feature unique among commercial online services is Parental Control, an option that gives you say-so over what your children can access on the Internet. That's an important consideration, for while the Net offers a cornucopia of valuable information, it's also home to lots of material that most people would consider unsuitable for viewing by minors. Only AOL makes it simple to control what sort of newsgroups and conferences your children can join, as well as prevent downloading of files from newsgroups (where many images of a sexual nature are posted).

The last thing you should consider before settling on America Online as your Internet provider is access numbers. While AOL does have a fairly extensive list of nodes across the country, many smaller towns (and some not-so-small towns) only have 2400-baud numbers—a transmission rate that is simply unacceptable for

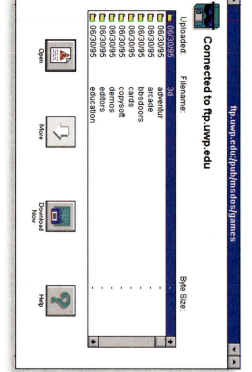

Figure 7: America Online's FTP menu takes the pain out of file transfer by presenting it in a format similar to what you see on other areas of the service.

nearly every Internet resource. Check to make sure there's at least a 9600-baud AOL access number within local calling distance, and preferably 14400; if you plan on viewing graphics on the World Wide Web, even 9600 isn't fast enough.

COMPUSERVE

Before America Online came into the picture, CompuServe was the king of the online services. Even today, it's various software libraries contain many more files than AOL's, and CompuServe is still the service of choice for companies involved in computer hardware and software looking to make their software and tech support available to end users. CompuServe first started offering limited Internet access in 1994, and now has a suite of features that, while not identical to AOL's, is

certainly comparable.

Currently, CompuServe offers menu-based access to USENET newsgroups, Telnet login, and FTP downloading and uploading; use the GO INTERNET command on log on to get the service's Internet menu.

Once there you'll also find links to the Internet New Users Forum, Internet Resources Forum, and *Internet World* magazine, all of which offer invaluable information for the Net newbie.

To jump on the WWW, however, you need to download a couple of additional programs: CompuServe's Web-browsing utility, called NetLauncher, and the Internet Dialer, a communications program based on TCP/IP.

If you log on to the Web directly using the Internet Dialer, you can then use third-party software to access Gopher and IRC servers, or even use the Web browser of your choice. Because of that capability, CompuServe's array of potential Internet resources—FTP, WWW, newsgroups, Telnet, Gopher, email, and IRC—is

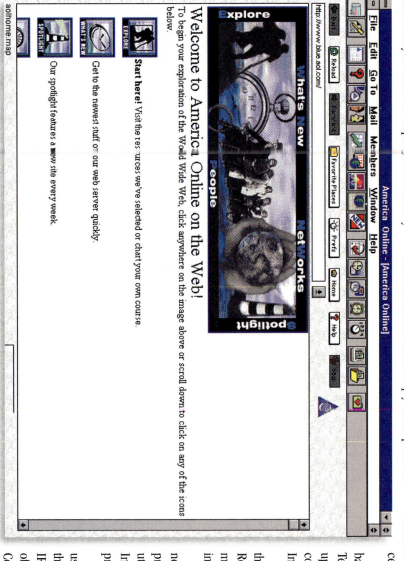

Figure 8: America Online's Web browser has many features you find in stand-alone browsers, including an option to set a cache on your hard drive to remember certain Internet sites you've already visited, thus speeding up data transfer rates when you return.

Welcome to America Online on the Web!

To begin your exploration of the World Wide Web, click anywhere on the image above or scroll down to click on any of the icons below.

Start here! Visit the resources we've selected or chart your own course.

Get to the newest stuff on our web server quickly.

Our spotlight features a new site every week.

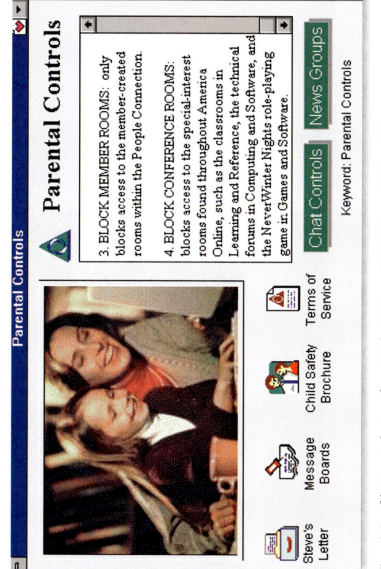

Figure 9: One of the strongest advantages of America Online is its Parental Control features, which let you block messages, access to newsgroups, certain files transfers, and more.

greater than any of the other major commercial online services.

ADVANTAGES AND DISADVANTAGES

Users who intend to invest a lot of time in learning and using the Net will find that the major services change pricing to be competitive. As with America Online, a Standard CompuServe account carries a monthly charge. That gives you unlimited access time in over 100 "basic" CompuServe areas and several free hours of Internet time, but if you want to use features exclusive to CompuServe (called Extended and Premium services) you'll pay per hour, starting as soon as you go to one of these areas (for more on CompuServe's pricing and features, see the "The Online Family" earlier in this book).

For a Standard membership, any time spent on the Internet beyond the first three hours is billed at $2.50/hour; at that rate ten hours of Internet connect time runs $27.45 month, 20 hours would cost $54.45, and 30 hours would run $77.45.

IRC server of your choice, as well as participate in MUDs that require a Telnet connection.

But that versatility also means you'll have to spend more time learning how to use those third-party programs. If you want to find a file at an FTP site on AOL, for instance, accessing an Archie server to do a file search is a simple matter of navigating a couple of menus; since CompuServe's menu-based FTP interface doesn't include a built-in link to an Archie server, you'll have to load your own Archie client software to do a name search. The same goes for searching Gopher servers using Veronica.

CompuServe's Net Launcher software is actually a stand-alone Web browser called Spry Mosaic, and it's a fast, powerful tool that's at least the equal of AOL's integrated Web-browsing interface. One especially nice feature of CompuServe's WWW browser is its "kiosk" mode, which removes all icons and menu bars from the top of the screen, thus providing you with the largest display possible; a keystroke can bring back all that stuff back should you need it.

CompuServe does have some drawbacks. If you're using a supplemental network like Tymnet to reach CompuServe, you have to pay a surcharge in addition to your monthly membership and usage fees, something that AOL doesn't charge for. Another drawback is the lack of built-in parental control devices: where AOL has a powerful Parental Control option to help prevent your children from accessing material you consider obscene or pornographic, CompuServe only has a disclaimer warning you of the possibilities of encountering questionable material on the Internet. (As the Internet grows, however, you can expect to see

Those prices are competitive with AOL's; but CompuServe also has an option for members with Standard accounts called the Internet club that's highly attractive when compared to America Online: $24.95 a month gets you 20 hours of Internet time, with additional time costing $1.95/hour, so instead of paying $77.45 for 30 hours you'd pay $44.45.

Another plus is the fact that CompuServe offers direct Internet access; if you use their Internet Dialer program, you can then switch to other third-party Internet software. If you don't care for CompuServe's FTP interface, for instance, you can use your own; if the newsgroup viewer supplied by CompuServe isn't to your liking, then you can use another one. It also means you can log on to the

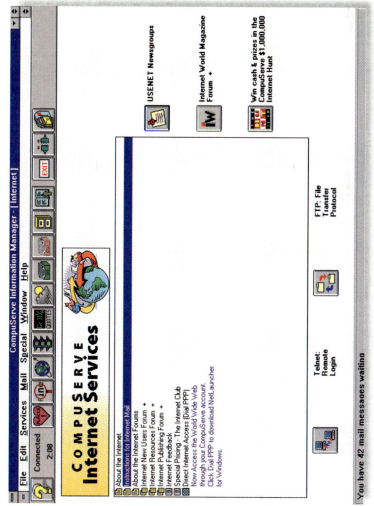

Figure 10: While not as eye-catching as America Online's Internet Connection, CompuServe's Internet Services offers you access to just as many Internet resources, and because you can use third-party software with CompuServe's Internet Dialer, CompuServe actually lets you see more of the Net than AOL.

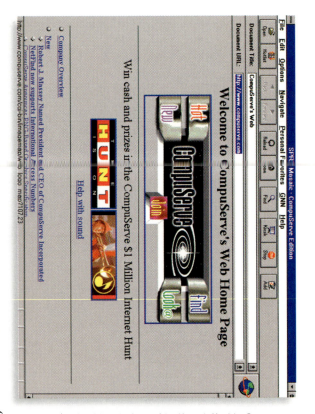

Figure 11: *CompuServe's Web browser, a specially designed version of Spry Mosaic, is an efficient program that brings the graphical power of the World Wide Web to your desktop. A "Kiosk" option turns off the menu bar at the top to allow you to see even more of a Web page. Also, CompuServe's Internet Dialer program offers direct Internet access, so if you don't care for their Web browser you can use your another one.*

Spy — Mosaic - CompuServe Edition
File Edit Options Navigate Personal Favorites GNN Help
Document Title: CompuServe's Web
Document URL: http://www.compuserve.com

Welcome to CompuServe's Web Home Page

Win cash and prizes in the CompuServe $1 Million Internet Hunt

Help with sound

○ Company Overview
○ New
◇ Robert J. Massey Named President and CEO of CompuServe Incorporated
◇ NetPad now supports International Access Numbers

---

doesn't have quite as much to offer as AOL and CompuServe, but it's still an easy and affordable way to get online.

Like America Online, Prodigy's Web browser is integrated into the service's interface, but unlike AOL the browser program is also the only interface provided for FTP and Gopher services as well. If you want to access an FTP site or Gopher server, you manually enter the address into the URL section of the Web browser (strictly speaking, you could also use AOL or CompuServe's Web browsers in the same way, but it's easier to use the menus provided). There's no support for Internet chat or Telnet log in, limitations that put Prodigy a full step behind CompuServe and AOL. Prodigy uses a menu-based interface to access USENET newsgroups.

Perhaps the biggest drawback to CompuServe is in its aesthetics. Sure, you can access newsgroups, FTP sites, and Telnet sites through menu selections, but the interface is downright ugly and primitive compared to the polished point-and-click design of American Online's Internet menus. Still, they get the job done, and the flexibility that CompuServe's approach offers can pay off in the long run for users willing to invest a little time in understanding the basics of various Internet protocols.

stand-alone software packages designed to block offensive newsgroups, FTP sites, etc.)

PRODIGY

For many years, Prodigy has lagged behind CompuServe and AOL in terms of speed, features, and interface; in fact, the Prodigy service itself is still being revamped in order to make it more faster and more visually attractive. The same can be said for Prodigy's Internet features. Prodigy

ADVANTAGES AND DISADVANTAGES

Of the three major online services we've examined, Prodigy offers the most attractive pricing for people who plan to spend a lot of time on the net: Their 30/30 plan gives you 30 hours a month to cruise cyberspace for $29.95, with any time beyond that billed at $2.95 an hour.

If you do settle on Prodigy, the 30/30 plan is really the only way to go. The Basic Prodigy membership gives you five hours of access for $9.95, with additional usage billed at $2.95 an hour; at those rates ten

---

hours would cost $24.70, only five bucks less than the 30/30 plan.

Prodigy's Web browser is highly similar to CompuServe's, and has nearly all the same features except for the Kiosk mode. The big difference is that on Prodigy the Web browser does double duty as an FTP and Gopher interface, and as a consequence you won't find a collection of popular FTP or Gopher sites that can be accessed through menus like on AOL or CompuServe to help you get started. That in itself makes using those resources more difficult than need be, since you have to manually type in FTP and Gopher sites in the URL section of the Web browser.

Prodigy also lags behind CompuServe and AOL in terms of high-speed access numbers. While that's probably not a problem in large metropolitan areas, other cities that have 14400bps AOL and CompuServe numbers may only have a 9600bps Prodigy access number, and as we mentioned before that's just too slow if you plan to enjoy the graphical presentation of Web pages.

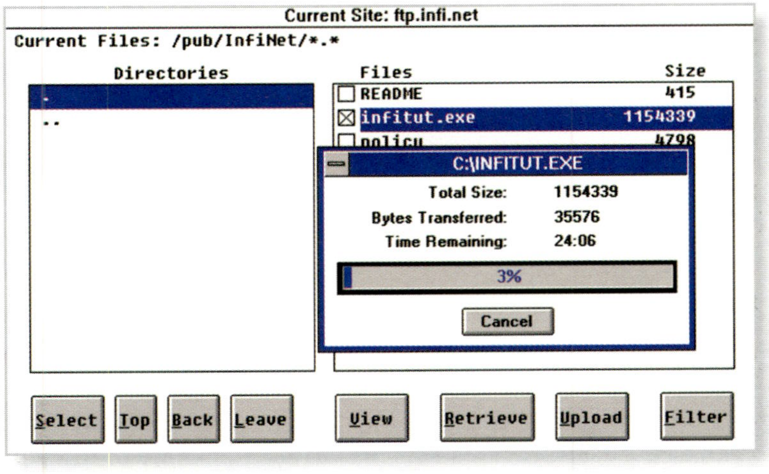

DIRECT INTERNET ACCESS

If you're willing to spend a little time setting up software packages and don't mind a few bumps and detours along the way, direct Internet access is definitely for you. Yes, it will take you longer to get up and running than if you use a commercial online service, but the rewards in the end are quite substantial.

First, you need to find out if there's an internet provider in your area; if not, you may have no choice but to use one of the online services to cruise the Net. But as the Internet continues to experience explosive growth, more and more Internet providers are popping up in smaller towns and cities; in fact, there are even a few 800 numbers for users in remote areas can dial in case they don't have an Internet provider within local calling distance.

Internet providers usually charge some sort of startup charge to open your account, but in return

---

Figure 12: *CompuServe's FTP interface gets the job done, but it's not exactly pleasing to the eye.*

Current Files: /pub/Infinet/*.*

Current Site: ftp.infi.net

Directories
..

Files   Size
README   4/5
infitut.exe   1154339

Select Top Back Leave View Retrieve Upload Filter

C:\INFITUT.EXE
Total Size: 1154339
Bytes Transferred: 35576
Time Remaining: 24:06
Cancel
3%

PRODIGY @ Web Browser
File Edit Options Navigate Help
Back Forward Home HotList Save Reload Load Images
Document Title: Prodigy Home Page
Document URL: http://antares.prodigy.com/welcome.htm

[Browse News] [Search Tools] [Help] [Viewers] [Internet Groups] [MarketPlace]

Welcome to the PRODIGY Web Browser.
Get ready! You're about to get caught up in the World Wide Web. The "Web" is continuously spanning new information, fresh ideas, cool people to talk to and much more. And we connect you to it all! Newcomers, click on PRODIGY Help Index for an Internet Tutorial and other Web-learning resources.

Hot Spots
Want to be Informed? Intrigued? Entertained? We've put the spotlight on the hot sites you won't want to miss.

Scavenger Hunt - WIN Prizes! Have Fun! Be a winner in August
Totally - Be part of an online zine
New York Prodigy - Cool Music
Arts & Entertainment - Zany Humor
Yahoo - It's not, then a Search
Dignline - It's an in depth Internet Directory
Jerry Garcia - Rock and Roll loses a legend. Read the latest about his untimely passing
Irving Digital - The WEB Magazine

Figure 13: *Prodigy's Web browser is similar to CompuServe's in many ways, but because it's built into the Prodigy service it's the only one you can use to surf the Web.*

take. For starters, rates for direct Internet access are usually much lower than through a commercial online service, particularly if you plan to spend a lot of time online. A typical SLIP or PPP account (see sidebar) might cost between $20 and $30 a month, but for that you get 40 or 50 hours of connect time—and once you start really surfing the Net for vital information or files, you'll find that it's not too hard to use up 30 or 40 hours a month.

Another consideration is speed. If you're accessing the Net through Prodigy or AOL, for instance, the data transmission rates can be affected by traffic indigenous to those services; in other words, if there are a lot of people on America Online, it can slow down how fast data comes to you, even if they aren't on the Internet. And while CompuServe has direct Internet access, you can still experience network slowdown if you're dialed into through a CompuServe node; you can avoid that by using a supplemental network like Tymnet or Sprintnet, but then you're paying surcharges.

A final advantage is flexibility. With a direct Internet account, you can choose which software you like best for email, FTP, Gopher, the World Wide Web—you name it, and you can probably find it for free or at a fairly low price somewhere on the Internet. The best Web browser available, Netscape, can't even be used through AOL or Prodigy.

But users with low frustration levels might want to stay away from direct Internet access. Many people accustomed to commercial services have a problem grasping the idea of a suite of software tools for online productivity; they're used to logging onto a service and performing every task by clicking on an icon or a pull-down menu, all from an interface that's relatively static. Indeed, it can be a little confusing to log on to your Internet provider, then minimize the window for the communications software and open a different item in a Program Group in order to read email (or use FTP, or access Gopher menus, etc.).

In truth, however, the hardest part about using different applications for different Internet resources is the initial configuration; once that's done, everything else is usually self-explanatory. And individual programs frequently are more powerful than the interface integrated into commercial online services. Take newsgroup readers, for instance. Binary files (pictures, programs, sound clips, etc.) are often posted in ASCII format (called UU-encoded, or UUE) to newsgroups, which are designed to only handle text; what's more, a single binary file may require the posting of several text files. On AOL, CompuServe, or Prodigy, you must download these files, then use a decoder program to change them back to their original binary format; most stand-alone newsgroup readers, however, have a function built in that will automatically decode these files, removing the headaches of learning how to decode, or even what UUE is.

In almost every instance, in fact, a stand-alone program offers you much more power and versatility than the built-in, menu-driven choices you find on the online services. It all boils down to how much time you want to invest getting up and running.

I'M ONLINE—WHAT NEXT?

The Net's a mighty big place, with millions and millions of documents at your fingertips. How do you find what interests you?

It's a problem that's faced cybernauts for years, but now it's easier than ever to hone in on just the information you need, whether it's the location of a patch file, a Web site where you can post a sound clip of your band's recording, or a

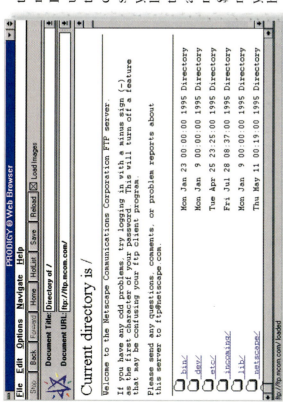

Figure 14: *Prodigy's Web browser does double duty as the FTP interface. It works fine, but the lack of an FTP menu means you'll have to find FTP sites on your own.*

for that fee you receive the software you need to get online and start exploring; also, most larger Internet providers have their own WWW pages where you can go for pointers in how to start surfing the Net, and where to find software that lets you make full use of all the Internet has to offer.

Because dedicated Internet providers don't force you to go through an interface like on the commercial online services, you have complete freedom as to where you go online and what you can do there. AOL doesn't have Telnet login, but you can easily do that through a dedicated Internet provider; Prodigy doesn't support Internet chats, but you can access every IRC server in the world through an Internet provider. It's all there: It's simply a matter of learning where stuff is located and how to use the software you need to get there.

ADVANTAGES AND DISADVANTAGES

Users who want to fully exploit the resources of the Internet—by downloading free software and shareware, subscribing to newsgroups, browsing the Web, accessing databases through Telnet login, participating in Internet chats—will probably want to go the direct Internet access route.

There are a couple of reasons why direct Internet access may be the route you want to

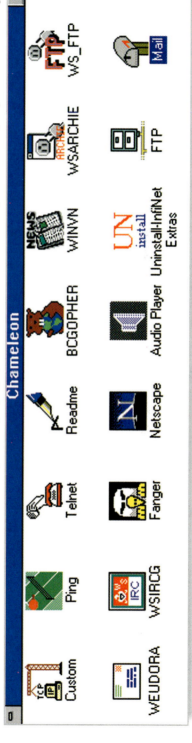

Figure 15: *If you choose to use a dedicated Internet provider, you'll probably use a suite of programs like these, opening and closing them as needed.*

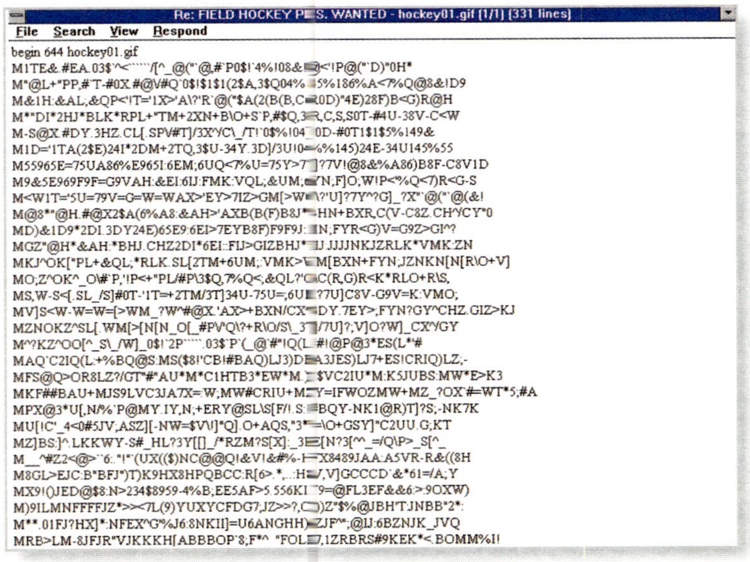

Figure 16: *This stand-alone newsgroup reader, called WinVN, can take the gobbledygook you see in the middle of the screen and automatically decode it into a binary file, such as a JPEG image or WAV audio file.*

list of menu choices from Gophers around the world. We'll begin with the two easiest and most powerful methods of locating information—indexes and search engines—and then touch on tools that are a little harder to use, but which might come in handy later. And don't forget: Whichever method of Internet access you choose, you're sure to find pointers that will get you headed in the right direction.

Indexes: These are one of the first tools an Internet novice should use. Constantly updated and categorized for easy use, indexes make navigating the Internet almost as easy as cruising through America Online or CompuServe (sometimes easier!).

Indexes are organized just as you'd expect, with headings for various topics—computing, entertainment, health, education, and so on. Each topic is broken down into more specific categories; click on computing, for example, and you might get a menu listing games, graphics, hardware, magazines, operating systems, etc. And the beautiful thing about indexes is that they very often include listings for other indexes, giving you instant access to even more options.

You'll find indexes all over the Internet, but two good ones to start with are on the World Wide Web. The Whole Internet Catalog (URL http://nearnet.gnn.com/wic/newrescat.toc.html) is a fantastic jumping-off point in your search for more specific information, and might be the most complete index online. Also worth looking into is the Yahoo Web Index (URL http://www.yahoo.com). It's not quite as extensive as the Whole Internet Catalog, but it's still a great place to start your Internet journey.

Search engines: Indexes are wonderful if you don't mind going through menu after menu in search of your information needs, but sometimes you want to get right to the meat of the matter—and that's where search engines come in. A search engine allows you to search by keyword, so the results that are returned only deal with the specific subject you want to know about. Even more impressive is that these search engines actually look *inside* a document—if you use the keyword "Liberia," for example, the search engine will show you every document that contains that word, whether it's in the document name or embedded somewhere in the text of that document. And while all these search engines are part of the World Wide Web, they will return results that point you to Gophers, FTP sites, newsgroups, and more.

But search engines aren't perfect. Use a fairly generic phrase like "computer," for instance, and you'll get back thousands of "hits" (addresses for documents that contains that word). And even though search engines allow you to limit the number of hits that are returned, there's often no way of knowing which document has the info you need.

Perhaps the most practical search engine is the WebCrawler (http://webcrawler.com), once privately run but now owned and operated by AOL. While its database is somewhat limited, it returns results very quickly, and often is all you need to locate that elusive Web page or FTP site.

If you don't mind waiting for results to your inquiry, you'll want to use the Lycos search engine (http://lycos.cs.cmu.edu). Its database has over five million documents (there's a smaller Lycos search engine with fewer documents that will obviously return results faster), and you can also choose to get an extract of each document that shows how your keyword was used. While this option makes it simple to decide which documents or Internet addresses are worth exploring, it comes at a price: Lycos searches are notoriously slow.

Two other search engines that will prove useful are the **Yahoo Search** (http://www.yahoo.com/search.html) and the **WWW Worm** (http://www.cs.colorado.edu/home/mcbryan/WWWW.html). Also, the home pages (i.e., the starting points for information pertaining to the search engine) for these search engines often have links to yet other search engines, so once you find one you'll eventually find them all.

FTP searches: Both Prodigy and AOL have an Archie server to help you find files, and both are easily accessed through menu buttons; CompuServe does not. Typing in the full name of the file will narrow the results of an Archie search, but if you don't know the exact name you can use part of the filename and wildcards (typing in DOOM*.* will return a list of files that have DOOM in their name). Keep in mind, however, that Archie searches can take a while, especially if you use wildcards. In addition, many Internet sites have lists of popular FTP sites to help you get started, and many WWW sites and Gopher menus have databases of FTP sites.

CompuServe users and those with direct Internet access don't have automatic access to an Archie server, but in both cases you can use a third-party Archie client to access one of the many Archie servers around the world (see Table 1). Be sure to use one that's geo-graphically closest to you for best response times). Remember: Archie databases only have data on files at anonymous FTP servers. That means that files at sites requiring you to log in even if login is publicly available won't be included in Archie databases.

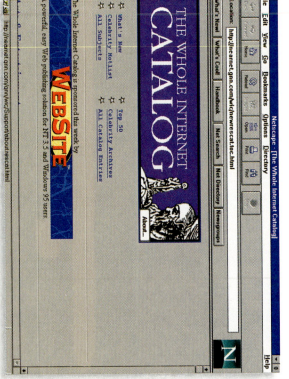

Figure 17: *The Whole Internet Catalog is a fantastic resource that groups Net resources by category. Start your journey here, and chances are you'll soon find what you're looking for.*

Newsgroups: Finding the newsgroups you'd like to participate in is easy. The first time you

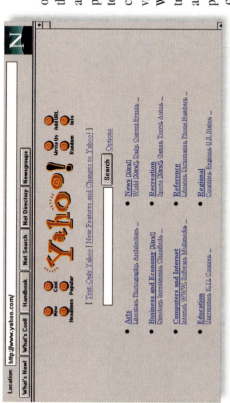

Figure 18: Another popular catalog is Yahoo, started originally by two college students as a part-time project but now one of the most widely accessed indexes on the Internet.

access your Internet provider's news server, you can get an entire list of the newsgroups they carry; since there are over 16,000 USENET newsgroups alone, however, it can take a while to get the whole list. Once you have it, though, you can scroll through at your leisure and pick only the one's you're interested in. On the commercial online services, you can type in a keyword—computers, sports, music, etc.—and view a list of newsgroups with those words in the title, making it simple to find only those groups that you care about.

Gopher searches: Veronica is similar to Archie—you log on to Gopher servers that have Veronica in order to search for a topic—except it searches for words and phrases that are found in menu selections from Gophers all over the world, rather than a file name. AOL's Gopher feature has a link to a Gopher server with Veronica; Prodigy claims to have Veronica searches, but when you access it you find only an Archie server.

IRC: There are many networks of IRC servers, so the best way to find the one you'd like is to use one of the search engines listed above. Here's a list of IRC networks; enter them into a search engine, and you should find receive more information on each of the networks and what you need to do to get involved in this exciting, fascinating world.

Efnet	NetherNet
Undernet	IdealNet/MTSUnet
LinuxNet/SysNet	Japanese IRC
Iaonet	QuestNet/Taiwan Big5
Chiron	ZAnet/South African IRC
KidLink	Australian IRC
DalNet	University of Cincinnati

THE FUTURE OF THE INTERNET

What does the future hold for the Internet? Well, it can be summed up in one word and one acronym: business and WWW. From manufacturing to retail, companies are realizing just how important a presence on the Internet can be—and a WWW site means they can show customers their products, provide them with an order form to buy those products, and even make it possible for them to contact customer service via email. A World Wide Web site is truly an interactive advertisement: potential buyers can download images and information about a product, then place an order for said product, all with a few simple mouse clicks.

But thanks to the Internet's links to colleges, universities, and research organizations, you can still find plenty of practical information online, and even commercial sites will have to include plenty of freebies if visitors are expected to return. After all, there's too much that's being given away on the Net for someone to spend money and time unnecessarily, and the interaction that's made possible by newsgroups, IRC servers, MUDs, and more will only serve to foster the worldwide community that is the Internet.

One thing's for certain: The Internet is here, and will only get bigger with every passing day. And for a very small amount of money, you can tap into this incredible resource. How you do it, though, is up to you. Isn't freedom of choice a beautiful thing?

WHAT DOES IT ALL MEAN?

The first time you sign onto the Internet, you might be overwhelmed by all the acronyms and phrases people are bandying about. Here's a few of the more common acronyms and words and what they mean, but be forewarned: Once online, you'll probably run into a few that will leave you clueless. That's okay, though, because the key thing to remember about using the Internet is that you can learn at your own pace and still be very productive.

Archie: An Internet service (originally developed at McGill University) that lets you search indexes of available files on anonymous FTP sites (at anonymous FTP sites, you log in with a user name of "anonymous" and your email address as a password—if you are "User15" on America Online, for instance, your password would be user15.)

There are several ways to access an Archie server, but the easiest is either through Gopher menus or an Archie application such as WSArchie, which lets you type in the name of an Archie server and the name of the file that you need. See the list of Archie server addresses and the geographic locations they serve in Table 1.

ARCHIE SERVERS	
archie.internic.net	U.S.
archie.rutgers.edu	Northeast U.S.
archie.rutgers.edu	Northeast U.S.
archie.sura.net	Southeast U.S.
archie.unl.edu	Western U.S.
archie.ugam.ca	Canada
archie.funet.fi	Europe
archie.doc.ic.ac.uk	United Kingdom, Ireland
archie.hensa.ac.uk	United Kingdom
archie.au	Australia
archie.edva.uni-linz.ac.at	Austria
archie.mcgill.ca	Canada
archie.th-darmstadt.de	Germany
archie.rediris.es	Spain
archie.ac.il	Israel

Table 1

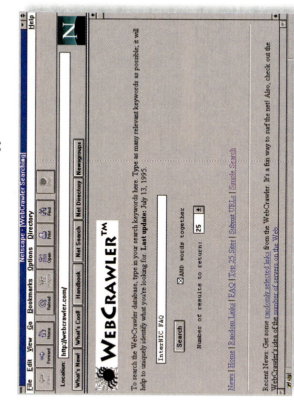

To search the WebCrawler database, type in your search keywords here. Type as many relevant keywords as possible, it will help to uniquely identify what you're looking for. Last update: July 13, 1995.

InterNIC FAQ

Search   Number of results to return: 25   ☒AND words together

News | Home | Random Links | FAQ | Top 25 Sites | Submit URLs | Simple Search

Recent News: Get some randomly selected links from the WebCrawler. It's a fun way to surf the net! Also, check out the WebCrawler's idea of the number of servers on the Web

Figure 19: The WebCrawler search engine is fast and easy to use, but doesn't have as many Internet documents indexed as some other search engines.

Client: The software used for a particular Internet protocol. To use an Archie server, for instance, you could use Archie client software; to log on to an Internet Relay Chat site, you'd use an IRC client.

FAQ: Frequently Asked Questions. Found at many Internet locations, FAQs are designed to help new users learn the basics of various services such as newsgroups and MUDs. But FAQs are also available on almost every topic you can image, from Linux (a free Unix-based operating system for Windows-based 386 and higher PCs) to *FX Fighter* (a one- or two-player beat-'em-up game designed solely for home use) to the lowdown on how to decode files that are posted in ASCII format in newsgroups (in UUE, or Unix-to-Unix Encode). If you're about to enter a new area of the Internet, try to locate the FAQ; it could save you a lot of nasty hate mail from people who expect you to have read it before you go posting questions.

FTP: File Transfer Protocol, or the way binary files are transferred between computers on the Internet. It's basically the same as uploading or downloading a file on a commercial online service or modem-to-modem. But when you're using FTP you can actually see the entire directory structure of the computer to which you've connected (except for anything that's been hidden purposefully, that is).

Gopher: Gopher is an Internet protocol that lets you access information resources, download files, log in with Telnet, send mail, and more; Gopher software (here are several types available online for free) lets you use a mouse to point and click your way through the menus, which are often found on Gopher

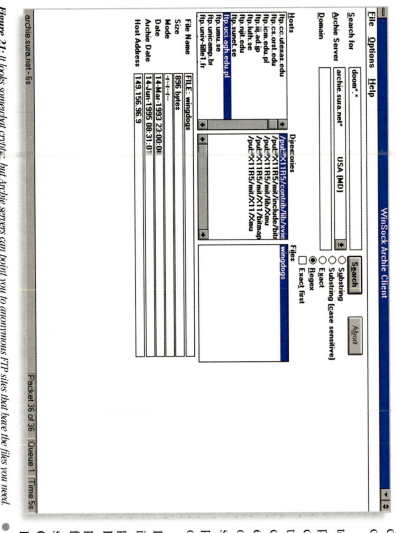

Figure 21: It looks somewhat cryptic, but Archie servers can point you to anonymous FTP sites that have the files you need.

servers are Internet sites designed to be accessed with Gopher. It's similar to the Web, in that choosing a menu option may connect with you an entirely new computer. Gopher is an especially good way to cruise the Internet if you have a looking for general topics of interest. Also known as gopherspace.

Newsgroup: Similar to privately run electronic bulletin boards where you can post messages and files, except that the newsgroups on the Internet are accessible by millions of people around the world. Similar to the forums you find on America Online and Compuserve.

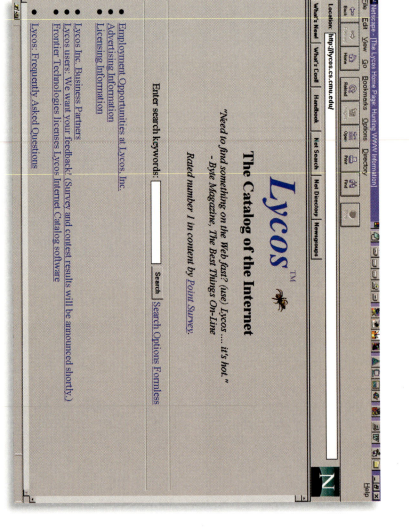

Figure 20: The Lycos search engine is much slower than the WebCrawler, but if you're trying to do a very thorough search for documents relating to a certain topic, this is the to go—Lycos has over five million documents on file!

Newsgroup viewer: A program that allows you to read and post message in the various Internet newsgroups, or forums. It's often built into the Internet features of commercial online services such as CompuServe and America Online.

PPP: Point-to-Point Protocol. It's similar to SLIP but better, especially if data is constantly being sent back and forth between the two connected computers.

SLIP: Serial Line Internet Protocol, which lets you use a modem to connect to the Internet. If you use an Internet provider instead of a commercial online service, you can usually choose between SLIP and PPP.

Telnet: An Internet protocol that allows you to log on to other computers and running programs on the machine to which you've connected; also refers to the software that does the connecting. You can use Telnet to access the card catalog of the Library of Congress, for example. While Telnet isn't as widely used as it once was, it's still necessary for certain tasks, such as participating in a MUD. Telnet will also play a key role in graphically rich multi-player online games.

URL: Uniform Resource Locator. This is an Internet "address," the string of characters you type into your Internet software to connect to a particular computer. For example, the URL for the FTP site of Netscape Corporation, maker of a popular Web browser (see below) is ftp://ftp.ncom.com. The part before the colon specifies what type of Internet protocol—FTP, Gopher, Telnet, HTTP (Hypertext Transfer Protocol), etc.—but you only need to enter that part

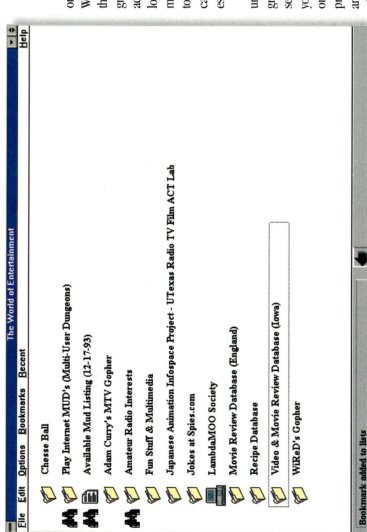

Figure 22: *Gopher is a menu-based Internet resource that works much like the Web. Click on a folder icon, and you may be taken to another menu on another server thousands of miles away.*

if you're using a Web browser to access a site. And case does matter when you're typing in a URL—ftp://ftp.Mcom.com wouldn't work. Here are a few examples.

Gopher
gopher://sunsite.unc.edu
World Wide Web
http://www.origin.ea.com/osi.html
Telnet
telnet://dra.com
FTP
ftp://oak.oakland.edu

Veronica: A database that lets you search Gopher menus (also known as "Gopherspace") using a keyword; like Archie, Veronica databases are stored on various computers around the world. Once Veronica returns a list of menu items containing the word you entered, you simply click on the menu choice and are then connected directly to the Gopher server where that menu choice actually resides.

Here are the addresses for several Gopher servers that feature Veronica searches:

gopher://info.psi.net
gopher://veronica.unikoeln.de
gopher://veronica.sunet.se
gopher://veronica.uib.no
gopher://empire.nysernet.org
gopher://dragon.dgsca.unam.mx

WAIS: Wide Area Information Server, an automated Internet search system that allows users to locate documents containing keywords or phrases. Most often accessed through Gopher menus.

World Wide Web (WWW): A collection of millions of documents that are interlinked using HTTP (Hypertext Transfer Protocol), an Internet protocol based on HyperText Markup Language, or HTML. You've probably seen HTML used on a small scale in the Help files of Windows programs: Clicking on an underlined word brings up an entirely new document about the word, or takes you immediately to a portion of the original document relating to that word. On the Internet, clicking on an underlined word or on a highlighted picture may bring up a document that is stored on the computer you're already connected to—or it may take you halfway around the world and connect you to another computer.

Besides allowing instant access to documents on computers all over the Internet, the World Wide Web has one other important feature: It supports the inclusion of multimedia elements such as graphic images and digitized audio files. The advantages to this are obvious, with Web sites looking more and more like sophisticated magazines in their design. But there's a downside, too—documents that contain large graphic files can take a long time to be sent to your computer, especially if you're connected at 14400 bps or less.

Web Browser: A type of software that understands HTML and displays hypertext links, graphics, and can even play files. There are several types of Web Browsers available, but if you access the Internet through a commercial online service you'll often have to use the one provided by that particular service. If you choose an Internet provider to go online, you can choose whichever Web Browser you like the best.

Currently, the most popular stand-alone Web browser is Netscape; others include Spry Mosaic, Internet Works, and NCSA Mosaic. When properly configured (and assuming you have a few "helper" applications, such as a Telnet program), a Web browser is all you need to navigate the Net. ◖

Stephen Poole *has been involved with personal computers since 1987. In addition to heading up the Technical Support group at the national online service USA Today Sports Center, he has served as Editor of PC Entertainment and PC Gamer.*

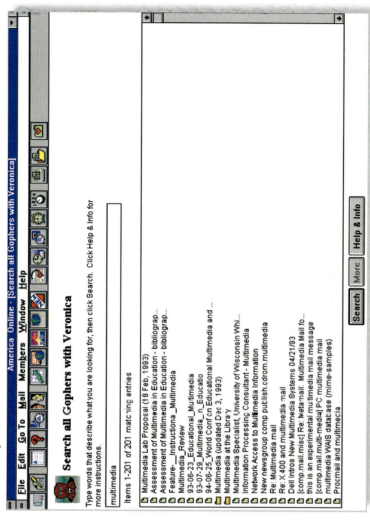

Figure 23: *How do you find what documents are on which Gopher servers? Why with Veronica, of course! Veronica is an index that allows you to enter a keyword, then searches Gopher menu selections for any matches.*

THE 100 BEST INTERNET SITES FOR FAMILIES

The Internet has something for everyone. It's a particularly rich source of information and entertainment for families and children.

By David Haskin

The sites we'll look at here are appropriate for every member of your family—many are even aimed specifically at kids. Some of the sites focus on a narrow subject, while others are gateways to a world of information, providing links to a variety of other related Internet resources.

A **link** on the **Internet** is a highlighted word, phrase or picture that you can click. This takes you to another section within the same site, or to an entirely new site. Clicking on links to maneuver around the Internet is often called **surfing**. Links are sometimes also called **hyperlinks**.

Most of the sites listed here are on the **World Wide Web** (**WWW** or the **Web**, for short). The Web is the easiest part of the Internet for non-technical people to traverse. A Web site typically consists of a **home page** (the screen you first see). There might be information on that page or, more typically, there will be links on which you click with your mouse to go either to additional information on that site or to another Web site.

Tip: You'll know your cursor is positioned over a link when it turns into a little hand. When that happens, clicking your left mouse button takes you to that information or site. Links are also usually underlined or in a different color than the rest of the text.

A few words of caution are in order, however. First, the World Wide Web practically begs you to hop around from site to site. Virtually every Web page has links to other sites—but those other sites might not be a place you want your kids to visit. So if you want to be absolutely sure that your child doesn't wander into one of those sites, it's best to stay around as he or she explores.

Second, on the Net nothing is forever. All these sites were active at the time of this writing, but Web sites have a way of coming and going on

short notice. We didn't include many otherwise excellent sites that indicated that they might be moving in the future.

Next, some of these sites may be slow to connect and display information. The faster your modem, the better. Patience is required on the Internet, and particularly on the Web, during peak evening hours or when accessing popular sites.

Also, beware of sites that are overly self-serving. Many organizations have Web home pages that aim only to entice you to buy their services or products. In this list, we avoided such sites. We did, however, include commercial sites, but only if they provide extensive and useful information beyond merely advertising and marketing.

Finally, be very careful about how you type Web addresses in your Web browser. Getting a single character wrong makes it impossible to make the connection. Similarly, only capitalize

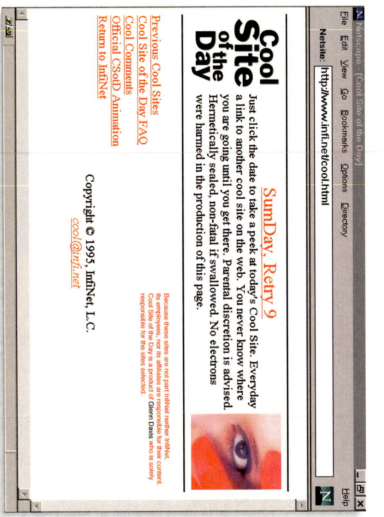

Figure 1: *They're sometimes off-beat and strange, but the sites highlighted on Cool Site of The Day are almost always interesting.*

characters if they are capitalized in this listing. Otherwise, stick with lowercase. Even if we break an address into two (or more) lines in this article, you'll need to type it into your computer on one line with no internal spaces between characters.

With those rules in mind, hop on your Internet surfboard and have fun!

GETTING STARTED ON THE WEB

The World Wide Web has an enormous number of interesting sites, and many of them are great fun. Sometimes just getting started is the toughest part. This section lists some sites that are not interesting in and of themselves, but are essential because they provide links to other sites to start you on your way. There are many such sites available; this first section lists nine of the better ones.

EASIEST WAY TO STAY THERE.

OVER 420 HOURS FREE EACH MONTH!

NetCruiser Service

EASIEST WAY TO GET ON THE INTERNET.

FOR WINDOWS

everything you need for [fast, easy, direct] **internet** access

FREE

NETCRUISER

NetCruiser Software

Plus NetCruiser includes World-Wide Web, IRC, Gopher, FTP, Usenet, Telnet, E-mail—all the most popular Internet resource discovery tools.

Best of all, with NetCruiser service you get NetCruiser software FREE. It's fun. It's easy. And, with simple point-and-click icons to guide you along the way, it can have you up and running in only minutes.

Order now and we'll even give you FREE activation too. So call us today. It just doesn't get any easier than this.

NETCOM
The Leading Internet Service Provider

"NetCruiser...the hands-down favorite of our first-time Internet users."
PC World

"...NetCruiser from NETCOM is one of the most comprehensive Internet packages available. This one-stop interface will have you on the Internet within minutes..."
LAN Times

"NetCruiser—best Internet front end."
Online Access Magazine

"NetCruiser is great for people who are intrigued by the Net but intimidated by the commands usually required for access."
PC/Computing

ONLY $19.95 A MONTH!
- FREE ACTIVATION—SAVE $25!*
- 420+HRS/MO. AT NO CHARGE!

800-353-6600

How can you get the best Internet access software and the best nation-wide Internet service? Easy. Just pick up the phone and order NetCruiser™ for Windows™ from NETCOM.

NetCruiser Internet Service gives you 40 prime-time hours, and hundreds of week-end and off-peak hours, every month for under $20. That's enough access time for just about anybody who's planning a stay on the Internet.

THE FEDERAL WEB LOCATOR
The Villanova Center for Information Law and Policy

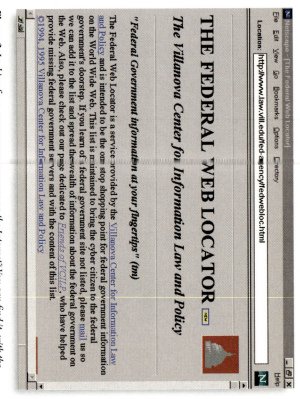

The Federal Web Locator is a service provided by the Villanova Center for Information Law and Policy and is intended to be the one stop shopping point for federal government information on the World Wide Web. This list is maintained to bring the cyber citizen to the federal government's doorstep. If you learn of a federal government site not listed, please mail us so we can add it to the list and spread the wealth of information about the federal government on the Web. Also, please check out our page dedicated to the content of UCILP, who have helped provide missing federal government servers and with the content of this list.

©1994, 1995 Villanova Center for Information Law and Policy

Figure 2: *Looking for a government resource on the Internet? You can find it with the Federal Web Locator. It has links to just about every U.S. government Internet site.*

"Federal Government information at your fingertips" (tm)

COOL SITE OF THE DAY
http://www.infi.net/cool.html

This Web Page is justly famous for tracking down and displaying some of the most interesting Web sites. Best of all, it is an invaluable resource because it maintains links to cool sites from the previous several months, which makes this page a must for new surfers. The sites are often offbeat, sometimes serious, but almost always entertaining.

THE FEDERAL WEB LOCATOR
http://www.law.vill.edu/fed-agency/fedwebloc.html

Federal government agencies provide many informational Web sites. Some of them are highly specialized, such as those of specific state or local government agencies. But many federal sites are of broader interest. If you are interested in what your government is up to, or if you're looking for specific information about a government agency or program, this is the place to come.

HOT LINKS
http://gagme.wwa.com/~boba/hotlinks.html

This is a comprehensive set of links to other sites. This site is relatively easy to get into (some sites with many links to other sites are so popular that it seems to take forever to connect). And, it is very well-organized, with links sorted into categories and subcategories that make it simple to find fascinating locations of special interest to you.

ONLINE DICTIONARY OF COMPUTING
http://wombat.doc.ic.ac.uk/

If you hear a lot of computer jargon and don't know what it means, this site can help. You type a word or phrase and press the *Enter* key and the site displays more information on than you may have wanted to know! Many definitions also have

WORD OF INTEREST
http://woi.com/woi/

This is yet another site full of links. This one

WEBCRAWLER
http://webcrawler.cs.washington.edu/WebCrawler/WebQuery.html

This was one of the first—and is still one of the best—places to search for specific Web sites by subject. You simply enter a keyword and click on a button. WebCrawler finds sites that match your criteria. This is an excellent way to find the precise site you want out of the many thousands that are available.

THE WHOLE INTERNET CATALOG
http://gnn.digital.com/gnn/wic/index.html

This is one of the most comprehensive of all sets of links, with connections to thousands of other sites. Also, the site is well-organized, making it one of the best places to start your Web journeying.

SPECIAL INTERNET CONNECTIONS
http://www.uwm.edu/Mirror/inet.services.html

This is one of the oldest and most thorough of the collections of links to other Internet sites. While most other sites with many links send you only to other WWW pages, this site provides links to virtually every type of Internet resource, including FTP (file transfer protocol—a way to send and retrieve pictures and other non-text files) and gopher servers (search utilities for locating things on the Internet). This site is well-organized and complete.

WORLD WIDE WEB WORM (WWWW)
http://www.cs.colorado.edu/home/mcbryan/WWWW.html

As you can see above, there are many sites from which you can search for other topic-specific Web sites, but many people consider Worm, along with WebCrawler, to be the best. It enables you to search by keyword so, for example, searching for "children" results in an extensive list of sites of interest to younger people.

UNCLE BOB'S KIDS PAGE
http://gagme.wwa.com/~boba/kidsi.html

The problem with surfin' the Web is that not all the sites are of interest to, or appropriate for, kids. You needn't worry with the links from this page, however. Every one of the hundreds of sites to which you can jump is kid-friendly. This compendium is quite well-organized, too.

links to other definitions, which means you can end up learning a whole lot more than you expected to. Despite the threat of getting too much information, this site is quite useful for those learning their way around computers and the Internet.

is more organized than most and is also noteworthy because of its complete collection of travel-related sites and its section on links to areas of interest to kids.

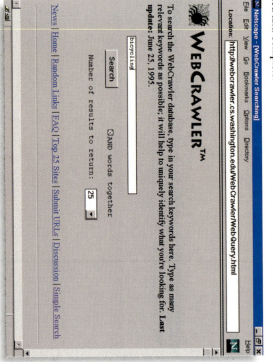

WEBCRAWLER™

To search the WebCrawler database, type in your search keywords here, type as many relevant keywords as possible; it will help to uniquely identify what you're looking for. Last update: June 25, 1995.

bicycling

Search

☐ AND words together

Number of results to return: 25

News | Home | Random Links | FAQ | Top 25 Sites | Submit URLs | Discussion | Simple Search

Figure 3: *Finding what you want on the World Wide Web can be an exercise in patience. WebCrawler lets you search quickly by keyword for Web sites of specific interest.*

KIDS AND THEIR FAMILIES ON THE WEB

While some Internet resources aren't appropriate for kids, the following most assuredly are. The sites in this section will entertain and inform your kids while giving them a chance to interact with other kids from around the world. Also listed here are some resources for families and sites that list hundreds of other resources for kids and parents.

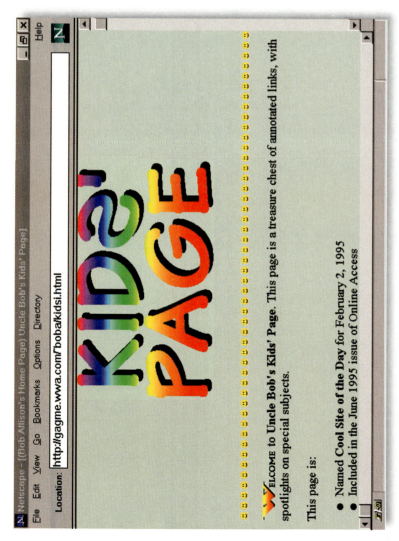

Figure 4: Uncle Bob has put together one of the most comprehensive jump sites *that lead to pages of interest to kids and their families.*

CHILDREN'S LITERATURE ON THE WEB

http://www.ucalgary.ca/~dkbrown/index.html

This is a comprehensive page with links to all manner of information about literature for kids. It includes reviews of children's books, discussions about movies adapted from children's books and lists of upcoming children's publishing events. It even has links to text of children's stories that you can download and read to your kids. This is the most comprehensive guide to children's literature that we've found.

CYBERKIDS

http://www.woodwind.com:80/cyberkids/

This is an online magazine created for kids, by kids. It includes stories, articles, puzzles, artwork and much more. Many of the features include links to related sites. All told, this is one of the best online magazines we've seen for any age group. Besides the excellent magazine, there also is a discussion area in which kids can comment on various issues.

FACTS FOR FAMILIES

http://www.med.umich.edu/aacap/facts. index.html

The road of parenthood isn't, alas, without its bumps and unexpected turns. This isn't the jolliest Web site, but it does provide some essential information. A service of the American Academy of Child and Adolescent Psychiatry, it provides descriptions and information about emotional and psychological issues faced by children and their folks. These issues range from autism, to handling grief, to chronically skipping school.

Along with viewing the submissions of others, you also receive instructions about submitting your own items.

KIDS AND PARENTS ON THE WEB

http://www.halcyon.com/ResPress/kids.htm

This is another comprehensive collection of links both to kid-tested sites and those that provide important information for parents. Whether you want to learn about dancing or get information about parenting children with disabilities, this is a great place to start. There's also a link to a variety of projects that enable your kids to meet and correspond with email pen pals. Like any good Web link site, it is updated regularly. The last time we looked in, there were more than 500 links to other places.

LEGO INFORMATION

http://legowww.homepages.com/

Kids love Legos (and adults do too, of course!). The Lego Home Page is sponsored by the company, but this isn't a typical self-serving corporate home page. Rather, it features photos of unique Lego constructions, information about new Lego products, access to the Lego Builders Club and information about games and projects that involve Legos. It's the place to be for people who love those wonderful snap-together blocks.

KIDPUB

http://en-garde.com/kidpub/intro.html

This is the site for young authors on the Internet. Basically, two things happen at this site. First, young people submit their stories for others to read; as part of the submission, you can include a biography and an email address in case readers want to contact you. Second, this site is a collaborative writing project—people who log on write a story together. You read what others have written before, then add a paragraph to move the action along. Besides being fun, this is a great way for kids to practice self-expression.

FAMILY WORLD

http://family.com/indexGX.html

This is a superb compendium of information from *Family World Magazine*. It provides many activities that parents and kids can do together as well as important information to help you be a better parent. This is an excellent site, but it's popular so it can be slow to appear on-screen.

GLOBAL SHOW-N-TELL

http://www.manymedia.com/show-n-tell/

This is a great site for kids who get nervous about standing up in front of their class at Show-and-Tell time. Obviously, this is aimed at younger kids, but it's quite interesting for adults, too.

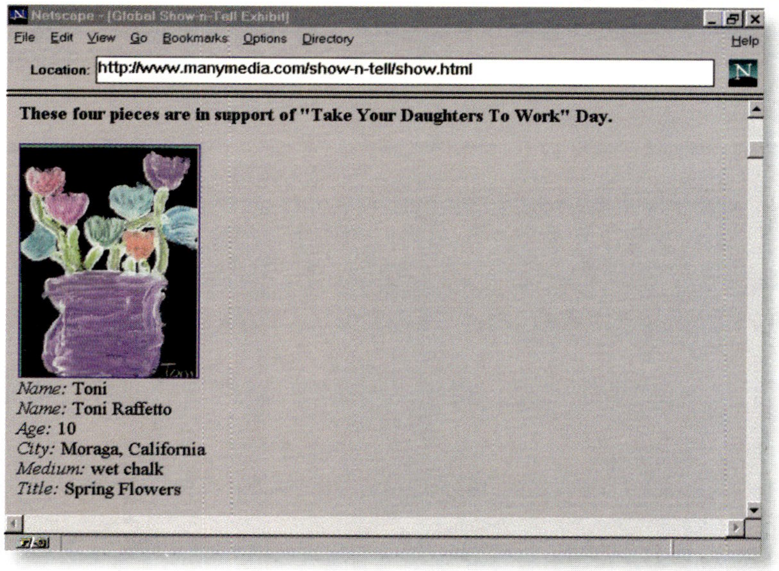

Figure 5: This Web site is like show-and-tell in kindergarten, but on a global scale. Kids submit pictures and descriptions of things that are important to them for all the world to see.

MIGHTY MORPHIN' POWER RANGERS
http://kiip.media.mit.edu:8001/power/homepage.html

If your kid is a Power Ranger fan, she or he won't want to miss this page. It has everything you'd ever want to know about the Power Rangers and has pictures you can download and view at your leisure. Also, there's a lot of information about the Power Ranger movie and the actors who play the Power Rangers.

PARENTS HELPING PARENTS
http://www.portal.com/~cbntmkr/php.html

There's nothing fancy about this page, but it can be an invaluable resource. You'll find links to dozens of resources for parents, ranging from Internet sites that will entertain your kids to places to go to get information about topics as diverse as disabilities and creating good health habits for kids.

SANTA'S HOME PAGE
http://ottawa.net/santa.html

You know that the Internet and the World Wide Web are widely accepted when even Santa Claus has his own Web page. You can read special messages from the elves, the reindeer and even Jolly Old St. Nick himself. You can also get instructions about how to email Santa and receive your own "I emailed Santa" button. But be warned: This site gets awfully busy around Christmas time.

CREATE A SPIROGRAPH
http://juniper.tc.cornell.edu:8000/spiro/spiro.html

Spirographs are fun to create—they are intricate designs based around circles. Toys that create spirographs are popular, but now you can create a spirograph online. You can tell the site how big you want the circles to be and the computer does the rest. When you finish, you can download your masterpiece and print it or use it as Windows wallpaper.

STRING FIGURES FROM AROUND THE WORLD
http://www.ece.ucdavis.edu/~darsie/string.html

Ever make a "cats cradle" with string? Here's a whole Web page devoted to various types of string figures that you and your kids can make. This is a fascinating page, complete with descriptions of the different figures and diagrams showing what they look like. The page starts with the basics and then helps you create fascinating new string figures that you've probably never seen before.

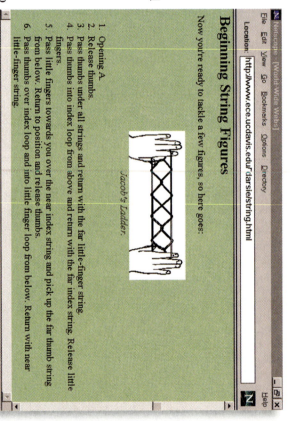

Beginning String Figures

Now you're ready to tackle a few figures, so here goes:

1. Opening A.
2. Release thumbs.
3. Pass thumbs under all strings and return with the far little-finger strings.
4. Pass thumbs into index loop from above and return with the far index string. Release little fingers.
5. Pass little fingers towards you over the near index string and pick up the far thumb string from below. Return to position and release thumbs.
6. Pass thumbs over index loop and into little finger loop from below. Return with near little-finger string.

Jacob's Ladder.

Figure 6: This site brings an old-fashioned pleasure—string figures—to the Internet. This is a delightful, slow-paced site that teaches you the basics of string figures and how to create a variety of different figures.

WOODEN TOYS
http://www.pd.astro.it/forms/mostra/mostra_i.html

This is a lovely page located in Italy. Back in the days before plastic toys transformed from one thing into another, or looked like cartoon action heroes, there were simpler toys made of wood.

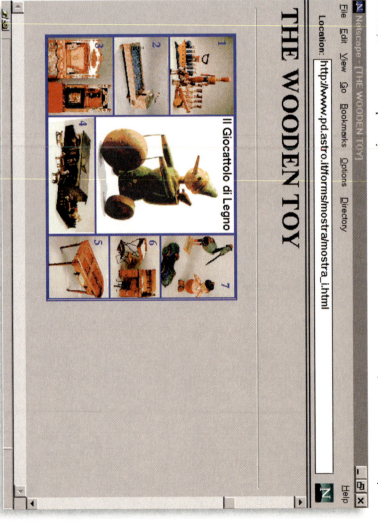

THE WOODEN TOY
Il Giocattolo di Legno

But these toys were beautifully made and could spur kids' imagination. This site shows pictures of some of the best of the old-style toys. Kids and parents who love toys will love this page. One warning, though: It sometimes takes a while to get

Figure 7: Even in our fast-paced, high-tech world, there's something comforting about wooden toys. This page has many photos of these old-fashioned toys.

CRAYON (CREATE YOUR OWN NEWSPAPER)
http://sun.bucknell.edu/~boulter/crayon/

There are commercial Internet services available that scan many news sources and give you only the specific news you want. Crayon isn't one of those sites, but it still is a handy way to collect news that interests you. First you name your "newspaper," as in "The Bobby Gazette." Then you select from a list the Internet news sources you want reviewed. When you finish, it creates a customized list of

NEWS OF THE WORLD

One important advantage of the Internet is that it's immediate. An-other advantage is that it's huge. That combination makes it an ex-cellent place for gathering all sorts of news and information. Here are several sites from which you can collect news and information.

on this page. The faster your modem, the better.

those news sources that you can then access and use again. Of particular interest is the international news section because it provides access to information from many countries around the world.

CURRENT WEATHER MAPS
http://wxweb.msu.edu/weather/

This site would be interesting even if it only told you about the world's weather at any given moment. You can view national or international weather or weather in your local area—much of the information is updated hourly. But this site is also fascinating because you can view and download a variety of maps taken by weather satellites. Besides being interesting to look at, these maps help teach about the earth's geography as well as about weather formations. Note, though, that as so often is the case, the faster your modem, the happier you'll be with this site. Some of the maps are rather large and can take a long time to appear on-screen if you use, say, a 9600BPS or slower modem.

THE INTERNET GOLDPAGES
http://www.goldpages.com/news/

This is an excellent jumping off point for a variety of newspapers, magazines and recreational sources. More and more, local newspapers are setting up Web pages and this is a good place to find out if there is one for the paper in your area or another town of interest. Also, you can jump from here to pages for

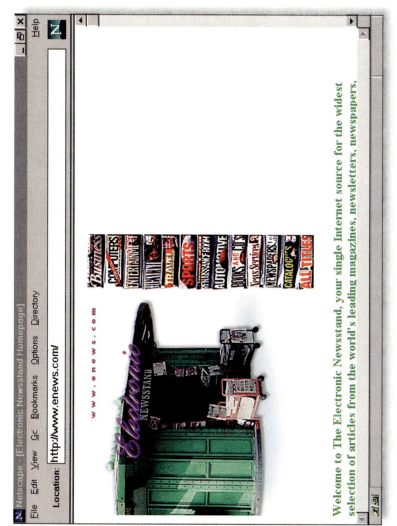

Location: http://www.enews.com/

Welcome to The Electronic Newsstand, your single Internet source for the widest selection of articles from the world's leading magazines, newsletters, newspapers,

Figure 8: The Electronic Newsstand provides online access to hundreds of magazines.

national news publications like *Time Magazine* and *USA Today*.

THE ELECTRONIC NEWSSTAND
http://www.enews.com/

This remains the largest and, for some, most useful Web site for accessing online news and periodicals. It is well-organized, making it easy to find the specific publications you want. Note, though, that each publication takes a different

approach to making information available to you. Some freely distribute the contents of their publications while others hold their contents closer to the vest, encouraging you to subscribe. Still, this site leads to lots of news on virtually any topic.

NEWS UPDATE
http://www.fyionline.com/infoMCI/update/NEWS-MCI.html

This is the place to come if you want up-to-the-minute news. Sponsored by MCI and the Reuters news service, it has today's news, updated three times a day. It also has sections for late-breaking news, weather and sports stories.

TIME MAGAZINE DAILY
http://www.pathfinder.com/@@EdNdtgAAAAAADX0/time/daily/time/1995/latest.html

This is a wonderful site if you want to keep up with the news of the world in some depth. It's an encyclopedia of contemporary events, an ideal tool for adults and for young researchers.

WELCOME TO THE WHITE HOUSE
http://www.whitehouse.gov/

Do you wonder what the president and his family do in their spare time or what the most recent policy papers are? This site describes the President's activities and schedule, and also provides background about various issues.

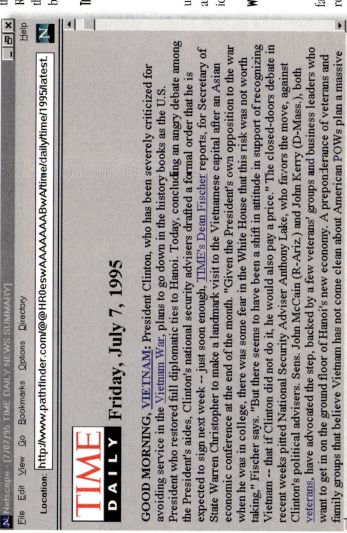

Location: http://www.pathfinder.com/@@HR0eswAAAAAABwAWtime/daily/time/1995/latest.

TIME
DAILY Friday, July 7, 1995

GOOD MORNING, VIETNAM: President Clinton, who has been severely criticized for avoiding service in the Vietnam War, plans to go down in the history books as the U.S. President who restored full diplomatic ties to Hanoi. Today, concluding an angry debate among the President's aides, Clinton's national security advisers drafted a formal order that he is expected to sign next week -- just soon enough, TIME's Dean Fischer reports, for Secretary of State Warren Christopher to make a landmark visit to the Vietnamese capital after an Asian economic conference at the end of the month. "Given the President's own opposition to the war when he was in college, there was some fear in the White House that this risk was not worth taking," Fischer says. "But there seems to have been a shift in attitude in support of recognizing Vietnam -- that if Clinton did not do it, he would also pay a price." The closed-doors debate in recent weeks pitted National Security Adviser Anthony Lake, who favors the move, against Clinton's political advisers. Sens. John McCain (R-Ariz.) and John Kerry (D-Mass.), both veterans, have advocated the step, backed by a few veterans' groups and business leaders who want to get in on the ground floor of Hanoi's new economy. A preponderance of veterans and family groups that believe Vietnam has not come clean about American POWs plan a massive

Figure 9: The Time Magazine Daily site not only provides up-to-the-moment news, it also enables you to search back issues of Time Magazine for virtually any topic.

Figure 10: What's the President up to today and where does he stand on a particular issue? That's the sort of information you can get from the White House's home page.

FAIRY TALES

gopher://ftp.std.com/11/obi/book/Fairy.Tales/Grimm

This is a gopher site, not a World Wide Web site. Still, it is extremely useful because it contains a comprehensive collection of fairy tales you can read to your kids. After you find the fairy tales you want, you can save them to a file by selecting *Save As* from the *File* menu of your Web browser. Or, you can print them by selecting *Print* from the *File* menu. Either way, these tales are sure to delight the children of the electronic age just as they have children of many generations before.

FRACTAL EXPLORER

http://www.vis.colostate.edu/~user1209/fractals/index.html

This page is for the mathematically and artistically inclined. It provides a basic lesson in fractals, those beautiful designs on the border between chaos and symmetry. This page shows fractal drawings; you can zoom in on one section of the drawing seemingly endlessly for more and more beautiful detail. You can save the drawing on your computer by clicking on a button while viewing.

ARTS AND LITERATURE

The number of arts-related Web pages is astounding—we can only skim the surface. Here is a number of art-related pages that should appeal to practically everybody, from youngsters to adults. And don't forget to look for links to additional sites.

CARLOS' COLORING BOOK

http://robot0.ge.uiuc.edu/~carlosp/color/

This is a unique site: an online coloring book. You select a line drawing, then you select a color. The section of the drawing on which you click is filled with that color. When you finish, you

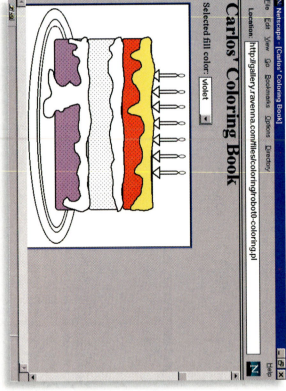

Figure 11: Young Internet surfers will love Carlos' Coloring Book. You first select a color, then click on the area of the drawing in which you want to place that color.

can download the picture to your computer. It's quite engaging and younger kids love it.

THE INTERNET MOVIE DATABASE

http://www.cm.cf.ac.uk/Movies/search.html

If you want information about a movie, stars, studios or the Academy Awards, this is the place. You can search for information by movie title or just about any other type of information. This site is heavily hyperlinked. So, for example, if you are viewing information about a movie, you can click on the name of one of the stars and view the other movies in which that person appeared. The depth of information is astounding—it even lists memorable quotes from movies. You can also rate movies yourself and your ratings are averaged with the ratings of other users. Movie buffs can become lost here.

ARTSOURCE

http://www.uky.edu/Artsource/artsourcehome.html

This is an excellent source of links to many art-related Web sites. Of particular interest are links to online exhibitions. Most of these links lead to places where you can view the work of the artists and learn about them. The exhibits are always changing and they are always surprising. For example, some exhibits have audio clips of the artist talking about their works. This is a great site for the budding art researcher.

BOOK STACKS UNLIMITED

http://www.books.com/

This is an extremely useful commercial site. It's true that the vendor's goal is to make money selling books—you can order them online if you want. But this site also provides access to many other book-related resources. For example, it has many book reviews and a library of uncopyrighted books that you can access at no charge. It also has sections where you can discuss books with others and find excerpts from newly released books.

and still images from those movies. You also can see how your favorite movies are doing at the box office.

MUPPETS HOME PAGE

http://www.ncsa.uiuc.edu/VR/BS/Muppets/muppets.html

Any parent will tell you that one of the best things about having kids is getting to watch great kids' movies and television shows without being embarrassed. In the 70's and 80's, one of the best shows was *The Muppets Show* developed by the late Jim Hensen. This home page tells you everything you want to know about those lovable Muppets, including descriptions of each episode of the show. Whether you were a fan of Kermit, Miss Piggy or the Swedish Chef, there's something for you on this page.

PHOTO PERSPECTIVES

http://www.i3tele.com/photo_perspectives_museum/faces/exhibitions.html

This is an online gallery specializing in photographic exhibits. When we logged on recently, there were exhibits of photography of the American Ballet theater; from the agony of the former Yugoslavia; and on endangered species. All were powerful—the best of photographic art brought to you over the Internet.

PROJECT GUTENBERG

http://jg.cso.uiuc.edu/pg_home.html

The goal of Project Gutenberg is highly laudable: to make classic works of literature available for free on the Internet. Project Gutenberg, named after the inventor of the movable type press, is a true online library. The amount of literature crowding the cyber-shelves of this library is mind-boggling. Fortunately, this page is well-organized, making it easy to find precisely the book you want.

SAMPLE DIGITAL IMAGES

http://www.kodak.com/digitalImages/digitalImages.shtml

Kodak is a pioneer and moving force behind digital imagery—photos that are stored and manipulated by computer rather than the traditional film-and-development photographic processes. This site has a beautiful selection of digital images. You can download them using your Web browser software and create your own computer photo album or use them as Windows wallpaper.

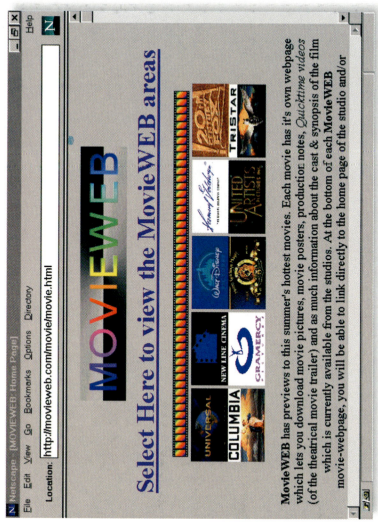

MovieWEB has previews to this summer's hottest movies. Each movie has it's own webpage which lets you download movie pictures, movie posters, production notes, *Quicktime videos* (of the theatrical movie trailer) and as much information about the cast & synopsis of the film which is currently available from the studios. At the bottom of each MovieWEB movie-webpage, you will be able to link directly to the home page of the studio and/or

Figure 12: MovieWeb has movie information from all the studios and access to tons of information from many other Internet sources.

THE LATE SHOW WITH DAVID LETTERMAN

http://cbs-tv.tiac.net:80/lateshow/lateshow.html

Did you go to sleep early and miss last night's Top 10 list? Come to this page and get the inside scoop on the Late Show, including archives of past Top 10 lists, photos from the show and

Dave's best lines. There's no need to stay up late as long as this Web site is available.

THE MOVIEWEB HOME PAGE

http://movieweb.com/movie/movie.html

This is another fascinating movie-related page. It provides video previews of hit movies

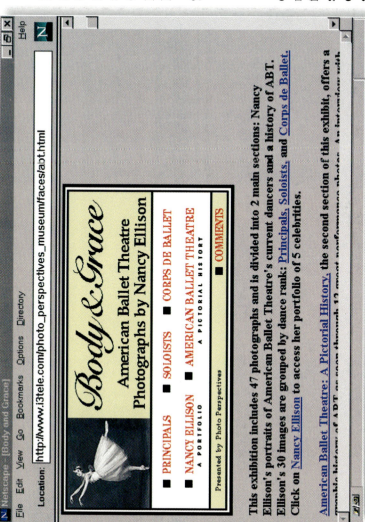

This exhibition includes 47 photographs and is divided into 2 main sections: Nancy Ellison's portraits of American Ballet Theatre's current dancers and a history of ABT. Ellison's 30 images are grouped by dance rank: Principals, Soloists, and Corps de Ballet. Click on Nancy Ellison to access her portfolio of 5 celebrities.

American Ballet Theatre: A Pictorial History, the second section of this exhibit, offers a

Figure 13: The exhibits at this online photo gallery are often quite beautiful. This exhibit is on the American Ballet Theater.

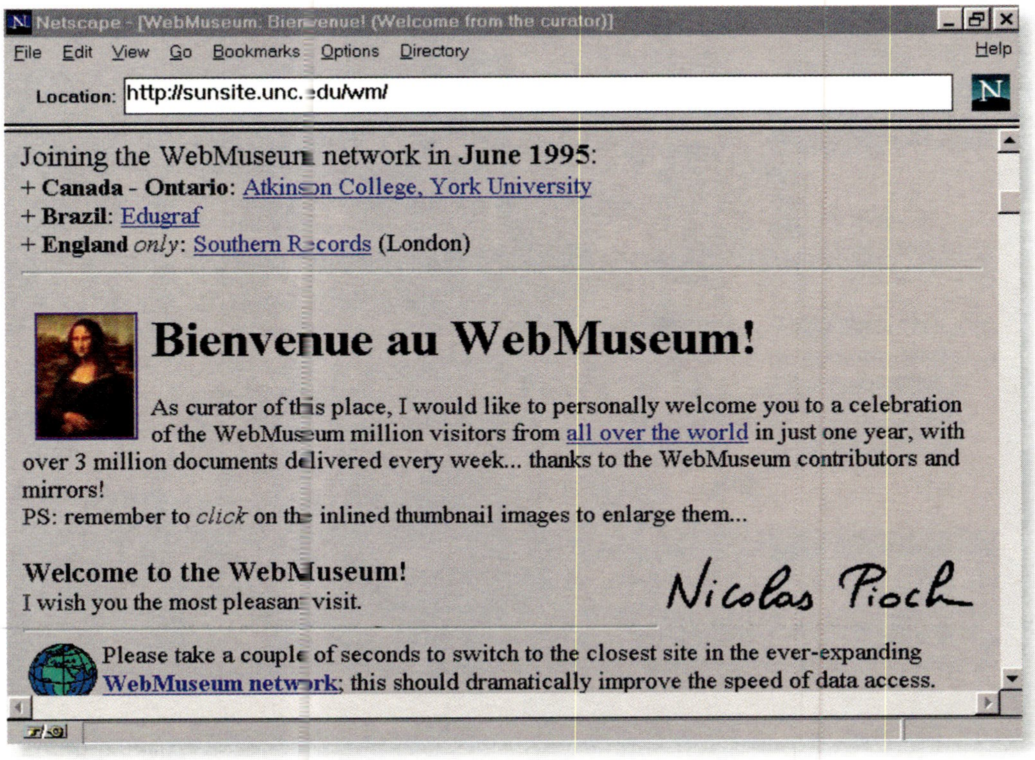

Net. In this section, we'll describe some of the more interesting educational sites.

THE CIA
http://www.odci.gov/

This is the home page for the Central Intelligence Agency (CIA), but no, going to this site isn't just for spies. It does give you access to many CIA publications like the *World Fact Book*, which is jam-packed with information about every country on earth. That makes this site a must-stop for kids writing geography reports as well as people of any age who are simply curious about these topics. And, of course, you can learn about the CIA (well, some things, anyway).

DINOSAURIA
http://ucmp1.berkeley.edu/expo/dinoexpo.html

What kid doesn't love dinosaurs—or what adult, for that matter? This page provides some general background about dinosaurs and links to other pages created by the University of California about these fabulous creatures. This is fascinating and educational stuff. However, it's a very popular site, so you may have to wait a while before the Web page loads.

THE ELECTRONIC ZOO
http://netvet.wustl.edu/e-zoo.htm

If it has to do with animals, you can get to it from this page. There are dozens of links to

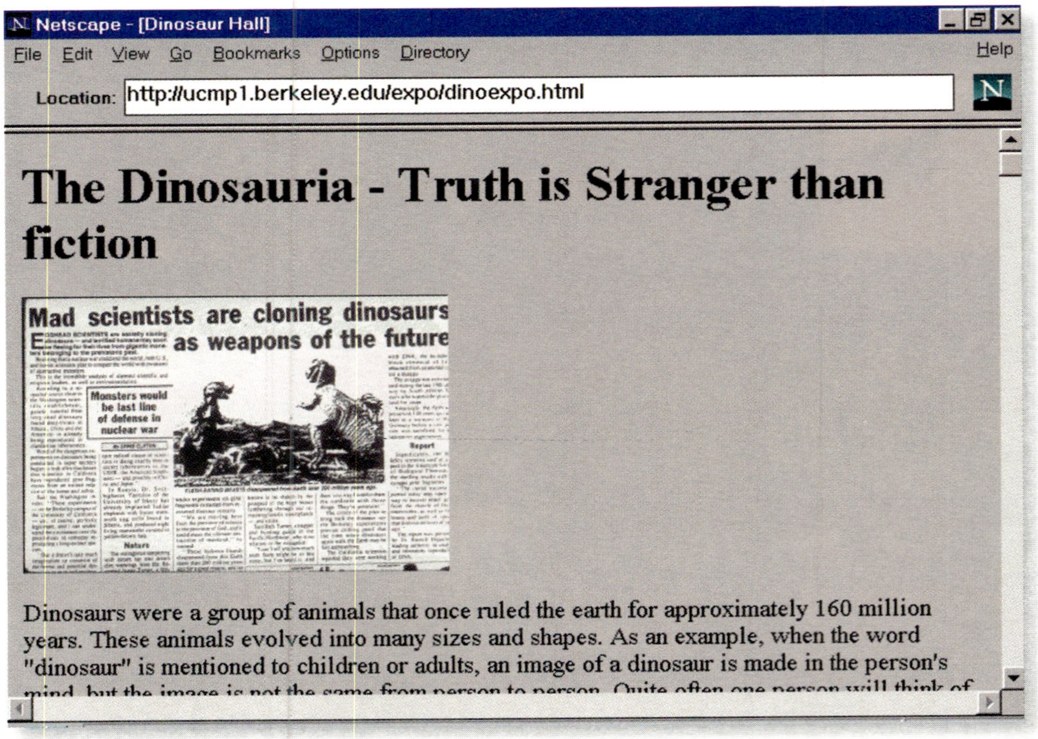

N Netscape - [WebMuseum: Bienvenue! (Welcome from the curator)]
File Edit View Go Bookmarks Options Directory
Location: http://sunsite.unc.edu/wm/

Bienvenue au WebMuseum!

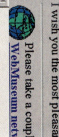

As curator of this place, I would like to personally welcome you to a celebration of the WebMuseum million visitors from all over the world in just one year, with over 3 million documents delivered every week... thanks to the WebMuseum contributors and mirrors!
PS: remember to *click* on the inlined thumbnail images to enlarge them...

Welcome to the WebMuseum!
I wish you the most pleasant visit.

Nicolas Pioch

Please take a couple of seconds to switch to the closest site in the ever-expanding WebMuseum network; this should dramatically improve the speed of data access.

Figure 14: The WebMuseum lets you visit the Louvre on the Internet—without leaving home.

Joining the WebMuseum network in June 1995:
+ **Canada - Ontario:** Atkinson College, York University
+ **Brazil:** Edugraf
+ **England** *only*: Southern Records (London)

this site is at the University of North Carolina, not Paris, but it is identical to the Louvre site. Mirror sites are necessary when a site becomes so popular that it becomes impossible to log on.

LEARNING

When your child learns on the Internet, you accomplish two things at once. First, of course, is the learning process itself—there's plenty of information for kids on the Internet. But your child also learns to use a computer and to traverse the

TEEN MOVIE CRITIC
http://www.skypoint.com/members/magic/roger/teencritic.html

This page is maintained by a young man who is a movie fanatic. He writes well and in a way that other teenagers can appreciate. Since he's not pretending to be an all-knowing, all-seeing film critic, his reviews are direct and refreshingly to the point.

SHAKESPEARE'S HOME PAGE
http://the-tech.mit.edu/Shakespeare/works.html

This page is an online collection of the works of William Shakespeare. But it is more useful than a simple substitute for the "collected works." You can search the entire collection for specific words or phrases. It also teaches about Shakespeare, his life and times, and has links to other Shakespearian resources on the Internet.

WEBMUSEUM
http://sunsite.unc.edu/wm/

Visit the Louvre on the Internet. This site is one of the most popular of all Web sites. You can view much of the artwork in the famous Louvre museum in Paris. There are both temporary exhibits—we recently checked in on an exhibit of Gothic art—and permanent exhibits. From this site you also can take a brief tour of Paris. This is a so-called "mirror" site. It provides, on another computer the exact information provided by the originator of this site. In other words,

N Netscape - [Dinosaur Hall]
File Edit View Go Bookmarks Options Directory
Location: http://ucmp1.berkeley.edu/expo/dinoexpo.html

The Dinosauria - Truth is Stranger than fiction

Mad scientists are cloning dinosaurs as weapons of the future

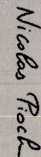

Dinosaurs were a group of animals that once ruled the earth for approximately 160 million years. These animals evolved into many sizes and shapes. As an example, when the word "dinosaur" is mentioned to children or adults, an image of a dinosaur is made in the person's mind...

Figure 15: This is an extremely popular site because it is about an extremely popular subject: dinosaurs. There's a lot of knowledge to be gained from this site.

currently on display, this one provides a lot of online substance. It is full of ever-changing exhibits and information about many different topics in natural history. Favorite exhibits include those about dinosaurs and early civilizations. During a recent visit to this site, we learned about the era before dinosaurs and watched an animation of how dinosaurs moved. About the only thing missing from this virtual museum are the snack bar and the museum store.

FRANKLIN INSTITUTE SCIENCE MUSEUM
http://sln.fi.edu/

This is another great educational site on science for kids and their parents. This museum features an ever-changing series of online exhibits—we just got back from a tour of the human heart. For some, though, the most useful part of this site will be the institute's Educational Hotlist. This is an extensive list of educational sites on the Internet covering virtually every topic. The sites on this list are all kid-friendly and, of course, educational.

HELPING YOUR CHILD LEARN SCIENCE
http://www.ed.gov/pubs/parents/Science/index.html

Provided by the U.S. Department of Education, this location is full of activities you can enjoy with your children to help them learn about science. It has activities you can try in the home and field trip suggestions. The information at this

Figure 17: Want to visit Chicago's fabled Field Museum? Now you can get there on the Internet.

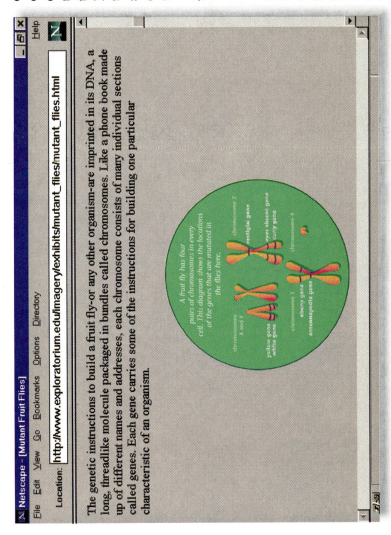

The genetic instructions to build a fruit fly-or any other organism-are imprinted in its DNA, a long, threadlike molecule packaged in bundles called chromosomes. Like a phone book made up of different names and addresses, each chromosome consists of many individual sections called genes. Each gene carries some of the instructions for building one particular characteristic of an organism.

Figure 16: Just as the Exploratorium pioneered hands-on museums for kids, this Web site provides hands-on experiments kids can try while at their computer.

information about specific animals. But it has much more, too, such as information about veterinary science.

THE ELEMENTS OF STYLE
http://www.columbia.edu/~svl2/strunk/

Most folks who are serious about writing know about William Strunk Jr.'s *Elements of Style*. This is the quintessential writer's manual and it is online in its entirety. The manual starts with the basics of grammar and usage and also goes in depth about creating compositions. Generations of writers have kept this book beside them as they write—now it's available free online in searchable form.

experiments work the way they do. Fun for adults, too.

THE FIELD MUSEUM OF NATURAL HISTORY
http://www.bvis.uic.edu/museum/

One of the greatest "kid" museums is the Field Museum in Chicago. While many sites sponsored by museums only describe the exhibits

Tip: Books aren't going to be replaced by online text anytime soon—it's too hard to read text on screen for hours. But traditional *indexes* are much inferior to computer-assisted searching. So when you're looking for a particular topic—get onto the Internet and you'll find tons of information, and find it fast.

EXPLORATORIUM EXHIBITS
http://www.exploratorium.edu/imagery/exhibits.html

San Francisco's Exploratorium was one of the pioneering museums where kids learned not by viewing, but by doing. Now the Exploratorium has put many exhibits online on this wonderful Web page. It includes experiments you can try while sitting at your monitor and explains why the

A Photo Gallery of the Universe

Hubble Space Telescope evokes a new sense of awe and wonder about the infinite richness of our universe in dramatic, unprecedented pictures of celestial objects. Like a traveler sharing...

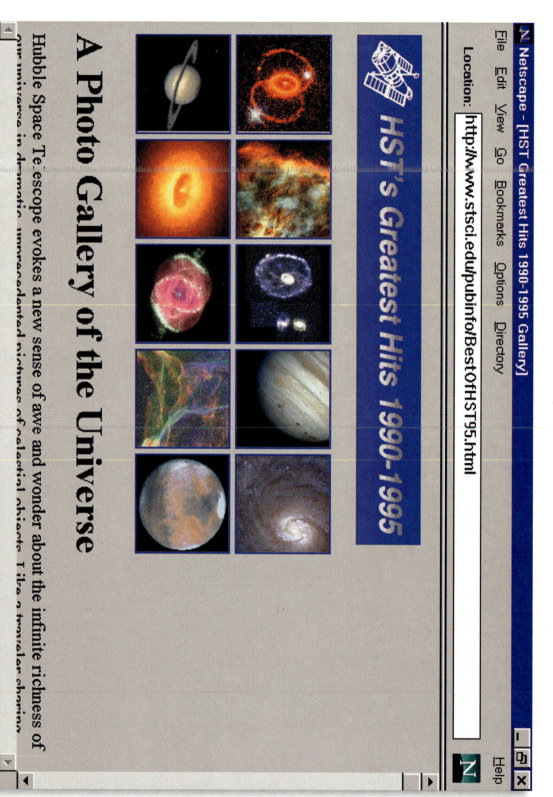

Figure 18: *This site, related to the Hubble Space Telescope, is a treasure trove both for information about astronomy and for some of the most beautiful pictures you've ever seen.*

site isn't the prettiest to look at—it's almost entirely text with just a few supporting pictures. But it will keep you and your kids busy with enjoyable science activities for a long time.

HUBBLE SPACE TELESCOPE'S GREATEST HITS
http://www.stsci.edu/pubinfo/BestOfHST95.html

It's hard to know whether this should be grouped with the learning sites or the art sites. This is a "best of" collection of photos taken of deep space by the Hubble Space Telescope. Along with the beautiful photos, which you can download to your computer by selecting *File/Save As* in your Web browser, there are lengthy text captions that describe what you're seeing.

THE JASON PROJECT
http://seawifs.gsfc.nasa.gov/JASON/HTML/JASON_HOME.html

The Jason Project is engaging and educational. Every year, Robert D. Ballard, the man who discovered and explored the Titanic on the ocean's floor, leads a virtual field expedition somewhere on the earth. Kids can participate as the expedition progresses. The 1995 expedition, for example, explored the volcanoes of Hawaii and the 1996 expedition will explore marine habitats off the coast of Florida. The rest of the year, you can come to this site to view the results of previous expeditions, including photos and other multimedia items.

INTERACTIVE FROG DISSECTION
http://curry.edschool.Virginia.edu:80/~insttech/frog/

Your kids may initially respond with "Gross" But this site is an excellent place to learn biology.

MATHMAGIC
http://forum.swarthmore.edu/mathmagic/index.html

This is a great educational page that teaches mathematics. It provides math challenges for kids of all ages, from kindergarten through high school. The problems are tough, but there's help available. The help comes from members of your team and from instructors who participate in this program. If you love math, or if you find math difficult and want to improve, this is an excellent site.

NASA HOME PAGE
http://www.gsfc.nasa.gov/NASA_homepage.html

This page is your gateway into NASA and, if you dig a bit, it provides much good information about space exploration. You can learn more about specific shuttle missions and other NASA projects. You can learn more about NASA itself

Figure 19: Kids love Shamu the whale will also love this Web site provided by Sea World. It covers many different types of wild animals.

and its various centers around the country. This page also has links to many other aerospace-related pages, including pages created by space agencies in other countries. This page and the links it provides will be interesting to nearly everybody, and it is a superb resource for research projects by both young and old.

SEA WORLD

http://www.bev.net/education/SeaWorld/homepage.html

Shamu, the much-beloved whale from Sea World greets you when you enter this page. This site does much more than simply tell you about this popular tourist attraction. The folks at Sea World have packed it with data about many different land and sea animals ranging from gorillas to many varieties of whales. It also teaches how to keep an aquarium as a hobby.

SMITHSONIAN GEM AND MINERAL COLLECTION

http://galaxy.einet.net/images/gems/gems-icons.html

This is a must-see Web page for anyone who loves gems and minerals. It features pictures (that you can download) of a wide variety of gems and minerals and detailed information about them. Many of the Smithsonian pages focus on simply describing current museum exhibits. This one has a lot of useful information for rock hounds and those creating school reports.

Galapagos Islands. Also, the images you can download are astounding and you'll also find detailed information about recent eruptions.

THE VIRTUAL TRAVELER

The Internet makes it possible to travel the world without leaving your desk. Here are a few sites in which you can learn more about the world.

FODOR'S WORLD VIEW

http://gnn.digital.com/gnn/bus/wview/index.html

Fodor's is the publisher of some of the bestselling guidebooks. This site skims the surface of its topics a bit, but it still provides useful information about many destinations around the world. It's definitely worth a look-see if you're about to leave for somewhere new and exotic.

GORP (GREAT OUTDOOR RECREATION PAGES)

http://www.gorp.com/

If your interest is in outdoor adventures, this is a great page to start from. It lists extensive resources on topics as diverse as our national parks and backpacking equipment. It has links to pages providing easy and nutritional recipes for outdoor camping adventures; groups that organize trips; and publications that write about outdoor adventures.

VOLCANO WORLD

http://volcano.und.nodak.edu/

Sure, many kids need to know about volcanoes for school projects. But this site does much more than just provide information for reports. It's full of interesting information about various active volcano sites, such as the

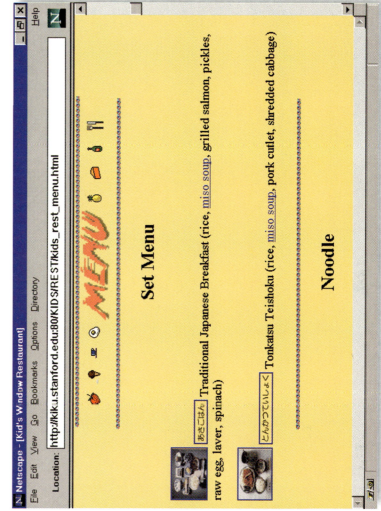

Set Menu

あさごはん Traditional Japanese Breakfast (rice, miso soup, grilled salmon, pickles, raw egg, laver, spinach)

とんかつていしょく Tonkatsu Teishoku (rice, miso soup, pork cutlet, shredded cabbage)

Noodle

Figure 20: Kids travel to Japan from this Web site. Here they learn what Japanese kids like to eat.

HAWAII VISITOR'S CENTER
http://www.hawaii.net/hawaiihome/vis.html

Hawaii is a place to dream about during long, cold winters—and even hot, sticky summers! This is Hawaii's official home page, providing loads of information for potential visitors. The images alone, which you can download, make this site worth visiting. But it also covers in detail what to see and do during your visit and even provides a virtual tour of this multi-island state.

KID'S WINDOW ON JAPAN
http://kiku.stanford.edu:80/KIDS/kids_home.html

This is a lovely site where you can learn all about what it's like to be a kid in Japan. You can learn the language and what kids in Japan like to eat. You also can learn the traditional Japanese craft of *origami*. This site provides a lot of wonderful information that is aimed specifically at younger children.

NATIONAL FLAGS
http://155.187.10.12/flags/nation-flags.html

As the name implies, this is a comprehensive collections of images of national flags. It's interesting to see how other countries' flags look. Plus, you can download the images, print them and add them to school reports about specific countries.

THE NEW SOUTH POLAR TIMES
http://www.deakin.edu.au/edu/MSEE/GENII/NSPT/NSPThomePage.html

One of the harshest and most exciting places for scientists and kids alike is the South Pole. This is the Web site for researchers located there. But it is also a great learning site for kids located anywhere. This is a bi-weekly newsletter from Amundsen-Scott South Pole Station located at South Pole, Antarctica. Besides reading the current and past issues of the newsletter, you can learn about polar exploration and even ask questions of the scientists via email. Talk about making contact with faraway places!

THE VIRTUAL TOURIST
http://wings.buffalo.edu/world/vt2/

Want to know about tourist sites in Singapore or learn about the geography of Australia? You'll start with a world map. Then click on a continent to view a more detailed map. Then click on a particular region or country and you'll see information about it. This site is a must if you or your kids are curious about the world or if you are planning to travel. It's also a great source of information for geography class. Besides general background about countries, there are also many maps and photos.

WINDOW TO RUSSIA
http://www.kiae.su/www/wtr/

Whether you are a child, or a parent who grew up during the Cold War, this is a fascinating page full of links to Russian resources. This page provides extensive information about Russia, a Russian-to-English dictionary and a series of

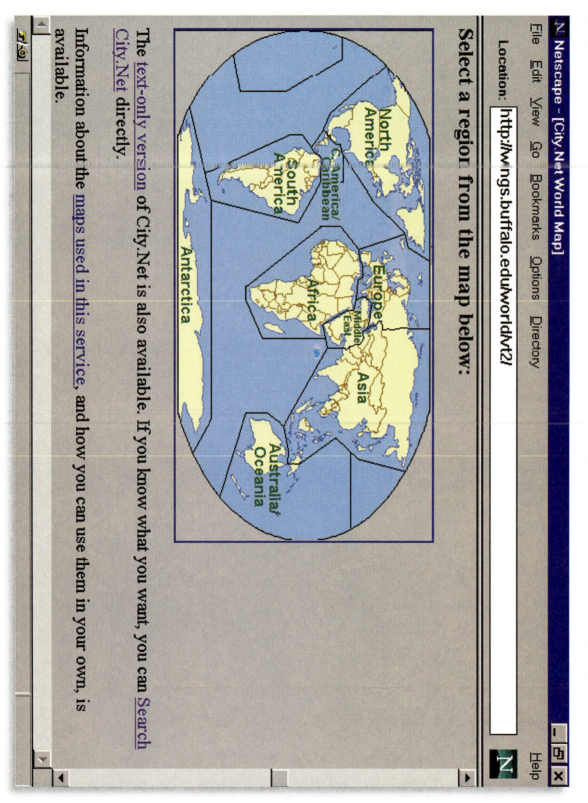

Netscape - [City.Net World Map]

File Edit View Go Bookmarks Options Directory

Location: http://wings.buffalo.edu/world/vt2/

Select a region from the map below:

North America • C. America/Caribbean • South America • Antarctica • Africa • Europe • Middle East • Asia • Australia/Oceania

The text-only version of City.Net is also available. If you know what you want, you can Search City.Net directly.

Information about the maps used in this service, and how you can use them in your own, is available.

Figure 21: Click on a spot in the world and learn more information about it—that's how the Virtual Tourist works.

online exhibitions of Russian art and photographs. Don't miss the exhibit about the Kremlin. As with most Web sites located on far-away computers, this one may take a while before pages load.

SPORTS, GAMES AND HOBBIES

Do you like sports? If you can't be out there watching or playing, the Internet is the place to be. This section lists some of the more interesting sports-related sites, many of which provide links to even more sports-related pages.

BACKCOUNTRY HOME PAGE
http://io.datasys.swri.edu/

Some folks believe there's more to life than football, baseball, hockey and other spectator sports. This home page is an excellent resource for those who like to hike in the woods. It provides access to information about backcountry journeys and organizations that give you the information you need to begin your journey, including reviews of hiking and backpacking-related products. To whet your appetite, it includes photos taken on backcountry expeditions.

BASEBALL LINKS
http://ssnet.com/~skilton/baseball.html

Unlike professional football, basketball and hockey, Major League Baseball doesn't yet have its own home page. But it does have this page that provides a comprehensive set of links to other baseball sites. Those sites provide schedules, statistics, history—just about everything you'd want to know about baseball. It also provides links to the home pages of individual major league baseball teams. This is a page that baseball fans won't want to miss.

ESPN SPORTSZONE
http://web1.starwave.com:80/

Some sites sponsored by large companies are essentially extended advertisements. But this one is jam-packed with up-to-date sports news about most popular sports. Besides news and statistics, this site also provides longer features and in-depth previews of coming events. It also gives you a chance to chat with other sports fans about nearly any sports-related issue. You can even submit questions that you want ESPN sportscasters to ask sports celebrities whom they will be interviewing.

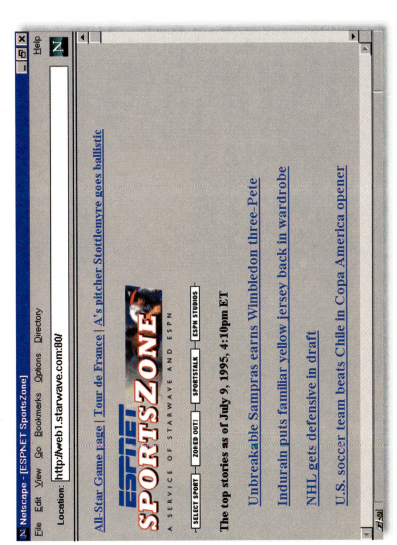

Figure 22: Get the lowdown on all the latest sports news from this Web site.

EVERYTHING EXTREME
http://www.duke.edu:80/~cperhun/

Does the thought of skydiving, hang gliding or rock-climbing excite you? Then come over to the Everything Extreme page. Here you'll find information about so-called "extreme" sports as well as photos and even video and audio clips. This is a great page because it captures the thrills of extreme sports but is a heck of a lot safer.

MODEL RAILROADS
http://www.he.tdl.com/~colemanc/model.html

Most parents and even grandparents remember model railroads from their youth. It's kind of comforting to know that toy trains still remain popular. As a testament to that popularity, this page has dozens of links to Internet resources related to model railroading. It's not the prettiest site around (it's actually a small part

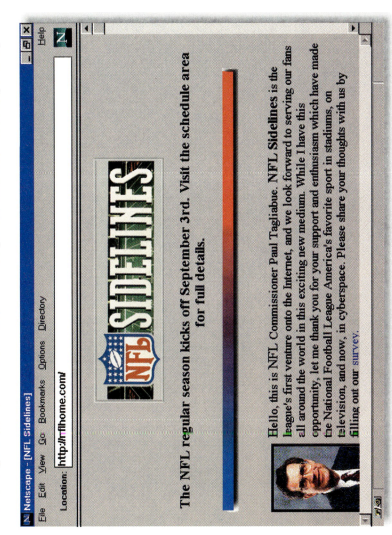

Figure 23: Block that pass, kick that ball. Pigskin fans won't want to miss all the latest events on the official NFL Web home page.

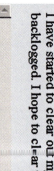

Browser Notice

I am programming this for netscape 1.1, because of this some feature might not work. Examples of things that might not work include anew backgroud, centering, and some of the tables I have built.

Important Notice

I have started to clear out my backlog of requests to add clubs, races, and other URLs that are backlogged. I hope to clear them out in the next two weeks.

THE TENNIS SERVER

http://arganet.tenagra.com/Racquet_Workshop/Tennis.html

This page is packed with useful information about tennis, whether you are a beginning or experienced player, or if you simply want to keep track of the sport and recent tournaments. It includes tips to improve your game; links to other Internet tennis resources; and information about equipment, common tennis-related injuries and training. It even has pictures of the top tennis players in the world.

THE TRIATHLETE'S WEB

http://www.iac.net/~miller/triweb.html

Triathalons are a specialized sporting event—you must be in top-notch shape and not afraid of pain. But The Triathlete's Web serves more than just those who participate in these events. It also has links to other information about sports and well-being. Not surprisingly, it has links to Internet information about running, swimming and bicycling—the three events in a triathlon. But it also has links to information about nutrition and medical issues. All told, this is quite a useful Web site.

Figure 24: No matter how serious a runner you are, you'll find something of interest on The Running Page.

scene, The Running Page is for you. While not as visually attractive as many Web pages, it provides many links to a wide variety of running information. You can learn, for example, about running clubs in your area or about track and field results.

The WWW Bicycle Lane

Table of Contents:

WWW: Cool Links | Bicycle Commuting | Magazines | Lists of Sites | Companies | Organizations and Clubs | Rides and Touring Information | Racing Calendars and Information | Mountain Biking | Bicycle Safety | USCF Teams on the Internet

Other Resources: Online Forms | Gopher Sites | FTP sites | Biking Pictures | Mailing Lists

Figure 25: Bicyclists on the Internet will find links to all kinds of information on the WWW Bicycle Lane.

THE NFL HOME PAGE

http://nflhome.com/

Football fans, unite! This is the official home page of the National Football League. You'll find schedules; facts about players and teams; and more in-depth information, such as information about the last college draft. There's also a trivia game and interesting features. For example, one recent feature discussed fathers and sons who have both played in the NFL.

THE NHL HOME PAGE

http://www.nhl.com/

Ice hockey may not have big network television contracts, but many people love its fast, rugged action. This is the National Hockey League's official Web site. It includes the basics, like schedules, statistics and trivia, but it has much more, such as photos of hockey action and hockey stars.

THE RUNNING PAGE

http://sunsite.unc.edu/drears/running/running.html

Running is more than a sport for many people—it's an obsession. If you or family members want to learn more about the running

sites that will elicit smiles and grins.

THE COMIC PAGE
http://www.missouri.edu/~c617145/comix.html

This page has links to practically every comic strip available on the Internet. Comics on the Internet? Well, the more things change, the more they stay the same. Many of the comics to which you can jump from this page are created only for consumption on the Net and, to put it politely, some may not be ready for prime time. But others you may have seen in your daily newspaper. This is a great page to come to for laughs and it's particularly useful if you love a specific comic strip but your regular newspaper doesn't carry it. A few of the comics are even from foreign countries.

HUMOR ARCHIVES
http://www.ugcs.altech.edu/~nathan/humor.html

Want a good laugh? This site has links to almost every humor resource on the Net. It starts with lists of jokes about political leaders, then moves into nearly endless topical jokes like

lightbulb jokes. This is well-organized and the developer of this page has done a good job of keeping it clean, but it is still recommended children be accompanied by parents when perusing this site since the links to other sites are less predictable.

THE KEEPER OF THE LISTS
http://www.dtd.com/keepers/

This is a collection of humorous lists about various subjects. When we last checked in, there were masterpieces like "The Top 40 Signs That You Smell Stinky," and "The Top 120 Places Elvis Has Been Sighted." Educational? Hardly, but a lot of fun.

MADLIBS ON THE NET
http://www.mit.edu:8001/madlib

You may have thought they were just for the car, but this site will teach you otherwise. Kids love Madlibs, in which you create a funny story by adding random nouns, verbs, adjectives and adverbs. This site is an almost limitless supply of Madlibs. It can become quite addictive for the young ones (and their parents!).

STEREOGRAMS
http://fmechds01.tu-graz.ac.at/heidrun/3d/3dpic2.html

The biggest risk you run with this site is that, when you're done, you'll have to clean

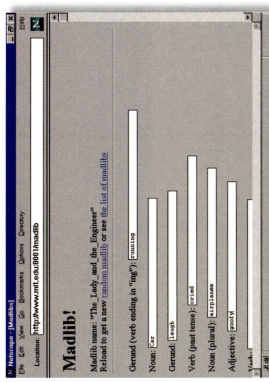

Figure 26: Madlibs are fun for the entire family. You can create Madlibs at this Web site.

THE WEB CHESS SERVER
http://www.willamette.edu/~tjones/chessmain.html

Want to play chess online? Then this is your site. At this writing, it is the only Web chess site available—the other sites all require more confusing Telnet connections. After you reach this site, you can either start a game against somebody who is waiting for an opponent (if nobody is waiting you must wait for an opponent) or you can watch a game in progress. You have the option of stating your ability level so that you only get into games with people of similar abilities.

THE WORLD WIDE WEB AVIATION SERVER
http://aviation.jsc.nasa.gov/index.html

Are you interested in learning to fly or do you just want to know more about aviation? This Web site provides access to most everything you could want to know about flying, from where to get weather information, to the steps you must take to learn to fly, to history and lore. This is an interesting stop whether you are an aviation fanatic or are just curious.

WWW BICYCLE LANE
http://www.cs.purdue.edu/homes/dole/bike.html#Cool

There are several bicycle-related Web pages, but this one is unusually thorough. It provides links to many bicycle-related Internet resources, whether you are a mountain biker or prefer riding on paved roads. This site is a must whether you are just getting started in bicycling or if your interest is in racing or touring.

JUST FOR FUN

The Web isn't all serious stuff—you can also play. Other sections of this book cover games. Here, however, you'll learn about Web

Figure 27: It doesn't translate well from the screen to this book, but this is a stereogram. If you look at it in a certain way on-screen, it appears to be three-dimensional.

Welcome to the NEW Chocolate Lover's Playground!

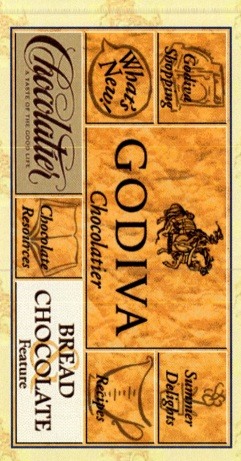

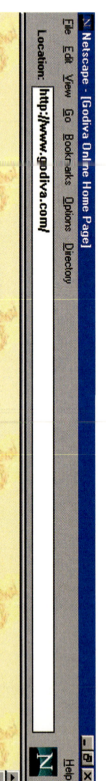

Figure 28: *Godiva not only makes some of the finest gourmet chocolate around, but it also has the best chocolate Web page on the Internet.*

Godiva Chocolatier and Chocolatier Magazine, two of the most noted authorities on the sumptuous subject of chocolate. Continue to satisfy your cravings for knowledge, fun and self-indulgence. Bake up batches and batches of decadent recipes...

HOME, HEALTH AND FINANCE

Here are some pages that adults will particularly appreciate. They cover important topics like health, finance and subjects to help you run your home more efficiently.

40 TIPS TO GO GREEN

http://www.ncb.gov.sg/jk/env/greentips.html

As the name implies, this page provides helpful hints for living your life with less impact on the Earth. The best thing about these tips is that most families can utilize them easily. Since this list comes from Singapore, you'll have to adapt some of the tips (such as the tip to slow down your driving on highways to 80km per hour), but all are useful no matter where you live.

THE GARDEN GATE

http://www.prairienet.org/ag/garden/homepage.htm

This site has loads of information about gardening and links to other garden-related sites. There is information (and links) both for outdoor gardens and houseplants. It's updated regularly.

It's interesting and it varies widely—a recent stop here found free soap, free diskettes for your computer and even free CD-ROM disks. Most offers expire after awhile, so the list is ever-changing.

FIRST AID ONLINE

http://www.synnet.net/Users/afoster/safety

This page is quite serious—and quite important. It provides first aid tips and treatments for a wide range of problems. True, if you have a household medical emergency, you probably won't think to run to your computer and wait until you can get onto the Internet. But this is still an excellent source of information for those who want to learn first

FREE STUFF

http://www.getnet.com/~xinh/freestuff.html

This page is, at the very least, interesting and will be addictive for some. It's a comprehensive list of free stuff you can obtain from a variety of vendors.

WHY ASK WHY?

http://www.eng.auburn.edu/~rudolmc/why.html

Why do we drive on parkways and park on driveways? Questions like these may be silly, but they're also fun. They're also more than fun—they teach kids to think critically and ask questions. This web site has dozens and dozens of questions like these to challenge and intrigue kids of all ages.

nose prints off your monitor. Here you'll find a catalog of stereograms, tho e images that create a three-dimensional illusion. You select an image, which then displays on-screen. You place your nose near (not cut!) the monitor, relax your focus and then slowly pull your head away until the stereo effect appears. If you haven't done this before, it can take a bit of practice. Also, displaying the images on-screen takes some time, so this site rewards those with faster connections. That's particularly true for the larger-sized images that typically provide a better effect.

rec.food.recipes USENET news group. It is a listing of hundreds of recipes for virtually every type of food you can imagine. For the most part, these aren't your run-of-the-mill meatloaf-and-potatoes recipes. The recipes have a decided gourmet and international flavor. To save them as a text file, select *File*, then *Save As* in your Web browser. Depending on your browser, in the ensuing dialog box, select *Text* from the *Save Files As Type* drop-down list.

WINE ON THE INTERNET
http://wines.com/wines.html

Fine wines are wonderful and there are many good wine-related pages on the World Wide Web. This one is less a vehicle for winemakers than an information resource for consumers. Also, you'll find lots of variety here. Particularly useful is the Virtual Wine Tasting Room. No, you can't actually taste the wine, but you can read about specific wines and what various reviewers had to say about how they taste.

YAHOO ENTERTAINMENT FOOD
http://www.yahoo.com/Entertainment/Food/

This is a compendium of food-related resources on the Internet. Want to learn how to make bagel chips or Turkish mucver? Well, this site has links to dozens of other sites that will provide such recipes and tips. For adults, this site also has links to pages that discuss fine wines. It's an excellent page to consult before you entertain.

David Haskin is a writer specializing in computer-related topics. Formerly a newspaper journalist and software executive, David is a regular contributor to PC Magazine, Computer Life *and* Computer Shopper. *He is the author of six books about computers including* The Complete Idiot's Guide to Multimedia, The Complete Idiot's Guide to PC Games *and* Using PC Tools for Windows.

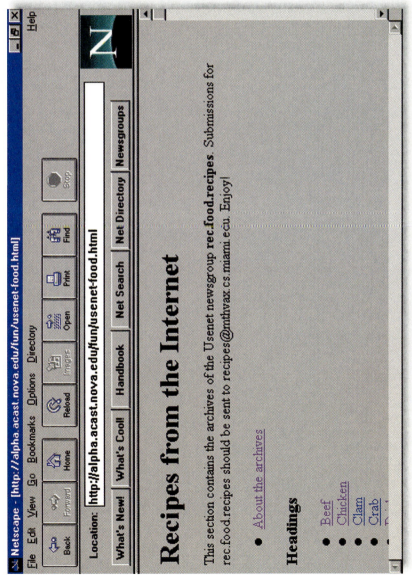

Figure 30: *Not the most graphically stimulating place on the Internet, this site will still stimulate your taste buds. It's an extensive collection of recipes.*

Netscape - [http://alpha.acast.nova.edu/fun/usenet-food.html]

File Edit View Go Bookmarks Options Directory   Help

Back | Forward | Home | Reload | Images | Open | Print | Find | Stop

Location: http://alpha.acast.nova.edu/fun/usenet-food.html

What's New! | What's Cool! | Handbook | Net Search | Net Directory | Newsgroups

Recipes from the Internet

This section contains the archives of the Usenet newsgroup rec.food.recipes. Submissions for rec.food.recipes should be sent to recipes@mthvax.cs.miami.edu. Enjoy!

- About the archives

Headings

- Beef
- Chicken
- Clam
- Crab

aid basics. It also has many links to other sources of medical information.

MUTUAL FUNDS MAGAZINE ONLINE
http://www.mfmag.com/

Mutual funds have become an extremely popular way for individuals to invest their money. This Web page, sponsored by *Mutual Funds Magazine*, will teach you about mutual funds and how to invest in the funds that are most appropriate for you. It also has performance rankings and information about thousands of funds. Before investing, you should gather as much information about a fund as possible; this site is a great place to start that process.

PC QUOTE
http://www.spacecom.com:80/Participants/pcquote/Welcome.html

Tracking your stocks is easy with this tool. You simply type the ticker symbol for your stock and its current trading information, such as price and volume, is displayed. If you aren't sure of the ticker symbol, PC Quote helps you find it.

FINE FOODS AND ENTERTAINING

We all love good food. Well, here are a few sites that are only in the best of taste!

GODIVA CHOCOLATE HOME PAGE
http://www.godiva.com/

If you think chocolate deserves to be considered one of the essential food groups, this is the place for you. It not only tells you about Godiva's luscious chocolate products, but it also provides a wealth of information about this particular nectar of the gods, ranging from the history of chocolate to some truly stupendous recipes. It also provides many helpful hints about chocolate for those who want to become chocolate fanatics. There's no help here for those trying to quit, though!

RECIPES A LA ALF
http://www.cs.fsu.edu/projects/group12/recipes.html

This isn't the most visually lavish Web page, but it might be the tastiest. It's an excellent database of recipes. Best of all, you can search for specific ingredients or recipe names. When you finish, you can save the recipes by selecting *File*, then *Save As* from your Web browser's menu.

RECIPES ON THE INTERNET
http://alpha.acast.nova.edu/fun/usenet-food.html

This is another excellent collection of recipes. It actually is the archives from the

A CHILD'S GUIDE TO COMPUTING:
SPECIAL RESOURCES FOR YOUNG PEOPLE

By Peter Scisco

If you're a kid, this one's just for you. We'll tell you everything you need to know to get the best software—games and educational programs that you'll want to play again and again. And some of the ideas here might interest grownups, too.

You probably already know as much about personal computers as your parents, maybe more. You probably know as much and maybe more about computers than many of your teachers at school. Raised on television, weaned on Nintendo, and understanding about the **Internet** and **multimedia**, you adopted the new technologies as your own.

But with the huge selection of **software**, books, and magazines all dealing with computers, how do you make the right choice? If you save your allowance for a game, you don't want to waste your money. And if your parents give you a program or a book as a gift, you want to make sure they get what you want, and that they feel comfortable with their choice.

So let's talk some about software, books, magazines and **online services**. After that, we'll talk about how you can use your computer at home to do research, and how I can help you with your homework. And finally, we'll talk about how you can use your computer to have fun and to learn.

SOFTWARE

What is software? Who cares? This isn't computer class. There aren't any pop quizzes or extra credit. The questions you should be asking are: What can I do with software? What does it do?

You can have fun. You can learn. You can challenge yourself and others. You can paint, create cartoons and write. Today's software programs—which mix graphics, sound, animation, narration and music—make it fun to do all of these things. Programs—believe it or not—can even make school and homework fun.

There are technical reasons why software does what it does. If you want to be a software designer when you grow up, you can seek out those answers at a library or at school or in magazines and books. But at home with your computer, you'll find out something quick

enough: Software is different from many other things you use every day.

Software isn't a movie. It's not television and it's not a videotape. It's not a set of wooden blocks, an open field under blue skies, a bicycle ride down a long hill or a fast set of rollerblades. But all these things are part of your world, and in a sense they are all tools that can entertain, teach and help you with whatever task you want to accomplish.

The key to really good software (and what makes using a computer so much fun) is that software programs are *interactive*. That means that you respond to the ideas, pictures, and sounds that the software presents, and your response results in more pictures, sounds, and ideas. Start putting those ideas together and you're on your way to places you've never dreamed of. All this means that you don't just sit in front of a computer screen like a week-old potato. Computers aren't for nerds and geeks—they're for dreamers and doers. You don't just watch events unfold, you become part of the event yourself. In some of the most exciting computer games, you direct the action of players on a stage, making your own movie and story as you go along.

Television, to use an example you're familiar with, doesn't really let you interact with it, unless you count using the clicker to channel surf. But that's not really interactivity. Deep down, you know that most television isn't very interesting, and most of it isn't really much fun. Stories from the tube feed images right into your brain, bypassing the most powerful computer that will ever be designed—your own imagination.

Not all software is better than television. Software is either good or bad depending on how well it encourages you to interact with the computer—which means you'll be having fun, learning and creating, not wasting time. A bad software program that's pretty much just like

watching television isn't worth your time. You're better off taking a walk or riding your bike or talking with your friends. You'll have more fun and you're more liable to learn something, too.

Good software, on the other hand, lets you move at your own pace, explore different paths and have experiences that are impossible any other way. How many times do you get asked to plan and design a city? Software programs like *SimCity 2000* and *SimTown* (Maxis, (800) 336-2947) let you do that. How often do you get to visit an astronomy lab or travel through the solar system? Run a farm? Run a country? Solve a murder? Paint a masterpiece? There are all kinds of software programs that let you do all of these things and more.

But remember, not all software is equal. Some programs are very simple, but are still very good at what they do. A game of chess or a matching game isn't as dramatic as a flight through space, but if the software does its job right, a game can be just as enjoyable as space travel. It just depends on what you want to do with your computer and where you want to go in your own imagination. It depends on whether you're playing a game, learning, or using a reference or some other electronic tool.

That means that there are all kinds of software programs out there, some good and some bad. Each one tries to do something a little differently than the others. Some are entirely different from one another—like a game versus a word processor. So to figure out the differences so they make sense, let's talk a little about the different types of software.

While we talk and think about those differences, remember one thing—no matter what kind of software you're interested in, look for a lot of interactive possibilities. Good software should encourage you to explore. It should

engage your imagination in a dramatic way, with great characters and writing and action. It should be easy to use. And it should be a lot of fun to use over and over again.

JUST YOUR TYPE

It's a rainy afternoon. Your best friend is out of town. You're looking for a good game to occupy your time and give you an entertaining way to spend the afternoon. If that's what you need, then you'll want to pick a software program that's much different from what you would need if you had to write a school report. On the other hand, if you're in the mood for learning and exploring, then you'll want something other than a game. Or maybe you want to make a gift for a friend.

Just about anything you want to do or need to do can be done by one software program or another. The trick is to know what you want to do and to be able to find the program that will help you do it.

Software and computers are radically different from anything your parents had when they were kids. So, it's likely they will be as confused as you are when it comes time to find the right program at the software store. But once you know the types of programs out there, it will be easier for you to spot the most helpful, interesting, entertaining and educational titles.

LEARNING GAMES

Software learning games include everything from the *Putt-Putt and Fatty Bear* series (Humongous Entertainment, (206) 485-1212)

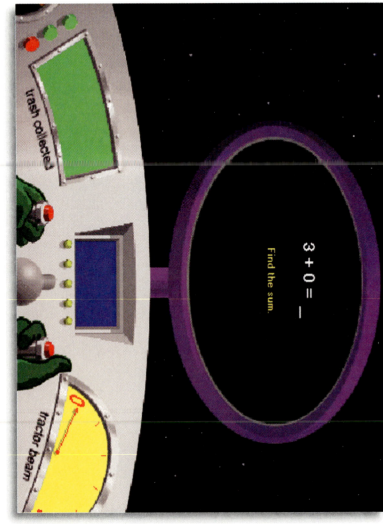

Figure 1: Learning games like the Math Blaster series from Davidson keeps you up-to-speed on your essential school skills.

for young children to the *Carmen Sandiego* series (Broderbund, (800) 521-6263) for older kids. These programs, and others like them, can teach you a lot of things—but they also are great games that are a lot of fun to play. These programs in particular share a clever design and use appealing characters.

Games that also teach are examples of the term **edutainment**. The *Carmen Sandiego* series is probably the best known collection of games of this type. All the *Carmen* games are favorites among computer-smart teachers. The *Carmen* games are also a comfortable choice for parents. But just because the adults in your life

like them doesn't mean that they're no fun to play. Just sit down with some of your friends—or even by yourself—and try to solve one of Carmen's mysteries, and you'll see how much fun using a computer can be.

Playing a game like *Carmen* (there are several in the series) gives you a chance to use what you've learned in school, but also teaches you how to find answers. We are all rapidly entering—willingly or not—the information age. If you know how to find answers to questions, then you'll have mastered an important skill. Besides, wouldn't it be great to know how to find the answers to any questions you have without having to run to an adult for an answer?

SKILL BUILDERS

Another kind of learning software concentrates on specific skills. While many of these titles are aimed at preschoolers or kids in the earliest grades, there are also plenty of programs designed to help older kids with school subjects ranging from math to social studies.

Mario's Early Years CD ROM Collection (Mindscape, (415) 883-3000) is one good example of a program designed for preschoolers. This CD combines several activities that help little kids learn to recognize colors, numbers and letters. And it uses characters that are familiar from the world of video games.

Playing games and picking colors are fine activities for your little brother or sister. They have no idea what real school is like. But how can your computer help you if you're already in school? What if you're having trouble with a specific subject—biology or spelling, for example? Your mom and dad might remember flashcards from the time they were in school, and that tool has been updated for the computer

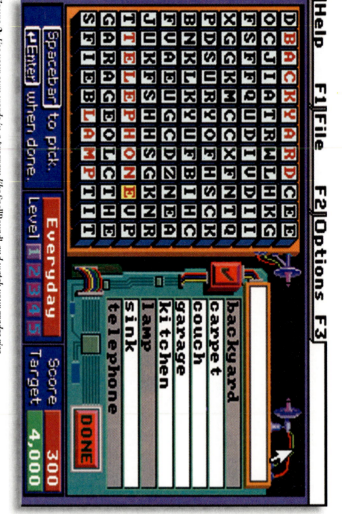

Figure 2: Use your own words in a program like SpellBound! and watch your grades rise.

172

Center can handle everything from a term paper to a personal journal. It will also help you design your reports to make them easier to read and more informative. And the way the program handles all those nasty endnotes will make your mom and dad jealous. They'll wish they'd had this great tool when they had to write endnotes! The CD-ROM version of the program also includes hundreds of pieces of clip art you can use in your reports. It all boils down to a better grade. And that means smiles from mom and dad.

REFERENCE

You can hardly buy a computer these days without a CD-ROM drive built in, along with multimedia attachments like speakers, phone answering machines, fax machines and all the rest of it. You might not have much use for everything that comes with the multimedia computer that you helped mom and dad set up in the family room, but you'll certainly get your time's worth out of some of the excellent CD-ROM references that are available.

These silver discs are packed with video and sound, and are quickly replacing the dozens of books and the encyclopedia that your parents used for reference when they were in school. Encyclopedia CD-ROMs from Grolier or Compton's New Media are a must-have for many families, and sometimes are included free with new multimedia computers or multimedia upgrade kits. Both are excellent references, and can be used for research or just for satisfying your curiosity. Even if your parents think they know it all, you'll be able to teach them something new from what you learn by spinning one of these references. Microsoft's

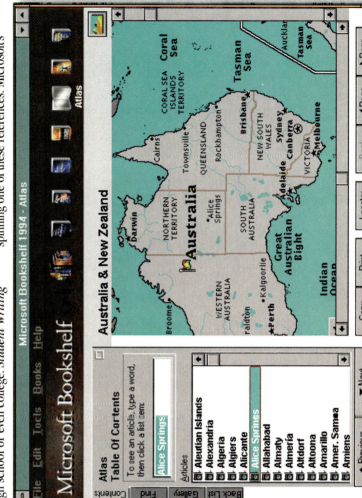

Figure 4: A reference 'ile like Bookshelf is great for getting your homework done right and on time.

using the really excellent *Multimedia Workshop* (Davidson & Associates, (800) 545-7677) or *Kid Pix Studio* (Broderbund, (800) 521-6263) to combine photos, animation, narration, audio and special video effects in very artistic ways.

Even dull-sounding programs like word processors are getting livelier, with all kinds of tools to help you create school reports that

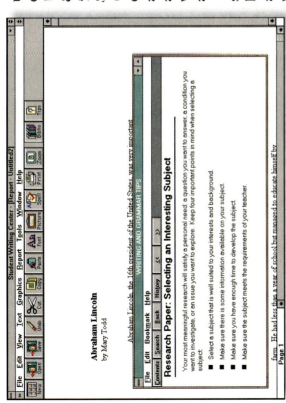

Figure 3: A word processor like Student Writing Center will help you create top-notch term papers and book reports for school.

generation with what is commonly called *drill-and-practice* software.

your parents and your teachers won't believe. Instead of sticking together pictures and graphs with glue and tape (like your mom or dad had to do in their reports for history or science class), you can use a program like *Creative Writer* (Microsoft, (800) 426-9400), which comes with an one-armed automatic spinning idea generator to kickstart your imagination and give you something really worth writing about.

The Learning Company's *Student Writing Center* isn't as flashy as *Creative Writer*, but it's an effective writing tool that gets the job done and lets you concentrate on what you want to say—not on how to get the computer to work. It's one of the best word processing programs any student could have, whether they're in middle school, high school or even college. *Student Writing*

Drill-and-practice programs are especially good, and especially plentiful, for kids who need to boost basic school skills. For extra help in spelling class, try *Super Solvers Spellbound!* (The Learning Company, (800) 852-2255). Or, if you need to boost your math skills, load up a copy of one of the *Math Blaster* games (Davidson & Associates, (800) 545-7677). Both these companies have kept their classic programs up-to-date with the newest technology, and they continue to make new multimedia learning programs.

CREATIVITY TOOLS

School is important, and you need to master subjects like math and geography to be successful, to keep learning and to get the most out of life. Some kids make fun of other kids who like to learn. But many of the kids who laugh at education will regret it later. When you're driving your new car to your new home from your great job, they'll be flipping burgers at some joint on the expressway.

Besides a great learning tool and a great place to play games and have fun, your computer is also a powerful creativity tool. With the right software, you can make your own animated videos, publish your own newspaper or design and print greeting cards.

A program like *Nickelodeon Director's Lab* (Viacom New Media, (212) 258-6000), for example, lets you make little movies using professionally designed clips from the Nickelodeon archives. *Art Center* (Electronic Arts, (800) 245-4525) and *Magic Theater* (Knowledge Adventure, (800) 542-4240) give you all the tools you need to make colorful slide shows of your own computer art. You can get even fancier results

What Makes A Good Software Program Good?

Walking into a software superstore crammed to the rafters with programs can be pretty confusing. You've been saving your allowance and working extra chores to get the money for a new software program. But how can you tell which programs are really good and which ones stink? Here are some guidelines that will get you on the right track.

Fun

No kidding. Any software program designed for a kid that isn't fun to use isn't worth the cardboard it comes boxed in. Even sophisticated homework programs with powerful tools like Davidson's *Multimedia Workshop* can be fun to use. Most of all, a kid's program should light a light in your imagination. If you can spend the better part of an afternoon with a simple video game like *Super Mario*, then a computer game with different characters and animated special effects ought to be able to hold your attention.

Challenge

Just because a computer game is fun to play doesn't mean it can't have any challenges. In fact, solving a puzzle and achieving a goal are what make so many computer games so much fun to play in the first place. The payoff is as important as the game and the story. The best kids' software you'll find strikes a balance so that the game is fun to play and the challenges are within reach. You don't want a game that's so hard that you toss it under the bed with last year's toys and last week's clothes. Remember that a challenge doesn't mean that you should never lose, or that you never ask for help. After all, sharing your experience of the game with someone else—even when it's getting the better of you—is part of what makes software so fun to begin with.

Easy To Use

Face it. Compared to video games, computers are still hard to use. And they're almost impossible compared to hitting the "on" button on the television. But software is getting better. Besides, all this computer stuff can be pretty simple to kids who seem to have been born with a computer mouse in one hand and a Nintendo controller in the other. Still, when you get a new computer program, it should be easy to set up on your computer. It should be able to figure out when I sound card you're using, and be able to copy all the files it needs onto your hard disk without messing up all your other programs. Also, the game manual should include all the information you need to fix any problems that come up, and should be written in plain English so you know exactly what to do at each step.

Lifespan

A really great software program is one that you come back to again and again. It's hard to know whether a program will have this kind of staying power when you buy it. But if you try to keep the other ideas we've talked about in this chapter in your mind when you go to the store, chances are you won't be stuck with a clinker when you get home. If you don't like a program that you bought, some stores might let you return it. Or, you could trade it to a friend for one of their programs that they have gotten tired of playing. But please—don't just copy the disks and give them to your friends. That's called software piracy. It's against the law, it steals money away from the people who created all these great programs and it keeps the cost of software high.

Value

Value is another tough thing to judge when you go to buy a software program. Take a hard look at the price of the software, and at what it does. If a program is a simple racing game, maybe it isn't worth $70. If it's a racing game with state-of-the-art sound and graphics and makes you feel like you're sitting in a real stock car, then maybe $70 isn't such a bad price, especially if you think about how many quarters you'd drop into the arcade game out at the mall for the same thrills. Of course, only you can really judge how much you think a program is worth, depending on your own likes and dislikes and how much use or fun you think you'll get out of it.

Encarta is another electronic encyclopedia that is as entertaining as it is informative.

You might not need a full fledged encyclopedia for your schoolwork each time. So make sure you have a "desktop" reference set like *Bookshelf 95* (Microsoft, (800) 426-9400) or *Complete Reference Library* (Mindscape, 415-883-3000). Both of these programs provide a dictionary, a thesaurus,

- plus quotation sources and an atlas to meet many of the needs of a student paper. You might never go to the library again.

In addition to CD-ROM encyclopedias and dictionaries, you can also stock your PC with specific references. Think of your computer as the ultimate traveling vehicle, capable of taking you inside the human body to examine human anatomy or back in time to learn about the

American Civil War or deep into space to check out black holes and quasars.

In fact, think of any subject you're interested in learning about, and odds are that you'll find a disc that can show you just about everything you would want to know. It doesn't matter whether you want to learn about Beethoven, bugs or baking—you'll find a CD-ROM reference to help.

ENTERTAINMENT

By now your folks have looked over this chapter and they're pretty happy that you're learning how to use the computer at home to do your schoolwork. So now we can talk about all the pure *fun* you can have with your computer.

Computer games cover all kinds of subjects. There are sing-along discs that let you pretend you're a musician, and there are cartoon adventures that let you act like a comic book superhero. You can chase villains, create wacky tools, solve puzzles, make paper airplanes—just about anything you can imagine.

If you're really into adventure, and you like the animated movies that come from Walt Disney and those other studios, then you might really like the classic *King's Quest* series (Sierra On-Line, (800) 757-7707). There are seven programs in the series, and they tell the story of a faraway kingdom. In each story, you get the chance to control the action. You have to solve riddles, unravel puzzles, battle demons and villains, and outsmart the kingdom's enemies to emerge victorious.

If science fiction is more your style, take a look at some of the games coming from LucasArts, such as *Rebel Assault*, *X-Wing*, and *Dark Forces*. Or jump aboard the U.S. Enterprise with Spectrum Holobyte's latest release, which takes the crew of our favorite starship from the TV screen to the computer screen. The fate of the galaxy is in the balance, and you must pick the right crew, negotiate well, and remain vigilant to keep the Federation intact.

TEACH YOURSELF

GREAT SOFTWARE

So, what do you want to do today? Just find the subject you're interested in exploring, and see what the world of computer software has to offer.

- **3-D Dinosaur Adventure** (Knowledge Adventure, (800) 542-4240)—Tour a dinosaur museum, match dinosaurs to their names and watch giant reptiles battle in ancient forests. This is one of many very good programs in this company's *Adventure* series.

- **AnnaTommy** (IVI Publishing, (800) 432-1332)—Imagine shrinking yourself to the

Kid's Software Selector Guide

Use this guide to select the right kind of software for you. Show it to your parents so they can see what kind of software they should be looking for to stock your shelves. If you have a little brother or sister, point out all the special programs that might appeal to them.

Preschool/Pre-readers

A child's work is play, so the best software for the youngest computer users takes that play seriously, with colorful screens, animated characters and plenty of room for kids to explore an electronic world in whatever way they like. The program's controls should be visual, using icons and pictures. Instructions should be spoken whenever possible. A helpful animated guide is also welcome.

School Age

Once kids leave kindergarten behind, they begin to trade their toys for tools. Lessons in math, science, geography, social studies and history build on basic reading and number skills. Software for this age group mirrors a growing maturity by featuring more sophisticated capabilities. The best of the crop takes advantage of your growing abilities by turning the computer into a creativity factory.

Teenagers

Entering the teenage years is an adventure for kids as well as parents. While kids are more eager than ever to assert their independence, parents are anxious about providing the right measure of guidance and support. If you're a middle-school kid at home using the computer, your parents will want to take advantage of your adventurous spirit by tapping into adventure games and more robust multimedia tools.

size of a microbe and traveling inside the human body. That's what's in store for you in this human anatomy journey.

- *Where in the USA is Carmen Sandiego?* (Broderbund, (800) 521-6263)—Just one of several *Carmen* titles. The well-known thief can be tracked across the United States while you learn about geography and important facts about different states.

- *Americans in Space* (Multicom Publishing, (206) 622-5530)—With video clips and a virtual museum, you can discover all the ideas and flights of the American space program, which has been

around much longer than the Space Shuttle. We've even put humans on the moon a few times.

- *Composer Collection* (Microsoft, (800) 426-9400)—If you're interested in classical music, bend an ear to this collection that includes works from Beethoven, Mozart, and Schubert.

- *Compton's Encyclopedia of American History* (Compton's New Media, (800) 862-2206)—A fascinating multimedia excursion into the American experience.

- *The Discoverers* (Knowledge Adventure, (800) 542-4240)—Take an endlessly fascinating journey from ancient history to modern times, from Ferdinand Magellan's wooden ships to the Magellan space probe.

- *Prehistoria* (Grolier Electronic Publishing, (800) 285-4534)—A super overview of the strange creatures that came after the dinosaurs, which are just as interesting as any giant lizard.

- *Recess in Greece* (Morgan Interactive, (415) 692-9596)—Help Morgan, a charming and way cool chimp, in his role as Odysseus in this electronic replay of Homer's *Iliad*.

- *Ancient Lands* (Microsoft, (800) 426-9400)—There's a lot more than the treasures of King Tut in this cool journey through ancient cultures. Take a video journey to Pompeii and watch a volcano swallow an entire city! (Don't forget the marshmallows.)

- *Oregon Trail II* (MECC, (800) 685-6322)—This remake of the classic *Oregon Trail* brings better pictures, more characters and new challenges to the old favorite.

- *Putt-Putt and Fatty Bear's Activity Pack* (Humongous Entertainment, (206) 485-1212)—Card games, matching games, logic puzzles, checkers, pinball and other great games all collected on one CD-ROM.

- *Mixed-Up Mother Goose* (Sierra On-Line, (800) 757-7707)—One of the first children's games for CD-ROM, this classic has been updated regularly and retains its charm.

- *The LucasArts Archives Vol 1* (LucasArts, (800) 782-7927)—Four great classic games from the people who made the *Star Wars* movies, plus screen savers and previews of coming attractions.

- *The Playroom* (Broderbund Software, (800) 521-6263)—An open-ended discovery program that encourages play and exploration.

- *Mickey's ABC's: A Day at the Fair* (Walt Disney Computer Software)—The familiar Mickey Mouse and other Disney characters lead young kids through alphabet games.

- *Tetris Gold* (Spectrum Holobyte, (800) 695-4263)—This CD-ROM carries all the favorites from the *Tetris* line, which makes for great puzzle-playing afternoons.

Figure 5: *The varied sources in Compton's Encyclopedia of American History reveal connections that help you learn the story behind the people and events.*

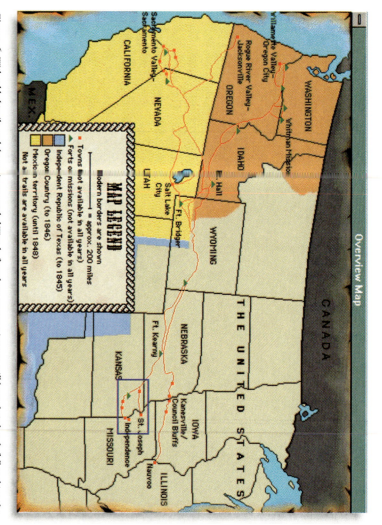

Figure 6: With added trails and the entire unsettled West before them, young pioneers will have their hands full making the overland journey to the new frontier in Oregon Trail II.

NEW GAMES

• **Where in the World is Carmen Sandiego? Junior Detective Edition** (Broderbund Software, (800) 521-6263)—Carmen's gang of ne'er-do-wells make their appearance in this entertaining edition for young sleuths.

• **Freddi Fish and The Case of the Missing Kelp Seeds** —Humongous Entertainment, (206) 485-1212)—Help Freddi and Luther rescue their friends from a variety of predicaments, and find Grandma Grouper's seeds in this game from the folks who made the *Putt-Putt* and *Fatty Bear* games.

• **SimTown** (Maxis, (800) 336-2947)—Build your own 'toon town in this junior edition of the classic *SimCity* program. Just try living in a house that looks like a pizza—you wouldn't have to go far for a snack!

• **BreakThru!** (Spectrum Holobyte, (510) 522-2584)—This colorful and entertaining puzzle will keep you amused for hours. And your mom and dad will like the fact that there's not a shred of violence anywhere in it.

• **The Incredible Toon Machine** (Sierra On-Line, (800) 7-7-7707)—Arguments about the comparative artistic merit of the Loony Tunes studios versus Animaniacs happen all the time on Saturday morning in America. Here's where the generations meet.

HOMEWORK HELPERS

• **Counting on Frank** (Creative Wonders, (800) 245-4525)—Guess how many candies are in the jar at Sherman's General Store in this game that stresses math and logic skills.

• **My First Incredible, Amazing Dictionary** (Dorling Kindersley, (800) 356-6575)—More than 1000 words to help young children gain the vocabulary they need.

• **Super Solvers OutNumbered!** (The Learning Company, (800) 852-2255)—Keep your basic math skills up to snuff while outwitting Morty, the Master of Mischief in this arcade-type game.

• **Super Solvers Spellbound!** (The Learning Company, (800) 852-2255)—Enter in your own words from your weekly school spelling list, then use those words in different games to boost your spelling skills—and your grades.

• **Math Blaster: Secret of the Lost City** (Davidson & Associates, (800) 545-7677)—Help Math Blaster and friends revive their crashed spaceship and unlock the secret of the Lost City. To do that, you'll have to solve several puzzles, all tied to math skills in such areas as addition, subtraction, multiplication, division, decimals, percents and fractions. But it's a lot more fun that any math class you ever took in school.

• **Zip Zap Map** (National Geographic, (800) 368-2728)—This fast-paced geography game is simple to play, but it takes real skill and knowledge—to win. And at its price (usually about $30 or so), it's a great value.

• **Cliffs StudyWare for the SAT** (Cliffs StudyWare, (402) 423-5050)—This electronic test-prep package combines practice exams, tutorials, drills, a comprehensive reference book and some solid test-taking tips. The software itself comes with two complete online exams modeled after the new SAT.

• **Mavis Beacon Teaches Typing for Kids,** (Mindscape, (415) 883-3000)—Proper keyboard technique can help you

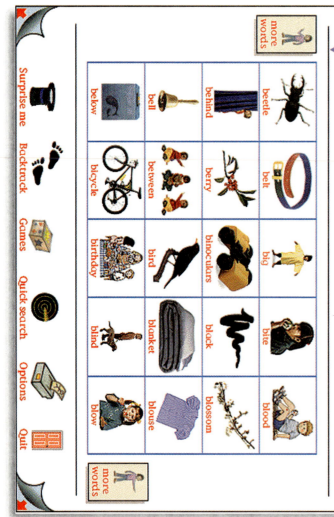

Figure 7: The Amazing Dictionary Catalog screens make it easy for very young children to find their way through this reference.

produce school reports more easily, and later protect you from work-related injuries. Mavis leads the way with basic typing lessons that start with single letters and progress to simple sentences.

- **The Multimedia Workshop** (Davidson & Associates, (800) 545-7677)—Everything you need for your budding media maven talents, and for the coolest school presentations anyone has ever seen. The program covers every facet of the multimedia creative process, from writing and publishing to illustration, photographs and video.

CREATIVITY

- **Creative Writer** (Microsoft, (206) 882-8080)—From generating ideas to attaching sounds and images to stories, this is the right tool for making everything from reports to greeting cards to newsletters.

- **The PrintShop Deluxe CD Ensemble 2.0** (Broderbund Software, (800) 521-6263)—This venerable publishing package has been around for years, for a variety of different kinds of computers. With the advent of CD-ROM, *The PrintShop*

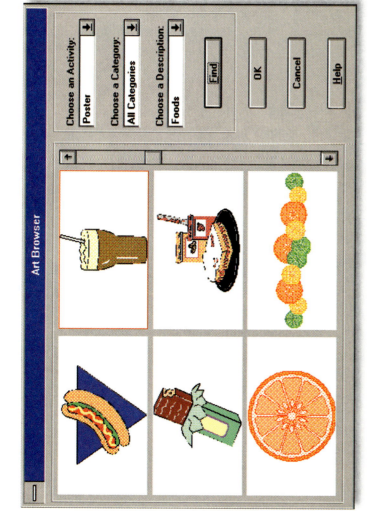

Figure 8: *The Art Browser in CardShop Plus! Deluxe saves you the trouble of scrolling through long lists of filenames, but it runs painfully slowly.*

Deluxe has become one of the best bargains around for making cards, signs, banners and calendars.

- **CardShop Plus Deluxe!** (Mindscape, (415) 883-3000)—Dedicated to greeting cards for all kinds of occasions, this program also lets you make posters, certificates and banners.

- **Better Homes and Gardens Cool Crafts** (Multicom Publishing, (206) 622-5530)—This program is so full of creative ideas that you'll never run out of fun things to do.

- **Kid Cuts** (Broderbund Software, (800) 521-6263)—This little creativity pack lets you make everything from masks to paper dolls. Print, color, cut, then glue.

- **Nickelodeon Director's Lab** (Viacom New Media, (800) 469-2539)—This creativity program contains every professional video studio tool a kid or parent might think of, from Nickelodeon video clips to sound effects, music, titles and graphics.

- **Storybook Weaver Deluxe** (MECC, (800) 685-6322)—Get your hands on the multimedia tools in this program to write books: electronic ones with music and sound effects to "read" on the computer or text-and-graphics-only ones to print out for your friends.

- **EA*Kids Art Center** (Electronic Arts, (800) 543-9778)—A traditional mix of coloring books, stamps and stickers and electronic drawing canvas. But it also boasts cool new tools, such as a screen saver maker that lets kids export their artwork into a unique application that mom or dad can run on the home machine or the computer at work.

- **Kid Pix Studio** (Broderbund Software, (800) 521-6263)—From animated puppets to whimsical paintings and stamps, this program lets you do it all.

- **Fine Artist** (Microsoft, (206) 882-8080)—There are plenty of paint and draw programs on store shelves. Many of them are suitable for kids as open-ended discovery toys. But few of them take the time to *teach* budding artists as well as this one does.

- **WiggleWorks** (Apple Computer/Scholastic, (800) 769-2775)—This program puts the "active" back into "interactive book" by encouraging kids to create and illustrate their own stories.

- **Little Kids ABC with Hickory and Me** (Western Publishing Company, (414) 633-2431)—Letter games and lessons for beginning readers, and a good value at a low price.

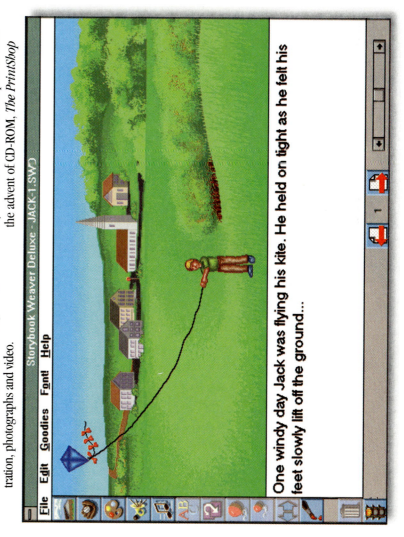

Figure 9: *In Storybook Weaver Deluxe, kids write the words to their stories at the bottom of the page beneath the illustration.*

Figure 10: Kids get a head start on school with lessons in Jump Start First Grade.

- **Alphabet Blocks** (Sierra On-Line, (800) 757-7707)—Great animation and playful characters that teach letters and sounds using the phone's method.

- **Busytown: The Busy World of Richard Scarry** (Paramount Interactive, (415) 812-8200)—A favorite children's author makes a graceful move to the computer, and snares young minds with a wonderful world they can call their own.

- **Jump Start Kindergarten** (Knowledge Adventure, (800) 542-4240)—With the talkative and helpful Mr. Hopsalot as a guide, even pre-readers can learn to tell time, recognize shapes, count to ten, order letters and numbers, recognize similarities and differences and even write simple sentences.

- **Jump Start First Grade** (Knowledge Adventure, (800) 542-240)—Frankie the dog guides rising first-graders in this skill-builder that mixes interactive play, age-appropriate activities and parental oversight.

- **Just Grandma and Me** (Broderbund, (800) 521-6263)—The first in the *Living Books* series, and still one of the best. An interactive storybook that encourages play and reading.

- **Putt-Putt Joins the Parade** (Humongous Entertainment, (206) 485-1212)—The little purple car charms young children in this caper to grab a place in the town parade. This is the first in the excellent *Putt-Putt* series.

Figure 11: The world of Tuneland is a great place for young kids to spend some time learning about the computer.

- **Tuneland** (7th Level, (214) 437-4858)—Great songs, great characters, engaging games and easy to use. Everything a young child could ask for in a computer program.

- **Thinkin' Things** (Edmark, (206) 556-8400)—All kinds of great learning activities that stress logical thinking and music skills. The first in a pair of *Thinkin' Things* titles.

GREAT ONLINE STUFF

You can't fully appreciate the power of your computer until you jack into the commercial networks, private **bulletin boards**, or the mysterious and all-powerful Internet. But once you do dial in, there's always a chance you might not be able to find where you need to go to find the very best stuff, to ask questions about school work, or to make and meet friends. Here's a quick guide to some interesting sites in the online world on the most popular information services.

AMERICA ONLINE

- **Keyword: National Geographic**—*National Geographic* Online hosts a section where you can download maps for school projects. If your mom and dad don't subscribe to the magazine, this is a great place to get the pictures you need to spice up a geography report.

- **Keyword: Disney**—*Disney's Adventures Magazine* comes to the online world with fun articles about everything from acrobats to whales. You'll find news about current movies, video game tips, and pictures of Disney stars and sports teams like the Mighty Ducks.

- **Stradivackius: The Counting Concert** (T/Maker Company, (800) 395-0195)—A unique visual design featuring three-dimensional graphics and an emphasis on musical instruments and the sounds they make set this disc apart from other learn-to-count programs.

Kid, Teach Yourself

You know that you can use your computer to write and design school reports. But did you know that the computer is perfect for teaching yourself about all kinds of things? Before you start thinking that all this sounds like another classroom you don't want to be in, think about all the other things you've learned outside the classroom.

For example, what about riding a bike? You didn't need a school for that, even though you probably had an adult teacher or an older brother or sister to give you a push and send you screaming and careening down your first hill. Or what about roller skating? Or kite flying?

Teaching yourself things on the computer is the same kind of thing. You only have to learn the things you want to learn, you can learn them as fast or as slow as you want—and you can have fun while learning.

The first thing you'll teach yourself about the computer is how the computer itself works. That doesn't mean you'll have to (or should!) pull the guts out of the machine. But you'll get to know how it all works by using it to play and work. When you get to school, you'll have an advantage in that you'll already know your way around the computers in the media lab. That means you can concentrate on the jobs your teachers give you.

But pretty quickly you'll be learning about all kinds of subjects—any idea or information that can be captured in a software program is wide open for your exploration. That's the key—you have to be free to explore, free not to worry where your journey is taking you. An atlas disc can take you on a trip around the world. An anatomy disc can teach you about how your body works. You can travel back in time, or ahead into the future. The list of games and programs you find in this article will help you blaze a trail in all those directions.

- **Keyword: *Tomorrow's Morning*—**This electronic version of the weekly newspaper written and designed just for kids covers world issues and entertainment news. There's even room for finance reports so you can figure out how to invest your allowance!

- **Keyword: *Image*—**A virtual gallery of artists' drawings, album covers and kids art designed for browsing and downloading. Dress up your computer with pictures of U2 and others. Post your own drawing in the Art for Kids gallery. You'll even find fun crafts and projects by clicking on the B.N. Explorer button. No more boring rainy days for you.

- **Keyword: *Encyclopedia*—**Open the covers of the cyberspace edition of Compton's Encyclopedia, with more than 34,000 articles and nine million words to help you with any term paper. It's all up-to-date, with sources for further exploration and research.

COMPUSERVE

- **Go: *STUFOA*—**The Kids & Teen Student Forum is one of the main hangouts if you want to meet other kids, exchange news and views and get information on everything from dating to English literature. And, no, they are not the same thing, although to check out what teachers are saying about students or to join in on discussions on how classrooms ought to be run. Some of it's stuffy, but there are some good discussions like "Why Johnny Can't Read" and "Single-Sexed Education" that can prove intriguing.

- **Go: *CNN*—**Keep up to date on current events—from the Bosnian War to the O.J. Simpson double-murder trial—by jacking in to one of the world's best news-gathering organizations. You can even join in the network's "Talk Back Live" show by posting messages here. Great photos round out an excellent forum.

PRODIGY

- **Jump: *Just Kids*—**Go here to find the entrance into the Kids Zone, where you can

Figure 12: *Share your drawings with other kids on America Online.*

they both can get pretty confusing from time to time.

- **Go: *GAM-212*—**Little kids will enjoy this cyberspace edition of the old paper favorite, Hangman, in which they must guess letters before they get strung up. The graphics aren't much to look at, but the software stays true to the spirit and fun of the paper game.

- **Go: *ASTROFORUM*—**Check out the late show from a million miles in space. NASA regularly furnishes the Astronomy Forum with new pictures, including views from the Galileo probe, the Hubble Space Telescope and other spacecraft. Talk about improving a science report!

- **Go: *EDUCATION*—**The Education Forum is the place to go for help with your homework, open doors to conversations, games, contests, jokes and other online amusement.

- **Jump: *Homework*—**The Homework Helper is like having a full library in your computer, but ask you mom and dad before you join. The service costs $2.95 an hour after the first two free hours that are included as part of your Basic Plan ($9.95 per month).

- **Jump: *Game Center*—**Get the latest news, rumors and reviews about the newest computer games in this section hosted by *Computer Gaming World* magazine.

- **Jump: *Nickelodeon*—**Your favorite television channel is now broadcasting in cyberspace. You can even help program the channel by letting them know which shows you like.

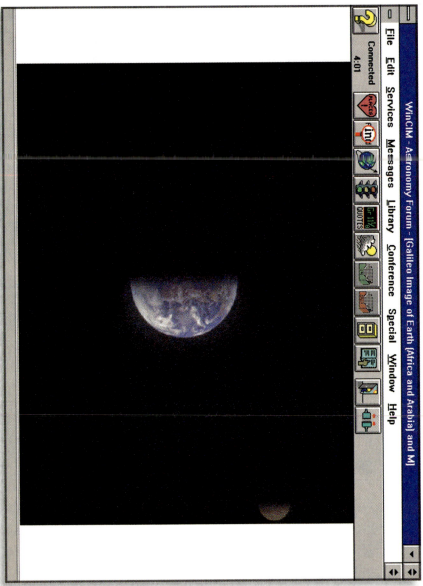

Figure 13: Take a trip through the solar system when you log in to CompuServe's Astronomy Forum.

Peter Scisco *has been writing about computers and technology for more than ten years. He is the former editor of COMPUTE! and Kids & Computers magazines. A father of three, Pete is a firm believer in, and advocate for, the potential of technology to positively influence the lives of children.*

museum without ever leaving your house. Examine the evolution of life on our planet Earth—and use some of the information in your next science course to really impress your teacher.

- **Jump: Sesame**—Meet all your favorite games and learning characters in the Sesame Street center.

interactive games, like mazes, or you can fool around with interactive toys, which don't really have a goal but are fun to play with.

- **The Museum of Paleontology at the University of California at Berkeley (http://ucmp1.berkeley.edu/welcome. html)**—Tour the halls of this virtual

WORLD WIDE WEB ON THE INTERNET

- **Uncle Bob's Kids' Page (http://gagme.wwa.com/~boba/kids i.html)**—This ought to be your first stop on the World Wide Web. There are seven sections with links to everything from games to dinosaurs to kid clubs. Get linked to Michael Jordan, Super Nintendo, outer space and everything in between.

- **Kids Club (http://bitizen.dds.nl:80/~ink/)**—Links to great and safe kids' stuff, and a chance to talk with other kids from ages 10 to 15. No adults allowed.

- **Kids Web (http://www.npac.syr.edu/textbook/k idsweb/)**—This is your digital library of the world, one of the coolest resources you'll ever have for homework and teaching yourself. You can literally travel the globe through cyberspace, although not all of the links are available at any one time.

- **Zarf's List of Interactive Games on the Web (http://www.cs.cmu.edu/afs/ andrew/org/kgb/www/zarf/games. html)**—If you came to the Internet to have fun, this is the place to start. You can play

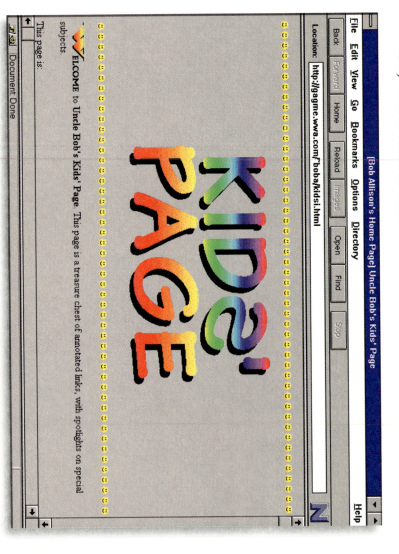

Figure 14: Uncle Bob has some great places to go if you're just starting to explore the Internet.

HELPING YOUR PARENTS ADJUST TO THE NEW COMPUTER

By Peter Scisco

Here are some ideas for cool things you can do with the new computer, and some tips on helping your parents adjust. (Don't squeal, it makes them nervous.)

Less than an hour after your family unboxed your new home computer, the adults around the house probably treated you to one of those boring lectures about the dangers of the Internet, and how you shouldn't stick paper clips into the floppy disk drive, and why it's not a good idea to switch the family financial CD-ROM with the latest Nine Inch Nails CD without telling somebody first.

Right. Like your mom or dad would know the difference between cyberspace and a parking place. But you can help them learn about computers if you take it one step at a time.

Before you jack into the Net (don't ever use that phrase around your parents—they'll probably call a congressman or something), start mom or dad off with some simple projects. You probably got some drawing software with your new computer. Try your hand at painting family portraits. Don't forget to let the adults have a turn. They'll get experience using the mouse and learn how to save and open files, and they'll also see that using a computer can be fun.

After your folks get the hang of a drawing program, show them that they can use their new skills on a special project. One of the simplest is to create a personal deck of cards. You don't need a lot of fancy equipment to

create cards on your family PC. A simple drawing program, like Windows's Paintbrush, will work just fine. You can even use a word processor if it allows you to create "frames," which most programs do. To make your deck, draw series of rectangles on the screen. Make the rectangles different sizes, then print them and choose the size that feels the most comfortable when you hold it.

Once you pick the size, go back to your program, select the rectangle you want and copy it to the clipboard. Open a new document and paste the rectangle to the page. Paste until you fill the page with rectangles. If you use a drawing program, you may be able to select a line of rectangles and paste the entire line, which will save you a lot of time.

Now comes the fun part. In each of the rectangles, you can paste a picture. Use different themes—whatever you're most interested in, like space or flowers. Decorate a Go Fish deck, for example, with pictures of sea creatures or with animal faces.

If you or your parents aren't comfortable drawing the pictures with the computer, this is a good time to introduce them to the concept of clip art. They can download a selection of pictures from an online service. Or, you can take them on a tour of the local software store to

select clip art collections right off the shelf.

Once you've designed your first set of cards, all kinds of possibilities suggest themselves. Who said cards have to be rectangles? Try making a deck of round cards, or a deck of triangular cards. You can also create specific decks for each game.

If you really want to score points with mom or dad, mention

that you can make flashcards for studying math and geography—that simple idea will get mom or dad nodding their head in a very "wasn't I smart to invest the money in this information machine" way.

There are a lot of other clever and interesting activities you can use your computer for. All of them will convince your parents that you're much better at using the machine than they will ever be, which means that sooner or later they'll start giving you free run of the machine and go back to their television set.

When that happens, you can start really exploring. And *that* means, among other things, going online. Now, while it's true that there are some unsavory characters out there in cyberspace, and that some of them disguise themselves to trick kids, you can stay safe by not giving out any personal information while you're online. It's fine to talk about hobbies or other interests—but nobody needs to know your full name or your age. And certainly no one needs to know where you live or what your phone number is. Think of your computer as a door to your house. You wouldn't let just anybody in, would you?

End of lecture. Promise. There are plenty of great places to explore online. Once you scope these places out, show your parents what you're up to—they'll feel better and they might even start learning about going online themselves.

On America Online, for example, check out the Kids Only section (*Keyword: Kids*; or, select it from the Main menu). If you're between the ages of five and 14, this is a place where you can meet other kids. Adults are free to visit the area, but are asked not to post messages or upload files. You can share stories and information about anything from Power Rangers to the Cartoon Network. There are also reference materials for helping you with school

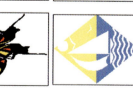

Figure 1: *Make your own deck of cards with your computer.*

Figure 2: *It's "Kids Only" talking in this America Online forum, but parents are welcome to look in any time.*

work, and a Suggestion Box for your ideas on making the service even better.

On Prodigy, visit the Kids Zone (*Jump: Just Kids*) for games, news, and conversation. You'll meet old friends like Carmen Sandiego, play word and number games, and get the latest lowdown on what's hot on TV and in video games. Some other interesting Prodigy places include Sesame Street (for younger kids), and Homework Helper—it's like having an entire reference library right there in your computer.

The CompuServe network isn't as "down home" as some of the other online services, but if your folks subscribe it's worth checking out the Kids & Teens Forum in the Education section (*GO:STUFOA*). Kids ranging in age from six to 18 meet in electronic discussion groups to talk about school, dates, parents, games and everything else happening in this so-called life. Like AOL and Prodigy, CompuServe also has plenty of resources

The Internet is known for its no-holds-barred discussions, and you should always check with an adult before diving in. You'll want to avoid some parts of the net, just like you'd avoid certain places in a strange new city.

You'll also want to check some places out right away. You'll need a **Web browser** like *Netscape*, or a link through one of the online services to make the most of your Internet explorations. One place you might want to start with, just to get your feet wet, is Steve and Ruth

Bennett's Family Surfboard (*http://www.sjbennett.com/users/sjb/surf.html*). This author/illustrator duo can link you to games and other fascinating web sites geared toward kids. There's even an Internet scavenger hunt for you scroungers out there.

Another site you'll want to visit is Web66, a cyber-crossroads where schoolkids all across the country share ideas and projects. You can dial up specific schools, or open the door to everything from NASA space archives to an interactive frog dissection. Yuck! Cool! Scalpel!

to help you with school work, and plenty of interesting professional people you can talk with and learn from.

All three of these services have links to the **Internet**, but finding your way around there takes time. It can be like exploring a dark castle without a torch.

Keep everybody interested with more creative ideas. You could show your mom or dad how to make a newsletter for the PTA. It's easy, and the word processor that came with your computer probably has a newsletter design already planned out (look for a "template" or model in the word processor's Help feature by pressing the *F1* key, then choosing *Search* and typing in *Template*).

Here are some other great ideas: Make your own party invitations. Make your own postcards with pictures you download from the Internet or one of the online services. Try your hand as the

All right. You've been online, and you've proved to your folks that you haven't been turned into some kind of drooling, pasty-skinned shut-in. In fact, right about now they're thinking it's really great that the home computer has somehow brought the whole family together for some quality time.

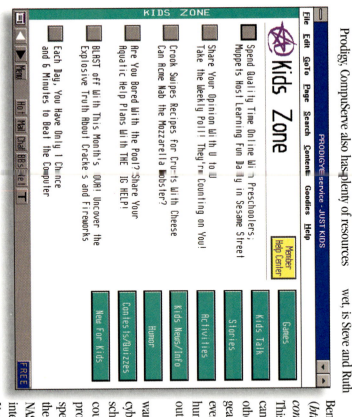

Figure 3: *On Prodigy, hang out at the Kids Zone for conversations, games and the latest news.*

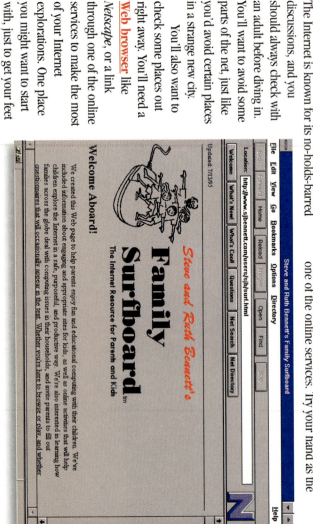

Figure 4: *Surf the Internet with Ruth and Steve Bennett's Family Surfboard.*

family weather reporter, gathering info and maps from online, printing them with your predictions, then putting them on the breakfast table for everyone to see.

When you unpack a new computer, there's a whole world of ideas waiting to be explored. But it's a different world than your mom or dad saw when they were kids. Don't be surprised if they seem a little scared at first. Be patient, and walk them through some of these ideas, then make up your own projects.

And don't forget to tell your parents: It's never too late to learn. ◗

Peter Scisco has been writing about computers and technology for more than ten years. He is the former editor of COMPUTE! and Kids & Computers magazines. A father of three, Pete is a firm believer in, and advocate for, the potential of technology to positively influence the lives of children.

EDUCATIONAL SOFTWARE: INTERACTIVE LEARNING

By Lance Elko

Your experience with educational software can be a dramatic success or an exercise in frustration. Understanding a few key concepts can make all the difference.

Can an educational software really enhance your child's learning experience? The answer is a qualified yes. Educational software really does work if it's designed well, developed to meet specific learning needs or enhance particular skills, and if it's used as intended. Another part of the equation is equally important: choosing the right software. Not all educational programs are created equal, and a little homework is a must for making the right decisions to meet specific learning needs.

In this chapter, we'll look at the world of educational software, examine the key ingredients you should look for in a learning program and offer tips on how to make wise purchases. We'll also study the advice and insights of leading experts and take a look at some of the best current titles available for selected age groups.

BETTER LEARNING THROUGH TECHNOLOGY

The quality of educational software today is a huge leap forward from even the best learning programs available at the start of this decade. Thanks to advances in computer hardware, today's software is far more engaging, livelier and much deeper. Lightning-fast microprocessors, generous amounts of computer memory, super-quick high-resolution video display cards, sophisticated sound boards that deliver digital audio and the CD-ROM (which holds as much data as 450 high-density diskettes) have all emerged in recent years to create a hardware environment capable of running software not even imagined just ten years ago. This convergence of digital audio, video and accelerated processing speed have led to a new kind of computing concept denoted by a term

Figure 1: Living Books are excellent "ooks for young readers. Children can choose to interact with the "bot spots" on the pages, or just have the story read aloud, with words highlighted as they are read. This screen is from Little Monster at School.

you've likely encountered, and one of the PC industry's favorite buzzwords in 1995: **multimedia**.

Most of today's PC educational programs are designed to take advantage of these new technologies. By offering faster and more colorful animation, audio narrative and feedback, video clips and often a huge variety of activities in one program, software publishers and developers are creating some truly groundbreaking learning titles.

TRADITION MEETS INNOVATION

The current crop of educational programs exploits not only cutting-edge technological advances in hardware, but also reflects a shift in

software design that started about five years ago. The educational software published throughout the first half of the 1980s was largely of the uninspired drill-and-practice variety. Leading educational software publishers took notice of the success of game software. They decided to enliven things in educational software by introducing concepts and designs borrowed from the game-development community.

Spearheaded first by Broderbund with its 1985 launch of *Carmen Sandiego*, then followed by other developers, the educational software category got a full "new set of clothes" by the end of the decade. Broderbund's *Carmen Sandiego*, Davidson's revamped *Math Blaster* series, and the *Super Solvers* and *Treasure* series from The Learning Company all demonstrated a new approach to teaching fundamental learning skills. (To launch its *Super Solvers* series, The Learning Company even created a marketing campaign to echo the shift: "Shhh! Don't Tell Them They're Learning.")

The new look and feel was a smashing success. Carmen got her own PBS TV show, board games and book line, and sales of the new breed of educational software climbed dramatically both to homes and to schools. The addition of entertainment to the learning software category was quickly emulated by educational developers everywhere. And, true to form, the computer industry coined another term to describe this hybrid software category: edutainment.

Initially, the "edutainment" label did not take hold. Many resisted because the new designation was a "play" on words which made light of "education," a revered word that one simply didn't refashion as a result of a marketing ploy. But the new label gradually gained acceptance. Today, even with game-like elements the rule rather than the exception in learning software, there is still a delineation between the two labels.

The use of "edutainment" in an advertisement or a review, or on a software package or in a software store, usually indicates that a title will have a game premise and sometimes a variety of activities geared simply towards having fun. The better edutainment titles manage to retain solid educational value while engaging the child. Others emphasize lighter, fun-filled play at the expense of teaching, enlightening, or encouraging creativity.

Many publishers still prefer the "education" label for certain titles when they want to underscore the learning benefit. This is particularly true with titles that teach, for example, foreign languages. Don't make any purchase decision, however, based on how a program is classified. There are more important things to look for.

CHOOSING SOFTWARE THAT WORKS

When choosing software, nothing is more important than making sure it's right for your child. Spending $50 on a program that gets used for 20 minutes is an exercise in frustration for both parent and child. There are a variety of criteria to consider before making a purchase.

The first and most obvious test is age range. Nearly every educational title states the appropriate age on the package. If you don't see it on the front of the box, check the spine and back of the box. If your child is near the low or high end of the age cutoff, study the program content description carefully, read a magazine or book review, talk to computer-savvy friends or ask your child's teacher.

Look also for specific educational benefits. What does the program attempt to teach, or what skills does it help to develop? While many educational programs offer an environment of activities that children can explore at their own pace, others are goal-oriented, designed to help children master a particular skill before progressing to the next, more difficult, phase.

You'll find that most programs designed to teach a particular subject or learning skill offer multiple levels of play. The language used to describe such a feature varies: *skill-*, *difficulty-*, or *multiple-levels*. Sometimes you'll see descriptions such as beginner/intermediate/advanced, or something cute like rookie/player/pro. Whatever the terminology, multiple play levels extend the usefulness of the product; your child can grow with the product. This feature also often benefits those with more than one child in the home. Your five year-old might start using the program just as your eight year-old has exhausted it.

KEY INGREDIENTS OF EFFECTIVE LEARNING SOFTWARE

The quality of educational software varies widely, although thanks to competition, the influx of top educators into the software business and huge strides in personal computer technology, the overall quality is much better than at any time in the past. There are dozens of good-to-excellent programs for every age group up to the mid-teen years.

But what makes good educational software? Are there particular components that make a program a truly valuable learning tool? We asked a variety of leaders in the field to name the key ingredients of effective learning software. By synthesizing all of their answers, we created the following list of ten essential components:

1. **Based On Proven Learning Theories.** Jan Davidson, founder and president of Davidson & Associates, adds that this key ingredient will not only develop a child's knowledge, but also, more importantly, will allow the child to gain an understanding of the material.

2. **High Engagement Value.** Universally regarded as a chief objective by educational software developers, engaging the child is a must for any effective learning program. In practical terms, how is this done? Susan Schilling, senior vice president, development and creative director for MECC, offers this observation: "Initially getting their attention can be done through the setting, graphics and story content. High levels of interactivity will keep them interested. Effective software allows the child to be part of the experience through decision-making, exploring, causing change, using creativity or attempting new things."

3. **Appeals To Different Learning Styles.** We all learn differently, notes Davidson. Some children learn best by hands-on experience, some are visually oriented, and others are more auditory or text-oriented. Good educational software should be designed with this in mind, making it appealing and useful to a variety of learning modalities.

4. **Empowers The Child.** This is the most important ingredient, says Marilyn Rosenblum, vice president of education sales and marketing for Broderbund. She notes that two questions should be asked by parents: Does the child feel that he or she is doing something important? Is there a product (such as a story; a printed result or a skill learned) derived from working with a product? If the answer to these questions is yes, that product is successful.

   Donna Stanger, vice president of product development for Edmark, states that the locus of control should be with the child. "From the earliest age possible, we want children to know that they can take charge of their own learning. With this control comes a sense of empowerment and a sense of responsibility."

5. **Easy To Use.** This is a fundamental rule in all tiers of consumer software, but it's profoundly important in educational software. If a program's design confuses or bewilders a child, it's of little or no use. A clean design and logical interface means that the child can interact with the content immediately. Contextual help—ideally a mouse click or key press away—is an important element in educational programs as well.

6. **Combines Fun With Learning.** The content may be superior, but if the presentation is dull and charmless, kids will want to move on. Making the experience fun holds the child to the program and facilitates learning.

7. **Intelligent.** This ingredient, offered in the most succinct fashion by educational software critic Warren Buckleitner, is made possible by smart programming. Intelligent software adapts and learns about a child, says Buckleitner. Astute programmers and designers can build a kind of artificial intelligence into a program to monitor responses from

JumpStart a genius.

JumpStart your children and there's no telling how far they'll go. This award winning **CD-ROM software** provides the essential head start on education. Each grade includes a full year's curriculum of teacher developed, fun-filled games and activities such as reading,

language, math, science, art, music and more. Our unique programs also adjust to individual needs and let you measure progress.

Call **1-800-848-4886** for where-to-buy and discover how to give your little genius a JumpStart.

Hours of animated creative learning activities.

JumpStart will improve your child's performance in school or your money back.

The JumpStart Series™
GETTING A HEAD START ON EDUCATION

KNOWLEDGE ADVENTURE

Bargain Software? Think Twice

Some businesses flourish by catering to the impulse buyer in all of us. Who isn't tempted by bargains? But when it comes to software, think twice. You can find bargain programs at software retail shops, in mail-order catalogs, and as program collections on diskette bundles or on CD-ROM. Ideally, it would be wise to read a review or talk to software-knowledgeable friend who buys educational software. But we're talking about an impulse buy and a small amount of money.

Is it really worth the time or effort to investigate an inexpensive program? Probably not. Generally, you won't find a lot of quality in educational software bargain buys. They often include older titles offering limited color palettes, minimal interactivity, little or no use of sound or music, and so on. If the copyright is more than two year's old, stay away. As we've said, there's been a world of improvement in the past few years. Also, most collections consist of has-beens, although there are some reasonably good software programs found in some collections.

Two educational shareware CD-ROMs to consider are *Learning Heaven 2* and *The Best in Educational Software*. Each is a collection of hundreds of programs ranging from preschool reading and counting to high-school science and algebra. These CD-ROMs are available for less than $20.00 each, and if you find only a handful of programs useful, you'll be getting good value. These discs may be ordered by calling 1-800-242-4775 or via CompuServe at 71355,470.

When using shareware, be sure to register the programs you want to use with the author (prices are found in each program.) Shareware is an honor system, and by registering and paying a small fee for those programs, you'll not only encourage future efforts, but might also receive notices about updated versions of the program.

A good rule of thumb for software shoppers: if you're not sure about what you're getting, don't waste your time or money on bargain buys.

---

children and adjust the program accordingly. If a child is clearly in command of one skill area, but providing incorrect answers or taking an inordinate amount of time to respond in another, the program can adapt.

8. **Offers Positive Feedback.** *A sense of reward is important, especially for younger children.* All learning programs should at least verify when a correct answer is given or a goal is reached. Strong positive responses—particularly important for preschoolers and elementary school students—should be used to help create self-esteem. This also encourages children to move on to the next stage or level of challenge.

9. **Encourages Lifelong Learning And Exploration.** *Microsoft's K-12 Marketing Manager Ellen Mosner says that children should be able to take what they learn from an educational software experience and apply it beyond the computer experience to other facets of their life.* Much of today's educational software is designed or developed by educators merely to complement teaching in the classroom.

10. **Gets Used.** *It's quite obvious that an unused program is of no benefit to a child,* says Bill Gross, president of Knowledge Adventure, but there's more to it than that. "An educational program must pose some challenge, some overriding goal, some reward, something to make you want to go forward, and then provide you with the tools to succeed in getting to that goal. You must also have obstacles in your path that you can overcome to achieve the goal. The masterful trick that's mastered by very, very good software is in making those obstacles right on the teetering edge between frustration and satisfaction. Make the challenges too hard, too fast or too frustrating, and you give up. Make them too easy, too simple, and you give up for lack of challenge. So an effective, successful title has figured out just how to properly increment the challenge, and properly create a goal that's desirable enough to keep you motivated. The very best titles blend the educational aspects with the goal seamlessly."

> "*An informed parent is a child's best learning advocate. The more parents understand about how their child learns, the more they can help.*"
>
> —Donna Stanger, Edmark

to describe the richness of a product on a ten by eleven-inch piece of cardboard on the back of a box." He echoes other experts advising that you try the product before you buy, "When you go to a movie, you've probably seen something about it. You've seen a preview or an interview with the actor on TV, and a clip, something that shows what the experience is like. Sure, those clips are often sensationalized, but they're way better than what we get now when we make a software

---

BEFORE YOU LAY YOUR MONEY DOWN: EXPERT ADVICE

Buying software is an educational experience in itself. There are many places that sell it, hundreds of titles available, and, of course, a limit to the number you can afford to purchase. But armed with a little knowledge you can be a wise shopper.

All of the experts agree that before you buy any educational program, you should know something about what you're getting. Reading a description of a program's highlights on the back of the box can help, but, Bill Gross notes, reading ad copy can be far too limiting. "It's very difficult

purchase at a store. I really recommend seeing the depth and execution of the product to ensure that your children will love it. This, of course, is a lot of work, but it's well worth it."

One bit of extremely useful information included on software packages is the description of hardware requirements. Usually placed in small type on the spine or at the bottom of the back, these *specs* will explain whether your computer system will run the software. Most companies list minimum requirements, so it's important that you know your system specs before you walk into a software store.

Talking to computer-literate educators is also a good idea. Broderbund's Mary-lyn Rosenblum suggests that parents ask teachers what software is being used in the classroom. Microsoft's Ellen Mosner goes a step further, advising that parents talk to the school or district technology coordinator or library media specialist. Susan Schilling of MECC suggests that you check to see if your school offers a Technology Night, events often sponsored by PTA groups. Attending one of these can give you a heads-up on software that's both educational and engaging for children.

Reading reviews is a must. Some experts suggest popular computing magazines. Rosenblum, however, says that for many parents, the more appropriate coverage is found in the "nontechnical, kid-oriented publications like *Parents Magazine*,

Child and *Parenting*." She also advises a trip to the library to look at educational publications that review software such as *Technology & Learning, Electronic Learning* and *Teaching K-8*.

Reading reviews in popular magazines is a good way to get a good sense of a program's content and design. But, Shelley Day, president

parents helping their kids with blocks or books, says Marylyn Rosenblum. She advocates sitting beside your young child and stimulating discussion about what's happening on-screen. If the experience is good, discuss it with siblings or friends as well.

However, too much parental intrusion can have a negative impact. Shelley Day believes in giving kids a generous amount of freedom to explore: "Back off! Only help when asked for help. When asked, give help, but not the answer. It can be hard to watch your child struggling with a new concept, especially when you can see them heading for the wrong answer. You want to step in and spare them the disappointment. But if you let them work it through on their own, they'll do two things: learn the material better and gain a higher sense of self-esteem, which is the most important thing you can give."

With these points in mind, it's clear that knowing your child is of utmost importance. Every youngster has a particular learning style, a unique threshold for frustration and a complex blend of growing independence and parental dependence. As your child develops and matures, so will the nature of your interaction with him or her."

Jan Davidson offers three key points of advice to shoppers. First, purchase software with a "satisfaction guarantee" plan; some companies will allow you to return software for a full refund if it doesn't meet your needs. Second, purchase programs from publishers that have a reputation for developing high-quality software. And third,

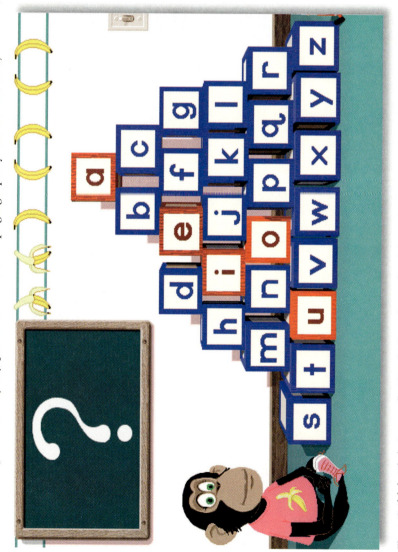

Figure 2: *Alphabet Blocks is an excellent introduction to the sounds and shapes of letters. The program is friendly, musical, and good-natured.*

of Humongous Entertainment, warns, "Read a magazine that you can trust. Some magazines seem to give everything a glowing review. Others are more selective." Day adds that an effective way to "test" a program is to use a demo program. Many companies, including hers, offer free or nominally priced demo CD-ROMs that show off interactive samples of entire product lines. Demos can also be found on discs bundled with magazines such as *KidSoft* or *CD-ROM Today*.

There are many other simple ways to become informed: talking with other parents who buy educational software, joining a local user group and participating in an online discussion about learning software are a few.

Buying programs at your local software store, where you can often get good advice, is the most obvious and convenient place to make a purchase. But, says *Children's Software Revue* editor Warren Buckleitner, "Don't forget about using mail-order services to buy software. You avoid local and state sales taxes, and can often get the software the next day." He also cautions to check first to see if they have a return policy in case, for example, you don't have a compatible sound card.

purchase software from companies that offer toll-free technical support.

PARENTAL INVOLVEMENT: HOW CLOSE DO YOU GET?

Once you're home with a new program, you want to be sure your child gets the most out of it. Should you sit with your child throughout each session? Or is it better to let them freely explore without your intervention? That depends, say the experts. When to get involved and when to stay away hinges on your child's age and maturity. But complete uninvolvement, at least initially, is not desirable. As Donna Stanger notes: "An informed parent is a child's best learning advocate. The more parents understand about how their child learns, the more they can help."

Encouragement and assistance-as-needed are key, especially for younger children. Bill Gross says that while it's not necessary to sit with children during an entire computer session, it's important to continually encourage and show interest in the child's success with the software. Parents working with children and their educational software should be no different than

SPECIFIC QUESTIONS TO ASK

When deciding what kind of software is appropriate for your child, Jan Davidson suggests that you first identify the objectives for the desired outcome. You can do this by asking five questions:

• Do you want to encourage a child to develop a skill or creative area that he or she has an aptitude for?
• Do you want to strengthen a weak area or an area in which your child lacks confidence?
• Do you want to supplement the learning going on in school?
• Do you want to teach your child something that's not being taught in school?
• Do you want to enrich an experience he or she has or is going to have (i.e. exploring an area before or after a vacation)?

Once you're able to answer these questions, selecting a software title will be much easier, says Davidson.

MECC also includes a list of questions in its Software Buying Tips guide for parents. The questions found here dovetail nicely with Davidson's list. MECC admonishes that parents start with their child in mind, then ask:

- What interests or excites your child?
- What are their strengths, and where do they need help building skills?
- How do they like to express themselves?
- Do they like to discover new things?
- What type of software is most appropriate for meeting their needs? (Basic skill programs? Simulations? Creativity tools? Interdisciplinary problem-solving programs?)

Once you've made a purchase and installed your software, be sure to check for any notes to parents in the manual or in a Help feature within the software. These notes are almost always helpful, and in many cases are imperative reading for parents wanting to maximize the effectiveness of the program. You'll find tips or program use, suggestions about noncomputer activities for complementing the program's content, and, most importantly, information on how to modify or add questions or problems and select targeted skill areas. All the leading educational software publishers include notes for parents.

SOFTWARE FOR ALL AGES

There are dozens of excellent educational programs on the market, and new titles are arriving every month. The programs we're recommending here are all available now, but are by no means the only good ones you'll find. Instead, we've selected titles that represent a cross-section of age ranges and topics. We've used all of these programs and can recommend each one without hesitation. For ease of reference, we've created age groups, but a number of the titles here also apply to adjacent age categories as a result of multiple skill levels or broad-ranging activities within a program. So if you're looking, for example, for programs for your nine-year-old, be sure to read both the Elementary Grades' and Middle Schoolers' sections.

PRESCHOOL (AGES 3 TO 5)

Most of the educational software designed for this age group falls into two areas: reading titles and basic skill-builder programs (designed to hone a group of skills such as pattern and shape recognition, counting, matching, problem-solving and so on). You'll find very few programs devoted exclusively to science or math skills for this age group.

Alphabet Blocks (Sierra). Ages 3 to 6, early reading. Bananas and Jack serve as hosts in a friendly environment that includes three skill levels and four classrooms. Skills taught include letter identification (by letter name and sound), and simple word construction. User modifications are a strong suit: Letter styles can be changed to upper- or lowercase, or cursive, and new skill levels are only a couple of mouse clicks away at any time. A playroom lets children explore objects and listen to songs.

Bailey's Book House (Edmark). Ages 2 to 6, early reading. With five engaging activities and plenty of charming cartoon characters that hold kids' attention, *Bailey's Book House* is a solid program for youngsters. Skills taught include letter recognition, rhyming and basic phonetics. An art activity gives kids the tools to create posters and cards and print them out.

Beginning Reading (Sierra). Ages 4 to 7, early reading. This program is structurally and graphically designed just like *Alphabet Blocks* (described above). As a follow-up program to its younger cousin, *Beginning Reading* teaches phonics as building blocks for assembling letters into words. It starts with two-letter consonants and vowel sounds, moves to rhymes, progresses to building words from word parts, then teaches sight reading. The Storybook Room, where kids listen to a story and fill in missing words, is an excellent reinforcement activity.

Bill Cosby's Picture Pages: Numbers and Shapes (Take 2 Interactive). Ages 3 to 7, introduction to counting and shape recognition. Based on the popular TV show, this friendly program asks kids to pair objects that have a relationship rather than an exact match (good for critical thinking). A nice feature: a game in which the child swims underwater to catch fish while avoiding

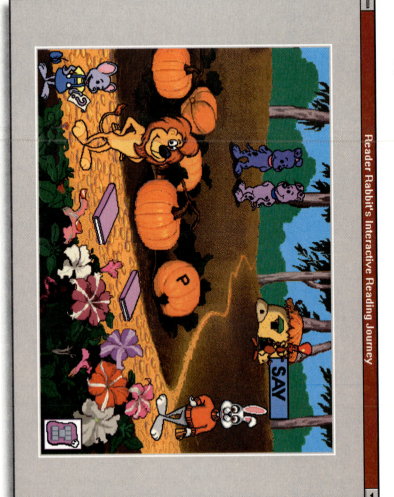

Reader Rabbit's Interactive Reading Journey

SAY

Figure 3: *The most comprehensive reading program available, Reader Rabbit's Interactive Reading Journey takes children step-by-step, from letter recognition to complete sentences.*

enemies and obstacles. If the child progresses, he or she must find numbered fish to match the answer to a simple math problem.

Early Math (Sierra). Ages 3 to 6, basic counting and arithmetic skills. Hosted by a funny little alien named Loid, *Early Math* features four rooms, each with a unique activity. Skills are honed in counting (1 to 100), shape recognition, place values (1s, 10s, and 100s), and simple addition and subtraction. Advanced levels offer practice with more complex math and geometry. An abundance of activities make this a good math program for preschoolers.

How Many Bugs in a Box? (Simon & Schuster Interactive). Ages 3 to 6, counting and basic arithmetic. Based on the best-selling pop-up book, this lively CD-ROM cleverly introduces preschoolers to the numbers 1 through 10 through a combination of games, exercises, and songs. Using a host of comical bugs to entertain and teach, the program also hones skills in early reading and memory building, and important areas such as sorting and sequencing. The program can grow with your child, too — the games offer three levels of difficulty.

Jump Start Kindergarten (Knowledge Adventure). Ages 3 to 6, basic learning skills. This cartoon schoolhouse holds 11 play areas that teach everything from relative sizes, counting, and telling time to shape recognition and matching. It's a charming program hosted by a spirited bunny named Mr. Hopsalot, who

never runs out of encouraging comments. As the title implies, this program will help preschoolers get a leg up on their first year.

Kid Phonics (Davidson & Associates). Ages 4 to 7, pre-reading. Using animated characters and musical themes, *Kid Phonics* features two activities that help attune children's ears to language. In the Sound Buster Game, children graduate from one level to the next by identifying sounds with characters, working with rhymes, and engaging in other activities. Once mastered, kids move to Word Builder, where they learn to build simple sentences. The animation, songs, and rhymes make *Kid Phonics* a gentle, fun, and effective tool for pre-readers.

Living Books (Living Books, a Random House/Broderbund Company). Ages 3 to 8, reading. All *Living Books* titles are based on popular children's books with which many youngsters may already be familiar. You won't go wrong with any of these titles, authored by some of the best names in children's literature.

The company name—Living Books—is a perfect description of the product. Pages come to life with a multitude of hot spots that children can click on to animate. Full of humor, excellent art, sound, and music, Living Books let children take their time to explore and move to the next page when ready. Text highlights include narration, so kids can see the word they are hearing. Every Living Book is loaded with clever humor; jokes (that adults will appreciate) and plenty of surprises. They're bilingual as well, with English and Spanish being the most common combination. Titles include: *Arthur's Birthday, Arthur's Teacher Trouble, Harry and the Haunted House, Just Grandma and Me, Little Monster at School, Ruff's Bone, The Berenstain Bears Get In a Fight* and *The Tortoise & the Hare*. Next in line: a Dr. Seuss title, which should be available now.

Millie's Math House (Edmark). Ages 3 to 6, basic math skills and pattern recognition. While not the newest of the programs described here, *Millie's Math House* is a classic example of a solid educational tool that kids happen to like—a lot. Using cartoon-style graphics, the program features six activities, five of which can be approached in the Explore and Discover mode. In that mode, kids just have fun with numbers. In the Question and Answer mode, they need to find a single answer. Cute, comical and full of charming characters, *Millie's Math House* offers a sound introduction to math concepts and loads of kid-appeal.

Reader Rabbit's Interactive Reading Journey (The Learning Company). Ages 4 to 7, reading. When this program was launched in late 1994, the publisher was so convinced of its

Figure 4: Children learn how to put letters into words with the help of Muppet characters in Sesame Street: Let's Make a Word

strength that a guarantee was issued: your child will learn to read with this program—or your money back. Without a doubt this is the most comprehensive reading program available. As a teacher, it's progressive; children move from one activity to the next after meeting certain goals. All in all, this CD-ROM features 40 storybooks and 100 reading-related exercises. The animated characters keep kids interested and smiling throughout.

Safety Monkey (IVI Publishing). Ages 3 to 8, everyday safety. Not a topic that normally comes to mind when we think of educational software, everyday safety is the subject of this colorful, animated trip through Swingland. Hosted by a young primate, whose name the program carries, Swingland features 15 hazard-filled environments (rooms at home, the school playground, the woods and other similar familiar scenes). Kids

Figure 5: The somewhat static graphics and animation of the Sound It Out Land series (Sound It Out Land 3 shown here) is balanced by effective phonetic exercises and outstanding original songs.

Hardware For Young Hands

Standard keyboards are adult-sized mice can be a bit intimidating for little hands. If you have a youngster at home, consider a couple of products that can make the educational computing experience a lot friendlier.

Big Keys, a specially designed keyboard for ages 2 to 6, features large (one-inch square) brightly colored keys in alphabetical order (left to right and top to bottom). Greystone Digital, the manufacturer, selected this design to reinforce learning of the alphabetic sequence. Big Keys is easy to use: Just disconnect your standard keyboard, and plug this one in—no software is required. An optional co-pilot cable allows simultaneous access to both standard and Big Keys keyboards. At retail stores, prices range from $90 to $115.

Also designed for ages 2 to 6, EasyBall from Microsoft is an alternative to the standard mouse. A large yellow ball is mounted in a stationary ring that doesn't slide around the desktop, and a big, blue button is positioned to the side for small fingers. Bundled with software (*Pointerland*, an animated farm environment that shows kids the full range of the device's use, and *Microsoft Exploraprdia: The World of Nature*), EasyBall works with DOS and any version of Windows. Also included is a multiple-input device driver for using both a standard mouse and EasyBall with your system. This allows activation of whichever mouse is in use without interference. The EasyBall package is available for approximately $55.00. For those with only one free serial port, Microsoft sells a MouseSwitch adapter ($14.95) to connect both EasyBall and a standard mouse.

Figure 6: Big Keys helps children ages 2 to 6 get around faster while learning the alphabetic sequence.

Figure 7: EasyBall, a mouse alternative, features a design for little hands—and it doesn't slide around the desktop.

Sammy's Science House

(Edmark). Ages 2 to 5, early science, sequencing, sorting and deductive reasoning. This exploration program features a variety of activities that teach basic logic concepts in a friendly manner. Kids can learn about the basics of weather; how to use critical thinking by categorizing objects (plants, rocks, and animals) by their characteristics, and how to sequence pictures to create a movie. A particularly enjoyable activity lets kids design their own toys either by following a blueprint or creating one from scratch.

Sesame Street: Letters

(Creative Wonders). Ages 3 to 6, alphabet. Using the familiar cast of the TV show, *Letters* invites kids into the homes of Bert and Ernie, Big Bird, and Snuffy. Here they're introduced to the shapes and sounds of the letters of the alphabet with the usual charming, innovative approaches of the Children's Television Workshop. Each home features a three-channel TV set that runs clips from the original TV show. An abundance of activities plus plenty of music and humor make this a warm, creative introduction to the alphabet.

Sesame Street: Let's Make a Word

(Creative Wonders). Ages 3 to 6, pre-reading. This graphically pleasing title is intended for kids who know their letters but not how to put them together. The theme is a game show in which the child is a contestant who selects one of six Muppet characters and one of four settings (farm, park, building site, or restaurant). At the chosen location, the child can click on objects to animate them and learn the spelling of the object's name. After a bit of exploration, the child is prompted to play a game, each one hosted by a different Muppet and designed to hone a different skill. *Let's Make a Word* is charming and engrossing for kids just learning reading basics.

Sound It Out Land series

(Conexus). Ages 3 to 6, pre-reading. Stressing phonics through activities and a strong soundtrack of original lyrics and music, the three-volume *Sound It Out Land* series is educationally solid if a little static in the graphics department. *Sound It Out Land* teaches letter sounds, then introduces three-letter words; *Sound It Out Land 2* teaches vowel and consonant blends, then builds to assembling letters into words and words into simple sentences. Finally, kids are instructed in the basics—or, for example, how to cross streets with traffic signals and how to handle a stranger at the door. Not heavy-handed and very friendly, *Safety Monkey* is probably best-suited for 3 to 5 year olds.

The Book of Shadowboxes (IBM Multimedia Studio).

Ages 3 to 8, pre-reading. Ignore the high-end of the age range here—preschool is the right target age for this introduction to the alphabet. Based on an award-winning book, *The Book of Shadowboxes* uses rhymes and matching games to teach the alphabet. Hosted by the friendly Shadow, who looks like a cross between the Pillsbury doughboy and Mr. Peanut, this program sends kids on a hunt to find objects that rhyme with a selected letter. Kids stay active with this title. And if they get lost, Shadow offers help. A well-designed art program is included as well.

3 Balloons: Alphabet, Numbers, and Shapes

(Swede). Ages 3 to 6, basic learning skills. The title of this program tells you exactly what skills are developed. What it doesn't reveal, however, are the wonderful graphics and animation that kids get when they start this one up. Never short on charm, *3 Balloons* lets kids pick from one of three characters who lead a scavenger hunt for shapes, letters and numbers. Youngsters are encouraged and rewarded throughout, and, like the animation, sound effects and music are outstanding.

Thinkin' Things

(Edmark). Ages 4 to 8, basic learning skills. An excellent way to introduce young children to a variety of important thinking skills, *Thinkin' Things* gives kids the freedom to approach problem-solving in their own way (a hallmark of Edmark's educational philosophy). Approaches to six fun-filled activities (which focus on memory enhancement, pattern recognition, spatial relationships, art, music and creative exploration) let kids learn by reading, listening, exploring and studying pictures and maps.

Tuneland

(7th Level). Ages 3 to 8, music appreciation. While not strictly educational, *Tuneland* is a delightful environment for kids to explore and discover 40 outstanding songs. Host Lil' Howie (the voice of Howie Mandel) takes kids on a game of hide-and-seek through a barn, farmhouse, train station and more. Cartoon animals guide children to new spots in this free-form 'toon land. There's no goal, just exploration and discovery. It scores high on charm and technical wizardry. Your kids might not learn a lot from *Tuneland*, but they won't want to stop playing and listening.

What Is a Bellybutton?

(IVI Publishing). Ages 3 to 8, human anatomy. An animated storybook, this program steps kids through a series of questions and answers about their introduced to that lifelong annoyance, the silent "e" rule, three-letter combinations (like "tch") and longer, multisyllable words in *Sound It Out Land 3*. The series has charm and solid educational value for pre-readers.

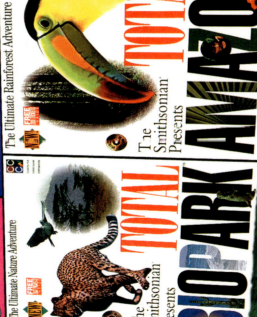

bodies. The language is carefully constructed so kids can understand the message. They learn why they need to brush their teeth, why men can't give birth and so on. Each screen contains a doorknob that kids must find to enter an activity area which reinforces what they've learned. It's a gentle, friendly introduction to anatomy that parents will likely appreciate.

Creative Endeavors

Children love to draw and paint, write, color, and make letters, posters, and special notes for parents, teachers, and friends. There's a wide selection of good programs available designed to let them exercise their creativity. We didn't include them in our recommendations since they're not in the education category. They *are*, broadly speaking, educational, but they're not designed to teach specific skills.

Here are some of the titles we recommend:

Creative Writer (Microsoft). Ages 8 to 14. At its heart, this is a word processor for kids. All the standard writer's tools are here—spell checker, thesaurus, cut and paste, a selection of fonts—but there's much more. Kids can use templates to create and print out letters, newsletters, banners, posters and more. Those who need aid from the muse can visit such places as the Idea Workshop, Project Workshop, and the Library.

Flying Colors (Davidson). Ages 8 and up. A wonderful concept, *Flying Colors* gets its name from the cycling of colors in a piece of on-screen art that kids create. It's an impressive, even *dazzling* graphic. And there are plenty of backgrounds, tools and pieces of clip art (more than 1,000) so kids (and adults, too) can create some truly magnificent animated art.

Kid Pix 2 (Broderbund). Ages 3 to 12. Kids can be multimedia artists armed with the tools and devices in *Kid Pix 2*. Essentially a drawing and painting program, this one includes hundreds of rubber stamps and a host of wacky tools that create all sorts of interesting, often comical, effects. The program also lets kids create slideshows and insert video clips. Despite its large arsenal of tools, it's very easy to use.

Kid Works 2 (Davidson). Ages 4 to 10. Children can create and illustrate their own stories, then hear them read aloud. *Kid Works 2* uses a text-to-speech technology that scans words and pronounces them through your sound card and speakers. Kids get very excited when they hear their story read back in a human voice. The program includes paint tools, stamps and ready-made backgrounds. Like *Kid Pix 2*, it's a studio for artistic expression.

Magic Theatre (Knowledge Adventure). Ages 6 and up. Using drawing tools with a variety of brushes, a special-effects library, clip art and sounds, kids can create impressive movies. They can work in short spurts and then string their saved files together, but they can't be rearranged once they're "committed." Even younger children can create impressive doodles. Older or more experimental kids can make some impressive free-form art.

Nickelodeon Director's Lab (Viacom New Media). Ages 8 and up. If your kids are ambitious, let them loose with this multimedia authoring system. Based on the familiar images and style of the Nick kids TV network, *Director's Lab* is not for the uninitiated. In fact, most kids under 10 will be overwhelmed. The program, though, is well-organized: Graphic Studio, for creating and painting images; Video Studio, for animation; Title Editor, for creating titles and credits; Music and Sound FX Studio, for recording and editing sound; and finally, the Director's Lab, a multitrack editing facility for putting all the media together for presentation. There's plenty to work with in the image, art and sound libraries, and the ambitious can import their own.

Student Writing Center (The Learning Company). Ages 10 and up. The ideal word processor for late elementary- and middle-school kids, *Student Writing Center* offers an unbeatable combination of elegance and utility. It includes preformatted document styles for reports, newsletters, journals, letters and signs. It also features writer's aids such as grammar tips and a bibliography maker. The CD-ROM version includes 400 images that can be dropped anywhere in a document.

Kid Pix Studio Kid Pix
File Edit Toolbox Goodies
New
Open a Picture
Save a Picture
Import Picture
Print
Printer Setup...
Return to Studio

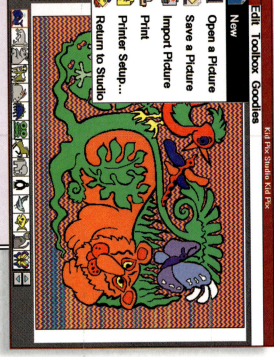

Figure 9: Targeted to ages 3 to 12, KidPix 2 *offers a huge arsenal of tools for creating art or for just having fun.*

The Elementary Grades (Ages 6 to 9)

Once children are school-aged, it's much easier for both parents and teachers to recognize their strengths and weaknesses. Exposure to a variety of activities and subjects in a structured learning environment reveals native skills and potential problem areas. As a result, many programs designed for this age group have a more specific focus than does software for the preschool set. There are also a variety of programs for this age group that provide entertainment while subtly honing logic and reasoning skills. Some of these programs, like those from Humongous, are suitable for older children in the preschool age range as well.

Student Writing Center - [Report - NATESCI]
File Edit View Text Graphics Report Tools Window Help
New Open Save Undo Cut Copy Paste Font Picture Spell Print Zoom Biblio Tips
NOVA
by Rachel Kline
Nova means "new" in Latin. Before modern astronomy, novas were thought to be new stars being born. This was not true because the stars had been there for a very long time, but only just being seen because of the special thing that was happening to it.
A nova is a star that suddenly gets very bright because of an explosion then slowly fades. The explosion causes the star to become 10,000 to 100,000 times brighter than the Sun. The nova hurls huge masses of gas and dust into space. This is a nuclear reaction caused from a build up of Helium gasses on its
Page 1

Figure 8: Ideally suited to kids ages 10 and up, Student Writing Center *is an outstanding word processor with preformatted document styles for reports, newsletters, journals, letters and signs.*

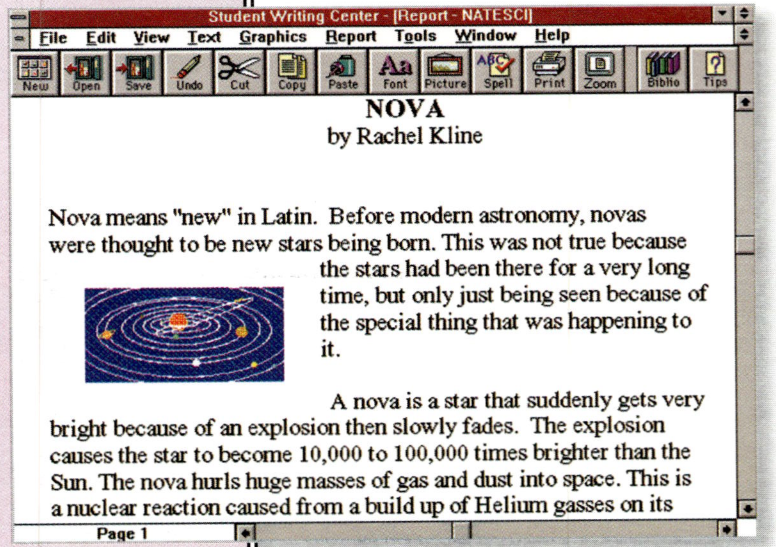

Adventures with Oslo: Tools and Gadgets (Science for Kids). Ages 5 to 14, science and logic. How to use six simple tools—the inclined plane, wheels and axles, pulleys, screws, wedges and levers—is the subject of this CD-ROM. It may sound a bit strange—it's not. The functions of these objects are taught in elementary school science. Seeing how and why they work can't be better illustrated than through interactivity and animation.

There are many clever and engaging activities. In *Oslo*'s Maze Mania, for example, children guide a ball through a series of mazes

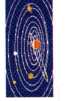

Lives Upstairs uses clever games to teach musical concepts, such as how to distinguish staccato from legato, allegro from adagio, and so on. Other games help kids learn how notes make up measures, or how instruments are classified and grouped in orchestras. Using a rich mix of audio, video, and animation, the program encourages free exploration of environments. Lots of clever activities, as well as a paint program and on-screen personal journal, make this program unique and highly recommended.

Fatty Bear's Birthday Surprise

(Humongous Entertainment). Ages 3 to 7, deduction and problem-solving. Like all Humongous titles, *Fatty Bear* leans towards the entertainment side of edutainment. This program is a story with a problem that needs solving, and there are lots of steps along the way, as well as plenty of fascinating diversions. There's no timer, so kids can explore and have fun as much as they like. The program tells the story of Kayla,

Figure 10: While not purely educational, Freddi Fish and the Case of the Missing Kelp Seeds is an award-winning interactive children's program with some of the best animation and music available. Children are entertained as they solve problems using logic, deduction and memory skills.

by using each of the six tools. In Dolly's Dilemma, children try to free a klutzy llama by—that's right—using the six tools. *Oslo* is appropriate for kindergartners through middle school, but kids in the 6 to 10 age group are the most likely beneficiaries.

Alien Tales (Broderbund). Ages 6 to 12, reading. In this intergalactic game show, players must prove that aliens didn't really write classic children's literature. They do this by reading from any of 450 passages selected from 30 books to show that they know more than the aliens do. Challenge rounds include true/false questions, crossword puzzles, code-solving and matching games. *Alien Tales* is a clever, highly effective CD-ROM that will probably encourage a few trips to the library.

Alistair and the Alien Invasion (Simon & Schuster Interactive). Ages 5 to 10, reading and problem solving. As part of Simon & Schuster's "Read, Explore & So Much More" series, this animated reading adventure offers a unique twist. While moving through the story, children can pause to explore screens (some are complete 360-degree environments) or play the Alien Plant Quest game, which meshes with the storyline. Brainy Alistair offers comments while kids investigate and discover; and he'll provide hints for the game. A solid reading and thinking skill builder, Alistair also gets high marks for charm and kid-appeal.

Beethoven Lives Upstairs

(BMG Interactive). Ages 7 to 12, introduction to musical concepts. A delightful surprise-filled program with an abundance of creative activities, Beethoven

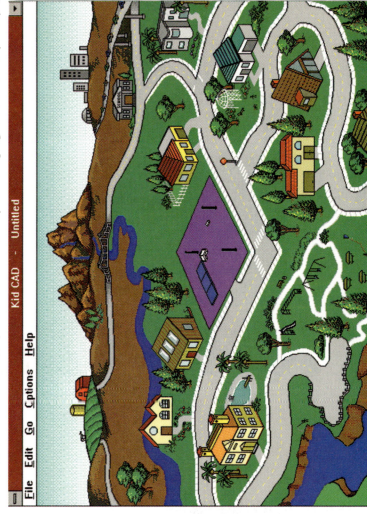

File   Edit   Go   Options   Help

Kid CAD - Untitled

Figure 11: Choosing a farm, city or town scenario, children 7 and older can play architect with KidCAD. There's a learning curve with this program, but once children understand how to use the variety of tools, they can create sophisticated structures, furnish and color the interiors—even insert people.

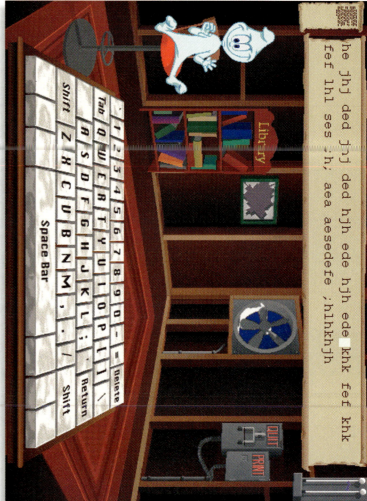

explore a storyline—trying to help Freddi find Grandma Grouper's missing kelp seeds—any number of ways and at their own pace. A wonderfully original soundtrack with first-rate animation and plenty of smart cinematic techniques make this a technological leader as well as darned good edutainment. Kids will have to figure out where objects are located and how to use them in order to solve this puzzle. If kids stumble, Freddi can be generous with clues. It's a big world to explore, and kids will play this one again and again.

KidCAD (Davidson) Ages 7 and up, logic and creative challenge. CAD is a word from the working world of adults. As an acronym for Computer-Aided Design, CAD is not something most kids will be familiar with. But if you have a would-be engineer or architect around the house, this is an excellent tool that introduces important skills and lets kids play with computer tools they might use later. Kids design their own 3D structures and add them to farm, city, or town landscapes using tools such as rotate, move, clone, copy, color and so on. The interface and abundance of tools may present a challenge to younger users, but once they've mastered the program, they'll love the worlds they can create.

Kid's Typing (Sierra). Ages 7 to 10, typing skills. A typing tutor with charm as well as

excellent feedback make *Kid's Typing* an excellent choice to improve keyboard skills. Detailed reports at every progressive level reveal areas that need work, and incentives for speed and accuracy are offered throughout. The program environment is a house in which kids must progress through different levels (rooms) with a unique reward upon the completion of each. The tailored, personal approach and clever humor of *Kid's Typing* make it as effective as it is rewarding for elementary-age children.

Mario Teaches Typing (Interplay). Ages 6 to 10, typing skills. The second of two typing tutors we're recommending for this age group, *Mario Teaches Typing* features the famous Italian plumber your kids doubtless know well from their Nintendo machines. Via progressive skill levels, kids are rewarded for accurate and speedy typing by helping Mario (they can also choose Luigi or Princess Toadstool) reach his goals by navigating through a sea of sharks, maneuvering through the hallways of a castle and the like.

Figure 12: Kid's Typing provides incentives for kids to hone typing skills. The program offers regular reports on individual typing strengths and weaknesses in accuracy and speed.

Freddi Fish and the Case of the Missing Kelp Seeds (Humongous Entertainment). Ages 3 to 8, deduction and problem-solving. In the world of kids' software, this is the closest thing yet to an interactive cartoon. A wide-open environment lets kids

a little African American girl whose birthday can only be a success if Fatty Bear can find some items and figure out a few problems. Kids direct Fatty Bear on his many quests. Beautiful graphics and wonderful music make this program a must for kids up to age seven.

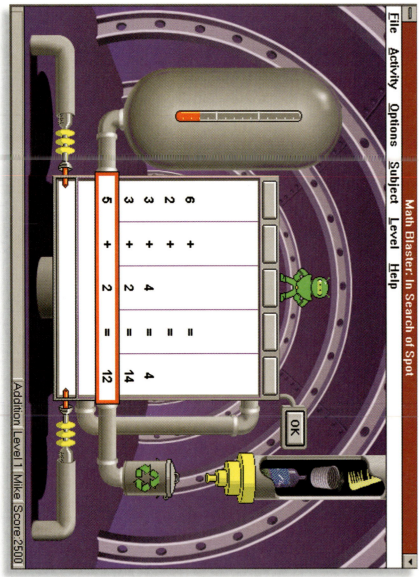

Math Blaster: In Search of Spot

File Activity Options Subject Level Help

Addition | Level 1 | Mike | Score: 2500

Figure 13: In Math Blaster: In Search of Spot, an outer-space scenario puts kids on a mission to find and rescue pet droid Spot. Increasingly difficult math problems must be solved to win the game.

Each lesson culminates with a report on accuracy, speed and trouble areas. For serious Nintendo fans, this may be all the inspiration they need to improve typing skills.

Math Blaster: In Search of Spot

(Davidson). Ages 6 to 12, math skills. This CD-ROM, the latest in Davidson's venerable *Math Blaster* series, finds Spot kidnapped by an alien. Starting with simple addition problems at the easiest level, kids move ahead in their quest to free Spot by tackling progressively more difficult math problems. At each of the six levels, kids can choose to work with addition, subtraction, division, multiplication, estimation, number patterns or a group that includes fractions, decimals and percentages. While *In Search of Spot* moves a little slowly and may bore some kids after awhile, it offers good value for those who need to bone up on math.

Math Workshop

(Broderbund). Ages 6 to 12, math skills. Teaching the fundamentals of basic math operations, fractions, logic and pattern recognition, *Math Workshop* is an excellent tool that teaches as it entertains. Hosted by Poly Gonzales, who instructs kids on what to do and is ever-present for help, the program offers every activity as a game with a goal. The more a child plays, the harder it becomes. Three difficulty levels make *Math Workshop* appropriate for a wide range of skills.

The Way Things Work

How It Works

MICROWAVE OVEN

MAGNETRON • TIMER • CONTROL PANEL

COOK • FAN • MICROWAVES • FOOD • TURNTABLE

A MICROWAVE OVEN cooks food in a fraction of the time it would take in a conventional oven. Microwaves, produced by a magnetron, penetrate the food, transferring heat to the water molecules in it by radiation. Heat then passes to the rest of the food by conduction.

Workshop • Machines • Principles of Science • History • Inventors • Back • Index • Options • Help

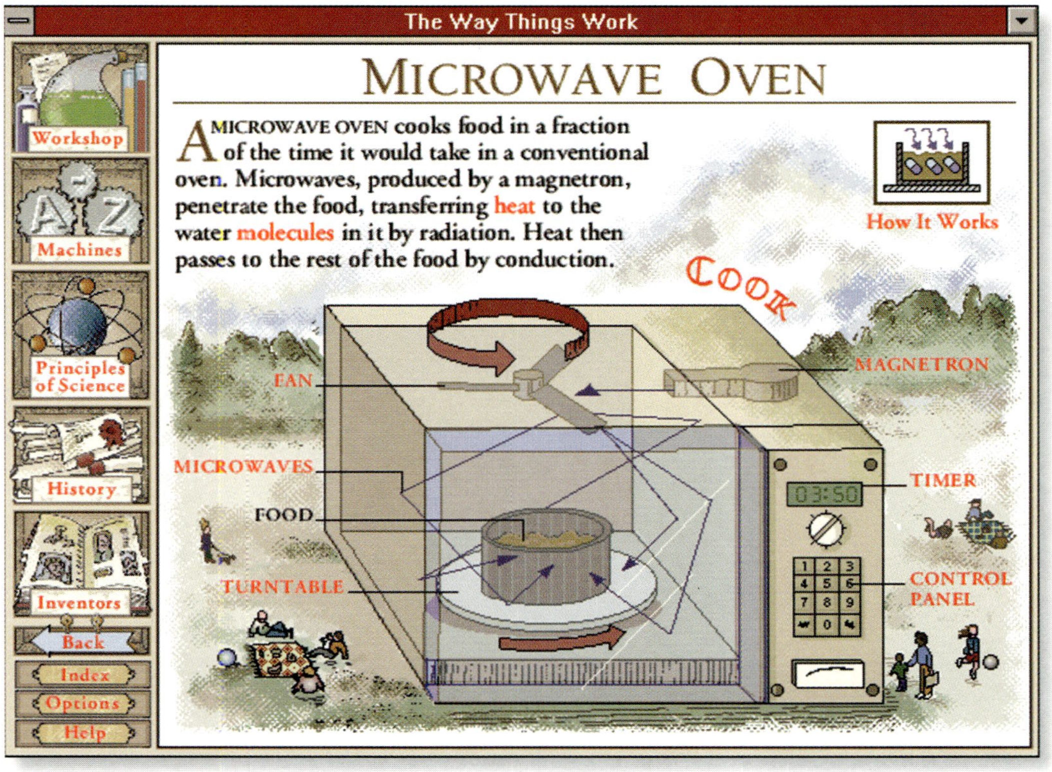

Figure 14: Based closely on the best-selling book of the same name, The Way Things Work explains scientific and mechanical concepts with lively animation, sound and plenty of humor.

This is guaranteed not to bore your kids; it's effective as a teacher.

Putt Putt Goes to the Moon

(Humongous). Ages 3 to 8, deduction and problem-solving. A sequel to a program discussed below, this edutainment title is typical of Humongous programs; kids can play it over and over. Putt Putt, an animated little car with a lot of personality, is launched to the moon as a result of a snafu. The child's job is to guide Putt Putt around lunar land to recover parts needed to construct the spaceship that will return him to earth. Finding the parts involves exploration and deduction as kids visit many sites filled with amusing diversions and no time limits. Cute, friendly and funny, *Putt Putt Goes to the Moon* is probably suited best for 5 to 7 year olds.

Putt Putt Joins the Parade

(Humongous). Ages 3 to 8, deduction and problem-solving. The program that launched Humongous into the limelight as a leading-edge children's software publisher, *Putt Putt Joins the Parade* might be a couple of years old, but it's as charming as most new edutainment titles on the market. The child's goal is to help Putt Putt make it to Cartown's parade by solving puzzles and taking mini-adventures to find objects. Along the way, clues

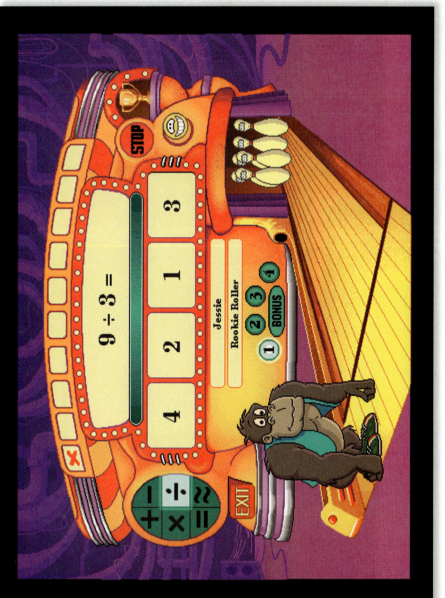

Figure 15: The colorful and humorous Math Workshop offers a host of activities covering calculations; pattern and shape recognition; and various types of problem-solving.

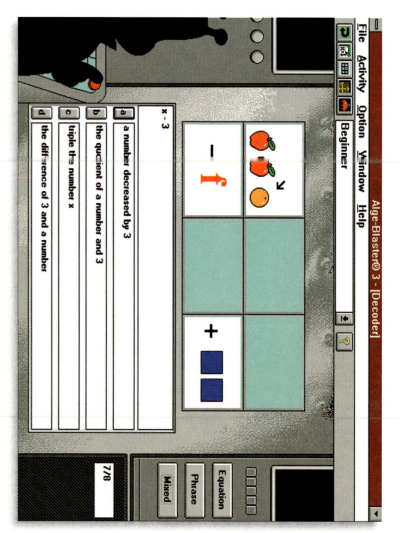

Figure 16: Alge-Blaster 3 includes puzzles and an outer-space game theme to teach algebra to kids ages 12 and older.

anatomy and biology. Based on the popular elementary school science book from Scholastic, this program takes a cue from the 1960s film hit, *Fantastic Voyage.* Mrs. Frizzle's class travels through the human body in a magic school bus. Each of the 12 locations (nothing too gross here) includes an educational game that teaches something about the function of an organ or bodily system. Animation, audio and the 3D environment are all first-rate, and there are plenty of jokes and hotspots to click on. Kids will be entertained while learning about themselves.

The Way Things Work (DK Multimedia).
Ages 7 and up, science. Modeled closely after the best-selling book by David Macauley, *The Way Things Work* is a multimedia *tour de force* packed with animation and sounds that bring scientific concepts alive. It's not a goal-oriented program in which the user is directed toward certain activities. Instead, kids—and adults, too—can explore how helicopters fly, how computers display images on a screen, and what makes air conditioners cool the room. All in all, there are over 150 machines explained, 22 scientific principles examined and more than 75 inventors covered. From 7000 BC to present, every major and minor scientific event or discovery is explored. Loaded with hyperlinks for seemingly endless variety, *The Way Things Work* is an outstanding reference that dynamically and effectively teaches scientific ideas.

Thinkin' Things Collection 2
(Edmark). Ages 6 to 12, high-level thinking skills. Designed for an older age group than

spelling of 1000 words (the program lets parents and teachers add another 3000). In a progressively more difficult sequence of spelling bees (three computer contestants challenge the user), kids must first win the class bee, then move up to all-school competition and ultimately to the White House for the national championship. This is a solid tool for kids who need help with learning proper spelling.

The Magic School Bus Explores the Human Body (Microsoft). Ages 6 to 10,

Eyewitness History of the World

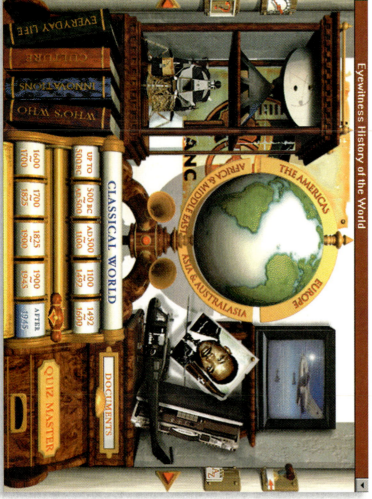

Figure 17: The interface for Eyewitness Encyclopedia of History features 27 different points of entry. All operation is point and click, and the program is loaded with hypertinks and multimedia components.

and suggestions are given. Technical values—interface graphics, animation, voice and music are outstanding, as in all the humongous titles.

Recess in Greece (Morgan Interactive).
Ages 7 to 12, Greek mythology, history and art. Morgan, a cartoon monkey, is stuck in Ancient Greece and must pass a music of tests to return to the twentieth century. By helping Morgan, kids learn about *The Iliad,* the Olympian gods, important Greek cities, and tackle a math and logic game that was actually played by the children of ancient Greece. One valuable educational game challenges kids to build contemporary words by blending Greek prefixes and suffixes. There are plenty of fun activities that are carefully mixed in with the educational components, making this program a friendly, solid introduction to an important historical era.

Sitting on the Farm (Sanctuary Woods).
Ages 7 to 11, reading, music. A single musical story that kids can read straight through (in English, French or Spanish) or explore. *Sitting on the Farm* tells the comically charming story of a little girl whose outdoor picnic is interrupted by one critter after another, each bigger than the one before. It's not terribly interactive, although a music section of the program lets kids select from eight instruments to play with the theme song (with a mike plugged into the sound board, they can sing along). There's also a storybook section where children can write whatever they like about the story. The target age range skews high—ages 7 to 8 is more appropriate.

Spellbound! (The Learning Company).
Ages 7 to 10, spelling. Using word games to teach spelling, *Spellbound!* provides kids with an entertaining environment for learning the correct

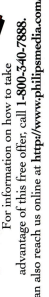
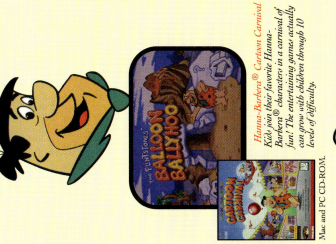
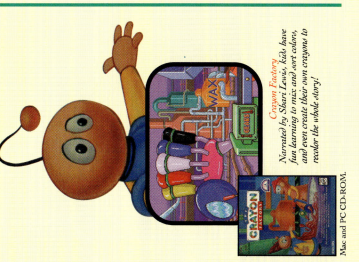

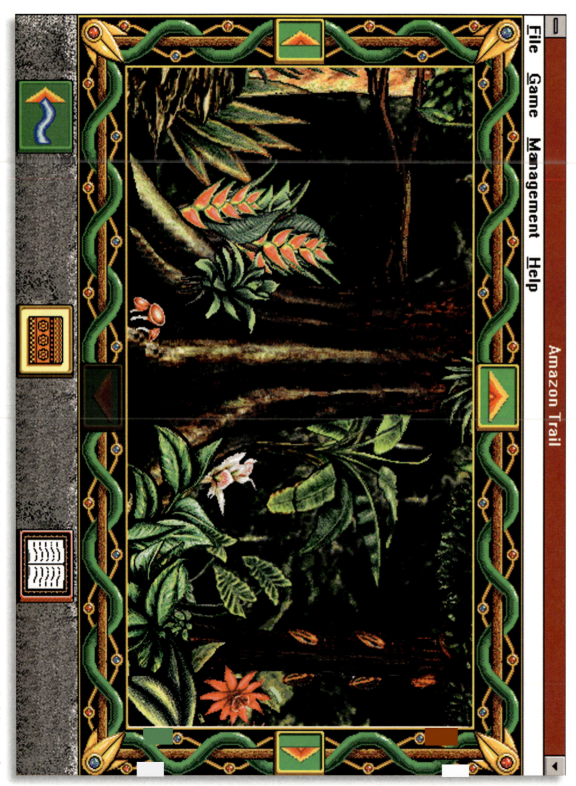

Thinkin' Things (see discussion in the Preschool section), this collection of five highly imaginative activities helps kids develop critical-thinking skills important to school studies as well as to creative pursuits. Activities range from musical explorations in which kids fine-tune listening skills, compose and save tunes and write their own increasingly complex rhythms, to exploratory environments that offer play with dimension, depth, perspective and optical illusion. This is a very smart and unusually innovative program.

Treasure Galaxy! (The Learning Company). Ages 5 to 9, math. With three skill levels, *Treasure Galaxy!* launches kids into an outer-space scenario where they embark on a quest for stolen crystals. By solving puzzles, kids progress through the game. The trick is that each puzzle requires that the master a mathematical concept—in an area such as fractions, weights and measurements, and geometry—without the language that normally accompanies these subjects in the classroom. As kids get closer to resolving the storyline, the problems increase in difficulty. *Treasure Galaxy!* isn't the best math program available for this age group, but it's an effective teaching tool that kids enjoy playing.

Treasure MathStorm! (The Learning Company). Ages 5 to 9, math. Like the preceding program from the same company, *Treasure MathStorm!* hones math skills as kids are challenged—here to scale a snow-covered mountain. The fantasy setting includes elves whom kids must capture. The elves pose math problems which, when answered correctly, earn needed money in the quest. The farther up the mountain kids proceed, the harder the questions. Six difficulty levels provide practice for a wide range of abilities. Specific math skills include money changing, weights and balances, telling time, and counting by fives, tens and hundreds.

Undersea Adventure (Knowledge Adventure). Ages 3 and up, marine biology. Packed with an information video and photos, *Undersea Adventure* lets children explore at their own pace. Probably best suited for 7 to 10 year-olds, the program is divided into several main areas: Undersea Reference, which features photos, sound and text for a large variety of sea creatures; Ocean Tours, a look at coral reefs, marine mammals, sharks and "odd couples"; The Seacology Lab, an inside view (literally) of sea creatures; and the 3D Deep Sea Hunt, in which you maneuver through a 3D environment in search of treasure and sea life. This program offers an exciting and informative view of the mysteries of ocean life.

MIDDLE SCHOOLERS (AGES 10 TO 14)

The bulk of today's educational software is targeted to preschoolers and children in the elementary grades; age groups in which critical skills must be developed. There are far fewer programs for ages 10 and higher, but there are good ones. It's worth repeating that age delineations are general guidelines. Your child may be below or ahead of his or her age group; consider programs in adjacent age clusters if this is the case.

Figure 18: A trip down the Amazon teaches kids about wildlife in the rainforest. Game elements coupled with exploring modes make Amazon Trail an entertaining and enlightening trek.

Figure 19: The Adventures of Hyperman uses animated cartoons to teach basic scientific concepts. It's full of wit, humor, and plenty of kid appeal.

Alge-Blaster 3
(Davidson). Ages 12 and up, algebra. Like other titles in Davidson's Blaster series, this program uses an outer-space game metaphor to pose algebra problems. It's not for kids who aren't already acquainted with algebraic concepts. It should be used as a supplement to classroom instruction. A clear tutorial is included for first-time users of the program, and the various games and puzzles engage students. Increasing levels of difficulty as well as a timer for those who feel confident make Alge-Blaster 3 a program that students can use for a long time.

Amazon Trail (MECC). Ages 10 and up. South American history, geography and ecology. Starting from the headwaters of the Amazon, students must navigate the length of the river on a quest posed by an Inca king. His people are suffering from a plague and the cure lies somewhere in the river's region. Exploration consists of stopping at various points on the banks of the river to examine the exotic flora and fauna, as well as bartering with natives and other travelers. By the time students find the necessary ingredients to create the needed medicine, they've completed a long journey and learned a great deal about one of the most important rainforest regions of the world.

Eyewitness Encyclopedia of History
(DK Multimedia). Ages 10 and up, world history. Each CD-ROM in the Eyewitness series features an interface that invites exploration. In fact, there are 27 different points you can click on to explore the major events, people and places in recorded history from anywhere around the world. Every operation is a point-and-click affair with layers of pop-up screens, nearly all of which include hyperlinks taking you to another location related to the word or phrase that's highlighted.

Audio first-person accounts add drama to events from every century and from all parts of the globe. There is no linear movement or no skill-level selection. Instead, students can zoom in to a particular subject and study related topics that provide context, or simply browse. This is a first-rate reference with educational value.

Eyewitness Encyclopedia of Nature
(DK Multimedia). Ages 10 and up, natural science. Another multimedia-packed program from the Eyewitness series, Encyclopedia of Nature serves as both an excellent reference tool and as an educational resource. Video, audio and animation—often synchronized for maximum effect—are used to illustrate concepts not possible with text and photo alone. Topics include: plants, fungi, birds, insects, amphibians, reptiles, invertebrates, fish, mammals, microorganisms and prehistoria, as well as explanations of energy flow, symbiosis, the biosphere, pollution endangered wildlife and much more. Encyclopedia of Nature has appeal for all ages.

Eyewitness Encyclopedia of Science
(DK Multimedia). Ages 10 and up, science. As an educational reference tool covering chemistry, math, physics, the life sciences and astronomy, this program uses a multimedia melange to explain scientific concepts and to bring eminent scientists, and their discoveries and inventions, to life. The theories of relativity, nuclear fusion and so on are explained with words, colors and animation that make often obtuse material easy to understand. Like all Eyewitness titles, this program can be used over and over for years to come.

Operation Neptune (The Learning Company). Ages 9 to 14, math. One of the first math educational programs that borrowed from the steer-and-shoot action in some videogames, Operation Neptune hones both math and pre-algebra skills. The student operates a mini-sub in a search-and-recover mission, navigating through underwater passages and around dangerous sea creatures to recover data canisters fallen from a failed space mission. Math problems are presented as the student progresses, and correct answers allow him or her to proceed. The focus of the math exercises is on problem-solving (many are word problems) rather than cut-and-dried calculation. Also, the kinds of math problems (calculations, geometry, number series, etc.) can be customized by parent or teacher to hone particular areas of weakness.

Oregon Trail II (MECC). Ages 10 and up, U.S. history. Starting from Independence, Missouri, in 1848, students journey west with nothing more than a used wagon, supplies and four computer partners. An updated version of MECC's award-winning Oregon Trail, this CD-ROM let kids choose an occupation, then face the hazards faced by the pioneers. They can choose any number of trails, each with a unique set of

Resources

If you're interested in exploring the world of educational software at a deeper level, there is a wide variety of resource materials. All of the larger online services, like America Online and CompuServe, include forums dealing with educational software. For print-based material, we recommend the following:

Magazines:

Home PC (CMP Publications) and *Family PC* (Ziff-Davis/Disney). Both monthly publications are available on newsstands and by subscription, and each regularly devotes space to educational software. Most issues of either magazine offer features and reviews on educational programs, as well as information on upcoming titles.

Books

Kidware: The Parent's Guide to Software for Children by Michael Perkis and Celia Nunez (Prima Publishing, 1995), $11.95. Coverage is mainly a rundown of educational software titles, divided into age groups as well as subject categories. Each review includes a "Tips on Use" section. Plenty of advice is offered to parents on hardware and software purchases.

That's Edutainment! A Parent's Guide to Educational Software by Eric Brown (Osborne McGraw-Hill, 1995), $29.95, coverage includes several chapters of background information for parents, with topics including why edutainment works, edutainment in the schools, getting involved with your child's education, and setting up a multimedia system. A large section of the book is devoted to 100 rated software reviews. Regularly updated editions are planned.

Newsletters:

Children's Software Revue. Published bimonthly, this newsletter covers new releases, offers opinions, and explores educational computing issues. Panels of kid testers report on what software they like. Subscriptions: $24 per year. For more information, write Children's Software Revue, 520 North Adams St., Ypsilanti, MI 48197-9998.

---

scenery and difficulties. Staying healthy, trading for goods, hunting and replenishing supplies must be kept in mind throughout the journey. Photos of historical sites and native scenery add realism to this excellent educational product.

The Adventures of Hyperman (IBM Multimedia Studio). Ages 7 to 14, science and problem-solving. This animated cartoon cleverly teaches basic scientific concepts by

---

drawing children into an interactive adventure that's engaging, lively, and very funny. Hyperman, a square-jawed antihero, speaks before he thinks. His foil, Emma C. Squared, a no-nonsense teenager with a brain for science, keeps him pointed in the right direction; gives chalkboard demonstrations to illustrate scientific concepts; and offers suggestions. Lessons in magnification (via an electron microscope), wind current, thermal properties, leverage and trajectory, light refraction, and genetic and evolutionary principles are taught with wit and humor.

The Discoverers (Knowledge Adventure). Ages 6 and up, science and history. Based on an award-winning IMAX film (which was itself based on Daniel Boorstin's book of the same name), this CD-ROM hops across time and cultures to explore the interrelatedness of various discoveries. For example, the accidental discovery of cave paintings in Nineteenth Century France is linked to a report on research on the intelligence of dolphins. The work of Magellan, Newton, Copernicus and many more great thinkers is explored. The emphasis, however, is not on the people, but rather on the significance of their discoveries and how these discoveries relate to contemporary world knowledge. *The Discoverers* is a fascinating program. Children ages 6, 7, and perhaps even 8 may find this a bit over their heads.

The Island of Dr. Brain (Sierra). Ages 12 and up, math, science, logic. As Dr. Brain's lab assistant, students embark on an

inventive island quest to retrieve an object for the good doctor. The proceedings consist of one mind-boggling puzzle after another. There's also an adventure component, as students must gather objects that must be used for later puzzle-solving. Kids will be challenged by problems in math, logic, chemistry, physics and even foreign languages. *Dr. Brain* is a fun-filled romp that's guaranteed to stimulate the gray matter.

Where in the U.S.A. Is Carmen Sandiego? (Broderbund). Ages 9 and up, U.S. geography and history. This classic educational title puts kids in the role of detective. The mission: find the thief Carmen Sandiego and her band of renegade accomplices. They're elusive, moving quickly from one state to another. Clues consist of facts about U.S. history, geography and culture, so, as kids pursue, they assimilate facts. The software package includes *The World Almanac of the U.S.A.* book, which can be used to help track down the elusive Carmen. Parents will likely enjoy this—especially the humor—as much as kids.

Where in the World Is Carmen Sandiego? (Broderbund). Ages 9 and up, world geography and history. Like the *Carmen U.S.A.* program (above), students play detective, tracking Ms. Sandiego across the globe. Excellent photos from every continent, along with appropriate foreign accents, provide a sense of the various nations and cultures visited. First appearing in 1985, this is a true educational classic. The newest version is on CD-ROM and offers multimedia features and more play

---

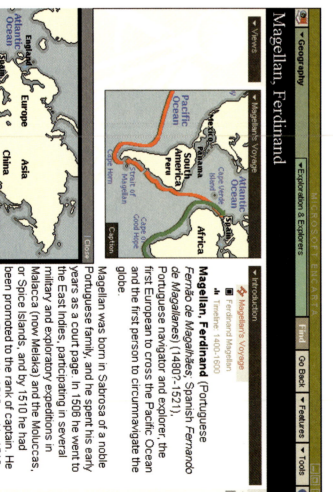

Magellan, Ferdinand

Magellan, Ferdinand (Portuguese *Fernão de Magalhães*; Spanish *Fernando de Magallanes*) (1480?-1521), Portuguese navigator and explorer, the first European to cross the Pacific Ocean and the first person to circumnavigate the globe.

Magellan was born in Sabrosa of a noble Portuguese family, and he spent his early years as a court page. In 1506 he went to the East Indies, participating in several military and exploratory expeditions in Malacca (now Melaka) and the Moluccas, or Spice Islands, and by 1510 he had been promoted to the rank of captain. He returned to Portugal in 1512 and in 1513 was stationed in Morocco, where he received wounds that left him lame for life.

Figure 20. *For households with students, a CD-ROM encyclopedia is a must. Microsoft Encarta, shown here, is one of several good choices that offer a wide variety of animation, diagrams, video, photos and audio.*

Foreign Language Software

Using software to learn a foreign language is the next best thing to visiting the native land itself. Thanks to advances in technology, you can hear a language spoken, learn at your own pace, test yourself, and even have your pronunciation evaluated by the software (you'll need a microphone for that feature).

There are several good foreign-language programs, all on CD-ROM, and you can find versions for English, Spanish, French, German, Japanese, Italian and Russian.

Four publishers dominate the foreign-language software market: Bayware, HyperGlot (now owned by, and published under, The Learning Company label), Syracuse Language Systems and Transparent Language. All of their products are commendable. Although each publisher employs a unique approach to their subject, each product is an effective teaching tool. In fact, foreign-language software is the sole product of each of these companies.

Because language study is "progressive," all the titles from these groups can be used from ages 9 or 10 through adult. They start with the basics and let you move ahead when you're ready. Bayware's titles include *Power Japanese* and *Power Spanish*, both comprehensive and immersive programs that do an excellent job of teaching.

The Learning Company offers a wide range of titles. Their latest are found in two series: *Pronunciation Tutor* and *Vocabulary Builder*. All titles in these lines are available in Spanish, French, and German versions, and they allow pronunciation comparisons with native speakers. Syracuse Language Systems' *TriplePlay Plus!* programs (in English, Spanish, French, German, and Hebrew versions) use three levels of game activity to teach vocabulary and phrases. They also include a voice input feature for comparing your pronunciation with that of the program host (a microphone is included with the software).

With titles in Spanish, French, German, Italian, Russian and Latin, Transparent Language also offers pronunciation comparisons with voice input. These titles present several stories with speech by a native speaker, and windows which reveal the meanings of words, phrases and sentences, as well as grammar notes.

Two other titles of note from entertainment publisher Sierra On-line are from the *BerlitzLive!* line, which to date includes Japanese and Spanish versions. They offer voice comparison, vocabulary and grammar exercises, and also provide information on the country's culture, with an emphasis on everyday situations you might encounter as a visitor.

Text Drill: la cocina

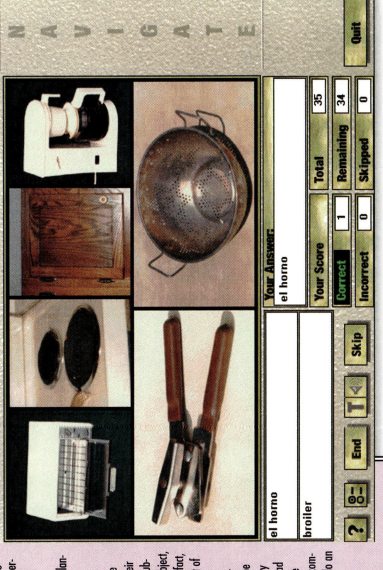

| el horno | | |
| broiler | | |

| Your Answer: | | |
| el horno | | |

Your Score	Total	35
Correct	Remaining	34
1	Skipped	0
Incorrect		
0		

Figure 21: *Multimedia foreign-language programs are highly effective teachers. Titles such as The Learning Company's Vocabulary Builder (Spanish version shown here) will even evaluate your pronunciation — if you have a microphone plugged into your sound card.*

the best site for prospecting, and how to pan for gold. Students meet historical figures, such as Jack London, and learn not only history and geography, but also gain a sense of what life was like in those rough-and-tumble times. An online journal is included for keeping notes of their experiences in the wild northlands.

A FAMILY AFFAIR

Think of some of the most popular kids' movies—*Beauty and the Beast*, *Home Alone*, *The Lion King* and *Pocohantas* are good examples—and consider the age mix of people who paid to see these films. Although created primarily for children, these movies drew people from every age group. Many current edutainment titles enjoy the same wide appeal. They're targeted to children, but they can attract users of any age when well-designed and developed using

state-of-the-art technology. A number of the titles discussed above are good examples. Most of the titles in the Middle Schoolers' section are, to one degree or another, appropriate for all family members of any age, and all the DK *Eyewitness* programs are valuable for the same reasons that entire families use encyclopedias.

during the Klondike Gold Rush of 1897, students are faced with immediate decisions: choose a traveling companion, find supplies, and purchase goods. Traveling north, practical lessons are learned: how one builds a boat, how to find

We didn't include multimedia encyclopedias in this section because they are generally considered reference works. If you don't own one, however, you're missing out on one of the best values in software for the home. *Compton's*, *Grolier's*, *Microsoft Encarta* and *Future Vision's Infopedia* are each published annually (*Infopedia's* publishers may be updating quarterly), and are available for well under $100. While each has its own unique design and content, any of them is a useful tool for any age. They're reference works, but they offer outstanding educational value, providing good research material for homework assignments. Each is also packed with video, animation, audio and hyperlinks, making it difficult to stop browsing and exploring. 🌐

value than its floppy-disk ancestors. It's bundled with *The Kingfisher Reference Atlas* paperback for following up on those more obscure clues.

Yukon Trail (MECC). Ages 10 and up, history and geography. Setting off from Seattle

Lance Elko has served as editor of five magazines covering personal computing since 1983, and is founding Editor of CD-ROM Today. His column, "The Education Connection," appears in Computer Entertainment News.

AN INTRODUCTION TO GAMES AND ENTERTAINMENT

By David Haskin and William Trotter

You've finished sending email to your sister in Boise. You've balanced the household checkbook. You've planned the family vacation. You've organized five years of correspondence. Time for a little R & R. All of this personal productivity stuff is great, but a lot of people use their PCs for entertainment. In this section we'll explain everything you need to know about games: the different major categories, hardware needs, rating systems and a lot more.

There are games, and then there are games...

To the newcomer, the "games" section at the local software store can look chaotic: Box after colorful box depicting sword-wielding heroes, dog-fighting jets, intricate miniature cities and empires—all clamoring for your attention.

How do you decide which game to buy? How can you find out—before you plunk down your hard-earned cash—which games are turkeys and which are thoroughbreds?

It's not as bewildering as it seems. There are only four basic types of computer games, and there are reliable sources of information—

consumer guides, if you will—that can really help you get the most for your gaming dollar.

First, the basics: a look at the main categories.

ADVENTURE, ARCADE, ACTION, SIMULATION: WHAT'S THE DIFFERENCE?

Once upon a time, in a land not far away at all, there was a game named *Adventure*. It wasn't the first computer game, but it certainly was the first to become widely popular. *Adventure* surfaced in the 1970s among users of mainframe computers, particularly in university computer science departments.

Adventure was a free game to which young programmers could add their own twists and turns. In the game, you were in a strange, magical and dangerous place. You collected clues and, if you were lucky, avoided pitfalls, wild beasts and other horrors and eventually found your way back to safety.

ADVENTURE BEGOT...ADVENTURE GAMES

Does the premise of *Adventure* sound familiar? *Adventure* is rightly regarded as the

ancestor of many of today's most popular games and, whether by coincidence or not, a broad genre of games available today is called **adventure games**. An adventure game is one in which you assume the role of a wayfarer on a journey or quest, usually in a place full of strange and interesting inhabitants. To succeed in the quest and return to safety, you must find objects, solve riddles, use magic and slay the occasional beast. The trappings and conventions are generally medieval; the monsters, wizards, and game stories all seem to take their cues from *Lord of the Rings*.

We take it for granted these days that games have amazing graphics, animation, sound and even video. *Adventure* had none of these. It was a text-only game: You typed instructions to pick up objects

Figure 1: Return to Zork is a recent incarnation of this classic adventure series which continues the original Zork's tradition of magic and mystery.

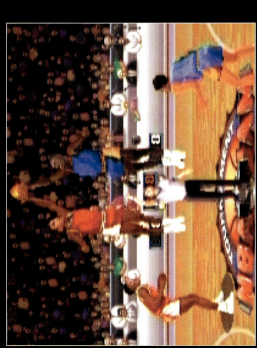

Figure 2: This is a popular arcade game called Alien Carnage. In this case, the hero is flying around a building site trying to save the world from an alien invasion.

or move in a specific direction and the game responded by describing, again in typed words, what was around you and what you could do.

The first best-selling personal computer game was *Zork*, which was a respectful and direct descendant of *Adventure*. *Zork's* premise was similar. You are lost in a great underground empire, a place both mysterious and magical. Like *Adventure*, *Zork* was a text-based game, but it had a richer cast of characters and was wittier than its predecessor.

Zork was so successful that it led to the introduction of many similar games. One early best-selling game was *King's Quest*, which was groundbreaking because it was not only one of the first games to introduce graphics into the action. In *King's Quest*, you actually saw scenery and people. Of course, the graphics and sound were crude by today's standards, but it was an important step forward.

Adventure games appeal most strongly to adolescents, who respond to the fantasy-like elements in the games, and to older players who enjoy puzzle-solving. Preadolescents will like the *"Dungeons and Dragons"* aspect of adventure games, but the sheer size and complexity of the more elaborate games may be too much for them.

Another term for this genre is "role-playing games" (RPGs for short) or fantasy role-playing games because the player usually controls a party of adventurers, each with different abilities and character traits. Part of the fun comes from figuring out how to get the most out of each member of your party—never send a wizard to do a warrior's job!

ARCADE GAMES

About the time that adventure games were starting to flower, video machines started

springing up throughout the nation. In bars and convenience stores across the land, players shoveled quarters into machines. *Pong* was one of the earliest hits. Remember that one? The game was embedded in a "table top" set-up, with two players sitting opposite one another and moving paddles to hit the image of the bouncing ball back and forth. Electronics had come to the land of pinball machines. Then came *Donkey Kong* and *PacMan*. Atari, Coleco and Matel all introduced limited purpose gaming systems: the Atari 2600, Matel's Intellivision and the ColecoVision. The migration of these games to a real computer really began with the introduction of the Atari 400 and 800. The new Atari systems used

computing power to enhance graphics and create action that was stunning for the time. These Ataris really set the stage for "dedicated" game machines like those from Nintendo and Sega.

While adventure games made you solve puzzles, these arcade games were faster-paced and less intellectual—they tested reflexes more than reasoning power. Inevitably, arcade games migrated to PCs, and today there are a wide variety of them available. These games retain their original character—the story lines (when they have them!) are thin, but the action is fast, fun and exciting.

Figure 3: While DOOM has gotten a lot of attention, Castle Wolfenstein 3D was one of the first popular action games.

204

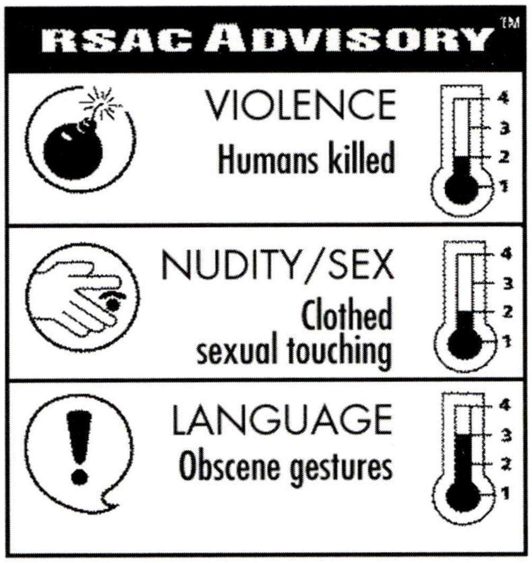

Figure 4: A sample of rating icons from the Recreational Software Advisory Council.

RSAC ADVISORY™

VIOLENCE
Humans killed
4 3 2 1

NUDITY/SEX
Clothed sexual touching
4 3 2 1

LANGUAGE
Obscene gestures
4 3 2 1

Arcade games usually require quick reflexes to shoot, pummel or at least elude bad guys. In an arcade game, you often jump into hidden places and collect weapons, tools and energy pellets (called power-ups). The end goal is often to save a lovable creature or damsel. Some arcade games are even more direct: You fight against an opponent, sometimes using martial arts.

Due to their fast action, arcade games typically appeal to younger kids and older people who simply want to check out of reality for a while. Many people find beating up on on-screen bad guys a great way to vent some steam: Walk into an arcade at lunch time in any downtown area and you're likely to see off-duty doctors, lawyers and other professionals playing alongside the kids.

Figure 5: If a title receives a score of zero in all areas, RSAC gives it an "All" rating.

RSAC ADVISORY™

ALL SUITABLE FOR ALL AUDIENCES

ACTION GAMES

Blurring the line between arcade games and adventure games is a more recent genre, action games. In these games, the puzzles are more difficult than those in arcade games, but less complex than in adventure games. Similarly, the speed of the action falls between the two extremes.

Action games have been around for a long time, but *DOOM* is the one that has received the most attention. The increased difficulty of the puzzles makes action games attractive to those who are easily bored by arcade games but who still prefer fast and furious action.

Note, though, that the action in many of these games is violent and sometimes quite graphic. While violence in arcade games is more cartoon-like than realistic, the trend in action games is toward more realistic blood and gore. In *DOOM*, when you shoot a creature, the creature is blown back and viscera are strewn about the area. For better or worse, this vivid violence, too, is one of the attractions of action games.

Not that all action games are violent. In some, like *Descent* (see *The Gamers Hall of Fame*), you shoot at objects, such as robots, instead of other people. But when you think about buying action games for your kids, consider whether you find the level of violence in a game appropriate for their ages. The newly developing rating systems can help.

RATING THE RSAC WAY

RSAC rates solely on the basis of content. Stephen Balkam, RSAC's executive director, says the organization's ratings emulate food labels, which provide information but not judgments.

RSAC rates games on three broad categories:

- Violence
- Language
- Nudity and sex.

For each game, RSAC rates each of these categories from zero to four, with zero being the "cleanest." If the ranking in each of the three categories is zero, the software receives an "All" rating, indicating that it is suitable for all audiences.

Besides rating each category, RSAC adds a tagline to each category. For example, two taglines in the Language category are "inoffensive slang" and "strong, vulgar language." Two taglines in the Violence category are "harmless conflict; some damage to objects" and "wanton and gratuitous violence."

The RSAC says it won't make judgments about age suitability because every child, and every parent, is different. For example, some parents may have strong feelings about violence but fewer objections to vulgar language. The RSAC's believes that it is not its role to make such judgments for parents.

THE ESRB APPROACH TO RATINGS

The ESRB feels equally strongly that, like the movies, games should have age-based ratings. According to Arthur Pober, executive director of ESRB, parents do prefer guidance about what is suitable for different age groups.

Game Ratings: What Parents Need to Know

As technology has exponentially improved our ability to show imagery and action, the level of realism and gore in some games has increased as well. The nature of graphic violence, and concerns over inappropriate sexual or racial stereotyping, have been concerns in gaming since game characters were first introduced. Just as these issues have become a focal point in children's television programming, they are an increasing concern in gaming. Most parents wouldn't think of taking their kids to an unrated or X-rated movie. But while the movie rating system is firmly entrenched, a similar system for PC games is still in its infancy.

The good news is that there are two separate organizations that rate computer games and place rating icons on packaging. The bad news, though, is that these two organizations, the Recreational Software Advisory Council (RSAC) and the Entertainment Software Rating Board (ESRB), are at odds. While many observers, including several members of Congress, believe that a single rating system would compel more vendors to submit their software for rating, it seems unlikely that the two ratings boards will cooperate any time soon. That's because each board disagrees with the way the other does business. The ESRB's ratings are age-based and are similar to movie ratings. The RSAC ratings are based on content and make no age recommendations. Another difference is that each board claims that they use only independent evaluators who are not tied to the software gaming industry. However, each organization maintains that the other is in fact dominated by industry. Also, each organization claims to have the most popular standard for PC games. ESRB, which grew out of the video cartridge game market, says that it has rated more than 700 products, about 200 of which are for desktop computers. RSAC, which grew out of the computer software industry, claims that it, too, has reviewed about 200 desktop computer game titles. In short: these guys don't like each other.

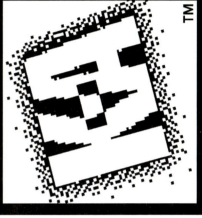

KIDS TO ADULTS

A G E S 6 + ™

Figure 6: A sample of the Entertainment Software Rating Board's rating

EARLY CHILDHOOD (3+)
MILD ANIMATED VIOLENCE
COMIC MISCHIEF

KIDS TO ADULTS (6+)
ANIMATED VIOLENCE
REALISTIC VIOLENCE
ANIMATED BLOOD AND GORE
REALISTIC BLOOD AND GORE

TEENS (13+)
SUGGESTIVE THEMES
MATURE SEXUAL THEMES
STRONG SEXUAL CONTENT

MATURE (17+)
MILD LANGUAGE
STRONG LANGUAGE

READING SKILLS
FINE MOTOR SKILLS
HIGHER LEVEL THINKING SKILLS
GAMING
USE OF TOBACCO AND ALCOHOL
USE OF DRUGS

ADULTS ONLY
NO DESCRIPTOR

Figure 7: Samples of descriptive phrases that go along with ratings.

As a result, ESRB has five rating categories:

- Early Childhood (EC): Children three and older.
- Kids to Adult (K-A): Age six and older.
- Teen (T): Age 13 and older.
- Mature (M): 17 and older.
- Adults Only (AO).

Like the RSAC ratings, ESRB's ratings also include taglines with each rating, such as "animated violence," "realistic blood and gore" and "mature sexual themes."

WHAT PARENTS CAN DO

Like movie ratings, game ratings are voluntary. Game vendors don't *have* to submit their wares to either ratings body. However, virtually all movies are rated, while many games are not. Why is this?

In both industries, retailers are the key to adopting and accepting ratings standards. Few theater owners will show unrated movies, which guarantees that those movies can't attract large audiences. However, only a few large retailers (such as Wal-Mart) are refusing to carry unrated games—and those retailers don't care which organization does the rating. The majority of retailers still don't require game ratings.

Although game ratings are gaining in acceptance only slowly, an increasing number of games are, in fact, being rated. Those games include best-selling titles like *Dark Forces* and *DOOM II*. Two ratings systems are better than none—both systems provide guidance to parents and to other adults who simply want to know what they are buying. But it's unlikely that computer game rating will be widely accepted until customers and retailers make an issue of it. Wal-Mart, for example, informed software developers that as of June of 1995, they would no longer carry unrated games.

SIMULATION GAMES

A final category of games, simulations, teach and entertain at the same time. The game creates a lifelike situation in which you must exercise skills and decision-making to achieve success.

The first popular simulation game was Microsoft's *Flight Simulator*, which puts you in the cockpit of an airplane. Your job is to learn to fly and then go from city to city. One of the reasons that *Flight Simulator* has been an enduring classic is that it is so realistic—you must really understand the principles of flying before you can be successful.

Another simulation game that became popular relatively early in the PC era was *Sim City*. In this game, you are the mayor of a city. For your city to grow and prosper, you must make difficult decisions on issues ranging from planning public transportation to whether to build a sports stadium. Other games simulate sports, wars and even the building of civilizations.

Simulation games keep you engrossed because any wrong choice can have severe consequences. In *Flight Simulator*, wrong decisions result in crashes; in *Sim City*, wrong decisions lead to a foundering economy, neighborhoods going downhill and, worst of all, the taxpayers turning you out of office.

THE RIGHT STUFF: GETTING THE RIGHT HARDWARE

Now that you know what kinds of games are out there, it's time to make sure your system has the capacity to play them. Do you want your home computer to be a top-flight, or even middle-of-the-road, game machine? If so, it needs enough power or it may not run some of the newest games. Some games won't even load without enough

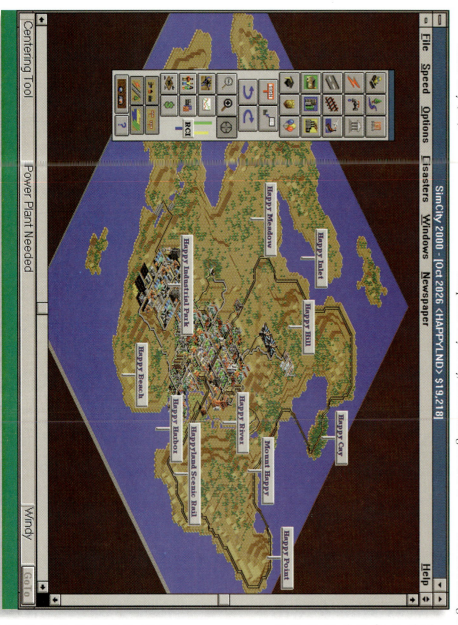

Figure 8: In Sim City, you run a city. You succeed if you get re-elected—so you better not anger the voters.

Do I Need A Joystick?

Joysticks are hardware devices used to control games. They're patterned after the joysticks used to control airplanes, which explains why they first became popular with flight simulation games. When playing a flight simulation game, you bank your plane to the right or left by moving the joystick in those directions, and move it down or up by pushing the stick forward or backward.

Nowadays, you can use joysticks to control a vast array of action, adventure and arcade games. Most PCs and sound cards have a special port where a joystick can be plugged in. A wide variety of joysticks are available at price points between $15 and $150, and most computer retailers have a broad selection for you to test and evaluate. One main difference between cheap and expensive units is the number of buttons on the joystick panel for doing things like shooting weapons in your games.

Low-cost joysticks have only one or two buttons while high-end models can have dozens that you can program to perform specialized actions. Having more buttons on a joystick means you need to move your hands less frequently to the keyboard or mouse to perform actions, so the flow of many games is less disrupted. Also, better joysticks let you adjust the tension of the stick itself according to your preference.

For flight-related games, joysticks remain the easiest and most fun way to navigate. For other games, though, joysticks aren't as essential—many people prefer using the keyboard to move and some prefer using the mouse. Low-cost game pads, similar to those used to control dedicated gaming units like Nintendo and Sega, are also available for PCs.

Seeing It In Three Dimensions

They're quite pricey, but virtual reality (VR) gadgets that give your games a three-dimensional feel are starting to appear in the market. These devices create a more encompassing, lifelike experience than you get from a regular computer monitor.

Typically, VR gadgets are headsets that you wear over your eyes. They plug into your PC, usually to the computer's game or serial ports or to a special add-in card. This is exciting new technology, but it would help to win the lottery before you buy: prices for these devices start at about $700.

Random Access Memory (RAM) or hard disk space. Others can even cause underpowered PCs to have a system crash.

Let's look at some minimum guidelines to ensure your computer is up to the task of playing games. These suggestions are meant to help whether you are buying or upgrading a PC. As of this writing, virtually every game available will run satisfactorily if you follow these recommendations. Don't despair, though, if you own an older PC that doesn't meet some of these minimums. Depending on its capabilities, it likely will work with most games that run in DOS, and with many Windows games as well.

When buying a game, check the minimum hardware requirements on its box or ask a salesperson if your system can play the game. The first thing to consider is this one inviolable (and costly) rule of computers and software: As PCs become ever more powerful (meaning faster CPU's, more memory, better graphics accelerators, and faster CD-drives), developers will continue to create great new games that push the envelope of capability. While the future is unknown, one certainty is that you'll always eventually need even more power.

AT THE VERY LEAST ...

As of this writing, any new or upgraded PC should include (at the very least):

- A 75MHz Pentium central processing unit (CPU), or a 100MHz 486 CPU.
- 8MB of RAM. Some new games won't work with less.
- A video adapter and monitor that support 800 × 600 resolution at a refresh rate of at least 76Hz. 800 × 600 is the minimum resolution for some new games, and a refresh rate of less than 76Hz will produce a flickery image that will give you a headache.
- A 15" monitor. Many systems come with 14" monitors, but 15" models aren't much more expensive.
- A quad-speed (4X) CD-ROM drive. You can buy double-spin (2X) CD-ROM drives for a song, but some games now require quad-spin drives.
- A hard drive with at least 500MB of storage space. Games are getting bigger and bigger, so you'll need ever more storage space.
- A 3.5" floppy drive. Few games come on 5.25" floppy disks anymore so don't worry about that type of drive.
- A 16-bit sound card. There are still eight-bit sound cards on the market, and they're cheap, but they produce mediocre sound. In fact, some new games won't work with those older sound cards.
- As good a set of speakers as you can afford. It's tempting to skimp with PC speakers, but high-quality audio equipment is worth the additional expense.

Expect to pay about $2000 for this basic, "game-ready" PC. If some of the equipment described here is unfamiliar to you, you can find explanations of what it does and why you need it elsewhere in this book.

THE ULTIMATE GAMING PC

Are our basic requirements too basic for you? Do you want to have the neighborhood PC-gaming hot rod? If you have money that's burning a hole in your pocket and you want to buy a PC that will play top-of-the-line, power-hungry games for a year or two or even three, here are the specs for a gamer's dream machine, the "ultimate" gaming PC:

- A 133MHz Pentium CPU (expect to pay a premium over a 75MHz Pentium).
- 16MB of RAM.
- A hard drive with 1GB (or more) of storage capacity.
- A video adapter card with at least 2MB of on-board VRAM to speed up the display of graphics.
- A 17" or 21" monitor.
- A six-speed (6X) CD-ROM drive.
- A sound card that provides 16-bit wavetable music playback.
- Depending on where in the pricing/technology curve you leap into the market to buy these options, your dream machine may cost you an extra $1000, $2000, or more. But you'll never have to go to the arcade again—and those quarters do add up.

David Haskin is a writer specializing in computer-related topics. Formerly a newspaper journalist and software executive, David is a regular contributor to PC Magazine, Computer Life *and* Computer Shopper. *He is the author of six books about computers including* The Complete Idiot's Guide to Multimedia, The Complete Idiot's Guide to PC Games *and* Using PC Tools for Windows.

William R. Trotter has been Senior Writer and reviewer for PC Gamer *magazine since 1987. He has published hundreds of articles and reviews on personal computer gaming, and has written the monthly* PC Gamer *column, "The Desktop General," since 1989. He is the author of eight published books.*

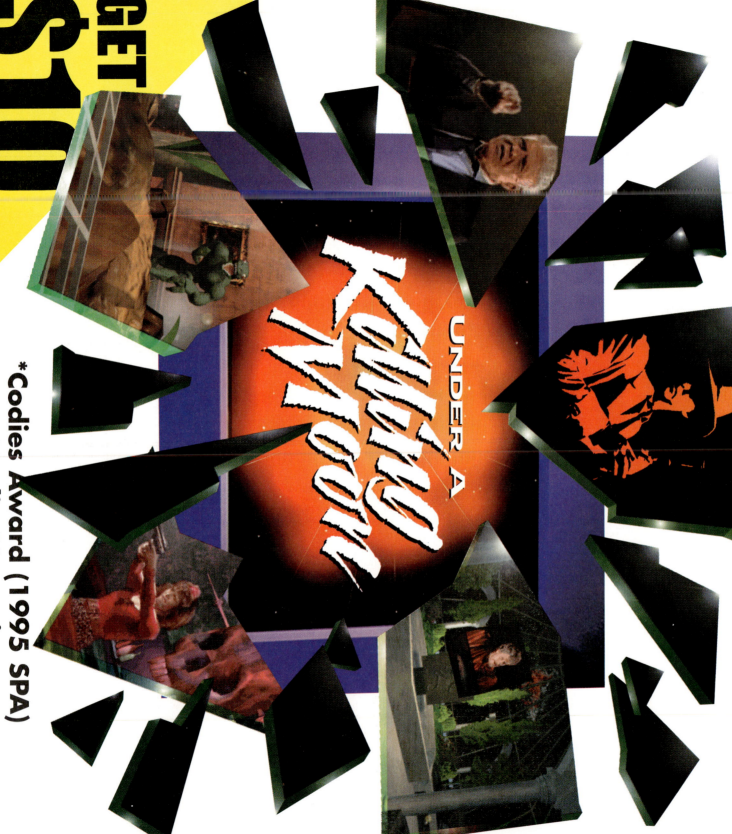

WINNER!
BEST ADVENTURE GAME*

UNDER A **Killing Moon**

GET **$10** OFF NOW!
AT YOUR PARTICIPATING RETAILER

*Codies Award (1995 SPA)
*NewMedia Magazine
*CD ROM Today
*Interactive Gaming
*Strategy Plus

ACCESS SOFTWARE INCORPORATED
4750 Wiley Post Way, Bldg. 1 Ste. 200 SLC, UT. 84116 1-800-800-4880

THE PC GAMERS GUIDE TO RESOURCES:
HOW TO FIND GREAT GAMES

By David Haskin and William Trotter

With great advertising and gorgeous packaging, game makers can make every game seem like the one you've been waiting all your life to play. With all of the games out there, how do you know which one really is the one you've been waiting for? While most software outlets will have some in-store demos running, chances are you won't find a store that actually lets you take the shrink-wrap off a game and try it before buying. Considering the investment a new game represents, you'll want the best possible consumers' information you can get before deciding what to buy.

The best source for that information is found in the PC gaming magazines. In these specialized publications, you'll find informed and generally nonpartisan reviews, written by people who have a deep knowledge of the field. From reading these reviews, you'll gain a clearer understanding of what's out there, how the different games within a genre stack up against each other, and what titles to avoid like the plague.

Computer Gaming World and *PC Gamer* are the two magazines that have dominated this field. Both have been around for a long time and both are staffed by experts. You can trust what you read in their pages. (Their addresses and other information can be found in the appendix at the end of this book.) Individual copies of these and other gaming magazines can be bought at software and computer stores as well as at many newsstands.

When looking at these magazines, you'll quickly notice that some are substantially more expensive per issue than others (*PC Gamer* is $4.00 more than *Computer Gaming World*, for example). The discrepancy in price is explained by the fact that *PC Gamer* includes a "free" CD-ROM with each issue, containing at least a dozen demos of current and forthcoming games—a valuable feature that

will pay for itself if it prevents you from wasting money on even or a lame game.

SHAREWARE: THE TEST-DRIVE METHOD

It's not often that you get to try a product at home before you buy it, but that's precisely what shareware is all about. Shareware was one of the earliest methods of distributing PC software and, for games, remains one of the most popular.

The idea behind shareware is simple: you obtain it for free and use it for a while, essentially previewing it at home in much the same way as the vendors' demos described above. However, with shareware, if you choose to continue using the "demo," you must register and pay the shareware vendor. If you don't continue using it, you simply erase it from your disk and that's the end of it.

Shareware relies on the honor system. By contrast, if you buy a commercial game from a retailer and decide you don't like it, you can only hope that the store and software vendor have liberal return policies. Few permit refunds on software for the obvious reason that a workable copy of the program now exists on your hard drive. Shareware vendors trust you to remove their programs from your hard drive if you decide you don't like them enough to pay for them.

Some of the most popular games today are shareware. The original *DOOM*, for example, was shareware. Other popular titles include *Jazz Jackrabbit*, *Heretic* and *Descent*. The shareware system remains a common and popular way for small companies and even individuals to market software, and will probably continue to be so in the foreseeable future.

Where do you get shareware games? Most often, you **download** them from online sources. All of the major online services, like CompuServe, GEnie, Prodigy and America Online, have massive collections of shareware. You can also

download shareware games from many Internet **FTP sites** (see "The 100 Best Internet Sites" elsewhere in this book).

Another great source of shareware games is friends. Unlike commercial games, shareware vendors encourage users to share their games with others. You can also buy low-priced CD-ROM discs of shareware games at virtually any software retailer. Remember, though, that even though you must pay for these discs, you must still pay later for any specific shareware programs you decide to "keep." For more information about shareware and to obtain a disc with hundreds of titles, call the *Association of Shareware Professionals* at (616) 788-5131.

Unlike those large software makers' demos, most shareware games are scaled down until you pay for them, so that what you get free is like the trailer advertising a movie. For example, the shareware version of *Descent* that you can download from online services has seven levels of play, but the upgraded version you get after registering has 30 levels and access to additional weapons.

It's tempting to forget to pay shareware vendors for their games even if you continue to use them. But remember, shareware vendors are professionals who depend on registration fees for their income. If you like their product and would like to see more from them, it's in your best interest (as well as theirs!) to pay the shareware producers for what you use.

Another reason to support shareware is that it is typically less expensive than similar commercial games that must be bought from retailers. Shareware vendors usually spend very little on marketing and pass those savings on to users. That, however, is changing; some larger shareware game vendors now aggressively advertise their wares, which may well drive up prices over time.

A more practical reason for paying is that the license that accompanies shareware games states that you must pay after using the product for a specified time. Failing to do so is rightfully considered software piracy and is against the law.

ARE HINT BOOKS WORTH THE MONEY?

Once you've bought a game and have begun to play, what happens if you get "stuck?" Aside from some hair-pulling, you might want to consider the purchase of a hint book. A **hint book** is a volume of clues and strategy tips that is marketed separately from the game it describes. Until recently, most hint books were published by the game companies themselves—if you wanted one, you had either to order it from the software developer by mail or locate it on the shelves of your local software outlet or bookstore.

In big, elaborate fantasy role-playing games, hint books are primarily of assistance as a source for help in solving puzzles, finding hidden stuff and working through mazes. Beyond the role-playing genre, the books are usually strategy guides, and can be found for everything from flight simulators to arcade-style games.

A typical strategy guide/hint book will set you back anywhere from $10.00 to $20.00 (on top of the $40.00 to $60.00 you paid for the game to begin with), so buying one is no casual investment. Are they worth the price?

Alas, there is no hard and fast answer to that question. It boils down to this: If you're so obsessed with a particular game that you're losing sleep trying to figure out a certain puzzle, then a book might be a reasonable investment for you.

But if a game company has done its job properly, all the information you really need should be in the original documentation. Unfortunately, there have been a few instances where companies have published inadequate, incomplete game documentation followed by a more expensive "complete" manual in book form, complete with separate price. Fortunately, this approach brought thunderous condemnation from the gaming community, and there's little sign of it becoming a standard.

If you're stumped, and you want a hint book, buy one—only you know when you've reached the point where ending your frustration is worth the cost of the book. The most extensive lines of strategy guides are published by Prima Publishing

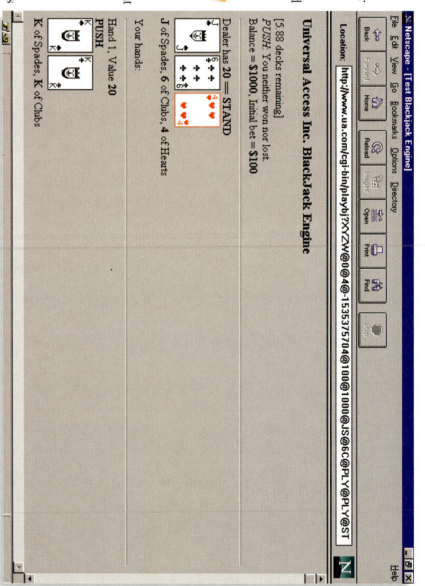

Figure 1: Try to beat the dealer in online blackjack.

Universal Access Inc. BlackJack Engine

[5.88 decks remaining]
PUSH. You neither won nor lost.
Balance = **$1000**, Initial bet = **$100**

Dealer has **20** — STAND

Your hands:

J of Spades, 6 of Clubs, 4 of Hearts

Hand 1, Value 20
PUSH

K of Spades, K of Clubs

and Sybex. Content quality can vary, so look any book over carefully before you buy it.

ONLINE GAMING

The idea is compelling: playing games against live opponents from around the world. With large online services like CompuServe and the **Internet** becoming quite popular, this idea is already a common reality.

However, online gaming is still in its infancy. That's largely because of the limited speed with which most people connect to the online world. Today's fastest modems operate at 28,800 **baud** (or **BPS**), and most people still have modems operating at 14,400 or even lower baud. At these speeds, it takes many seconds (or even minutes at 2,400 baud) to display a single image. As a result, most single-user games, which are often graphics-intensive, would bog down due to slow communications if played with multiple players online.

INTERNET AND ONLINE SERVICES GAMES

Online games don't currently feature fast action or many graphics. There are two broad categories of games you can play online: board and card games and puzzles are in one category, and the other includes adventure games and MUDs and MOOs (we'll explain these a bit later). While not graphically stunning, these games can still be fascinating and even addictive.

If you want fast, exciting games against real online opponents, many popular single-user games let you play either with or against a colleague using a modem. A description of that

process is included later in this chapter. This section, however, describes a representative sample of games you'll find on the Internet and on the leading online services.

BOARD AND CARD GAMES AND PUZZLES

The central question about online board games and puzzles is: Why not just get the old-fashioned board game or puzzle and play it on the dining room table?

This question arises especially when you realize that each time you or any other player makes a selection or move in these online board, card and puzzle games, the host computer must process it, which takes a few seconds. This same delay occurs each time, so playing these games can be somewhat frustrating if you're feeling less than patient.

Among the advantages, though, is that you can test your skills against either a computer or, in some cases, live opponents. And, of course, you always have somebody with whom to play. Let's face it, your family and friends may not share your fanatic addiction to chess or tic-tac-toe.

BATTLESHIPS
http://monoxi.york.ac.uk/cgi-bin/start_bships.sh

In this Internet adaptation of a classic game of strategy, you click on the square on which you want to fire. By firing on enough squares, you eventually figure out the location of your opponent's (in this case, the host computer's) battleships so you can destroy them. To win, you must finish off your opponent's fleet before he sinks all of yours.

http://arachnid.cm.cf.ac.uk/htbin/AndrewW/Puzzle/puzzle4x4image?art+12549637DA0BEFC8+3+

This has a complex Internet address but is a simple puzzle game. It consists of a broken-apart image that you put back together by sliding the squares around. This is the kind of game that you used to play in the car on long trips.

TIC-TAC-TOE

http://www.bu.edu/Games/tictactoe

This is, to understate the case, a classic game that needs no introduction. The online version retains all its fundamental charm. Fortunately, this game server moves things along quite quickly, so you won't have to wait very long for your turn.

YAHTZEE

http://wwwcgi.umr.edu/cgi-bin/cgiwrap?user=mneul&script=webyahtzee.pl

This site appears mostly gray, so it's not too exciting visually. But the game's action is still as addictive as the old board game's.

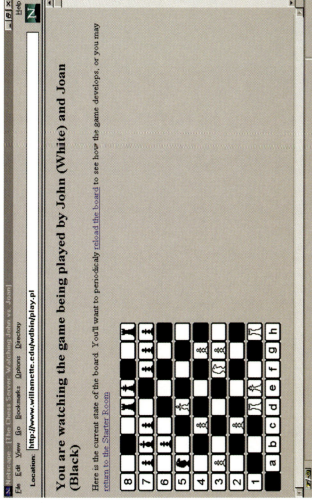

Figure 2: You can get into a chess game with another player or watch others' games in progress on the chess server.

The biggest danger here is that you will run up large online fees and lose your patience—this game is on a host computer in the United Kingdom and access can sometimes be slow.

BLACKJACK

http://www.ua.com/blackjack/bj.html

This is a lively version of the casino classic. Beat the dealer (a.k.a. the host computer) and earn virtual (not real!) money. This site usually offers fast access so you won't wait a long time between plays.

CHESS SERVER

http://www.willamette.edu/~rjones/chessmain.html

This is the place to be if you're a fan of one of the very first adventure games: chess. You can play against live opponents or watch other people's games in progress. It's a great place to test your chess skills.

MANCALA

http://www.astro.wisc.edu/~casey/mancala/mancala.shtml

This is a new online game, but it's based on an old game from Africa. The idea is to move your seeds into your winning pit while preventing your opponent from doing the same. This is another of those games whose simple form disguises its enormous potential for complexity.

THE PEG GAME

http://www.bu.edu/htbin/pegs

This is one of a classic type of game in which you and an opponent remove pegs from a board. You can only remove pegs that are next to or diagonal to the last peg removed. Like all good classic board games, the rules are simple, but the action is difficult to master.

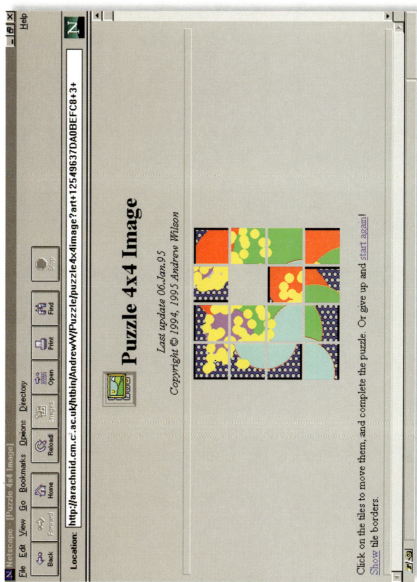

Figure 3: Piece a puzzle back together with this online game.

ADVENTURE GAMES, MUDS AND MOOS

Adventure games, as you learned in "An Introduction to Games and Entertainment," are the oldest computer games. Unfortunately, in the online world, these are still text-based games. You

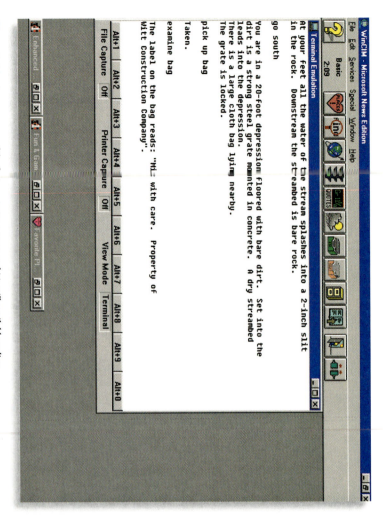

Figure 4: Adventure was one of the first computer games and it's still available online.

```
go south

You are in a 20-foot depression floored with bare dirt.  Set into the
dirt is a strong steel grate mounted in concrete.  A dry streambed
leads into the depression.
There is a large cloth bag lying nearby.
The grate is locked.

pick up bag

Taken.

examine bag

The label on the bag reads: "Wi.. with care.  Property of
Witt Construction Company".
```

THE UNENDING ADVENTURE
http://www.adventure.com/adventure/game2/

This game lives up to its title: It is an adventure game that you play online and then add material to yourself. As an adventure game, this one isn't bad. It's a throwback to the original adventure games since it's entirely text, but adds a welcome element of creativity. (Note to parents: We found no inappropriate material in this game, but that doesn't mean that other players won't add such material.)

WHIMSY
http://monet.uwaterloo.ca/john/whimsy/start.htm

This is an amiable MUD, suitable for older kids. It is built and maintained by the University of Waterloo. Like most MUDs, you create a name and identity for yourself. You then travel to different rooms and meet the other inhabitants of this world. You can also build your own rooms. Eventually, you'll get to know the inhabitants of this site and will feel right at home. But give it some time; navigating this online world takes some practice.

AMERICA ONLINE, COMPUSERVE AND PRODIGY

The commercial online services are rich veins of information and support for PC games.

---

read descriptions of your situation and then are presented with a series of choices. You type a response which determines the game's next step.

MUDs (Multi-User Dungeons) and **MOOs**?

This sounds like a dairy farm after a heavy rainstorm, but these are actually online worlds in which you interact with other real (like you) people. But it's a bit more complex than that.

You also create a new persona for yourself within the game. These worlds are typically full of magic and whimsy, humor and, when many people log on, interesting and sometimes intense "real time" interaction. (Note to parents: Some sites also have adult behavior.)

You still get at most MUDs and MOOs using a form of Internet communications called **Telnet**. But Telnet is a complex way to communicate and takes a long time to learn. Happily, MUDs and MOOs are starting to show up on the **World Wide Web**, which is much simpler to learn and navigate.

online game—it's been online for many years. In this game, you enter a deep and forbidding cave. You must solve puzzles and slay demons to get out. There's lots of good adventure game action in this classic and, best of all, it is a multi-player game—other sojourners join you in the Wumpus' caves.

HUNT THE WUMPUS
http://www.bu.edu/htbin/wd

This is both a classic adventure game and a classic

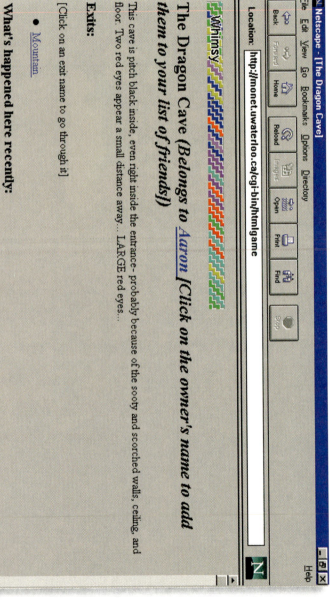

Figure 5: This is an example of a MUD, or online world in which you interact with other players.

Location: http://monet.uwaterloo.ca/cgi-bin/htmlgame

The Dragon Cave (*Belongs to* Aaron *[Click on the owner's name to add them to your list of friends]*)

This cave is pitch black inside, even right inside the entrance– probably because of the sooty and scorched walls, ceiling, and floor. Two red eyes appear a small distance away... LARGE red eyes...

Exits:

[Click on an exit name to go through it]

• Mountain

What's happened here recently:

• On Fri Jul 14 12:35:30 1995, *Flyheaver* arrived.
• On Fri Jul 14 12:36:03 1995, *Flyheaver* said: "Hello, all"

Say: | "Hello?!!" | or | Greetings, Flyheaver | Say it .

Services like America Online, CompuServe and Prodigy all have extensive sections devoted to specific games. Addresses, phone numbers and rate information for all three services can be found in the appendix at the end of this book.

AMERICA ONLINE (AOL)

No other online service is as user-friendly and easy to use as AOL; the only commonly encountered problem is the sometimes overlong response time due to the huge number of people using the system.

On AOL, the place to be is the *PC Games Forum*. To get there, open the *Go To* menu and search for, logically, *PC Games*. Once there, you'll find message boards for posting messages. These message boards cover pretty much anything related to games: problems, mini-reviews, issues and comments. Another excellent source of general gaming information is the *Games Forum*. At *Go To/Keyword*, simply type *Games* and you'll see a list of topics to browse through. In addition to a fairly large number of simple arcade time-fillers that you can actually download and play, the *Games Forum* also provides reviews, demos and discussions about games by both players and designers. You can pick up some good tips here, as well as obtain advance notice of new games that might be of interest.

For information from specific vendors, go to the *Industry Connection* within the *PC Games Forum*. *Industry Connection* has an extensive list of companies that provide problem-solving hints from commercial game vendors. As with all online services, though, not all game vendors are represented.

For four or five years running, the most popular game on AOL has been the multi-player fantasy role-playing adventure *NeverWinter Nights*. It uses the enormously popular *Advanced Dungeons and Dragons* system to provide all the questing, spell-casting and slay-the-monsters combat you could ask for.

While *NeverWinter Nights* does not offer the fabulous graphics and sound of the newest stand-alone computer RPGs (Role-Playing Games), it does have one overwhelming attraction: you join a party of *real* people and share a communal adventure with them. You'll get to know their role-playing characters and abilities, and you'll learn how to cooperate to achieve your goals.

Communicating with other players is easy: You can post messages to all members of your party, send private messages to any one player or broadcast "telepathic" messages to the entire population of the online game world. Newcomers should have no trouble finding experienced questers to show them the ropes—fans of this game love to bring in converts. Over the years, guilds and societies have been formed, alliances made and broken, and some evil characters have even had bounties placed on their heads. Be warned: this game can suck you right into its world.

AOL also provides more down-to-earth gaming fun at *Rabbit Jack's Casino*, where you can chat with others while you all play a friendly game of bingo, blackjack or five-card stud. Up to four players can participate in a single poker game or more than 20 can sign up for a round of bingo.

In Broderbund's *MasterWord*, between two and eight players take turns trying to guess each others' secret words. It's a fast-paced yet low-key game, just right for a brief spell of online gaming.

Broderbund's *MasterWord*, *NeverWinter Nights* and the casino games do require downloading some simple graphics software, but there's no charge and it's simple to do.

COMPUSERVE

On CompuServe, most of the game-related action is in the *Gamers Forum* or in the forums maintained by specific game vendors. To go to the former, type *Go Games*. Once there, you can download shareware games and hints or post questions and comments about specific games. Two of the better games you can access through CompuServe are *Classic Adventure* and *Enhanced Adventure*. These are similar versions of the original text adventure game. The enhanced version has more puzzles and challenges, so you might want to try *Classic Adventure* first. You know what? *Adventure* is still a good game. It starts with those immortal (to gamers, anyway) words: "You are standing at the end of a road before a small brick building."

Another good one is *British Legends*. This is a classic role-playing game in the spirit of *Adventure*. You wander through the countryside meeting many creatures, good and bad. Some of those creatures are other live players. You collect points and advance through the ranks, becoming ever more powerful as you go. This is a well-written and designed game but beware: It will cost you extra online fees to play it.

If you're looking for help, finding the forum run by the vendor of your specific game is trickier. One good way to find that vendor's forum is to use the *Find* capability in the *Services* menu of CompuServe's *Information Manager*. Type the name of the vendor; if that vendor has a CompuServe forum, this utility will find it. You can also check the game's documentation to see if the vendor has a forum on CompuServe or any other online service.

PRODIGY

If you're one of those people who reach for the channel-zapper when a particularly obnoxious commercial appears on your TV set, Prodigy may drive you crazy with its intrusive on-screen advertising. Still, more than two million Americans subscribe to it, and a lot of parents feel comfortable with it because the service has a strict no-pornography policy.

On Prodigy, all the game support is focused on the *Games* bulletin board. To get there, simply type *Jump Games BB*. You'll find discussions about virtually every popular game and also support provided by game vendors.

Many of the games found on Prodigy are playable only against the computer, but they do include some all-time favorites: *Where in the World is Carmen Sandiego?*, *Fantasy Baseball* and *Sports Illustrated for Kids*. One of the best gaming features on Prodigy is *Game Point*, which provides the software necessary to connect with *The Imagination Network*, where gamers can find a host of excellent games, including a multi-player version of *Red Baron* and a jolly kids-oriented puzzle game called *Boogers*.

PLAYING WITH OTHERS VIA MODEM

If you crave faster, more graphical action than the online games, but still want to play with other people, play a modem game. As the name implies, these games enable you to play either alone or with another person via modem.

The number of games you can play with modems is growing. Among these games are *DOOM*, *Descent* and a wide variety of flight simulations. This is different from online gaming since it's just you and one other player (at a time). Since both players load the same game, there's much less busy-ness going through the modems and phone lines, which enables both faster play and the playing of more graphical games.

Most modem-ready games assume that you aren't a communications expert, so they're simple to set up. Typically, you set up the game for modem play in the same way you set the other game play options (such as selecting the correct sound board). For many games, you access these options from within the game itself. Other games have a separate program for setting options, including modem options. Read the program's documentation to learn whether it is modem-ready and, if so, how to set it up for communications.

The setup program usually requires that you know only a few things. Typically, you will need to tell it:

- The brand and model of modem you're using.
- The communications port to which your modem is attached.
- Whether you will initiate the modem connection by calling your friend or whether you will receive the call.
- If you are initiating the connection, you'll need to provide your colleague's phone number.
- Depending on the game, you may need to type a modem command before the phone number. For tone phones, that command is usually *ATDT*. For pulse phones, the command is *ATDP*.
- Some games require you to decide whether you are playing cooperatively (with) or competitively (against) the person at the other end of the modem line.

If you have trouble connecting, it's a good bet that one of these settings is incorrect. One final caution: If you have call waiting, disable it before you start playing. There's nothing worse than being in a really tight spot in a big battle, only to have call waiting ring and end your modem connection.

Here is a list of things game players can do online to improve their gaming life:

- Download shareware games. There are thousands of shareware games that you can try before you buy.
- Download demos of commercial titles. Have you heard about the latest hot game? Chances are good that the vendor has a demo you can play.
- Communicate with other people who play the same games you are interested in. This enables you to share tips and get help when you become stuck.
- Download files containing hints and walkthroughs for when you can't figure out your game yourself. Walk-throughs walk you through a game and should be considered a last resort when you get stuck.
- Get computerized images of games you like to play.

In the next few sections, you'll learn about the places you can go for these items.

GETTING SUPPORT ONLINE

If you have questions about your games or want to try new ones, you're never alone. If you have a modem and access to the Internet or online services, the amount of game-related information you can get online is truly mind boggling.

GAME VENDOR BULLETIN BOARDS

Many game companies maintain their own bulletin board services (BBSs). Similar to the vendor forums on the online services described above, these are good places for getting tips and hints when you get stuck and can't progress in a game. These BBSs can also provide technical support when you can't get through on the company's (voice) phone lines. And, if a game doesn't work because of a bug, you can download patches to fix the problem.

Unlike joining a service like CompuServe, you don't have to pay online fees to the game vendor to use a vendor's own BBS, but you will have to pay toll charges to the telephone company. One thing to remember, though, is that hints and tips on these BBSs are usually provided by the company. That's good, but ironically enough, this "official" collection of information isn't usually as complete as you can get from users on the Internet and online services. Other game-players can be your best resources, whether you find them in newsgroups, the games forums of online services or in your neighborhood.

To find out whether a vendor has its own BBS, read the documentation that came with your game. If the vendor does have a BBS, the documentation should tell you what number to call and how to log on.

GAME SUPPORT ON THE NET

The richest source of information about games is the Internet. However, like so much on the Internet, this information is scattered in thousands of places, so you must know where to look. There are several specific types of game-related information you can easily obtain; the next few sections describe them.

GAME INFORMATION ON THE WORLD WIDE WEB

No matter what type of support or information you need, the best place to find it is the World Wide Web (WWW). WWW sites come in several categories:

- General game sites. These sites are developed by gaming fans and have links to many other game-related sites.
- Sites related to a single game. These sites are usually created by fans (or fanatics) of a specific game. These are good places to get hints, walk-throughs and links to the site maintained by the game's vendor.
- Vendor sites. These are home pages developed by specific game vendors.

You might expect that locating these sites would be difficult. Fortunately, however, there are a handful of mega-sites that provide links to all these different types of resources. Perhaps the best place to start is Happy Puppy Games Onramp (*http://www.misha.net:80/games/link/index.html*).

This WWW site has a mind-boggling array of games-related information and the most comprehensive set of links to other game-related Internet resources. You can download shareware and game demos, link to many other Web pages and find out what are the most popular games. It also has reviews of games.

Another good site for starting your search for information is The Yahoo Entertainment Games Page (*http://www.yahoo.com/Entertainment/*

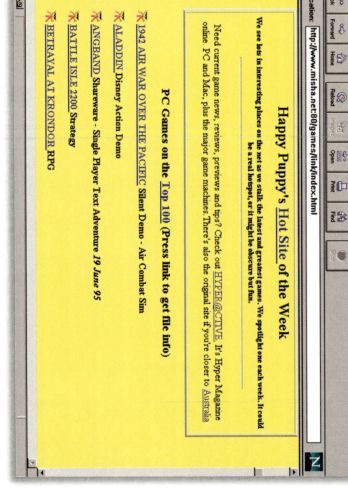

Netscape - [Happy Puppy Software Games: Onramp Home Page]

File Edit View Go Bookmarks Options Directory

Back Forward Home Reload Images Open Print Find Stop

Location: http://www.misha.net:80/games/link/index.html

Need current game news, reviews, previews and tips? Check out HYPER@CTIVE. It's Hyper Magazine online. PC and Mac, plus the major game machines. There's also the original site if you're closer to Australia

PC Games on the Top 100 (Press link to get file info)

Happy Puppy's Hot Site of the Week
We see lots in interesting places on the net as we stalk the latest and greatest games. We spotlight one each week. It could be a real hotspot, or it might be obscure but fun.

1942 AIR WAR OVER THE PACIFIC Silent Demo - Air Combat Sim
ALADDIN Disney Action Demo
ANGBAND Shareware - Single Player Text Adventure 19 June 95
BATTLE ISLE 2200 Strategy
BETRAYAL AT KRONDOR RPG

Figure 6: The Happy Puppy Games Onramp is the most extensive listing of game-related resources on the Internet that we've seen.

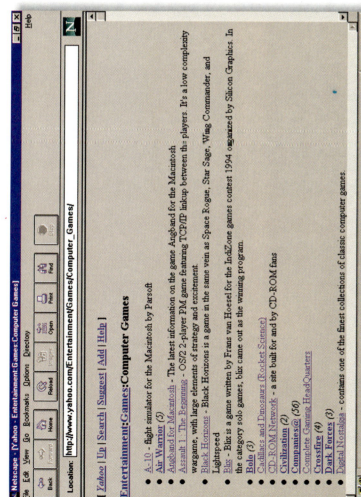

Figure 7: *The Yahoo Entertainment: Games Page is another excellent place to begin your online search for information about your games.*

Games/Computer_Games/). Yahoo is a huge collection of links to Internet resources and this is just one of Yahoo's many pages. But it still provides an extensive collection of links to all manner of game-related sites.

Game Support USENET Newsgroups

Finding people to talk to about the things that interest you is always great, and on the Internet it's even easy: Just log onto the USENET newsgroup of your choice. Newsgroups are ongoing conversations about very specific subjects. Somebody posts a message and anyone who checks into the newsgroups can read that message and respond, either to the group as a whole or to the individual alone.

Even if you only read newsgroup messages, you'll learn a lot. But if you ever have any questions, newsgroups provide hundreds and often thousands of people with similar gaming interests who can provide answers.

Many popular games have newsgroups dedicated to them. But if you can't find the newsgroup dedicated to your game, use *rec.games.misc*. This newsgroup is open to discussion about virtually any game, and can lead you to a more specific newsgroup if one exists.

FTP Sites

FTP sites enable you to download shareware games, hints, patches and add-ons. For example, one reason for *DOOM*'s enduring popularity is that, with just a little programming skill, fans can create their own episodes. That means that after you finish the regular *DOOM* episodes, you can keep playing new user-created ones. There are several FTP sites that are popular largely because they contain thousands of these "amateur" episodes.

Similarly, other FTP sites provide a potpourri of games you can download, while others are maintained by specific game vendors and they only have download-able files related to that vendor's games. Again, a great place to start your quest for FTP sites is the large, generalized WWW sites such as Happy Puppy or Yahoo.

David Haskin *is a writer specializing in computer-related topics. Formerly a newspaper journalist and software executive, David is a regular contributor to* PC Magazine, Computer Life *and* Computer Shopper. *He is the author of six books about computers including* The Complete Idiot's Guide to Multimedia, The Complete Idiot's Guide to PC Games *and* Using PC Tools for Windows.

William R. Trotter *has been Senior Writer and reviewer for* PC Gamer *magazine since 1987. He has published hundreds of articles and reviews on personal computer gaming, and has written the monthly* PC Gamer *column, "The Desktop General," since 1989. He is the author of eight published books.*

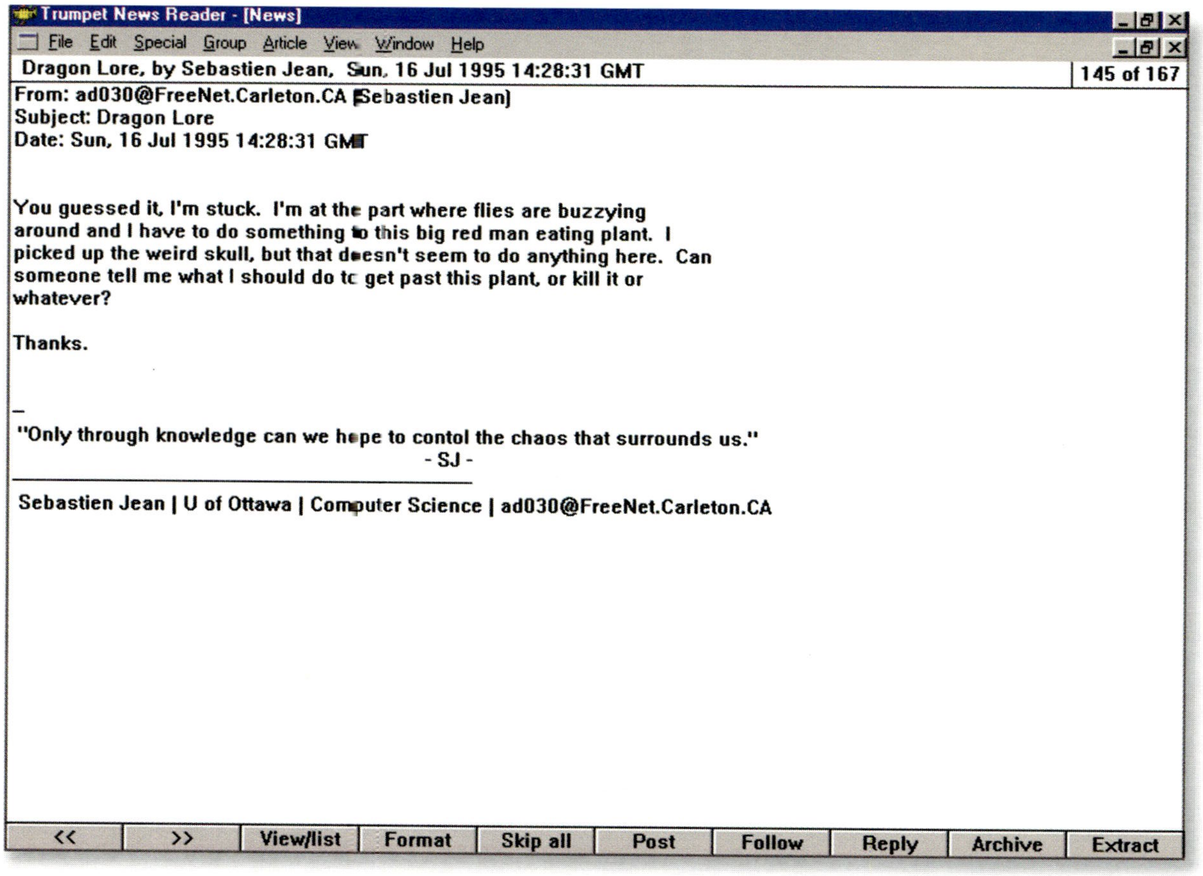

Figure 8: *USENET newsgroups are a great source of help.*

THE WHOLE PC GAMERS HALL OF FAME

By William Trotter and David Haskin

While PC games are rarely considered works of art, creating a great game requires mastery and integration of animated action, plot, music and sound. That explains why great games are in short supply and why, like movies, most are quickly forgotten soon after their release. Like the movies Casablanca and Star Wars, however, some terrific games endure. Here's our short list of the best computer games ever:

The games on our list cover every genre and are often radically different from one another, yet they do have some things in common: each is a title that set a new standard for "state-of-the-art" when it first appeared; each established a new hurdle for the industry as a whole; and each is addictively playable and re-playable. While some of these games pushed the limits of technology; others stood out for their superior design, intelligence and wit. We have chosen games on the basis of their merit, not their age: A game that was great fun to play in 1987 must still be great fun to play in 1995 to make its way onto our list of classics.

There's one other thing all really great PC games have in common: they induce a state called "game-lock," in which the player seems to become wired to the monitor screen, oblivious of time, phone calls, spousal imprecations and all other distractions; a hypnotic state that can be recognized when you see someone glued, glassy-eyed, to the keyboard, muttering at one o'clock in the morning, "Just one more turn... just one more turn..." The games we've listed for you have given us hours of escapist entertainment, and we hope you enjoy flying fighter jets, conquering planets and saving damsels-in-distress in these games as much as we have.

CIVILIZATION (MICROPROSE)

As is true with authors and directors, certain creative individuals consistently produce excellence in PC gaming. Designer Sid Meir has one of the best track records in the business, regularly turning out games that are both challengingly complex and addictively playable. In

economic decisions: what inventions does your fledgling society really need, what social institutions will serve your goals best? Do you feel comfortable with a constitutional monarchy, or do you secretly long to be a ruthless tyrant? Play it one way, play it another—no two games are ever alike. You'll be competing with Napoleon, Attila the

Hun and various other famous conquerors, and every choice you make in the game has subtle ramifications. The competing needs of your society create a game experience that is exquisitely balanced, and there is a sense of vast pageantry in the onward march of civilizations, from the age of the stone ax to the age of space travel.

When *Computer Gaming World Magazine* inducted *Civilization* into its Hall of Fame, the

Civilization, first published in 1991 and still going strong, Meir out-did himself.

In this *magnum opus* of "world conquest" games, the player gets to romp across whole centuries and continents, starting out with a simple tribe of barbarians yet aspiring to the conquest of space. Exploration, diplomacy and military strategy play a big part, but the really crucial decisions involve technological and

Figure 1: Another one bites the dust in Descent. However, instead of blood and gore, in this fast-paced action game you kill only robots.

editors stated that, "Though we have only anecdotal evidence to support us, we would guess that more hours have been invested in conquering the world of *Civilization* than in any other computer game in the hobby's history." That sums it up nicely.

DESCENT

Descent is arguably the best example of a relatively new subspecies of game—three-dimensional, first-person action games. This type of game was first popularized by *DOOM*, but *Descent* is faster, more riveting and less violent.

Like *DOOM*, *Descent* takes place off-planet. In this case, you are hired to rid mining stations of, not surprisingly, an evil enemy. However, there's no gore in *Descent* because instead of killing living creatures, you fly through the mine shafts destroying robots left behind by your enemy. As you get further into the game, the robots become both more difficult to "kill" and more focused on killing you. Fortunately, you'll find ever-more-powerful weapons and power-ups along the way.

While all this may sound like *DOOM*, the resemblance is only superficial. The first thing you'll notice about *Descent* is the speed at which the action occurs—you can really zip through those mine shafts. But the most important difference is that this is truly a three-dimensional game.

Descent achieves this startling effect by taking an entirely different approach to spatial basics like up and down. In games like *DOOM*, you usually move forward and backward and from side to side. In *Descent*, you fly your vehicle down mine shafts that take off at dizzying angles. The shafts themselves twist and turn like a roller coaster ride gone berserk. Initially, you'll be disoriented; eventually, you literally won't know which way is up—and it won't matter.

You'll also like *Descent*'s outstanding soundtrack and its graphics. "Best" is always an arguable assertion, but many folks think that *Descent* is the best of the three-dimensional, first-person action games.

EMPIRE (INTERSTEL; NOW PUBLISHED BY NEW WORLD COMPUTING)

Originally designed for break-time amusement on big mainframe computers in the early 1980s, this conquer-the-world strategy game made the transition to home PCs in 1987. Year after year, it continues to make every critic's best-of-all-time list.

Empire is a game of planetary exploration, expansion and all-out war. You start with a single city on a blacked-out map, explore to discover and capture other cities, and then set up production schedules for various types of weapons. You'll need these weapons to triumph over the human or computerized opponents who are vying with you for control of the planet. Cannon-fodder units such as infantry can be cranked out quickly; battleships and carriers take much, much longer.

Empire has the internal harmony and precision of a Swiss watch, arresting game-play and seemingly inexhaustible user permutations. The game is equally capable of generating short, bloody conflicts that play out with all the frenzy of a closet full of starving Rottweilers, as it is of producing truly Homeric epics than can last for days and days and days...

By the time this sees print, the long-heralded *Empire II* will be on the market, and it promises to incorporate not only state-of-the-art graphics, but years' worth of suggestions and input from *Empire* addicts.

FALCON 3.0 (SPECTRUM HOLOBYTE) AND CHUCK YEAGER'S AIR COMBAT (ELECTRONIC ARTS)

The very term computer simulation (or sim) signifies a realistic re-creation of an experience too dangerous, or too expensive, for most ordinary folks to know firsthand. These two exceptional flight sims are beyond compare even within this highly popular genre—not many of us will ever get to fly a combat mission, or for that matter would really want to, but these programs give you a taste of the danger, the white-knuckled excitement, the adrenaline rush, of the real thing.

In *Falcon 3.0*, the emphasis is on technological and tactical accuracy — "military correctness," so to speak. You can jump right into a dogfight using the Instant Action option, but the game is really designed to give you the whole experience of mastering the F-16 Falcon, from basic training to long, grueling campaigns in which the outcome of one battle affects the ongoing situation on the ground.

You'll undergo training at Nellis Air Force Base, get a squadron assignment, drill exhaustively in BFM (Basic Fighter Maneuvers), learn teamwork and even learn how to follow orders.

This program is, after all, a civilian version of a program Spectrum Holobyte actually designed for the military—if *Falcon 3.0* were any more realistic, it would be stamped "Classified."

The price you must pay for this level of authenticity is the hard work ahead of you before you really learn to fly. Fortunately, the documentation is excellent, and once you've mastered it, *Falcon 3.0* yields hundreds of hours of intense aerial adventure.

Chuck Yeager's Air Combat, on the other hand, is easy to get into, and allows you to fly a host of great airplanes, from the mighty P-51 Mustang to the Focke-Wulfe-190 to the MIG-21. Fantasy scenarios abound, if you want them, so that you can fly a Sabre Jet against ten B-52s... just to see what might happen.

While the graphics are admittedly dated, they more than adequately convey the swooping,

Figure 2: *Empire is the classic abstract war game, every bit as addictive and playable today as it was when it first debuted on the PC in 1987. The sequel, Empire II, features new state-of-the-art graphics. This game's system is easy-to learn, difficult to master and fiendishly addictive.*

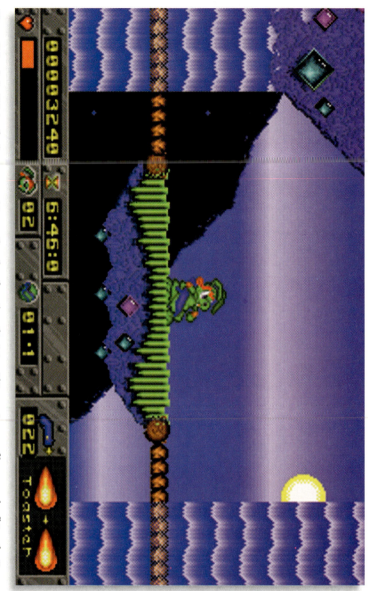

Figure 3: *Jazz Jackrabbit is a fearless bunny out to save the galaxy from the evil tortoises. This game's sense of humor and well-paced action makes it one of the best arcade games ever released.*

holler-happy excitement of the game, and there simply is no cozier, more user-friendly flight sim to be had.

JAZZ JACKRABBIT (EPIC MEGAGAMES)

You don't play arcade games to think deep thoughts. These games are pure escape—they draw you in with their fast action and keep you in by becoming increasingly challenging the further into the game you go.

Jazz Jackrabbit from Epic MegaGames isn't exactly an arcade game for intellectuals, but it is particularly noteworthy for its wit. The premise of the game is that the ages-old battle between hares and tortoises has spread across the universe. Evil turtle terrorists led by Devon Shell have kidnapped the beloved rabbit princess, Eva Earlong, and placed thugs on every planet, asteroid and moon. You are Jazz Jackrabbit, hare hero, and your job is to rid the universe of this evil menace and, of course, save the princess.

You're likely to appreciate the wit in this game, which extends well beyond its animal premise. As you move through menacing and alien worlds, you are taunted at every turn by tortoise impertinence such as billboards that announce "Rabbits Stink."

Parents will particularly like how the game doesn't take itself too seriously. While the violence and fast pace of many arcade games can be upsetting to younger kids, *Jazz Jackrabbit* is much more amiable. Combined with its humor, the clear message is that you can battle for Truth and Justice and still have good, clean fun.

KING'S QUEST (SIERRA ONLINE)

The original *King's Quest*, released in 1984, was one of the first adventure games for PCs as well as the first graphical adventure game—its predecessors were all text-based. This in itself made it unique, but *King's Quest* and its sequels (*King's Quest 7: The Princess Bride* is the latest) remain popular classics because of the superior quality of their lyrical, graphically-innovative storytelling and engaging characters.

Much of the credit for the quality of this series belongs to Roberta Williams, who, along with her husband Ken, founded Sierra Online. Roberta created the first *King's Quest* and has been in charge of the series ever since, earning that company a well-deserved reputation for producing intelligent, whimsical and highly entertaining games with memorable characters.

The initial *King's Quest* introduced the Kingdom of Daventry and the early star of this series, Sir Graham. Sir Graham was off on an adventure with kingship as his (and your!) reward for success. With the release of the six subsequent *King's Quest* titles, other characters have come to the fore, creating a richly complex dramatic tapestry.

The initial releases seem quite crude by today's standards, with hunky-chunky movement by the characters and no music. Each new title offered increasingly sophisticated storylines, graphics and sound. The most recent version features absolutely stunning **cel graphics**, animation and a full orchestral score.

There are many graphical adventure games available, but none has captured the imagination of as many people for as long as has the *King's*

Figure 4: *The King's Quest series features beautiful graphics, lovely storylines and compelling characters. This scene is from King's Quest VI.*

Figure 5: *Here's the first hole at the Banff Springs Resort Club, in Access Software's* Links 386 Pro—*you can almost smell that fresh mountain air!*

Quest series. These games are loved by family members of all ages.

LINKS 386 PRO (ACCESS SOFTWARE)

Since its release in 1992, *Links 386 Pro* has acquired a fanatical following among desktop duffers. Using breathtakingly beautiful, photo-realistic Super VGA graphics, atmospheric sound effects and an interface that allows full control over stance, club-facing and swing-plane, it recreates, as no other golf sim does, the experience of actually setting out to play a round on a championship course. It also contains a useful save-shot replay feature, so you can finally prove to your friends that you really did make that hole-in-one at Pinehurst.

The game has become so popular that it can be found in pro shops and sporting goods stores as well as in PC game outlets. Pro golfers play it and exchange notes about it via email; thousands of weekend golfers keep the game on their hard drives at work for lunchtime practice; and every year, Access faithfully releases a couple of new championship courses that dovetail into the basic program.

That, in fact, is one of the chief delights of the game. How many golfers will actually get to stroll the greens at Harbor Town (Hilton Head), Barton Creek, Pebble Beach, Big Horn, Castle Pines and

the Firestone Country Club—all in one lifetime? With this game, you get a vicarious experience that is very close to the real thing: before issuing any add-on program, Access takes fanatical pains to reproduce the look and feel of every hole on these courses, even down to the placement of individual trees and the mountains in the background. What you see on your screen is exactly what you would see from that spot on the real course.

You can savor the sunlight and the breeze, hear the birds chirping near the fairways, feel the solid contact of a perfect drive, or the sweet tap of a just-right putt... all without leaving the comfort of your study and without paying any fees beyond the basic, and very reasonable, price of the game.

Links 368 Pro has become a phenomenon; it is probably the most successful sports simulation ever developed. No PC owner who loves a good game of golf should miss it.

FLIGHT SIMULATOR (MICROSOFT CORPORATION)

After its introduction in the early 1980s, Microsoft's *Flight Simulator* quickly became the first popular flight sim game. And although there now are many other flight simulation games—most of which are more combat-oriented, like the two we mentioned earlier—*Flight Simulator* remains extremely popular.

As with any good simulator, *Flight Simulator's* focus is on reality: You learn how to take off, navigate while you are in the air and then land, hopefully without incident. You must fully understand the fundamentals of flight or face a dire consequence—the crash of your plane. For example, if you climb at too steep a rate without enough power, your plane will stall.

Through the years, *Flight Simulator* has endured and grown in popularity for two reasons. One reason is its leisurely pace. Yes, the consequences of mistakes are severe, but there is nobody trying to shoot you out of the air. Nor are you trying to gun down an airborne enemy. *Flight Simulator* often appeals most to people whose interest in flight is for relaxation and exploration rather than the thrills-and-chills of the other flight simulators in our Gamers Hall of Fame.

Second, this game has kept pace with new audio and video technology. The result is that it looks and sounds very realistic. If you hook up a joystick and turn down the lights, you can leave the world behind and become fully immersed in the world of flight. *Flight Simulator* is so realistic that reports of air sickness are common. Also, over the years many people have taken their first steps toward becoming real pilots by playing this game. No, you must still learn how to fly the regular way, with book learning and time in a real cockpit—but, Microsoft's *Flight Simulator* is a great place to start.

MYST (BRODERBUND SOFTWARE)

Myst is to adventure games what the *New York Times* is to newspapers—the brainiest and most sophisticated around. Like many others in our list, *Myst*, a relatively recent introduction, set a new standard for the industry. Even a year after its launch, *Myst* was selling over 100,000 copies a month at retail outlets—a pretty impressive record for this industry.

You begin on a deserted Island. No-one is to be found and you quickly discover that something on the island is terribly wrong. As you wander around, you discover clues about the island's former inhabitants and what became of them. To correctly piece your clues together, you must carefully read every bit of information you can find. The conclusions you draw from these clues help you decide what to do next.

Myst's graphics are gorgeous—this is one of the most visually stunning games ever developed. But besides being brainy and beautiful, *Myst* is noteworthy for several other reasons. First, nobody gets killed, a rarity in adventure games these days. There aren't even weapons and nobody ever sneaks up behind you. Second, the pace is much slower, reflective and thoughtful, than in most games. While fans of seek-and-destroy arcade games may miss shooting the bad guys, *Myst*'s appeal to many is its emphasis on intellectual challenge.

Myst is a game in which you luxuriate, appreciating the fact that its developers give you credit for intelligence. However, *Myst* enthusiasts find themselves just as addicted to it as arcade fans become to their faster-paced favorites. The good news is that *Myst II* is on its way.

Figure 6: Myst is a brooding, thoughtful game in which you must examine all clues carefully. It also has beautiful graphics.

SIM CITY (MAXIS)

Fed up with traffic congestion, urban blight, pollution, high taxes and crime? Had it up to here with those clowns in City Hall? Ready to bulldoze a few hundred square blocks, put in a mass transit system that really works and beautify your city with some new parks? *Sim City* gives you a chance to do all that and more.

You begin with about 100 square miles of virgin land and water. You control zoning and development, striving to balance commercial and residential needs. Lay out the road network, position the police and fire stations, and find that just-right spot for a new airport or sports stadium. Don't neglect the ever increasing need for power, either. While you're designing your urban utopia, the Sims (your citizens) are busily erecting houses and factories, clogging the roads with traffic, and constantly griping about what they want the mayor—you—to do next.

In a century or two of Sim-time, you can build a thriving metropolis, rendered in beautiful detail: tiny cars move on the freeways, microscopic football teams scrimmage inside the stadium, little planes take off and land, and houses sprout in newly developed suburbs. Of course, there can be disasters: air crashes, nuclear plant melt-downs, and, if you're playing the Tokyo scenario, a literal walk-on by Godzilla, who flattens a block or two with each step he takes and starts raging fires with his dragon breath. The game even lets you test your crisis management skills by tackling real-life disasters such as San Francisco's Earthquake of 1906.

Sim City depicts the dynamics of urban planning so successfully that the program is used as a teaching aid in many universities. It is quite simply one of the cleverest and most addictive "computer toys" ever designed—more fun than the best model train layout you ever dreamed of owning!

The original game has spawned a host of fascinating sequels, including the futuristic *Sim City 2000*, *Sim Farm*, *Sim Earth*, *Sim Tower* (design and manage your own high-rise monument) and the whimsical *Sim Ant*. *Sim City* is a landmark game in every respect, and fun for the whole family.

TETRIS (SEVERAL VERSIONS BY DIFFERENT PUBLISHERS)

Sometimes simple games can be the most fascinating—and the most addictive. That is certainly true of *Tetris*, a seemingly straightforward yet endlessly fascinating game.

Tetris, an import from Russia, is, quite simply, a game about falling blocks. There are several different shapes of blocks and the goal is to arrange them so that they create solid horizontal lines with no gaps. Once you accomplish this, the filled-in line disappears.

Sound simple? Well, it isn't. While you can rotate and move the blocks as they fall to create a solid row, the varying shapes offer almost infinite possibilities. Turning a shape one way might enable you to create a near-solid line in one row but it could also make filling in an underlying row more difficult or altogether impossible. That means that you must think—and act—quickly; yet be planning ahead for future rows. Once a shape hits a row of blocks, it can no longer be maneuvered.

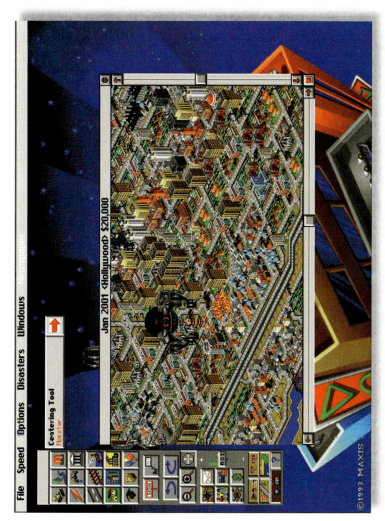

Figure 7: In this SimCity scenario, Hollywood is ravaged by one of its own back-lot monsters. As mayor, your job is to return Tinseltown to all its former glory.

The game becomes more difficult with each success, and you'll find it speeds up considerably. The result is a game that starts off with a pace that's deceptively reasonable, but eventually becomes frantic. This game was so successful that it is one of the rare programs to migrate across many **platforms**. You'll find it in arcades, on PCs and on **dedicated game machines**.

UNDER A KILLING MOON (ACCESS SOFTWARE)

At a time of great debate within the PC industry over just what an **interactive movie** really was or could be, Access introduced a breakthrough product that defined the genre and re-defined the limits of what was technologically possible in PC games. The result was *Under a Killing Moon* (*UKM*), a whimsical take-off on hard-boiled detective movie classics. This time, the crime takes place in Twenty-first Century San Francisco and our hero is a bumbling private eye named Tex Murphy.

This was the first interactive movie to make use of actual movie actors (Margot Kidder, Russell Means and Brian Keith) rather than amateurs. The actors were filmed against a neutral background, then placed inside computer-generated "sets" of astonishing realism. The game's designers set out to create what they described as "a world so realistic, players would feel that if they could only remove that thin glass monitor screen, they could actually step inside this world, travel around in it, and converse with its inhabitants."

To a remarkable extent, that goal was achieved. With your mouse, you can walk the streets, explore rooms, unearth clues and solve the puzzles found in Tex Murphy's zany world. As

you move through the computer-generated environment, lights and shadows change just as they would in reality. Numerous dialogue choices and branching plot-lines keep the game fresh through multiple replays.

UKM is a very big game—it comes on *four* CDs—and it can use all the RAM and processing power you've got under the hood. But it packs more than 70 hours' worth of game-play (on average), challenging but not impossible puzzles, very sharp dialogue, hilarious gags and considerable action.

Some mild violence and a few naughty dialogue bits would earn it a PG-13 if it were a movie, but a lot of PC owners have enlisted their kids as assistant clue-finders, and the kids seem to love the game as much as do the adults.

WING COMMANDER (ORIGIN SYSTEMS)

When Origin Systems first showed *Wing Commander* at the 1990 Summer Consumer Electronics Show in Chicago, the industry was knocked off its collective feet: it was PC magic, a defining moment when the programmers' ability to suspend our disbelief and kindle our sense of wonder approached the level of Art.

Conceived by designer Chris Roberts (who has never made any secret of his desire to become the Cecil B. DeMille of computer games), *Wing Commander* was basically the hottest outer space dogfight simulator ever developed, with eye-popping graphics, sizzling velocity and the most sophisticated use of sound of any PC game to that point. The game was given added depth by movie-like cut-away scenes that established vivid characters and carried forward a larger story which formed the context of the intense battle scenes.

Devotees of the game became fanatically addicted to it, and it zoomed to the top of the bestseller charts. Origin has not only maintained the original's quality in its sequels, but has made good use of every technical advance to improve on the quality of the original game. *Wing Commander III*, for instance, features intense performances by veteran actors Malcolm McDowell, John Rhys-Davies and Mark Hamill,

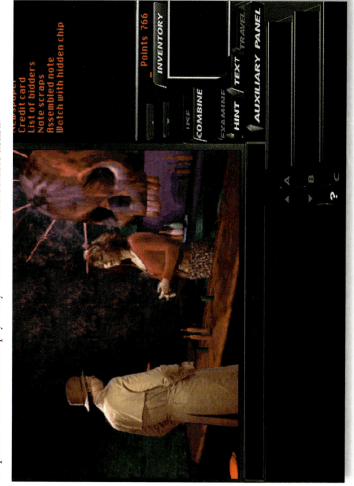

Figure 8: In this scene from Under a Killing Moon, that's Margot Kidder behind the bar, talking to down-on-his-luck private eye Tex Murphy. If you're interested in the "interactive movie" phenomena, this game is the perfect place to start.

221

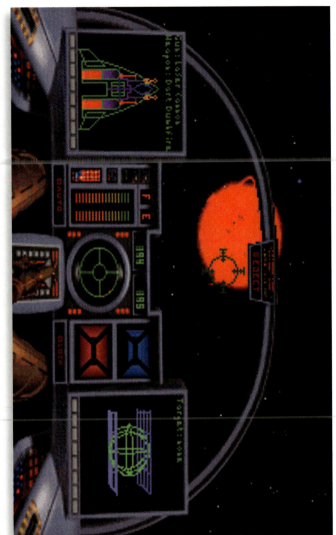

Figure 9: An in-your-face experience of in-the-cockpit action is what the Wing Commander series delivers. These remarkable games also pioneered the use of movie-like plots to further the action.

and movie-quality graphics that make the battle scenes almost unbearably intense.

The original game, however, still delivers plenty of excitement, and can be had for a bargain price. The *Wing Commander* series has been described as "the ultimate in action games," a hard-won title indeed considering the quality of the competition, but one that is certainly deserved.

ZORK AND RETURN TO ZORK (ACTIVISION/INFOCOM)

Zork was a groundbreaking game. Besides being one of the first widely-selling PC games, it was also unusual due to its off-kilter wit. The developer, a small company named Infocom, designed this game for thinkers with a sense of humor.

This is a text-based game in which you type instructions and receive answers displayed on-screen. At the start, you find yourself deposited in the Great Underground Empire of Zork. Infocom spent considerable time creating the details of this empire, including its economic, social and political history, and a monetary system. The world of *Zork* is amusing because its creators include subtle satire of our own world, often found in responses to questions you ask of Zork's inhabitants.

Zork's richness of detail, as much as its puzzles and humor, make it addictive. The original

game was something like listening to a radio drama in that you had to create pictures in your mind as you proceeded. It also required that you do your homework: The best way to find your way through the underground empire was to make a map with tried-and-true pencil and paper.

Zork was so successful that it spawned five sequels from Infocom as well as copycat adventure games from other vendors. But as the computing world became more graphics-oriented, Infocom faded away until it was

purchased by Activision, a larger games company. Activision recently released *Return to Zork*, a graphical adaptation of the original and a worthy successor to it—it is as funny and as well-paced as the original, and its puzzles are every bit as good, too.

William R. Trotter *has been a senior writer and reviewer for PC Gamer magazine since 1987. He has published hundreds of articles and reviews on personal computer gaming, and has written the monthly PC Gamer column, "The Desktop General," since 1989. He is the author of eight published books.*

David Haskin *is a writer specializing in computer-related topics. Formerly a newspaper journalist and software executive, David is a regular contributor to PC Magazine, Computer Life and Computer Shopper. He is the author of six books about computers including The Complete Idiot's Guide to Multimedia, The Complete Idiot's Guide to PC Games and Using PC Tools for Windows.*

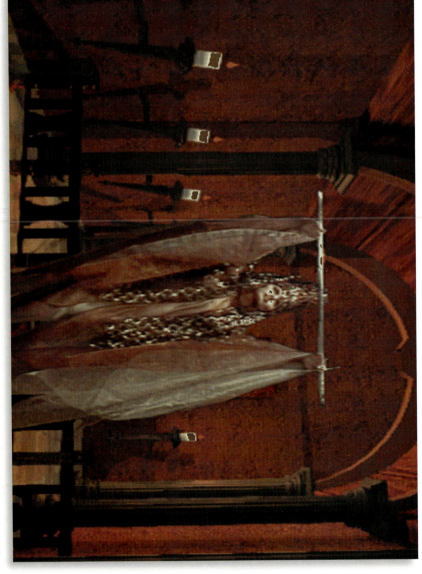

Figure 10: The Great Underground Empire is just as complex and funny in Return to Zork as it was in the original text adventure—but it also has beautiful graphics, sound effects and music.

THE PERSONAL COMPUTER
vs THE DEDICATED GAME MACHINE

By Vince Matthews

Are dedicated gaming machines the ultimate answer? Will your PC outstrip the tabletop gaming box? Are the two platforms becoming one—or going in different directions? Should you have one or more of each? We'll explore these questions and more in this article.

Personal computers and **dedicated game machines** are quite similar under the hood—though PC users and videogame players may not care to admit it. One of the very first computer games inspired Nolan Bushnell to create the videogame *Pong*, and Trip Hawkins, the founder of the 3DO company and ex-president and chief executive of Electronic Arts, believed so firmly in the PC he dismissed videogame consoles as a passing fad.

So what makes a dedicated game machine so great? With today's PC, users can play games, but also watch movies and television programs, play audio CDs, interact with online services and even connect to worldwide networks. Sure, PCs are still used to process spreadsheets, organize written documents and even design homes, but now the personal computer is also a multimedia superstation offering a world of possibilities.

ROUND ONE: THE DIFFERENCE

While PCs are generally **backward-compatible** (meaning that consecutive generations of new hardware can frequently continue to run earlier software), expandable and offer some great gaming experiences—both **shareware** and commercial software—several major problems plague the PC as a games machine.

- The PC has many, many different standards. When a company such as Nintendo or Sega manufactures a videogame machine, the machine is produced under specific standards. All the units under that brand name are produced using the same quality control and board configurations so, in essence, every user is using the same machine.

  For instance, a Nintendo 8-bit game will work on any Nintendo 8-bit machine—and so will any game produced by a Nintendo licensee. Nintendo has given the licensee the information they need to make sure the

title is compatible with the NES (Nintendo Entertainment System). PC-game developers are generally not the same companies that build PC systems. When PC-game developers are involved in a game project, they have to take into consideration that the machine they are developing for is constantly changing. Since the development of a major game may take over a year, the PC **platform** may change several times during the course of development. Developers must foresee this problem and then take steps to make sure their finished product is both compatible and playable on a variety of PC systems from different manufacturers with different configurations of hardware.

- Frequently, the developers' primary concern is creating a state-of-the-art product, and if that means the product has to play on the most cutting-edge hardware (such as a Pentium-based system right now), so be it. Unfortunately, many consumers are unaware of what kind of hardware they have or what they'll need to make a game run at its full potential. Consider the case of *The Lion King* from Disney. Many consumers who had a multimedia PC thought that was all they needed to run the program. In truth, they also needed a special sound card that may not have been supplied with their machine. As a result, many consumers returned both the game's CD-ROM and the computer to the store, not knowing how to make the product run or what was "wrong" with the machine.

- PC games are limited to the machines they run on and, in my opinion, can never match dedicated videogame machines for bringing the arcade experience into the home. A videogame console can be plugged directly into your home entertain-

ment system or home theater, making the whole experience much more of a family affair than you can create on your PC. Even the presentation is cleaner and more polished—it's as close as any consumer will come to the arcade experience without lugging a thousand-pound coin-operated machine into their living room.

- Major game titles will remain exclusively on console machines. Nintendo and Sega are videogame companies; their systems will always support their major and arcade-related titles. These titles won't always be shared with the PC game developers because the videogame companies recognize the advantage of having exclusive rights to their popular titles and characters. In simpler terms, aside from perhaps *Mario Teaches Typing*, don't expect the pudgy little plumber to be appearing on your PC anytime soon.

Personal computers have taken some big steps toward being more user-friendly. With *Windows 95*, they will hopefully begin to take on the characteristics of a true **Plug & Play** machine and solve some of the compatibility problems discussed above. Even so, the PC still lacks the community atmosphere and family involvement that videogame systems have always been able to provide. After all, videogame machines are hooked up to the one piece of electronic equipment that the family uses most—the television.

ROUND TWO: SYSTEM OVERVIEWS

There are basically two types of videogame systems: cartridge-based systems and CD-based systems. Both cartridges and CDs are merely storage devices that supply information to the game machine. Cartridge-based games are limited by chip sizes, but CD-based games are only limited by the space allowed on the disc. Not enough space? No problem, add another disc. CD-based

MORPHEUS

INTERACTIVE™

Many of the current 32-bit videogame machines feature custom graphics and sound chips that enable the machines to duplicate more advanced arcade-like features. PCs have dedicated chips, too, but you're more likely to find a custom graphics chipset in a graphics work-station—like those used to create computer-generated movie effects—than in a standard PC. Sound cards or sound drivers are another issue. While a dedicated game machine has a dedicated sound chip or processor, most PCs must have a sound card installed to enable the machine to produce high-quality, arcade-like sound. A PC will also

need speakers to produce the sound, while game machines use the speakers in the television that they are connected to. To produce full motion video (FMV), an **MPEG board** is required. Most multimedia PCs and

Figure 1: *CD-based games like VR Stalker for 3DO offer nail-biting cinematic intros.*

machines also have an advantage over cartridge-based machines because CDs are much cheaper to produce and duplicate than cartridges. And because a CD has much more storage space than a cartridge, it's easier to store memory-hungry elements like full-motion video and cinematic intros. These add to a game's appeal and storyline.

Several companies produce videogame systems. Among them are Sony, Sega, Nintendo, 3DO and Atari. And while they're almost all rooted in cartridge-based machines, the 3DO and Sony PlayStation are CD-exclusive and have no cartridge-based versions.

unit. In many cases, videogame machines even share some of the same **chipsets** that PCs use—but it's the way that these chips or chipsets are configured that give a machine its playing power.

ROUND THREE: HOW THEY WORK

Videogame systems are a lot like a VCR: you plug the video source and audio source into the back of your television. There are no mouse drivers to install and no sound cards to buy. You simply place a CD or cartridge in the machine and turn it on. Within seconds, the machine is doing exactly what it was intended to do—display a game ready to play. Personal computers, on the other hand, may require that you **configure** the system, or go through a lengthy and aggravating installation process.

FINAL BATTLE: PROCESSING POWER—WHO'S GOT MORE?

Videogame machines, like personal computers, are defined and driven by one major component—the **CPU**, or central processing

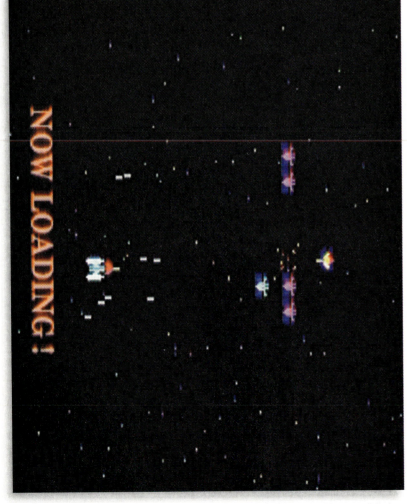

NOW LOADING!

Figure 2: *No installation required. Just place the CD or cartridge in the machine and almost instantly the game is ready; Some games that require some loading time offer players entertaining diversions, like this scene from Namco's Ridge Racer.*

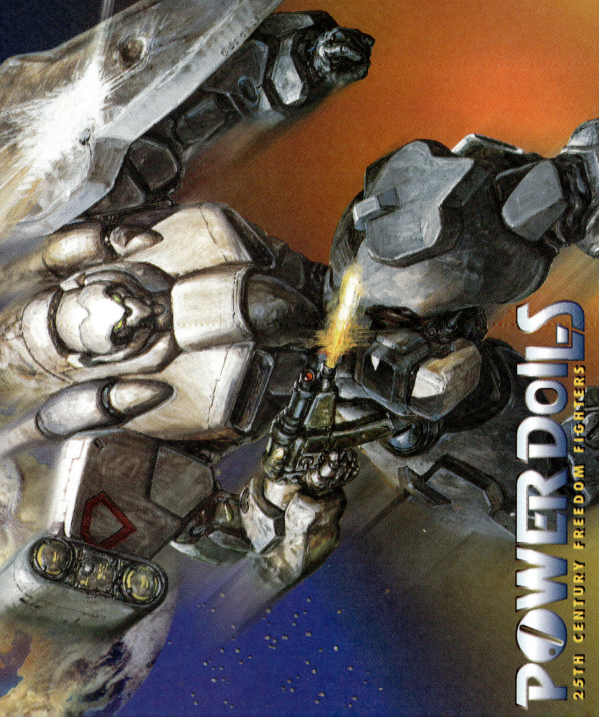

Citizens of Planet Earth:

You Are the Enemy.

POWER DOLLS
25TH CENTURY FREEDOM FIGHTERS

"You traveled across the galaxy to attack us. You claim our parents freely chose to colonize this world for you! No. This is our world! You drew first blood. Now you must die!"

A Futuristic Paramilitary Simulation: Plan and lead a realistic rebellion. At your command is an elite force of highly trained, extremely deadly, female cyberwarriors ready to kill and die to defend their planet!

DOS CD-ROM

AP ALL PLAYERS

KOGADO Software Products

Minimum Requirements: O/S - DOS 5.0, Ram - 4MB, Video - VGA, CD-ROM - 2x, Hard Disk - 5MB, Sound - Sound Blaster & MIDI, Input - Mouse

Catch us on the Web: http://www.megatech-software.com

To order, call 1-800-258-MEGA

MEGA TECH

© 1995 Megatech & Design, Inc., Torrance, CA 90501 • All rights reserved

The NEW Systems

When choosing a videogame system, it's important to remember that any machine is only as good as the software that runs on it. The best systems usually have a variety of good titles in different categories. Also remember that a particular arcade favorite or character's game may only be available on a single system.

Sega's Saturn: Running Rings Around The Competition.

Prompted in part by Sony's entry into the videogame arena, the Sega Saturn shows a noticeable improvement over previous Sega systems, although the system has gone through a lot of retooling to get where it is today.

With the Saturn, Sega offers incredible CD-based games, many through a unique first-person, virtual-esque viewpoint. Sweeping camera angles and lifelike rendered or polygon-based characters highlight many of the games, which easily rival any past or present PC titles. With Sega's strong arcade tie, games like Virtua Fighter and Daytona USA—almost direct arcade translations—are exclusive to Sega, and upcoming titles like Virtua Fighter 2 and Sega Rally will offer even better gaming experiences. Still, the Saturn is one of the more difficult machines to program on, and it's graphically weaker than the PlayStation, so don't expect to see truly amazing third-party titles until developers get a better grasp of the system. Finally, the Saturn, like most 32- and 64-bit game machines, is not backward-compatible. Expect the Saturn to be heavily supported by Sega's legendary marketing campaigns and guerrilla packaging tactics.

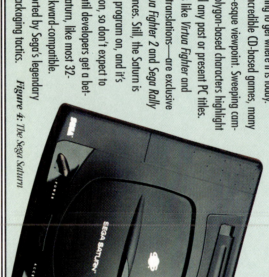

Figure 3: Games like Daytona USA show off The Saturn's processing power. Notice the detail and lifelike backgrounds.

Figure 4: The Sega Saturn

THE GAME SYSTEMS
THE EVOLUTION OF THE GAME MACHINE

new 32- and 64-bit videogame machines retail for around $300 to $400. It wasn't always this way, though. Before videogame machines began to take on PC characteristics like CD-ROM drives and mice, the PC was by far the superior machine, both in processing power and game experience.

1962 *Spacewar* is created by MIT graduate student Steve Russell. The game—one of the very first computer games ever made—eventually makes its way into several universities computer labs where it has a profound influence on several students, including a University of Utah student, Nolan Bushnell.

1972 Atari is founded with just $250 by Nolan Bushnell, now a University of California engineering graduate. After trying to market *Computer Space*, an unsuccessful version of *Spacewar*, Bushnell designs and builds a small prototype for a game called *Pong*. The game is a surprising success. Bushnell then hires a small staff of engineers, among them Steve Wozniak and Steve Jobs, the future founders of Apple Computer. They produce additional *Pong* units on Bushnell's homemade production line.

all CD-based game systems are supplied with some version of the MPEG board before they leave the manufacturing plant. And finally, most videogame systems come prepackaged with controllers; PCs do not. A PC user will have to buy any additional peripherals needed separately, such as a game pad or joystick, unless they are provided in a "package deal." (some computer stores offer such incentives).

The 3DO, Sony PlayStation and Sega Saturn are already supplied with all the major components they need to make games play. Only the 64-bit Jaguar requires that you buy a CD attachment if you want to play CD games.

In a nutshell, depending on what types of games a PC user desires to play, how fast they want the applications to run and what type of sound quality they desire, they might need to customize or configure their PC accordingly to be able to equal the processing power of a dedicated videogame machine. This could require as much as $300), while the

Figure 5: 3DO's M2 technology rivals high priced PCs. This M2 demo shows off the machines incredible graphics power.

1973 The arcade rights to *Pong* are sold to Bally Midway, although pirated versions of the game are everywhere. Companies like Magnavox produce *Pong* machines for the home. All versions of the game are incredibly successful. Atari introduces *Sprint*, the first coin-operated machine that uses a CPU to control the game action.

1975 With the backing of Sears and a major television ad campaign, Atari's home version of *Pong* racks up $40 million.

1976 Looking for major investors to launch his new system, the Atari VCS 2600, Bushnell pursues Disney and MCA. They decline but Warner Communications does not, and it buys Atari for $28 million dollars. Atari introduces the Atari 2600 to the public, and the very first "set-top" mass-market videogame console is born. For the first time, arcade games can be played at home, on this revolutionary new system. Nolan Bushnell remains the company chairman.

1978 The home videogame market has grown to a $200 million dollar business. Atari accounts for half of Warner Communications income, but due to internal differences, Nolan Bushnell leaves Atari. The game business continues to boom, though, as *Space Invaders* marches into arcades across the country.

1981 Mattel introduces the Intellivision, as Atari's 2600 and the ColecoVision go head to head for their share of the $1 billion home videogame market. Meanwhile, Coleco negotiates with Nintendo and gets the home rights to its incredibly successful arcade title, *Donkey Kong*. With the profits from *Donkey Kong*, Nintendo's president, Minoru Arakawa, purchases 27 acres of land in Redmond, Washington—on which Nintendo of America sits today.

1982 Subsequent licensing efforts for *Donkey Kong*, including breakfast cereal, cartoons and pajamas, add to Nintendo's coffers. Arcade sequels such as *Donkey Kong Jr.* are also popular. Nintendo begins to eye consumer electronics, and *Pac-Man* eats up the arcades.

1983 With the $3 billion dollar videogame market flooded with low-quality products and staggering inventory problems, the industry reaches its peak and sales begin to plummet. Atari posts record losses in excess of $500 million, Coleco is dissolved and a year later Mattel sells

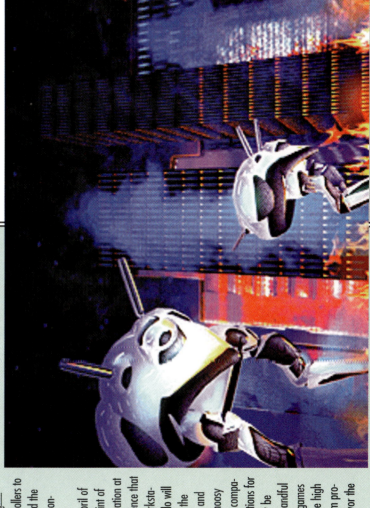

Figure 7: SGI images like this one will be easily produced on the Ultra.

Nintendo Ultra 64: Now You're Playing With Power!

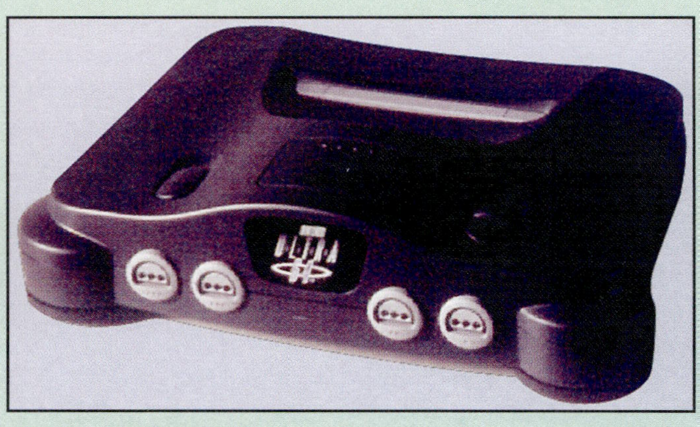

Developed in conjunction with Silicon Graphics—the company whose graphics workstations are responsible (and probably better known) for the special effects in *Jurrasic Park* and *Terminator 2*—Nintendo's Ultra 64 promises to be one of the most amazing videogame systems ever created.

Figure 6: The Nintendo Ultra 64.

The 64-bit cartridge-based system boasts 3D, real-time **rendered graphics**, incredibly realistic sound, a memory expansion port and an SGI-based chipset that will enable the machine to do things its competitors, the PlayStation and the Saturn, must do via software—which eats up processing power. Expect the controllers to be the real surprise, though. Nintendo redesigned the standard joypad to work well for 3D game environments, instead of just the standard 2D.

The machine won't be available until April of 1996, but even then, with a promised price point of $250 (much cheaper than Saturn or the PlayStation at launch), the machine will offer a game experience that before could only be witnessed on graphics workstations costing a hundred times as much. Nintendo will still control developer and third-party access to the machine, much like it did in the Nintendo 8-bit and SNES days. But while Nintendo remains very choosy about whom they grant third-party licenses to, companies like Paradigm, which designs flight simulations for the military and NASA, are rumored to already be completing Ultra 64 games. Currently, only a handful of companies have been signed on to develop games for the Ultra system. Many developers claim the high cost of Nintendo chipsets will prohibit them from producing games for the cartridge system, and favor the cheaper CD medium.

Sony PlayStation: The Next Walkman?

Not a hardened veteran like Sega or Nintendo, Sony's first entry into the videogame arena is the PlayStation. Although Sony is new to this particular corner of the electronic neighborhood, they've been in the electronic neighborhood longer than anybody.

The PlayStation was born out of a relationship Sony had with Nintendo to develop a CD system for the Super Nintendo. However, when Nintendo decided to go it alone, Sony was left having devoted a substantial amount of time—and development dollars—into a game machine. Instead of selling the technology, Sony decided to enter the videogame business. The result is the Sony PlayStation.

Since the announcement of the machine in 1991, the PlayStation has undergone a variety of changes, including a down-sizing of the machine's output devices to achieve a less expensive price point. The PlayStation now boasts a mouse, a memory card, its signature black disc and the innovative connector cable that allows two monitors and a pair of machines to be linked together for simultaneous two-player action—without a split-screen. Other game machines like the Jaguar and Saturn offer this feature, but the PlayStation is the only machine that already has as many as five titles that utilize the feature.

With a wide range of titles being developed in the US and Europe, and with additional titles coming from Japan, the PlayStation will have one of the most powerful game libraries available. Sony was also careful to cultivate key relationships with companies like Namco and Psygnosis to make sure the PlayStation was capable of providing arcade-like gaming experiences at launch. The PlayStation is more powerful than most high-end PCs and is definitely a player.

Figure 8: The Sony PlayStation.

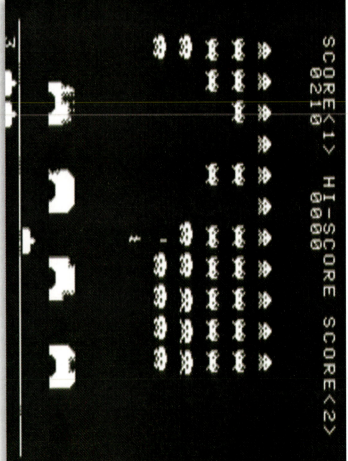

videogame market seems dead.

1984 Atari is sold to Jack Tramiel, founder of Commodore Business Machines. Atari is renamed Atari Corporation.

1985 Nintendo introduces the Nintendo Entertainment System at the Consumer Electronics Show in Chicago. The NES is a cartridge-based American version of the Japanese Famicom—also made by Nintendo—but recently burned buyers and retailers are still weary of the word *videogame*. Yet the NES, backed by a $30 million ad campaign and Nintendo's commitment to quality, manages to win over the skeptics.

1987 The Nintendo Entertainment System enjoys strong sales, and Nintendo remains unchallenged in the home videogame market. Acclaim is formed to produce games exclusively for the NES, and other companies follow. By the end of 1987, some 25 third-parties have signed on to produce games exclusively for the Nintendo Entertainment System.

1988 Understanding that entertainment value and quality are what sold the systems and kept players hooked, Nintendo sells another seven million NES units. Games like *The Legend of Zelda* and *Mike Tyson's Punch-Out* sell two million copies apiece. *Super Mario Bros. 2* is released.

1989 The NEC TurboGrafx-16 is released. It boasts a 16-bit processor, enabling it to produce

1990 The Sega Genesis is launched in the US at $199. Using the same 6800 processor that ran the Macintosh computer, the 16-bit Genesis machine has more impressive graphics power than any home videogame system before it.

1991 Feeling the pressure from Sega's growing market share and the dying 8-bit market, Nintendo unveils its Super Nintendo

better sound and graphics than the NES, but the games are of poor quality, and less than a million units are sold. Nintendo maintains its market share dominance, with one out of every four American families owning a NES.

Figure 10: Space Invaders is one of the most popular videogames of all time.

Figure 9: Wipeout pushes the PlayStation to its limits.

3DO: Setting The Standard

While the Sega Saturn, Sony PlayStation and Nintendo's Ultra 64 are exclusive to the respective companies manufacturing the hardware, the 3DO lives by a very different set of

Figure 12: The Goldstar 3DO machine.

rules. Unlike the previously mentioned machines, 3DO is a standard, much like VHS is a standard, and anyone who buys a 3DO license can produce a 3DO machine.

Currently, machines are produced by Panasonic, Goldstar and Sanyo. In addition, a 3DO Blaster card for PC users is available from Creative Labs. With the card and a CD-ROM drive, PC users can play a variety of 3DO titles on their PC—no other gaming platform has ever offered such a unique feature. And although the system was poorly supported at first, the 3DO now boasts a wide variety of titles, including some of the best sports games available for any games system. John Madden Football from Electronic Arts and Slam and Jam from Crystal Dynamics show off the 3DO's scaling and rotation abilities in outstandingly playable games.

The 3DO standard is the brainchild of Trip Hawkins, former head of Electronic Arts, who ironically developed the 3DO concept upon the same principles on which the PC was built. The machine is both expandable and backward-compatible, with the latest version of the 3DO technology, called M2, plugging directly into the existing 3DO. The M2's impressive PowerPC 602 chip is supported by ten co-processors, 6MB of memory and built-in MPEG1—which also makes the 3DO one of the most powerful game machines available.

Figure 13: Total Eclipse, one of the first 3DO titles, uses texture-mapped backgrounds for realistic flight terrain—the effect is now evident in most games.

---

some of the ways game machines are expanding their horizons below. Even the meek little PC mouse has managed to break its way into videogames.

THE VALUE OF HAVING BOTH... OR SEVERAL... IN THE HOME

While videogame systems can teach kids hand-eye coordination, and some problem-solving skills, they offer little in the educational department. Multimedia PCs, on the other hand, have an abundant number of educational or <u>edutainment</u> titles. These titles can teach children how to read or solve math problems, and are almost always more entertaining and educational than just sitting the child down in front of a television set.

Videogame systems are more involving than television: a fair amount of activity may entertain, but too much of anything can be harmful. Parents should always properly regulate the use of any such device, and never be afraid to use the power button.

Entertainment System or the SNES. The Genesis is now in 2.3 million homes, partially due to the success of a Mario-like game called *Sonic the Hedgehog*.

1992 The videogame industry surpasses $5 billion in retail sales.

1993 The videogame business is 21 years-old. The 3DO multiplayer is introduced, and just before the year's end, the Atari Jaguar is launched. It is the world's first 64-bit game machine.

1994 Sega and Nintendo continue their aggressive head-to-head marketing campaigns. The Atari Jaguar and 3DO battle for any kind of market share. The revolutionary *Donkey Kong Country* changes the way videogames are perceived.

1995 Sega fires the first shot of the 1995 videogame wars by launching the Saturn—Sega's 32-bit, CD-based next-generation gaming super system—months before the intended release date. Sony, entering the videogame playing field for the first time, launches the PlayStation, also CD-based.

1996 Nintendo unleashes the Ultra 64.

CONVERGING AND RELATED TECHNOLOGIES

While dedicated game systems can't process spreadsheets or word documents, they are becoming more versed in performing some tasks originally only associated with the PC. We've listed

---

Figure 11: Mario made 'em millions. At one time, Mario was more recognizable to children than Mickey Mouse.
(Trademark of Nintendo of America, Inc., courtesy of Nintendo of America, Inc.)

GAME COMPARISONS—GENRES

Every videogame falls into a particular category or genre. Game genres can be influenced by a variety of topics from a programmer's opinion to a revolutionary programming "trick." But for the most part, most game genres stick to the same uninspired formulas. However, as processors become more powerful, they enable machines to produce more appealing graphics, and more difficult playing fields. These make videogames all the more challenging and exciting.

We've listed below several genres and examples of each category.

The Atari Jaguar: The Cat With Nine Lives

Aside from its slow retail start and initially high price tag, the struggling Atari Jaguar still lacks a variety of good software to drive the system. Hardly any American developers have signed on to produce software for the machine, and the software that is available makes poor use of the Jaguar's tremendous processing power. Still the only true 64-bit game machine, the Jaguar offers a CD-ROM drive, an MPEG upgrade and a virtual reality helmet in its bag of add-ons, but few of the games in the current Jaguar catalog take advantage of any of these extras. Atari also has the right to cross-license up to five Sega titles a year due to a legal settlement, but has yet to do so.

Still, the Jaguar may yet get a chance to roar. Rumors persist that Atari has a Web Browser in development for the machine that would allow players access to the World Wide Web. This would be a major advantage for the Jaguar, although we're no aware that any plans currently exist for a keyboard, mouse or storage device—which would seem to be essential items for logging onto the web.

Atari remains firm in its belief that it can win the videogame wars looming ahead. But with a variable consumer reputation that dates all the way back to the 2600 days, an uneven history of product management—its Lynx hand-held machine, but again lacked the software to drive hardware sales—and poor marketing support, Atari may not be able to equip the Jaguar with the muscle and stamina to be a long-term contender against the likes of Sony, Nintendo and Sega.

Figure 14: The Atari Jaguar and CD attachment.

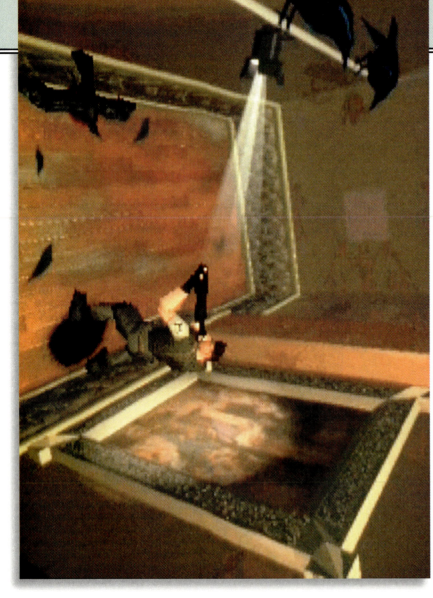

Figure 15: Redefining the Genre: Games like Capcom's Resident Evil for PlayStation redefine players' expectations of platform games.

PLATFORM GAMES

Ever since the birth of this genre in 1981 with the creation of this arcade classic *Donkey Kong*, *platformers* (or *side-scrollers*) haven't changed much. More popular games, such as *Sonic the Hedgehog* and *Super Mario Brothers*, have expanded the genre—offering more goals to achieve and more complex terrain to traverse—but still the tried-and-true formula—running from right to left gathering power-ups or bonus items needed to reach an ultimate goal—survives today. This is another area in which dedicated game machines are better than PCs. While first-person games like *Doom* and *Magic Carpet* are all the rage on PCs, platform games are almost nonexistent, partially due to the PC's sluggish scrolling rate—which has only recently improved. Sadly though, many platformers now seem to be little more than a licensing launching pad for the next *Mario*, with content losing to flash and style.

SHOOTERS

Again started in the arcades, this time with the coin-op classic *Space Invaders*, *shooters* offer a simple premise: kill or be killed. Shoot-'em-ups like *Galaxian* and *Zaxxon* have expanded on the genre,

but have done little to change the format since the first invaders marched across the screen in 1978. Konami's *Nemesis* was the first to offer multiple weapons, end-of-level bosses (those ever-so-difficult bad guys you must overcome to get to the next level), and power-ups—a formula that's still used widely today. Other variations on the genre include *Star Blade* and *X-Wing*, where you control only the gunner and fly along a predetermined path.

ONLINE SERVICES

Currently the Sony PlayStation and Atari Jaguar are rumored to have online devices in development for their machines. The devices would allow videogame players to log on an online service like the Internet and download, retrieve or post information.

The XBand Modem, already available for the Genesis and Super Nintendo, should be available shortly for the PlayStation and Saturn. The modem allows players to compete over the phone line with another player (who must also have an XBand Modem) in a videogame that supports the XBand Modem). Currently games like Mortal Kombat and NBA Jam are available for play on the system. There is also a PC version of the device.

now they boast incredibly realistic 3D-polygon graphics, and view points that "change on the fly," giving players the ability to move the camera perspective in, out and around the car while the game is in progress.

There are three types of simulations. First, the flight simulation. This type of simulation offers realistic in- and out-of-cockpit viewpoints in a variety of aircraft. One of the most popular flight simulators is the Microsoft *Flight Simulator*. Other popular flight simulators include *F15 Strike Eagle* and *Strike Commander*.

The second type of simulation is the strategic simulation. The very first strategy game to be played via computer was chess. Since then the genre has expanded to include military simulations like *V for Victory* and popular sports-management games. Another type of strategic simulation, or *God simulator*, offers players control over a universe, city or other manageable community. Games like *Sim City*, *Populous* and *Civilization* are included in this category.

Finally, there are sport simulations. One problem with sport simulations is that the game, such as football, never really changes. Innovation in the simulation must come from the developer. In short, it's up to the programmer to portray it in an unusual or interesting way. Most of the innovations

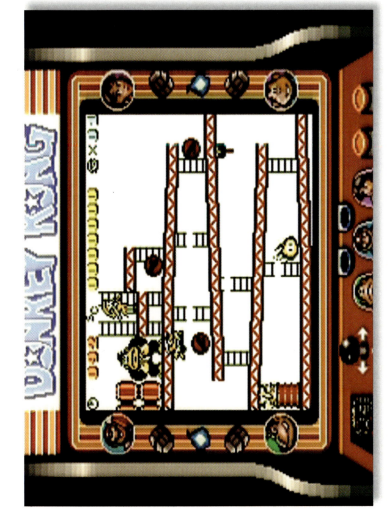

Figure 16: Donkey Kong—one of the first and still one of the best.

FIGHTING GAMES

International Karate, *Fist of the North Star* and *Kung Fu Master* are probably a little lesser-known than their younger siblings, *Double Dragon* and *StreetFighter II*. Their concept is simple: defeat your opponent in a one-on-one street fight. Later versions of the fighting genre, like *Final Fight*, offer players the option to pick up weapons, and *Mortal Kombat* gives players the opportunity to perform special moves or combos in order to complete their task.

DRIVING GAMES

Atari's *Pole Position* was the first to offer a 3D, head-on, first-person perspective of driving. It's the same game design which is still used primarily today. Earlier racing titles such as *Super Sprint*, *Night Driver* and *Spy Hunter* offered a top-down view of the action. Driving games haven't changed much in design or concept, but

ROLE-PLAYING GAMES OR ADVENTURES

Role-playing games (RPGs) began meekly enough as text-only adventures, with the enormously popular *Zork* leading the way. Players read a description of their situation, then typed in a response or "solution" on the keyboard. It wasn't until Sierra introduced its groundbreaking menu system, and 2D maps gave way to stunning 3D worlds, that the genre really began to take off. Popular titles like *Zelda* and the *King's Quest* series brought the genre into the mass market. Today, a simple point-and-click interface, beautifully shot movie introductions, animated game play and CD sound are taking the genre into an whole new era. Still, the basic formula remains the same: solve the puzzles, stay alive and (in some games) kill whatever attacks you.

Figure 17: Sim City offers players the opportunity to run a city. Sims like this one are very popular.

HotWARE

No matter what kind of processing power a piece of hardware has, it's only as good as the applications or games that run on it. And because great games are so hard to find, here's a short list of some of the best HotWARE and the game systems that support them.

Daytona USA (Saturn) — The videogame conversion of one of the most impressive arcade racing games to date. Not as pretty as *Ridge Racer*, but just as playable.

Demolition Derby (PlayStation) — The name says it all.

FIFA Soccer (3DO) — More than just another sports title, the game really shows off the 3DO's capabilities.

Gex (3DO) — A well-done platform game with tons of character.

Mortal Kombat 3 (Saturn/PlayStation/Ultra 64) — The videogame conversion of the highly successful arcade fighting game. Impressive graphics but too violent for children.

Panzer Dragoon (Saturn) — A shooter for all intense purposes, but graphically amazing. A 3D virtual roller coaster.

Pilotwings 2 (Ultra 64) — Flight simulation. A highly anticipated sequel.

Ridge Racer (PlayStation) — The ultimate racing title. The computer intelligence is limited, but this doesn't take away from the overall game.

Tekken (PlayStation) — Another fighting game, but done with impressive visuals and set in a 3D environment.

Tempest 2000 (Jaguar) — A remake of the arcade classic, one of the few Jaguar titles worth buying.

Virtua Fighter / Virtua Fighter Remix (Saturn) — A 3D fighting game. The videogame conversion of the arcade game of the same title. Remix offers graphically better characters but the same playing fields.

War Hawk (PlayStation) — A shooter that really exploits the PlayStation's potential.

Wipeout (PlayStation) — A high-speed futuristic racer with exceptional graphics and sound to match.

---

in this genre have followed in the footsteps of television—games often come now offer players spoken commentary and instant replays. Popular titles from Electronic Arts like *John Madden Football* and *NHL Hockey* dominate the genre.

THE VIDEOGAME RATINGS SYSTEM

The Interactive Digital Software Association (IDSA) videogame rating system was established in April of 1994 by an independent group of software manufacturers in an effort to help parents make more informed software-buying decisions. The ratings were prompted by a congressional inquiry on videogame violence.

Although there are other types of videogame rating systems in use, the IDSA system is the most widely used videogame rating system. Currently, the IDSA system is used by Sega, Nintendo and a wide range of software manufacturers. Other systems in use by the Software Publishers Association and by 3DO are similar but not as explanatory. Brief content descriptions may accompany the main rating. It is important to pay close attention to these descriptions; often they will give a consumer information about a product that is not apparent on the packaging.

HOTWARE: PC GAMES AND THEIR VIDEOGAME COUNTERPARTS

Part of the attraction of bringing a PC title to the videogame platform relates to the sheer

KIDS TO ADULTS

AGES 6+ TM

Figure 18: Parents should look for a symbol like this one to determine if the product is suitable for their children.

KEYBOARDS AND MICE

A keyboard is in development for the Saturn. However, there are no titles available (or planned) to support the peripheral.

The PlayStation, Saturn and 3DO all have a mouse that can be purchased separately. Only a limited number of titles support the mouse.

volume of sales and potential revenue that software manufacturers can achieve in the videogame market. A popular title may sell as many as 500,000 units or more. Some of the better conversions are those games that have retained their PC quality. Games like *Sim City* offer players the same options they had in the original PC version, but the videogame version is much easier to play and control. But this isn't always the case; due to the limitations of the 16-bit machines, some PC conversions have to make sacrifices. For example, the videogame version of *Wing Commander* offers the same play mechanics as the PC version, but doesn't offer the same visual appeal.

Probably the most popular PC game to make its way to the videogame platform is *Doom*. Videogame versions of the game have appeared on the Sega Genesis and Atari Jaguar, and soon the game will be available on the Ultra 64. All versions of the game retain the basic formula that made *Doom* such a popular PC title. Interplay's *Descent* also promises to be one of the stronger PC conversions when it appears on the Saturn and PlayStation this fall. It follows in *Doom's* footsteps

Figure 15: Doom is a violent and addictive first-person shoot-'em-up.

PC Game Controllers

PC players are no longer confined to their keyboard as a game input device. In addition to the mouse, there are several types of game controls available for the PC. Among them are standard game pads that resemble videogame controllers, steering wheel attachments for driving games, flight yokes and pedals for flight simulations, trackballs and even a light gun for some CD-ROM-based shooters.

Controllers often make a substantial difference in game play, and almost all the controllers allow players to customize their weapon of choice. Several companies manufacture game controllers for the PC. Some of the best are listed below. Remember the quality of the controller is often reflected in the price.

- **The Gravis Joypad.** Until the Gravis Joypad, there were no controllers for PCs similar to those for videogames. Now it has almost become a PC-gaming standard. The pad resembles a standard videogame controller with one directional pad and four action buttons. Before the Joypad, PC players either used a joystick or the keyboard for game input.

- **The Virtual Pilot Pro.** This, used along with the Pro Pedals (both are manufactured by CH Products), make flight simulations even more realistic. The yoke works with amazing accuracy just like the control yoke on a real airplane, and the pedals are the only ones of their kind to feature forward and backward rudder control, again just like a real airplane. The pedals can also be used in driving games.

- **Flightstick Pro.** Also by CH Products, this sturdy joystick offers realistic flight controls in games like *Wing Commander*. Its reaction time and calibration are exceptional.

- **The PC Game Gun.** Manufactured by American Laser Games, the PC Game Gun is compatible with American Laser Game titles like *Who Shot Johnny Rock* and *Crime Patrol*. The gun sends an infrared signal to the PC indicating whether or not you've hit the intended target.

Figure 20: *The Gravis JoyPad.*

Figure 21: *The Flightstick Pro resembles a real fighter pilot's flightstick.*

as a first-person search-and-destroy game. Still games like *Shadow of the Beast* and *Flashback* blazed the conversion trail long before *Doom* was even a twinkle in a programmer's eye.

Almost as long as the systems have existed, videogames have been stealing games and game concepts from the PC and vice versa. In fact, as the CD-based, next-generation videogame systems become more popular, expect to see even more titles crossover between the platforms. With the tremendous processing power of the new CD-based game machines, they'll be able to produce stunning intro sequences, polygon-based characters and worlds, plus other unique gaming experiences that have been the rage on the PC for years.

Vince Matthews is the former Senior Game Tester and Associate Publisher of Game Players magazine, a national video game publication. He has also written for CD-ROM Today, PC Gamer and Computer Entertainment News. He has been playing video games since 1976.

SYSTEM EXPLANATION

EC *Early Childhood*—Titles rated EC are suitable for children ages three and older. These titles contain no inappropriate material.

KA *Kids to Adults*—These titles are for persons six and older. These titles have a wide appeal but may contain some violence in the form of comic mischief or crude language.

T *Teen*—The titles are suitable for persons 13 and older. Titles in this category may contain violent content, mild or strong language, and/or suggestive themes.

M *Mature*—Persons 17 and older. Titles with this rating may contain one or more of the following: intense violence, strong language or mature sexual themes.

AO *Adults Only*—Titles with this rating are suitable for adults only. These products may include graphic depiction of sex and/or violence. AO titles are not intended for rental or purchase by any person under the age of 18.

INTERESTING AND USEFUL THINGS YOU CAN DO WITH YOUR COMPUTER NOW

By Gary Meredith

We've surveyed the current software scene and chosen some of the very best. Looking to learn the guitar; turn your family history into multimedia, design a house or save a life during an emergency? It's all here, and much more.

A cartoon some years back titled "Alternate Uses for That Expensive Computer You Just Bought" made a satiric swipe at the first wave of personal computers. With suggestions that ranged from paperweight to doorstop to planter, it hit far closer to home than a lot of people in computing would have cared to admit. Then, as now, the big selling point with personal computers was the promise of all the wonderful things to be done with a PC. But the sad truth was that neither the hardware nor the software of the day were up to all that much.

In those days, "state of the art" for most computer users meant an 8085 microprocessor

drive bigger than 30MB. Sound boards had made their appearance, but there was very little software to support them.

How things have changed. Today, there's hardly a vocation or avocation that hasn't been touched, and usually enriched, by the PC. The capabilities of the computer have finally caught up with its promise. There were perhaps a few hardy souls back in the old days who would drag out their computer to utilize a cooking or home repair program that consisted mainly of hard-to-read text. But today's new laptop computers let a shade-tree mechanic take the computer out to where he's working and access information in ways that put the

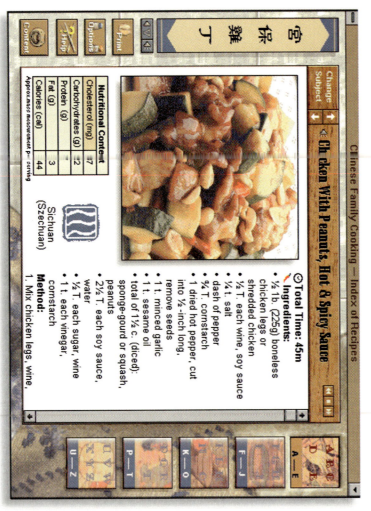

Figure 1: *Chinese Family Cooking (SunMedia)*

(Screen shown in Figure 1:)

Chinese Family Cooking — Index of Recipes

◁ Chicken With Peanuts, Hot & Spicy Sauce

Total Time: 45m

Ingredients:
- ½ lb. (225g) boneless chicken legs or shredded chicken
- ½ T. each wine, soy sauce
- ¼ t. salt
- dash of pepper
- ¾ T. cornstarch
- 1 dried hot pepper, cut into ½-inch long, remove seeds
- 1 t. minced garlic
- 1 t. sesame oil
- total of 1½ c. (diced): sponge-gourd or squash, peanuts
- 2½ T. each soy sauce, water
- ½ T. each sugar, wine
- 1 t. each vinegar, cornstarch

Method:
1. Mix chicken legs, wine,

Sichuan (Szechuan)

Nutritional Content

Cholesterol (mg)	37
Carbohydrates (g)	42
Protein (g)	3
Fat (g)	3
Calories (cal)	44

Approximate measurement per serving

computers was the promise of all the wonderful things to be done with a PC. But the sad truth was
(or at best, a 80286), 640K of memory; video that asked 16 colors to do the work of the whole spectrum and, if you were very fortunate, a hard

venerable old Chilton automotive manuals to shame.

Okay, so now we have the technology. But have the software designers kept up? To be sure,

---

The Right Stuff

Computer equipment is covered much more completely elsewhere in the *Encyclopedia*, but we'd like to point you to just a few things to look for. First of all, make sure you get the fastest computer, with the most memory, you can afford. Look for at least a 486DX2-66 with a minimum eight megabytes of RAM (memory). The 486 is far from dead, and with the right peripherals, a 100MHz 486DX4 can give one of the base model Pentiums (60 or 66MHz) a run for its money. Also, if you can swing it, upgrade to 16MB of memory. Despite the minimum memory requirements for Windows 95, you'll still need all the memory you can pack in, especially because software in general continually becomes ever more demanding of a computer's resources.

An SVGA video card, preferably a 64-bit Windows accelerator model with 2MB of VRAM (Video RAM) is essential, as is a 16-bit wave table sound board. With the tremendous drop in the prices of hard drives, even a modest outfit is likely to have an adequate amount of disk storage, so that shouldn't be much of a worry for the shopper. Also, Windows 95 includes a disk compression utility that greatly expands hard drive capacity.

The must-have peripheral is a CD-ROM drive, but be careful to pay close attention to the speed of the drive you're getting. By all means avoid a single-speed drive, and it probably makes sense to steer around a double-speed drive (2X) and just go right up to one of the quad (4X) models. You'll need to exercise caution even with these, however, as there are some quad drives which, owing mainly to their small data buffers, perform no better than some top-end double-spin offerings. While there are still several programs available on floppy disk, they're becoming rarer every day, making a CD-ROM drive almost as essential as a keyboard.

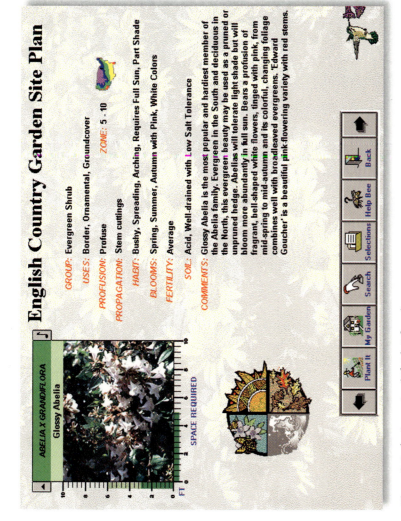

English Country Garden Site Plan

ABELIA X GRANDIFLORA
Glossy Abelia

GROUP: Evergreen Shrub
USES: Border, Ornamental, Groundcover
PROFUSION: Profuse
PROPAGATION: Stem cuttings
ZONE: 5 - 10
HABIT: Bushy, Spreading, Arching, Requires Full Sun, Part Shade
BLOOMS: Spring, Summer, Autumn with Pink, White Colors
FERTILITY: Average
SOIL: Acid, Well-drained with Low Salt Tolerance
COMMENTS: Glossy Abelia is the most popular and hardiest member of the Abelia family. Evergreen in the South and deciduous in the North, this evergreen beauty may be used as a pruned or unpruned hedge. Abelias will tolerate light shade but will bloom more abundantly in full sun. Bears a profusion of fragrant, bell-shaped white flowers, tinged with pink, from mid-spring to mid-autumn and its colorful, changing foliage combines well with broadleaved evergreens. 'Edward Goucher' is a beautiful pink-flowering variety with red stems.

SPACE REQUIRED · FT

Plant It · My Garden · Search · Selections · Help Bee · Back

Figure 2: Garden Companion (Lifestyle Software)

there's still some garbage on the market, programs that make little or no effort to exploit the capabilities of the PC. But competition has a way of weeding these pretenders out, and what we have today are programs that will change your mind as to what computers can really do. And the best of them work not because they do everything for you, but because they help you to be better at whatever you're doing.

AROUND THE HOME...AND ELSEWHERE

HOME COOKING

The ancient culinary arts would seem to have little in common with the digital domain of the computer, but they actually have one of the older relationships of the PC era, going back well before the advent of DOS machines. Some of the earliest programs were recipe databases with which the forward-looking chef could create, modify and index mouthwatering masterpieces. About the only advantages these text-based programs had over the traditional cookbook was the quick indexing and, with some of the more sophisticated programs, the ability to modify a recipe to serve a given number of people. Recipes and shopping lists could also be easily printed out or copied.

Today's programs do all that and a great deal more. The addition of video and high-resolution graphics has turned the cooking program into a dynamic classroom where the very best cooks share their trade secrets.

Chinese Family Cooking (SunMedia) offers some intriguing recipes spanning the vast range of Chinese cuisine. Technique is usually the toughest part of learning to cook any new foreign food.

Each cuisine has its own special techniques, and Chinese cooking is particularly inventive and unusual. Even stir-frying is a mystery to some, but it's all covered in *Chinese Family Cooking*. Using the cleaver is essential for some cuisines, but unless you can coax Martin Yan into your kitchen for a private lesson, the next best thing is *Chinese Family Cooking's* video lesson on wielding a cleaver without losing a thumb.

One of the most dramatic innovations found in the newer cooking programs is their exploration of cuisine beyond the kitchen. Adding

a cultural frame of reference can cause a chef to approach cooking from a new direction, thus enhancing the eventual dining experience. That's the tack taken by *Four Paws of Crab* (Live Oak Multimedia), which features a myriad of Thai recipes and cooking techniques, all couched in a fascinating exploration of the way Thai food defines Thai culture.

Is there a name more synonymous with cooking than Julia Child? Even now, in her eighties, she's still a whirlwind of activity, bringing the best of today's culinary creators to the fore with her latest PBS program, "Cooking with Master Chefs." A CD-ROM of the same name is now available from Microsoft; it follows the same path of the television show but also goes a little farther. There are a lot more recipes, but the accent remains on technique, with hundreds of cooking tips, along with step-by-step video lessons that illuminate what in many cases are quite advanced cooking techniques.

GREEN THUMBS GALORE

Unlike cooking, over and done with in a relatively short period of time, gardening requires constant, if sometimes low-level, attention over days, weeks, months and seasons. The storage and indexing capabilities of the computer make it a natural for providing both a database for plant varieties and a means for tracking the slow, incremental growth of those plants. Add to the equation contemporary computer graphics sophistication that can display even the most colorful species and you have a near-perfect marriage of the organic and the inorganic.

Books That Work - Garden Encyclopedia

New Plants from Cuttings

Perennials and shrubs can take a long time to grow from seeds, so many gardeners start them from cuttings. Seeds can also turn out different from their parent plants, whereas cuttings are identical clones.

Your cutting should be 4 to 6 inches long, preferably from a stem without flower buds. You can root it in vermiculite, finely ground perlite or sterilized potting soil. If you use a rooting hormone that contains fungicide, wear gloves or be sure to wash your hands afterward.

Keep your new transplant moist all the time by tenting it in clear plastic. A sawed-off plastic soda bottle can make a sturdy alternative to a plastic bag. A heat mat will hasten root growth by warming the soil. You'll know your plant has rooted if you feel resistance when you tug gently on the stem.

Main · 1 · 2 · 3 · 4 · 5 · AB · CD · EF · GH · IJ · KL · MN · OP · QR · ST · U-Z · Glossary · Help · EXIT · Back

Name Search · Photo Album · Search · All Plants · Plant Lists · Plant Names

Figure 3: Garden Encyclopedia (Books That Work)

Garden Companion (Life-tyle Software), for example, functions as both a plant encyclopedia—covering over a thousand varieties of flowers, trees and other plants—and a plant management database. The encyclopedia lists the usual plant characteristics such as soil type required, growing season, cultivation requirement, and the like. The encyclopedia's database allows you to go about it from the other direction as well: You specify the parameters you wish it to consider, from available light levels to general appearance, and the encyclopedia lists the plants that fit your parameters.

Another nice feature is the Garden Type screen, which contains templates for different kinds of gardens, including an English Country garden, a Formal garden, or even a Japanese garden. You can modify these to fit your own particular plot of land.

Garden Encyclopedia (Books That Work) covers much of the same territory as Garden Companion, but with a style all its own. The usual plant listings and cross-indexing capabilities are there, but with the added element of video. Many plants require special handling—bulbs, for example—so a step-by-step video reference is particularly helpful. You can also keep a mini-diary for each plant, chronicling its

progress, whatever treatment it may have required and so on.

These two programs, along with several others, have a couple of useful features in common. If you have even a passing acquaintance with horticulture and gardening books, you've probably seen those often-confusing zone maps

plants for your dream garden, you can print out the list to take with you to your local garden center. You can even have both common and botanical names listed, along with any sub-varieties, and whatever you may require in the way of fertilizer or pest and disease control products.

File Edit Bookmark Preferences Help

The Frank Lloyd Wright Companion

CONTENTS GO BACK STRUCTURE

Early Usonia Years
1923 - 1935

KAUFMANN RESIDENCE
PICTURES & PLANS
1935 Mill Run, Pennsylvania

Kaufmann Residence
Fallingwater
S.230

Fallingwater is perhaps the best-known private home for someone not of royal blood in the history of the world. Perched over a waterfall deep in the Pennsylvania highlands, it seems part of the rock formations to which it clings. Reinforced-concrete cantilever slabs project from the rock band to carry the house over the stream. From the square living room, one can step directly down a suspended stairway to the stream. Immediately above, on the third level, terraces open from sleeping quarters, emphasizing the horizontal nature of the structural forms; "the apotheosis of the horizontal" it has been called. Robert Mosher did the early supervision of Fallingwater. Edgar Tafel, who had arrived at Taliesin but four years earlier, completed the work from the second level and above.

Fallingwater's features are too many to describe in a few paragraphs, but a few must be listed. The stone is known as Pottsville sandstone; the ridge from which the stone is quarried starts in Pottsville (between and slightly north of Harrisburg and Allentown). Nonstructural wood is North Carolina

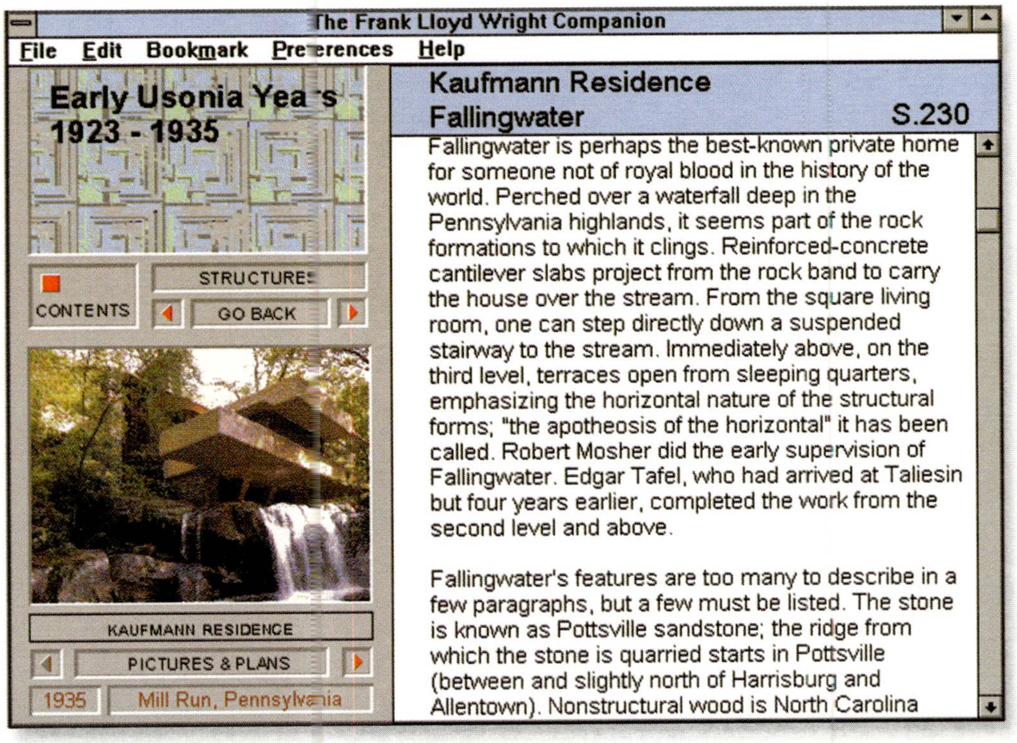

Figure 5: The Frank Lloyd Wright Companion (*Prairie Multimedia, Inc.*)

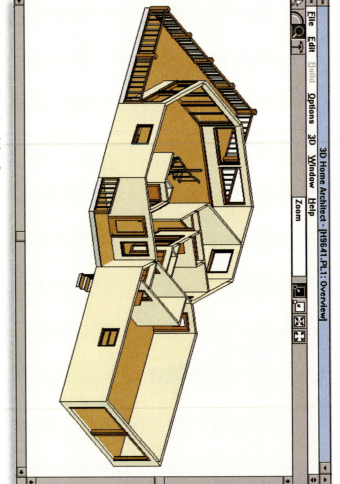

File Edit Build Options 3D Window Help

3D Home Architect - [H9641.PL1: Overview]

Zoom

Figure 4: 3D Home Architect (*Broderbund*)

which tell you which plants will or will not thrive in your area. With these gardening programs, you can bypass that confusion by simply typing in your zip code or area code, which automatically establishes the correct climatic zone for your area. It then lists all the plants that will flourish there. Another feature is a bit more mundane, but handy nonetheless. Once you've picked out all the

One program, Forever Growing Garden (C-Wave), approaches horticulture on a more humorous level, and is perhaps geared more towards younger gardeners or the less-serious gardeners among us who have decidedly non-green thumbs. Using colorful cartoons and some off-the-wall humor, Forever Growing Garden still manages to spade up a rich helping of botanical advice.

HOME-BUILDING AND REPAIR

Only a few years ago, CAD (computer-assisted design or computer-assisted drafting, take your pick) systems were mostly for engineering professionals who had the money to afford both the expensive programs and the expensive computers required to run them. Most computers simply didn't have the number-crunching power required, and the price tags for the software were as high as the learning curve for mastering them. Now every PC owner can utilize design programs that out-render anything available five years ago, and without taking a year's sabbatical to learn them. Of course, most of us have little use in everyday life for the sort of precision CAD offers, unless we're thinking of building a house or renovating.

Check out the plethora of home design magazines at any newsstand; there are house plans for any budget, size requirement or taste. But all these magazines share three shortcomings: First, the drawings are two-dimensional, and even when a effort has been made to present a three-dimensional view, there's still something missing. Second, these plans are set, and can be changed only by an architect or, at the very least, someone with better-than-average drafting skills. Finally, what if no plan you see captures what you envision as

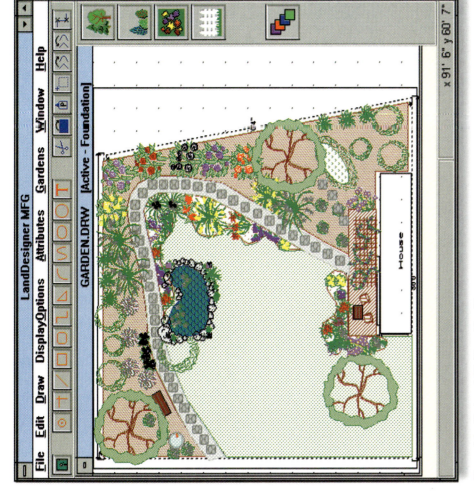

Figure 6: LandDesigner MFG (*Green Thumb*)

your dream house? That's where the latest home architectural design programs enter in.

Along with other such programs, *3D Home Architect* (Broderbund) contains hundreds of pre-drawn plans which you can easily modify to suit your purposes. If you want to get a feel for what the house will be like once it's finished, you need not only access the 3D mode, which not only provides a static three-dimensional view from whatever camera angle you choose (even from underneath the house, but also lets you walk through your house. Being able to see the various structures and the relationships among them makes it much easier to come up with a design that suits your lifestyle. If none of the pre-drawn designs catches your fancy, you can start over with a clean "sheet of paper," turning your own vision into dimensional drawings. These can also be viewed in 3D.

3D Home Architect is not just about house plan drawings, however; there's a wealth of advice included as well. Gerry Connell, the Bob Vila of the Learning Channel, shows up to share, in several video clips, answers to the most frequently asked questions concerning home design and construction. Beyond that, you can browse through the huge library of articles from *American HomeStyle* magazine.

Perhaps the most useful feature of these programs, once you get past the design stage, is their ability to calculate material costs. As you create or modify a house design, the program keeps track of the material used, from floor joists to shingles. You'll need to contact your local lumber yard or hardware store to get per-piece costs for the materials involved, but once you enter those, the program will automatically compute subtotals and a grand total.

But what if you don't see anything you like in the pre-drawn designs, and your creative talent is vacationing in the Bahamas? Maybe you just need a little inspiration, and where better to get it than from the archives of the quintessential American architect Frank Lloyd Wright

The Frank Lloyd Wright Companion (Prairie Multimedia, Inc.) is a compendium featuring every Wright design with over 700 floor plans and more than 1,000 photos of the realized designs. And while most of us have neither the financial resources nor the specific landscape for a home like the gorgeous and still-radical Fallingwater; almost anyone can glean useful design information from this encyclopedia.

Divided into chronological periods, the *Companion* is cross-indexed so that nearly any search criteria can be applied. There are also notes on the design and building of each structure, often describing any problems that might have been encountered with a particular structure or sub-structure.

Now that your house is built, you might want to think about landscaping. The going price for professional landscape architects might be enough in itself to send you in search of a PC program to do the job. It's only later that you discover how much fun it is to lay out the design yourself.

LandDesigner MFG (Green Thumb) takes all the guesswork out of landscape design by providing the beginner with templates that can be used "as is" or modified to fit your land's topography. It also lists over a thousand different plants, from tiny accent flowers to towering trees, along with the growing patterns, care requirements and placement options for each. One of the biggest problems encountered when landscaping is knowing how much room to give particular plants. That problem is a no-brainer here.

Like the home architecture programs, *LandDesigner MFG* will compute costs once base prices have been entered into the database. And like the gardening programs, your plant selection is growing-zone-based, minimizing major planting mistakes.

Okay, your dream castle's built and you've got a lawn they'd die for at Versailles. A life of leisure and quiet reflection on the grounds of your estate seemingly stretches out to the horizon—until the

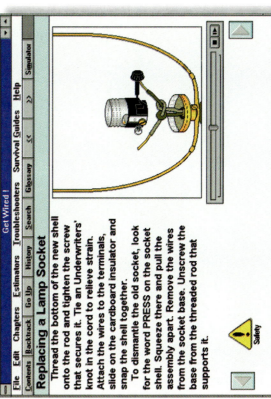

Figure 7: Get Wired (*Books That Work*)

first insidious drip of a leaky faucet interrupts your meditations. If you thought the software designers left you at the threshold after your house was built, think again. The market is loaded with do-it-yourself repair manuals that skillfully utilize graphics, video and text to simplify even the

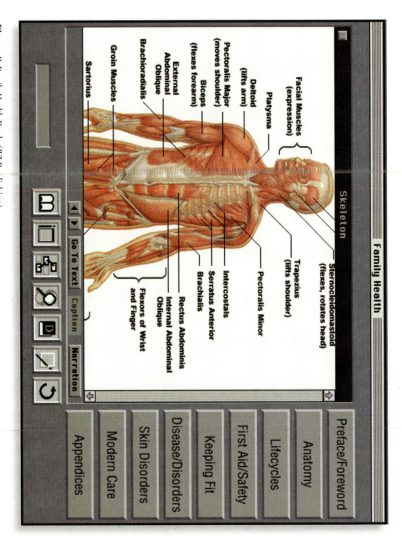

Figure 8: Family Health Book (IVI Publishing)

Health Book, for example, common maladies and their remedies can be researched, often with only a few clicks of the mouse. The information is fairly deep, but written simply and with no ambiguity, a definite plus during a minor medical emergency. Long-term issues for illnesses are covered along with immediate care. And most importantly, you're always told when a visit to your doctor is in order.

Somewhat differently, *The Family Health Pack* (MM Publishing) breaks up its medical advice into four modules: a medical dictionary and family health guide; a drug reference; a guide to symptoms, illness, and surgery; and a family health database with which you can track the health history of every family member.

There seem to be about as many different drugs as there are people to take them, so a pharmacological compendium is always a handy item for anyone's medical library. The problem is, most printed drug guides are so ungainly, with so much superfluous information, that using one could eventually drive you to the acetaminophen or salicylic acid bottle. *PharmAssist* (Software Marketing) brings all the information down to a manageable and usable state. You want to know about a pill? Click. Now you know.

Full-color pictures of practically every tablet or capsule a doctor might prescribe keep you from taking the blue when you should have taken the yellow. Interactions with other drugs or foods can be called up, along with who should or should not be taking the medicine, plus any possible adverse reactions, however improbable or rare.

Homeopaths and traditional medicine advocates have also discovered the convenience of using the computer. A couple of programs by Hopkins Technology, *The Herbalist* and *Traditional Chinese Medicine*, both explore the ancient art of healing with natural compounds, with a little philosophy and history thrown in for context. Both programs explain just how herbal remedies supposedly work, what to expect from each and, perhaps most critically, where to find the often rare ingredients.

ARCHIVING MEMORIES

Can there actually be a family without at least one photo album? A family album stuffed with visual memories has been *de rigueur* in most homes since Eastman perfected his first Brownie. A typical gathering would nearly always entail dragging out the ponderous volume for yet another peek at days and lives gone by.

It's certainly easy enough to find simple photo album programs, either commercial or shareware, but most of them are just thumbnail image repositories. The old photo album was a tangible, tactile experience that, in most cases, was

---

then that home medical software is experiencing a rapid growth of its own. Certainly there are still a great many things for which a visit with your doctor may be the only course of action, but that still leaves many areas where good advice dispensed in an entertaining and

Figure 8: Family Health Book (IVI Publishing)

trickiest home repair problem. *Get Wired* (Books That Work) is a complete guide to the nervous system of your home, the electrical wiring. While some things are better left to a trained electrician (and the program tells you which are, in no uncertain terms), there are a multitude of

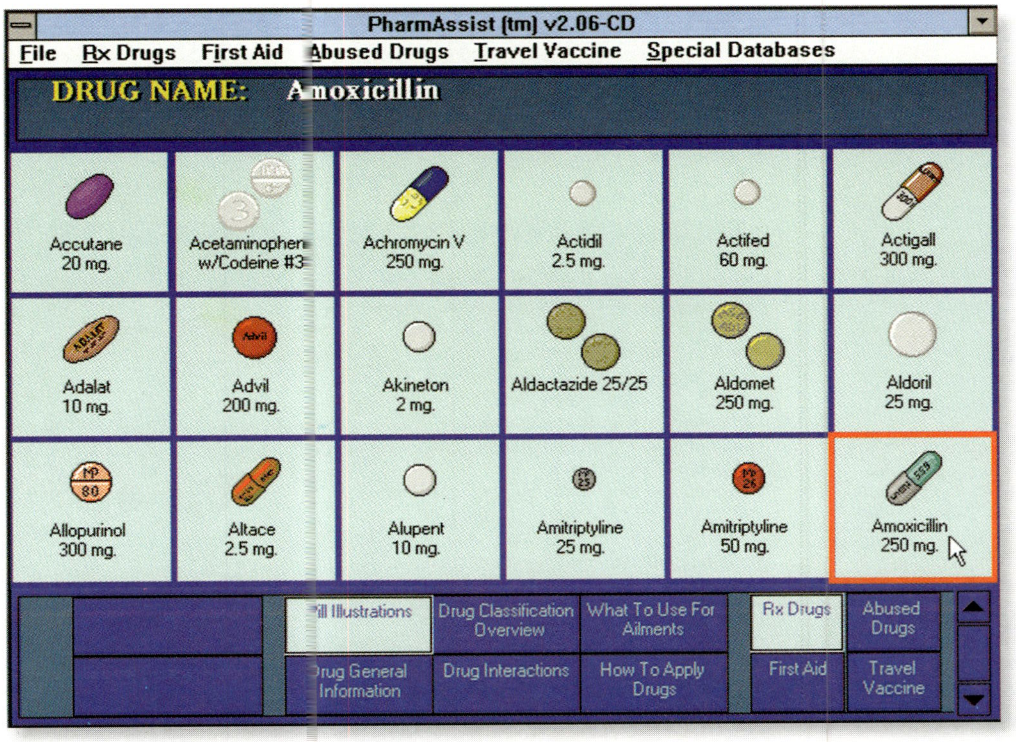

File   Rx Drugs   First Aid   Abused Drugs   Travel Vaccine   Special Databases

PharmAssist (tm) v2.06-CD

DRUG NAME: Amoxicillin

Accutane 20 mg.	Acetaminophen w/Codeine #3	Achromycin V 250 mg.	Acidil 2.5 mg.	Actifed 60 mg.	Actigall 300 mg.
Adalat 10 mg.	Advil 200 mg.	Akineton 2 mg.	Aldactazide 25/25	Aldomet 250 mg.	Aldoril 25 mg.
Altace 2.5 mg.	Alupent 10 mg.	Amitriptyline 25 mg.	Amitriptyline 50 mg.	Amoxicillin 250 mg.	
Allopurinol 300 mg.					

Drug Illustrations · Drug General Information · Drug Classification Overview · Drug Interactions · What To Use For Ailments · How To Apply Drugs · First Aid · Rx Drugs · Abused Drugs · Travel Vaccine

Figure 9: PharmAssist (Software Marketing)

HOME MEDICAL CARE

Medical costs continue to rise dramatically, resulting in part from the escalation in the complexity of medical treatment. Small wonder

electrical jobs that you can complete with a few tools and the program's tutorial.

insightful way can save you from those year-old waiting room *Newsweek* and *National Geographic* magazines.

The Mayo Clinic Health Library series from IVI Publishing presently consists of three programs—*Family Health Book*, *The Total Heart* and *Family Pharmacist*. With the *Family*

as far from orderly as it could possibly be. And more importantly, it was not just a book with photographs, but a companion to the narrative that always accompanied the page-turning. So how do you simulate that feeling, that ongoing family narrative, with impersonal electrons on a screen?

Well, with *Echo Lake* (Delrina) you do it by including a personal narrative along with the pictures, or the sounds, or the videos. Using visual and text cues, *Echo Lake* jogs the memory, bringing out stories about people and events, stories that you may have completely forgotten. It works so well, in fact, that it's not difficult to imagine *Echo Lake* as a teaching tool in writing classes. Indeed, the program teaches multimedia composition, too, since you're asked to bring together different kinds of media to tell your story. The warm, woody interface helps to put you in a reflective mood, or at least more reflective than you normally are sitting at your computer.

LEARNING OPPORTUNITIES

Learning on the computer would seem to be a natural. After all, you can proceed at your own pace, going back to previous material a second time for reinforcement when you need to. The computer's a teacher that never tires, never forgets, and hardly ever loses its temper (for all of you who were still wondering what a General Protection Fault really is!). Well, the truth is that learning on the computer succeeds only to the extent that the programmers are able to mask the inherent lack of true interaction. Sure, there's gobs of interactivity in most programs, at least interactivity as defined by computer standards. But so far, there have been no computer programs that can even approach the total immersion techniques of the best foreign language classes. Similarly, no music program as yet has the subtle judgment or the years of experience that even an average human music teacher can provide. At best, these learning programs should be thought of as augmenting other learning experiences. But at their best, they can provide foundations for learning that will accelerate the overall process exponentially.

It's a shame we can't all regress to childhood when we want to learn another language. Our brains are never nearly as adept, never as "programmable," as they are when we're young. Still, we all have the capacity to learn new languages after we cross the puberty line if we're given the right environment and lessons. Total immersion is accepted as the best way to learn a language, since it forces us to think in another language rather than translating a word in one language into its English equivalent. Unfortunately, most of us don't have the luxury of spending a year in France just so we can eventually order dinner in Paris with confidence. Computerized language-learning programs can overcome that, usually more successfully than a couple of hours a week in an evening class at the local community college. And there are a multitude of programs from which to choose.

Power Spanish (Bayware) takes a fairly traditional approach to language learning, using examples along with video clips of native speakers in a modified rote method. This is great for learning the basic phrases you need to get by on vacation in Spain, but doesn't allow to begin really thinking in Spanish. One feature many will appreciate is Voice Stretch, which lets you slow down a word or phrase (without lowering the

Figure 10: Echo Lake (Delrina)

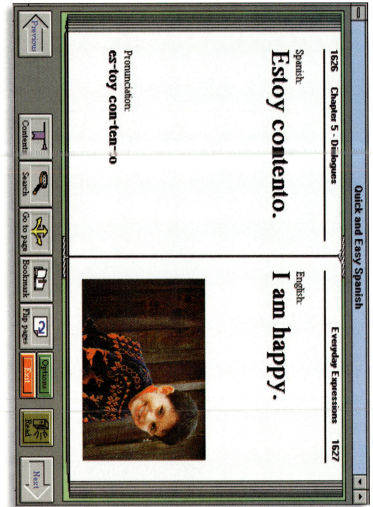

Spanish:
Estoy contento.

Pronunciation:
es·toy con·ten·o

English:
I am happy.

Figure 11: Quick and Easy Spanish (Softbooks)

pitch) so that you can hear subtle nuances. *Quick and Easy Spanish* (Softbooks) features a similar design, although more attention is paid, through video clips, to proper mouth, tongue, and lip movements, letting you master, among many other things, the troublesome "th" sound of Barcelona.

The Triple Play Plus series (Syracuse Language System) for English, French, German, Hebrew or Spanish, takes language acquisition to a higher level by actually listening to what you say and critiquing it. A feature called Automatic Speech Recognition can record your voice input, then give you immediate feedback on pronunciation. It's still not the same as interacting with another speaker, and it will only comment on your pronunciation, but even that's an improvement over some of the teachers you may recall from your high school days.

While learning French or German can be tough, at least you don't have to learn a new alphabet, or harder yet, a new way of speaking. Learning sign language, for example, requires a totally different mind-set because it's visual rather than aural. True, fingerspelling in sign language is based on the English alphabet, but basic American Sign Language (ASL) is much more than just fingerspelling. *The American Sign Language Dictionary* (HarperCollins Interactive) is not simply a dictionary. By extensive use of video, a great deal of the vast ASL vocabulary is presented in easy-to-understand fashion. The Hint feature is particularly fascinating, giving you both a mnemonic to remember a word and providing insight into why the word takes its form. Sign language etiquette is covered, and you can also

look up a word in English, French, German, Italian or Spanish.

There is, for now, no substitute for a good human teacher when learning a musical instrument. Yet PC software and hardware have progressed to the point where they can, at the

ASL   Go To   Dictionary

computer 2 (kəm pyoo′ tər), n.

The thumb of the right "C" hand touches the forehead or the temple, and the hand twists slightly up and down.

HINT Reference to the mind.

Figure 12: The American Sign Language Dictionary (HarperCollins Interactive)

very least, provide a good musical foundation. For years now, the *Miracle Piano System* (Mindscape) has brought basic keyboard skills to thousands using a mixture of rote learning and challenging games to test and reinforce the lessons. The program never forces you to go

understand, progress in computerizing guitar has been much more painstaking than for keyboard. So the few interactive programs that are available can still leave a lot to be desired. That doesn't mean you can't learn an instrument besides keyboards from a PC program, though.

faster than you're able, and in some areas, such as time keeping and fingering technique, it is a more exacting taskmaster than even the strictest knuckle-rapping human teacher. You can purchase the software as part of a package that includes an electronic keyboard which connects to your computer through the port on your sound card, or you can use any MIDI-capable (Musical Instrument Digital Interface) electronic keyboard instrument. *Piano Course* (Musicware) is another worthwhile program, albeit a bit more serious in its approach.

Interactively learning other instruments with the PC is not quite as straightforward as it is for piano study. Electronic versions of wind or string instruments are not nearly as common. Consider that keyboards—organs, pianos, harpsichords, etc.—are (along with drums) by nature the most computer-ready and essentially binary of instruments. A key is pressed or it isn't. A drum is struck or not. Other instruments involve techniques such as sliding fingers and special mouthing to achieve their various sounds. The electric guitar, however, comes after keyboards on the list of instruments enjoying an active, ongoing development of MIDI interfacing. Because the interface has to take an analog signal—in this case a metal string vibrating in the magnetic field of a guitar pickup— and convert it to a digital signal the computer can

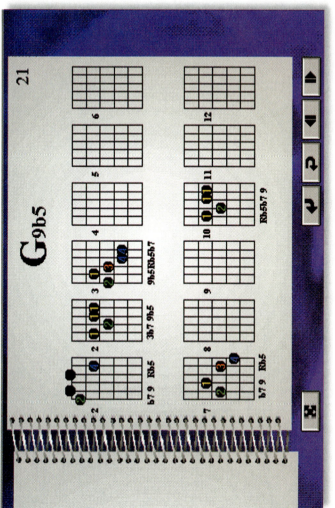

Learn to Play Guitar (Cambrix) uses a method already proven on another platform, the VCR. For years, guitarists and other instrumentalists have been making instructional videos that teach an instrument visually, with close-ups, slow motion and stop action, accompanied by the artist's own voice. *Learn to Play Guitar* takes short snips of playing, either lead lines or chords, and breaks them down. You can play a clip, try to emulate it on your guitar, then go back for more reinforcement. Guitarists used to learn their licks by slowing down vinyl records to make a complex line easier to copy. You can go them one better with this and several other programs which let you dissect even the trickiest pull-offs and double-stops.

Soloist (Ibis) is a more generalized music program that lets you use any instrument along with a microphone plugged into a Sound Blaster-compatible sound board. This is a pretty basic program, more a series of note-recognition exercises than anything else, but it does help develop your ear for relative pitch. Besides, it includes a chromatic tuner, and as any oboist knows, you can't be too in tune.

(RELATIVELY) PAINLESS VACATIONS

How many times have you heard the homily, "To know where you're going, you have to know where you've been?" Well, knowing both has become a lot easier in the past few years with the

Figure 13: Learn to Play Guitar (*Cambrix*)

goodies inside the Apple. You pick a couple of spots on the globe and the distance between them is calculated. Pretty slick for its day (did anyone ever think to check the accuracy?), but the new mapping programs are a lot slicker. The best of them not only tell you distance and time traveled at a given speed, but warn you of all speed limits along your route, along with any other traffic regulations you should know about. On top of that, they'll make a list of all attractions

Map'n'Go (DeLorme) is one of the most sophisticated trip planners that covers the continental US. You begin by entering your starting point and destination. If you're headed for a large city where there's a ten- or 15-mile difference between, say, the eastern and western city limits, you might want to opt for specifying a zip code, which gives you an extra measure of accuracy. With start and end points entered, the quickest route is displayed, with mileage, time and way points to consider. Using the Map-it! feature, you can add points of interest that are within a specified distance of your route (the default is five miles). Then, just print out the complete itinerary, pack the car—and don't forget to stop the paper delivery.

Atlas stalwart Rand McNally offers *TripMaker*, which expands its scope to include Canada and Mexico along with the US. It will also let you figure your costs for a given trip, and even though it can't take into account all the variations in gas, food and lodging costs, it's close enough that your nervous system will be prepared when the final tally does come due.

City Streets (Road Scholar) goes the others one better by including support for Global Satellite Positioning (GPS). Using the new PCMCIA GPS cards that work with most new laptop computers, you can access any one of 24 geostationary satellites. This link, along with the software, provides you with continuous information on your location, right down to seconds of latitude and longitude, as well as your direction of travel and speed. So if you still manage to get lost—try taking the train next time.

PERSONAL MULTIMEDIA

If there's one area where recent personal computer developments have resulted in truly

Figure 14: Map'n'Go (*DeLorme*)

within a given driving distance of your route, and tell you where to eat, sleep, gas up and use the rest room. About the only thing they can't do is give your kids a satisfactory answer to the question "Are we there yet?"

advent of sophisticated mapping programs for the PC. Anyone who's ever played around with a Macintosh (go ahead, admit it—we won't snitch on you) has probably had a ball with the little distance map feature hidden with all the other

Drawing Vs Painting

Just as with natural media, there's a big difference between a drawing and a photograph on a computer. A digital drawing is called a *vector-based* graphic because it is made up of lines of varying vectors. A square, for example, consists of four vectored lines, each of which possess attributes defining color, width, position, etc. Think of this as the equivalent of a traditional drawing.

A digital photograph, by contrast, is called a *bit-mapped* graphic because it is constructed of hundreds, thousands or even millions of tiny dots, or *pixels*. Each of these pixels is mapped, or linked, to one or more information bits which determine its location, intensity and so on.

Of course, you can have a photo of a painting or drawing. The essential distinction is that vector graphics are *descriptions* of how an image should be constructed on the fly—mathematical descriptions of position, size, texture, color and so on. They end up looking like cartoons, nice paddies or topographical maps—layers of superimposed zones. On the other hand, a bit-mapped graphic is a point-for-point copy of the original. It looks like a photograph—with considerable greater detail and shading than is possible via vector techniques.

Photos are more easily manipulated than drawings because they are comprised of individual pixels. When you apply change to a vectored-based graphic line, you affect the entire line. A bit-map ed line, on the other hand, can be edited pixel-by-pixel. A disadvantage of bit-mapped graphics is that, at extreme magnification, seemingly smooth lines and curves appear jagged. The same thing happens if you blow up a photo—you begin to see the noise, the "grain," within what seems, at normal viewing distance, a smooth, clear space. Vector-based graphics retain their smoothness at all sizes, which is why scalable computer fonts, such as PostScript fonts, are vector-based.

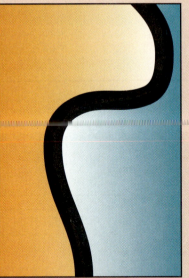

Figure 16: Vector-based curve

Figure 17: Bitmap-based curve

2D DRAWING AND PAINTING

It was the Macintosh which first showed just what a computer could do graphically. The PC was something of a late bloomer in this area, but today the two **platforms** are on pretty much equal footing from a graphics-creation standpoint. In fact, the PC is actually a bit ahead of the Mac as far as entry- and mid-level graphics programs are concerned.

The programs fall into two areas—drawing and painting—with some programs, such as Corel's *Graphics Suite*, covering both territories.

DRAWING PROGRAMS

There's a lot of competition between the creators of the top drawing programs, with the consumer being the real winner. With everyone playing "Can You Top This?" with both features and pricing, nearly every top program will do what you ask of it. Still, if there's one program that seems a bit ahead of the rest, it's probably *CorelDraw*, now in its fifth incarnation. Over the years, *CorelDraw*, with its ever-growing suite of tools, has become the Swiss army knife of graphics programs. While other programs are better at specific drawing tasks, *CorelDraw* is adequate for most all graphics activities, with additional modules for tracing, animation, graphing and presentations.

CorelDraw 5.0 itself lets you create extremely complex drawings, even if you have little or no innate drawing talent. By drawing freehand, combining so-called primitive shapes (square, circle, triangle, etc.), or using Corel's vast library of clip art (included with the

starting progress, it's multimedia. For years, we've all been able to see the results of multimedia development, primarily in computer games, but in other areas, too. Television and film, after something of a rough start, have taken computer-created visions to their collective heart. Just witness programs such as *Babylon 5* or the various *Star Trek* sagas, where nearly all special effects work has made the transition from hand-built models to computerized techniques. Even your local news program, with its spiffy flying logos and video effects, has embraced the new technology. But until recently, some parts of the multimedia experience, namely 3D rendering and animation, were the provinces of professionals with complex and expensive equipment. Other areas, such as multimedia authoring, grudgingly admitted the amateur, but only at a certain level. Even sound-editing programs, which had been around in various forms since the first generation of sound boards, didn't come close to offering the sophistication of their professional brethren. But—you guessed it—all that has changed.

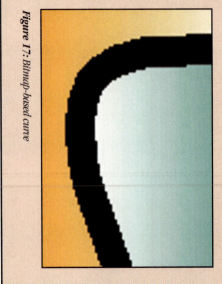

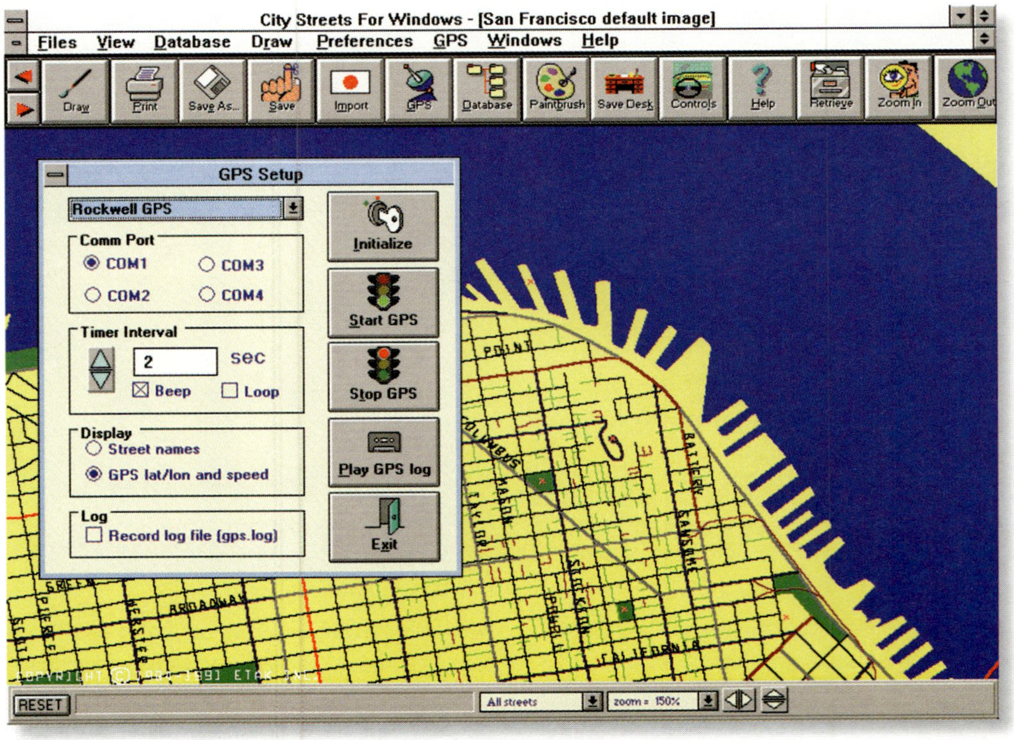

Figure 15: City Streets (Road Scholar)

mistakes. Beyond that, it can do something even *CorelDraw* can't: edit drawings with some of the same flexibility of photo-retouching programs. *SmartSketch* is perhaps the first program where the traditional demarcation line between drawing and photo-retouching has blurred.

Measured drawings are often required for technical applications. If you're interested in these, you might try *Designer* (Micrografx) or *Canvas* (Deneba). Both allow you to create complex designs which come with their own dimensioning information. *Canvas* even has a Mouse Cursor option that customizes the way the cursor reacts in certain situations involving line dimensions.

PHOTO-RETOUCHING PROGRAMS

Photo-retouching programs have become so numerous that it really is hard to tell all the players without a scorecard. It seems every graphics company worth its salt has some sort of photo program, although many refer to their offerings with the somewhat more nebulous appellation, "Image Enhancement Utility." Many of these programs can certainly do amazing things with digitized photos, but most are equally useful for just painting or drawing.

Ask any digital artist to name just one paint or image-enhancement program and probably eight out of ten will say Adobe's *Photoshop*. It's hard to recall when *Photoshop* wasn't at the top of the graphics heap, and its designers have worked hard to keep it there despite some really tough competition. There is a suite of excellent, professional-quality graphics tools included, and dozens of plug-in filters (third-party add-on software) add new capabilities to *Photoshop*. *Photoshop* can modify photos radically—it probably signals an end to the old adage, "Seeing is believing." Remember the flap a few years ago about the *TV Guide* cover that had Oprah Winfrey's head attached to Ann-Margaret's body? This sort of optical sleight-of-hand is child's play for *Photoshop*.

There are other graphics applications that will perform many of *Photoshop*'s tricks as well as a few unique ones of their own. *Picture Publisher* (Micrografx) features nearly all the tools of *Photoshop*, is less expensive and may be easier for the average user to learn. In fact, it beat *Photoshop* to the line in featuring layered editing, which permits the artist to work on an object in a picture without affecting other parts of that picture (though *Photoshop* now includes this faculty too).

Picture Publisher offers an extensive built-in set of image-enhancement filters. With just a few clicks, you can turn an average digitized photo into an exciting charcoal drawing or pastel. After accessing the Image/Effects menu, a list appears

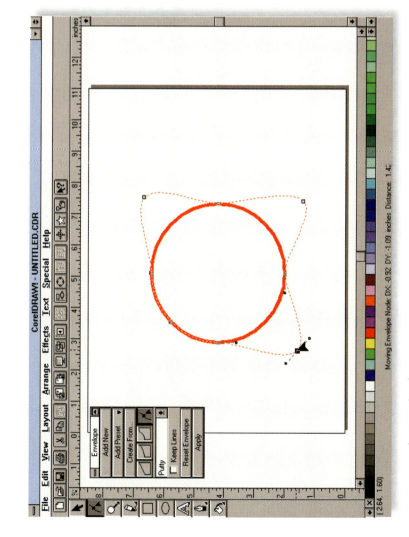

Figure 18: CorelDraw 5.0 (Corel)

program), you build and modify your drawings. Drawings can then be edited in a number of ways, including extrusion for 3D effects, and enveloping, where a figure's shape can be altered. Node editing places a series of points along the perimeter of a drawing, which can then be

perhaps we might consider *SmartSketch* (FutureWave) as a Honda Accord with an automatic transmission. It'll still get you there, maybe not with as much style but with a lot less work. The drawing program for people who can't draw, *SmartSketch* takes some of the features of

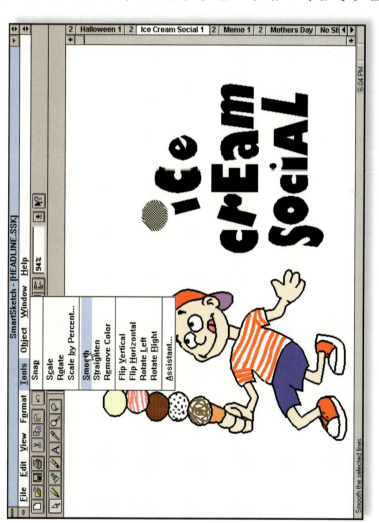

Figure 19: SmartSketch (FutureWave)

manipulated individually or in combinations to produce new shapes.

If *CorelDraw 5.0* can be likened to the Ferrari of drawing programs—glamorous, with lots of power but a manual transmission—then

the more sophisticated programs—in particular the smoothing and shaping capabilities—and automates them. So when you draw something resembling a circle, the program figures out what you were really aiming for and corrects your

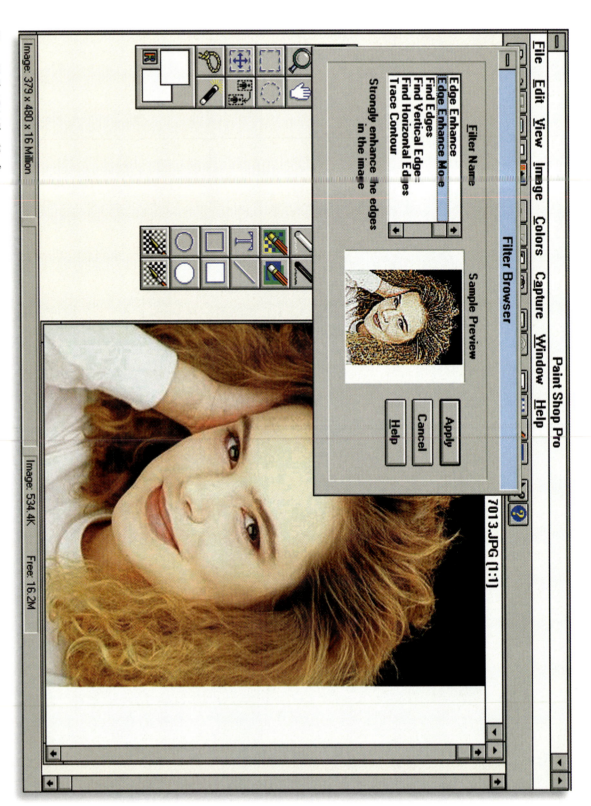

Figure 20: PhotoPaint Plus (*Corel*)

along with a small preview window that lets you see the changes in your picture before you apply them to the full photo. There are many user-adjustable settings, too. Using the charcoal filter, for example, you can specify the length of your strokes as well as their density. Often a very detailed original photo will turn into a jumbled mess with these filters, so until you've got your feet wet, it may be best to use simple pictures, such as portraits. Speaking of portraits, there's actually one filter that overlays a dark mask around the periphery of a picture, a mask with the center cut out. The edges of the cutout are feathered, creating the look of an old-fashioned portraiture. To further enhance the feel of an old photograph, you can use the colorizing tool to give a sepia tint to the photo.

One of *Picture Publisher's* most useful features is its unlimited Undo. You can go back through a list of all the actions you've taken against a photo, and selectively eliminate any action that you now regret—without having to start over from scratch. It also has a useful macro recorder and a customizable button bar. *PhotoShop* will doubtless take notice of these excellent features and we'll see them in a future version of that program as well.

PhotoPaint Plus (Corel) is an even less expensive alternative to *Photoshop* that will do the job for probably 90% of all amateur computer artists. One of *PhotoPaint Plus's* strongest features is its Brush Management module. Brushes in computer paint programs can be just about anything you want. There are, of course, the standard brush shapes, but often these can't easily produce the effect you're seeking. *PhotoPaint* and most other paint programs will let you create your own brushes, either from scratch or from part of an image. You could even type out your name, turn it into a brush and paint with it.

At the low end in price, though certainly not in capabilities, is *Paint Shop Pro* (JASC), a very robust paint program that also functions as a nifty image-management utility. You have practically every tool the big boys have, along with a generous collection of filters. You can do quick and simple batch conversions of graphics files, a handy thing when you have several images that are, for example, in the TIFF format but need to be compressed to GIF files for quick uploading via modem.

While nearly all the programs covered in this article are Windows-based, there is at least one DOS-based program that deserves consideration. *Neopaint* (Neosoft) is a nicely executed collection of painting tools that is a far cry from the original DOS painting programs such as *Paintbrush* and *Deluxe Paint.* With *Neopaint,* you can do the requisite photo enhancement, plus there are some unique features like an extrusion utility, which gives a three-dimensional look to text.

Finally, for all of us who suspect that somewhere down deep we possess a bit of artistic talent but just don't know how to bring it to the surface, there's *Dabbler* (Fractal Design). With the same approach as its more sophisticated sibling, *Painter* (Fractal Design), *Dabbler* uses the computer's resources to create a "natural

Personal Image Scanning

By Richard Mansfield

Nothing adds more to letters, invitations, flyers and other desktop published documents than photos. Until now, your only options were touchy hand-scanners or expensive flatbed scanners. With Storm Software's new EasyPhoto Reader, adding photos is a breeze.

Storm Software has come up with a clever solution to a common problem. If you want to add a photo of your family to paper letters or email, you have to scan the photo. Scanning transforms a photo into a digital format that is then stored as a file on your hard drive and can be inserted into a document. Unfortunately, until now hand-scanning was a difficult process: you had to slowly pull the scanner across the photo in a perfectly straight line and at a constant rate of speed. This was quite tricky.

Now, though, Storm has developed a motorized hand scanner and it works quite well. You just place your color photograph on the scanner bed and press the Start button. The only adjustment you have to make to the Reader is a light/dark wheel you can use to compensate for photos that are under- or overexposed. The Reader then slowly and accurately feeds the photo under its scanner, resulting in a perfectly scanned digitized image. The digital file is a high-quality 24-bit, 600 DPI (1200 enhanced) graphic that you can then simply drag and drop into any text document in any contemporary word processor. (If you have an older word processor, you might have to copy and paste rather than drag and drop.)

Once scanned, your photo is automatically added to a "Gallery" that looks like a film strip. The EasyPhoto software includes this effective photo-database program that's both easy to use and yet fully capable of managing a large number of images.

Making it Easy

Fortunately for those of us who don't have graphic arts degrees, the EasyPhoto software also makes it simple to scan, store and retouch photos. The software includes a special built-in tone-balancing feature that automatically brightens dark areas within any photo and also helps reduce any noise. And if a photo has a scratch, you can usually get rid of it with a single mouse-click on the "Remove Scratch" button.

Ever been plagued with those pink lights that seem to appear in people's eyes when you take their picture, making them look like smiling zombies? No problem. EasyPhoto has a button for that too: Remove Red-eye. And if you really like the results of your retouching efforts, there's even an option on the software's File menu that

instantly makes your picture into Windows wallpaper.

The automation and simplicity isn't limited to scanning and reading. Files are saved in compressed (JPG) format so you avoid eating up your hard drive space with large

Figure 1: You can collect photos from disk, cd, the EasyPhoto Reader, or a digital camera, then add them to the "Gallery" database shown on the right.

image files. Also, when you go to print a photo, EasyPhoto's "ClearPrint" technology checks your particular printer and automatically makes adjustments for optimized results—you'll get the best quality that your printer can produce.

Additional Features

EasyPhoto works with Windows 3.1 or 95. You can create custom computer slide-shows, and provide captions for each photo. There's "viewer" software that allows you to send a photo collection to your aunt so she can see the slide-show without any effort on her part. You can even turn a favorite photo into a personal screen-saver.

Any drawbacks? Like any hand-scanner, you can't scan huge photos. You're limited to photos five inches wide or less. Also, you can't use the motorized scan on a graphic from a book, magazine or newspaper unless you cut it out—a single page must be fed into the unit. Nonetheless, the scanner is detachable from the motorized base—so you can then use it as an ordinary hand-scanner.

Setup is a snap: just plug the scanner into your printer (parallel) port on the back of your computer, then plug the printer into the scanner plug. It only takes a minute—no internal expansion card is used. At $269 for the motorized scanner hardware (including EasyPhoto software and 100 digitized images) or $69 for the software alone, EasyPhoto offers a complete digital photo solution, making it possible for anyone to get high-quality results effortlessly.

EasyPhoto, from Storm Technology, is available from retailers nationwide.

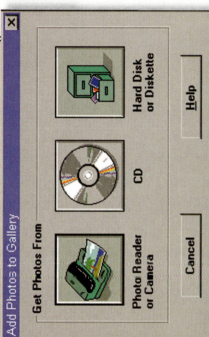

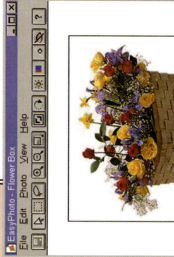

Figure 2: The Photo WorkShop retouching program has provisions for cropping (cutting off unwanted areas), resizing, rotating, flipping, and adjusting brightness, contrast and color.

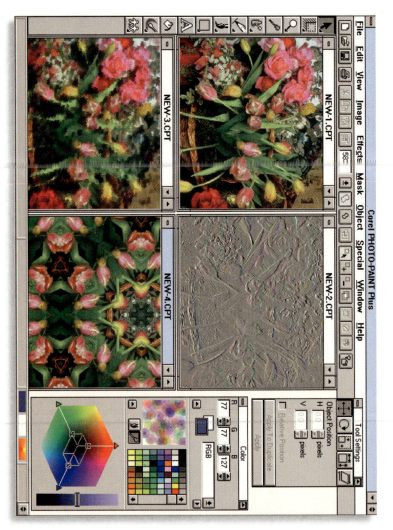

Figure 21: Paint Shop Pro (JASC)

media" environment. The main screen consists of little "wooden" drawers like you might find in an artist's studio, which contain different media (paint, chalk, pencil, crayon, etc.) along with "natural" tools like a gum eraser. On top of that, you can select, for example, textured paper for authentic-looking charcoal drawings. Even the sounds of an artist's studio are there, so that when you're using a pencil, you can hear that little "scritch, scritch" as you draw. Combine this with a good digitized drawing tablet (which, in fact, you might want to consider for good results with any drawing or painting program) and you have the artistic experience encapsulated, minus the turpentine aroma. The program also includes a tutorial that leads you through the basics of drawing and painting, so that you'll soon have no need for canned clip art—right?

3D ART

The three-dimensional look has taken computer graphics by storm. It seems as though every game these days is rendered in 3-D, though sometimes with mixed results. And with three-dimensional rendering an integral part of the virtual reality vision, 3D art applications will only continue to proliferate. But is there a place in the 3D world for the average computer user? Until recently, the answer would have been a resounding no.

Traditionally, 3D programs were among the most difficult applications to master in the PC universe. By its very nature, three-dimensional art is considerably more complex than two-dimensional art, and the programs to create 3D have mirrored that. Fortunately, that has changed to a great degree with the introduction of new,

more intuitive applications which are not only easier to use, but less expensive as well.

One good one is 3D F/X (Asymetrix), a streamlined rendering and animation program that dispenses with all the jargon about splines, metaballs, bump mapping and what have you.

import graphics from other paint programs, or access the extensive catalog of pre-designed objects which range from common household items to human figures, from ships to planes to cars—even the Sydney Opera House. Add your own background, or again, select one of the catalogued scenes, then set up your lighting (one of the most intuitive aspects of the entire program) and, if it's to be an animated sequence, overlay one of the many animation paths included with the program. Then let the program render (build) the final object or animation. It's a simple program that is nonetheless very sophisticated, so even grizzled 3D vets can find a great deal to enjoy in 3D F/X.

If you'd like to get a fuller taste of what industrial-strength 3D software is like, but don't want to bankrupt either your wallet or your patience, you might take a look at Imagine L/T (Impulse). It's an only-slightly simplified version of an industry-standard 3D program. While not nearly as easy to use as 3D F/X, it's not impossibly difficult either, and you may soon find yourself appreciating the greater flexibility you have with this program. It works the way most of the high-level programs do, in a wireframe mode with separate windows for side, top and front views. There are several modules within the program for designing the basic object, modifying it, applying

Figure 22: Dabbler (Fractal Design)

Instead, you just drag and drop objects (not wireframe representations but solid objects) and effects onto the screen and let the program do the hard stuff. You can create objects from the basic shapes included (sphere, cylinder, cube, etc.),

attributes (such as a metal or wood surface texture) and then creating an animation sequence.

Finally, if you have the money, trueSpace 2 (Caligari) will do just about anything you can ask of a 3D application, and do it all without

control was minimal at best, usually involving volume and perhaps some effect on timbre (the quality of tone that distinguishes a trumpet from a piano when both are playing the same note). The newest programs, however, give you the power of a studio recording engineer. And they work marvelously in conjunction with the latest 16-bit sound boards.

You can input voice (from a microphone) or music (either analog-to-digital sound conversions, CD input or direct MIDI) to be recorded directly into your hard drive, where it can then be manipulated by your sound-editing program. Just remember that even a few seconds of sampled sound can result in a huge file on your hard drive and make sure you have plenty of free disk space available.

Because sound files are relatively easy to manipulate, there are dozens of applications on the market that will do the job for you. They have, in fact, all begun to look alike, differing mainly in the number of features and the fineness of control they allow you over your sound files. Although there are dozens of audio file standards, most PC applications work primarily with wave files (.wav), a Microsoft file standard which has become more or less *de facto* for the entire industry, and with General MIDI (.mid) files. With most programs, the file is visually displayed as a waveform, although the displays with the low-end programs are useful for judging a wave's amplitude (volume), but not its frequency (pitch) or actual waveform (sound characteristic).

Sound Forge (Sonic) is representative of the editing capabilities found in today's mid-level programs. While the interface is little different from dozens of other applications, some of its editing options are unique. Any editing program will give you a fairly decent waveform representation at normal magnification, but sometimes you need to magnify the image to see and edit tiny sections of a sound wave. The waveform representation will often break apart into near-meaningless dots, making accurate cutting and pasting, for example, impossible. Sophisticated applications like *Sound Forge* prevent this breakup.

Most of *Sound Forge*'s features can also be found in the Audio Editor module of *MediaStudio Pro* (Ulead Systems). With this package, you can take a wave file of music or voice and modify it in a number of ways. There is, for example, near-infinite control of echo, so that you can range from giving a dry-sounding file a bit of "presence," to adding enough stadium echo

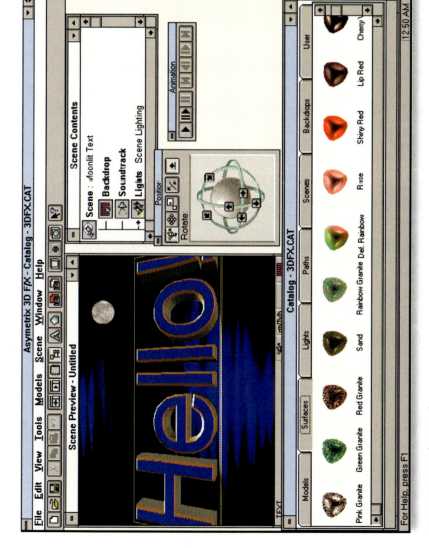

Figure 23: 3D F/X (*Asymetrix*)

terminally taxing the patience of the user. For a high-level program, the interface is remarkably intuitive, and the results will have you feeling you can give Industrial Light and Magic a run for its money. This program produces

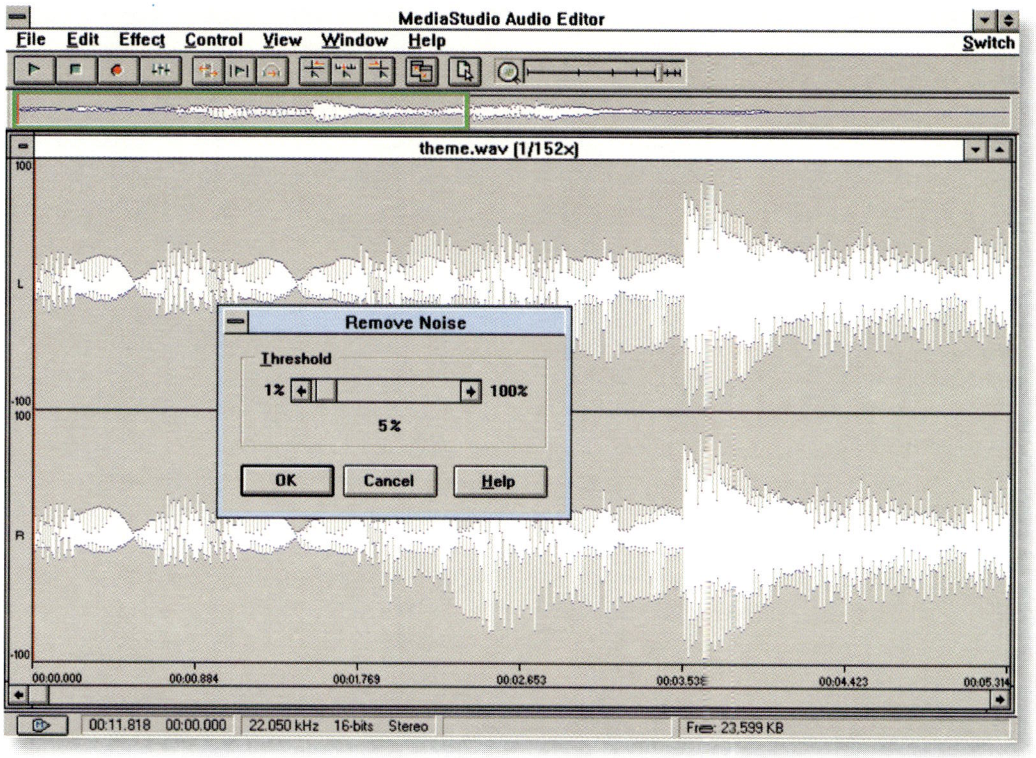

What *PhotoShop* is to photo-retouching, *trueSpace 2* is to 3D art—they both set the industry standard and are the choice of many professionals.

Figure 24: MediaStudio Pro's Audio Editor (*Ulead Systems*)

professional-quality results yet the process is generally painless and understandable even for the novice. As well as being extremely flexible, it also includes sets of extraordinary textures.

SOUND EDITING

Since the appearance of the first sound boards, computer users have used programs that offered some control over sound. Early on, the

to rival Lou Gehrig's famous farewell speech. Or perhaps you have a voice recording on tape which you've converted to digital form, and you discover that the tape hiss you barely noticed on the original recording has come along for the ride and is a lot more obvious than it once was. With Audio Editor's Noise Reduction menu, you can cut out most of that hiss while leaving the recording sounding sharp and clear. Some care should be taken to avoid overdoing noise reduction, though, because too much will often clip parts of the primary signal, leaving your speaker with an odd case of hiccups.

VIDEO EDITING

Of all the aspects of multimedia, video is undoubtedly the least standardized today. True, new standards pop up in other areas from time to time, but you can still be fairly certain that, a year or two from now, most graphic artists will be saving to TIFF files, most 3D artists will still be working with DXF files, and most audio editors will have hard drives full of Wave (.wav) and MIDI (.mid) files. Unfortunately, the computer video world doesn't yet enjoy that sort of stability. There are standards, of course—such as the AVI (Intel Video for Windows) and MOV (Apple Quicktime) formats, but even they change specifications with disconcerting regularity. And that's without considering the dozens of

compression codec schemes (code/decode) that programmers have developed to manage the storage and presentation of video files. The problem is that no one has yet perfected a compression scheme that the video industry will accept. If computer audio files are considered huge, then video files must be on the order of gargantuan. Ten seconds of video can eat up 30MB or more of disk space, and that's just a tiny image running at a jittery 15 frames per second.

Still, video editing continues to grow, and with the right program you can join in. If Adobe's Photoshop is the bellwether of the graphics community, then the company's Premiere enjoys that same reputation among video editors. There are indeed many programs that will out-perform Premiere in selected areas, and there are prohibitively expensive professional editing suites that will put it to shame. All that aside, Premiere still ranks as the most effective overall editing program for the great majority of computer video fans.

At first sight you'll probably be intimidated by all the editing modules and options, but it's really a very simple program to use. If you have a video capture board, you can bring in video directly from a VCR or camcorder. The board converts the video signal to a digital format which you can then edit. Imagine that you have two or three clips that you'd like to splice together seamlessly. Once the files are loaded you can

select a transition—say, a wipe or a fade—and paste it onto your editing board in Premiere. The video clips can be placed in separate channels, allowing you to lay the beginning of one clip over the ending of another, resulting in a smooth fade from the first clip to the second. Audio tracks can also be introduced, edited and synchronized with the video, and you can overlay other studio tricks such as floating titles or color changes.

If Premiere's price tag scares you (and it just might), take a look at MediaStudio Pro (Ulead Systems), a multimedia editing suite that's built around the very capable

Video Editor. This program can do nearly everything Premiere can, if perhaps not quite as smoothly. Still, it has more than enough features to satisfy most amateur video producers, including a library of transitions that can add an expert's touch to any home video. A further consideration is that Video Editor is part of a full suite that includes audio, graphics and morphing editors which you can switch among easily.

AUTHORING

Once you've finished acquiring and polishing all your images, sounds and movies, what will you do with them? Repeat showings of that short video clip—even with the neat iris-out transition—can get old very quickly. Well, once you've come to this point, you're ready to tie all your creations together and make them say something. And you do that with an authoring program.

Authoring is another one of those terms that gets thrown around and applied to any number of seemingly different activities. In fact, an authoring program be anything from a simple application to produce slide shows to a full-blown authoring suite that you can use to create the next Myst. But the best authoring systems share a few important features: they accommodate a wide range of types of media, they offer tools to integrate these media and they produce a smoothly running finished product.

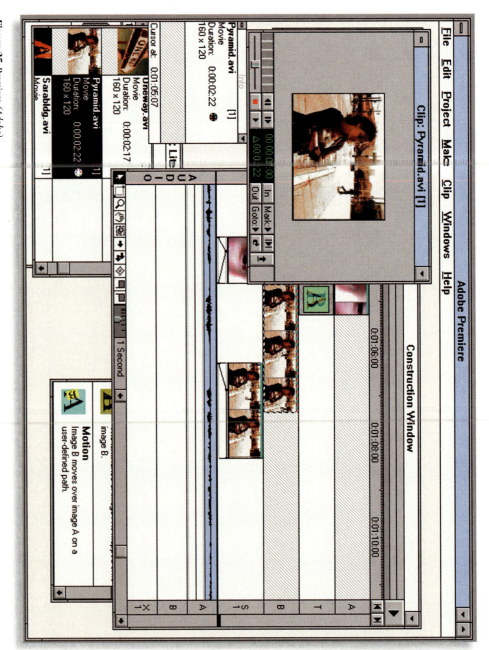

Figure 25: Premiere *(Adobe)*

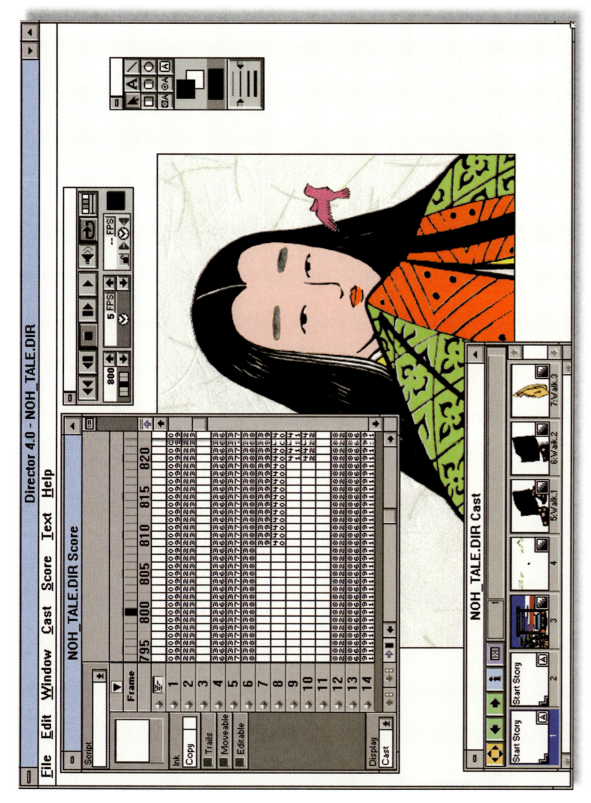

Figure 26: Director 4.0 (*Macromedia*)

Interactive (HSC) is probably as representative of the state-of-the-art as any program in the entry-level market. First off, it benefits from some impressive lineage, taking its basic system from *IconAuthor*, one of the top applications in multimedia authoring. As you might have guessed, both *IconAuthor* and *Interactive* use icons to design multimedia presentations. You're supplied with an extensive library of icons which cover everything from simple pauses and transitions to advanced audio and video. You might, for example, want to design a presentation that uses some video you have. All you need do is find the Video icon from the library and drag it onto the screen. The screen will show the different "pages" of an application, along with whatever items or actions are associated with each page. The whole thing ends up resembling a flow chart, which makes debugging a glitchy application a lot easier. You also have access to some fairly nice audio- and image-editing tools, eliminating the need to drop out of your authoring program to do a little touch-up work on a photo.

While *Interactive* uses the icon/flowchart method, the ubiquitous *Director 4.0* (Macromedia) resorts to a film metaphor. You place the various elements, called Actors, onto *Director 4.0*'s stage. You "direct" the entrance, exit and actions of the Actors using a timeline that's synchronized to the stage. This method is not nearly as intuitive or most people as icon-based applications are, but it offers a more flexible way of editing if you're willing to scale the learning curve. The fact that so many of today's multimedia applications are created with *Director 4.0* speaks well for its capabilities. On the other hand, it does cost about three times as much as *Interactive*.

As with graphics software, capable DOS multimedia authoring applications are rare. You can, however, produce some very acceptable presentations using *Neobook* (Neosoft). From a very simple interface, you build pages for your presentation. To create a button that will display a picture, play a sound or display some scrolling text, you simply draw a picture of your button. A menu then pops up, offering you a number of actions you can apply to that button. You can

even chain together several actions. *Neobook* is about as straightforward as authoring gets, plus you have the advantage of working in DOS which, in some instances, is still less of a hassle than using Windows (at least prior to Windows 95).

IT'S ONLY THE SURFACE

We've hardly scratched the surface. The number of things you can do with your computer increases almost continually as new products are introduced while other products are improved. The problem these days is not whether you'll find enough interesting things to do with your computer. No, your problem might well be finding the willpower to occasionally get up from the computer and go for a walk. ✪

Gary M. Meredith is the former CD-ROM Editor for both PC Gamer and CD-ROM Today magazines. He is a freelance writer as well as a multimedia applications developer, and recently authored a strategy guide for the MicroProse game Colonization.

249

PERSONAL FINANCIAL SOFTWARE, STOCK QUOTES AND RESEARCH

By Jason R. Rich

Your PC provides access to an incredible variety of software and information resources for investment research and stock tracking. This article will help you get started.

If all you needed to strike it rich on Wall Street was a personal computer, a modem and some financial software, everyone who made an investment would become a millionaire. While the financial software available to PC users is as powerful as what many professional financial analysts and stock brokers use, having these tools at your disposal doesn't give you the knowledge needed to become a financial wizard.

Before making any type of investment, it's vital that you have a strong understanding of how various types of investments work. Unfortunately, there are no quick answers when it comes to learning the fundamentals of investing. Time, research and patience are required, but using a PC can make the learning process easier and far less time-consuming. And a computer does offer many long-term benefits when it comes to managing your investments and portfolio.

Before investing, carefully read the prospectus and all related information, ask questions of the salesperson or broker, and look to independent research firms, financial advisors, investment clubs and financial publications for additional advice, especially if you're a novice investor.

When it comes to investing and personal finance, your computer can be used for a variety of tasks, including:

- Portfolio Management
- Online Trading
- Obtaining Access to a Brokerage or Mutual Fund Account
- Research
- Fundamental and Technical Analysis
- Personal Finance / Electronic Banking

Before you purchase any type of financial software, define your financial goals and determine what types of investments you plan on making. You might want to consult a financial analyst, accountant or stock broker when making these decisions. However, if, like millions of Americans, you want to dabble in the stock market or invest in mutual funds, your computer will prove to be a powerful tool for helping you identify and analyze investment opportunities, make actual trades and manage your portfolio.

INVESTING USING ONLINE SERVICES

The types of financial services available on the commercial online services, such as Prodigy, America Online, for example, offers an option called Personal Finance (*Keyword: Finance*) which acts as a gateway to hundreds of easy-to-use financial services, news sources and databases.

As part of an AOL membership, users have instant access to the service's financial newsstand which offers articles from a variety of financial publications, such as *Investor's Business Daily, The New York Times* business

AMERICA ONLINE

The Main Menu of America Online, for example, offers an option called Personal Finance (*Keyword: Finance*) which acts as a gateway to hundreds of easy-to-use financial services, news sources and databases.

America Online (AOL), CompuServe, The Microsoft Network and Dow Jones News/Retrieval are extremely diverse. Some are designed specifically for the novice investor, while other services and databases are highly specialized, cost a considerable amount of money to access and are targeted to professional investors. For novice investors interested in using a PC for investing, an online service is, in fact, the best place to begin. These services are available 24 hours a day, seven days a week, using a PC equipped with a modem. And most of the information a novice is likely to want is included in the service's basic price.

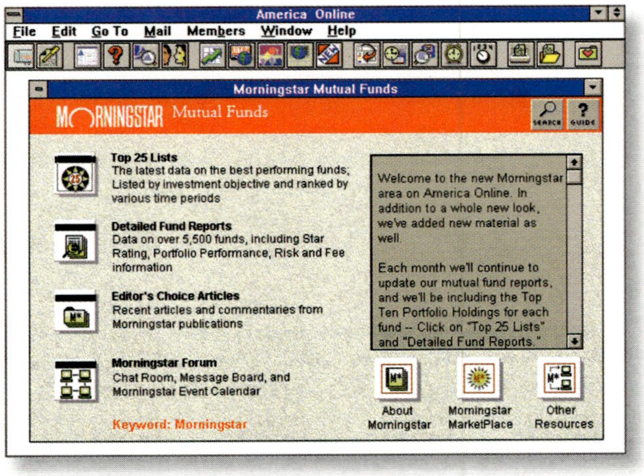

Figure 1: From AOL's Personal Finance area, users can access all types of financial information, raw financial data and investment-related services. AOL offers an easy-to-use graphic interface with point-and-click icons.

Figure 2: In AOL, mutual fund investors have instant access to Morningstar's complete database of mutual fund rankings, along with other services offered by Morningstar (Keyword: Morningstar)

section, *Business Week* and *Worth* magazine. By accessing the Quotes and Portfolios area, it's possible to obtain stock quotes on a 15-minute delay, manage a stock or mutual fund portfolio online, obtain market news, or look up specific stock symbols.

While on AOL, you can also access the Research module of the Personal Finance area, and obtain raw historical financial data and up-to-the-minute news, along with other business-related information. If you're interested in discussing your investment strategies with other AOL members, there are a variety of forums available on AOL (and on all of the popular online services) that offer live chat rooms, message boards and information on a wide range of topics, ranging from general investment discussions to technical analysis and tax questions.

COMPUSERVE

CompuServe also caters to personal investors with its large and ever-growing list of resources available online. Using CompuServe's WinCim software, this information is just a few keystrokes away after choosing the Finance option from CompuServe's main menu. CompuServe divides its online financial information into two categories. The first category falls under the Basic Financial Products heading and is included in the basic membership fee for the service. Additional features, under the Extended Financial Products heading, are available for an additional charge.

PRODIGY

The financial information offered on Prodigy includes stock quotes (delayed 15 minutes), and charts (updated throughout the day) of the key economic indicators. Dow Jones Company News offers the last seven days' worth of articles on publicly traded companies. The PC Financial Network is Prodigy's online discount broker. Personal portfolio management is also possible on Prodigy using the Quote Track service. This feature allows users to retrieve stock quotes, calculate the market value and gain or loss of a portfolio. Along with this information, Prodigy offers access to the latest news stories.

Like AOL and CompuServe, Prodigy is an excellent service for casual investors who want access to news and financial information, but don't want to pay high fees for specialized information.

DOW JONES

Dow Jones News/Retrieval Service (DJNS) is Dow Jones & Company's online source of business news and financial information, which includes over 1,750 online resources for corporate managers, financial professionals, personal investors and professional information searchers. DJNS offers an electronic library of more than 1,400 full-text international, national and regional publications, including *The Wall Street Journal* (domestic and international editions), and *Barron's*.

DJNS also features news from Dow Jones' real-time newswires: *Dow Jones News*, *Dow Jones International News Services*, *Capital Markets Report*, and *Professional Investor Report and Federal Filings*. In addition, DJNS carries *PR Newswire*, *Business Wire*, *Canada Newswire*, *Japan Economic Newswire* and *Investext*

reports. You'll also find business and general services, such as online travel information.

This service can be extremely useful for obtaining current and historical financial data and news you might need. This information can be sorted and gathered based on your specific search criteria, so you won't be bogged down with information which isn't pertinent to your specific interests.

DJNS is designed for those who are serious about business, finance and investing. The cost of the full service is higher than other major online services, but the information offered on this service is specialized and much of it isn't available elsewhere.

The Dow Jones News/Retrieval service can be accessed using almost any telecommunications software. Dow Jones & Company also offers several specialized software packages designed for use with their online service.

MARKET MONITOR

Between 8:01 p.m. and 6:00 a.m. weekdays, and all day on weekends and holidays, the Dow Jones Market Monitor service is the least expensive way to access portions of the Dow Jones News/Retrieval service. For a flat monthly fee of $29.95, users have unlimited access to the many Dow Jones News/Retrieval services.

The Market Monitor (after hours) plan provides daily and historical news and quotes, forecasts and analyses via a personal computer and a modem. Under this plan, investors can access news from five Dow Jones newswires, *The Wall Street Journal*, *Barron's* and more than 500 other publications, plus obtain quotes for all of the companies listed on the major US stock exchanges (including quotes for more than 3,900 mutual funds). Financial "snap shots" of securities including earnings per share, P/E ratios and yields are also available using the Market Monitor plan.

Most investors and business people read *The Wall Street Journal*, *Investor's Business Daily*, *Barron's* or another financial newspaper to keep up on the latest trends and business news. The drawback to these traditional publications is that you have to flip through the entire publication and find the articles that are of direct interest to you.

PERSONAL JOURNAL

Now, Windows users can have a electronic financial publication created for them each day that caters to their specific interests. *Personal Journal* is the first financial newspaper published for a circulation of one—you. This customizable edition of *The Wall Street Journal* allows you to read editorials, business and worldwide news summaries, and full-text news

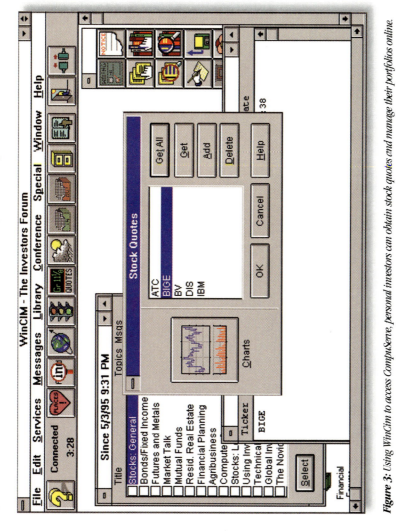

Figure 3: Using WinCIM to access CompuServe, personal investors can obtain stock quotes and manage their portfolios online.

HERE ARE JUST A FEW POPULAR WEB SITES WORTH EXPLORING:

Figure 4: Whether you're heading for the ice cream parlor, an island in the Caribbean, or just exercising your curiosity, corporate home pages can provide a lot of information... and just plain fun.

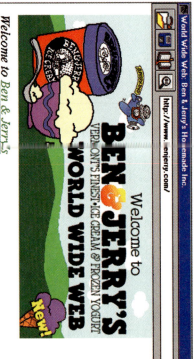

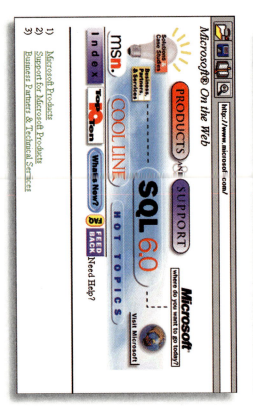

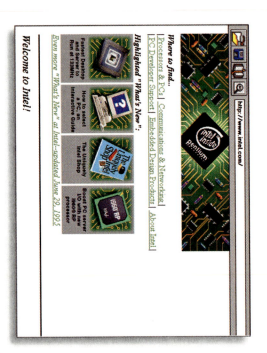

articles that relate to topics you pre-select. You can choose the companies, stocks and mutual funds you want to track, and read everything that pertains to those selections each day right on your computer screen.

Personal Journal is updated continuously and is available for $12.95 per month (which includes one edition each business day; additional updates during the day are $.50 each). Special software, Windows and a 9600bps (or faster) modem are required to receive *Personal Journal* on your PC. To subscribe, call (800) 291-9382. A similar service, called NewsPage, is available on the Internet (http://www.newspage.com). NewsPage filters over 500 news sources and categorizes the news stories and articles based on topics that you pre-select.

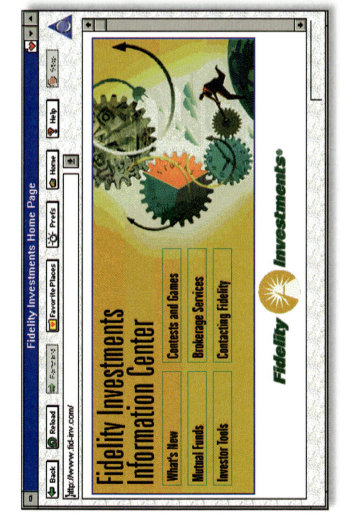

Figure 5: From Fidelity's World Wide Web site, computer users can learn about investment opportunities and mutual fund offerings from Fidelity Investments.

$$$ ON THE INTERNET

As if the financial data, information and resources available on the commercial online services aren't enough, the Internet and World Wide Web offer dozens of sites that are of interest to investors. The corporate home pages like those shown in Figure 4 offer some general information. Companies concerned with investing, like Fidelity Investments, also have an online presence, on both the commercial services and on the Internet. With access to Fidelity's World Wide Web site (http://www.fid-inv.com), users can analyze data on the company's mutual fund offerings, order prospectuses and applications, learn about investment opportunities, and use online worksheets to analyze personal investment goals.

SOFTWARE FROM YOUR BROKER

Several well-known discount brokerage firms, like Fidelity Investments and Charles Schwab & Co., offer stand-alone software packages that are designed to be easy-to-use, yet extremely powerful tools for personal investors.

FIDELITY INVESTMENTS

Fidelity's On-Line XPress (FOX) 2.1 software is a DOS-based program that provides computer users access to their Fidelity accounts, plus allows them to perform actual online stock or mutual fund trades (with a 10% commission discount). Users connect directly to Fidelity's computer system and can perform a variety of portfolio management tasks. The *FOX* software retails for $49.95, and is available directly from Fidelity Investments by calling (800) 544-0246.

CHARLES SCHWAB

Charles Schwab's *StreetSmart 2.0* package is Windows-based and offers its customers many of the same features as Fidelity's *FOX* software. Using the Research module, the *StreetSmart* software acts as a gateway for connecting to specialized online services, such as Dow Jones News/Retrieval or Standard & Poor's MarketScope and Company Reports. Users can buy and sell stocks, mutual funds, bonds and options; obtain market news; monitor account balances; create performance graphs; print performance reports for a portfolio or specific investment; and access information about Schwab's other products and services.

StreetSmart 2.0 for Windows is priced at $39.00, and is available directly from Charles Schwab & Co. by calling (800) 334-4455.

COMMERCIAL SOFTWARE

Even with stand-alone software packages designed for investors, you'll still need to import raw real-time, delayed and/or historical financial data (i.e., stock quotes, etc.). This data can be obtained from newspapers and entered manually, or you can access an online service, like those described above, that provides financial data live or on a delay. There are also devices that connect to a PC and receive financial information sent via radio waves. Since some software is only compatible with specific data providers, it's a good idea to determine what financial software you'll be using, then decide what raw data you'll require, and the best way to obtain it.

STOCKTRACKER

If your brokerage doesn't offer its own software package, one easy-to-use portfolio management package for Windows is available from Virgil Corporation. For casual and novice investors who have begun building up their portfolio, but do not have the need to perform their own technical analysis, *StockTracker* helps investors manage their portfolio easily and inexpensively.

Figure 6: Use this site to locate public companies with their own Web pages.

StockTracker is designed to work exclusively with CompuServe to download financial data. This package uses the standard Windows point-and-click interface, and allows investors to automatically obtain stock quotes, company news, reports, and charts from CompuServe.

According to Virgil Corporation's president, Robert Simon, "Investors want late breaking news,

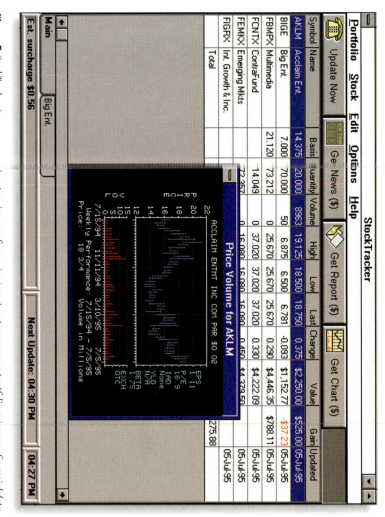

Figure 7: *StockTracker is an easy and inexpensive way for novice investors to manage a portfolio using real financial data provided by CompuServe.*

information on price swings, quick access to financial data and more control over their portfolios. Combining *StockTracker* with the in-depth financial information provided by CompuServe, general computer users can now easily and conveniently stay informed and in control of their investments."

StockTracker operates in the background, logging onto CompuServe every hour, half-hour or at any other interval you specify. It thereby continuously updates securities prices, calculates the value of the portfolio, and alerts you if a price falls above or below preset triggers. With the click of a button, all the current news can be retrieved on all of the companies in a portfolio. *StockTracker* will also retrieve a Company Report from Standard & Poor's database.

Obtaining current stock quotes is a service provided free-of-charge under the CompuServe Basic Services Plan (in which the member plays a low, flat monthly fee for unlimited access to CompuServe's basic services). To obtain historical prices, company news, charts and/or Standard & Poor's reports, there is an additional fee for online service usage and connect-time.

The main *StockTracker* screen provides instant access to all of the program's features. The user's portfolio is displayed on the screen and provides each security's ticker symbol, name, basis (purchase price), quantity owned, volume, day's high, day's low, last, change, value and gain/loss.

A full working demo of the *StockTracker* software can be downloaded directly from CompuServe (*GO VIRGIL*). Using the software's built-in registration module, the demo version of

the software can be upgraded to a full-licensed and working version within hours, when payment for the software is made with a major credit card. The latest version of this software, *StockTracker 1.5*, is priced at $59.95. The software can also be ordered on disk by calling the Virgil Corporation at (800) 662-8256.

WINDOWS ON WALL STREET

Investors who want to take an active role in performing their own fundamental and technical analysis can use a software package like *Windows On Wall Street*, which has been designed for novice and intermediate investors interested in learning more about investing while, at the same time, managing their own portfolio. This single software package transforms a PC into a powerful investment center for monitoring both individual stocks and entire portfolios.

In addition to making fundamental and technical analysis faster and easier, this software offers an extensive Help feature and tutorials designed to teach users how to use the software, and the fundamentals of investing.

The analysis of market and security movements play a critical part in an investor's ability to manage risks. Being able to consistently determine when to take profits can be just as important as deciding what security to purchase. Thoroughly analyzing movements will help an investor do both. *Windows On Wall Street* includes the technical analysis and charting tools needed by most personal investors.

The software's built-in telecommunications module allows users to log onto one of several popular online services, such as Dow Jones News/Retrieval or CompuServe to access the

historical and current data needed to perform analysis. Using *Windows On Wall Street*, gathering this data is almost totally automated and requires just a few simple keystrokes. *Windows On Wall Street* neatly combines end-of-day downloading and charting into one powerful software package.

With this software's built-in formula builder, users can create over 5,000 indicators containing multiple plots, trend lines and buy/sell signals, and can combine multiple securities into custom composite indices. Learning to accurately read and understand what an indicator represents is an investment skill that is acquired with practice and training. The more indicators that confirm a trend, the more weight any results should be given in the buy/sell decision-making process.

Simply by downloading data on a security and then clicking the mouse on the Charts icon, you can create a colorful and detailed chart in seconds, not hours. The time you spend working with your investments can be used to study the charts you create and making educated buy/sell decisions.

Even if you're already using a software package, such as *Fidelity's On-Line Xpress* or *Charles Schwab's StreetSmart*, to keep tabs on your mutual fund or brokerage accounts and perform online trades, using a tool like *Windows On Wall Street* will help you make informed decisions using the most recent financial data (as well as historical data) available.

Priced at $149.95, *Windows On Wall Street* is the flagship product of MarketArts, Inc., a company dedicated to creating and producing financial investment software with a special emphasis on the individual investor's needs. The software is available from major computer retailers or directly from MarketArts by calling (214) 783-6792.

METASTOCK

Another software development firm specializing in software specifically for investors is Equis International. Their current product line includes a series of DOS-based packages designed to help investors perform comprehensive end-of-day or real-time technical analysis and charting.

MetaStock was created to address the needs of a wide audience, from beginning investors to Wall Street professionals. The software's unique layered design allows the program to grow as the user's level of experience expands. Equis International reports that approximately 25 percent of their customers are professional money managers, stockbrokers, investment advisors, financial planners or research analysts.

MetaStock is a powerful technical analysis tool with extensive charting capabilities. While it is not a Windows-based software package, it nonetheless offers a user-friendly, intuitive graphical interface that includes an on-screen toolbar providing users with instant access to many of the software's features.

More than 75 technical indicators and studies have been incorporated into the software. Using the package's Custom Formulas module, users can create their own indicators using a spreadsheet-like language that allows for "if-then" statements. In addition to using indicators, another powerful research and analysis tool involves testing. *MetaStock* offers a powerful system tester that permits users to write and test trading systems using their own trading rules. Users can examine how much money they would have made or lost if they had followed their rules. *MetaStock* will also automatically optimize each trading system to maximize profits.

For retrieving end-of-day, real-time or historical financial data, *MetaStock* is compatible with over 40 different data services, including: Dow Jones News/Retrieval, CompuServe and The Signal (Data Broadcasting Corporation). Two versions of the *MetaStock* software are available. Which version personal investors should use depends on the type of investments they'll be making. The standard *MetaStock* package is ideal for analyzing end-of-day financial data while the *MetaStock RT* (Real-Time) package is a comprehensive real-time and intraday technical analysis charting program for stocks, bonds, commodities, futures, indices, options and more.

Using *MetaStock RT*, users can chart securities in any time period. Tick charts, one-minute bars, two-minute bars and five-minute bars are just a few of the available options. In real-time, *MetaStock RT* automatically updates and recalculates all charts, formulas and indicators as new price information is received. It's also possible to backtest a personal trading system using intraday price data. One useful feature of *MetaStock RT* is the Quick View of the Top Performers option. This provides an overview of the markets. From the Most Actives Screen, users can instantly see the top gainers, losers and volume leaders on the major markets. Using this feature, it is possible to instantly spot emerging opportunities as they happen.

By defining a customized quote screen, *MetaStock RT* allows users to instantly see current quotes for up to 500 different securities that they are interested in following. When connected to a real-time data service, investors can also view news headlines and other data while using the software. The *MetaStock RT* software incorporates many additional features designed to help investors analyze data quickly.

Because *MetaStock* is designed with all investors in mind—ranging from novice or first-time investors to professionals—the software takes what the developers call a "layered" approach. The "outer layers" of *MetaStock* consist of simple analytical tools that most investors take advantage of as part of their buy/sell decision making process. The "inner layers" of the software provides the more technical and advanced tools that more experienced investors will want to take full advantage of. All of the software's commands and options can be accessed from pull-down menus or on-screen command icons.

The *MetaStock* package is priced at $349.00. A demo disk and tutorial booklet package is available for $5.00 by contacting Equis International directly. *MetaStock RT* is priced at $495.00. The *MetaStock* software is available directly from Equis International by calling (800) 882-3040.

GENERAL FINANCIAL SOFTWARE

Along with specialized software packages designed to assist in specific aspects of investing, there are several more general applications that provide modules to handle just about every aspect of personal finance, from managing a checkbook or obtaining stock quotes to performing fundamental analysis on potential investments.

QUICKEN

Quicken for DOS or Windows is the most popular personal finance package on the market. *Quicken* is designed to print checks, pay bills, update your register and reconcile your bank accounts in much less time than it takes to do these tasks manually. This package will manage all bills, bank accounts, investments, credit cards, loans, budgets, assets and liabilities and keep accurate tax records. *Quicken* also automatically categorizes spending and can create colorful and easy-to-read graphs and charts, allowing the user to have a vivid view of his or her budget.

For personal investors, the *Quicken* package allows users to manually enter in financial data and then automatically keep track of a portfolio's performance by printing graphs and reports or using the built-in investment calculator. When *Quicken* is combined with the *Quicken Companion* package (sold separately), users can take advantage of the software's home inventory, tax estimation and additional personal investment applications. The Companion product (when used with *Quicken*) allows users to access information and financial data for over 8,000 stocks with the click of a button. Users can automatically retrieve the latest mutual fund and options prices and link this information directly into their *Quicken* records. There's also a handy ticker symbol look-up feature.

To obtain the latest quotes, *Quicken Companion* is compatible with CompuServe's Quick Quotes feature (a CompuServe membership and modem is required.)

Quicken for Windows CD-ROM Deluxe Edition takes full advantage of CD-ROM's considerable storage capacity by offering personal investors several additional features not found in other versions of the software. In fact, for novice investors, the investing tutorials offered in the CD-ROM edition alone are well worth the price of the entire package.

Quicken For Windows CD-ROM Deluxe Edition includes: the latest edition of *Quicken For Windows, Quicken Home Inventory; Quicken Tax Estimator; Quicken Tips*, plus *The Wall Street Journal Video Guide to Money and Markets CD-ROM Version, The Wall Street Journal Personal Finance Library; Tradeline; Electronic Stock Guide, U.S. Government Personal Finance Publications*, and a complete online user's manual (with tutorials) for the *Quicken* product.

The Wall Street Journal Video Guide to Money and Markets CD-ROM Version allows users to use their PC to learn the basics about stocks, bonds, foreign exchange markets and more by watching full-motion video multimedia presentations shown on the computer's monitor. Answers to popular investment questions are answered in *The Wall Street Journal Personal Finance Library*, an interactive application which incorporates hundreds of articles previously published in *The Wall Street Journal*. Using a series of electronic worksheets, users can apply their new investment knowledge to real-life financial situations.

The various versions of *Quicken* from Intuit are available wherever computer software is sold or by calling (800) 624-8742.

GET RICH QUICK?

There are no quick and easy get rich schemes when it comes to investing on Wall Street. But at least the average investor now has tools available only to professionals just a few years ago. Combine that with a solid knowledge of what investment opportunities offer, and you can now make educated investment decisions using your PC. You may not get rich quick (or even slowly), but at least the playing field has become more level.

Jason R. Rich has been writing about computers for the past ten years. He currently works as a contributing editor for Computer Entertainment News, and as a columnist for Disney Adventures magazine and Family PC magazine. Each week, he showcases the latest interactive entertainment titles and technology on the JX cable network's "Breakfast Time" show. He has also authored more than 20 computer and video-game-related books.

HOME BANKING:
THE CUTTING EDGE OF TECHNOLOGY

By Thomas Kitrick

Fifteen years ago, if you had told your banker that someday he or she would have a PC sitting on their desk, eyebrows might have been raised. Now in a virtual community where commerce is an event increasingly taken for granted, major institutions are rapidly moving to create the true virtual bank. A bank as close as your desktop...

A NEW FACE OF BANKING

Today, customers insist on individual treatment. They expect stellar service, and they want that service to be better, faster and cheaper than ever before. In every kind of business, companies have had to stop what they're doing and start listening to their customers—or risk losing them to companies who will.

The business of banking is no different. In fact, banking has undergone one of the greatest transformations of any industry. Banks have had to change. They no longer refer to themselves as just banks—now they're financial institutions. Banks of yesterday didn't have the ability to offer mutual funds, brokerage services, 24-hour banking and Internet access. The financial institutions of the future will. They will have to cater to the needs of customers who demand convenience—including instant access on the customer's schedule, as well as a broad menu of products.

Customers want different things from financial institutions. Customers are more mobile than ever and are constantly moving in new directions, moving to new cities and moving toward new ideas. They want banks of today to take them there. As all kinds of information and services become instantly available twenty-four hours a day, many customers get farther away from the idea of wanting a traditional walk-in bank branch and move closer to a world of electronic, remote banking.

BATTLING FOR THE CUSTOMER

Many financial institutions are working hard to build and fortify existing customer relationships while developing new ones. Stronger customer relationships lead to increased loyalty, reduced account turnover and opportunities to sell new and additional products to existing customers. The customer benefits by this competition for a "life-long" relationship, and the

financial institution benefits by finding new sources of revenue and loyal, stable customers.

PC technology presents a significant opportunity for personal customer service. As a way of being readily available to customers, it can't be beat. Customer-selected online access offers the ability to bring full-service to the customer, whether it be home, office or car. It's wherever you want it to be.

This shift has been occurring ever since the introduction of Automatic Teller Machines (ATMs) in the mid 1970s. Imagine a customer actually making deposits into an unknown piece of machinery. In fact, ATM transactions are growing at a rate of 12% a year—three times faster than in-branch transactions. Today, 49% of consumers use ATMs exclusively for cash withdrawals.

Figure 1: More convenient than a trip to the bank, more pleasant than voice-mail, online banking offers speed and efficiency.

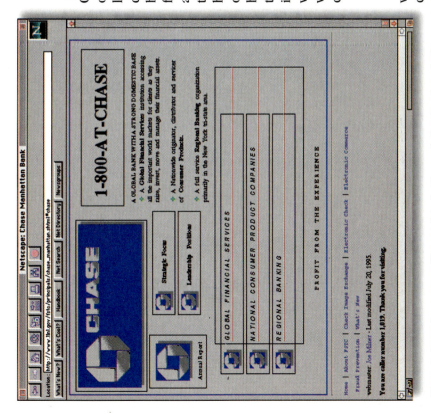

Figure 2: Currently a quarter million people in the US are actively using a home banking program.

The "Branch-Bank" of the future will be anything that can deliver exactly what customers want when they want it, whether it is a telephone, a PC, an interactive television, a screen phone or some form of Internet access.

Nationally 62% of consumers like the idea of being able to bank from home, according to a survey conducted by Mentis Corp., Salisbury, Md. The more affluent a person is, the more likely he or she is to want to bank from home. Among those with incomes over $75,000, 78% look favorably upon home banking.

All evidence points to a building consumer desire for home banking as an integral part of full-access PC service. Hectic lifestyles, increasing affluence and professional demands mean less time for teller lines and the resulting inefficiency in response time. The '90s customer wants access to financial information at the touch of a finger. The book "Overworked American" concludes that the free time of working Americans has decreased by 40% in the last 20 years. Home banking for some of us may become more of a necessity and less of a high tech luxury sooner than once thought.

Home banking offers a customer the ability to view multiple accounts, including checking, savings, credit cards and investments, place stop payments on checks, order new checks, pay bills, and to apply for installment loans, mortgages and lines of credit.

HEADING TOWARD HOME

Customers can chose one of several roads leading toward the do-it-yourself home bank. Some major financial institutions are already traveling the many roads to home banking and others are just beginning to realize the vast opportunities it can bring. Here are various home banking vehicles customers can chose today:

BANK BY PHONE

The telephone wins the popularity contest among remote banking options. When you look at the 160 million phones in the United States and the fact that almost 97% of all households are equipped with them, it's easy to see why the phone comes out ahead. Today, toll-free numbers are a dime a dozen for most large financial institutions—almost 93% provide a toll-free number according to the ABA's Retail Banking Survey.

Telephones allow customers to call in and, with the help of a touch-tone phone, input enough information, such as account number and/or Social Security number, to access their accounts 24 hours a day. Toll-free numbers enable customers to be served quickly and efficiently no matter where they are, which helps branch personnel retain and enhance financial relationships with mobile customers.

THE SCREEN PHONE

Screen phones entered the market several years ago and now many banks have pilot programs in place to distribute them to customers for free. Screen phones offer customers the ability to perform ATM banking from home. The phones have small screens attached so customers can actually see their account information and conduct ATM-type transactions from the comfort of their easy chairs. The cost of the screen phone ranges from $75-$125.

A more advanced version, the "smart phone," allows customers to conduct their financial business off-line and then transfer batches of information to their bank online. The smart phone is also more expensive—it costs $300-$600.

THE PERSONAL COMPUTER

If the phone is the most prevalent tool for customers today, the personal computer (PC) is the most probable ace-in-the-hole for home banking tomorrow. Computers are no longer just interesting toys for techies. They're now viable household tools for anyone interested in making more efficient and effective use of their time. About 36% of all households have PCs and that installed base is growing rapidly.

Using a PC, consumers can track accounts, make transfers and pay bills electronically. Banks expect to handle electronic payments to anyone with a bank account, from the local community group to the telephone company.

In a recent article by the ABA Banking Journal, Richard Crone of KPMG Pete Marwick LLP said, "The single greatest desire of people in this nation today is to know where they're spending their money and to be able to manipulate their own financial information. That is the one thing PC programs do better than phones and screen phones."

Right now, only about 250,000 people in the United States use a PC banking program. Crone also notes that "PC people" are members of the 40/40/40 group—40 million Americans who are 40 years old and control about 40% of intermediary assets—the time-poor, money-rich baby boomers.

The evidence points to a growing acceptance of the PC for home banking and possible dominance a decade from now. One of the main roadblocks to PC banking is the cost, which includes the monthly fees banks charge consumers to access the various services. Fees can range between $8-$20.

PC banking comes in different packages. Now interested participants have various options to chose from as the scope of the home banking playing field expands. Here's a look at the PC banking menu selections.

DIRECT DIAL ACCESS

Customers are given proprietary software from their financial institution. The software enables customers to perform various account functions and pay bills simply by dialing into their bank's online computer system. With direct dial access banking, the customers can view the changes or transactions made to their accounts as soon as they are received by their bank. Most major financial institutions offer a direct access product.

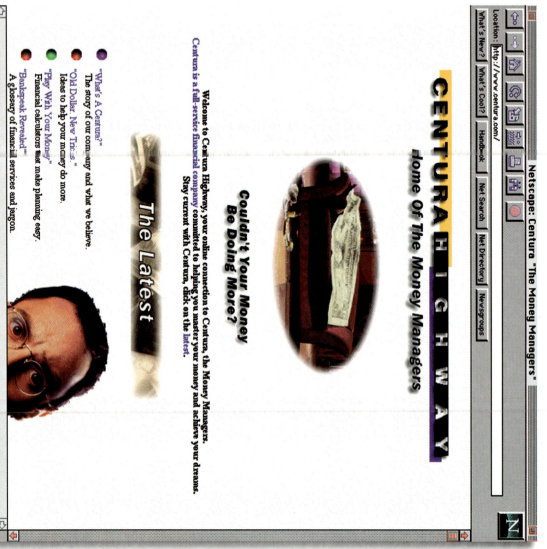

Figure 3: You'll find many banks accessible via the Internet, along with financial planning and other services. This is the Internet home page of a money manager.

OFF-LINE BANKING/THIRD-PARTY ALLIANCE

Off-line banking is the customer's alternative to direct communication with their bank. The customer can choose to set up an account with a third party software provider. The customer performs his transactions then dials into the mainframe of the third party to download all the changes made to his account. Off-line transactions are transferred once a day to the third party so account information is updated every night rather than instantly. The third party then transfers the batch file to the customer's bank.

For banks to remain competitive in the home banking arena they will have to establish relationships with third party software companies and offer their own software packages, or risk losing customers who are interested in one vs the other.

THE INTERNET

With PC popularity gaining momentum, it will drive more and more consumers to merge onto the Internet to conduct their financial business.

The Internet is a network of more than 44,000 computer networks linked together for the purpose of sharing and exchanging information.

The World Wide Web, the most rapidly growing part of the Internet, lets consumers browse their way through the home pages of various financial institutions and other points of interest. Point and click software helps consumers move through the Internet easier and faster while they are doing things like ordering goods and services, reading an electronic magazine or trading shares of stock.

Several financial institutions have built their own "billboards" on the Internet to advertise their goods and services to potential customers who visit the "Net" on a regular basis. The home page is the company's site on the Internet that lists a menu of information, which includes product and service information, general financial information, promotional items, community news and even a shopping mall. Nearly 400 banks have established home pages and some of these offer varying degrees of home banking functions.

INTERACTIVE TV

With a keypad resembling a TV remote control and a computer mouse application, customers can conduct banking transactions from their TV sets. The mouse offers point and click capability to move from each transaction quickly. Although 100 million homes have TVs, interactive television has not yet hooked home banking advocates who prefer using their phones or PC to conduct business.

HOME BANKING IS HERE NOW

Home banking is no longer a futuristic ideal developed by back office brainstormers. It's here right now.

The financial institutions that will serve you in the year 2000 will be actively and effectively using home banking applications to enhance customer relationships and build new ones. The companies that fight and win the technology revolution will also win the battle for the customer.

The scope of business and financial services is changing. Non-bank competitors, like software and brokerage companies, stand on the doorstep of every large bank in the country threatening to take their share of customers. Banks are challenged by customers whose face and pace are very different from 10 years ago—even five years ago. The customer isn't an 8 to 5 businessman or woman with spouse and kids at home. The customer is any individual who wants to use the right technology to save time and make money—from any place any time of the day.

Banks are finally delivering. Phone banking, PC banking and the Internet are the inroads to succeeding in a very different world, with very different people that have very different lifestyles. Banks are getting used to change and to making changes.

As J.P. Getty said over 50 years ago, "In time of rapid change, experience is your own worst enemy." IC

Thomas Kitrick is Vice-President of Internet Marketing for First Union National Bank, headquartered in Charlotte, North Carolina. He was previously responsible for marketing financial instruments and securities at Goldman Sachs & Co. and Mastercard International. He is a frequent speaker at international electronic commerce conferences.

THE HOME OFFICE

20 QUESTIONS TO ANSWER BEFORE YOU SET YOURSELF UP AT HOME

By Steven Anzovin

Working at home is one of the fastest growing trends in the American workplace. Labor researchers estimate that as many as 15 million Americans work out of a home office—either a business they own themselves or as telecommuters working part-time at home and part-time in a traditional office environment. If you become part of this trend, here are some common-sense guidelines that will help you succeed.

WHAT IS A HOME OFFICE?

Ten years ago, you were a rare bird indeed if you had a home office. But times have changed—and PCs have made all the difference. With a powerful home computer you can do many kinds of work at home in comfort, leaving your car in the garage and your suit in the closet. Your PC itself can provide new and novel self-employment opportunities. Or it can merely increase your efficiency with work you already do. A PC is a true power tool—it can be as versatile and useful as you want it to be. All you need is the right PC, the right software and a bright idea.

IS A HOME OFFICE RIGHT FOR ME?

Anyone can have a home office. Kids and grandparents, men and women, people with disabilities, computer novices or data professionals—when you are working in your own home, the only barriers are the ones you bring with you. You can start small, using your computer to supplement your existing income, or go full time into a new venture. For some, a home office is merely a satellite center supporting their corporate or traveling careers; for others, it is the start of a new career, an expression of independence and a step toward the integration of work life and home life.

However, no matter what your career and expectations, you'll be more likely to succeed as an at-home professional if you:

- are self-motivated and confident
- enjoy your work
- work best without supervision
- can persevere despite distractions, isolation and setbacks
- are a flexible, creative problem-solver

WHAT KINDS OF WORK CAN I DO AT HOME?

Most kinds of computer-based work fit well into a home office. The top businesses for people who work entirely at home include:

- word processing and resume services
- writing, research and editing
- telemarketing
- desktop publishing
- graphic arts
- operating a commercial BBS (bulletin board service)

Sales reps, repair workers, consultants and many others work out of a home office as an adjunct to their traveling careers, using their PCs to organize their schedules, arrange their travel plans and serve as a home base for email and messages.

A home office is also essential for people who **telecommute**. Jobs that involve routine computer tasks, such as data entry and forms processing, are good candidates for conversion to telecommuting. Other possible telecommuting careers include:

- computer programming
- social-service work
- medical or legal paraprofessional

WHAT'S THE PSYCHOLOGICAL IMPACT OF WORKING AT HOME?

Some people love the freedom—from distractions, rigid schedules, meetings and the dozens of rules against napping, music, comfortable clothes, etc. Others find adjusting to working at home hard at first. Typical problems include:.

ISOLATION

Working alone for long periods can lead to feelings of isolation. Fight against them by getting out of the office at least once a day—take lunch with a client, do library research, attend a business class.

LOSS OF CONTACT

At-home workers often sacrifice the face-to-face contact that builds close relationships between workers in an office. If you are still connected with a corporate office, come in for meetings and special events and keep in touch daily by phone and email. Call your clients regularly "just to check in."

WORKAHOLISM

Because your home office never closes, some people are always tempted to squeeze out "just one more bit of work." Result: Exhaustion and family problems. Set reasonable work hours and try not to exceed them. Don't be your own labor slave.

DISTRACTION

You may have trouble applying yourself to your work because "there are too many other

Figure 1: *With the power of the PC, your home office can connect to other computers anywhere in the world.*

Convincing The Boss

Many companies already have telecommuting programs in place—but yours doesn't. How can you convince your boss to let you work at home?

Draft a written explanation describing why you want to telecommute and how it will benefit the organization. Cover these issues:

- The reasons why—family, health, travel, etc.
- What your on-site and at-home schedule will be.
- How and when you'll report to your boss.
- Who will supply, and be responsible for, the PC and other hardware involved, and who will pay for supplies, maintenance and computer insurance.
- Whether expenses such as phone calls and express courier service will be reimbursed.
- Will your employer extend the same benefits package to you even if you work part-time at home? If not, what will change?

Be sure to mention these advantages:

- Telecommuters cost less than in-house employees.
- Home-based workers are generally more productive than workers who perform similar tasks in a typical office environment.
- Telecommuting reduces absenteeism, enhances an organization's ability to retain experienced personnel (reducing the need for expensive job-training programs) and attracts talented new personnel.

Present your plan coolly and objectively, and answer all questions honestly. Be willing to try it for a couple of weeks without a firm commitment, but make sure that you can get an evaluation in writing from your supervisor. If things don't work out, find out why and offer an alternative plan that will work.

---

things to do." Fight distractions by keeping a strict work schedule and routine.

HOW WILL MY FAMILY HANDLE IT?

Because your home office is in your home, it affects the lives of your family. That can cause problems—and lead to new opportunities.

THE "YOU'RE NOT REALLY WORKING" SYNDROME

The first thing your family will have to get used to is that your home office is really a business, and that you're really working at a job even though you're not "going to work." It may take some time for them to accept that you're

---

not available for playtime, chauffeur service or homework help during business hours—but they will.

DEALING WITH A LOWER STANDARD OF LIVING

If your home business is a startup, it may be a while before you start to earn a significant income. The early days may be hard for your spouse, especially if he or she still has an outside job and is earning the bulk of the family income. Be firm about your commitment to your new business; when the earnings start rolling in, spousal resentment usually disappears.

INVOLVING YOUR FAMILY IN THE BUSINESS

The real key to home office success is to involve your family members in the business. Small kids can sort, stuff envelopes, file, recycle and do other office chores. Teens can gain valuable work experience by typing, answering phones and doing research. Get your spouse into the act, too. Married couples often complain that their careers and their home lives are always in competition, and that the home life usually loses. Why not go into business together?

Tip: Dealing With Windows... The Glass Kind
The window that lets light and air into your home office and gives you a view of the outside world can also be a productivity-killer if it casts glare onto your PC screen, making it hard to see your work clearly and leaving you with a headache at the end of the day. Some tips for reducing window glare and easing the strain on your eyes:

- Position your screen so it's perpendicular to the window. Never position your screen so a window is behind your back or behind your PC.
- Place a room divider—hanging fabric will do—so that it blocks glare from windows without blocking indirect light.
- Wear a baseball cap to keep glare out of your eyes. This is especially helpful for people who catch glare on their eyeglasses.
- If necessary, pull down the blinds or install shades that let in a soft, glare-free illumination.

Figure 2: Berkeley system's LaunchPad gives kids an enjoyable interface while protecting your home office software.

Let's say you'll be doing more demanding home-office work—handling very large database files, crunching numbers in big spreadsheets or running complex business management software. You'll want to step up to a faster machine with more storage. Faster means:

- 100MHz, 486DX4-class CPU or a 60 to 75MHz Pentium CPU
- 16MB of memory
- 500MB hard disk or larger
- CD-ROM drive
- 15-inch color monitor

Expect to spend under $2000 for this level of computing power.

You'll need even more machine for desktop publishing, multimedia authoring and advanced graphics. In these fields, time is very definitely money, so purchase the fastest PC you can afford, with plenty of hard disk storage and memory. Today's top-of-the-line is:

- High-end Pentium—100MHz or faster
- 16MB of RAM or more
- 1GB (gigabyte, or 1000 megabytes) hard disk
- Quad-speed CD-ROM drive
- 17- or 20-inch color monitor
- High-speed, **accelerated video card** with millions of colors and 2MB or more of on-card RAM memory.

A desktop PC with these specs can cost more than $3000 at today's prices. But it will quickly pay for itself in the time you save.

Will travel be a major part of your home business? Then you'll need a **notebook** (or **laptop**) computer or PDA (personal digital assistant). See "Can I Take My Home Office on the Road?" below.

WHAT PERIPHERALS DO I NEED?

Your home business PC system will also need some basic **peripherals** (add-ons to perform special tasks). Most small offices can get by with just a printer and a fax/**modem**/voicemail system for handling the business's telecommunications needs. Depending on what kind of work you do, you may also need a scanner, a device for bringing information on paper into your computer.

THE PRINTER

People buying their first home office system often treat the printer as an afterthought. That's a mistake. Your clients and potential customers won't see the new top-of-the-line PC on your desk, but they will see the letters, resumes, bids and brochures you've printed on your printer.

If you want your printed communications to have a slick, professional look, don't consider

---

Figure 3: Visioneer's PaperPort is a simple, low-cost scanner that can help you keep all your home office files and papers on your PC.

CAN I SHARE MY HOME OFFICE PC WITH MY KIDS?

Your kids will see you working diligently at your home office PC and want to use it, too. While you don't want to discourage them from learning computer skills, it's also not a good idea to let your kids use your home office PC for entertainment and homework. Not only will you be competing with them for PC time, and probably resenting it, but they may accidentally trash your business files and programs.

If you can't afford a second PC just for the kids, put strict limits on when they can use your computer—for example, only in the evenings and on weekends. Get a disk security program that lets you lock kids out from your software and files. Or try Berkeley system's *LaunchPad*, a Windows program that gives kids access to their own programs while making yours invisible to them.

DO I HAVE ROOM FOR A HOME OFFICE?

Many home offices don't require much room—enough for a small desk, chair and bookshelf. But even that can be hard to find in a small apartment. In a pinch, your kitchen table, counter-top, or dresser can be pressed into service, but it's much better to have proper computing furniture and an office that doesn't have to do double duty as a dining area.

Even homes with adequate room rarely come equipped with the perfect space for a home office, so expect to make some compromises. Ask these questions:

- Is the space dry and cool?
- Is there adequate electricity for my PC and peripherals?
- Is there a phone jack?
- Is there good lighting and a window for ventilation?

- Will I have privacy and quiet for work—a door I can close on the world?

When you've picked out likely sites, call a family meeting and reach a consensus about the location. They'll appreciate having the input, and you'll encounter less resentment down the road.

WHAT'S THE PERFECT HOME OFFICE PC FOR ME?

Buying a desktop PC for your home office can be a bewildering and anxiety-ridden experience, but it doesn't have to be. Peace of mind comes from first defining what kind of work you plan to do and then picking the right PC to get the job done. One general rule: if you're working with graphics—desktop publishing, design, art work in general—you can opt for a Macintosh. Many visual artists use that machine, though in the past year there's been a trend toward PCs (IBM-compatible machines) because the graphics capabilities of today's PC now match the Mac. However, for any other kind of work, an IBM-compatible machine is the *de facto* standard in the business world. About 90 percent of all computers sold today are PCs, and this marketplace dominance is growing.

Basic office tasks—such as word processing, managing mailing lists and sending email—call for a basic PC. Today that means, at minimum:

- 66MHz (megahertz, a measure of micro-processor speed) 486DX2-class CPU (central processing unit, the main part of the PC)
- 8MB of RAM (random access memory).
- 400MB hard disk for storage
- CD-ROM drive

At the time of this writing, a good system with these specifications costs under $1500.

The Healthy Home Office

Flexible beings that we are, we tend to adapt ourselves to the work conditions imposed by computers, rather than fashioning offices that meet the needs of our bodies. We strain our eyes squinting through glare; twist our necks and backs working in unnatural positions for long hours; and suffer new kinds of hand injuries caused by the repetitive motions that computing requires.

Fortunately, many of the negative health effects of computing can be avoided or reduced via relatively simple measures. You can help yourself to more healthy computing by following these rules:

- Take regular breaks to reduce the chance that you'll damage yourself by the constant repetitive motions of computing. Every hour or so, get up from your PC and stretch. Walk around.

- Reduce eyestrain by adjusting lighting conditions in your office. Look away from the screen at regular intervals and focus on a distant object.

- If you feel numbness or shooting pains in your hand, wrist or forearm, stop typing immediately. Stretch your hand gently and keep away from the keyboard for an hour or more. Check to be sure that your keyboard is low enough. When typing, your forearms should be parallel to the floor. And your palms should be resting on something so that your hands, too, are parallel to the floor. It's not only fatiguing if your hands are held in a claw-like position while you type—it can also lead to serious injury. Rest your palms on what? Most computer stores sell palm rest pads, or you can consider upgrading your keyboard by buying the Microsoft Natural Keyboard, which has a built-in palm rest.

- If you continue to experience pain, get medical attention. Don't wait until problems get so bad that you need surgery or other extreme measures. And don't let people tell you it's all in your head. PC-related health problems are real and can be treated.

anything but a **laser printer.** Other types of printers just can't produce the same high quality. With low-end lasers costing as little as $500, the price is not too difficult to swallow, either.

FAX/MODEM

Faxing, email, and access to **online services** and the **Internet** may also be important for your home business, so you'll also need a device called a fax/modem to handle those chores. Many PCs come with one already installed, so you may not have to purchase

anything more. But ask these two questions before you consider yourself satisfied:

- Is the fax/modem fast enough to handle the requirements of the Internet and today's multimedia-oriented online services? Check the baud rate, a measure of data transfer speed. If it operates at less than 14.4K (14,400) baud, you should definitely upgrade to a 14.4K or an even faster 28.8K modem.

- Does the fax/modem also handle voicemail? A good voicemail system makes your home office seem more professional. There are several popular voicemail systems on the market that come complete with the proper hardware and software for setting up multiple voicemail boxes and recording messages for each onto your PC's hard disk for later playback. One advantage of such a system is that it eliminates the need for an answering machine or service.

SCANNER

Scanners work something like office copiers, but instead of making a copy on paper, they take a paper original—either art or text—and copy it into a file that can be stored on your PC's hard disk. You don't have to be a desktop publisher or graphic artist to make good use of one. A scanner can help you keep all your paper documents, from letters to invoices to contracts, neatly filed in your PC, ready for instant access. A new class of low-cost scanner (under $400) is designed for just this purpose. It includes OCR (optical character recognition) software that converts the scanned image to text that you can edit, search and otherwise manipulate within the computer. (Without OCR, scanned documents remain merely *pictures* when stored in the computer.)

ALL-IN-ONE PERIPHERALS

A new type of peripheral does it all: printing, copying, scanning and faxing. Several printer manufacturers offer at least one model of this all-in-one machine, at prices ranging from $700 to $1800. Space-saving all-in-ones may seem like a good solution for home offices. But they tend to be less capable at each task—slower or producing less professional results—than stand-alone peripherals. And if it breaks down, you've lost the use of three or four machines, not just one.

Figure 4: Hewlett-Packard's Officejet combination printer, copier and fax machine can save you several hundred square inches of desk space.

WHAT SOFTWARE DO I NEED?

Your home office needs the right software to run efficiently. At a minimum, that typically means a word processor, a personal information manager (PIM), telecommunications software and a simple accounting program. Depending on the nature of your business, you may need additional software, anything from a spreadsheet to a desktop publishing program to a custom inventory manager. Here we'll look at just the basics.

SOFTWARE COMPATIBILITY

The first issue to consider is whether your software needs to be compatible with software used at your corporate offices or by your major clients. Are all the people you work with creating business documents with the same word processor? Are they all using one service for email? Then it's probably a good idea if you do, too.

ALL-IN-ONE SOFTWARE

Many new PCs come bundled with an all-in-one software program that includes a word processor, a personal database, a spreadsheet for crunching business numbers and telecommunications for accessing online information. If your computing needs are modest, look no further: an all-in-one will get you started.

WORD PROCESSING

Writers and other professional communicators need heavier-duty word processing than can be found in an all-in-one program. Get demonstration copies of the top word processors and choose the one that best suits you. For many years, *WordPerfect* dominated this market. However, in the past couple of years, Microsoft *Word* has become the leader.

PERSONAL INFORMATION MANAGER (PIM)

You may not be able to hire a secretary, but you'll get many of the advantages of one with a personal information manager (PIM). A PIM is a

AVERAGE ENERGY COST OF A HOME OFFICE OPERATING 9 HOURS PER DAY, 240 DAYS/YEAR.

Electrical device	kWh/yr	$/yr
	($0.07/kWh)	
PC	300	$21.00
Laser printer	260	$18.00
Modem	22	$2.00
Fax machine	150	$11.00
Copier	1500	$105.00
Two 100W incandescent lights	430	$30.00
Two overhead 40W fluorescent lights	175	$12.00
Answering machine	40	$3.00
Total	**2877**	**$202.00**

Note: One kilowatt/hour equals the electricity consumption of ten 100-watt lightbulbs operating for one hour.

Source: EPA; American Council for an Energy-Efficient Economy; US Dept. of Energy.

Table 1

mini-database that keeps all your rolodex files and contact lists in instantly accessible form, and links them to a day-by-day calendar of your appointments and things to do. Few at-home professionals can afford to be without a PIM.

TELECOMMUNICATIONS

Windows 3.x comes with a basic telecommunications program called Terminal that can perform simple file transfers, connect with bulletin board services and access online databases. Some home businesses need more than this, however. Windows 95 includes a sophisticated email system, but you may need truly heavy-duty telecommunications software if you plan to send large graphics files directly to and from clients' computers. (Smaller text files can be sent as email through online services such as CompuServe, The Microsoft Network or America OnLine.) If you need industrial-strength telecommunications, consider the best-selling program—Intuitive Communications's **Procomm**.

You'll benefit from having an account with one of the big commercial services, such as America Online, CompuServe or Prodigy, which provide

manage your accounts payable and receivable, keep track of your expenses, print your checks, and generally put you in good shape when tax time comes around. Most personal money-management software can do a perfectly adequate job of

managing the finances of a small home office. Each service has its own custom software, which you can get for free almost everywhere—bundled with PCs, tucked into magazines, stashed on sampler CD-ROMs and directly from each service.

MONEY MANAGEMENT

Your home office is a business, and it should be run like one. Accounting software will help you

email and a vast amount of online information. Each service has its own custom software, which you can get for free almost everywhere—bundled with PCs, tucked into magazines, stashed on sampler CD-ROMs and directly from each service.

component of your business—you. To do your best, you must be comfortable, and that means purchasing good-quality office furniture.

- Get a real office chair—it's worth every penny you spend on it. It should include a swivel base, adjustable height and tilt, thick padding on chair and arms, and adjustable lumbar support.

- Next, get the right desk. Most writing desks are about four inches too high for comfortable computing. You may have to invest in a desk with a lower, slide-out typing shelf, or install one on your current desk. But desks designed with computer ergonomics in mind are sold everywhere. Well-made computer desks are available from companies such as ScanCo.

- Properly light your workspace. Install overhead lights to provide an even overall illumination and desk lights by your PC to direct bright light where you need it. (But remember not to shine a light directly on your monitor—avoid glare.)

- Provide adequate storage—bookshelves, filing cabinets, whatever your office requires. The value of a natty and orderly workspace is a matter of personal preference. But if you're one of those who's uncomfortable in cluttered, antique-shop settings, take the time to keep things clean. A well-organized work area provides a sense of orderliness that can be a real psychological boost for some home workers. Evaluate your entire work area. Is everything easy to reach? Rearrange shelves and storage areas so you don't have to strain your back retrieving needed materials. And make sure you have room behind your desk to move your chair back and stretch.

WHAT ABOUT OFFICE FURNISHINGS?

You've spent thousands of dollars on a new PC, peripherals and software. Now your home office is complete, right? Not quite. You've forgotten to take care of the most important

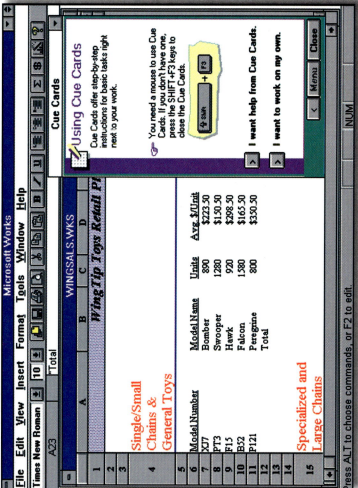

Figure 5: Microsoft Works is the standard Windows all-in-one software program. It may be all you need for your home office.

THE BUDGET HOME OFFICE

You don't have to take out a second mortgage to get your home office underway. If you're willing to use older hardware, you may be able to get away with an initial outlay of only a couple of hundred dollars—or maybe nothing at all.

BUDGET PCs

Let's say most of your home office work will involve basic word processing and telecommunications. An older computer—say, an 80386-based CPU, a standard monitor, a low-speed modem and an old printer—can do the job, but not as quickly or as professionally. (PCs based on the 8086, 8088 or 80286 processor can't run Windows, so they are not recommended, unless you're willing to live with DOS only.) A simple setup can be purchased for two or three hundred dollars through your local paper's classifieds. Or talk to your local PC user groups—members may have older machines for sale. You'll find announcements of their meetings in local papers. PC brokers will also help you find the right "pre-owned" PC for you, anywhere in the country, at significant savings. Remember, though, that some home office work *requires* the professional look that only a laser printer (minimum $500) can provide.

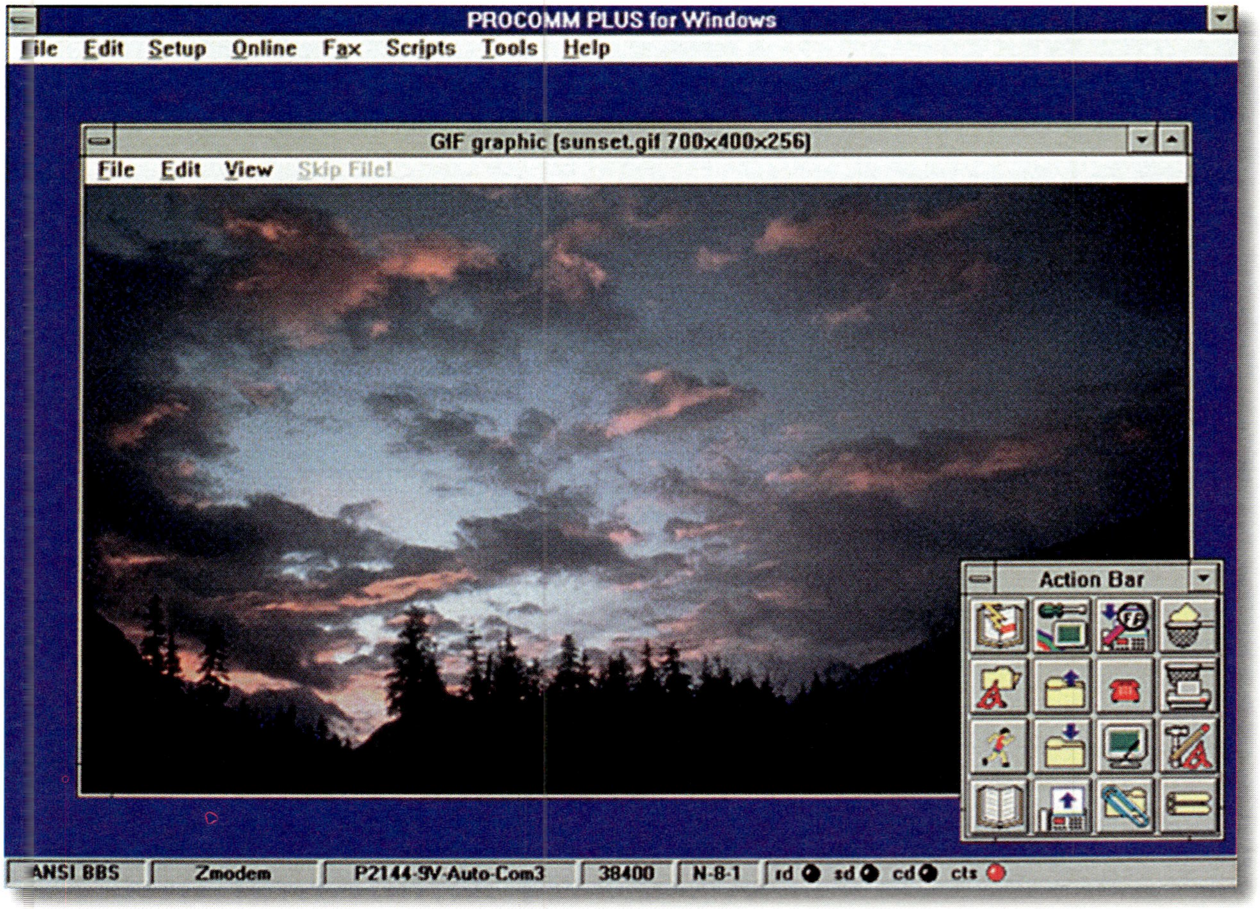

Don't have even a couple of c-notes to invest? You might be able to get a donated PC from a business in your community. Also ask around about hand-me-downs among your friends and relations—many people have older PCs in their closets that they'd love to hand on. Have a disability? The National Christina Foundation donates PCs to help physically challenged people telecommute or set up small businesses.

BUDGET SOFTWARE

One good source of low-cost programs is your local PC user group. Most distribute basic word processors, personal database managers and telecommunications programs on individual floppy disks that may cost as little as $5. Many of these programs are shareware; that means if you decide to use them you send a modest fee, usually $25 or less, to the developer. Business shareware is also available from every commercial online service and BBS (bulletin board service). Don't spurn low-end commercial software, either. There are lots of programs for $50 and under that provide much of the functionality of their better-known but more costly competitors.

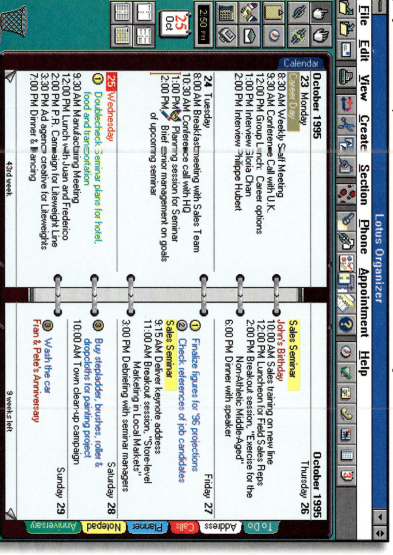

Figure 6: Lotus Organizer is a popular personal information manager (PIM) and scheduler—it's especially good if your home office needs to stay coordinated with a corporate office.

Figure 7: Datastorm's ProComm Plus is a top-rated telecommunications program that handles fax, data and voice calls—it even includes a graphics viewer

264

The Five All-Time Best Time Savers

Here are five tips that can potentially save you hours every workday.

- Organize your business communications for maximum efficiency. Get up early and take care of your email. Call before 8 a.m. and be first in the queue to leave voicemail messages and send faxes—at lower phone rates, too. During the main part of the work day, get your work done and don't answer the phone (assuming your work isn't telemarketing, that is). Let your voice mail take the calls. Return urgent messages only. Schedule a final phone session at the end of the day, when everyone wants to keep conversations short and sweet.

- Use a telephone headset. You'll be able to type and do other computer chores with both hands while on the phone taking orders, doing interviews or extolling your virtues to your clients.

- Read business news online instead of in paper form. You'll have access to a wider range of news and spend less time getting it. Cancel your business newspaper or magazine subscriptions to pay for the extra online time.

- Keep social interactions to a minimum. Avoid those long, friendly conversations and surprise dropovers that eat up precious work time. Save socialization for after-hours.

- Be picky about your clients. If it takes twice as long to satisfy one client for the same pay, find another who's more reasonable. Working for half the pay and twice the aggravation is a definite waste of time.

HOW CAN I SAVE MONEY ON ELECTRICITY?

Paying to power a basic home office can cost you about $200 a year (See Table 1). For the typical consumer, every hour of power saved is seven cents you're not paying to the power company. The less power you use, the less your energy bill affects your home business.

Some hints for energy saving:

- Turn off your PC, monitor, peripherals and other devices when you're not in the office.

- If you must leave your PC running to receive faxes or maintain contact with a network, at least turn off your monitor, printer and lights. They use more power than the PC itself.

- Plug all your components into an inexpensive strip outlet with an on-off switch. When you turn off the master switch, all your components will power down simultaneously, eliminating the possibility that you'll leave one or more components running all night or all weekend.

- Choose hardware that is energy efficient. If you're in the market for a new machine, get an Energy Star computer. Most PC manufacturers offer newer models that are compliant with the Environmental Protection Agency's Energy Star specifications, which means they automatically enter a low-power, low-cost "sleep mode" when they are inactive for a period of time (that you can specify). Look on the packaging for the Energy Star logo—a picture of the Earth with a neon star and the word *Energy* on it.

Figure 8: You can create a home office on a budget.

not down. Here are five simple ways to save trees and cash, too:

- Use email whenever possible
- Don't print drafts (instead use the Print Preview feature found in many applications.)
- Use a smaller type size and decrease the space between lines of text
- Leave narrower margins
- Print on two sides of the paper using one of the many PC print utility programs.

Tip: When you are copying files from your main computer into Briefcase, the two computers must be connected, either over a network or by a cable. If this isn't possible, you can create a briefcase on a floppy and move it from one computer to the other.

Feeding printers can be expensive, too. Save money by:

- Re-inking ribbons
- Refilling your own inkjet cartridges
- Recycling toner cartridges for a savings of 30 to 50 percent over new ones.

WHAT ABOUT SECURITY AND INSURANCE?

When you're working out the budget for your home office, don't forget about insurance and security. While it is possible to put your PC on your homeowner's or tenant's insurance policy, it's best to get a separate insurance policy specifically tailored to the home office. Your insurance agent will be able to direct you to the right coverage and perhaps the best deal. Make sure the policy includes an itemized list of all your home office equipment, and update that list as your needs change. (Most policies don't cover the value of software, only hardware.) Expect to

Figure 9: Time equals money when you're your own boss.

SUPPLIES ON THE CHEAP

You'll need budget furnishings and supplies, too. Rather than making do with the kitchen table and an old wooden chair, try finding something a little more business-like at flea markets and used-furniture outlets.

HOW CAN I SAVE MONEY ON PC SUPPLIES?

Another place to save home office dollars is in consumables—paper, printer supplies and other items that you use and eventually discard.

Paper is the single biggest waste product in most offices, and the cost of paper is going up,

spend as much as $200 a year, depending on the value of your equipment, amount of your deductible and other factors.

Your security needs will vary with your location and the value of your home office equipment. Full-fledged alarm systems and attack-trained guard dogs are probably overkill, but consider something as simple as bolting your PC and peripherals to the desk. Kits for this purpose are available from office supply catalogs. Also, if you have lots of kids passing through your home, you might want to keep the PC locked when you're not working so it can't be commandeered by junior hackers. If your PC doesn't have a lock, lock away the power cord or the keyboard.

CAN I TAKE MY HOME OFFICE ON THE ROAD?

Many at-home professionals spend lots of time traveling. If you're a road warrior, you can use a PC to make your business more efficient while maintaining your mobility.

TAKE YOUR PC WITH YOU

For travel, you need a notebook (also called a laptop) PC—a small, portable computer. In the opinion of many road warriors two qualities are most important in a notebook: light weight and a readable screen. Some would add a comfortable keyboard and long battery life to that list. And don't forget to get a fast portable fax/modem. Consider models that offer a docking station with additional ports for a monitor, full-sized keyboard, printer and other peripherals. Use the docked notebook as your desktop PC; when it's time to hit the road, pop out the notebook and leave the docking station at home.

HOW DO I KEEP IN TOUCH WITH MY HOME OFFICE PC?

There's no need to lose touch with your home office computer while you're on the road. To stay connected, you'll need a modem in your notebook PC or PDA and another modem inside the desktop PC at home, plus remote control software such as Symantec's PCAnywhere. Here's how it works:

1. Install the remote-control software on both your home and notebook PCs.
2. Begin a Windows session on your home PC and turn on your modem before you leave. Leave your monitor off to save energy.
3. On the road, connect your modem to a phone line. Dial your home modem's phone number from the remote-control software.
4. You'll see your home PC's screen on your notebook. You can work with it just as if you were sitting at home.
5. When you're done, hang up.

Don't want to leave your home PC on while you're away? Get a device that turns on your PC

Figure 10: At-home professionals can shop for office products through America Online.

OfficeMax OnLine

From Your Keyboard To Your Door!™

SHOP OUR STORE

CUSTOMER SERVICE

SPECIAL VALUES

BUSINESS RESOURCE CENTER

PACK A PDA

Increasingly, business travelers with modest computing needs are packing PDAs (personal digital assistants) instead of notebook PCs. These small, inexpensive (typically under $500) handheld computers are good for keeping your calendar and to-do lists, taking notes, sending email and doing on-the-spot calculations. Linking cables and software let you transfer information between your PC and PDA.

SYNCHRONIZE FILES

Keeping files up-to-date on multiple PCs can be a hassle. File synchronization software can help. These programs look for your most recent files and make sure they are the same on all your machines. See the sidebar "The Windows 95 Briefcase."

USE THE COMPUTER RESOURCES AT HAND

Many hotels have fax machines that can double in a pinch for a printer—just use your fax/modem to fax yourself a copy of the document you want to print. Need a real printer and other computer services? Try Kinko's, a nationwide chain of copy shops. You can rent time on desktop PCs, use laser printers, scanners and other peripherals, and work with popular business software for a few dollars a session.

whenever a call comes in, and shuts it down when you hang up. You can find these remote power devices in most computer catalogs and retail stores.

IS MY HOME OFFICE TAX DEDUCTIBLE?

Home office expenses can be tax-deductible, just like the expenses of any other business. That can include the cost of your computer and peripherals. However, the IRS rules for the deductibility of home office expenses are strict and change each year. It's best to consult an accountant or professional tax preparer on this matter.

Here are a few general principles to keep in mind that will make it easier for you to claim a deduction.

• Generally, you have to be able to prove that the home office is either your primary place of business or that it is indispensable to your work and not merely a convenience. If you have a job out of your home and merely take work home occasionally, the IRS will probably not allow a home office deduction.

• Use your PC and peripherals exclusively for work, or keep exact records of how much time they are used for work and how much for entertainment, kids' homework, etc. You can depreciate only the work-time percentage of the cost of the PC. (The cost of software cannot be depreciated under IRS rules at the time of writing, but it may be deductible in other ways.)

• Don't mix work and living areas. You may be able to deduct a proportion of certain home office expenses, such as utilities, that corresponds to the percentage of your home devoted exclusively to the home office. But if your office space is also used for living, the IRS may disallow such deductions.

• Keep scrupulous records of all your home office expenses, and do not mix them with your living expenses. For example, install a separate phone line for your office and do all your work-related calling and online research on that line only. Likewise, keep a credit card just for business expenses.

• Study the instructions for IRS Form 8829, Expenses for Business Use of Your Home, and get IRS Publication 334, Tax Guide for Small Business.

WHAT ONLINE RESOURCES ARE AVAILABLE FOR HOME OFFICES?

The world of online information can be a lifesaver for the at-home businessperson. You can find everything from general business advice to free tech support for specific software programs to online ordering of office supplies. All these services can help your home business compete with others in your field. You can even chat with other home workers all over the country.

The first place to look for help with questions about hardware and software are the industry forums on the commercial online services. If you are on America Online and have a question about Microsoft software, for example, use Keyword: *Microsoft* to go to the Microsoft Resource Center, where you can find extensive information on every Microsoft product and technical support for any problem you may have. Even more useful are the forums on home offices, communications and on-the-road computing. Here you can pick up tips from veterans and talk with other at-home professionals who are grappling with the same problems you are. For example, America Online hosts a Strategies for Business forum that can help home operations get started, as well as Mobile Office Online with tips for home office workers on the go. CompuServe and Prodigy also have business help, mobile computing and working from home forums.

Steven Anzovin *is a contributing editor for* Computer Entertainment News *and* CD-ROM Today *magazines. He is the author of 22 books, including* The Green PC, *a guide to reducing the environmental cost of computing.*

The Windows 95 Briefcase

by Evangelous Petroutsous

After some serious research and investment in computer and telecommunication equipment, you managed to create your ideal office at home. You have your own schedule and work at your own pace. But there's a special problem when you share files with clients or others outside your home. In some cases, you can just send them a few files which they simply copy onto their hard drive and that's it. But all too often you *exchange* files—they do some editing and return the file to you; you make further changes and send it back, etc. Keeping such files *synchronized* is not trivial. This predicament is sometimes called *the version problem* because there can be several copies of the same document. Which is the most current (the one with everyone's most recent editing)?

Consider the simple case where you take some work home, or on the road. You copy a few files from your company computer on a diskette, move them to your notebook computer, work with them and when you return you copy the files back onto the company computer. As simple as it sounds, there's always the risk of overwriting a new file with an older version, or copying an unmodified file over the one that a co-worker spent hours fixing up and improving.

Figure 11: *First copy to the Briefcase any files you want to take home. The Briefcase can also "contain" whole entire folders (directories).*

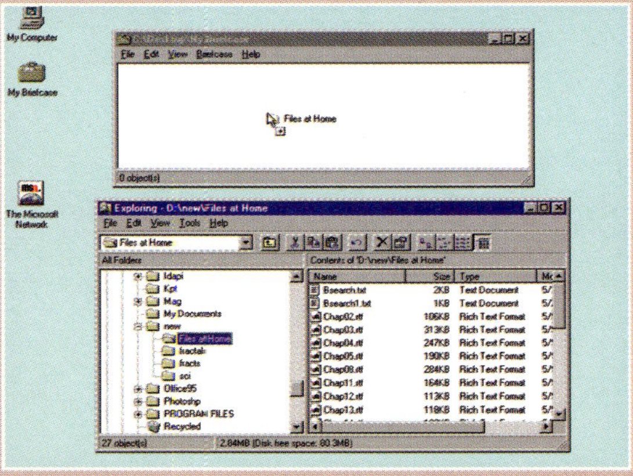

One simple mistake while copying files, and the hours spent over the weekend on a project are wasted. Even worse, this kind of problem is usually detected when it's too late to be fixed—that is, after the wrong, badly edited or un-spellchecked file was printed and mailed to someone outside the company.

Sharing files between computers is a disaster waiting to happen. To help avoid this problem, Microsoft included a special tool in the Windows 95 operating system called Briefcase, which automates file synchronization. The Briefcase is a metaphor for a physical briefcase, where you would put documents you want to work on later at home.

The electronic version of the briefcase is a special folder where you drag and drop (or copy) documents (files) you need. Then you copy the same documents onto a floppy, or onto your notebook's hard disk over the network. After you return to the office and are ready to copy the now-modified files back into the company's computer, all you have to do is run the Briefcase application, which will automatically synchronize all the files.

How are the documents synchronized? The computer finds out which documents have been modified since the briefcase was created, or last updated, and overwrites the old versions with the newer ones. This way, every time you synchronize with the Briefcase, you have an identical set of files on two computers (or on a computer and a floppy disk).

The easiest way to share files between two computers is to connect the computers, either over a network, or with a cable connecting their serial ports. If that's not feasible, you can always share files by copying them onto a diskette. The process of moving files from one computer to another and keeping them up-to-date is illustrated in Figures 11 and 12. Here are the steps you follow:

1. Drag the icons of the files you want to take home from your main computer to the Briefcase icon on your portable computer.
2. Modify the files in the Briefcase folder on your notebook while you're away from the office.
3. When you're back at the office, reconnect to your main computer, and then select the Update All command in the Briefcase utility. Briefcase will automatically replace the unmodified files on your main computer with the modified files in your Briefcase.

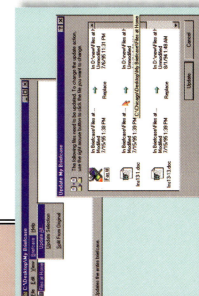

Figure 12: *When you're ready to return edited files, chose* Update All, *and let the computer do the work for you.*

Here are the steps for keeping files synchronized if you can't physically connect your portable to the main computer:

1. Insert a floppy disk into a disk drive on your main computer.
2. Copy the files you're interested in to the Briefcase.
3. Move the entire Briefcase to a floppy disk.
4. Insert the floppy disk into a disk drive on your portable computer, and then edit the files within the Briefcase folder.
5. When you are back at the main computer and ready to synchronize the files, reinsert the floppy disk containing Briefcase into a disk drive on your main computer, and then double-click the Briefcase icon (on the floppy).
6. When you see the Briefcase menu, click Update All.

There is, however, one situation that the Briefcase can't handle: If both versions of a file (the one on the main computer and the one on the portable computer) have been modified, the Briefcase can't synchronize them. Briefcase will, though, detect this problem and let you know that both files have been modified. Then it will give you the option to overwrite either one or leave them as they are until you can somehow merge the changes in both files (outside Briefcase) to create one "latest version."

DESKTOP PUBLISHING

By Ralph Roberts

Recent rapid advances in technology have resulted in powerful and affordable personal computers. These wonderful machines easily let you do things today that could only have been accomplished by an expensive print shop just a very few years ago. The equivalent of thousands of dollars in equipment and people with decades of experience is now on your desktop, and for a bit less than the print shop owner had to pay. Here's how to take advantage of all that publishing power sitting on your desktop.

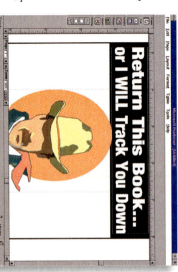

Figure 1: Many desktop publishing programs help you design professional-looking documents quickly, easily, and without much experience at all. This illustration shows a Microsoft Publisher Wizard—a small program that does all the real work for you.

DESKTOP PUBLISHING AND WORD PROCESSING

Let's look at fast and easy, yet professional ways to create:

- business cards
- newsletters
- flyers
- brochures
- ads
- labels of all sorts
- greeting cards
- pamphlets
- and much more

We'll use only inexpensive programs—including some that come free with Microsoft Windows. Desktop publishing programs (abbreviated as "DTP") allow you to typeset words, insert graphics, then print out the resulting document. Just as word processing programs supplant a typewriter, DTP programs replace scissors, paper, and messy pots of glue.

A small business can save hundreds or thousands every year by producing their own brochures, letterheads, invoices, statements, advertisements, business cards, and all those other constantly needed pieces of paper. The difference between ordering from an expensive business forms dealer or taking a "camera-ready" piece down to the corner copy shop represents a significant cost savings.

Home users, too, save money by being able to make their own greeting cards, personalized notepaper, yard sale signs, club newsletters, and much more.

With the power of desktop publishing at your beck and call, you can design forms and publications that are exactly right for your purposes. The creativity-enhancing aspects of DTP enable the home user to provide that wonderful personal touch in correspondence as well.

Tip: Bookplates and other labels: None of us likes lending our books and not getting them back. Use a desktop publishing program to make up some nice-looking bookplates ("This Book Stolen From...," etc.) and print them on adhesive paper with peel-off, stick-on backing (such as Avery #5353). You can make very nice labels for other items you own using this method also. More about this in the section below on labels.

Yes, desktop publishing can be and should be fun, but only if it's easy. Luckily, technology is now to a point where you don't have to be a Parsons graduate to create and publish professional-looking documents. In fact, pushing a mouse to move an arrow around on the screen and clicking a button is about the highest level of computer expertise required. You will, however, need Microsoft Windows on your computer—either the older version 3.1 or the new Windows 95. Windows is a graphic user interface (GUI, pronounced goo-ey) which displays and prints text and images. Almost all the new and powerful programs coming out these days require Windows.

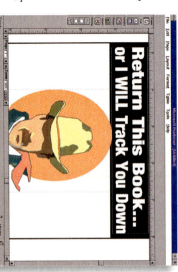

Figure 2: This bookplate is one example of using DTP to produce labels.

Most of us have little experience with desktop publishing, page layout, or using a computer in general. This is no hindrance since a desktop publishing program helps you to do simple page layout jobs such as business forms, greeting cards, newsletters, envelopes, stationery, and a lot more with a minimal investment in money and learning time. What's more—it's both fun and satisfying.

So let's look at practical uses of desktop publishing for you.

We'll explore some handy tricks using the word processing software included with Windows, and give you an overview of what each Windows applet does.

WORD PROCESSING: WORD MANIPULATION

What is the single most important program for any computer user, whether at home or in business? Spreadsheet? Database manager? Inventory? Money management? Project scheduling?

No, none of those. Most important of all is word processing software, and for some very obvious reasons.

In many cases, the only thing people may see from you are words on paper or on a computer screen. Change that to "words and images" and

268

Household Productivity and the PC

<a> Desktop Publishing and Word Processing

Recent rapid advances in technology have resulted in powerful and affordable personal computers. These wonderful machines easily let you do things today that could only have been accomplished by an expensive print shop just a very few years ago. The equivalent of thousands of dollars in equipment and people with decades of experience is now on your desktop, and for a *lot* less than the print shop owner had to pay.

Using inexpensive programs—including some that come free with Microsoft Windows—this section shows you fast and easy, yet professional ways to create:

<bl>
business cards
newsletters
flyers
brochures
ads
labels of all sorts
greeting cards
pamphlets
and much more
<bl end>

you now have desktop publishing, which is both an extension and an augmentation of word processing. Pictures and artwork might not be worth a thousand words, as the old adage goes, but they sure entice people into reading your words.

Quickly and efficiently producing correspondence and documents—mail, fax, and electronic mail (called **email**)—is one key to success in the Information Age. A good letter plants a foot solidly in the doorway; a shoddy one can cause that door to be forever slammed. The appearance of professionalism (especially in correspondence) is often more important than being professional.

WHAT YOU SEE IS WHAT YOU GET

The typewriter, outdated though it may be, had much in common with today's new generation of word processing programs—they are both WYSIWYG (What You See Is What You Get, pronounced *wizzy-wig*) devices. As you typed a page, you saw exactly what the final result was, mistakes and all, and filled up the trashcan next to your desk with crumpled failed efforts. Still, limited as it was, you did see the final results.

The first generations of computer word processing programs *were not* WYSIWYG. Format codes and other esoteric computer commands had to be embedded in the text. Only by actually printing the document were you able to see what it really looked like. Wastepaper basket manufacturers enjoyed continued prosperity.

Now, thanks to graphical user interfaces like Windows, what you see is really what you get. And, while the typewriter was limited to only one **typeface** at one size, Windows-based word processing programs offer hundreds or even thousands of faces in many different sizes and styles. These styles of type are more accurately referred to as *fonts*. **Typestyle** simply refers to whether a particular font is bold, italic, underlined, or has some other special attribute. Selecting the proper fonts requires both art and skill, but is tremendous fun.

WHAT'S AVAILABLE AND WHAT'S BEST

Depending on their complexity, WYSIWYG word processing programs allow rudimentary to sophisticated desktop publishing. Overall, however, word processing software is simply a necessary adjunct to a good DTP program. The word processor allows editing and spell-checking of the edited text. Moving or *importing* your text into the desktop publisher is the next step. DTP software gives you much more control. In short, word processors edit words, DTP programs edit or *lay out* entire pages, providing a means of adding artwork or photos and instantly seeing how your final product looks.

Two quite adequate word processors come included with Windows 95 for free—NotePad and WordPad. NotePad is best for very simple text, while WordPad is a more full-featured word processor. WordPad is not intended for long documents, but works exceptionally well for letters, short reports, faxes, and elementary DTP. WordPad is an elaboration of Windows Write, the free word processing program included in Windows 3.1. It can read a number of other word processors' formats including Write (.wri), Microsoft Word 6.0 (.doc), Rich Text Format (.rtf) and text documents (.txt).

OTHER WORD PROCESSING PROGRAMS

WordPad is certainly worth the money you paid for it (nothing), but longer documents, such as that Great American Novel, call for a bit more power. There are plenty of choices out there. The prices run from $60 or so for "competitive upgrades" to several hundred dollars.

One of the more powerful word processing programs is Microsoft Word for Windows 95. Word has the advantage of being created by the same people who do Windows, and thus has generally better integration with other Microsoft products such as spreadsheets, databases, and so on. In effect, this means it's easy to copy and paste between these various programs.

WordPerfect for Windows, now a product of Novell, the leading network providers, also has a lot going for it, including having been around for so long that many people already have some basic familiarity with it.

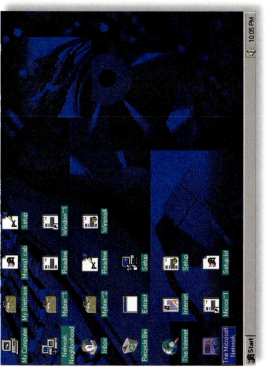

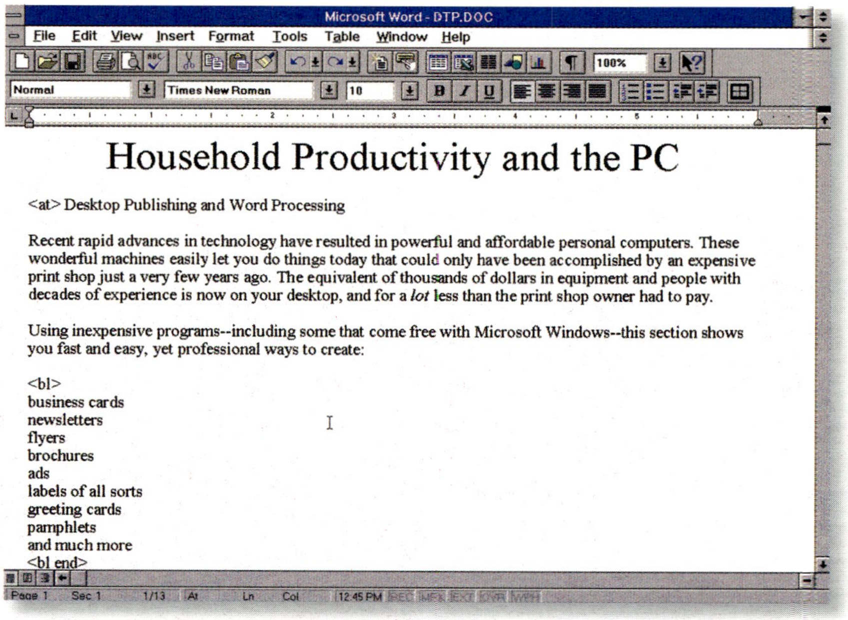

Figure 3: The Windows 95 desktop looks quite different from older versions of Windows, but you'll like its speed and efficiency doing desktop publishing in this new environment.

Figure 4: Steps 1 and 2 when Doing a Quick Business Card Using WordPad

Figure 8: This section was written using Microsoft Word. The letters in the arrow brackets provide information for the typesetter.

The two packages named above are the leading contenders, but lots of other good word processing software abounds in the marketplace. Read reviews and ask computer stores to show you these packages in action, and find the one that best fits your needs.

TYPESTYLE AND FONTS

The characters that your printer uses in printing a document on paper are defined by two attributes—their *typestyle* and their *font* (or *typeface*).

Typestyle is one major factor governing the look of text. It includes bold letters, underlines, and italics.

A font is a set of letters, numbers, punctuation marks, and other characters that are designed to look similar to each other. For example, the lowercase letters in the Times Roman font are all the same height and have small curlicues.

First, let's consider typestyle.

Superscripts are characters: words, or items like copyright and trademark symbols that go slightly above ordinary characters. Footnote numbers and asterisks are other examples of superscripts, as are square, cube, and other exponential roots in mathematical formulae. Subscripts are any words, characters, or symbols that go slightly below the base of the current line.

USING FONTS

Fonts are styles of type, the entire alphabet and other characters all of the same design. The more sophisticated dot-matrix printers offer several fonts, but inkjet and laser printers (with a combination of built-in and downloadable fonts) let you choose from hundreds—the product of centuries of the type designer's wonderful art. These fonts may all be in various sizes; a far cry from the single fixed-pitch typewriter-like font that is all you find on older printers.

Professional typesetters have over 30,000 styles of type or fonts to choose from, using them for different purposes and effect. The use of fonts on a reader may be likened to the effect of a speaker's voice on a listener. Some styles suggest strength, others delicacy. Some styles are formal or legalistic, while others are informal or adventurous. Many (if not most) of these fonts are now available for personal computers.

Fonts are divided into four general classifications—**Roman**, **sans serif**, script, and black letter. The Roman styles, having serifs or finishing strokes (little extensions to the letters),

Doing A Quick Business Card Using WordPad

You can create a nice business card without even buying a desktop publishing program. Just use WordPad in Windows 95 (you can do essentially the same thing in Windows 3.1 using Windows Write).

1. In Windows 95, click on the Start icon.

2. Move to Programs, and the Programs menu pops up. Move the arrow right (it's not necessary to click) to Accessories. The Accessories menu pops up. Move the arrow over and down to the bottom and onto WordPad. This time click. Once.

3. When WordPad's window appears, click on File in the upper-right corner. Move down the menu that drops down and click on Page Setup.

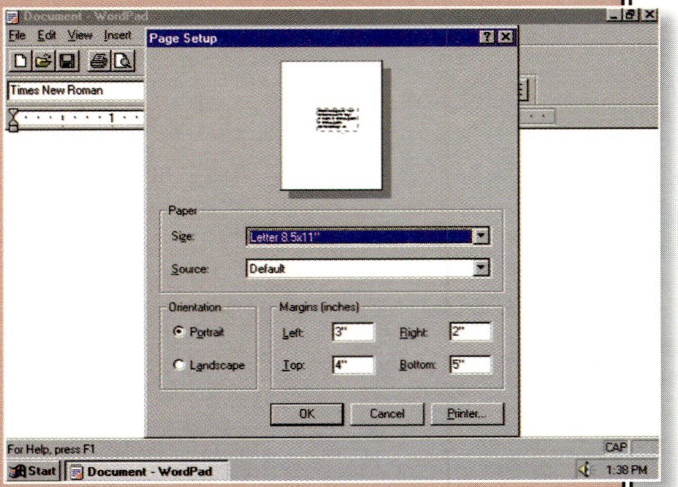

4. In the Margins (Inches) box, set the Left margin to 3 inches, the Right margin to 2 inches, the Top margin to 4 inches, and the Bottom margin to 5 inches. This sets up a standard business card layout of 3.5 inches wide by 2 inches high. Click on OK at the bottom of the dialog box.

5. Type in your name, or the name of your company, such as our example, "Joe's Lawmowing Service."

Figure 5: The Page Setup dialog box is where you set margins as described in step 4.

6. Select the text by holding down the right mouse button and moving the up and down bar across the text (it should change from black on white to white on black). Look for the size control on the bar at the top of the window. It is approximately at the center, just above the ruler, and probably shows "10," meaning 10 points. Click on the downward arrow to its right and select 22 from the drop down box. The size of your text should have gotten larger.

7. On the next line, type in your name and address. Select that text and make it smaller. Around 10 to 12 points works well.

8. Select all the text and center it (clicking on Help on the top bar of the window lets you look up WordPad's commands).

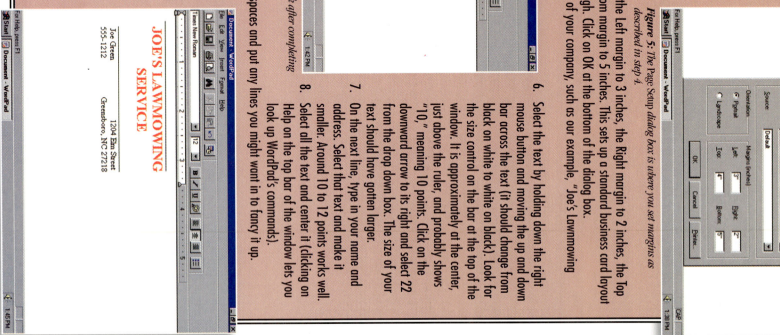

JOE'S LAWMOWING
SERVICE

1204 Elm Street
Greensboro, NC 27218

Joe Green
555-1212

Figure 6: Here's how your card should look after completing steps 6 and 7.

9. Adjust the look of the text with spaces and put any lines you might want in to fancy it up.

10. Print the card out on your printer. Measure to make sure everything fits within 3.5 inches wide by 2 inches high.

11. Take it to a quick print shop and tell them you have a "camera-ready" card. You can probably get 500 for well under $20.

Figure 7: The completed card with a dash of color added.

JOE'S LAWMOWING
SERVICE

1204 Elm Street
Greensboro, NC 27218

Joe Green
555-1212

are often best set in a sans serif font. Helvetica Black is an excellent font for headlines, if you have it—nice, thick, bold, solid letters, much thicker than normal fonts.

Besides choosing the right font, you also need to select the proper size for the job the text has to accomplish. Body text should be somewhere in the range of 9 points to about 14 points maximum. If it is too big or too small, you lose readability. Overly large is just as bad as text that's tiny—either way, people won't make the effort to read it. Headlines can and should be larger. The range between 20 to 40 points, depending on the number of words, is usually good. If you have a short, pithy headline on the order of one or two words, then you can get away with inch-high (72 points) or larger type depending on available space.

Naturally, if you have more than one headline on a page, the more important ones should be larger. Newsletters should have lead stories, and so forth.

Tip: In newsletters, reports, and other lengthy text, use shadowed boxes for callouts. You've seen callouts often in magazines. They are the little bits of exciting or controversial text set in a larger font size than the body text of the article to entice the reader to read the whole article.

In newsletters, reports, and other long text, use shadowed boxes for callouts.

PAGE AND IMAGE MANIPULATION

Now we move up a step from word processing. Various elements—words, graphics, headlines, colors, etc.—can be arranged on each page of a document to create a pleasing effect that entices the reader into examining the material at greater length.

The words "a pleasing effect" are important. Some publishing professionals such as typesetters and graphic designers have a derisive term for the DTP efforts of us beginners— "ransom notes." This term comes from the hodgepodge of cutout and pasted-on letters kidnappers have traditionally used for decades to hide their handwriting.

There are some basic rules for typesetting and page layout that mark the difference between amateur and professional. As mentioned, a simple rule of thumb is two font families per page. A font family would be like Helvetica, Helvetica-Narrow, Helvetica-Condensed, Helvetica-Black, and so forth. These are similar appearing fonts but differ enough in thickness, spacing, and general appearance to add dimension and snap to your page.

As to the more complicated rules, and for tasks such as centering, alignment, import of text

TYPESTYLES

Bold - - - - - - When letters are printed thicker and darker than normal body text. Used for titles or to emphasize words such as the names of products.

Italic - - - - - - Slants the letters and makes them more script-like (the effect varies from font to font). Used to show emphasis, and is the correct style for titles of books, magazines, newspapers, the names of ships, and so forth.

SMALL CAPITALS - - - - Converts all letters, both upper- and lowercase, into capitals just slightly smaller than regular-sized capitals. Makes an nice looking effect for titles when the first letter in a word is a regular-sized capital, and the rest of the word is small capitals.

ALL CAPITALS - - - - Converts all letters in the selected block of text to regular-sized capitals.

Underline - - - - Puts a line under all the characters and spaces in the area of text so defined. Was used during the typewriter era to indicate italics. Rarely used nowadays.

Word Underline - - - Underlines only characters, not blank spaces, so that words are not joined by underlines.

Double Underline - - If your printer supports it, puts two lines under everything in the selected block of text.

Dotted Underline - - If your printer supports it, puts dots under everything in the selected block of text.

are the ones we're all most familiar with and are used in most modern publications. Typewriters also have a Roman typestyle, the Courier font being very common. Times, Baskerville, Garamond, Bodoni, Caslon, and Century are some widely used Roman fonts.

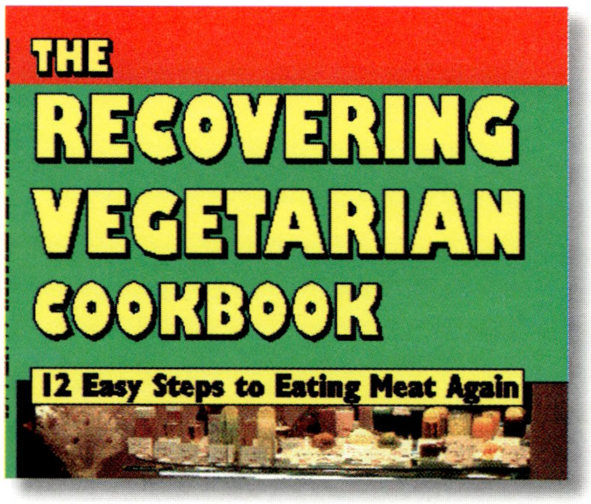

Figure 9: A combination of font selection and typestyle attributes is used to create fancy effects like this one for a book cover.

Sans serif simply means that the font has no finishing strokes on the letters. Book titles and

headlines are often printed in this style of type. Examples of sans serif fonts are: Futura, Univers, Arial and Helvetica.

Script typestyles look like very neat, fine handwriting with the letters joined together. Commercial and Bank are two script fonts. This style of lettering, though, is used today generally only in wedding invitations and on the menus of French restaurants.

The last of the four major classifications, black letter, is like the German manuscript handwriting in Gutenberg's time (Johann Gutenberg invented movable type around 1450 and made printing possible). Gutenberg's first type was of this style. Printers in Germany and other Northern European countries still occasionally use this style of font, but it is seldom used elsewhere because it's hard to read. Fraktur and Schwabacher are black letter fonts.

Font sizes are measured primarily in **points**. A point is equal to 1/72 of an inch. Most commercial type falls between 4 points (extremely small print) to 144 points (letters 2 inches high). Newspapers usually use 8- or 9-point type, while newspaper major headlines are 36 to 72 points (½ to 1 inch high).

Serif fonts, those having little extensions on the letters, are easier to read in large blocks of text. In your documents, any body text such as paragraphs, lists, or columns should almost certainly be a serif font.

Larger, but shorter sections of text—such as titles, headlines, or product names in ads—

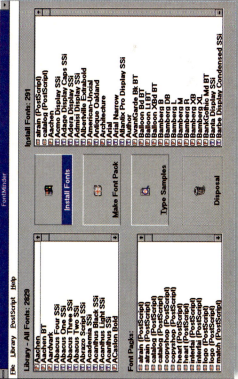

Figure 10: You might have a lot of fonts on your system—this author has 2,829—but don't overuse them. One or two fonts per page is a good rule of thumb.

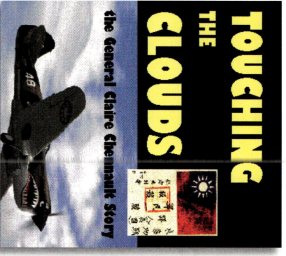

Figure 11: *Sans serif fonts are excellent for titles and headlines, such as this example on a book cover (using the Gill Sans typeface family).*

DTP software packages such as *Microsoft Publisher*, NEB's *Page Magic 1.01a*, and the *PagePlus Publishing Suite 3.05* by Serif Inc. all offer important features that "walk you through" the more complicated page layout designs. You get lots of help features, tips, and design tools that let us neophytes turn out slick, professional-looking results from the very first.

Microsoft Publisher 2.0 (now available also in a CD-ROM edition) is an excellent example. *Publisher* uses automated design helpers called **Wizards**. Choose the *Newsletter Wizard*, for instance, and *Publisher* guides you

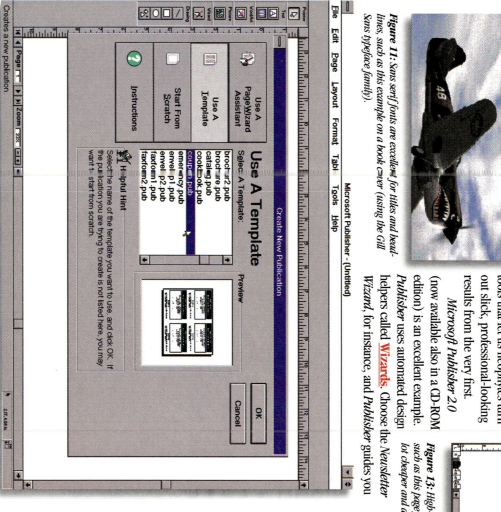

Microsoft Publisher - (Untitled)

File   Edit   Page   Layout   Format   Table   Tools   Help

Create New Publication

Use A PageWizard Assistant
Start From Scratch
Use A Template
Instructions

Use A Template
Select A Template:

broct2.pub
brochure.pub
catalog.pub
cookbook.pub
coupon1.pub
emer-toy.pub
envel-p1.pub
envel-p2.pub
faxform1.pub
faxform2.pub

Preview

Helpful Hint
Select the name of the template you want to use, and click OK. If the publication you are trying to create is not listed here, you may want to start from scratch.

OK   Cancel

Creates a new publication   Page   Zoom 33%

Figure 12: *Templates are included in almost all desktop publishing programs. A template is simply a sample document such as a business card, coupon, or whatever you need. Just edit them to fit your particular purpose.*

There are two very definite levels in word processing software. The top level consists of the so-called "professional" packages used by publishers to produce books and magazines. Such programs as *PageMaker, FrameMaker,* and *QuarkXPress* provide loads of advanced features and cost hundreds of dollars.

Until recently, the lower level of DTP programs was just abbreviated versions of the big guys. Short on features, but requiring just as much knowledge to use effectively. Things have changed very much for the better, however,

and graphics, and so on, most of the inexpensive "entry-level" desktop publishing software provide guides that perform these jobs for you.

through the process of setting up the pages of the newsletter, placing frames for text and graphics, formatting a banner, and creating headlines. In only a few seconds, the size and positions for all your newsletter components are ready. Then you can import or type in the actual text for each article and put photographs or artwork where they belong. Even when you use a Wizard, you'll still have to tailor the final product to your specific publication, but this approach is still many orders of magnitude easier than starting with nothing but a blank page.

Serif Inc.'s *PagePlus Publishing Suite 3.05* CD-ROM Edition also offers similar on-screen aids for designing and creating documents.

NEBS Inc.'s *Page Magic 1.01a*, is new but has several advantages if you're interested in

printing business forms which might appeal to you. NEBS is an old company, long-known as a source of business forms. *Page Magic* includes a number of templates that are designed specifically to work with NEBS forms.

In general, *Microsoft Publisher* seems to be getting the highest ratings currently as an entry-level desktop publishing program. But, you'll want to test-drive a few and see which best fits your requirements.

Now, let's look at some enjoyable and useful projects you can do.

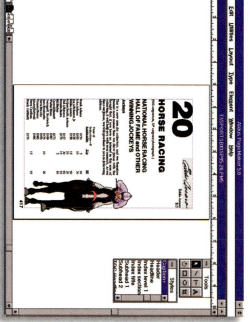

Aldus PageMaker 5.0

File   Edit   Utilities   Layout   Type   Element   Window   Help

20 HORSE RACING
NATIONAL HORSERACING HALL OF FAME and OTHER WINNING JOCKEYS

Figure 13: *High-end desktop publishing programs allow very precise editing, such as this page from an autograph price guidebook. Entry-level programs are a lot cheaper and do most jobs just as well.*

Tip: People like buttons. Any desktop publishing software or even just a word processing program gives you all you need to create designs for striking buttons to advertise your goods or services (for $29.95, you can get a "Badge A Minit" kit from that company in LaSalle, Illinois—1-800-223-4103). Many people don't throw away buttons you give them, so your message stays with them, working for years. Any message you can get into a 2-1/4 inch circle will work as a badge. With an inexpensive color printer or even a black and white printer using colored paper, professional-looking badges are truly a minute or so away.

THINGS YOU CAN DO

We hope you find the following projects both useful and thought-provoking. They should give you both an introduction to what desktop publishing can do for you, and also spark your creativity in thinking up other useful projects.

AWARDS

There's nothing like a pat on the back to perk up friends, significant others, and fellow employees. You can make customers remember you or reward someone who has been especially

Various award certificates are available as clip art that you can import from other applications, or you can use such aids as *Microsoft Publisher's* BorderArt option on the *Layout* menu and create your own.

You might want to buy some special paper for awards. At most any stationery store, you'll find a wide selection of colors and qualities of paper. A buff-colored, high rag-content paper will give your certificates a very expensive-looking parchment effect. Fanfold paper in colors is available for **dot-matrix** printers also. Actual certificates with fancy borders already in place are also available from office supply stores.

If you are creating an award that's being presented to someone by your business, be sure to get your company logo and a tasteful but subdued advertising message (maybe in the form of a slogan) on the certificate. People like getting awards, and they hang them on the walls of their offices or stores for others to see. You could not have bought that space for advertising purposes at any price, yet your ad will be hanging there for years.

For the crowning effect, buy an inexpensive frame and present it already framed. Or go to a quick print shop that will seal documents in plastic. Giving an award enhanced in these ways makes it look professional, and not like something that took a minute to call up and type their name on.

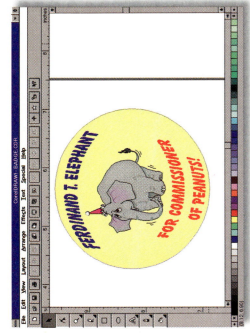

Figure 14: Using a desktop publishing program, a cheap color printer, and a badge-making kit such as that offered by the Badge A Minit company, making badges for fun and profit is a snap!

BUSINESS CARDS

You should carry the first key to success in your pocket or purse.

No, not money (although that's always nice), but business cards. Business cards help you earn more money, or gather more support or membership for your organization, or just let you make a personal statement. People are generally friendly if you talk to them but, without some reminder, they may not be able to recall your name or company after you leave.

Business cards, when done in *Publisher*, are also so fast and inexpensive to produce that you can print special versions for various promotions or sales. You can have cards for all sorts of purposes.

If you don't want to use a copy service, just put a card stock in your printer (most lasers will print a reasonably stiff piece of paper; check your printer's manual for how thick you can go). In the print dialog box, type in the number of cards you want divided by eight (you would need 10 sheets of cardstock to print 80 cards, etc.). Print out the cards and cut them apart.

Voila. Instant business cards.

There are even commercial packages of blank card stock scored with perforations to make separating a sheet of finished cards easy. Look for Avery 5371 at your local office supply store, for example. We use it with great success.

That's the inexpensive end of the spectrum. You can also use a DTP program such as *Microsoft Publisher* to make really fancy cards, having several colors, and even color photographs on them. These will require the assistance of a commercial print shop to do the four-color separations and actual printing, but you can still do all the design, leaving a frame for the picture. Even for a multicolor card without a picture, however, expect to pay perhaps several hundred dollars depending on design. But they *are* nice.

So your business card costs can run anywhere from maybe a cent or two per sheet of eight for those you print yourself to 15 or 20 cents or more for fancy multicolor cards on heavy elegant linen card stock. It all depends on the kind of image you are trying to present, and what you are willing to pay.

> *Tip:* **Colorful paper: Stock up on several colors of regular 8.5 × 11 inch paper at your office supply store—you'll find constant and wonderful uses for all these colors. Just having a selection of colors often will spur creativity. Pastels are best; they provide good contrast for the text, pictures and other objects you'll be printing out. You can never have too many colors of paper. If you want even more selections than your local stores have, call Paper Direct at 1-800-A-PAPERS. They have one of the largest and most unique selections of papers you'll find anywhere. Ask for their free catalog.**

BROCHURES

One type of brochure is a single sheet of paper (usually 8.5 × 11 inches) that can be folded in thirds and used as a mailer, or put in literature racks for interested people to pick up. In this latter case, you'll want to put something colorful and snappy on the front to make it interesting.

> *Tip:* **While three-fold brochures fit neatly in a regular business envelope, you might want to consider just folding them, then sealing them with a bit of tape or a staple. Add the customer's address and a stamp, and drop them into the mail that way—they will go just fine. This technique saves money on envelopes and eliminates the tiresome job of stuffing brochures into envelopes. Also, for a slight additional charge, the copy shop where you have your master reproduced can give you the copies already folded, so all you have to do is address, seal, and stamp them.**

The second kind of brochure is more fancy, printed on glossy paper with four-color photographs. Often this style features several sheets. You can produce the masters for these using a desktop publishing program, but you'll need to go through a commercial printing company to have them printed. Still, you'll easily save hundreds of dollars in setup costs, and maintain greater control over the finished product as well.

If color photographs are to be included, just leave an empty frame where they go. The print shop people will have to make color separations

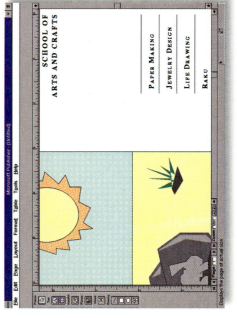

Figure 15: Many of the desktop publishing programs in all price categories offer templates for the production of brochures. The one pictured here comes with Microsoft Publisher.

for the photographs and put them in place during the printing process.

Alternatively, if you have access to a color scanner, place the photographs where they go in the brochure electronically and discuss supplying the brochure on disk to your printer. That means the printer takes your desktop-publishing file and outputs it directly to their film output device from which the plates for the printing press are actually made. This process saves you money but does require some technical know-how, and not every printer can or will handle files from the lower-end DTP packages (although most of them now accept PageMaker and Quark-Xpress files).

Large brochures are expensive, so you'll want to call around and get quotes from printing companies before investing your time in creating one. You'll need to know how many color photographs are to be included, since there is a separation charge for each, the total number of colors (which will be four for color photographs), and the type of paper.

You may also be asked are any questions such as "are there any bleeds in the brochure?" A bleed is when the printing or a color box goes all the way to the edge of the paper. This can be a pattern, an overprinted color, or whatever, but it does entail an extra charge because of the way the piece has to be handled on the press (it has to be printed on oversized paper and trimmed to the correct size). You can save money by avoiding bleeds.

To create a multi-page brochure, use a guide such as *Microsoft Publisher's* Newsletter PageWizard, but specify only one or two columns. That way you'll get the benefit of the headings and page numbers for each page, but it can create a layout in the format of a brochure.

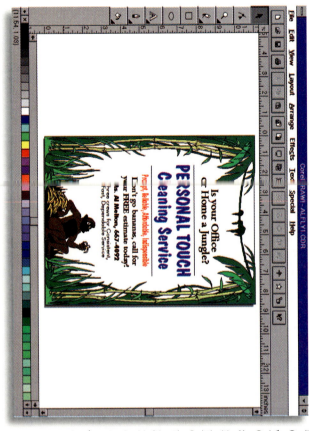

Figure 16: A nice colorful flyer attracts attention... and new business! This one was produced in Corel Draw and has worked very well for a service specializing in cleaning homes and offices.

Tip: Thank you notes: Modify one of the memo templates that come with most DTP packages (in Publisher, Memo and Memoz) to serve as a thank you note, or use something like Publisher's Greeting Card PageWizard to make a card.

FLYERS

Flyers are one page, unfolded, brochures. They are the most overlooked yet one of the cheapest and most highly effective forms of advertising.

A flyer is really just a big ad. You can use *Microsoft Publisher's* Ad PageWizard or the Coupon PageWizard to make it (draw a box as large as the margin guides on the page).

Flyers work very well for seasonal-related events or sales—Memorial Day Blow Out, July 4th Clearance, Halloween Sale With Prices So Low It Scares Us, The Mother Of All Yard Sales, and so forth.

Don't try to get too much information on a flyer; they work best if uncluttered (brochures and newsletters are better for imparting larger amounts of information). The Ad PageWizard is a good choice because it lets you put a large, attention-getting slogan on the flyer, a striking but appropriate piece of clipart or other illustration, a minimum of explanatory text, and your company or organization's name, address, and phone number. Flyers get people in the store, or to the meeting. At that point, you can give out brochures, newsletters, and catalogs to those who are really interested. *Publisher*, by the way, includes a catalog template—press the *Template* radio button in the *Start up* dialog box and find the word *catalog* on the template list box to access it.

Figure 17: Another example of a flyer, this one created in PageMaker. It grew a lot of new business for this greenhouse company when mailed to local residents.

practically nothing, and that small percentage that gets you extra business is well worth the effort.

Why do companies keep sending out mailing after mailing when probably over 90 percent of it gets thrown away? Because the small percentage that *does* get read, not only pays for the mailing but makes a good profit.

No piece of correspondence should go out of your office, no bill should be paid, without including your flyer in the envelope. It costs you

In fact, now that you can produce desktop publishing documents so easily, consider putting together a coordinated promotion plan of your company or organization. You can plan everything from business cards and various forms, to flyers, brochures, and a regular newsletter.

MAKING YOUR OWN ADS

Every business, large or small, needs to advertise occasionally. Most publications charge extra for producing "camera ready" ads. A camera-ready ad is completely typeset, has the artwork in place, and is *exactly* the right size. The term *camera-ready* comes from the fact that layout sheets for each page of the publication are photographed and a plate for the printing press made from the photo. You can often save a respectable amount on advertising by providing camera-ready copy. *Microsoft Publisher* provides tools like WordArt which allow you to do camera-ready ads.

Tip: To Do List: Use a table template (or the Table PageWizard in Publisher) to make up a To Do list of the projects to be done for each day. For work, put inspirational slogans at the top, along with the company logo, and give them out to other company team members. Seeing what you have to get done, and being able to check each job off as finished is a great boost to productivity.

This both saves you money and gives more control over the finished product (you care a lot more about your business than some harried layout person on a tight deadline).

Use typographic effects such as placing a shadow behind letters to blast the main point of the ad out at the reader. **SALE. HUGE DISCOUNTS. SAVE.** And so forth.

A laser or inkjet printer is ideal for doing an ad, although the better dot matrix machines can provide some very acceptable results that will reproduce nicely. A trick to increase resolution is to make the ad slightly oversized, then reduce it on a copier to 96 percent or so of the original. Be sure the reduced ad is exactly the right size as we discuss below. The purpose of reducing the printed ad is to pull the dots in closer together; making it more near actual typeset quality. Most quick copy shops can handle the reduction for you for maybe 50 cents, as opposed to having the publication do it on their copy camera—tacking on another seven or eight dollars to your bill.

The ad sales person will tell you the exact size of the ad you are buying. Sizes for a quarter-page ad, for example, vary from publication to publication. A quarter-page for a tabloid-sized paper is usually something like 5-¾ inches high by 4-⅞ inches wide (although this varies slightly from paper to paper). Make the ad people specify exactly in inches or picas instead of 11.5 column inches (the area of the ad instead of its dimensions). A specification in "column inches" would be useless to you in producing the ad, but it is how they calculate how much the ad will cost you.

The first step is to draw a box the same size as the ad or, if you are going to have it reduced to improve resolution, whatever size when reduced 96 percent will be the correct ad size. Print the box out and measure it, then adjust as necessary until it's *exactly* the right size. Then save a copy of the file to use as a template the next time you need to create a quarter-page or whatever ad.

What you want in an ad (to justify the expense and make it effective) is something that jumps out at the reader. Choose an appropriate piece of clip art that emphasizes what your business does or points up some special event such as the Fourth of July or New Year's.

If you have a scanner, your company logo or other artwork should be scanned in as either a .PCX or .TIF file. Most DTP software can import and use either of those formats.

Use a nice bold font for your company name in the ad, and a smaller non-bold version of the same font for the address and phone number. The cardinal rule in creating an ad is to keep it clean and uncluttered. The most common mistake an amateur makes in constructing an ad is trying to put in too much. You might have six specials this week, but in a quarter-page ad, there isn't a lot of room. Choose the two best specials and tout those.

There are lots of little tricks to make your ads stand out from those around them. A shadowed effect will pop your ad up off the page. Just be sure that everything including the **shadow** fits within the size restriction of the publication. You can safely assume that no leeway exists—it

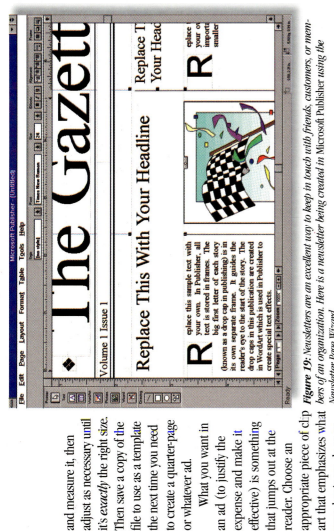

Figure 19: Newsletters are an excellent way to keep in touch with friends, customers, or members of an organization. Here is a newsletter being created in Microsoft Publisher using the Newsletter Page Wizard.

course of a year in production costs by producing their own ads.

NEWSLETTERS

Another excellent and inexpensive way to get your message out—for your company, club, church, or school—is by publishing a regular newsletter. Think of it as a small newspaper, usually printed on 8.5 x 11-inch paper.

You can actually do everything needed for a newsletter, including writing the story, from right within most DTP packages. However, as you become more comfortable with the process, you might want to invest in a word processing application, a more sophisticated drawing program such as *Corel Draw*, and some sort of scanner.

> *Tip:* Do you spend a lot of time on the phone explaining to people how to get to your store, office, or home? Use your DTP software's drawing tools to draw a map to your place. Then just fax, hand, or mail them a map.

must fit, which means you may have to resize your box to allow for the shadow.

Usually a white background is best, but sometimes a light shade is effective or, for small ads, a total reversal of white on black (like a picture negative) can work.

Small businesses that advertise regularly can save hundreds of dollars over the

Desktop publishing is one of the best ways to get value out of your computer. And, thanks to excellent and powerful DTP software, today anyone can start his or her own personal publishing company. Even if you limit yourself to a single job—creating custom Christmas cards, say—you're likely to find the DTP experience rewarding. 📡

Ralph Roberts is the author of over 50 books and thousands of articles in the personal computing field. He wrote the first book on computer viruses in the US, and is the author of the best-selling book The Official Book of Leisure Suit Larry. *Ralph's first article on personal computing appeared in* Creative Computing *magazine in 1978.*

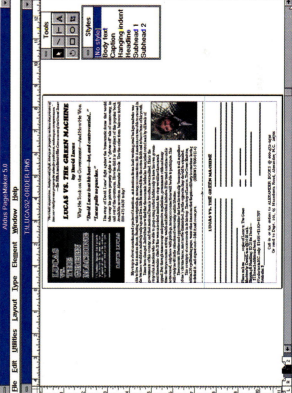

Figure 18: This flyer was designed to sell books, and it does the job quite well.

MOVING INFORMATION BETWEEN COMPUTERS
PC TO MAC & MAC TO PC

By Tom R. Halfhill

What used to be a formidable barrier—moving text between a PC and a Mac—is now an open door. This article explains what to do.

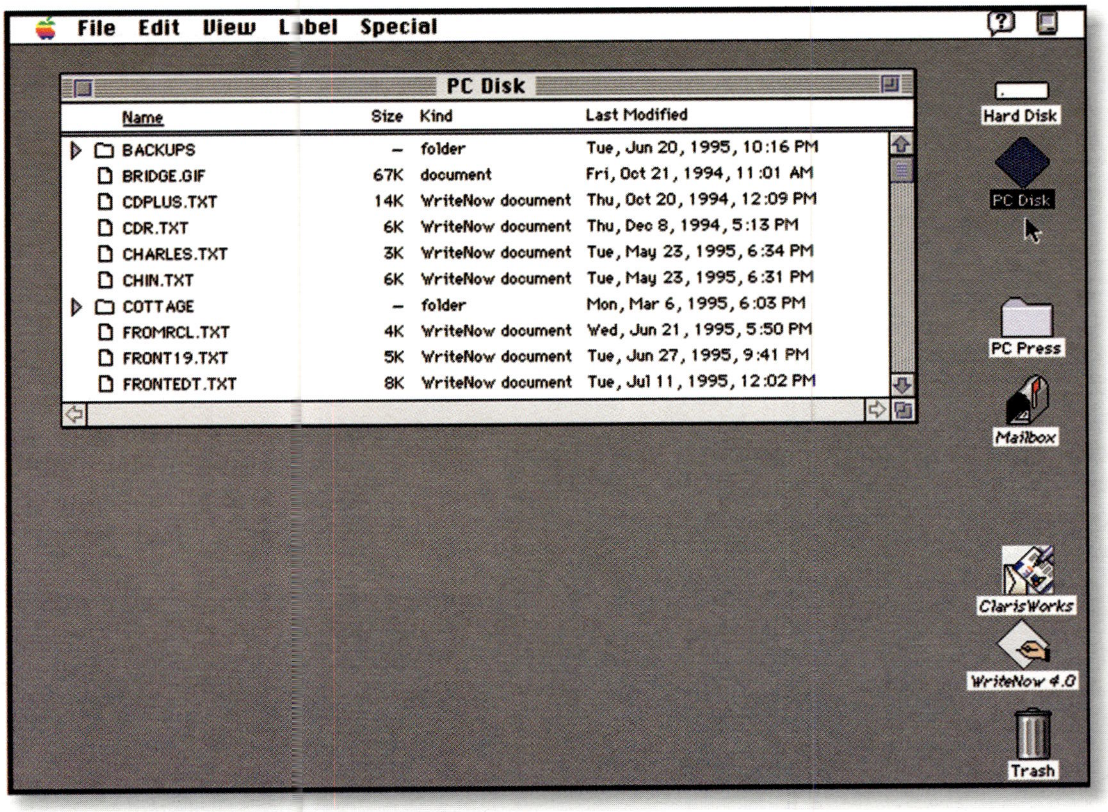

Figure 1: *With a program such as Macintosh/PC Exchange or Access PC, Macs can read, write, and format PC disks just like Mac disks.*

File Edit View Label Special

PC Disk

Name	Size	Kind	Last Modified
BACKUPS	–	folder	Tue, Jun 20, 1995, 10:16 PM
BRIDGE.GIF	67K	document	Fri, Oct 21, 1994, 11:01 AM
CDPLUS.TXT	14K	WriteNow document	Thu, Oct 20, 1994, 12:09 PM
CDR.TXT	6K	WriteNow document	Tue, Dec 8, 1994, 5:13 PM
CHARLES.TXT	3K	WriteNow document	Tue, May 23, 1995, 6:34 PM
CHIN.TXT	6K	WriteNow document	Tue, May 23, 1995, 6:31 PM
COTTAGE	–	folder	Mon, Mar 6, 1995, 6:03 PM
FRONIRCL.TXT	4K	WriteNow document	Wed, Jun 21, 1995, 5:50 PM
FRONT19.TXT	5K	WriteNow document	Tue, Jun 27, 1995, 9:41 PM
FRONTEDT.TXT	8K	WriteNow document	Tue, Jul 11, 1995, 12:02 PM

Hard Disk · PC Disk · PC Press · MailBox · ClarisWorks · WriteNow 4.0 · Trash

Here's the problem: Your kid wants to write a report using your IBM PC-compatible at home and then finish the paper at school, but the school has Apple Macintoshes. Or maybe you're facing the opposite problem: You own a Macintosh and you want to bring some work home from the office, where you've got a PC. Everyone knows that PCs and Macs are incompatible, right?

Well, not exactly. It's true that Macs and PCs are based on different microprocessors and therefore are incompatible with each other's software. Normally, a program designed to run on one kind of computer won't run on the other. (The only exception is emulation, where a PC can pretend to be a Mac and vice versa, a topic we won't discuss here.) But that doesn't mean you can't exchange information between the two types of machines. The document files you create with your software—text documents, graphics, spreadsheets, databases and so forth—are easily portable between Macs and PCs. In fact, there are several ways to bridge this gap, depending on what you're trying to do.

It is somewhat easier to move information from PCs to Macs than from Macs to PCs. Macs are less popular, so they must bend over backward to be a little more accommodating. (Indeed, one of Apple's advertising slogans is "Stand out, fit in.") But either way, the problem is easy to solve with the right software.

First there's the job of physically moving the files from one machine to the other. We'll discuss three ways to do this. Then, once you've successfully moved the files, you have to manipulate them using the software on the other computer. It's often such a surprisingly simple process that you might even forget you're dealing with two "incompatible" computers.

MOVING FILES ON FLOPPIES

The easiest way to move a document file from a PC to a Mac or vice versa is with a floppy disk. You merely save the document onto a floppy, carry it to the other computer, insert it into the disk drive and then copy the file off of the floppy as usual. (The computer slang for this casual form of "networking" is **sneakernet**.)

Almost all PCs and Macs sold during the past several years have floppy disk drives that use the same kind of disks: 3.5-inch **floppies**. They fit easily into a shirt pocket and are protected by a hard plastic shell with a sliding metal cover. (Modern floppies don't feel very floppy, but the name was retained from older, larger floppy disks that didn't have a hard plastic shell.)

Since all recent PCs and Macs use the same kind of floppy disks, it's easy to share the disks between computers. There's only one catch: Although the disks are physically identical, PCs and Macs record their information in different **data formats** that are normally incompatible. Fortunately, this problem is easy to solve with the right software.

This software comes free with all current Macs and is available separately for older Macs. If the Mac has the latest version of Apple's **operating system**—System 7.5—it includes a program called *Macintosh/PC Exchange*. This

Figure 2: Amazingly, it's easier to format a PC disk on a Mac than it is on a PC!

program allows Macs to read, write and **format** PC-standard disks. (It can also read, write and format ProDOS-standard disks for Apple II-series computers, which are still common in many schools.)

Macintosh/PC Exchange is so easy to use that you might not even realize you're using it. When you insert a PC disk into the Mac's floppy drive, the Mac automatically recognizes it as a PC disk and mounts the icon on the desktop just like a Mac disk. You can do everything with the PC disk that you could do with a Mac disk: copy files, delete files, rename files, create folders (**subdirectories**) and so on. It's totally transparent.

Tech Tip: Any Mac with a SuperDrive floppy disk drive can read PC-format disks by using a program such as *Macintosh/PC Exchange* or *Access PC*. Older Macs cannot read PC disks. If the Mac was made in the 1990s, it almost certainly has a SuperDrive.

Even if the Mac doesn't have System 7.5, it might still have *Macintosh/PC Exchange*. The program was included free with many versions of System 7.1 that were sold in the home and educational markets in recent years. Before that, Macs came with a program called *Apple File Exchange*. This program isn't as easy to use, so it's worth replacing with *Macintosh/PC Exchange* or a similar program sold by another company, such as *Access PC* from Insignia Solutions. (*Access PC* is faster.)

What if you're moving files in the other direction—from a Mac to a PC? The answer isn't quite as simple. PCs don't come with any software that lets them read Mac disks. Frankly,

the best solution is to use the Mac to create a PC-format disk, rather than try to read a Mac disk on a PC. But if you can't do this, you can buy a program called *MacDisk* from Insignia Solutions. *MacDisk* lets you read, write and format high-density (1.44MB) Macintosh floppies on a PC.

Another alternative is a **shareware** program called *MacSee* from ReeveSoft. You can **download** *MacSee* from popular **online services** such as CompuServe and America Online. Like *MacDisk*, *MacSee* lets you use high-density Macintosh disks on PCs.

Floppy disks aren't the only kind of disks you can move back and forth between PCs and Macs. If both computers are equipped with a removable hard disk drive, such as a Syquest drive or an Iomega Zip drive, you can transport files on those disks, too. This is especially useful if the file you're moving won't fit on a 1.44MB floppy. Again, you'll need a program such as *Macintosh/PC ExcEange, Access PC, MacDisk* or *MacSee* to read the disk on the other computer.

Tech Tip: It's easier to exchange floppy disks between PCs and Macs if the disks are formatted to a capacity of 1.44MB (high density). All recent Macs can also read older PC disks formatted to 720K, but PCs are physically incapable of reading older Mac disks in 400K and 800K formats.

MOVING FILES BY MODEM

Another relatively simple way to exchange files between computers s to send them over a phone line via **modem**. To make this work, each

computer needs a modem and **communications software** for sending and receiving files.

This can be a little trickier than carrying floppy disks back and forth. Communications software is finicky, and a computer-to-computer transfer normally requires someone at each end to make the phone connection and run the programs.

The best approach is to send the file by **email**. For example, some schools are giving their students online accounts and email addresses on the **Internet**. Many office workers have email addresses, too. You can exchange files between PCs and Macs merely by sending the file as an email message to yourself or another person. **Upload** the file on one computer, and download it on the other.

The easiest way to email a file is over CompuServe or America Online or some other online service in **binary format**. This preserves all the special formatting in your file. For example, CompuServe gives you the option of sending a *file* (as opposed to a text) document. From the WinCIM (Windows Compuserve program) *Mail* menu, choose *File*. From the AOL Windows program, choose the *Mail* menu, *Compose Mail*, then click on the *Attach* button. Other online services have similar options. If you are sending email via the Internet, you must use a method known as **UUcoding**. Unfortunately, these subjects are beyond the scope of this article.

A third method of transferring files between PCs and Macs is to use a direct physical connection between the computers. In an office or a school computer lab, you can use a **local area network (LAN)** for this purpose—assuming the network has both PCs and Macs. With a LAN, moving files from computer to computer is almost as easy as copying them from a floppy disk, and you can transfer very large files at very high speeds. To learn more, talk to the network administrator (the person in charge of the LAN).

You can set up a temporary "LAN" of your own by hooking two computers together with a **null modem cable**. This is an inexpensive cable that connects the **serial ports** of two computers—two PCs, two Macs, or a Mac and a PC. The null modem cable simulates a pair of modems and a phone connection. On each computer, you run an ordinary communications program that allows you to transfer files. You set up these programs just as if you were establishing a phone connection, only without the phones. Since there are no modems involved, you can transfer files at the highest speed the serial ports can handle.

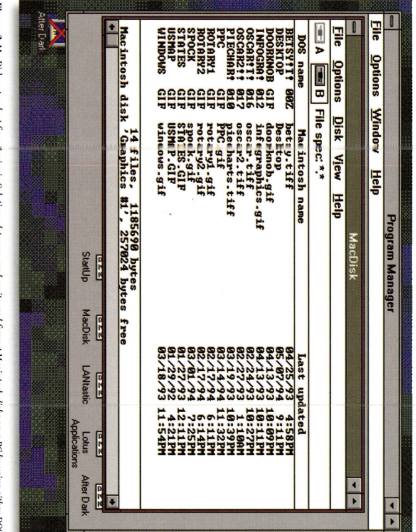

Figure 3: MacDisk, a product from Insignia Solutions, lets you read, write and format Macintosh disks on a PC by using either DOS or Windows. Notice how it automatically translates the longer Mac filenames into legal DOS filenames.

ASCII text, be aware that the file will not contain any special formatting you may have used. Only the raw text will be saved. Page margins, italics, type fonts, font styles, graphics and other elements will be removed. Tabs may be ignored or converted to spaces. So be sure to save another copy of your file the usual way. (Give it a different filename, or save it on a different disk or in another folder.)

ASCII text files are admittedly limited, but that's not necessarily a problem. For example, students who are preparing reports can write the text on their home computer, save the document on a floppy disk in ASCII format, carry the disk to school, load the document into a word processor on the school's computer and then add all the special formatting there. Formatting is usually the last thing you do, anyway.

Still, there are times when you don't want to lose the formatting. Ideally, you should be able to create a document on a PC or a Mac, dress it up any way you want and transfer the document to another computer without losing any work.

Luckily, this is much easier today than ever before. It's especially straightforward if both computers are running their own versions of the same software.

For instance, almost all Macs sold in the home and educational markets in recent years come with free software called *ClarisWorks*. *ClarisWorks* is an **integrated software package** that includes a word processor, a spreadsheet, a database manager, a drawing program, a paint program and a communications program. There is also a Windows version of *ClarisWorks* for PCs. The PC and Mac versions of

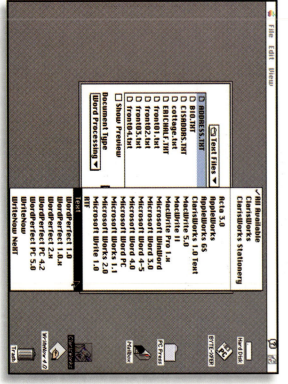

Figure 4: Most programs can open and save document files in a wide variety of file formats. This list is found in the Mac version of ClarisWorks.

ClarisWorks are so similar that documents can be moved easily between PCs and Macs. When all is said and done, the simplest way to move files between PCs and Macs is to carry them on a floppy disk.

This method, too, is a little tricky. And, of course, it requires the two computers to be located within a few feet of each other. When all is said and done, the simplest way to move files between PCs and Macs is to carry them on a floppy disk.

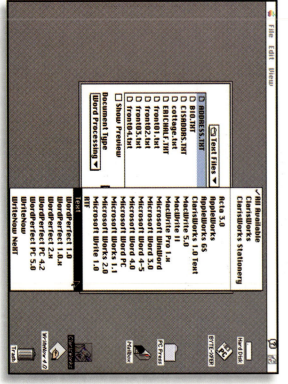

Tech Tip: You can turn almost any serial cable into a null modem cable by adding a null modem adapter, which costs a few dollars at Radio Shack. Bring your cable to the store to make sure you get the right adapter.

Coping With File Formats

By far the easiest kinds of files to exchange between PCs and Macs are plain text files. All computers recognize the same basic alphabetic characters and symbols, known as **ASCII characters**. ASCII text files are the lowest common denominator and are therefore the most portable.

Virtually all word processors have an option to save your document as ASCII text, although it's probably not described that way. On Macs, and on PCs with Windows or OS/2, this option is generally found under the word processor's *File* menu. Look for a menu item called *Save As*.

When you choose this menu item, the computer will ask you to assign a **filename** to the document you're saving. Somewhere on this screen (usually near the bottom) will be a list of options for different file formats. Look for an option called *ASCII*, *Text*, *DOS Text*, *Text With*

Line Breaks or something similar. All of these are ASCII text formats. (See your word processor manual for more information.)

Tech Tip: Sometimes you can't avoid an ASCII option that adds carriage-return or linefeed characters to your text. When transferring ASCII files from PCs to Macs, sometimes the text will appear double-spaced on the Mac. You can fix this by deleting the extra carriage returns and linefeeds. Check your word processor manual or help screens for information on finding and replacing special "hidden" characters.

If your word processor gives you a choice of ASCII formats, pick *ASCII* or *Text* instead of *DOS Text* or *Text with Line Breaks*. The latter two options may add a **carriage-return** or **linefeed** character to the end of every line of text. These characters will probably make the text look funny on the other computer unless you manually delete them.

When you save your document as

Even if both computers don't have the same software, there's still a very good chance they can exchange documents in a common file format. Microsoft *Word* is such a popular program on both PCs and Macs that almost all word processors can save documents in *Word* format. You can take advantage of this even if you don't have *Word*. For example, you could use *WordPerfect* on a PC to save the document in *Word* format, then read the document on a Mac with *ClarisWorks*, which also understands *Word* format.

Another common file format for text documents is **RTF** (Rich Text Format). Many

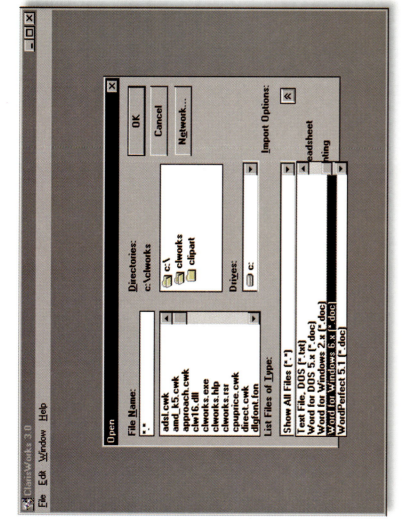

Figure 5: *Even if you don't have Microsoft Word, you can save documents in Word format to exchange files between different word processors. This menu appears in the PC version of ClarisWorks.*

ClarisWorks can read each other's document files with no loss of formatting. You can move formatted text and graphics back and forth without a hitch.

Likewise, many best-selling programs these days are available for both PCs and Macs. Examples include Microsoft's *Word, Excel,* and *PowerPoint;* Novell's *WordPerfect;* Adobe's *PhotoShop* and *PageMaker;* Claris *FileMaker;* and Quark's *QuarkXPress.* All of these programs can share files between their PC and Mac versions.

word processors on PCs and Macs can save and load documents in RTF format.

Look for these options under the *File* menu of your word processor. There should be a menu item called *Open, Open As,* or *Import.* This will bring up a screen that lets you choose from a list of file-format options, much like the options found under the *Save As* menu item.

System 7.5 for Macs includes a free program called *Easy Open,* which is also available

Tech Tip: When sharing documents between the PC and Mac versions of the same program, you may encounter a problem if one computer doesn't have the latest release of the software. Almost always, however, newer releases give you the option of saving documents in an older version of the file format. Try Save As *under the* File *menu.*

separately. When you try to open a document that was created with a program not installed on the Mac, *Easy Open* figures out which programs (if any) *can* read the file and asks you to pick one.

Easy Open also works with special translators available from a company called DataViz. If you frequently transfer formatted files between PCs to Macs, however, consider purchasing an even more versatile product from DataViz called *MacLinkPlus.* This amazing Mac program can translate almost any kind of file. A similar product is Mastersoft's *Word for Word,* which is available for both Macs and PCs.

Tech Tip: If you're transferring a formatted text document that uses type fonts and styles, try to pick a font that's available on both computers. Both PCs and Macs come with a few similar TrueType fonts. Courier is a rather boring typewriter-like font, but it's the same on any computer. Times or Times Roman is another safe choice. Don't always judge a font by its name; some fonts with different names are virtually identical.

MOVING GRAPHICS FILES

Of course, you're not limited to sharing text documents between PCs and Macs. You can also exchange graphics, digitized photos, sounds, spreadsheets and databases. Again, it's easy if both computers have the same software or a program that can read common file formats.

One common format for digitized photos and other **bit-mapped graphics** is GIF

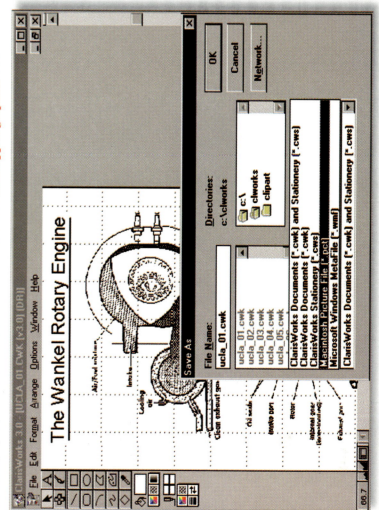

Figure 6: *PCs and Macs share many common graphics formats. This screen shows how the PC version of ClarisWorks can save a graphics file in Macintosh PICT format.*

(Graphics Interchange Format). GIF is particularly good because it compresses the file to save space, an important consideration when moving files on floppy disks or by modem. One of GIF's limitations, however, is that it can't handle more than 256 colors or shades of gray.

Another popular graphic file type is TIFF (Tagged Image File Format). TIFF files can handle millions of colors. TIFF originated on the Mac but has been adopted by many PC programs. Be aware, though, that there are numerous flavors of TIFF. Even if you have a graphics program that reads TIFF, it might choke on some variations.

On PCs, a similar file type is BMP (Bit-Mapped). Some Mac programs can read BMP files. Another file type common to both computers is EPS (Encapsulated PostScript), which stores vector-graphics images. Both computers also have metafiles; on Macs, they're called PICT files, and on PCs, they're called Windows Metafiles (WMF). Still another graphic file type is JPEG (Joint Photographic Experts Group), which can compress an image to smaller sizes than GIF, though there can be some loss of quality.

To keep things simple, stick to GIF if you can. Otherwise, try JPEG or TIFF. If you find yourself transferring lots of graphics files, consider buying a translation program such as DeBabelizer Lite from Equilibrium Technologies for the Mac. It can translate almost any graphics file, including odd ones such as Unix and Amiga formats. The equivalent program on the PC is Hijaak.

Another useful tool is PaintShop Pro, an excellent Windows shareware program from JASC. In fact, all the popular online services have numerous shareware and freeware programs that can translate among GIF, JPEG, TIFF, and other formats.

Sharing information between PCs and Macs has become so routine that some people scarcely notice they're switching computers. As Macs continue to accommodate themselves to the larger world of PCs, and as PCs continue to acquire more Mac-like features, the process is becoming almost seamless. Fanatics may argue over which kind of computer is best, but what's certain is that neither a Mac nor a PC will limit your ability to move your work back and forth between your home, office, or school.

Tom R. Halfhill is a senior editor at BYTE Magazine and has been writing about personal computers since 1981. He was previously the editor of COMPUTE! and Game Players magazines and has co-authored and edited numerous books on computing and other topics.

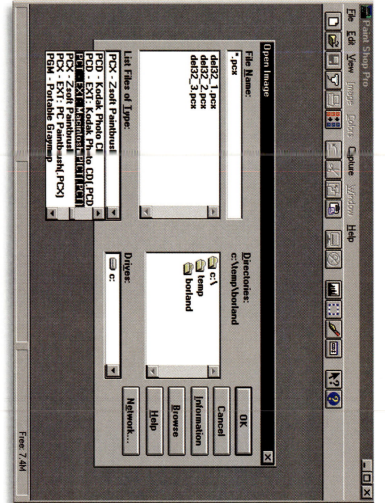

Figure 7: *PaintShop Pro for Windows, a shareware program, can open and save graphics files in numerous different formats.*

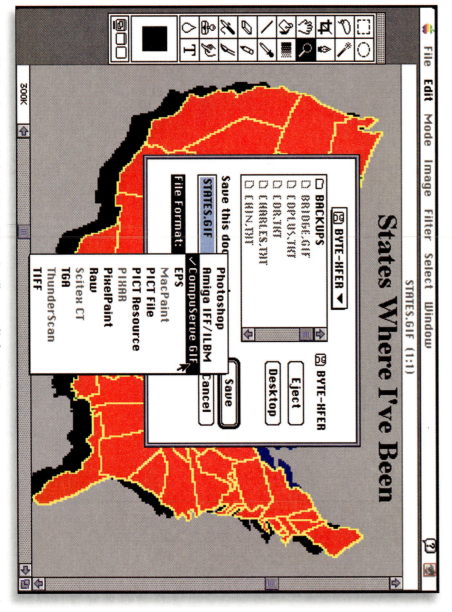

Figure 8: *Adobe PhotoShop, available for both PCs and Macs, also offers many file-format options.*

SHOULD WE BUY ONE FOR GRANDMA?

By Lisa Iannucci

The online world is filled with active retirees sharing information, chatting and communicating via email with their families all over the world. If you're thinking of getting a computer for an older relative, here are some good reasons why that might be an excellent investment.

Marjorie Hujsak uses CompuServe to keep in touch with her family. She sends email messages to her five children who are scattered across the United States, and to her ten-year-old granddaughter who lives in Florida.

"Usually you would wait to call the family on the weekend, but this makes it easier," says Marjorie, a Maine resident. "Some of my family is in California, so the time difference also makes it difficult to call. Now we keep in touch through these little messages."

Marjorie are using online services to keep in contact with their families. What some older Americans don't realize, however, is that using online services can be much more than just a vehicle for family communications.

WHAT'S IN IT FOR ME?

Sure, keeping in touch with family is a terrific reason to use online services, but it isn't the only one. Thousands of seniors are moving into cyberspace thanks to specialized forums discussions in live chat areas. They can also learn how to participate in various governmental issues that affect them and thereby have their voice heard. Seniors also have access to many organizations that offer information for older Americans as well as discounts on various products and memberships.

FINDING SENIOR FORUMS

Once you've subscribed to an online service, conduct a search to find the various forums specifically for seniors. For example, in CompuServe, use the FIND feature and type in SENIOR. For America Online (AOL), do a KEYWORD search and type in SENIOR.

HOW DO I GET AROUND?

In addition to private email messages, there are several other ways to communicate with other senior members. Each CompuServe forum is divided into three parts: a message/bulletin board, a library and a conference center. The message/bulletin board area is a public area that allows forum members to respond to existing topics, leave questions for other members to answer, or start discussions on new topics. In the library, subscribers can download (or upload) information on many topics listed in that forum. Conferences are opportunities to engage in live conversations with other forum members. Periodically, forums host special conferences on a particular topic, travel, for example, with expert guests.

One of the largest senior areas on CompuServe is the Retirement Living Forum

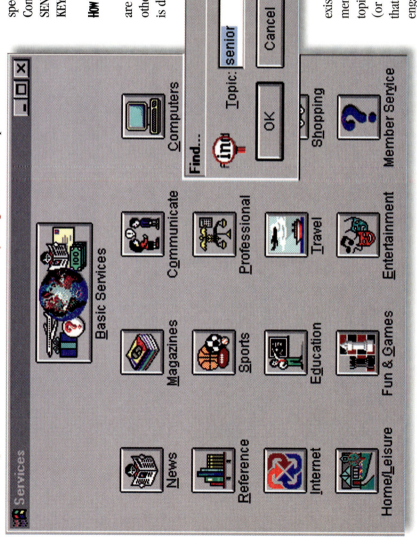

Figure 1: CompuServe forums and services available for seniors.

Marjorie believes that using CompuServe has kept her close to her family, especially her granddaughter who likes being remembered with these special notes. Many grandparents like

that appeal specifically to their interests. Topics in these forums include retirement, travel, cooking, grandparenting, and aging issues. Seniors can socialize and join online friends for

Welcome to the best years of your life!

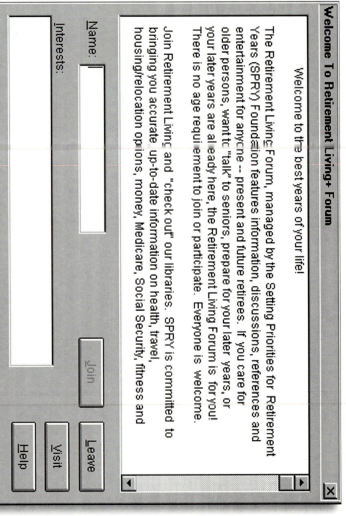

The Retirement Living Forum, managed by the Setting Priorities for Retirement Years (SPRY) Foundation features information, discussions, references and entertainment for anyone -- present and future retirees. If you care for older persons, want to "talk" to seniors, prepare for your later years, or your later years are already here, the Retirement Living Forum is for you! There is no age requirement to join or participate. Everyone is welcome.

Join Retirement Living and "check out" our libraries. SPRY is committed to bringing you accurate up-to-date information on health, travel, housing/relocation options, money, Medicare, Social Security, fitness and

Name:

Interests:

Figure 2: SPRY (Setting Priorities for Retirement Years) is an active CompuServe forum.

consumer-oriented information and resources for seniors; for people planning retirement; for adult children seeking information on caring for elders; and for professionals serving older people and their families.

The Retirement Living Forum is operated by the SPRY Foundation, a non-profit organization designed to enhance the quality of life for older Americans. SPRY is the acronym for Setting Priorities for Retirement Years. SPRY works with many Federal agencies and national associations to provide literature for the forum members on such topics as health, finances, Social Security and Medicare. Some of these organizations include the National Institute on Aging, the National Institutes on Health, and the Social Security Administration. There are also special public sections of the American Society on Aging (ASA). If you're a member of ASA, you can access the private message center and library as well.

CompuServe also has senior sections within certain forums. For example, in the ISSUES forum, there is a VILLAGE ELDERS section. But of course older adults are not limited to senior-only forums. They can visit any forum they are interested in and meet others with the same interests.

To access one of the largest senior forums on AOL, use the KEYWORD search and type in SENIORNET. SeniorNet is a non-profit organization for older adults interested in using

America Online
File Edit Go To Mail Members Window Help

MEMBER SERVICES

GO TO MAIN MENU

Main Menu   Welcome,

SeniorNet Online
The International Community of Computer-Using Seniors

- Welcome to SeniorNet Online
- Announcements
- About Buick/SeniorNet
- Buick Celebrates V-E Day
- What's New & Events
- SeniorNet Membership Application
- SeniorNet Sourcebook
- White House Conference
- Senior Resources

Host: SeniorNet
Keyword: seniornet

SeniorNet Forums

Computer Learning Center

Community Center

Showcase & Exchange

Figure 3: SENIORNET is a non-profit organization and is among the largest forums on AOL for seniors.

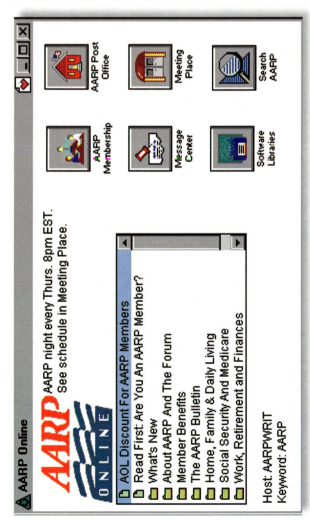

Figure 4: *The American Association of Retired Persons is represented on CompuServe, AOL and elsewhere on the information highway:*

computers, and includes many areas such as a computer learning center, a community center for live chat, and special forums for discussing topics on subjects unrelated to computers. SeniorNet offers sections on language clubs, household hints and repairs, and participation in "actual world" gatherings of SeniorNet members who have met online. There are also special areas such as the World War II section, and Generation-to-Generation, an area that links seniors and schoolchildren.

Many organizations contribute to the SeniorNet libraries, including Caring Grandparents of America, The Gray Panthers, and The Older Women's League. Forum members have participated in the White House Conference on Aging and other such important conferences that link the voice of the senior population with the right people in government who need to hear these views.

THE AARP

The American Association of Retired Persons is now online and appears in many online services, including CompuServe and America Online. This special forum can be accessed by typing in AARP at the GO commands and KEYWORD commands. This association provides access to the AARP bulletin, an AARP online social hour and resource information on topics including health, aging, and retirement. You don't need to be a member to access the forum, but if you would like the AARP discounts, you should contact them directly for membership information.

DISCOUNTS

Some forums offer special online discounts for seniors. For example, you can access SeniorNet on AOL using different pricing options.

If you become a member of SeniorNet you can choose a plan that allows you unlimited access to the SeniorNet online area and one hour of use outside of the SeniorNet area. AARP provides their AOL users a one dollar discount off the monthly rate for seniors. Check each individual online service for senior discounts available.

Remember, you're not limited to senior forums when you're online. There are many other forums and thousands of databases, magazines and shopping services online. These services are terrific for the home-bound older relatives who want to educate themselves or socialize. If you've never used a computer or online service, the information highway can be mysterious. With a little knowledge, you can solve the mystery quickly and then you're on your way.

In today's active environment, it may be difficult to stay close to your children and grandchildren. Unfortunately, not many letters are written to grandparents anymore, and children are so busy with their own activities, many don't have time to send a picture, a card or even a thank-you note. However, kids love computers and getting email messages, so computers offer a perfect opportunity to enhance your relationship with your grandchildren and keep in touch with your own kids.

HOW TO SEND EMAIL

On CompuServe, choose CREATE MAIL, while you are offline. A box will appear on the screen. Type in your family member's name and user ID number (UID). Type in your message in the message box and click on SEND if you want to post it immediately, or put it in your outbox if you want to send it later. On AOL, select COMPOSE MAIL, and add your family member's screen name.

You can also choose to send now or later. Add all of your family member's UIDs to the address book to make sending email messages easier.

Don't worry if a family member is overseas or on a different online service than you are. Through the Internet, messages can be sent from one online service to another and even reach worldwide. To learn how to do this, check the online documentation found on your service's main menu screen.

OTHER IDEAS

- Create a newsletter and email it to your family members. Have them send you updates on each family member to include in the next edition. Let a grandchild name the newsletter and have his or her own column.

- Start an ongoing letter. Tell what's happening in your life. Ask the next person to add to the letter and send it on. When it returns to you, you'll know all about the lives of your family members. When you start the letter again, you can ask questions or send notes or thoughts on favorite topics.

- Tell your child or grandchild when you will be online and agree to meet for a live chat. You won't be charged for a long distance phone call.

- Visit your grandchild's favorite online area. Learn about their favorite hobby, television show or books. Keep them up-to-date on their favorite subjects and tell them a little about yours.

- Download a computer game that can be played interactively. Challenge your grandchild to a tournament. If they win, send them a special winner's announcement. If you win, send them a special email message or prize through postal mail anyway.

- If either of you have a scanner, scan pictures or artwork and send them to each other. They can be added to the newsletter or just used to share long distance fun.

Lisa Iannucci has published in Parenting, Practical Homeowner, New Body, Home Mechanix, Writer's Digest, Bride's, American Health *and* Weight Watchers. *She is Executive Editor of New York's Westchester Health Review. She began computing ten years ago. A member of The American Society of Journalists and Authors, she regularly reviews software for ASJA and the Compuserve Journalism forum.*

RESOURCES: GET IT WHILE IT'S FREE

By Stephen Poole and Evangelos Petroutsos

Buying a computer is only the first step: you'll want new software, answers to your questions, maybe just a place to chat with other computer users. Look to books and magazines, on-line services, user groups and other sources of information that will keep you and your computer up-to-date.

Computers aren't cheap. A PC is one of the more expensive purchases you can make, especially when you consider the money you spend on it *after* you get it home. Even budget-priced software starts at around $20-$25 a pop, with high-end desktop publishing and paint programs soaring into the hundreds of dollars.

And the spending doesn't stop there. If you've ever called a technical support number trying to get assistance with a computer-related problem, you know just how high the bill can climb for a single call. What's more, you often have make more than one call to get a solution to a problem.

But there are steps you can take to diminish the financial bite of owning a computer. In fact, you might be surprised at just how much stuff you can get for free or at a greatly reduced rate, including software.

Do you buy computer magazines in order to get expert opinions before you make a new hardware purchase? Well, you can find that very same advice online, without the expense of a subscription or a monthly trip to the newsstand.

Ever bought a computer game, only to have to drive back to the store to return it after you found you didn't like it? There are dozens of places on the Net where you can access reviews of games that'll let you know whether or not you're interested in the game's subject matter, as well as any known compatibility problems. If you're still not sure, you can post a message in a USENET newsgroup to find out how the product you're thinking of purchasing will run on your system.

And thanks to the success of shareware games like *Doom* and *Descent*, as well as shareware productivity applications such as *Paint Shop Pro* and *PKZIP*, you can often "try before you buy" for only the cost of connect time while you download the product. Once you've learned how much time, money, and frustration all these things can save you, you'll never shop for software the same way again.

Let's take a look at all the resources available to the new computer owner. We'll start with the most immediate source of assistance, the store where you bought your equipment.

COMPUTER STORES

If you bought your new system at a computer store, you can always turn to your dealer for help. One of the benefits of buying a computer locally is that there are salespeople and technicians available to assist you. Sometimes, a local salesperson may not be able to answer every question. Don't be surprised. No one person can solve every problem you may encounter. However, many retailers, from small local stores to national chains, have service departments staffed with people who tackle computer-related problems on a daily basis. If you run into a roadblock, give them a call. If that doesn't solve it, take the machine back to the store so they can give it a close look. Most any problem can be solved this way.

TECHNICAL SUPPORT BY PHONE

Sometimes, you may have to seek help from the company that sold you the computer. If you purchased your machine from a local store, go there first. If you bought it mail order, call the mail order company first. But if all else fails, try the technical support department of the manufacturer. Most major computer manufacturers have an 800 number for technical support. The tech support engineers are usually quite knowledgeable and helpful. You just have to put up with the inconvenience of 800 numbers (voicemail mazes leading to the inevitable "waiting room" while you hold for "the next available representative").

Before you call, you should have at hand the serial number of your computer (usually found on the warranty card that comes with the machine and also stamped on the back of the machine). If your problem involves a peripheral, such as a CD-ROM device, or just a question about software, you should still be prepared to provide the serial number. With so many illegal copies floating around, software companies aren't eager to help non-registered users. And, in general, the serial number helps the tech support person identify the particular version or model that's giving you problems.

You can also provide the version number for software directly—it's almost always displayed in the About window. Just run the application, open the Help menu and click on "About." Also be prepared to describe your computer: for example, a 486 system at 66 MHz, with 8 MB of RAM and 340 MB hard disk. If you are using special programs, like a RAM Doubler, or a disk compression utility (both described in the section Upgrading Your System), be sure to mention them too.

And of course, be next to your computer when you call, ready to explain what the problem is and ready to *recreate* it step-by-step while the tech person asks questions. This will ensure that your description of the problem is precise and the guru on the other side of the phone can guide you to the solution.

MAGAZINES

Magazines dedicated to computers, software, and going online are an industry unto themselves. A visit to a newsstand reveals row after row of such publications, aimed at everyone from novices to power users. With single-issue prices between $2.95 and $4.95, most of these are a decent value—assuming that you've bought one that's useful to you.

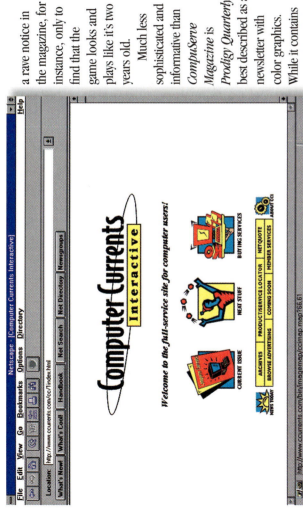

Figure 1: The largest free computer magazine is Computer Currents, *but it's only available in print format in major metropolitan areas. Fortunately, anyone with Internet access can enjoy a national online edition of the magazine.*

The high cost of materials, printing, and hiring artists and writers means that except for local tabloids, free computer magazines are extremely rare (unless you count online editions of printed magazines, which we'll discuss later).

FREE MAGAZINES

Computer Currents is one of the few free computer magazines available, but unless you live in California or one of a handful of major metropolitan areas (New York, Chicago, Boston, Dallas/Fort Worth, Houston) you've probably never heard of it. With most of the pages given over to advertisements, it's sort of a pared-down version of the mammoth *Computer Shopper* magazine, though it also contains news, columns, editorials, and letters. If you live in an area where *Computer Currents* is published, it's definitely worth a look; after all, it's free!

Aside from *Computer Currents*, though, about the only "free" computer-related periodicals are those you receive automatically when you join one of several online services. Of these, the most professional and useful is *CompuServe Magazine*, delivered each month for as long as you remain a CompuServe member. It contains tips on how to save time and money online, the location of new downloadable files, special-interest features (online tax filing and Christmas shopping, celebrities on CompuServe, and so forth), and announcements of new CompuServe features and enhancements.

One thing you should remember when reading *CompuServe Magazine*, however, is that in spite of the fact that it shows you how to be more efficient online, the ultimate goal is to get you online more often. You may jump online to download a 1.8MB shareware game after reading a rave notice in the magazine, for instance, only to find that the game looks and plays like it's two years old.

Much less sophisticated and informative than *CompuServe Magazine* is *Prodigy Quarterly*, best described as a newsletter with color graphics. While it contains many pointers to areas of the Prodigy service, the small size (the New Member Edition is only eight pages) means you won't find extensive feature stories like the ones in *CompuServe Magazine*.

Members of The ImagiNation Network (INN) receive the *INN Quarterly*, similar to *Prodigy Quarterly* but even less substantive or attractive. Because The ImagiNation Network is devoted exclusively to games and social interaction—and also because INN doesn't have program files available for downloading—about the only useful things you can glean from the *INN Quarterly* are announcements of new features, rate changes, and tips on how to use the service more efficiently.

FREE STUFF INSIDE MAGAZINES

While there aren't many free magazines, there are a lot of magazines with free stuff inside, especially software. The bundling of floppy disks or CD-ROM discs in computer magazines is the latest trend, and while these publications may cost you a little more for a subscription or a single copy, the software that you pick up for free can make up for that extra cost many times over.

The monthly magazine *CD-ROM Today*, for instance, includes a CD-ROM full of "demos"—software that has been stripped down in one form or another. These demos let you try out expensive programs before you buy them. The CDs also include shareware and freeware programs. One nice feature of the *CD-ROM Today* disc is that there's a little bit of everything on it—games, reference tools, productivity packages, utilities, and almost anything else under the sun.

Strictly speaking, the CD in *CD-ROM Today* isn't really free; one look at the single-issue price of $7.95 makes that pretty obvious. But subscribing ($49.95 per year) reduces the per issue cost significantly, and the sheer bulk of titles that you get to preview at your leisure makes it a fairly good deal, especially if the software you're taking for a test drive is something you've been considering buying.

Games are one of the most popular types of software to put on disks accompanying magazines because it's fairly simple for programmers to put a limited portion of a game into a demo, yet still let you experience the look and feel of the product. The most popular magazine dedicated to computer games, *PC Gamer*, is bundled with a CD-ROM packed full of demos, as well as bug fixes for existing games and front-end software for online services such as GEnie and The ImagiNation Network. It carries the same newsstand and subscription rates as *CD-ROM Today*.

These aren't the only magazines carrying CDs full of demos, of course, but they have been doing it longer than any of the other computer-related publications. Most other

Figure 2: PC Gamer *magazine comes bundled with a CD-ROM full of playable demos of the newest computer games.*

computer magazines will occasionally feature a CD (*Electronic Entertainment* now features a monthly CD, but a large part of the magazine is dedicated to videogame systems), so the only way to find out what's available is to go to your local bookstore or newsstand and look for computer magazines sold in plastic bags.

Demo disks and CDs can be a very cost-effective way to try out new games, but you need to keep a few things in mind before you go out and start grabbing magazines featuring them. A lot of these demos and shareware titles are easily available on the Internet or one of the online services, so it's possible you could download the ones you're interested in for the cost of a few minutes of connect time. Since demos are previews of upcoming games, they've usually been designed to run on the highest-end machines; if you're using a 486/33MHz, you won't get much fun out of free demos designed to run on a 486/66MHz or faster computer. And if you don't enjoy the magazine that comes with the CD, you might want to consider looking elsewhere for free software. And there's plenty of places to find free software as we'll see later.

ELECTRONIC MAGAZINES

Thanks to the growth of commercial online services and the Internet, going online for all the stuff you used to have to look for in magazines is not only feasible, it can also be done cheaply, efficiently, and conveniently. While

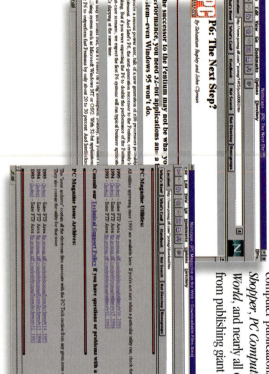

Keywords "computer magazines," and voilà!—a simple mouse-click will take you directly the magazine you'd like to read.

CompuServe also has a fairly extensive list of computer publications, including *Computer Shopper*, *PC Computing*, *Internet World*, *PC World*, and nearly all of the computer magazines from publishing giant Ziff-Davis. To get a complete list of all the computer-oriented magazines available on CompuServe, choose Services from the WinCIM menu bar, then select Find and type in "computer magazines."

The Internet is also a great place to look for online magazines—both electronic editions of traditional print publications as well as

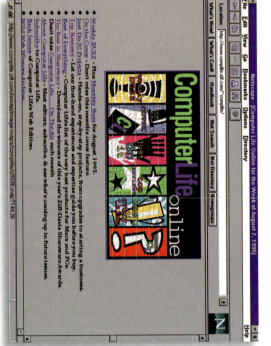

online editions of printed publications will never boast the same amount of information you find in their newsstand counterpart—sales would drop dramatically if that were the case—you can still get a lot of bang for your buck from online magazines. And because there are so many computer magazines online, chances are that one of them will have what you're looking for.

America Online features several popular computer magazines such as *PC Novice*, *PC Today*, *HomePC*, *FamilyPC*, and *Computer Life*. To get a list of all computer-related publications on AOL, choose Services from the Menu Bar, then select Search Directory of Services. Enter the

-
-
-
-
-
-
-
-

Figure 4, Figure 5: Online versions of newsstand magazines can be wonderful place to turn for informative articles and news stories—not to mention free utilities that you would normally have to buy the magazine to receive.

Figure 6: Computer Life online (http://www.complife.ziff.com/~complife) has a snazzy look and feel.

Figure 3: There are dozens and dozens of computer-related magazines available on the Internet. The MagNet Web page is a good jumping-off point. It boasted links to over 100 computer-related publications.

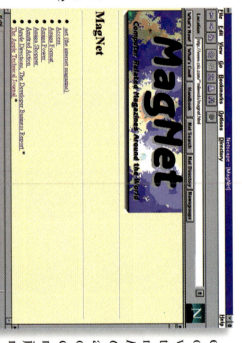

Tip: If you're not yet on the Internet, or are having problems using it, see the article "The Internet: What it is; how to connect; what it costs".

PC Computing Online (http://www.pc-computing.ziff.com/~pccomp), for instance, features bug patches (files to correct problems with retail software) and an archive of freeware and shareware; in August, they also had a very timely list of 1,001 keyboard shortcuts for Windows 95. *PC Magazine On the Web* (http://www.pcmag.ziff.com/~pcmag) has an extensive list of articles touching on almost every conceivable aspect of PCs, from the future of OS/2 to product analysis of various programs. Retrieve stories from past issues, download utilities that came on disks bundled with newsstand editions—there's even a file you can download with hundreds of troubleshooting tips that could save you an expensive call to a tech support department.

And while you may not be able to find a print version of *Computer Currents* in your home-town, you can always read the National Edition, *Computer Currents Interactive*, by visiting http://www.ccurrents.com/cc/1index.html.

If you're a fan of computer games, you'll find plenty of places to turn for reviews, previews, and feature stories on the latest titles; nearly all the major computer game magazines from the U.S. and England are represented on the Web.

The Nuke Home Page (http://www.nuke.com) is where you'll find the online version of *Computer Game Review*, featuring reviews, previews, demos, and other game-related

-
-
-
-
-
-
-

electronic magazines (e-zines) that are only found online. With Netscape or whatever internet software you use, go to—MagNet (http://www.cris.com/~mileski/magnet.html). *Computer Life*, *Home PC*, *Internet World*, *PC Computing*, *NetGuide*, *PC Magazine*, and *Windows Magazine* are just a few of the computer-related magazines that can be accessed via MagNet with a single mouse-click. And you'll be amazed at just how much these electronic magazines have to offer: They're a veritable goldmine of information and free programs. If you're looking for general interest magazines, you might also want to look into the Electronic Newsstand (http://www.enews.com/).

Figure 7: The online edition of Computer Gaming World is an excellent source of free information and software.

information. *Computer Gaming World's* Web site (http://www.gamingworld.ziff.com/~gaming) offers reviews, feature stories, bug patches, walkthroughs, hints, cheats, and an archive of back issues.

Unfortunately, there's no search engine to locate articles or files of interest—you must manually scan the table of contents of back issues in hopes of finding something of interest.

One of the most exciting aspects of the World Wide Web is that it's international—you'll find online versions of magazines from all over the world. Of course, most of us can't read Norwegian or German, but you can enjoy several top English PC magazines by heading to http://www.futurenet.co.uk/computing.html or http://www.futurenet.co.uk/games.html. From these two sites, you can access the home pages for the U.K. version of *CD-ROM Today* (multimedia software and hardware), *PC Answers* (tips for home PC users); *PC Format* (aimed at intermediate users), *PC Guide* (PC jargon and technology made simple), *PC Plus* (for experienced users), *PC Sports* (remember—they call soccer "football" in England!) and *PC Attack* (arcade-style games for the PC).

E-ZINES

All the Web sites we've mentioned so far are online versions of newsstand magazines, but the Net is also home to e-zines, short for electronic magazines. E-zines only appear online. The GD Review (GD is short Games Domain), located at http://wcl-rs.bham.ac.uk/GamesDomain/gdreview, is updated frequently and is a good source of reviews, previews, news, and opinions on computer and video games (the Games Domain itself leads to dozens of other computer-gaming related sites, too, and is one of the busier sites on the Web).

The Digitale (http://www.umn.edu/nlhome/m447/reinb001/digi/digitale.html), is less extensive than The GD Review, but it can still prove useful in helping you make the best buying decision when it comes to computer games. And like the GD Review, The Digitale encourages budding writers by accepting unsolicited reviews of games for publication.

The Computer Sports Edge (http://www.mcs.net/~dan66/edge.html), an

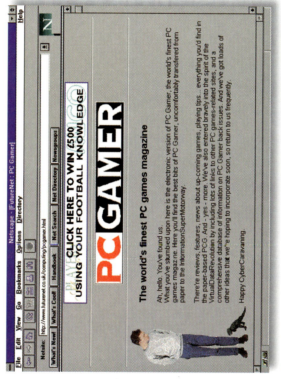

Figure 8: Check out the Web site for the British version of PC Gamer. It's updated weekly, and has links to many other useful computer-related sites on the Internet.

online magazine dedicated to computer and tabletop sports games, is created by people who love sports but who aren't professional writers. Because of the narrow scope, there aren't a lot of reviews available at this site right now, and the number of files for downloading is pretty skimpy, too. But the folks running it seem to be real enthusiasts, so it's probably worth dropping in every so often to see what's been added.

Which magazines should you visit on the Web? Well, despite sounding obvious, a good rule of thumb is that if you enjoy the paper version, you'll probably like what you find online. *Computer Life*, for instance, is aimed at novice users, so PC veterans who visit that Web site will probably be disappointed (actually, there's not much there even for beginners). Even if you're not familiar with the print versions of these publications, a few minutes at each site should be all it takes to decide whether there's enough free, useful stuff to warrant a return trip. And there's one other way these Web sites can save you money: After visiting one, you'll know whether or not the newsstand version of the magazines is to your liking *before* shelling out four or five bucks.

TRADITIONAL MAGAZINES

One of your best sources of information are classic (ink-on-paper) computer magazines. Reviews and articles are of obvious interest, but don't neglect the ads. Yet, reading ads has a downside too. You'll soon find a computer that's better than yours, and costs less. It will happen, maybe within weeks of your purchase, but just ignore it. Computer technology evolves so fast that by the time you buy a brand new computer, someone's already creating new features to antiquate it. Today's new computers are designed to be building blocks, and with the new Plug and Play technology under Windows 95, expanding your system is easier than ever before.

Here's a list of many popular family and home computing magazines found in almost every computer store and bookstore.

FAMILY PC

Family PC is dedicated to family computing. It covers both PC and Macintosh computers, and multimedia topics are among the primary articles. You'll find a variety of topics for the computer novice and articles for all ages, along with general articles on computing,

hardware and software reviews, and regular columns on family computing, such as Creative Computing, Family Shopper, etc. The articles are jargon free, easy to understand and contain practical information, which the typical home user will find useful.

Price $2.95
Published monthly (10 issues per year).
For subscriptions call 1-800-413-9749

PC NOVICE

PC Novice focuses mostly on how-to articles. You'll find articles on both DOS and Windows, how to set-up new peripherals, how to recover files you deleted accidentally, how to set-up your printer, your modem, etc. Many of the articles won't apply to you, until you run into trouble. Then you'll be going through old issues to find that "how-to" article that seemed irrelevant at the time. Unlike other family-oriented magazines, PC Novice is not visually exciting, as are some of the other magazines discussed here, nor will it show you how to have fun with your new computer. However, it is filled with practical, down-to-earth advice and useful information. Its articles are more like short book chapters, independent of each other, so if you keep the old issues you'll end up with a very useful selection of tips and techniques.

Price $2.95
Published monthly
For subscriptions call 1-800-424-2900

THE PC NOVICE GUIDE TO BETTER WINDOWS

This is a special publication of PC Novice with articles on Windows. Whether you are new to Windows, or you want to make the best out of your operating system, check out this magazine. It features the same structure as PC Novice and the emphasis is on advice for the beginner.

Price $4.95

HOME PC

This magazine is dedicated to family and home computing and covers a variety of topics. Its articles are simple and easy to read, and they appeal to all members of the family. It contains hardware and software reviews, product tests conducted by Home PC's Consumer Lab and a section on kids software. There are also many general articles on computing as well as interesting Internet sites to visit.

The Do It Yourself section contains advice on hardware upgrades and step-by-step instructions, illustrated with photographs. You can't go wrong here. The Personal Productivity section contains articles for those who use their computer to set up a business from home. If your kids, or any other family member, uses the home computer, check out this magazine, even if you find it too simple for your skills and expertise.

Price $2.95
Published monthly by CMP.
For subscriptions call (510) 562-5750

PC COMPUTING

Here's another very popular computer magazine, addressed to a broad audience. This magazine is not targeted specifically to home users, but you'll find it useful in many situations, from selecting the proper software, to making the most out of your machine. It contains many reviews and side-by-side comparisons of competing products. Its "Decision Maker" charts list the best product according to the user's needs and will help you find the right product for you. A unique feature of this magazine are the PC Usability Lab tests, which provide valuable advice on the real-world practicality of the various software packages. Most programs today provide more features than you may need, but it's hard to find out how usable a specific program is without buying it first.

Price $3.95
Published monthly by Ziff-Davis
For subscriptions call (303) 665-8930

CD-ROM TODAY

Devoted to the multimedia aspect of Windows and Macintosh, this magazine will help you understand your computer's multimedia capabilities; sort your way through new multimedia titles and games; and keep up with exciting new technologies. There are lots of software reviews, with emphasis on games, graphics and video applications. A CD is included with every issue.

Price $7.95
Published monthly by Imagination Publishing, Inc.
For subscriptions call (415) 696-1688

PC UPGRADE

If you want to expand your computer, or find out about the latest upgrades and how to manage installation yourself, check out this magazine. Not for absolute beginners, but worth consulting before you install a new hard disk or CD-ROM drive. It contains comprehensive lists of products, with features listed by category and price, which you could consult before any new hardware purchase.

Price $4.95
Published bimonthly by Bedford Communication.
For subscriptions call (609) 488-1881

COMPUTERS & THE FAMILY

The last magazine in our list is a publication of Newsweek, targeted to family computing. You'll find a variety of information in this magazine, from general articles on computing, to suggestions about buying new hardware and software. The publication is filled with useful resources like online places to visit, interviews, and lists of popular computers and peripherals.

Computers & the Family is not published regularly. The latest issue, "Summer, 1995," will be available at bookstores into late 1995. Keep an eye out for the next issue.

Price $2.95
Published by Newsweek, Inc.

skills. However, you will always find useful information in them. PC Magazine is a typical example. It contains numerous reviews, technology updates and general computing articles. PC Magazine has established an excellent reputation for its product reviews. Each issue contains a comparative review of the most popular products in a specific category (like modems, video cards, etc.). If you are planning to buy a new video card, or a new modem, look for the most recent issue of PC Magazine that focuses on video cards, or modems. You may not understand all the technical jargon, or even some of the most exotic features, but you'll find complete comparison charts with features, as well as the Editor's Choice.

For those interested in the Internet, or other online information services and BBSs, there are quite a few magazines dedicated to computer communications, and we expect to see even more. Just like general computer publications, different magazines will eventually address the different market segments. Right now, they cover all aspects of the Internet.

ON-LINE ACCESS

This magazine contains lists and reviews of new Web sites, new BBSs, and in general interesting places to visit with your modem. It is addressed to people who know how to use their modems and communication software, and is more of a reference than a tutorial resource.

Price $4.95
Published monthly
For subscriptions call (800) 36-MODEM

NETGUIDE

Another magazine devoted to the world of electronic communications. In each issue you will find reviews of Internet sites, as well as the latest information about the on-line services. There are also general articles on telecommunications and the latest trends in computer communications.

Price $2.95
Published monthly by CMP
For subscriptions call (516) 562-5000

BOOKS

Although magazine articles contain timely information, books provide depth. There are books for absolute beginners, books for "dummies," advanced books, everything you can imagine. Most of the books we'll list here are for the novice. They only provide the very basic information to get you started, but they will ease your way into computing.

We've selected a few titles that we believe can help you in getting started with your new computer, or show you how to have fun with the

There are other, more advanced magazines, which you may find too technical for your taste, or

family. They are for beginners and we selected them based on the topics they address and their layout. Most of the following titles are easy to read, fully illustrated, that will appeal to the entire family.

Tip: By the time this Encyclopedia hits the market, some of these books will have been revised, especially after the release of Windows 95. If you are using Windows 95, or plan to upgrade from Windows 3.1 to Windows 95, look for books "written for Windows 95" or "Revised for Windows 95."

GENERAL COMPUTING

Let's start with a few titles on computing in general, which will help you understand how your new computer works.

HOW COMPUTERS WORK

This is one of a series of books for new users and has become a national bestseller. Fully illustrated, it explains the basic principles of computers and will help you develop an understanding of what's going on inside the machine and how the various components and the software interact. You can read this book even if you don't even know how to use your computer yet.

The book starts with the basics, i.e., how the computer starts up, the role of the BIOS and the operating system and then examines the basic hardware components (the chips that make up the computer, the microprocessor, memory, video card, etc.). Like all the other books in the series, it is very easy to read. The artwork is beautiful and informative and perfectly integrated with the text. Most of the information in the book is contained in the illustrations, rather than in the text itself.

By Ron White, illustrated by Timothy Edward Downs. Ziff Davis Books,
ISBN: 1-56276-250-8, Price $22.95
(A version with a CD-ROM costs $39.93)

HOW SOFTWARE WORKS

Here you'll find the same approach taken in *How Computers Work*. It starts by explaining the role of the BIOS and the operating system and then explains how the most popular types of programs work. Topics such as how the computer understands the characters you type on the keyboard and how your mouse movements work are covered. There are chapters describing how the computer handles databases, spreadsheets, how it formats documents, how it handles fonts, and more. In the last section of the book you will find out how Windows itself works—how it opens and closes windows, how it prints, etc.

It's a fresh look at the programs you use every day—not from your point of view, but from the computer's. Yet, it is a non-technical book that you'll enjoy reading.
By Ron White, illustrated by Pamela Drury Wattenmaker. Ziff Davis Books,
ISBN: 1-56276-133-1
Price $24.95

HOW MICROPROCESSORS WORK

This is yet another "How it Works" publication from Ziff Davis Books. It describes the most complicated component in your computer: the microprocessor. The book is thoughtfully and beautifully illustrated and very easy to read, despite the fact that it covers a complex topic. You needn't know how microprocessors work in order to use a computer, any more than you need to know how your car's engine works to drive it, but if you are curious about this amazing technology, this book is a good choice.

The book covers topics like bits and bytes, the binary numeric system, how the microprocessor communicates with the outside world (keyboard, mouse, disks, etc.), the various components of the microprocessor and more. Then it moves to the description of the popular 486 and Pentium processors, their internal architecture and their strengths. The last chapter is a general discussion on the future of microprocessors. Its an interesting read for anyone who's even remotely involved with, or interested in, computer technology. Even power users who never understood what the Floating Point Unit is, or wondered how Intel can fit a few million transistors into such a tiny space, will find answers in this book.

By Hammerstrom
Ziff Davis Books, ISBN: 1-56276-145-5
Price $24.95

There are more titles from Ziff Davis in this series, such as *How Modems Work, How Computer Graphics Work, How Multimedia Works*, etc. Check them out at your local bookstore. If you like the style of one title in the series, you'll probably buy more.

PCs FOR DUMMIES

This is a simple book for beginners who want to know more about their computer. It starts with a description of your computer's external parts and then it takes you through the setup process. It describes all the parts of your new computer, their role in its operation and most of the peripherals you'll need (printers, CD-ROM devices, etc.).

There's a general discussion on the role of the operating system, a look at DOS, Windows, and OS/2, and application software. You will also find practical advice on how to buy software and what to look out for (how to keep track of program versions, how to upgrade, and more). There's also a good deal of information on upgrading your computer. Finally, a good, witty description of computer acronyms will help you pick up the computer jargon quickly.
On the downside, it's not as richly illustrated as the previous titles.
By Dan Gookin and Andy Rathbone
IDG Books, ISBN: 1-56884-904-4
Price $19.99

PETER NORTON'S INSIDE THE PC

Already in its sixth edition and with over one million copies sold, this book is a valuable reference for every PC owner. Although significantly more advanced than the other books in this section, it is a source of useful information that you won't easily outgrow. It explains all the parts of your PC, their operation and how they interact with the BIOS and DOS. You will find information about the microprocessor and the keyboard, as well as more advanced topics, like how video and sound boards work, for example. The latest version of the book contains extensive coverage of the new Plug and Play technology, multimedia under Windows 95 and the latest software trends.

On the downside it doesn't contain many illustrations, but is intended to be used more as a reference, rather than an introductory book.
By P. Norton, Lewis C. Eggerbrecht & Scott H. A. Clark
SAMS, ISBN: 0-672-30624-7
Price $35.00

DOS FOR DUMMIES, 2ND EDITION

This is probably the best-selling DOS book for beginners and it's both easy to read and covers a lot of ground. It starts with the basic operations and explains the most common error messages and ways to avoid them, how to find (or reclaim) lost files and other topics. There's an interesting section explaining the most common mistakes beginners make—a timesaver for all newcomers to DOS. Take a look too at the section titled "What to do after you panic," to find useful advice on the most frustrating things that can go wrong. Toward the end of the book there's very useful advice on some rather advanced, yet quite common topics, such as how to diagnose problems, how to optimize your hard disk's performance and how to detect and disinfect viruses.

By Dan Gookin
IDG Books, ISBN: 1-878058-75-4
Price $16.95

THE WAY COMPUTERS AND MS-DOS WORK

This is another visually rich book, that explains everything a beginner should know about his or her new PC. It covers the basic DOS commands, how to manipulate files on your computer and the basic kinds of data processing. Every command is illustrated with examples and screen shots. You can actually learn a lot about the basic DOS operations by just looking at the pictures. In the process of teaching the basics of DOS, this book also provides an understanding of the way your computer works without going into extreme details about the hardware components. There are also lots of sidebars with tips and advice about dealing with errors.

The Way Computers and MS-DOS Work is the first in a series, called the WYSIWYG (What You See Is What You Get) from Microsoft Press. Other titles are *The Way Multimedia Works*, *The Way Word Works*, *The Way Excel Works*, and more.

By Simon Collin
Microsoft Press, ISBN: 1-55615-697-9
Price $19.95

THE ULTIMATE MICROSOFT WINDOWS 95 BOOK

One of the first books on Windows 95 is from Microsoft Press. It's a full-color book, yet it is not an illustrated guide, like some of the books we described previously. Its pages are filled with text and figures and the margins of most pages are crowded with tips.

The book covers the basics of the operating system, such as how to manipulate files, how to print, how to use the applications that come with Windows, and so on. The section on the desktop is called "The Metaphorical Desktop" and shows you how to treat the Windows desktop as an extension of your physical desktop. How to customize it and alter its default behavior to suit your taste and working patterns.

Despite being an introductory book, *The Ultimate Windows 95 Book* covers a few advanced topics, like OLE technology, how to use network resources and the Microsoft Network. There's also a large section on troubleshooting.

By Joanne Woodcock
Microsoft Press, ISBN: 1-55615-670-7
Price: $24.95

UPGRADING ON YOUR OWN

If you plan to upgrade your PC, especially by adding multimedia capabilities to it, here are two good books that can help you. *Inside The PC* (mentioned earlier) contains valuable information about your computer's components too.

UPGRADING AND FIXING PCS FOR DUMMIES

Although upgrading or fixing a PC is not a task for the absolute beginner, this book is written for beginners. It covers basic topics like what needs to be upgraded and when, the tools you need to get to the inside of the machine and the basic Do's and Don'ts. Then it describes the anatomy of your computer. You'll learn where the various components are located and how to identify them. The book describes all types of PCs, from the early IBM PC to today's 386/486 and PS/2 systems.

You will find procedures to help you identify the broken parts, advice on how to buy replacement parts and get estimated costs for the various fixes, or upgrades. The replacement process is also described step-by-step with illustrations.

Another thorny issue when upgrading a computer is how you tell it about the changes by editing the CONFIG.SYS and AUTOEXEC.BAT files. This is also explained in the book, along with the meaning of those numbers you see when you boot up the machine.

By Andy Rathbone
IDG Books, ISBN: 1-56884-903-6
Price $19.99

MULTIMEDIA AND CD-ROM FOR DUMMIES

Multimedia is a new technology and most users are not quite familiar with it. You probably know what to expect from a multimedia computer, but you'll need some expert advice to make the best of your multimedia computer. You'll need even more help if you are about to upgrade that plain old PC into a multimedia computer.

Multimedia and CD-ROM for Dummies will help you in either case. It covers both hardware and software issues, explains things like multi-session and Photo CD-ROMs and contains step-by-step instructions on adding a new CD-ROM drive, or a sound card, to your PC. Software set-up is also explained thoroughly.

The author covers all aspects of multimedia computers, the available hardware and the problems you'll encounter if you decide to add multimedia capabilities to your PC on your own. The parts of the books in which technical terms are explained and are marked as sidebars, and you can avoid them altogether.

By Andy Rathbone
IDG Books, ISBN: 1-56884-089-6
Price $19.95

GETTING ON-LINE

Here are a few good beginner books for those interested in connecting to on-line services, or exploring the Internet.

MODEMS FOR DUMMIES

If you bought your first modem and you don't know what to do with it, or you have been using a modem but haven't been able to do everything you were hoping to, then check out this book. It encompasses all aspects of the wonderful world of communications you may be interested in. The book starts with an introduction to modems, how to set them up, how to get them to work when they don't (and they don't always work the first time) and more. Then it goes on to explain the basics of the communications programs.

After things are working, two thirds of the book focuses on what you can do with your new modem (the really neat stuff). There are sections for all major on-line services, a collection of useful BBSs, how to communicate with MCIMail, even an introduction to the Internet. Unfortunately, the book lacks a diskette that would help you get started immediately. At the end of the book you'll find advice on how to buy modems and communication software, as well a long glossary with the terms you'll find in your modem's, or computer's documentation.

By Tina Rathbone
IDG Books, ISBN: 1-56884-223-6
Price $19.99

THE OFFICIAL AMERICA ONLINE FOR WINDOWS MEMBERSHIP KIT AND TOUR GUIDE

This is the best-selling title on America Online. It contains the America Online for Windows program on diskette, so that you can start using AOL immediately. The book explains how to install the software and get connected right away. It shows you how to exchange mail messages and files with other users, how to meet other users (People Connection) and describes the most useful and interesting resources on AOL, like news, weather, sports, entertainment, and more. There is also a good chapter on kid's activities, which is one of AOL's best implemented features. You will also find practical advice on how to keep track and control your connection charges, how to minimize connect time and more. If you want to get on the Internet through your AOL account, you will find an introduction to AOL's Internet Connection. At the end of the book you'll find a list of keywords for all the forums you can visit on AOL.

By Tom Lichty
Ventana Press, ISBN: 1-56604-128-7
Price $27.95

AMERICA ONLINE'S INTERNET

By the same author as *The Official America Online Membership Kit and Tour Guide*, this book explores the Internet Connection of AOL. If you are using AOL and want to surf the Internet, this book will help you. It explains everything you can do on the Internet through AOL, including the Web Browser, Gopher,

FTP and more. The book is thoughtfully designed, contains many tips and the author not only explains the basic terms, he also explains where they came from, and why some of them are so bizarre—a very helpful feature for new users.

By Tom Lichty
Ventana Press, ISBN: 1-56604-175-9
Price $24.95

HOW TO USE AOL

A fully illustrated book explaining how to get started with AOL, this one is addressed to people who hate reading big books. It doesn't contain the software you may need, but you can find it easily either by calling AOL or by buying one of the many magazines that bundle a free AOL trial subscription disk. This book is very easy to read and is a very good starting point for families. It includes a section on the various AOL activities for school kids and teenagers, and explains how to use the Parental Controls to restrict your kid's access to Internet, or other online areas you don't want them to visit.

It also explains how to use the Internet Connection to access the Internet for email and newsgroups, but there's no discussion of Web browsing in the current edition of the book.

By Christopher J. Benz
Ziff Davis Press, ISBN: 1-56276-258-3
Price $17.95

HOW TO USE PRODIGY

This book follows the same structure as *How To Use AOL*, with interesting chapters for family activities. The chapter that describes how to manage your family accounts is especially useful, since Prodigy is also an Internet provider. With Prodigy you can set up a family account, which will be used by all family members. The owner of the master account, though, can restrict the privileges of the other family members.

There's also a chapter on online banking, for those of you who can't wait for their monthly statements, or hate to wait in line at the bank.

By Douglas Hergert, illustrated by Steph Bradshaw
Ziff Davis Press, ISBN: 1-56276-257-5
Price $17.95

COMPUSERVE FOR DUMMIES

This is a good resource for CompuServe users and covers a lot of ground. You'll find everything you need to get started, how to send and receive mail and files, and CompuServe activities you'll want to check out, such as news, sports, and entertainment. There's also a chapter on the games people play on CompuServe, if you are interested in multi-user, modem games.

This book will also serve you well even after you have familiarized yourself with CompuServe, covering very interesting and practical topics, such as how to find a new job on CompuServe, get help in doing your homework, even how to use CompuServe for research. There's also advice on how to keep track of your charges and how to minimize them.

By Wallace Wang
IDG Books, ISBN: 1-56884-181-7
Price $19.95

INTERNET MEMBERSHIP KIT

If all you want is Internet access, but you just don't know how to reach the Internet (and don't want to pay monthly charges to an online service), check out this kit. It is a complete Internet kit from Ventana Media, which comes with everything you need to get started and make the most out of Internet. It includes free registration with the IBM Internet Connection, the software you'll need and two best-selling Internet titles from Ventana Press (*Internet Roadside Attractions* and *The Internet Tour Guide*). The software includes a Mosaic Web Browser, Eudora (an email program), Fetch (for fast file transfers), PCTCP or MacTCP and Turbo Gopher. You'll also find a CD-ROM with a collection of top Internet sites and fully hyperlinked text. PC and Macintosh versions of this kit are available. Like all other Ventana Media products, it's fully refundable, should you not be satisfied.

Ventana Media, ISBN: 1-56604-213-3
Price $49.95

THE "INTERNET FOR WINDOW" FOR DUMMIES STARTER KIT

This is another complete kit for Internet starters. It comes with the Chameleon software on diskettes, which is explained thoroughly in the book. However, you will have to select your own Internet provider (you'll find a list of Internet providers in the book). This book takes you from the program's installation all the way to Internet surfing. You'll find out how to connect to the Internet with Chameleon, how to use FTP, how to search for the resources you're interested in using, the Archie and Gopher programs, how to send and receive mail, and finally how to use WebSurfer to browse the various WEB sites on the Internet.

By John R. Levine and Margaret Levine Young
IDG Books, ISBN: 1-56884-237-6
Price $34.99

EASY WORLD WIDE WEB WITH NETSCAPE

This is another beautifully illustrated, all-color book for beginners who don't like reading books in a linear fashion. Instead of chapters, this book is made up of Tasks. Each Task is limited to only a few pages, and is illustrated with pictures of the Netscape browser. The first Task is how to get started with Netscape. If you don't have Netscape, you'll find out how to download it from an FTP server. Other Tasks deal with images, sounds and movies (where to find and what to do with them), email, how to subscribe to newsgroups, and more. Unfortunately, the book isn't accompanied by any software, which doesn't make it the first choice for new Internet users. However, its illustrations and how-to approach to each task make it a good reference book for Netscape users.

QUE, ISBN: 0-7897-0277-7
Price $19.99

BUYING SOFTWARE FOR KIDS

If your kids are using the computer at home, you'll have to invest a good deal of time selecting software for them. This may not be as simple as it seems. Kids see computers in an entirely different way: To them, computers are toys. They don't have to work with computers, they play with them. And they aren't going to play, or use computers at all, if you can't provide them with something exciting. Fortunately, most kids have a good idea of what they like from the games they've seen at school, or at their friends' home computers.

Your task is to make sure that the games they play have some educational content as well. Kids are also very picky with their software. Technical specifications don't make sense to them, neither will they settle for something useful, but boring. They know what they want, and they will spend endless hours with it if it interests them. A long list of (mostly unnecessary) features can make an adult buy the wrong program, but they will not fool a kid. The notion of "working" with computers, so familiar to adults, doesn't apply to kids. So, when you are buying software for your family, aim for immediate gratification. Visual stimulation is far more important than any other aspect of the program.

Here are two good sources to help you in selecting the appropriate software for your kids.

CLUB SOFTKID
718 UNIVERSITY AVE.
LOS GATOS, CA 95030

This is a software club specializing in kids' software. CLUB SOFTKID carries numerous titles from selected manufacturers and their catalog can be found at many computer stores. It contains useful descriptions of each program and target ages. You can also subscribe to the *Club KidSoft Magazine*, and/or their Club KidSoft CD, which is filled with demos, animated stories and art from club members. If you are reluctant about

CHILDREN'S SOFTWARE REVUE
520 NORTH ADAMS ST.
YPSILANTI, MI 48197-2482

A newsletter with reviews of children's software. You can subscribe, or read the reviews on AOL, in the HOMEPC section.

mail ordering software, notice that the Club offers a 30-day money-back guarantee.

COMPUTER CLUBS

If you live in a big city, chances are that there is a computer club nearby. A computer club is a place where you can go to meet other computer owners, ask for free advice, or vent your frustration. There are many types of computer clubs, ranging between those for the absolute novice to clubs filled with true experts. Computer clubs are great places to not only get answers to your problems (or to help others if you can) but also to meet people with common interests. If you want to find out what games kids enjoy, or share your concerns with other parents, a computer club can be the right place to start.

To find out the computer clubs in your town, or neighborhood, call 1-914-876-6678. (Macintosh users dial 1-800-538-9696). You'll get an automated answering system that will provide the names of computer clubs by state, area code, or zip code. This is the locator service for APCUG, the Association of PC User Groups. Not every group belongs to this organization however, so also ask about clubs at your local computer store. They'll probably have a list of clubs in your area as well. The famous Boston Computer Society, for example, one of the largest and oldest computer clubs in the country, is not a member of APCUG. Computer clubs operate basically thanks to the volunteer efforts of their members. They also have a monthly, or yearly fee, which rarely exceeds $100—in most cases it's between $10 and $50 per year.

FREE SOFTWARE

When people consider the cost of a computer, they usually only think of how much money it takes to get the machine home. But a PC is worthless without software. And while it's true that most new PCs come bundled with enough applications to keep you busy for a few weeks, inevitably the time will come when it's time to pay a visit to the local software retailer and pick up something new.

But if you're a member of CompuServe, America Online, or have direct Internet access, you don't necessarily have to pay retail prices for software. Thanks to the exploding popularity of freeware and shareware, particularly on the Internet, you can pick up meg after meg of all sorts of programs for free, from paint programs and compression utilities to the very latest in high-tech computer games.

GAMES

Computer games are without question one of the most common types of free software you can pick up online, so let's start by taking a look at the places you'll find them. Space doesn't permit us to list every single spot where you can find free software, so we're going to focus on what we consider the best download sites.

Finding free games on America Online is a snap: Just search for the Keyword "PC Games," then click on the Software Libraries icon. You can browse the software libraries, which are organized by category, title, and platform (DOS or Windows), or you can search for a specific game or type of game using additional Keywords. What's more, you can narrow the results that are returned by specifying that you want a list of games posted only in the past week or month. (A similar search engine is available for hunting for games that have been posted on AOL's forums and support areas—choose GoTo on the AOL menu bar, then select Search Software Libraries).

The PC Games Software Library is also home to numerous programs that allow you to "cheat" in a game by making your character invulnerable, providing you with unlimited ammo, and so forth, as well as files that provides clues and answers to many popular computer games. And if a game you've purchased isn't behaving correctly, you can check here to see if a bug patch to fix the problem has been posted for downloading.

The first place to look for games on CompuServe is in The Gamer's Forum place (GO GAMERS). This is where nearly every computer game publisher posts demos and shareware versions of their new products for you to download. And even if you don't find a certain game here you can probably learn where it is located by posting a message on the Forum's Message Board (a good place to find hints and tips on games). Like The PC Games Forum on AOL, products are grouped by category, and you may search the libraries using a Keyword and submission date.

If the game you're trying to find isn't in The Gamer's Forum software library, there's a simple way to find the location of all the forums that might have files in which you're interested. By selecting Services from the WinCIM menu bar, choosing Go..., and typing in Quick, you can use a search engine to get a list of all the areas on CompuServe that deal with a specific topic. To bypass menus altogether, type GO GAMEFF to

Even though you need to send in a registration fee to receive the full version of shareware programs (or to legally use the full version you downloaded beyond the trial period), these applications often cost half the price (or less) of similar retail packages. And this system has a distinct advantage over traditional retail software: You can pick up the program, test it out, and order the full version, all without leaving the comfort of your home.

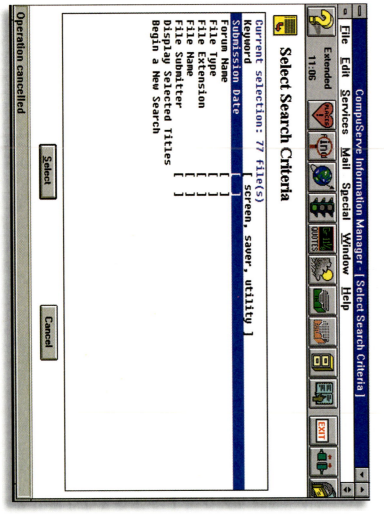

Figure 9: CompuServe's file finders return a list that you can narrow by using various search criteria (Keywords, file type, submission date, etc.).

magazines, USENET newsgroups devoted to computer games, and sites that offer hints, cheats, and walkthroughs for popular PC games. Between this site and the Happy Puppy OnRamp, you should be able to download enough free software to keep you gaming for many, many hours.

Figure 10: Interested in PC games, but don't feel like shelling out $50+ at your local software store? Try Happy Puppy Games Onramp (http://happypuppy.com) on the Internet.

access the Games File Finder. Here you can search for programs by Keywords (up to three), publisher, date of submission, filename extension, etc.; unfortunately, you can only use one of these filters at a time. After entering three Keywords, for example, you may get back a list of 400 files, at which point you could narrow those files down with another parameter such as submission date or publisher, then repeat the process a third time with yet another filter.

With AOL and CompuServe now offering full Internet access, a whole new world of freeware, shareware, and game demos has opened up for users. One place every game fan should visit on the Internet is the Happy Puppy Games Onramp (www.happypuppy.com); as of September there were over 125 shareware games and interactive demos available for downloading. But that's not all. Happy Puppy also features game cheats and hints, bug patches, previews of upcoming games, lists of FTP sites where you can download games, links to sites run by game publishers, and more.

You'll also find a link to Lord Soth's Games, an extremely comprehensive hypertext list (over 700 links) of FTP and Web sites where games can be found. To make things easier, the list is categorized by type of game as well as operating system (DOS or Windows), and if you're not sure which games are worthwhile you can check out the Internet PC Games Chart (Internet users from around the world vote on what games they like best) or a list of the 25 games most frequently downloaded at Happy Puppy.

Another great place to find free gaming software and information is at the aforementioned Games Domain (http://wcl-rs.bham.ac.uk/GamesDomain). Though not as expansive as the Happy Puppy OnRamp, the Games Domain is still a good place to check for links to FTP sites, Web sites run by game publishers, online gaming

what has been uploaded since the last time the Comprehensive List was updated. A database program is needed to view the Database, but AOL offers a free program called AOLDBF that you can download to view and search the database listings offline.

And there's certainly a lot to view. Choose Applications on the Computing menu and click on the Software Libraries icon, for example, and you'll see listings for Address & Phone, Business, Database, Desktop Publishing, Home Financial, Word Processing, and Productivity, to name a few. With categories this specialized, the same file may appear in more than one category, but this simply gives you a better chance of locating the program you're trying to find.

If you don't feel like wading through menus, you can use AOL's excellent file-search utility mentioned above to quickly retrieve a list of files related to a certain topic. Just select Go to, choose "Search Software Libraries," then type words that describe what you'd like to locate. Typing in "paint programs Windows," for instance, reveals a plethora of paint and graphics utilities, including the classic *Paint Shop Pro 3.0*, *ASL Painter!*, *Child's Play* (paint program designed for kids), ZZColor (paint-by-numbers), and many more—over 460 more, in fact. That may sound like a lot, but recall that you can narrow the hits by asking to see only files uploaded in the past week or month.

There are several ways to find out where free programs are located on CompuServe. Perhaps the simplest approach is to select Find

PRODUCTIVITY, UTILITY, AND OTHER APPLICATIONS

Games might be one of the most popular types of shareware, but there are plenty of "serious" applications on CompuServe, America Online, and the Internet just waiting to be downloaded.

Paint programs, screen savers, compression utilities, bug patches, video and sound card drivers are just a few of the gems you can find online. There's also one hitch: You have to find them before you can download them.

Thankfully, locating shareware applications on America Online and CompuServe couldn't be much simpler. AOL users can simply click on the

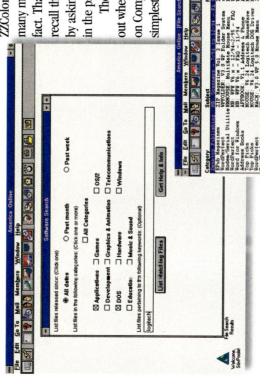

Figure 11. Figure 12: AOL's Software Search takes the pain out of locating software updates, shareware games and applications, and other free software.

Computing selection on the Main Menu to get a list of all the various forums and areas related to computers, divided into categories that will help point you in the right direction (DOS, Windows, Applications, Games, Graphics and Animation, Multimedia, etc.). If you've never used AOL's forums for downloading programs, your first stop on the Computing menu should be the Software Center; it gives you an idea of the sorts of utilities and programs are available in the various forums. There's also a Comprehensive File Listing, both in ASCII and a database format, that lists every file on the service, as well as a weekly update that shows

from the WinCIM Services menu, then type in a word or two—"paint program," or "screen saver"—that describes the application. You'll then be given a list of forums that contain information matching your criteria.

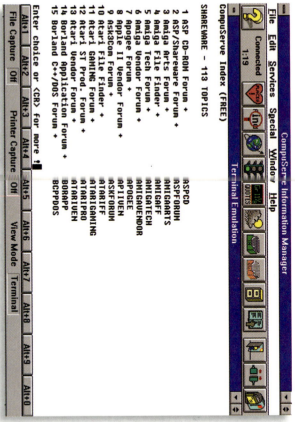

```
CompuServe Information Manager
File  Edit  Services  Special  Window  Help
Connected  1:19                    Terminal Emulation

SHAREWARE - 113 TOPICS
CompuServe Index (FREE)

1   ASP CD-ROM Forum +              ASPCD
2   ASP/Shareware Forum +           ASPFORUM
3   Amiga Arts Forum +              AMIGAARTS
4   Amiga File Finder +             AMIGAFF
5   Amiga Tech Forum +              AMIGATECH
6   Amiga Vendor Forum +            AMIGAVENDOR
7   Apogee Forum +                  APOGEE
8   Apple II Vendor Forum +         APIIVEN
9   AskSam Forum +                  ASKFORUM
10  Atari File Finder +             ATARIFF
11  Atari GAMING Forum +            ATARIGAMING
12  Atari ST Prod. Forum +          ATARIPRO
13  Atari Vendor Forum +            ATARIVEN
14  Borland Application Forum +     BORAPP
15  Borland C++/DOS Forum +         BCPPDOS

Enter choice or <CR> for more ↑
```

Figure 13: CompuServe's Quick Index allows you to search the massive service for forums relating to whatever topic you specify. You'll find message boards for posting questions, answers, and comments, as well as software libraries chock-full of shareware, demos, and bug patch files.

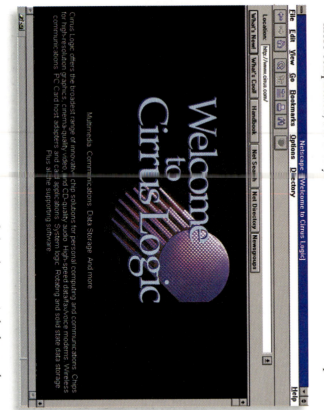

```
Netscape - [Welcome to Cirrus Logic]
File  Edit  View  Go  Bookmarks  Options  Directory
Location: http://www.cirrus.com/
What's New! | What's Cool! | Handbook | Net Search | Net Directory | Newsgroups

Welcome to Cirrus Logic

Multimedia Communications  Data Storage  And more
Cirrus Logic offers the broadest range of innovative chip solutions for personal computing and communications. Chips for high-resolution graphics, cinema-quality video and CD-quality audio. High-speed data/fax/voice modems. Wireless communications. PC Card host adapters. System logic. Rotating and solid state data storage. Plus all the supporting software.
```

Figure 14: As the Internet grows, you can expect to find nearly every major hardware and software vendor represented online—and that can save you a lot in long-distance calls.

To retrieve a file without going through menus, you can use one of CompuServe's File Finders: PC File Finder (GO PCFF), Graphics File Finder (GO GRAPHFF), Microsoft File Finder (GO MSFF), or the ZiffNet File Finder (GO ZIFLEFINDER). These work the same as the Games File Finder: Starting with a massive number of files, you use filters to progressively narrow down the number of files that match your search criteria.

Finding free applications on the Internet is more complicated, but once you learn where to look you'll be rewarded with more software than you can shake a mouse at. Most applications are distributed at a FTP (file transfer protocol) sites, though an increasing number of locations on the World Wide Web now include access to software libraries.

most popular ones as of mid-1995. We've noted in parentheses whether the site offers DOS or Windows software, but this isn't part of the site address, so when looking for these locations with your Internet software, don't type in the words within parentheses.

There are several ways to search for shareware, freeware, and public domain software on the Net.

You can use one of the Internet "search engines"—WebCrawler, Lycos, Yahoo, etc.—that allow you to look for documents on the Web by entering keywords; the "documents" that are returned are often FTP or World Wide Web locations where you can download files with the click of a button.

Another approach is to use a catalog, such as The Whole Internet Catalog or Yahoo, to go through several menus to find a program. You can also connect to an Archie server, but once there you'll be asked to type in at least part of the name of the file—not a good prerequisite if you're simply looking for free software and don't have any idea what the filenames are. Web sites dedicated to a particular topic such as graphics or sound will often have an FTP function, or at least hot links to place where you can download related files. For more information on Archie and other Internet features, see the article "The Internet: What it is; how to connect; what it costs".

Keep in mind, however, that the Internet is growing at such a phenomenal rate that new places to download software are coming online every day. And there are simply too many places on the Net to download software for us to list them all, but here are some of the

- ftp.cica.indiana.edu/pub/pc/win3 (Windows)
- http://www.acs.oakland.edu/oak/SimTel-msdos.html (DOS)
- http://www.acs.oakland.edu/oak/SimTel-win3.html (Windows)
- ftp://ftp.cdrom.com/pub (DOS and Windows)
- http://coyote.csusm.edu/cwis/winworld/winworld.html (Windows)
- http://www.pic.net/uniloc/uniloc.html (DOS and Windows)

FREE TECH SUPPORT

If you want to avoid wasting time or money waiting for tech support, the chances are very good that you can find the solutions to your computing problems online.

Before you go online for help, though, you need to do several things. First, make sure that your explanation of the problem you're experiencing is as detailed as possible. Second, make a note of the version number of the software and the type of hardware you have (i.e., sound card, video card, mouse, etc.). Third, be sure to have copies of your computer's CONFIG.SYS, AUTOEXEC.BAT, WIN.INI, and SYSTEM.INI files (if you use a multiple-boot configuration, just send the configuration that's being used when you encounter difficulties). Finally, be sure that the software didn't come with any related files, such as README.DOC or README, that might have the answer to your problem.

AMERICA ONLINE AND COMPUSERVE

Finding hardware and software support forums on AOL and CompuServe is as easy as locating files. The fastest method on AOL is to choose GoTo..., click Search Directory of Services, then enter the name of the company who manufactured the product with which you're having a problem. If that doesn't work, head over to the Industry Connection area (Keyword Industry Connection), where you can browse through menus categorized by subject. On CompuServe, you'll want to either use the Find feature (under Services on the WinCIM menu bar), or access the Quick Index (GO QUICK).

The levels of support you find on AOL and CompuServe vary wildly, from areas that only have bulletin boards for posting questions and answers—to full-blown software libraries with all the latest updates for that company's software. Still, chances are that at the very least you'll reach someone who can point you in the right direction to resolve your difficulties.

TECH SUPPORT ON THE INTERNET

Finding free tech support on the Internet is a little trickier, but as the Information Superhighway grows you can rest assured that every hardware and software vendor will eventually be online. Most of the major PC manufacturers, in fact, are already represented online, and their support areas are all quite thorough.

Compaq owners, for example, will want to visit http://www.compaq.com to check out the software library, which contains lots of useful programs and files ranging from display drivers,

Figure 15: Compaq owners in need of technical support can turn to the Compaq Service and Support Home Page on the Internet to find answers to frequently asked questions, ROM upgrades, and a wealth of files for downloading.

ROM upgrades, diagnostic and configuration utilities, and more. But before you start downloading files you should check the Compaq FAQ ("Frequently Asked Questions") file—it's divided into categories such as Laptops and Notebooks, Desktops, and Systems to make your search easier. You'll also find info on how to email the Tech Support department here, as well as troubleshooting tips.

At Dell Computer's Home page (http://www.dell.com) you can access all the files found at Dell's BBS Online Information System, and save yourself long-distance phone charges. It's similar to what's at Compaq's home page, with video and audio drivers, utilities, bios updates, network programs, etc. There's also a simple mail form for submitting tech questions, a list of Dell vendors and local BBS's carrying Dell files, an automated tech support area (highly similar to the phone-based automated tech support used by Dell), and a list of parts for upgrading your computer—identical to the parts program used by Dell's technicians to give you a part number.

You can use Yahoo or other Internet search engines mentioned above. But if you're in a hurry, the first place you'll want to try is the Computer and Communication Companies Directory, maintained by staff at the University of California's Lawrence Livermore National Library (http://www atp.llnl.gov/atp/companies.html). It has listings of over 1700 companies associated with computers, and you can browse through the lists by clicking

on a letter of the alphabet, or use a search engine to key in on the company you're interested in. This is definitely a link you'll want to add to your list of favorite place on the Net.

Two other outstanding ways to access tech support and file updates are Eric's List of Hardware Vendors on the Web (http://www.europa.com/~lahockey/hardlnks.html) and Harris Semiconductor Software support and Update sites (http://mtmis1.mis.semi.harris.com/dos_support.html) Using these resources, here's a smattering of the hardware and software vendors we found in just a few minutes on the Internet:

- Acer Computers (http://www.acer.com/aac/index.htm)
- Boca (http://www.boca.org)
- Creative Labs (http://creaf.com)
- Cirrus Logic Graphics chips (http://www.cirrus.com)
- Diamond Multimedia Systems (http://www.diamondmm.com)
- Epson Printers (http://www.epson.co.jp/epson/weleng.htm)
- Hewlett Packard (http://www.hp.com/home.html)
- IBM (http://www.ibm.com/Products)
- MediaVision (http://www.mediavis.com/mainmenu1.htm)
- Microsoft (http://www.microsoft.com)
- NEC (http://www.nec.com)
- NexGen (http://www.nexgen.com)
- Packard Bell (http://www.packardbell.com)
- Seagate (http://www.seagate.com)
- Sony CD-ROM (http://www.sel.sony.com/SEL/ccpg/drivers.html)
- Quantum (http://www.quantum.com)
- U.S. Robotics (http://www.usr.com)
- Western Digital (http://www.wdc.com)

Figure 16: Dell Computers has an excellent online support site on the World Wide Web, with downloadable upgrades, email for technical support, an automated troubleshooting system, and a sophisticated Parts List program that takes the worry out of buying a replacement part.

There are dozens and dozens of computer-oriented newsgroups, many of them dealing with PCs and PC software. Here are some of the busier newsgroups; a glance at the name is all it takes to determine whether or not it's worth a visit.

- comp.sys.ibm.pc.demos
- comp.sys.ibm.pc.digest
- comp.sys.ibm.pc.hardware.cd-rom
- comp.sys.ibm.pc.hardware.chips
- comp.sys.ibm.pc.hardware.misccomp.sys.ibm.pc.hardware.networking
- comp.sys.ibm.pc.hardware.storage
- comp.sys.ibm.pc.hardware.systems
- comp.sys.ibm.pc.hardware.video
- comp.sys.ibm.pc.misc
- comp.sys.ibm.pc.soundcard.advocacy
- comp.sys.ibm.pc.soundcard.games
- comp.sys.ibm.pc.soundcard.misc
- comp.sys.ibm.pc.soundcard.music
- comp.sys.ibm.pc.soundcard.tech
- comp.sys.ibm.pc.games.action
- comp.sys.ibm.pc.games.adventure
- comp.sys.ibm.pc.games.announce
- comp.sys.ibm.pc.games.flight-sim
- comp.sys.ibm.pc.games.misc
- comp.sys.ibm.pc.games.rpg

NEWSGROUPS

One of the easiest ways to find answers to computer or software questions is from users just like yourself who may have encountered the very same problem you've run into. No one knows for sure how many "USENET" newsgroups there are, but a large portion of them are dedicated to computers. By simply posting a detailed description of your problem and a thorough rundown of your system and its configuration, there's a very good chance that someone will know what's going wrong and recommend the steps you need to remedy the situation.

Evangelos Petroutsos has a degree in Computer Engineering from the University of California and works as an author and consultant. He is co-author of the best-selling book Visual Basic Power Toolkit.

Stephen Poole has been involved with personal computers since 1987. In addition to heading up the Technical Support group at the national online service USA Today Sports Center, he has served as Editor of PC Entertainment and PC Gamer.

16-bit card (see ISA) has the same 32-finger 8-bit card, but it's located against the back of the computer, and there's a second connector, half as large, located in the middle.

32-bit card Usually a VESA local bus or "PCI" card. A VESA local bus (VLB) card looks pretty much like a 16-bit card, but has 64 connector spots, and the first of the two lips is located about ¼" away from the back of the computer. A PCI card resembles an 8-bit card in size, but plugs into a special PCI slot on the computer's motherboard. Another type of 32-bit card is the MCA (Micro Channel Architecture) card, found only on IBM PS/1 and PS/2 computers. An EISA card is a special 32-bit card primarily used on network file servers and is rarely seen in desktop computers.

8-bit card (see ISA) an 8-bit card, look at the connector—you'll see 32 thin metal "fingers" on a protruding edge connector on the bottom of the card. This connector is in the middle of the card.

8086/80286/80386/80486/Pentium The family of microprocessors introduced by the Intel Corporation in the late 70's. The first IBM PC of 1981 used a somewhat handicapped version of the 8086, (the 8088) as its base, and all PCs since have retained compatibility with this original chip architecture while adding new features and capabilities. (The "80" is usually left off when referring to "386" and "486" based computers.) And, finally, numbers are ignored altogether with the advent of the Pentium (which would have been a "586").

access time The average time it takes for a hard disk drive or CD-ROM to move to any given piece of information on the surface of its disk.

action game puzzles are more difficult than those in arcade games, but less complex than in adventure games. Similarly, the speed of the action falls between those two extremes.

adventure game one in which you assume the role of a wayfarer on a journey or quest, usually in a place full of strange and interesting inhabitants.

Amiga A multimedia computer first introduced in 1985 by Commodore. Now manufactured by Escom, a German company.

analog a type of signal (information) that extends over a smooth range of continuous values. Analog information must be digitized into discrete chunks (see "Sample") before it can be processed by a computer. Similarly, digital computer data must often be converted into analog form for screen display or speaker output.

animation a rapid succession of static images, which produces the illusion of fluid movement.

applets jargon for mini-applications, such as the Windows Calculator applet.

arcade game faster-paced and less intellectual than adventure games—arcade games test reflexes more than reasoning power.

ASCII American Standard for Information Interchange; a now international standard that defines the common codes for alphabetic characters and symbols used by computers. For example, the ASCII value of "A" is 65.

AVI Audio Video Interleave. The standard Windows format for digital video movies (Microsoft Video for Windows format). AVI is so named because the sound track is mixed in between every frame of video.

backup to copy information from a primary storage device (like your hard drive) to a secondary storage device (floppy disks, backup tapes, another hard drive). The purpose of backing up is safety—you'll have a copy should you accidentally delete or otherwise corrupt the original. Normally, you back up only *data* (such as letters or reports you've written, or spreadsheets you've filled in, or pictures you've drawn). There's no need to back up *programs* (like your word processor) because you already have a backup of them—the original disks or CD that you got when you bought the program.

backup tape A minicartridge that contains spools of magnetic tape (similar to audio cassettes). The QIC-80 (Quarter Inch Cartridge) is the most common type of backup tape. And, recently, DAT (Digital Audio Tape) and 8mm videocassette tape have also been adapted for computer backup. Baud is a measurement of the speed at which data can be transmitted.

Baud A signal transition in an analog symbol. Loosely equivalent to "bits per second," although modern modems now pack many bits into a single baud, rendering this term confusing and obsolete. Baud is a measurement of the speed at which data can be transmitted.

BBS Bulletin Board System. A computer that hosts files and messages. You can access a BBS using a terminal program and a modem. A BBS is like a mini "Online Service" (which see) that's usually run by one person out of his or her home.

binary format A file format that preserves all of the special attributes of the original document, using all 8 bits of each byte. Example: A text document that includes type fonts, margin settings, footnotes, embedded graphics, and other features. Programs and graphics files are stored in this format (as opposed to simple text files which are *ordinary* letters in an alphabet). Sometimes you're asked if you want to transmit data over your modem in text or binary format.

bitmapped graphics A method of displaying pictures on a computer screen by individually addressing the location and color of each dot, or pixel. Sometimes called raster graphics. A bitmap is a one-for-one *copy* of the original graphic and, therefore, can display photo-realistic images. See "vector graphics."

BPS Today's modems can go up to 2,400 bits per second (or roughly 300 characters per second) and as high as 28,800 BPS (or 1200 characters per second) and as high as 28,800 BPS. The base speed of a modem is always described in bits per second (BPS), although many modems can multiply this basic rate using compression.

bundled sold with. For example, some software is usually bundled with a new computer.

bus architectures the pathways by which information is sent around inside the computer. The PCI bus is a fast 32-bit bus—as opposed to the slow 16-bit ISA bus.

cards A small circuit board containing electronic chips that you can plug in to add new capabilities to your computer.

carriage-return A special ASCII character that is often used to mark the end of a line of text, indicating to move to the start of the line. (In some cases, a *line/feed* character must also be included to actually advance to the next line. So the CR+LF combination moves the cursor on the screen, or the position of the printhead, to the start of the next line.)

CD Quality hi-fi sound. 44,000 samples per second

CD-ROM drive A device (similar to a disk drive) that can read computer CDs.

CD-R A rewritable CD.

CD-ROM Speed This refers to the actual speed a particular drive spins a CD, although it is more useful when shopping for a CD-ROM drive to examine both data transfer rates (150 Kilobytes per second for a single-spin drive, 300KBps for doubles spins, and so on) and access times (usually in the 180 to 200 ms range for good drives). Your best bet is to get a 4X drive or better, meaning that it goes four times as fast as the original CD-ROM units could. (Audio CDs are always played back at 1X speeds.)

cel graphics A type of animation that displays one frame (cel) after another, making a slight change in each frame to create the illusion of movements. Cartoons are a type of cel animation. (The term *cel* comes from the cellophane overlays used in traditional cartoon animation.)

clock The computer's clock controls the operations of the CPU and synchronizes the computer's electronic components. The faster the clock, the faster each instruction is executed.

CMYK The process of composing colors based on four primary colors: Cyan, Magenta, Yellow and Black. The most common

color Depth the number of colors that your computer's video card can display at one time. Today's video cards are capable of displaying either 256 (also known as "8-bit" color), 65,536 (16-bit, or "high color") or 16,777,216 (24-bit or "true color") simultaneous colors.

color model used in printing (vs. RGB used in video or YUV used for video movies).

communications software A program that works with a modem to give you access to other computers over telephone lines. A terminal program, a fax utility, or an online service navigator are all examples of communications software.

component an element of the total machine. For example, the video monitor is a component. Can also refer to individual chips on a motherboard or other card. Also see "peripheral."

compression A software technique for removing redundant information (think of squeezing a sponge to remove the air) and storing a file using fewer characters. Compressed files not only use less disk space, they also take less time to transmit via modem, or to move from disk into the computer. Many files are inherently compressed, such as AVI videos (their file format involves, by definition, a compression method). The PKZIP program can also collect and compress a group of files, to be uncompressed with PKUNZIP. Hard disk compression methods such as DoubleSpace, DriveSpace, and Stacker automatically compress and decompress files from your hard drive "on the fly," effectively doubling the useable size of your hard drive.

connect time How long you're online. Most online services charge for access by the minute, although rates are usually quoted hourly.

CPU Central Processing Unit—the "brain" inside the computer, the main (and largest) chip. Also called the "microprocessor." See 8086/80286/80386/80486/Pentium.

CPU upgrade A newer, faster CPU which takes the place of the existing one. An Intel 486DX2/66 OverDrive CPU nearly doubles the speed of a 33 megahertz 486 computer, whereas the DX4 OverDrive CPU triples the speed.

DAT Digital Audio Tape. A backup tape (or tape drive) that can store from between 2 gigabytes and 8 gigabytes of information for around $10. DAT drives are considerably more expensive than QIC-80 tape drives, and require a SCSI interface. However, over time, you can save money using DAT because the tapes are so inexpensive and hold such enormous amounts of data.

data buffer, or buffer Often a program can use more information than the computer or one of its peripherals is capable of supplying quickly. This is especially true of data streaming off of CD-ROM drives which, even now, are still relatively slow at sending information. When data supply is slow, a data buffer (a reserved section of memory) acts as a reservoir for data from the CD-ROM drive, insuring a steady stream of data to the computer's microprocessor when the drive alone cannot keep up with the demand.

data formats The particular way in which a program organizes the document files it lets you create. Different programs create different data formats that are sometimes incompatible with each other.

demodulation (see Modulation) The process of converting an analog signal back into digital data.

digital a type of signal (information storage or transmission) that consists of only on/off (binary) information in the form of zeros and ones. Computers can only process digital signals. By contrast, *analog* signals, such as those found on music cassette tapes, must be digitized (sampled) before they can be processed, using a device known as an ADC (Analog to Digital Converter). A DAC (Digital to Audio Converter) translates digital information into analog form. So the microphone input on your sound card converts analog information (your voice) into a digital "wave" file. Later, the process is reversed: The file can be played, converting it from digital form back into an analog waveform that can be reproduced through the speakers.

digital Video Video that has been captured and saved in the computer or on a storage device like a CD-ROM. ("Digital" is a

THE ANSWERS ARE HERE.

THE WHOLE PC FAMILY ENCYCLOPEDIA

- How can I help my kids learn on the PC?
- What can I do with my computer NOW?
- One huge easy-to-understand book.
- Many of the best authors in the PC field.

- Over 300 pages of rich text and color images.
- Suggested retail price only $16.95.
- The ONE computer book your family will use for months to come.

The Whole PC Family Encyclopedia ™
Pick it up at your nearest retailer or bookstore.
Or order additional copies by calling 1-800-556-9181 (Orders Only.)

reminder that the movie has been rendered into zeros and ones inside the computer.)

directory analogous to a file folder, a directory is a named location on your hard drive which can hold program files, data files, or other ("nested") subdirectories. The "root" directory is the hard drive itself, as in C:\. In Windows 95, the term *folder* is used instead of *directory*. See "sub-directory."

disk compression utility a program that squeezes the information stored on the disk, effectively increasing the disk's capacity. See Compression.

disk swap memory a reserved area of hard disk space that holds data that "overflows" because it can't fit into RAM memory (see Memory).

disk swapping occurs when there's not enough memory (RAM) on your PC to accommodate all open applications, and Windows has to temporarily store information on the disk. The computer might be trying to make room for a new application, or a data file. This can slow your computer down to a crawl.

documentation the instructions for using a program, either in a printed manual or stored in a computer file on your hard drive or on the installation disk. Look for files named "README" or any file ending in the extension .DOC to locate a program's documentation if it's not provided on paper.

DOS Disk Operating System. Microsoft DOS (MS-DOS) is a set of programs and utilities for managing information stored on your hard drive, floppy disks, and CD-ROMs. The functions of DOS are usually taken over by Windows 3.1 and especially by Windows 95, which does not require DOS except when initially starting up the computer.

dot pitch a measurement of the resolution (detail) capabilities of a monitor—measured by how closely together the phosphor dots are positioned.

download Transferring a file to your computer from another computer, usually by using a modem and a phone line.

driver special software used by the computer to communicate with a device. A CD-ROM driver adds a new drive letter (e.g. D:\) to MS-DOS for access to the disc.

DXF A file format standard for Computer-Assisted Design (CAD) programs that allows interchange between various software packages. Nearly all 3D rendering and animation programs can utilize .DXF files.

DX The full configuration of an Intel microprocessor CPU. DX2 means that the chip uses an internal clock that's two times as fast as the speed of the motherboard's (external) clock. The DX4 chip runs three times as fast; the "4" stands for "486."

EIDE Enhanced IDE (Integrated Drive Electronics). EIDE hard drives are typically faster than standard IDE drives. The EIDE interface can accept up to four devices (hard drives, CD-ROM drives, tape drivers), whereas IDE is limited to just two. Your computer must have both an EIDE controller card and one or more EIDE drives to get the full benefit of EIDE.

EISA Extended Industry Standard Architecture. Refers to a type of 32-bit expansion card.

email electronic mail. It is sent from one computer to another over telephone lines via modem or over a local-area network.

emulation A method of running software on a computer that is normally incompatible with that software. An example is an emulator called SoftWindows, which allows the Apple Macintosh to run MS-DOS and Windows software.

enhanced parallel port (EPP) External CDs, the new Zip drives, some scanners and other peripherals plug into your computer's parallel port (daisy chained with the printer). External peripherals can be very convenient, because you can take them with you, and connect them to any computer, including your laptop. No expansion cards, no jumpers, no hassle. However, they are not as fast as internal ones, especially if your computer doesn't have an enhanced parallel port—and most older computers don't. EPPs are gradually replacing the older parallel ports which were used primarily for sending data to printers which are, by nature, slow to absorb information. An even better version of EPP is called ECP, for Enhanced Capability Port. An ECP port can transfer data without slowing down your computer.

ESDI (Enhanced Small Device Interface) A board that controls up to two hard drives (and two floppy drives). The ESDI standard predated SCSI and IDE.

filename A name assigned to a file that distinguishes it from other files saved on the same disk. Standard DOS/Windows 3.1 filenames are limited to eight characters optionally followed by a period and a three-character extension. Windows 95 permits long filenames with up to 250 characters.

FLI, FLC These three letter extensions designate a type of file that contains computer-generated animation. (For example, FLYCOW.FLC might show the cow that jumped over the moon.) These formats were established originally by Autodesk, and have become the de facto standard for storing animation sequences. Increasingly, the Windows .AVI format is replacing .FLI and .FLC files as the format of choice for both video movies and animation.

floppy drive a disk drive that accepts floppy disks.

floppy disk a 3.5-inch diskette in a hard plastic shell. Commonly referred to as a "floppy," which refers to the flexible media inside the rigid plastic shell. Older floppies were 5.25 inches square and weren't protected by a hard shell.

FM Synthesis A way of synthesizing the sounds of various musical instruments. It's now the most common technique for creating sound in today's sound cards. Not as good as "wavetable synthesis," which uses recordings of actual musical instruments.

format to lay down information and mark off zones on a blank tape or floppy disk, information and zones that are later used to help organize files that will be stored on the medium. Some floppies and tapes are sold unformatted, so you have to format them. Fortunately, formatted media are increasingly common, although you might still choose to format a floppy disk or tape if you want to erase it completely.

FPS frames per second, a measurement of how many different shots you see in an animated or motion picture. 24-30 is ideal, 15 FPS is acceptable, but anything less than that looks jerky. (The human eye retains images for up to 1/10th second before fading, so animation must run at least 10 FPS to fool the brain into believing it's viewing motion at all.)

frame grabber A video capture card that can capture still images from a video sequence.

freeware Free software, usually available on information services, computer bulletin boards, and CD-ROMs.

FTP File Transfer Protocol, a method used on the Internet to download files from a remote computer. (FTP can also be used to upload files from your computer to the remote computer, but this is much less common.)

FTP site A computer on the Internet (an FTP server) that hosts files for downloading into your computer. Accessed from DOS via the FTP command or via an FTP client program. You can also access an FTP site from a World Wide Web browser, e.g. ftp:\\ftp.microsoft.com is your gateway to Microsoft's FTP server.

graphics accelerator A optimized graphics chip on a video card that takes over the burden of graphics operations from the CPU, noticeably speeding up screen redraws. There are several types of graphics accelerators: Windows GDI, Video for Windows, and 3-D polygon renderers. Sometimes all are featured on the same graphics card.

hard disk, hard drive a "black box" containing a stack of rigid platters coated with magnetic media, spinning at over 3,000 RPM, that stores information permanently, even if you shut off your computer's power (in contrast to RAM memory chips, the contents of which is erased when you turn off the power). All your programs, documents, and other data are stored on your hard disk drive, although CD-ROMs take over some of the burden of data storage on modern computers.

hint book contains clues and answers to puzzles in a game. If you get stuck in an adventure game and can't proceed, turn to the hint book (sometimes sold separately, or is an appendix to the game manual) to find the solution.

IDE One of the three types of hard drives. IDE stands for Integrated Device Electronics and, as the name suggests, the controller is built into the drive. In other words, you can connect this drive directly to your system's motherboard.

information services (see Online Services)

ink jet printer A printer that creates a black and white or color image on paper, by spraying tiny particles of ink on the surface of the page. A bubblejet printer is similar, but instead of spraying ink, tiny boiling bubbles of ink burst off the printer's printhead onto the paper.

integrated software package a collection of programs designed to work together as a suite. For example, ClarisWorks includes a word processor, a spreadsheet, a database manager, a drawing program, a paint program, and a communications program.

interlacing whether or not a monitor redraws each line or only every other line while displaying a single frame of video. Interlaced video is jittery and unpleasant. See "non-interlaced."

Internet A worldwide network that links together millions of computers. In principle, the Internet is not owned or controlled by any single company, institution, or government, although it is increasingly becoming beholden to commercial interests. The Internet is the delivery vehicle for the World Wide Web, which see.

ISA Industry Standard Architecture. The most common (8 or 16-bit) type of expansion card (see "Cards"). Look for Plug and Play versions of ISA cards if you have a Plug and Play-ready computer, and Windows 95.

L1 & L2 caches L1 (Level One) is a small amount of memory actually built into a Pentium CPU; L2 (Level Two) is high-speed memory that buffers access to the slower main RAM of your computer.

laser printer A printer that uses a laser beam to "paint" a negative image upon a photoconducting drum, selectively erasing the static electricity charge on the drum. The remaining statically charged regions of the drum attract toner particles. The drum then rolls onto the paper and the toner is thermally fused to the page. (Some printers substitute a row of LEDs for a scanning laser, but the result is the same.) Laser printing is the highest-quality personal computer printing technology in use today.

linefeed A special ASCII character that is sometimes used to mark the end of a line of text, indicating to move down to the next line. (See "carriage return.")

local area network (LAN) a small network in an office or a school computer lab. With a LAN, moving files from computer to computer is almost as easy as copying them from a floppy disk,

main processors see CPU

math co-processor a chip that specializes in calculating math involving *fractions*. This chip is similar to the brain of a pocket calculator, and frees up the computer's CPU for other tasks. This co-CPU is now part of the CPU in some 486 and all Pentium CPUs. As we all know, calculations involving fractions are more difficult than arithmetic involving only "whole" numbers. The computer faces the same difficulty. It's not just us humans; fractions are inherently tough.

memory Chips in the computer called RAM (Random Access Memory) which temporarily hold information and programs while the computer's power is turned on. Other memory chips called ROM (Read-only Memory) cannot be written to, but hold information even while the power is turned off. Memory is measured in K (kilobytes, approximately 1,000 bytes), M (megabytes, approximately 1,000,000 bytes), even G (gigabytes, or billions of bytes.) This same memory size terminology is used for both your main RAM memory and storage "memory" like that on your hard drive, although the latter kind of memory is thousands of times slower than RAM or ROM chips.

metafile A special type of file that can store different kinds of data, such as text and graphics. See Vector Graphics. The Windows Metafile Format (WMF) is the most common type.

microprocessors The silicon chips that are the central brain of a computer, performing all or most logical and arithmetic functions. Also known as CPUs (Central Processing Units). IBM PC-compatible computers use microprocessors based on the Intel x86 standard; older Macintoshes use Motorola 680x0-based processors; Power Macs use PowerPC processors made by IBM and Motorola.

MID A file format for MIDI music files. For example, you could play a file called SWANLAKE.MID to hear some MIDI music.

MIDI A music description language, used by sound cards and synthesizers. The music is broken down into its components—the duration, pitch, and force of a note on a piano, for example. Then these symbols are stored in a .MID file for later playback. See "WAV."

modem A device that allows computers to communicate with other computers over ordinary telephone lines. The computers at each end of the link require a modem and the appropriate communications software.

modulation The process of translating a digital signal into analog tones for transmission via telephone lines. The inverse process at the other end is, understandably, called *demodulation* (translation of the analog signal back to digital). The term *modem* comes from this modulation/demodulation process.

monitor the video display device for a computer. Usually a CRT (Cathode Ray Tube), a TV-like unit, or an LCD (Liquid Crystal Display) on a portable computer.

monochromatic consisting of only a single color against white. Usually, but not necessarily, black and white—a monochrome monitor might display green text on a black (actually dark green) background. A black and white silhouette drawing would be monochromatic, as opposed to a *grayscale* photo printed in a newspaper that features various shades of gray for greater realism.

MOO Multi-Operator Options in a game where more than one person is playing simultaneously.

morphing a special effect whereby Michael Jackson is transformed into a panther, or one thing turns into another, smoothly. A technique for metamorphosing (transforming) one image into another one, in many steps.

motherboard Also "system board," the main (and largest) circuit board in your computer where your memory, your CPU and other components are plugged in.

mouse a handheld device that moves an arrow (pointer) on the computer screen to let you choose items and manipulate objects using the buttons on the mouse. A mouse consists of a rubber-jacketed steel ball resting against a horizontal and vertical roller. Photodetectors count the rotation speeds of the rollers to calculate the direction and speed of your movement. As an alternative to the keyboard, the mouse specializes in working with graphics. The keyboard, of course, is best for text entry.

MPC (Multimedia PC) A Personal Computer equipped to handle multimedia. This usually means a PC with a sound card and a CD-ROM drive. There are currently three levels of MPCs, each one increasingly more sophisticated.

MPEG Decoder A card that can decompress and play back digital video at reasonable resolutions. Specialized MPEG hardware helps you play good quality animation on your computer, although a Pentium machine is fast enough to decode MPEG data without additional hardware.

MPEG Motion Pictures Experts Group. MPEG is a software technology (often assisted by hardware) that displays high-quality video and audio on a computer, in full motion.

MUD Multi-User Dungeons is a role-playing game where more than one person is playing simultaneously (usually via the Internet).

multimedia a catch-all term for any presentation involving multiple kinds of media: sound effects, color graphics, animation, music. Multimedia is the merging of television and

wants to respond, and back and forth until there's a dialog of whatever length. (You need a type of Internet software known as a newsreader to take part, although many online services provide convenient access to newsgroups.)

multisync monitors unlike "fixed sync" models, a multisync monitor can display signals from various video cards, each of which repaints the screen at different speeds. Though a multisync monitor costs a little more, you'll be able to easily upgrade the quality of your video (by buying a new and relatively inexpensive video card).

newsgroups ongoing conversations on the Internet about very specific subjects. Somebody posts a message and anyone who wants to respond, and back and forth until there's a dialog of whatever length. (You need a type of Internet software known as a newsreader to take part, although many online services provide convenient access to newsgroups.)

non-interlaced an interlaced computer monitor is less expensive than a non-interlaced model, but causes annoying, wavy flickering. Non-interlaced is the most desirable kind of video monitor.

null modem cable an inexpensive cable that connects the serial ports of two computers—two PCs, two Macs, or a Mac and a PC. The null modem cable simulates a pair of fast modems and a telephone connection.

offline no telecommunications are taking place, the modem is not talking to another computer.

online the modem is talking to another computer's modem.

online service A commercial service that makes information available over phone lines to remote computers equipped with modems. Online access is usually billed by the minute based on hourly rates. Examples of information services include CompuServe, America Online, Prodigy, GEnie, Delphi, The Microsoft Network, and eWorld.

opening Screen The display shown when you first start a program or game running. It's usually a nice graphic and it stays up there are few seconds to distract you while the program loads in from disk and gets itself ready to actually work.

operating system A program that performs all the main control and management functions of a computer, allowing other programs ("applications") to run on top of the operating system. MS-DOS, Microsoft Windows, and IBM OS/2 are examples of operating systems for PC compatibles; the latest Macintoshes use an operating system known as System 7.5.

overdrive chip an Intel CPU upgrade that improves the performance of a 486 chip or, in the future, of a Pentium. (See "CPU Upgrades.")

PCI Peripheral Connect Interface. A high-speed alternative to local bus (see "32-bit card") for relaying data directly between peripherals like a hard drive and the computer's main brain, the CPU. PCI permits data transfers up to 233 megabytes per second, and is the interface of choice for high-end 486 and virtually all Pentium computers.

palette A set of 256 colors, chosen from the full range of 16.7 million possible colors, to display a particular 256 color (8-bit) image. If you display a picture that uses a custom palette, the screen colors of the background may change abruptly to match the custom palette. Increasingly, computers are getting beyond the limitations of the 256-color image and are capable of displaying many thousands or even the full 16-million color spectrum. How many colors can simultaneously be displayed on your monitor depends on your video card. (See "color depth.")

parallel port this connection on the back of your computer used to be devoted only to your printer. However, now many other peripherals are also gumming themselves onto this potentially high-speed connection (the bits in the data move all at the same time over the *parallel port*, as opposed to one-at-a-time over the *serial port*). For more on this, see "EPP."

parents' advisory Like the G, NC and R ratings of movies, an attempt by computer game manufacturers to self-police and provide parents with a general sense of the level of violence or adult content of a game.

parity bit a simple technique for checking the integrity of the transmitted information. One approach is to make the parity bit a one if the number of bits set to 1 is odd, zero otherwise. This particular byte, for example, would result in a parity bit of zero: 10011001. This special bit is then attached to each byte of information as a way of making sure the information made it across the phone lines intact.

patch if a program doesn't work because of a bug, you can sometimes find a "patch" from the software's creator to fix the problem.

performance the overall quality of the computer's behavior; primarily its speed, but also its capacity to run several programs at once, its memory size, its hard drive size and so on.

PhotoCD a technology patented by Kodak, which makes it possible to store high quality photographs on a CD. Instead of having your film printed on paper you can have the images recorded on a CD, which you can view on a television with a PhotoCD player, or you can open them from your CD-ROM drive on your computer.

pixel The smallest unit of a computer image (the "grain" of a computer image). Pixels are small dots that combine the red, green and blue phosphor elements of a computer monitor to display a particular color (Individual red, green, blue phosphors aren't pixels, just as single proton or electron shouldn't be mistaken for an atom.)

ports See parallel port or serial port. A port is a connection between the computer and a peripheral or peripherals.

power See performance.

printer resolution The number of dots the printer can place on the paper in an inch (Dots Per Inch, or DPI). 300 DPI is acceptable for a quality printed document, 600 is better and 1200 is quite sharp, near the professional typeset sharpness you see in magazines and books.

processor cache See L1 & L2 Cache.

RAM Random Access Memory. This is the electronic (solid state) memory a PC uses to perform most of its functions. It is volatile memory, meaning that whatever information it may be storing is lost when the computer's power is turned off. This is as opposed to ROM, or Read Only Memory, which consists of chips into which data is permanently "burned."

RAM doubling utility Not recommended for computers containing more than 4M of RAM memory, these new utilities compress data in RAM, in effect "doubling" the amount of RAM in your system, at the cost of some loss of performance.

redraw repainting the video image when something has changed; a window when you scroll text, the whole screen when you maximize a window, etc.

refresh rate The time it takes the electron guns inside your monitor to completely illuminate the entire screen. This is the vertical refresh rate. Typically, this measurement ranges between 60 and 72 times per second (expressed in a monitor's specifications as 60, 70, or 72Hz). The higher the refresh, the better. At 70 or 72Hz, annoying flicker virtually disappears.

rendering The generation, often in 3D, of a scene into either a bitmap file (for still pictures) or a video file (for animations). A 3-D rendering can be either flat, shaded, or ray-traced. A ray-traced image or animation usually boasts greater detail than a merely shaded scene, and includes shadows, transparency, and reflections.

resolution the amount of detail you can see, the *sharpness* of a computer monitor or a graphic being displayed on it. If you can see individual blades of grass in a landscape, that's high resolution. If the grass looks like a green blob, that's low resolution. Specifically, resolution refers to number of horizontal and vertical pixels—more is better. A 1024×768 screen is higher resolution than 800×600 or 640×480, although pictures and text tends to be smaller since they are made up of finer, tinier, pixels. Resolution depends on your video card. Also see "color depth."

retrace when an electron gun inside the computer monitor momentarily stops firing so it can move back to the left side of the screen and then draw the next line of light.

RTF Rich Text Format. A file format designed to retain word processor formatting and some layout information for embedded graphics. Perhaps most important, RTF files retain formatting like *italics*, so when you give someone an .RTF file they'll see your italics when they load the file into their word processor. Microsoft Word, Lotus Ami Pro/Word Pro, and WordPerfect all use a unique file format, requiring translation between word processor documents. The Rich Text Format is an attempt to create a semi-universal standard for text document files. RTF documents can be also be created and edited with the Windows 95 WordPad applet.

samples taking a digital "snapshot" of a brief moment of audio or video, then translating it into numeric codes so it can be stored on CD or tape or disk or whatever medium. Samples represent the values of the actual sound or video at regular intervals. (See "CD Quality" or "Telephone Quality")

sampling rate The number of samples taken per second, or "frequency." Expressed in kHz (kilohertz) One kHz is 1,000 samples per second.

SCSI One of the three types of hard drives SCSI (Small Computer Systems Interface) drives are the fastest, but they require a SCSI interface card or port. (SCSI is standard on most Apple Macintosh computers.) If your computer doesn't have a SCSI port, you will have to install a SCSI adapter (another expansion card) as well. A SCSI adapter lets you connect up to seven devices to your computer. The devices are "daisy-chained," connected in a serial fashion, one after the other.

serial port Input/output connectors that allow a computer to communicate with external devices, such as modems, scanners, and a mouse. See "parallel port."

shareware Software that you can try out before purchasing. (However, you are expected to pay the registration fee if you continue to use the software after the evaluation period.) Shareware is usually available on information services, computer bulletin boards (BBS's), and CD-ROMs, and unlike commercial software, you're encouraged to "pass it along," and share it with others.

SIMM (Single Inline Memory Module). These tiny circuit boards fit into special slots, and there are only a few SIMM slots in your computer. The amount of memory on each SIMM board ranges from 1MB up to 16 MB.

simulation Games or other software that endeavor to imitate real life. Flight simulators are quite popular and, according to pilots, quite realistic. Except for the consequences of the crash.

sneakernet Computer slang for exchanging files between computers by carrying floppy disks back and forth. Copying a file onto a floppy disk and carrying it physically to another computer user, via the high-tech networking physics of your sneakers.

software drivers small program-like files that won't run by themselves, but that assist other programs with "libraries" of short tasks, data and other information. Also see "driver."

sound card A card that allows your computer to record and play back sounds and reproduce music from MIDI files.

spell checker A utility program, usually part of a word processor, that looks through what you've written and asks you about words it doesn't find in its dictionary—and offering suggestions of alternative spellings as well.

stop bit Not all bits transmitted over the telephone via modems (two computers talking to each other) carry information. Following each byte (a series of 8 bits) there is always an extra bit, called the stop bit. It is used to synchronize the transmitting and receiving modems. When the receiving modem sees the stop bit, it knows a byte has ended and a new one begins.

subdirectory A directory within another directory. With Windows 95, the terminology has shifted from *directory* and *sub-directory* to what are now called *folders* (and folders within folders—subfolders). It's all relative, however—all folders are subfolders of the root directory (the drive letter or drive name itself, as in C:\). See "directory."

Super VGA or SVGA A video card standard that can display 256 or more colors at a resolution of 640×480, or higher.

surge suppresser A device that protects electronic equipment plugged into it, by diverting dangerous power surges safely to ground. A surge suppresser does not "condition" your power signal, however, nor does it protect you from brownouts and power outages, as can a UPS (which see). And nothing short of rooftop lightning arrestors can protect you from a direct strike.

SX A processor model that lacks some of the features of the DX version, which reduces its cost. The 486SX processor doesn't have a built-in math co-processor. The 386SX chip processes information in 32 bit chunks, but it moves information around in 16 bit chunks.

tape see "backup tape."

TCP/IP a transmission protocol that allows any kind of computer to send and receive data from any other kind of computer over the Internet. Transmission Control Protocol/Internet Protocol, or TCP/IP for short.

telephone quality The quality of a sound recorded at 8,000 samples per second, with 8 bits per sample. Low fidelity sound, but sound that doesn't take up too much disk space.

Telnet MUDs and MOOs (which see) use this form of Internet communications, which let you "type" on a remote computer console. But Telnet is a complex way to communicate and can take a long time to learn.

TGA, BMP, TIF Some of the most common image (picture) file formats. Pictures and other graphics are stored in these formats on disk.

transfer speed the rate at which data can move from a hard drive or CD-ROM (or indeed any storage device) into your computer's RAM memory, once the data has been located on the media. (The time it takes to locate the data is called the access speed, which see.) Together, transfer speed and access speed describe the quality of the performance of a storage device, with transfer speed usually being the more important specification.

True Color The highest quality computer visual display. It uses three bytes per pixel, one for each primary color, red, green, and blue.

Unix An operating system commonly used on minicomputers and workstations, and often used for Internet programming (but not used to merely access and maneuver around on the Internet). An alternative to DOS or Windows or the Mac's OS, Unix is still popular with academics, but is nonetheless used by only a small fraction of the total computer-using population.

upload Transferring a file from your computer to another computer, usually by using a modem and a phone line. (as opposed to *download* which means that you bring a file into your computer from another computer elsewhere.) Remember the distinction by thinking of yourself communicating with the big outside world "above" your modem. This way, you *down*load to the "little you," and *up*load to the big outside world.

UPS Uninterruptible Power Supply. A device that can power your computer for a while from lead-acid batteries if there's a power outage or when voltage is reduced during a brownout (brownouts are particularly harmful to PC power supplies).

Uucoding, UUEncoding A method of sending binary files over the Internet or between different email systems. Binary files require 8 bits of data, but many email systems can only transfer 7 bits at a time, so the binary data is converted into streams of seemingly nonsense characters, which can fit into 7 bits at a time.

vector graphics A method of displaying graphics on a computer screen by drawing the lines and shapes that make up the image (as opposed to just copying, bit-by-bit, each dot of the original). See "bit-mapped graphics," which are direct copies. An advantage of vector graphics is that they can easily be *scaled* to different sizes, merely mathematically, resulting in a smooth image. A disadvantage is that vector graphics can never look photographic and resemble cartoons or drawings. Only bitmap graphics (which see) can produce photo-realistic images.

vertical refresh rate how many frames of video per second are displayed on a computer monitor

VESA or VL-bus a special kind of connector called "local bus" that speeds things up by being able to "talk" directly to the computer's microprocessor. Before buying a VESA expansion card, check your manual or with your computer's manufacturer to see if your machine accepts this kind of card. Most modern machines, including Pentium computers, use PCI cards instead.

video capture card a peripheral that displays (and captures) videotape images or regular TV images on the computer monitor.

video card a relatively inexpensive "controller" that feeds a signal to your computer's monitor. It's the rough equivalent of the "tuner" in an ordinary TV.

video grabber see Video Capture Card.

video RAM Just as your computer has RAM memory (see "Memory" or "RAM"), so too does a video card need a way of storing information. A video card stores the next frame of a video image that you'll see on your screen. As you might expect, the more video RAM your card has, the better. 1M is typical, 2M is better, 4M and you're sitting pretty. (Not necessarily the same as VRAM, which is a special high-speed version of Video RAM; many video cards use standard DRAM, dynamic RAM.)

video standards Today's lowest-common-denominator video standard is over a decade old. Known as VGA (for Video Graphics Array), this standard specified that a color monitor be capable of displaying 16 colors simultaneously, at a resolution of 640 by 480 pixels. Super VGA (SVGA) is a superior, and now very popular, video standard, supporting at least 256 colors at 640×480, with resolutions up to 1600×1024 using up to 16.7 million colors, depending on the video card and the features supported by the monitor.

virtual reality Virtual reality is an attempt, via computer, to reproduce reality. Those rides where you get into a room on rollers and watch a movie of a car race while machines tilt the room in concert with the curves in the track—that's virtual reality as we know it today. Reality, as most of us experience it, includes a lot more than computers can currently simulate, but the gap is closing. The goal of VR is to make you feel that what you're experiencing is, in fact, real, or at least pretty close.

VOC a sound file format (an alternative to the .WAV file). The .VOC file format is used by the Sound Blaster sound card.

VR See Virtual Reality

WAV a sound file format short for waveform, and popular for sound effects and voice mail. This is the file format used by most Windows applications to hold sound and music recorded digitally. For example, QUACK.WAV, when played, might reproduce the sound of a duck quaking. Also see "MIDI."

wavetable A way of reproducing the sound of a musical instrument, based on actual samples of the true sound (as opposed to an artificially *synthesized* sound). A wavetable is a collection of pre-recorded digitized sounds of the various instruments of the orchestra and band, stored on ROM (memory) chips.

Windows an operating system (which see) developed by Microsoft Corporation that is highly visual (color, high detail, 3-D effects, overlapping zones, etc.) based on a desktop metaphor. Windows is a considerable improvement over the way we had to interact with computers using the DOS operating system during the 80's, and Windows 95 is a considerable improvement over Windows 3.0 and 3.1 that we had to use until 1995. It's likely that we'll now see a new version nearly every year.

World Wide Web or, usually WWW or simply "the Web," the popular face of the Internet. Technically, the WWW is an online hypertext system (highlighted words—links—take you elsewhere when you click on them, to another Internet site described by the hypertext). The WWW is an immense set of screens ("pages"), documents connected together by these links. You use a WWW "browser" such as Mosaic, Netscape Navigator or Microsoft Internet Explorer, to interact with the Web.

3M CD-ROM
3M Center
St. Paul MN 55133
612-736-3838

7th Level
1771 International Pkwy. #101
Richardson TX 75081
214-437-4858

Absolute Entertainment Inc.
10 Mountainview Road
Upper Saddle River NJ 07458
201-818-4800

Access Software Inc.
4910 West Amelia Earhart Drive
Salt Lake City UT 84116
801-359-2900

Acclaim Entertainment Inc.
One Acclaim Plaza
Glen Cover, NY 11542
516-656-5000

Accolade
5300 Stevens Creek Blvd. Suite 500
San Jose CA 95129
408-985-1700

Activision Studios
11601 Wilshire Blvd.
Suite 1000
Los Angeles CA 90025
310-473-9200

Adobe Systems
1585 Charleston Rd.
Mountain View CA 94039
800-888-6293

Advanced Gravis
3750 North Fraser Avenue
Suite 101
Burnaby BC
Canada V5J 5E9
604-431-5020

Alliance Interactive Software Inc.
1859 North Pine Island Road # 103
Plantation FL 33322
305-423-4289

Allsop Inc.
4201 Meridian Street
Bellingham WA 98227
206-734-9090

America Online
8619 Westwood Center Drive
Vienna VA 22182-2285
800-827-6364

American Laser Games
4801 Lincoln Road NE
Albuquerque NM 87109
505-880-1718

ASCII Entertainment
366 A Lakeside Drive
Foster City CA 94404
415-570-6200

Asymetrix Corporation
800-448-6543

The Avalon Hill Game Company
4517 Harford Road
Baltimore MD 21214
410-254-6200

BAO
2004 Fox Drive Suite G
Champaign IL 61820
217-356-0796

BASF Magnetics Corporation
35 Crosby Drive
Bedford MA 01730
617-271-4000

Bayware
P.O. Box 5554
San Mateo CA 94402
415-312-0980

Berkeley Systems
2095 Rose Street
Berkeley CA 94709
510-540-5535

Bethesda Softworks
1370 Piccard Drive
Rockville MD 20850
301-926-8300

Books That Work
2300 Geng Road
Building 3, Suite 100
Palo Alto CA 94303
800-242-4546

Broderbund Software
500 Redwood Blvd.
Novato CA 94948-6121
800-521-6263

Caligari Corporation
1951 Landings Drive
Mountain View CA 94043
415-390-9600

Cambrix Publishing
6269 Variel Ave Suite B
Woodland Hills CA 91367
800-992-8781

Charles Schwab & Company
101 Montgomery Street
San Francisco CA 94104
800-334-4455

Chips & Bits Inc.
PO Box 234, Route 100
Rochester VT 05767
800-699-4263

Comfy Interactive
710 Lakeway Drive
Suite 25C
Sunnyvale CA 94086
408-733-3713

Compaq Computer Corporation
Post Office Box 692000
Houston TX 77269-2000
713-370-0670

CompuServe
5000 Arlington Center Blvd.
P.O. Box 20212
Columbus OH 43220
800-848-8199

Compton's NewMedia
2320 Camino Vida Roble
Carlsbad CA 92009
619-929-2500

Computer Express
31 Union Ave.
Sudbury MA 01776
508-443-6125

Concise
5252 Balboa Ave. Ste 605
San Diego CA 92117
619-268-3358

Corel Corporation
1600 Carling Ave.
Ottawa Ontario CANADA K1Z 8R7
613-728-3733

Creative Wonders
1450 Fashion Island Blvd.
San Mateo CA 94404
415-513-7436

Davidson & Associates Inc.
19840 Pioneer Ave.
Torrance CA 90815
310-793-0600

Delorme Mapping
PO Box 298
Freeport ME 04032
207-865-1234

Delrina Corporation
6320 San Ignacio Ave.
San Jose CA 95119
408-363-2345

Deneb
800-730-6322

Disney Interactive
1400 Way
Glendale CA 91201
818-567-5090

DK Multimedia
95 Madison Ave.
New York NY 10016
818-544-6575

Dorling Kindersley Publishing
95 Madison Ave.
New York NY 10016
212-213-4800

Dow Jones News/Retrieval
P.O. Box 300
Princeton NJ 08543-0300
800-451-1511

Edmark
6727 185th Ave. NE
Redmond WA 98052
800-426-0856

Electronic Arts
1450 Fashion Island Blvd.
San Mateo CA 94404-2000
415-571-7171

Equis International
3950 S. 700 East Suite 100
Salt Lake City UT 84107
800-882-3040

Fidelity Investments
161 Devonshire Street
Boston MA 02110
800-544-0246

Fractal Design
800-297-2665

Future Vision
300 Airport Executive Park
Spring Valley NY 10954
914-426-0400

FutureWave Software Inc.
619-637-6190

Gametek Inc.
2999 N.E. 191st Street
5th Floor
N. Miami FL 33180
305-935-3995

Graphix Zone, Inc.
38 Corporate Park Suite 100
Irvine CA 92714
714-833-3838

Green Thumb Software
303-499-1388

Greystone Digital
P.O. Box 1888
Huntersville NC 28078
800-249-5397

Grolier Electronic Publishing
Sherman Turnpike
Danbury CT 06816
203-797-3365

GTE Interactive Media
2055 Corte Del Nogal #200
Carlsbad CA 92009
619-431-8801

HarperCollins Interactive
800-424-6234

Headbone Interactive
1520 Bellevue Avenue
Seattle WA 98122
206-323-0073

HSC Software
800-800-0005

Humongous Entertainment
16932 Woodinville-Redmond Rd.
NE
Woodinville WA 98073
206-450-0965

IBM Multimedia Publishing Studio
1500 Riveredge Parkway, Suite 200
Atlanta, GA 30328
404-644-4881

Ibis Software
415-546-1917

Impressions Software Inc.
222 Third Street, # 0234
Cambridge MA 02142
617-225-0500

Impulse Inc.
800-328-0184

Intellimedia Sports Inc.
Two Piedmont Center, Suite 300
Atlanta GA 30305
404-262-0000

Interplay
17922 Fitch Ave.
Irvine CA 92714
714-553-6678

Intuit Software
P.O. Box 3014
Menlo Park CA 94026
800-624-8742

IVI Publishing
7500 Flying Cloud Dr.
Minneapolis MN 55344
612-996-6160

JASC
612-930-9171

Kidboard Inc.
6546 France Ave. S Suite 376
Edina MN 55435
800-926-7095

Knowledge Adventure Inc
1311 Grand Central Ave.
Glendale CA 91201
818-246-0400

Laguna Design Center
1088 North Coast Hwy.
Laguna Beach CA 92651
714-494-0772

Leading Edge Products Inc.
117 Flanders Road
Westborough MA 01581
508-836-4800

The Learning Company
6493 Kaiser Drive
Fremont CA 94555
510-792-2101

Lifestyle Software Group
800-289-1157

Live Oak Media
800-454-7557

Living Books
500 Redwood Blvd.
Novato CA 94948
800-776-4724

Lucasarts Entertainment Company
Post Office Box 10307
San Rafael CA 94912
415-721-3300

Macromedia
415-442-0200

Mag Innovision
2801 S. Yale St.
Santa Ana CA 92704
714-751-2008

Magnet Interactive Studios Inc.
3255 Grace Street NW
Washington DC 20007
202-625-1111

MarketArts Inc.
1810 North Glenville Suite 124
Richardson TX 75081
214-783-6792

MAXIS
2 Theatre Square
Orinda CA 94563
510-254-9700

MECC
6160 Summit Dr. North
Minneapolis MN 55430
800-685-6322

Merit Studios
13707 Gamma Road
Dallas TX 75244
214-385-2353

Micrografx Inc.
1303 Arapaho
Richardson TX 75081
214-994-6124

Microsoft Corporation
One Microsoft Way
Redmond WA 98052
206-882-8080

Mindscape Inc.
60 Leveroni Ct.
Novato CA 94949
415-883-3000

Morgan Interactive
160 Pine St. Ste. 509
San Francisco CA 94111
415-693-9596

Motion Works International
1020 Mainland Street
Suite 130 Vancouver BC
Canada V6B 2T4
604-685-9975

Multicom Publishing
1700 Olive Way # 1250
Seattle WA 98101
206-622-5530

National CD-ROM
11005 Indian Trail Suite 101-A
Dallas Texas 75229
1-800-CDROM-13

Neosoft Corp.
1861 Landings Drive
Mountain View CA 94043
503-389-5489

Netcom
3031 Tisch Way
San Jose, CA 95128
415-691-0600

Netscape
501 E. Middlefield Rd.
Mountain View CA
415-254-1900

New World Computing Inc.
20800 Agoura Rd. Suite 200
Agoura Hills CA 91301
818-889-5600

Origin Systems
12940 Research Blvd.
Austin TX 78750-3235
512-335-5200

PC Gamer
P.O. Box 5014
Pittsfield MA 01203-9418

Peachtree Software
1505-C Pavillion Place
Norcross GA 30093
404-564-5800

Prairie Multimedia Inc.
708-513-0978

Prentice Hall
1 Lake St.
Upper Saddle River NJ 07458
201-236-7112

Prima Publishing
P.O. Box 1260BK
Rocklin CA 95677-1260
800-776-3449

Prodigy
445 Hamilton Ave.
White Plains NY 10601
800-776-3449

Putnam New Media
11490 Commerce Park Dr.
Suite 130
Reston VA 22091
703-860-3375

Rand McNally
708-329-2316

Road Scholar Software
713-266-7623

Sanctuary Woods
1825 South Grant Street
San Mateo CA 94402
415-286-6000

Science for Kids
9950 Concord Church Rd.
Lewisville NC 27023
910-945-9000

Sierra Online
3380 146th Place SE
Suite 300
Bellevue WA 98007
206-649-9800

Simon & Schuster Interactive
1230 6th Ave.
New York NY 10020
212-698-7000

SNK Corporation of America
20603 Earl St.
Torrance CA 90503
310-371-7100

Softbooks
714-586-1284

Software Marketing Corp.
602-893-3377

Sonic Foundry
608-256-3133

Sony Computer Entertainment
919 East Hillsdale Blvd.
Foster City CA 94404
415-655-8000

Spectrum Holobyte Inc.
2490 Mariner Square Loop
Alameda CA 94501
510-522-3584

SRS Labs
2909 Daimler St.
Santa Ana CA 92705
714-442-1070

Storm Software
1861 Landings Drive
Mountain View CA 94043
415-691-6600

Strategic Simulations Inc.
675 Almanor Avenue
Suite 201
Sunnyvale CA 94086

Sun Media Inc.
2809 Main St.
714-756-9500

Sybex
2021 Challenger Dr.
Alameda CA 94501
510-523-8233

Take 2 Interactive Software
575 Broadway
New York NY 10012
212-941-2988

TDC Interactive
2716 Ocean Park Blvd.
Suite 3085
Santa Monica CA 90405
310-452-6720

Teen Talk Communications
719 E. Genesee St.
Syracuse NY 13210
315-478-6729

Time Warner Interactive
2210 West Olive Avenue
Burbank CA 91506
818-295-6600

Times Mirror Multimedia
One Maynard Drive
Park Ridge NJ 07656
201-307-8866

Transparent Language
22 Inman Lane
Hollis NH
603-465-2230

U.S. Gold
303 Sacramento St.
San Francisco CA 94111
415-693-0297

Ulead Systems
800-858-5323

Ventana Communications
P.O. Box 13964
Research Triangle Park, NC 27709
919-544-9404

Viacom New Media
1515 Broadway
New York NY 10036
800-469-2539

Vic Tokai Inc.
22904 Lockness Ave.
Torrance CA 90501
310-326-8880

Villa Crespo Software Inc.
1725 McGovern Street
Highland Park IL 60035
708-433-0500

Virgil Corporation
290 Green Street Suite #1
San Francisco CA 94133
415-433-4698

Virgin Interactive Entertainment
18061 Fitch Avenue
Irvine CA 92714
714-833-8710

The Wall Street Journal
P.O. Box 300
Princeton NJ 08543-0300
800-291-9382

Warner Multimedia
111 North Hollywood Way
Burbank CA 91505
818-840-6329

Westwood Studios
5333 South Arville Suite 104
Las Vegas NV 89118
702-368-4850

Wiley Computer Books
605 3rd Ave.
New York NY 10158
212-850-6000

WinWay Corp.
5431 Auburn Blvd. Suite 398
Sacramento CA 95841
916-965-7878

World Library Inc.
2809 Main St.
Santa Ana CA 92714
714-756-9500

Ziff-Davis
P.O. Box 57167
Boulder CO 80322-7167